European Revolutionaries and Algerian Independence 1954-1962

Revolutionary History, Volume 10, No 4
Socialist Platform Ltd
MERLIN PRESS

Revolutionary History

Founding Editor: Al Richardson (1941-2003)

Edition Editor: Ian Birchall

Editorial Coordinating Team: Ted Crawford, Paul Flewers, Esther Leslie, John Plant

Reviews and Obituaries Editor: John Plant

Website Coordinator: Alun Morgan

Editorial Board: Toby Abse, Ian Birchall, Tony Borton, David Broder, Barry Buitekant, Clarence Chrysostom, Mildred Gordon, Chris Gray, Simon Hardy, Dave Renton, Mike Jones, Stuart King, Richard Kirkwood, George Leslie, Sheila Leslie, Ben Lewis, Mike Pearn, Jim Ring, Alejandra Rios

Continental Contributing Editor: Fritz Keller

Foreign Advisory Board: Andy Durgan, Rick Kuhn, Staffan Lindhe, Jean Jacques Marie, Einde O'Callaghan, Tom O'Lincoln, Reiner Tosstorff

ISBN. 978-0-85036-665-5

Copyright © 2012

Web site: www.revolutionaryhistory.co.uk

E-mail: tcrawford@revhist.datanet.co.uk (editorial)

barry.buitekant@hotmail.com (business)

trusscott.foundation@blueyonder.co.uk (text processing)

Socialist Platform Ltd, BCM 7646, London WC1N 3XX

Merlin Press
6 Crane Street Chambers, Crane Street, Pontypool NP4 6ND
www.merlinpress.co.uk

Printed in the UK by Imprint Digital, Exeter

Contents

Editorial	6
Acronyms	8

European Revolutionaries and Algerian Independence, 1954-1962

I: Ian Birchall, Introduction	9
II: Sylvain Pattieu: The Comrades of the Brothers	15
Introduction	15
Chapter I: A Colonial War	16
Chapter II: The Far Left in the 1950s	17
Chapter III: In Face of the FLN	19
Chapter IV: What Kind of Support for the Algerian Revolution?	33
Chapter V: SFIO, PCF: The 'Betrayals': From 'Peace in Algeria' to Pacification	55
Chapter VI: The Days of the Networks	74
Chapter VII: The New Left	88
Chapter VIII: In the Service of the FLN?	89
Chapter IX: Facing Fascism?	91
Chapter X: Pieds-rouges	92
Chapter XI: Conclusion	94
III: Additional Material: The Far Left	98
Pierre Lambert, Let the Algerian People Speak: Part V — Independence by Stages and the Constituent Assembly	98
Pierre Lambert, Silence Becomes Complicity	101
Ian Birchall, A Note on the Committee for the Release of Messali Hadj and the Victims of Repression	104
Voix Ouvrière, Tail-Ending	107
Voix Ouvrière, Once There Was a Party…	109
Ian Birchall, Socialisme ou Barbarie and the Algerian War	113
IV: Aspects of the War	125
The Algerian War Seen from Renault-Billancourt	125
La Vérité des Travailleurs, Save the Reservists of the Gare de Lyon From Military Justice	144
Vérités Pour, A Reminder of Principles	149
Vérités Pour, Bernard Randon, The Great Refusal	152

Ian Birchall, A Note on the MNA	156
Ian Birchall, Mitterrand's War	168
V: Solidarity in Europe	175
Fritz Keller, Solidarity Action in Austria	175
John Plant, John Baird: A British MP Who Supported the Algerian Revolution	192
VI: Past and Future	206
Report to the Second North African Interfederal Communist Conference on 24 September 1922, Adopted Unanimously	206
Communism and the Colonial Question	211
Hadjali Abdelkader, Colonial Action	212
Robert Louzon, A Disgrace	215
Manus McGrogan, From the Algerian War to May 1968 and After: The Roles of Left Radicals and Their Press	218
VII: Bibliography	232
Some Further Reading	232
A Note on Some Novels Dealing with the War	235

Other Material

Work in Progress	239
Obituaries	246

Robert J Alexander — Robert Barcia (Hardy) — Jean-René Chauvin — Martin Conway Cook — Robert V Daniels — Sitanshu Das — Will Fancy — Georges Fontenis — Francisco Gomez Palomo — Hoàng Don Tri — Edmond Kovacs — Claude Lefort — Moshe Lewin — Bess Lomax Hawes — Bongani Mkhungo — Jakob Moneta — Hugo Gonzales Moscoso — William W Norton — Vinayak Purohit — Corin Redgrave — Friederike Schlesak — Irwin Silber — Mahendra Singh — Wilebaldo Solano — Richard Stites

Reviews	321
Georg Adler, Peter Hudis and Annelies Laschitza (eds), *The Letters of Rosa Luxemburg* (Mike Jones)	321
Ross Bradshaw and others (compilers), *Remembering Colin Ward, 1924-2010* (JJ Plant)	324

Gerd Callesen and Wolfgang Maderthaner (eds), *Victor Adler–Friedrich Engels Briefwechsel*, Dokumentation Verein für die Geschichte der Arbeiterbewegung (Fritz Keller) — 326

Gerd Callesen and Wolfgang Maderthaner (eds), *Victor Adler–Friedrich Engels Briefwechsel* (Fritz Keller) — 326

Richard B Day and Daniel F Gaido (eds), *Witnesses to Permanent Revolution: The Documentary Record* (Ben Lewis) — 329

Jean-Numa Ducange (Editor), Karl Kautsky and Jean Jaurès, *Le socialisme et la révolution française* (Jean-Jacques Marie) — 337

William J Fishman, *The Insurrectionists* (Robin Blick) — 340

Pierre Frank, *The Long March of the Trotskyists* (Harry Ratner) — 342

Daniel A Gordon, *Immigrants and Intellectuals* (Ian Birchall) — 355

John Gorman, *Stratford: Another East End* (JJ Plant) — 358

Ernst Hanisch, *Der große Illusionist: Otto Bauer (1881-1938)* (Fritz Keller) — 359

Annelies Laschitza, *Die Liebknechts. Karl und Sophie* (Theodor Bergmann) — 364

Deborah Lavin, *Bradlaugh Contra Marx: Radicalism and Socialism in the First International* (Terry Liddle) — 369

Dorian Lynskey, *33 Revolutions Per Minute: A History of Protest Songs* (JJ Plant) — 371

Merilyn Moos, *The Language of Silence* (Ian Birchall) — 376

David North, *In Defense of Leon Trotsky* (Cheney Longville) — 378

Joshua Rubenstein, *Leon Trotsky: A Revolutionary's Life* (Paul Flowers) — 382

Victor Serge, *Retour à l'Ouest: Chroniques (juin 1936-mai 1940)* (Ian Birchall) — 385

Alan Thornett, *Militant Years: Car Workers' Struggles of the 60s and 70s* (Julian Alford) — 387

Paul Trewhela, *Inside Quatro: Uncovering the Exile History of the ANC and SWAPO* (JJ Plant) — 392

Jürg Ulrich, *Kamenev: Der Gemäßigte Bolschewik. Das kollektive Denken im Umfeld Lenins* (Reiner Tosstorff) — 395

Ben Watson, *Adorno for Revolutionaries* (Sheila Lahr) — 399

Larry Wayne, *Union Bread. Bagels, Platzels and Chollah: The Story of the London Jewish Bakers' Union* (JJ Plant) — 404

Mary K Wilmers, *The Eitingons: A Twentieth-Century Story* (Bridget St Ruth) — 409

Alan Woodward, *Life and Times of Joe Thomas: The Road to Libertarian Socialism* (Bridget St Ruth) — 414

Letters — 417

EDITORIAL

A colonial war spearheaded by a 'socialist' politician; a national liberation movement strongly influenced by Islam; repression and torture on one side, terror tactics on the other. There is much about the Algerian war for national independence (1954-62) that seems all too familiar in today's world.

So, on the fiftieth anniversary of Algerian independence, we are publishing a collection of material relating to those organisations and individuals in France and the rest of Europe who acted in solidarity with the Algerian struggle. Internationalism has always been at the heart of the revolutionary socialist tradition, and these were internationalists who put their money where their mouth was.

The core of the issue consists of key chapters from Sylvain Pattieu's book *Les Camarades des frères*, which, on the basis of extensive documentary sources and interviews with the main participants, tells the largely unknown story of the French Trotskyists and anarchists who took up the Algerian cause earlier than the better-known networks headed by Francis Jeanson and Henri Curiel. While the bulk of the Socialist Party went over to backing the war and the Communist Party was, at best, ambiguous in its response, these activists saved the honour of the French left. Yet their political choices also raise many difficult questions, and we hope this study will enable a sober but critical reappraisal of this period.

Pattieu's book is complemented by other documents which illustrate the different positions adopted by sections of the French far left. We have concentrated not so much on theoretical analyses of the situation as on the concrete practicalities of solidarity, the mundane but often highly hazardous tasks of those who 'carried suitcases' for the FLN. There are also short sections on solidarity activity in Britain and Austria, and the final chapter shows the links between the left in the Algerian war and the new generation of activists in 1968.

The events of those tortured and violent years still arouse strong passions. (Hence it is important to stress that signed articles represent the positions of their authors, not of the *Revolutionary History* collective.) The unhappy subsequent history of Algeria had its roots in the independence struggle, and there is material here for a left critique of the FLN. History does not repeat itself mechanically, and there are no recipes here to solve our present problems. But a study of these remarkable events can certainly help to educate and inspire a new generation of anti-imperialists.

The Editorial Board gives its thanks to Ian Birchall, who not only assembled this issue of *Revolutionary History*, but also translated the material originally written in French and German.

The Editorial Board also gives its thanks to Harry Ratner for his generous financial donation to *Revolutionary History*.

Editorial Board
Revolutionary History

Copyright

The woodcuts of Otto Rudolf Schatz used on the cover are reproduced thanks to the permission of the copyright owners, Professor Michael Jursa and Dr Martin Jursa (both from Vienna/Austria). None of these woodcuts or any part of them may be reproduced, stored in a retrieval system, or transmitted in any form or by any means, electronic, electrical, chemical, mechanical, optical, photocopying, recording or otherwise, without the prior permission of the copyright owners. Otto Rudolf Schatz (1900-1961)[1] studied art in Vienna after the First World War and from 1924 belonged to the Hagenbund group of Austrian artists. He got to know Ernst Fischer, the Communist writer,[2] and became the most important Austrian representative of the *Neue Sachlichkeit* (New Objectivity) tendency in art. He produced woodcuts for the German translation of Upton Sinclair's novel *Co-op*. Schatz was in Austria when the Nazis took over; because of his reputation as the 'red painter' 1500 of his wood-blocks were burned. Because the Nazis denied him painting materials, which were only available on the black market at very high prices, he produced miniatures in order to make the best use of such materials as he could get hold of. In 1944, he was sent to a labour camp. In 1945, he returned to Vienna and portrayed the devastation of the city in woodcuts and coloured pictures. He contributed woodcuts to the Communist publication *Tagebuch*. His outspoken criticism of Social Democrats gave him a reputation as a troublemaker, and did not help his career; although his murals and mosaics decorated many schools and public buildings in Vienna, he was not given the title of Professor until 1955. One of his last projects, when he was dying of lung cancer in 1960, was to illustrate an article by Reimar Holzinger about Algeria. His woodcuts show the Foreign Legion as a machine destructive of all freedom.

Notes
1. This brief note on Schatz is based on information in Fritz Keller's doctoral thesis.
2. Best known for *The Necessity of Art* (1963).

Acronyms

Main acronyms used
AGTA: *Amicale générale des travailleurs algériens* — General Association of Algerian Workers (organised by FLN)
ALN: *Armée de libération nationale* — National Liberation Army
CFTC: *Confédération Française des Travailleurs Chrétiens* — Catholic trade-union federation
CGT: *Confédération générale du travail* — largest (then PCF-led) trade-union federation
CRUA: *Comité révolutionnaire d'unité et d'action* — Revolutionary Committee of Unity and Action
ENA: *Étoile Nord-Africaine* — North African Star (1926-37)
FA: *Fédération anarchiste* — Anarchist Federation
FCL: *Fédération communiste libertaire* — Libertarian Communist Federation
FEN: *Fédération de l'enseignement national* — main French teachers' union
FI: Fourth International
FLN: *Front de libération nationale* — National Liberation Front (Algeria)
FO: *Force ouvrière* — 1948 anti-Communist split from CGT
GPRA: *Gouvernement provisoire de la république algérienne* — Provisional Government of the Algerian Republic (1958-62)
MNA: *Mouvement National Algérien* — Algerian National Movement
MTLD: *Mouvement pour le triomphe des libertés démocratiques* — Movement for the Triumph of Democratic Freedoms (legal, electoral wing of PPA)
OAS: *Organisation de l'armée secrète* — Secret Army Organisation
OS: *Organisation spéciale* — Special Organisation (PPA paramilitary organisation, 1947-51)
PCF: *Parti communiste français* — French Communist Party
PCI: *Parti communiste internationaliste* — Internationalist Communist Party (Trotskyist)
PPA: *Parti du Peuple Algérien* — Algerian People's Party (1937 successor of banned ENA)
PSU: *Parti Socialist Unifié* — United Socialist Party (founded 1960)
SFIO: *Section française de l'internationale ouvrière* — French Socialist Party
SJÖ: *Sozialistische Jugend Österreichs* — Youth section of Austrian Socialist Party
SouB: *Socialisme ou Barbarie* — Socialism or Barbarism
UDMA: *Union Démocratique du Manifeste Algérien* — Democratic Union of the Algerian Manifesto (moderate organisation, founded 1946 by Ferhat Abbas)
UEC: *Union des étudiants communistes* — Union of Communist Students
UGS: *Union de la gauche socialiste* — Union of the Socialist Left
UGTA: *Union Générale des Travailleurs Algériens* — General Association of Algerian Workers (FLN trade-union body)
UNEF: *Union nationale des étudiants de France* — French national students' union
USTA: *Union des Syndicats des Travailleurs Algériens* — Association of Unions of Algerian Workers (MNA trade-union body)

Ian Birchall
INTRODUCTION

This issue of *Revolutionary History* focuses primarily on the solidarity shown by the French left with the Algerian independence struggle between 1954 and 1962. However, this has to be understood in the context of the war as a whole. So this introductory section presents a brief outline history of the Algerian war.[1]

* * *

The Algerian war (1954-62), alongside British withdrawal from India and Africa, and the Portuguese colonial wars which led to the downfall of Caetano, was one of the key episodes in the process of decolonisation which saw the end of the European empires in the period after the Second World War and the emergence of the so-called 'Third World'. The war raged for seven and a half years (though it was only in 1999 that it was officially recognised that it had been a war), and tore through the fabric of French society, leading to the collapse of the Fourth Republic. It put to the test the whole of the French left, the Communist Party (PCF), the Socialist Party (SFIO) and the smaller groupings to their left, including the tiny organisations of French Trotskyists.

France had colonised Algeria between 1830 and 1847; subsequently settlers from France (including those deported after the June 1848 rising in Paris) and other European countries took over the country. Unlike other French colonies, Algeria became an integral part of the French state, constituting three *départements*. But while the settlers had full rights as French citizens, such privileges were extended only to a very small minority of the native population, those who were willing to renounce their religion. (Muslim is probably the most accurate way to describe the indigenous population, since not all were Arabs.)

The indigenous population were legally French subjects, not French citizens. They were subject to the notorious *Code de l'indigénat*, which imposed a special set of laws and regulations, and which criminalised even the most minor forms of insubordination. France boasted of its 'civilising mission', but this was conceived in clearly racial terms — as former Prime Minister Jules Ferry put it in 1885: 'Superior races have rights because they have duties. They have the duty to civilise inferior races.'[2] But even in its own terms, France's civilising achievements were limited. In 1834, a French general reported that nearly all the native population could read and write, with schools for boys and girls in each village.[3] A century later only a quarter of the Muslim population could read Arabic; less than one in ten could read French. There were permanent food shortages.

There was a major rebellion against French rule in 1871, which was brutally crushed, and subsequent periodic revolts, but the modern movement for independence emerged after the First World War when Messali Hadj (then a PCF member in Paris) and others founded the Étoile Nord-Africaine (North African Star) from which subsequent movements for independence developed.

At the end of the Second World War there were hopes of change in French policy, but these were quickly dashed. In May 1945, celebrations of the Allied victory in Sétif, a market town in eastern Algeria, turned into a Muslim rising which was crushed in the most brutal fashion by French troops and settler death squads. Probably at least 15 000 died, though some claim as many as 50 000. Even on the lowest estimate, the Europeans killed 50 Muslims for every European life lost. Many young Algerians came to realise that they could not put their hopes in the French government; Ahmed Ben Bella, who had been decorated for courage in the Second World War, left the French army to devote himself to the nationalist cause. The 1947 Statute established an Algerian Assembly, but the elections in 1948 were blatantly rigged to prevent a pro-independence majority; this served only to make the nationalist forces more determined.

The year of 1954 was one of crisis for French imperialism. Following the catastrophic defeat at Dien Bien Phu in May, France had to withdraw from Indochina after a war lasting eight years. The Algerian nationalists realised that this was a conjuncture of which they could take advantage. But there were divisions within the nationalist leadership. A group of younger militants, impatient with Messali Hadj's leadership and his stress on electoral politics, broke away from the MTLD (Movement for the Triumph of Democratic Liberties) to form the FLN (National Liberation Front).

On 1 November 1954, the FLN launched a wave of synchronised attacks across Algeria, leaving nine dead and a large amount of damage to property. The French government considered them as criminals rather than as a political movement, but the ALN (National Liberation Army) continued to grow, sometimes using intimidation to extend its influence.

As guerrilla struggle spread, the French government was caught up in a process of escalation. The only solution was seen to be the sending of more troops. In 1955, 60 000 reservists were recalled, and 180 000 conscripts ordered to remain with their units. In some places reservists refused to board their trains.

Elections held at the beginning of January 1956 produced a victory for the centre-left alliance known as the Republican Front, and Guy Mollet of the SFIO became Prime Minister. (However, the level of violence in Algeria meant there was no voting there.) The centre-left parties undoubtedly got votes because they seemed to be promising a resolution to the Algerian situation. But when Mollet visited Algiers in February, he was met by a mob of angry settlers who pelted him with tomatoes, furious at any threat to their privileges. Mollet abandoned any attempts at making peace and instead set out to crush the rebellion.

This meant stepping up the repression, and in particular sending more troops; by the end of 1956 there were 450 000 French troops in Algeria. There was considerable resistance by the reservists and conscripts who were sent to Algeria. Officers were attacked, orders were ignored, and on the troop-trains soldiers pulled the brake cords repeatedly. But these revolts got no support from any section of the mainstream left.[4]

In March 1956, the National Assembly voted for 'special powers', which gave Robert Lacoste,[5] the Minister-Resident in Algeria, the right to rule by decree, and transferred police powers to the army, giving it the authority to detain and interrogate suspects. The Communist deputies, more interested in renewing a 'Popular Front' with the SFIO than in backing Algerian independence, voted for the special powers, causing considerable consternation on the left. Meanwhile Tunisia and Morocco gained independence, allowing the French government to concentrate on Algeria.

In October 1956, the French Air Force hijacked a plane carrying Ben Bella and other FLN leaders without government approval, thus sabotaging secret talks between the FLN and the SFIO. But the government was unwilling to confront the armed forces, and the FLN leaders were held in captivity until the end of the war.

In the autumn of 1956 came the Franco-British invasion of Egypt, ostensibly directed at Nasser's nationalisation of the Suez Canal. Mollet's enthusiasm for the action derived largely from his belief that the Algerian rebels were being incited from Cairo — he described the FLN as a 'handful of maniacs and criminals who take their orders from outside Algeria'.[6] The humiliating débâcle did not lead to any lessening of the repression in Algeria and it gave encouragement to the FLN.

In response to the French execution of prisoners, the FLN launched a wave of bombings in Algiers. In 1957, the French army set out to crush, by the most brutal means, the FLN's organisation in the capital. This was the so-called 'Battle of Algiers', depicted in Pontecorvo's movie *The Battle of Algiers* (1966). In military terms this was a major setback for the FLN, but the war continued in the mountains and rural areas, and the Muslim population felt even greater hatred for the French. By now 400 000 French troops were deployed in Algeria.

The French Army was guilty of systematic abuses, in particular torture and the killing of prisoners. By 1957, this was becoming widely known, and there were many protests, not only from the left, but also from Catholics and even a serving officer, Jacques Pâris de la Bollardière. Press censorship and seizure of publications became more common as the French government tried to suppress knowledge of the nature of the repression being exercised. Henri Alleg, a European Communist in Algiers, was tortured, but managed to smuggle out an account of his ordeal; when this was published it rapidly sold 66 000 copies before being banned, after which a further 90 000 were sold clandestinely.[7]

Though the FLN continued its struggle against French rule, the FLN leadership were also determined to have a monopoly over the struggle. Hence they set out to destroy the Mouvement National Algérien (MNA), the organisation of those still loyal to Messali Hadj. The MNA lost most of its support in Algeria after systematic attacks, notably the massacre of 300 villagers at Mélouza.

Mainland France was also important territory for the FLN. In 1954, there were 200 000 Algerian workers in France, and by 1960 350 000. For the FLN they were a vital source of support and especially finance (not always collected voluntarily). It was this money which the 'suitcase carriers' helped to transport. The MNA retained considerable influence among Algerian workers in France, and there were frequent armed clashes between the two organisations in which some 4000 people died in the course of the 'war within a war'.[8]

The tensions in French society produced by the war were too much for the structures of the Fourth Republic. The growing cost of war produced a balance-of-payments crisis. The constitution encouraged a multi-party system in which each successive government was based on a fragile coalition. In 11 years the Republic had had 21 Prime Ministers. In May 1958, there was a military-settler rising in Algeria calling for a de Gaulle government. The Fourth Republic collapsed amidst threats of 'civil war'. General Charles de Gaulle, a veteran right-wing military leader from the Second World War, took over the government at the price of a referendum which established a Fifth Republic with a new constitution, under which he got himself elected as President.

It was initially assumed, by left and right alike, that de Gaulle would be a strong supporter of keeping Algeria French. In June 1958, he visited Algiers and was cheered when he declared: 'I have understood you', though he carefully refrained from using the phrase 'French Algeria'.[9] But de Gaulle and the circle around him were not stupid, and their main aim was to defend the interests of French capitalism, for which the preservation of colonial rule in Algeria was no longer necessary.[10] His position began to evolve. In late 1958, he appealed directly to the FLN, offering a 'peace of the brave' and an amnesty. Then in 1959 he spoke of 'self-determination' and offered Algeria the choice of secession, integration or self-government in close association with France.

The right-wing elements in Algeria who had brought de Gaulle to power now realised they had been betrayed. In January 1960, settlers in Algiers, backed by some elements in the military, staged an insurrection, setting up barricades, but de Gaulle refused any concessions and the revolt collapsed. By showing the divisions between the government and the settlers, the rising gave encouragement to the FLN. Then in April 1961, four generals in Algiers staged a putsch, but de Gaulle called on conscripts to disobey orders, and again the rebellion failed.

Some leading military figures, notably General Salan, went underground to work with the OAS (Secret Army Organisation), a terrorist body that committed atrocities in both Algeria and mainland France, and attempted to kill de Gaulle.

In strictly military terms the FLN was not progressing. After 1957 it had little influence in the cities, and there were serious divisions within the leadership. By 1959, the French army was having considerable success; the National Liberation Army suffered heavy losses and defections, and morale was low.

But at the same time the war was rapidly becoming intolerable to more and more sections of the French population. By March 1959, 71 per cent favoured ceasefire negotiations with the FLN.[11] The number of people involved in direct support for the FLN, the so-called 'suitcase carriers',[12] was small, probably between 500 and a thousand.[13] But they made a considerable impact on public opinion, notably when Francis Jeanson, organiser of the main network, was put on trial in 1960 and sentenced *in absentia*. In September 1960, the Manifesto of the 121[14] was published, signed by a number of leading intellectuals and public figures, declaring support for those who refused to fight and those who 'offer assistance and protection to Algerians oppressed in the name of the French people'. Despite the victimisation of some of the signatories, this again had a significant impact on public opinion. Legal anti-war activities, notably among students, became more widespread.

In October 1961, the FLN called out its supporters for a peaceful demonstration in Paris in breach of the curfew imposed on Algerian workers. They were attacked by police and over 200 were killed, with the encouragement of Paris police chief Maurice Papon.[15] In February 1962, a PCF-led demonstration against the OAS was attacked by police and nine deaths ensued. This led to nationwide strikes and demonstrations.

By 1961, it had been clear that de Gaulle had no alternative to direct negotiations with the FLN. He made various concessions, notably dropping French demands for control of the Sahara. In early 1962, after secret talks, negotiations were held and in March an agreement was signed at Évian, near the Swiss border. This was put to a referendum in April and got 65 per cent support. The OAS launched a final vicious 'scorched earth' campaign of violence and destruction, but was unable to prevent the inevitable. Algeria became fully independent on 5 July 1962. Total French military losses were around 25 000, while some 300 000 Algerians had died.[16]

In September 1962, Ahmed Ben Bella became President, and there were widespread claims that he was taking the regime in a socialist direction, with the establishment of workers' self-management committees. But in 1965, Ben Bella was overthrown by another FLN leader, Houari Boumediène, with no popular opposition; this made clear the central role of the army. The FLN continued to rule the country until the rise of the Islamic Salvation Front led to the civil war of the 1990s.

France meanwhile enjoyed a period of economic growth. The French left was fundamentally transformed by the war. The SFIO went into long-term decline, losing its left wing which helped to form the PSU (Unified Socialist Party). The war had seen the emergence of a significant current to the left of the PCF and the SFIO, and many of the activists who had been radicalised by opposition to the war went on to play leading roles in 1968.

Notes
1. This account draws heavily on the valuable history of the war by M Evans, *Algeria: France's Undeclared War* (Oxford, 2012).
2. Speech in the Chambre des députés, 28 July 1885.
3. R Murray and T Wengraf, 'The Algerian Revolution — I', *New Left Review* I/22, December 1963, p 25.
4. M Evans, 'Mutiny by French Troops During the Algerian War', *Socialist Worker*, 27 May 2006.
5. Robert Lacoste (1898-1989): SFIO deputy for the Dordogne 1945-58, 1962-67; Resident Minister in Algeria from 9 February 1956 to 13 June 1957, then Minister of Algeria from 13 June 1957 to 14 May 1958 [*RH*].
6. Cited in Evans, *Algeria*, p 151.
7. Evans, *Algeria*, p 224; see also I Birchall, 'Algeria: Torture Last Time', *Socialist Review*, February 2008.
8. Evans, *Algeria*, p 217.
9. Evans, *Algeria*, pp 237-38.
10. Some right-wing figures, such as sociologist Raymond Aron and Raymond Cartier, editor of *Paris Match*, had already argued that French capitalism would be better off without an overseas empire.
11. Evans, *Algeria*, p 257.
12. The suitcases generally contained money rather than arms; the suitcase carriers also gave shelter to FLN militants and helped them cross frontiers.
13. Evans, *Algeria*, p 278.
14. It was always known as such, though it had at least 172 signatories.
15. Interview with Jean-Luc Einaudi, *Socialist Worker*, 15 October 2011.
16. Evans, *Algeria*, pp 337-38.

Sylvain Pattieu
THE COMRADES OF THE BROTHERS

Sylvain Pattieu's *Les Camarades des frères* was published in 2002 by Éditions Syllepse, and we thank Pattieu and his publishers for permission to translate. It was the first full history of the role of Trotskyists and anarchists in solidarity with the Algerian liberation struggle, based on the far-left press, internal documents and other material from public and private archives, and on interviews with a number of the key participants.

As Pattieu shows, the French far left in the 1950s was small and isolated, yet both in its understanding of events and in its practical contribution to the struggle, it was not insignificant. As historian and former FLN activist Mohamed Harbi wrote in the preface:

> On the far left only the libertarians and the Trotskyists recognised the events of 1 November [1954] as the start of a war and showed themselves to be ready to respond to it in the name of the principles of universal socialism, in the name of internationalism.

Pattieu's book consists of an Introduction, 10 Chapters, a Conclusion and some documents. We have translated in full Chapters III to VI, and the Conclusion. The other sections are summarised. Pattieu's notes are translated; additional notes by *Revolutionary History* are marked [*RH*]. Biographical notes on key individuals are taken from Pattieu's Biographical Notes; in a few cases dates of birth and/or death have been added.

* * *

Introduction

The Algerian war had a profound impact on French political life. On the left, Guy Mollet of the Socialist Party (SFIO) was the agent of repression, while the Communist Party (PCF) failed to live up to its traditions of opposing colonialism and imperialism. On the right, Gaullism emerged as a major current.

Meanwhile a New Left emerged from the opposition to the war. This included progressive Christians, many of whom went to the Parti socialiste unifié (PSU).

However, in the many works devoted to this subject, the Trotskyists and anarchists are often forgotten.

'Why should we take an interest in such small groups? First of all because the far left constitutes a true laboratory of ideas and theories, of education and practice. But it also had its own activity, and its results were sometimes disproportionate to its numerical size. The far left worked underground, its activity was sometimes subterranean, but that did not prevent it appearing on the surface. During the Algerian war it accumulated forces which would become fully visible at the end of the following decade, before and after May 1968, but this composite tendency survived the years of decline after the end of the leftist wave, and today in France it still represents a force which is certainly a minority but whose existence is established.'

This book puts most emphasis on the Fourth International, which took solidarity with the FLN furthest, and survived repression until the end of the war. It benefitted from having international support, and from choosing to back the FLN and not its rival, the MNA.

The book draws on very valuable interviews with activists. Written archives are unfortunately incomplete, and it has not been possible to consult police files. Hence this study is not exhaustive and some questions remain open.

Chapter I: A Colonial War

The year of 1954 saw two major events marking the end of France's colonial empire: the defeat at Dien Bien Phu and the outbreak of the Algerian war. It was also a period of economic prosperity and cultural change in music and the cinema. Initially the French press did not pay much attention to events in Algeria, and most of the population of mainland France took little interest in Algeria.

After Messali Hadj's Étoile nord-africaine was dissolved by the Popular Front, Messali formed the Parti populaire algérient (PPA — Algerian Popular Party). Following the massacres at Sétif and elsewhere in May 1945, a current in the PPA began to look to armed struggle. Massive impoverishment and unemployment in the indigenous population made French rule increasingly unpopular.

The PPA now became the Mouvement pour le triomphe des libertés démocratiques (MTLD — Movement for the Triumph of Democratic Liberties), but this was deeply divided. A moderate group known as the 'centralists' took over the central committee and put Messali into a minority. In March 1954, Boudiaf and other leaders formed the Comité révolutionnaire d'unité et d'action (CRUA — Revolutionary Committee of Unity and Action). In the summer of 1954, the MTLD split, with Messali's supporters expelling the CRUA, while the centralists held a separate congress. The CRUA leaders then formed the FLN and the National Liberation Army (ALN), which initially had less than 700 fighting men.

Neither Messali's followers nor the French state took the actions of 1 November 1954 very seriously. 'Only the Trotskyist and anarchist press believed the insurrection would endure and spread.' The PCF, on the other hand, failed to respond. Although the PCF had campaigned vigorously against the Rif war in the 1920s, and had taken a radical position on the Indochina war from 1947 onwards, its position on Algerian independence had always been ambiguous, calling for reforms rather than national independence. The PCF was distrustful of the FLN, which it did not control, and sought to reconcile the different sections of the population in Algeria. As François Billoux put it at a Central Committee meeting in 1956:

> In Algeria there are a million Europeans who were born in this country, who have lived there for generations, and the majority of whom consider Algeria as their homeland: this makes Algeria a special case… and requires us to find a solution that is specific to Algeria by taking account of the legitimate interests of all its inhabitants of different origins.

The SFIO was divided between those who supported a repressive colonial policy and those opposed to it. In this situation a left outside the PCF and SFIO began to emerge, with the foundation in 1955 of the Mouvement Uni de la Nouvelle Gauche (United Movement of the New Left). Among its leading figures were former Trotskyists such as Yvan Craipeau and Pierre Naville.

Repression was stepped up in 1955 and there were already reports of torture by the French authorities. The ALN grew stronger and the peasantry became active in the war. In the election campaign of December 1955, Guy Mollet described the war as 'an imbecile dead-end', but as Prime Minister in 1956 he intensified the repression. Despite French success in the 'Battle of Algiers', the war led to the fall of the Fourth Republic. De Gaulle's moves to end the war soon lost him the support of the far right in Algeria, but the anti-war movement grew, and in 1962 the Évian agreements gave independence to Algeria.

Chapter II: The Far Left in the 1950s

The far left is defined as that part of the left outside the national political consensus of republicanism and parliamentary democracy. The Communist Party, which remained within that consensus, exercised almost total hegemony, so that the far left was a tiny minority. In the period of the Algerian war the Trotskyist current had little more than a hundred activists throughout France, while the anarchist Fédération communiste libertaire (FCL) had two to three hundred. The far left had some support among intellectuals, but much less among workers. Those Trotskyists doing entry work in the PCF had to conceal their identity while still trying to recruit.

Moreover the far left was divided, with both Trotskyists and anarchists being split. The French Trotskyists had split in 1952, when Michel Raptis (Pablo) had put forward the perspective that 'capitalism is now moving rapidly towards war because it has no other way out in the short or medium term'. Revolutionaries would therefore have to defend the USSR in a process of 'war–revolution'. The majority of the French section of the Fourth International accused Pablo and the leaders of the FI of being 'revisionists and pro-Stalinist liquidators'. In France the Fourth International advocated clandestine entry into the Communist Party.[1] The majority of the French section refused to accept this, and went on publishing *La Vérité*, while the minority led by Pierre Frank produced *La Vérité des travailleurs*. There were thus two rival organisations, both called Parti communiste internationaliste (PCI).

Alongside these, *Voix ouvrière* had a very workerist orientation and scarcely existed during the Algerian war; *Socialisme ou barbarie*, which had come out of the Trotskyist movement, was more oriented to theoretical debate than to practical activity.

The Fédération anarchiste (FA), reconstituted in 1945, had a paper which in the 1940s sold between 20 000 and 30 000 copies. It was significantly influenced by a number of Spanish exiles. It too expected world war in the near future, but opposed East and West equally.

In 1953, the Fédération anarchiste changed its name to the Fédération communiste libertaire; a leading figure, Georges Fontenis, advocated working-class anarchism and the need for structured organisation. Those who opposed him revived the name Fédération anarchiste, and won the support of well-known singers Georges Brassens and Léo Ferré. The FCL's membership tended to be largely workers and teachers, while the FA consisted mainly of the self-employed.

Thus the far left was isolated, sectarian and inward-looking. Entrism carried the risk of loss of identity, but the only alternative seemed to be a purely declamatory denunciation of society. At the start of the Algerian war the far left's prospects seemed very poor.

Notes
1. For more on this, see Ian Birchall, 'Nineteen Fifty-Six and the French Left', *Revolutionary History*, Volume 9, no 3 [*RH*].

Chapter III: In Face of the FLN

The November 1954 insurrection was just as much a surprise for the far left as it was for the government. But with this significant difference, that for revolutionary activists it was a pleasing surprise, since they had long supported the demands for independence of the various colonies, and of the 'exploited' and 'oppressed' colonial peoples. And according to the principle of 'revolutionary defeatism', any blow struck against 'imperialism' in one's own country could only help to advance the revolution there. For all these reasons links between the far-left organisations and the independence movements developed.

The Fourth International was particularly concerned with this support for colonial liberation movements. But the national liberation struggles, whether in Vietnam, Algeria or elsewhere, were not led by Trotskyists, but by nationalists, or even by Communists supported by the USSR. The Fourth International's position was very clear:

> Our sections in the metropolitan imperialist countries and in all capitalist countries have a duty actively to defend the struggle for freedom from imperialism by the colonial peoples, even in cases where this struggle is led by nationalist and bourgeois-democratic elements.[1]

The Fourth International's position was not merely a statement of principle. The colonial question was one of its main concerns, and two issues of the journal *Quatrième Internationale* had been devoted to it as early as June and September 1945. Besides an 'Appeal to the dockers of Marseille and the French railway workers not to transport war equipment', these issues contained some very radical slogans: 'Not a soldier, not a gun against the colonial peoples'; 'Long live the colonial revolution!'; 'Total and immediate independence for all the colonies'. The PCI[2] developed these slogans and demanded independence for Algeria in 1945; it spoke out against the bombardments of Haiphong,[3] and it organised a protest meeting at the salle Wagram in Paris. The meeting was banned by the Interior Minister Édouard Depreux,[4] and three Trotskyists were injured during confrontations with the police during a demonstration which marched on the hall, led by Yvan Craipeau[5] and Messali Hadj.[6] The secretaries of the organisation were prosecuted for 'threatening the morale of the army and the nation' because of a poster opposing the Indochina war. The Trotskyists also ran an anti-colonialist campaign in various unions such as the FEN[7] and the CGT.[8] Thus a Trotskyist involved in trade-union activity, Dumont,[9] spoke in support of independence for the colonies at the national congress of the CGT in 1948. The Trotskyists also put their efforts into various committees, such as those set up to campaign for the release of Henri Martin.[10]

Finally, there were numerous connections between Trotskyist activists and militants from the colonial countries. These connections resulted from the fact that the Vietnamese Trotskyists, before being eliminated by the repression of the French authorities and then of Ho Chi Minh, had a certain influence, not only in Indochina, but also among Vietnamese immigrants in France. Jean-René Chauvin,[11] who was responsible for colonial matters in the PCI in 1947 and 1948 tells how, when he was called up into the army in 1940, he found himself in Agen after the armistice[12] and was friendly with the staff of a company of Vietnamese workers. When he spoke to them of Ta Thu Thau,[13] one of the Trotskyist leaders of the Vietnamese independence movement, he immediately won their sympathy.[14] Henri Benoîts,[15] a PCI militant from 1944, recalls how he became an internationalist at the time of the revolts by Vietnamese, who had been called up into the army in 1939, and then sent to the Sainte-Livrade camp in the Dordogne, and who in 1945 were demanding the right to go home. He demonstrated with them on May Day 1945, demanding independence for Indochina.[16]

Such connections also existed with Algerian pro-independence activists, but for different reasons, since there were no Algerian Trotskyists — or very few. But the presence of a large number of Algerian immigrants in France made it possible to have links with the MTLD.[17] So it was a case of links between the two organisations, but also of personal connections and indeed of connections between leaders. It was in the factory that Henri Benoîts met militants. He fought alongside them in the CGT and he was thus very sensitive to their demands for independence. Moreover, he worked with representatives of all the tendencies of the nationalist movement as well as with Algerians who were members of the French Communist Party (PCF). The workers' delegate[18] who was most widely known and most representative of the Algerians in the factory was a centralist[19] who worked in the foundry; he was arrested at the outbreak of the insurrection and interned in Algeria.[20] As for the leaders, Pierre Lambert[21] and Daniel Renard[22] knew Messali Hadj and had, for example, already sheltered him at the home of Annie Renard-Cardinal, Daniel Renard's wife, when he made a clandestine visit to mainland France.[23]

However, the far left was not well informed about the differences within the Algerian nationalist movement, and if activists more or less understood the divisions between centralist 'moderates' and Messalist[24] 'radicals', the formation of the CRUA[25] passed them by completely. In the summer of 1954, Jean-René Chauvin travelled in Algeria with his partner Jenny Plocki,[26] who was close to Cornélius Castoriadis and the Socialisme ou Barbarie group.[27] Though they had both left the PCI a few years earlier, Jean-René Chauvin had been responsible for the party's colonial commission and he had maintained contact with some

MTLD militants, in particular with Ahmed Mezerna, known as 'Lamine', who was one of Messali Hadj's lieutenants, and who had given him addresses where they could stay throughout the country. Their journey was tourism, but also political inasmuch as the two travellers were interested in Algeria. Jean-René and his partner soon observed in the course of their journey that the MTLD was using different rhetorics in different towns, and that although there was a shared sense of hospitality there were deep differences amongst the nationalist militants. But it was only when they returned to Paris that they learned of the split in the MTLD.[28]

To metropolitan eyes, even for Trotskyists who were well used to splits and all too familiar with the subtleties of congress documents, the internal political life of the Algerian nationalist movement was quite difficult to grasp. But the far left was unanimous on one point: both PCIs, the FCL, the FA and even the various groups and individuals who represented what was in process of organising itself as the 'New Left', all condemned with one voice the repression against Algerian militants. But this principled position in no way implied an opinion on the insurrection itself: should they support this new and unknown 'FLN' which was apparently conducting the operations? What action should they carry out in mainland France to persuade people of the demand, backed only by a tiny minority, of 'independence for Algeria'? Should they even adopt this slogan?

Moreover, for the far left as for other political forces, the Algerian war did not appear at the outset to be the founding event of a new political line-up in France. Support was therefore not immediately perceived as a priority even by the tendencies which subsequently would be most active. Thus in an internal report to the PCI in November 1954, Michel Raptis (Pablo),[29] one of the main leaders of the Fourth International and the person behind the first support networks for the FLN, declared that a 'new chapter has been opened in the struggle for the emancipation of these countries' and that this emancipation 'could no longer be blocked'.[30] But if he thus seemed to have understood in an almost prophetic manner the significance of the events of All Saints Day[31] in opening a new stage for the Algerian people, if he seemed to have correctly grasped the inability of the old empires to do anything but delay the inevitable moment of decolonisation, he nonetheless asserted that 'the struggle against German rearmament… will be the main political struggle for the whole European proletariat in the coming months'.

But the far left quite quickly took a firm position. On the concrete question of support for the FLN and the movement which was emerging in Algeria, there were widely diverging positions. For in fact if the whole of the far left could agree to condemn repression by a 'bourgeois' state whose authority it did not recognise, it was more difficult to situate itself in relation to the FLN: the organisation was unknown, its programme and its aims were clearly nationalist, and the reference to 'Islamic principles' in the FLN's original declaration seemed repellent to the atheist mentalities of most far-left militants. So political reticence with regard to the FLN was not at all on the same basis as that of majority of the population and the mainstream political forces: there was no attachment to the 'integrity' of the French nation,[32] no belief that 'Algeria is France', but there was suspicion about the authentically progressive character of the Algerian revolution.

Hence the FA refused to take any other position than to condemn the repression. In its view the real conflict was not between colonisers and colonised but between rich and poor: the FLN and the French state were thus lumped together. Looking back on the war, Maurice Joyeux,[33] leader of the FA during this period, wrote in 1988:

> The Algerian war was an episode based on the opposition between two bourgeoisies, the native bourgeoisie and the colonial bourgeoisie; certainly we had to fight to put an end to this war, which could provide an argument for the revolutionary struggle in the metropolis, but for Algeria freed from colonialism we had to reject the intermediate period that would bring the social problem back to its starting-point. The struggle against the war waged by colonialism in Algeria should under no circumstances have become a fight for the victory of the FLN, a bourgeois nationalist organisation which would take responsibility for the exploitation of the Algerian population, whose sons would have died for nothing, for the pleasure of acquiring a new master.[34]

Maurice Fayolle,[35] responsible for dealing with the Algerian question, expressed the position of the FA, which it would hold throughout the war, in the December 1954 issue of a monthly anarchist journal, *Défense de l'homme*:

> We are the only ones who can say it in a free journal: yes, those who today are shedding blood in North Africa as they did yesterday in Indochina are criminals. Yes, those who hope to maintain the French presence in North Africa through massive reinforcements of riot police and parachutists and through police manhunts are dangerous madmen. But we also say to the North African proletarians: we follow your struggles with sympathy, for we shall always be on the side of the oppressed against the oppressors; but beware: don't make a futile sacrifice of your new forces in pointless battles. You have better things to do than fight to change masters. Better things to do than fighting to replace the Gospels with the Koran. Going beyond racial prejudices, nationalist mirages and religious lies, the anarchists fraternally

invite you to join them in the only valid struggle: the struggle which aims to liberate all men — those of the colonised peoples and of the colonising peoples — from all exploitations and all tyrannies.[36]

There was a glaring discrepancy between the theoretical position defended in the article and the concrete struggles unfolding in Algeria. In practice it led to neutrality, certainly coloured with goodwill towards the 'North African proletarians', but the refusal to takes sides between the Algerian nationalists and the French state ended up, in short, with impotence: by being so anxious to stand 'above' they ended up 'outside'. Distrust, in some ways justified, towards the FLN became more important than 'internationalist solidarity'. This current of the far left was thus free from any illusions about the Algerian revolution, but was condemned to passivity throughout the entire Algerian war, and moreover was only slightly affected by repression, in any case not before 1957.

But when the other tendencies of far left had agreed to support the Algerian revolution, certain problems remained. There were two organisations claiming to lead this revolution, two rival groups whose differences were settled in insults and in blood: Messali Hadj's MNA, which had refused to recognise the authority of the FLN, and this same FLN which was hitherto unknown. How should support be organised? Should it consist of political support, propaganda directed at French public opinion to persuade it that the demands for independence were justified, an attempt to unite a part of the left, a part of the labour movement around progressive positions about Algeria and around the struggle against repression as far as France was concerned? Or was it possible to give concrete assistance to the Algerian revolution even if that meant crossing the boundary of illegality with all the dangers that involved?

The choice between the FLN and the MNA was difficult for French activists who did not always understand the reasons for the split. Several factors were involved, among which were the analysis of the political relations of forces and the analysis of each of the nationalist organisations, but also personal links with the Algerian militants.

The 'Lambertist' PCI adopted the most clear-cut position, not without causing problems within its own ranks. Leaders such as Lambert and Renard had known Messali Hadj for a long time, and at the time of the 1952 split they were the ones who maintained privileged relations with the 'historic' leader of the nationalists. Moreover, they represented his main base of support in France and were regularly in contact with him when he was under house arrest at Niort. And members of the 'Lambertist' PCI, organised in a 'Zimmerwald circle', were in contact with him.[37] In addition, the PCI ran a campaign for his release and took part in the demonstrations organised in mainland France by the MTLD.

And its press openly sided against the centralist faction of the MTLD and with the supporters of Messali Hadj who had created the MNA.

Some days after the All Saints Day insurrection, *La Vérité* headlined 'Not Another Dirty War!', and dealt with the Algerian question at length.[38] The centralists were sharply criticised while Lambert drew a hagiographical portrait of Messali Hadj. Support for the MNA was almost unconditional: a political note dated 23 November 1954 praised the 'firmness of class politics of the PPA leader Messali Hadj' and stressed the 'proletarian social composition of this organisation'.[39] Thus the PPA was a 'revolutionary proletarian party' in function of two criteria: its 'programme' and its 'social composition'.

This analysis was extended to the MNA and henceforth for the Lambertists the situation was clear: the Algerian revolution had a good chance of success because 'to defeat the Algerian independence fighters it will take a long time and a lot of soldiers'; the leadership of this revolution, which did not merely oppose colonised to colonisers, but was also based on the main contradiction between workers and bourgeois, fell to the MNA, an authentic proletarian organisation according to Bolshevik principles. Moreover a political resolution from 1954[40] spoke of 'the sole existing party, the PPA'; it was necessary to have a better 'understanding' of it and to go along with its 'evolution'; under these conditions any other organisation, such as the FLN, which might claim to be leading the revolution, could only be the enemy of the revolution and thus an instrument of the bourgeoisie. Hence denunciation of the FLN was a constant feature in the Lambertist position. The only FLN leader supported by this group was Ben Boulaïd, responsible for the Aurès region; through the Committee for the Release of Messali Hadj, in which the PCI was very influential, a petition for intellectuals was launched after the Algerian militant's trial, to campaign against the death sentence passed on him.[41] But Ben Boulaïd had remained close to Messali Hadj, and his relations with the FLN were so ambiguous that some people have even put forward the idea that he was murdered by the FLN. At all events the FLN played no part in the defence of Ben Boulaïd and this campaign was run by the MNA alone.[42]

There were three main themes in the denunciation of the FLN. The representative nature of the FLN was constantly undervalued in favour of the MNA; thus *La Vérité* claimed the MNA had the majority of the resistance forces, basing itself, for example, in May 1956 on reports by the journalist Claude Gérard in order to claim that a 'large number of independence fighters support Messali Hadj and the MNA and not the FLN controlled from Cairo'.[43] Suspicion was thrown on the FLN, so that in November 1955 Pierre Lambert could write that 'it is the French government's preferred negotiating partner' because 'the military operations of the FLN complement the political manoeuvres of the

French'.[44] Finally they denounced the conduct of the 'FLN killers'.[45]

So, for the Lambert PCI, the task was to support the MNA, but also to keep an eye on its authentically 'proletarian' orientation and to 'link together the revolution in Algeria and the revolution in France';[46] thus for Pierre Lambert the Algerian revolution could set in motion the revolution in France.

Some of the militants, around Michel Lequenne[47] and Marcel Favre-Bleibtreu,[48] challenged what they saw as unacceptable interference in the internal divisions of the Algerian nationalist movement.[49] In disagreement with Lambert on other questions, such as the analysis of the USSR, they did not believe that the Algerian revolution could be led by the Messalists alone and they preferred to work for the reconciliation of the different tendencies of the MTLD. They did in fact meet some of the leaders of the MTLD, which had been dissolved, for which they were sharply criticised by Lambert, who saw this as a serious breach of party discipline. The Bolshevik-Leninist Tendency (TBL) led by Lequenne and Favre-Bleibtreu did not want unconditional support for the MNA and put the emphasis on critical support.

Lambert expelled them in February 1955 for a further breach of discipline: the pretext for this expulsion was the questioning by the police of Lucien Rontanelle, managing editor of *La Vérité*, and of Michel Lequenne and Marcel Favre-Bleibtreu, members of the editorial board, about an unsigned editorial on Algeria in January 1955. Contrary to the decision of the Political Bureau of the organisation, they attended the interview and hence were expelled: the other members of the tendency followed them, and 15 to 20 militants left the PCI.

The Frank PCI adopted a more prudent attitude and took care not to side wholeheartedly with either of the nationalist organisations at the expense of the other. The privileged contacts with Messali Hadj were mainly with the Lambertists, and if the Frank PCI maintained contacts with militants from the dissolved MTLD, its members often found it hard to distinguish who was in the FLN and who belonged to the MNA, especially because every day cadres of the MTLD were going over to the FLN.[50] So to begin with the PCI supported the struggle of the Algerian people without giving support to any particular organisation, and opposed the repression while its members made contact with the Algerian militants that they knew. They tried to understand what was going on and what was represented by this FLN which had taken the initiative in the insurrection. Realising that the FLN was the real leadership of the revolution in Algeria, they henceforth gave preference to contacts with the organisation without thereby anathematising the MNA.[51]

It was certainly difficult to make contact with an organisation which did not have and had never had any legal existence. However, the problem was easier to deal with than it might seem because the cadres of the FLN were very often former cadres of the MTLD known as such by the Trotskyists militants: there were solid contacts after years of joint work, and the main difficulty was in distinguishing between the pro-FLN, the pro-MNA and the former centralists, who, moreover, were all affected by the repression which was indifferent to the finer points of Algerian nationalism.

So if priority was given to contacts with the FLN, it was for pragmatic and not ideological reasons: the PCI and the Fourth International fairly rapidly analysed the FLN as being the organisation that was leading the Algerian revolution. Thereupon the nature of the party, its social composition, the main lines of its programme and its organisation did not matter so much: these considerations were pushed into the background and the only thing that mattered was concrete action for independence and above all against French imperialism. This 'pragmatic' position, this support 'for those who are fighting', was totally opposed to the approach of the 'hostile brothers' of the other PCI and merely sharpened the tensions between the two organisations. But the Frank PCI managed to avoid the danger of exclusive support for one of the nationalist organisations and thus kept for itself room for manoeuvre by refusing to choose 'on behalf of the Algerian people'. However, the division of the Algerian nationalist movement was a fact of life which the militants of the Fourth International regretted and which could even cause them certain problems when they had good relations with both sides. This was the case with Henri Benoîts in the Renault factory who defended both an MNA militant who had been injured because he refused to pay a contribution to the FLN, and an Algerian in Force ouvrière[52] who was threatened for the same reasons.[53]

The FCL was active in supporting the MNA and Messali Hadj; adopting the same approach as the Trotskyists of the Frank PCI, it did not condemn the FLN. The specific situation of the FCL is that it was affiliated to the Libertarian Communist International (ICL), and so was in contact with a sister organisation, the North African Libertarian Movement (MLNA), founded in Algiers in 1954 and led by a man called Doukhan[54] who had been met by the French libertarian leaders through the youth hostel movement.[55] So *Le Libertaire* (no 403, 4 November 1954) declared its support for the Algerian revolution by asserting that the population was behind the insurgents,[56] which at the time was not wholly true, but anticipated the future situation, and declared that the MLNA was joining the struggle against colonialism. Certain anarcho-syndicalists in the CNT[57] came to the same position and published the following appeal in *Le Libertaire*, no 406, dated 25 November 1955:

> We should not lump together imperialism and the demands of the colonised peoples, but on the contrary we should, following Bakunin's example, be

in solidarity with the subject people, against the imperialisms... even if the desire for emancipation on the part of these peoples assumes, in some cases, a national character which will only be transient.[58]

The FCL supported the MNLA, but this organisation with limited influence could not aspire to lead the Algerian revolution and it remained a small component of the movement. So concretely it was the MNA to which the FCL gave its main political support, and press releases from this organisation were published regularly in *Le Libertaire*.[59] In no 432 on 26 May 1955, a special box inset was even devoted to Messali Hadj's birthday, and the National Committee of the FCL 'in the name of French revolutionary workers' addressed its 'fraternal revolutionary greetings' to the Algerian leader.[60] On 26 June 1955 in no 436, the contents of a discussion between Messali Hadj and Georges Fontenis[61] in a hotel near Angoulême were reported in an article headlined 'Messali Hadj Hails Our Struggle'. The MNA leader was presented in it as 'one of the most clear-sighted revolutionary fighters of the age'.[62]

Thus the FCL gave critical support to the MNA, though to a reader of *Le Libertaire* the support was more visible than the criticisms: the dynamic of struggle and hope engendered by the Algerian revolution and opposition to repression tended to lead to such support for the 'comrades' rather than to any criticism. At the same time, the presence in the FCL of Algerians living in mainland France, who were closer to the FLN,[63] preserved the FCL from making too final a judgement about the FLN. The FCL's support for the MNA was much more pragmatic than that of the Lambertist PCI: there was no definitive commitment to an organisation and no 'monopoly of solidarity'. However, because they had the same position of support for the MNA, the two organisations often found themselves side by side, notably in the Committees for the Release of Messali Hadj, of which they constituted two of the main political components.

There were thus three different attitudes on the part of the far-left organisations at the beginning of the Algerian war. The first was that of the FA, which in the name of sacrosanct 'principles' put the 'two nationalisms' of the Algerians and the French on the same level, and which despite opposing the repression in the end refused to take sides and condemned itself to a position of mere observation and revolutionary incantations. To a lesser degree, taking account of the fact that it scarcely existed as an organisation and that its means of action were in any event limited, this was also the position of the Trotskyist group *Voix ouvrière*.[64] The second attitude was that of the Lambertist Trotskyists, who supported almost unconditionally one of the Algerian nationalist organisations, the MNA, taking sides in the internal rivalries of the Algerian nationalist camp, and considering Messali Hadj's party as a proletarian party on Bolshevik-Leninist lines, thus applying preconceived schemas to a more complex reality. The third attitude was that of the Frank PCI and the FCL, both of which gave their main support to one of the nationalist organisations but without cutting themselves off irrevocably from the other. If the Trotskyists were perceptive enough to understand that it was the FLN, despite its small level of influence on immigrant workers in mainland France, which was leading the revolution in Algeria, the FCL was able to adopt a position of support for the MNA while still preserving a certain degree of flexibility, that is, without definitively condemning the FLN.

These choices indicate not merely different political and tactical estimates of the situation, but also different approaches and a greater or lesser flexibility not only in the application of revolutionary principles, whether based on Trotskyism, Marxism or anarchism, but also in the position to be adopted in face of a concrete situation. If the analyses were in opposition to each other, it was because these analyses were oriented by forms of militant activity which were themselves also different: we are therefore dealing with far-left organisations which did not share the same concept of articulation between theory and practice. These divergent analyses and practices allow us, in retrospect, to understand better the deep causes of the various splits which took place in the early 1950s. The various divergences become fully coherent when they are studied in the light of the reactions to the Algerian insurrection of 1954. The 'purists', the FA and the Lambert PCI, took positions in which principles, whether anti-authoritarian or Bolshevik-Leninist, were turned into dogma, while the 'pragmatists' took greater account of concrete elements and a certain political reality. The FCL supported a struggle although it was 'nationalist', and the Frank PCI supported the FLN, which was certainly not a Bolshevik or even a Marxist organisation. However, even if these positions are labelled as 'pragmatic', they were nonetheless faithful to certain principles, and they still had their share of illusions and disappointed hopes. Now, in order to understand them better, we have to look at the way these positions were taken up concretely by the different organisations, and how the support for Algerian independence shown by three of them was put into practice, as well as the reactions it provoked from the authorities.

Notes
1. International Conference of the Fourth International, April 1946, quoted in *La Question coloniale et la section française de la 4ᵉ Internationale* (François Maspero, undated), archive O Col 1615 at the BDIC at Nanterre. This is one of the 'Cahiers rouges' training pamphlets published by the Ligue communiste révolutionnaire, the later name of the PCI.
2. Parti communiste internationaliste. See summary of Chapter Two above [*RH*].

3. The shelling of Haiphong by French ships on 23 November 1946 marked the beginning of the Indochina War [*RH*].
4. Édouard Depreux (1898-1981): SFIO politician, later national secretary of the PSU [*RH*].
5. Yvan Craipeau (Auger, Francis, Car, 1911-2001): Trotsky's secretary in 1933, a Fourth International militant from its foundation in 1938, he led one of the Trotskyist groups during the the Second World War. He left the PCI in 1947 because he disapproved of the lack of openness in the organisation. A philosophy teacher, he was transferred to Guadeloupe and joined the New Left on his return to France in 1954. He later played an important role on the left wing of the PSU, where he defended the demand for Algerian independence.
6. Y Craipeau, *Mémoires d'un dinosaure trotskyste* (Paris, 1999), p 191.
7. Fédération de l'enseignement national, the main teachers' union. When the CGT split in 1948, it retained its autonomy from both federations [*RH*].
8. Confédération générale du travail, largest of the French union federations, at this time effectively controlled by the PCF [*RH*].
9. Probably René Dumont, a librarian (not to be confused with the ecologist René Dumont), later a Lambertist [*RH*].
10. Henri Martin (b 1927): a French Communist sailor imprisoned in 1950 for distributing leaflets against the Indochina War. There was a major public campaign around his case [*RH*].
11. Jean-René Chauvin (1918-2011): Trotskyist militant since the 1930s. During the Second World War he was deported for his anti-Nazi activities to Auschwitz and other camps. He left the Fourth International for the New Left and later was active in the Revolutionary Marxist tendency of the PSU. See also I Birchall, 'Death of an Internationalist', *Socialist Review*, April 2011 [*RH*].
12. The armistice signed on 22 June 1940 established the German Occupation of Northern France. [*RH*]
13. Ta Thu Thau (1906-1945): Vietnamese Trotskyist leader murdered by Stalinists. See Al Richardson (ed), *The Revolution Defamed: A Documentary History of Vietnamese Trotskyism* (Socialist Platform, London, 2003) [*RH*].
14. Interview with Jean-René Chauvin, Paris, 8 February 2000.
15. Henri Benoîts (b 1926): industrial draughtsman at Renault, member of the CGT, member of the Fourth International since the end of the Second World War, he took part in campaigns against the Indochina war. He was one of those in charge of assistance to the FLN in the PCI. He also gave constant support throughout the war to Algerian militants in his factory at Renault-Billancourt. With his wife Clara he was a witness of the savage repression against the peaceful demonstration organised by the FLN on 17 October 1961. Now retired.
16. Interview with Henri Benoîts, Issy-les-Moulineaux, 7 February 2000.
17. Movement for the Triumph of Democratic Liberties, formed 1946 as the electoral wing of the Party of the Algerian People (PPA) [*RH*].
18. In French workplaces staff delegates are elected and have certain legally defined roles [*RH*].
19. The name given to members of the PPA Central Committee who opposed what they saw as Messali Hadj's dictatorial style of leadership [*RH*].

20. Interview with Henri Benoîts, 7 February 2000; interview with Clara and Henri Benoîts (1993-94), 'The Algerian War Seen from Renault-Billancourt', in *Expression immigré(e)s-français(es)*, journal of the FASTI (Federation for Aid and Solidarity with Immigrant Workers), Paris, no 74, October 1993 and no 76, April 1994. [This interview is translated in full in Section 4 below —*RH.*]
21. Pierre Lambert (Pierre Boussel, 1920-2008): leader of the French Trotskyist group expelled from the Fourth International in 1952; until 1958 he gave consistent support to the MNA leader Messali Hadj. A candidate in the 1988 presidential election, he then became leader of the Parti des travailleurs (PT). [See obituary in *Revolutionary History*, Volume 10, no 1 — *RH.*]
22. Daniel Renard (1925-1988): Renault worker during the 1947 strike, leading ally of Lambert after the 1952 split [*RH*].
23. Interview with Michel Lequenne, Paris, 18 November 1999.
24. Followers of veteran nationalist leader Messali Hadj (1898-1974); see article on the MNA in Section 4 below [*RH*].
25. Revolutionary Committee of Unity and Action, from which the FLN was formed; see summary of Chapter 1 [*RH*].
26. Jenny Plocki (b 1925): of Jewish Polish origin, she was 15 when she was taken, with her parents and her 14-year-old brother, to the Vel' d'Hiv stadium during the round-up of Jews. She and her brother had French nationality and so they were released, but their parents died while deported. At the Liberation she joined the PCI, but left it quite soon because of disagreements about the nature of the USSR. She then joined the Socialisme ou Barbarie group. Now retired.
27. A 1949 split from the PCI which rejected Leninism and the workers' state analysis of Russia. See the article on Socialisme ou Barbarie in Section 3 below [*RH*].
28. Interview with Jean René Chauvin and Jenny Plocki, Paris, 8 February 2000.
29. Mikhalis Raptis (Michel Pablo, Speros, Gabriel, Pilar, Molitor, Jérôme, Jean-Paul Martin, Marat, Mike, Abdelkrim, Vallin, 1911-1996): born in Egypt in 1911, he went to Greece in 1916. Worked as an engineer after studying at the Athens Polytechnic; he became a Marxist in 1928 in a clandestine group. Arrested and tortured by the police in 1936 at the time of the Metaxas coup, he was expelled from Greece with his partner Hélène in 1937. Close to the Greek Trotskyist leader Pantelis Poulioupolos, he represented him at the founding congress of the Fourth International in 1938. Raptis lived in France during the Second World War, and was involved with one of the Trotskyist groups that published a paper addressed to German soldiers, *Arbeiter und Soldat*. But the German soldiers won over to Trotskyism were shot, as were some of the French organisers, and Raptis had to go into hiding. Organiser of the unification of the French groups at the end of the war, he was elected Secretary of the Fourth International in 1946 and held this position until 1960. He was one of the theoreticians of the organisation. The main organiser of Fourth International support for the FLN during the Algerian war, he was jailed for 15 months in 1961 for his activities. After independence he moved to Algeria and became an adviser to Ben Bella's government until Boumediène's coup in 1965. Expelled from the Fourth International in 1965, he and his supporters founded the TMRI IV (Revolutionary-Marxist Tendency of the Fourth International), which became the TMRI. Before 1968 he was one of

the theoreticians of workers' management along with Daniel Guérin. He took part in May 1968 in Paris although he was banned from French territory, and insisted on the importance of new social movements (blacks, women, students). He settled in Greece from 1974 and became a well-known journalist. Around 1990 he renewed his links with the Fourth International, which he considered to be the only framework able to bring together 'critical Marxists'. He opposed the Gulf War against Iraq and denounced the break-up of Yugoslavia. But in his home country he was also involved in the defence of Turkish families threatened with expulsion and of homosexual prostitutes. He died in February 1996.

30. Document Fo (Rés 137...), BDIC archives, Nanterre.
31. 1 November, the day the FLN insurrection started [*RH*].
32. The testimony of Henri Benoîts, in a letter written in 1979 at the request of his 'Algerian comrades' to explain the reasons for his commitment during the Algerian war, and kept in his personal archives, is revealing from this point of view: 'Class feeling must have precedence over national feeling. This war of Algerians against the colonial system, and not against French people, was therefore profoundly in tune with such aims. It fitted more generally with the struggle of all oppressed peoples who, since the end of the Second World War, had risen up against the domination of imperialisms in general, and mine in particular, which was committed to defending the remnants of the colonial empire. Since the class struggle has a universal content it seemed to me that the natural application of consistent internationalism was to support this struggle. So I didn't have any uneasiness or anguish when I had to commit myself. The ideals of my youth, my Marxist training based on Lenin and Trotsky, helped me to rise above the academic debates juxtaposing mass action to individual action. By definition, the struggle of the whole Algerian people was in itself a mass struggle. Finally, since the practice of unity is the basis of common action, it seemed to me that any blow against my enemy, French capitalism, could only help to weaken it and encourage the struggle of the working class against its exploiters.'
33. Maurice Joyeux (1910-1991): lifelong anarchist activist, imprisoned throughout the Second World War [*RH*].
34. Maurice Joyeux, *Sous les plis du drapeau noir, souvenirs d'un anarchiste* (Paris, 1988), p 181.
35. Maurice Fayolle (1909-1970): helped reorganise French anarchism after the Second World War; leading figure in founding of l'Organisation révolutionnaire anarchiste (ORA) in 1967 [*RH*].
36. Jacques Jurquet, *Années de feu, Algérie 1954-1956* (Paris, 1997), p 81.
37. Ibid, p 77; Benjamin Stora, *Messali Hadj, pionnier du nationalisme algérien* (Paris, 1986), p 213 (first edition 1982, based on a doctoral thesis submitted in 1978 at the École des hautes études en sciences sociales).
38. Jurquet, *Années de feu*, p 78.
39. For the following quotations, see political note no 7, 23 November 1954, Fo 278, BDIC archives at Nanterre.
40. Document Fo 278, BDIC archives at Nanterre.
41. This appeal against the sentence on Ben Boulaïd was signed by Albert Camus, François Mauriac, Laurent Schwartz, Marceau Pivert, Jean-Marie Domenach,

Merleau-Ponty, Henri-Irénée Marrou, Yvan Craipeau, and, for the far left, Georges Fontenis, Daniel Renard and Pierre Frank.

42. Stora, *Messali Hadj,* pp 237-38: 'Messali had not broken off contact with the leader in the Aurès, Ben Boulaid.' In these pages Stora defends the claim that Ben Boulaïd was murdered by the FLN.
43. Document Fo 278, BDIC archives at Nanterre.
44. Document Fo (Rés 137…), BDIC archives, Nanterre.
45. Document O Col 1615, BDIC archives at Nanterre.
46. Resolution on the Algerian revolution and the tasks of the party: document Fo 278, BDIC archives at Nanterre.
47. Michel Lequenne (b 1921): self-educated intellectual. With Marcel Favre-Bleibtreu he was a leading figure in the Bolshevik-Leninist Tendency which left the Fourth International in 1952, and then was expelled from the Lambertist PCI in 1956. He joined first the UGS (Union of the Socialist Left), then the PSU, which didn't prevent him rejoining the Fourth International in the early 1960s. In the PSU he was a leading figure in the extreme left tendency and was part of the 'Commission of wise men' set up to arbitrate between the seven tendencies during the PSU Congress in 1963. He left the PSU in 1965. He now [2002] contributes regularly to different reviews and in particular writes articles for *Politis* and *Critique communiste*, the LCR review.
48. Marcel Favre-Bleibtreu (1918-2001): Trotskyist leader, he left the PCI in 1953 and was active in the Bolshevik-Leninist Tendency, then joined the UGS and later the PSU. He was one of the main figures in the left wing of that party and at the same time rejoined the wing of the Trotskyist movement headed by Pierre Frank.
49. Interview with Michel Lequenne, 18 November 1999.
50. Interview with Simonne Minguet and Pierre Avot-Meyers, Paris, 17 November 1999.
51. Interview with Michel Fiant, Le Var, 8 November 1999; interview with Simonne Minguet and Pierre Avot-Meyers, 17 November 1999; interview with Henri Benoîts, 7 February 2000. In February 1956, responding to references to the Trotskyist advisers of the MNA in the book *L'Algérie hors-la-loi* by Colette and Francis Jeanson, *La Vérité des travailleurs* published a clarification from the PCI's Political Bureau: 'Our duty is to serve the Algerian movement, not to make use of it… It is not our place to indulge in attacks on Messali Hadj. As a metropolitan party, we respect his record as an anti-imperialist fighter and we are in solidarity with all Algerians who are victims of imperialism. Obviously those who are in the front line of the struggle deserve our maximum sympathy and support… Today no faction can be more revolutionary than that which is fighting the guerrilla struggle.' (Quotation taken from *La Question coloniale et la section française de la 4e Internationale*, p 34, document O Col 1615, BDIC archives at Nanterre) In March 1961, Pierre Frank wrote in a letter (document Fo Rés 569/4): 'We have supported the FLN not because we saw it as a Marxist formation, but because it was carrying out a genuine, effective struggle against French imperialism.'
52. Force ouvrière — a 1948 American-financed split from the main French union federation, the CGT. Despite its origins, FO remained a genuine trade union [*RH*].

53. Interview with Henri Benoîts 7 February 2000. [Fernand Doukhan, an Algiers teacher who had been active in the anarchist movement — RH.]
54. Georges Fontenis, *Changer le monde: histoire du mouvement communiste libertaire (1945-1997)* (Paris, 2000), p 91.
55. In the postwar period the lay youth hostel movement was a field of activity for the far left [RH].
56. Fontenis, *Changer le monde*, p 118.
57. The Confédération nationale du travail, a small anarcho-syndicalist union founded in 1946 [RH].
58. Fontenis, *Changer le monde*, p 119.
59. One only has to consult issues of the journal for the period to observe the important place given to MNA press releases and the absence of press releases from the FLN (archives of the CIRA — Centre international de recherche sur l'anarchisme — at Marseille).
60. CIRA archives.
61. Georges Fontenis (Fontaine, Grandfond, 1920-2010): syndicalist and anarchist militant, teacher, secretary of the FA from 1945 to 1951. In the early 1950s his positions won a majority and he transformed the FA into the Libertarian Communist Federation (FCL). As an advocate of the critical rereading of Marxism by the anarchist tradition, he earned serious enmities in the anarchist milieu. From November 1954 onwards he involved himself in solidarity with the Algerian revolution, and the FCL paper, *Le Libertaire*, was several times successfully prosecuted for his articles. Fontenis himself was questioned by the police and suffered fines and convictions. When the FCL was wound up, he spent a year in clandestinity and then became involved with *La Voie communiste* and wrote articles in the journal under the name Grandfond. After a short spell as a free-mason, he took part in various anarchist groups throughout the 1960s and 1970s, in which he defended the principles of workers' management and libertarian communism.
62. CIRA archives. See the obituary in this issue of *Revolutionary History*.
63. Fontenis, *Changer le monde*, p 131.
64. See the documents in Section III below [RH].

Chapter IV: What Kind of Support for the Algerian Revolution?

The far left was unanimous in condemning the repression against Algerian nationalist militants. But the attitude towards the FLN and the MNA, and above all the adoption of concrete positions, aroused much more controversy. With the exception of the FA, all the far left demanded independence for Algeria: but each organisation still had to determine the most effective means of participating in the revolution. What organisation should they assist, of course, but also in what way, legally or illegally, openly or clandestinely — such were the questions that the far left had to answer.

For in fact the Algerian war posed problems which went far beyond mere public political support, since the war was being extended into metropolitan France. Mainland France constituted what was, according to the FLN's division into regions, the notorious seventh *wilaya*.[1] The struggle in this seventh *wilaya* was crucial because the FLN had to collect the revolutionary 'contributions' from the tens of thousands of Algerians working in metropolitan France. The FLN's French Federation was an essential cog in the mechanism of the Algerian revolution, above all after 1958 when the FLN definitively imposed its authority among emigrant workers at the expense of the MNA.

The far left was therefore potentially able to offer direct concrete support to the Algerian revolution. But the risks were significant and such actions were necessarily clandestine. A mere breach of the press laws could be expensive in terms of fines and prosecutions, which could be fatal for small organisations. The far left was determined to defend its own slogans and to call for Algerian independence. But in view of its weakness, it could do so only in coordination with more moderate forces, those which gravitated around the New Left,[2] for these had a social and institutional base sufficient partly to 'protect' the far left and indeed to popularise its actions.

The far left thus turned to the rest of the left with the aim of pursuing the most radical struggles possible in the broadest possible framework. These two aspirations (unity and radical policies) were, however, in inverse proportion. The far left also appealed to the broader left to block repression. It broke its isolation by articulation between activity in its own name and united activity, as well as through the constant concern to call on the rest of the left to act as a witness and to make it accept its responsibilities.

The Trotskyists and the libertarians could not count on the solidarity of the PCF, which was much too hostile to any form of 'ultra-left adventurism',[3] nor on that of the SFIO, which was initially very timorous in its opposition to the war, and which subsequently conducted the repression during Guy Mollet's government. So it was the New Left circles which constituted a privileged and valuable partner. Privileged by the fact of their similar anti-colonialist opinions, even if the differences were very substantial about the means of achieving independence and about the support to be given to the FLN; but also because Trotskyists, sympathisers or 'lifelong ex-Trotskyists' in Laurent Schwartz's[4] words, had spread out within the New Left,[5] from Yvan Craipeau to Pierre Naville[6] via Jean Rous[7] and Roland Filiâtre;[8] valuable because of the intellectual and journalistic audience that these circles represented: prestigious intellectuals such as the mathematician Laurent Schwartz,[9] who was in fact a former member of the Fourth International, but also editors and leader-writers such as Claude Bourdet[10] or Gilles Martinet.[11]

The New Left, a heterogeneous and unstructured milieu of various tendencies, undeniably represented a significant element of public opinion. In its relations with the milieu, the far left, above all the Trotskyists, took advantage of its influence, played on its contradictions and tried to radicalise it by forcing it to take a position. In this way it hoped to influence or win over New Left activists, especially youth, whom it could not have addressed directly. For the New Left the links with the far left not only provided a proof of its left-wing credentials, but also a means of supporting certain excessively 'extreme' actions and positions which aroused sympathy and even secret approval.

Initially the far left defended the demands of the Algerian nationalist movement in its press: it was necessary to persuade the masses of the legitimacy of the aims of the Algerian revolution. But its press necessarily had a limited audience, and the far left attempted to bring together broad committees of struggle against the repression. The FCL created a Committee Against Colonialist Repression,[12] whose influence did not extend beyond the far left and which was wound up in June 1955 to be replaced by a Movement for Anti-Colonialist Struggle which also had little influence.[13] The Lambertist PCI strengthened its Committees for the Release of Messali Hadj, which had already existed before the insurrection and which also drew in the New Left.[14] Meetings were organised with Claude Bourdet, André Mandouze[15] and Yves Dechezelles,[16] the MNA's lawyer. On 16 June 1955, even the old socialist leader Marceau Pivert,[17] former leader of the PSOP,[18] put his head on the line by appearing at a meeting in Boulogne along with Daniel Renard and 'a North African worker'.[19]

As for the Frank PCI, a report by Mortier in *Internal Bulletin*, no 1, in June 1955 advocated the 'creation of a broad anti-colonialist front throughout the country'.[20] Such a front should include the SFIO, Force ouvrière (FO), the CFTC,[21] and the New Left, and action committees should 'collaborate closely with the nationalist movement... while not interfering in its internal disputes and strictly respecting its autonomy'. But this hope for a broad regroupment of anti-colonialists, which did not prevent a violent criticism of the exclusive attitude of the Lambert group, came up against the reality of public opinion which was hostile to the independence of Algeria.

The positions of the leaderships of the main parties in the working-class movement were such that claims about the breadth of such committees had to be scaled down; effectively it was only the New Left that became involved in such committees. As early as 8 January 1955, Pierre Frank wrote a letter congratulating Claude Bourdet for his contribution to a meeting against the repression[22] at the Vel' d'Hiv:[23] 'This will eventually bear fruit', wrote the Trotskyist leader in a letter which allows us to glimpse a definite respect for the leader-writer on the part of the revolutionary.

The Frank PCI and the Fourth International helped the Algerian revolution practically rather than politically: the organisational efficiency of the Trotskyists made up for their small political influence. The Frank PCI was the first organisation to be involved in concrete organised support: the Fourth International formed the first support network for the FLN. It was through Yvan Craipeau that the first contacts were made to this end.[24] Yvan Craipeau was a major figure of French Trotskyism: Trotsky's secretary in 1933, he was one of the leaders of the Trotskyist POI and organised the Trotskyist resistance during the Second World War. He was one of the initiators of the 1944 congress which founded the PCI from a fusion of the POI, the CCI and the October group:[25] he was elected General Secretary of the PCI in 1946. But his plan for a broad and open organisation clashed with the conception held by Pierre Frank and a good half of the party. The fusion with the Socialist Youth, which had been disbanded, and the ASR,[26] a split from the SFIO, was a failure. Craipeau had hoped to create thereby a revolutionary party of 10 000 members, and his disappointment was on the same scale as his hopes. He criticised the 'sectarianism' of the Frank tendency and left the PCI. For him, revolutionary hope could come only from a broader organisation, and from the early 1950s he involved himself in projects around the New Left while maintaining good relations with his 'comrades' from the PCI.[27]

Early in 1955 he was contacted by a leading figure in the FLN who asked him for 'concrete assistance'. Yvan Craipeau was known to the Algerian militants because he had given shelter to certain members of the MTLD who were threatened by the police. He explained that the New Left did not offer the most appropriate political framework for clandestine support, and he proposed organising a meeting with some of the PCI leaders.[28] Yvan Craipeau's action fitted into a double perspective. On the one hand, he saw the activities of the PCI and of the New Left in favour of the Algerian revolution as complementary. The New Left, through the audience it possessed, could popularise the denunciation of repression and defend the idea of the independence of Algeria. But this institutional credibility made it impossible for it to carry out more practical and illegal activities, of which in any case its leaders would disapprove.[29] Moreover, Yvan Craipeau believed in solidarity amongst far-left militants, believing that different forms of struggle were complementary; in a text of 1955 he even spoke of a 'freemasonry of the far left'.[30]

It was therefore quite natural for him to put the PCI and the FLN in contact with each other. This meant the Frank PCI, for he was on very bad terms with Lambert. So the encounter took place during the winter of 1954-55. Yvan Craipeau organised a meeting between a cadre of the FLN French Federation and Simonne Minguet[31] for the PCI, and Michel Raptis, known as Pablo, representing the Fourth International leadership.

A member of the Political Bureau of the PCI, Simonne Minguet had been won over to Trotskyist ideas during the Second World War when she was a student. She had opposed the Vichy regime and Nazism. She was a worker in the Caudron factories from 1944 to 1948, and she led strikes in the postwar period which were not only against the factory management, but also against the orders of the leadership of the CGT and the PCF: the factory saw one of the first attempts at workers' management.[32] She was one of the few women to have a leadership position in a Trotskyist party which had the same male over-representation as the rest of the political milieu.

As for the Greek Michel Raptis, he was one of the main leaders of the Fourth International, alongside the Belgian Ernest Mandel, known as Germain, the Frenchman Pierre Frank and the Italian Livio Maitan. He had been exiled in France for some years; he was a theoretician but also a tireless organiser. He had taken part in the Founding Congress of the Fourth International, and his analyses had influenced the World Congress of 1953. Those who split, French Lambertists or British Healyites, paid unconscious tribute to the importance of Raptis when they accused the Fourth International of Pabloism. So if Pablo was a top leader of the Fourth International, his links with the French section were particularly important: he had in fact been the chief architect and arbiter of the reunification of the various Trotskyist groups which gave birth to the PCI.[33] But it was also under his influence that the majority of the French section had been excluded in 1952, leading to the formation of the Lambertist PCI.

Simonne Minguet and Pablo offered the assistance of the PCI and the Fourth International. The FLN wanted to establish roots among Algerians living in metropolitan France and to persuade Algerian workers in France to assist the Algerian revolution. The Trotskyists' know-how could be very useful in distributing their propaganda. So the Trotskyists were entrusted with the task of printing and distributing a leaflet and the first FLN paper, *Résistances algériennes.*[34]

As far as distribution was concerned, this 'only' meant leaving packets of leaflets or papers with shopkeepers or in bars controlled by the FLN, just like any ordinary delivery of supplies. Sherry Mangan,[35] an American journalist and member of the Fourth International who was living in France, was one of those who carried out these 'deliveries': his nationality and also the respectable demeanour of this Harvard graduate were a double advantage for this sort of clandestine work.[36] But the real problem was printing: they had to find printers who were not very bothered about the nature of the work to be done. It was Pierre Avot-Meyers,[37] a worker member of the Political Bureau of the PCI and partner of Simonne Minguet, who took on this tricky task. He coordinated the clandestine activity. Henri Benoîts, a member of the Political Bureau of the PCI, was responsible for liaison with the Algerians for most of the 'material' activities, and in particular he took responsibility for 'publications'. As for Pablo, he regularly met leaders of the French Federation. Naturally pseudonyms and code-words were used: to begin with contacts were mainly with a former centralist, Cherchalli Hadj, but also with a student leader who had responsibilities for the press, Mohammed Harbi,[38] today a well-respected historian.[39]

Mohammed Harbi was one of the few FLN cadres who had a real Marxist culture, and it was he who decided to entrust the printing of publications to the Trotskyist group. He considered that the Socialisme ou Barbarie group had the most accurate analysis of the situation in Algeria, but it was mainly composed of intellectuals who were not very keen on action, and who above all were very distrustful of the FLN. The PCI had less prejudice against working with the FLN, even if it was at the price of certain illusions about the nature of the collection of various tendencies which made up the FLN and about the scope of the colonial revolution.[40]

Until 1956, numerous small print-shops were used; in return for money, the owners were prepared to keep their eyes shut, and Pierre Avot-Meyers even turned to a print-shop which specialised in pornographic publications. But this sort of printing rapidly became quite dangerous when the repression intensified and the police began to know more about the French Federation of the FLN. It became, to say the least, imprudent to do the printing in France. Henceforth it was the Belgian Trotskyists who took on the job. The printed copies were sent in packets to various 'addresses' of post-office boxes in the name of various militants or theoretical magazines.[41]

But a Trotskyist network was also formed 'at the base' in the factory where Henri Benoîts worked.[42] He thus went beyond what his organisation was telling him to do, since he didn't merely deal with 'publications' but kept in contact with FLN militants in his factory. Despite being advised to be careful and to 'compartmentalise' different activities, it was difficult for him not to lend a hand to comrades from the factory who were sometimes threatened by repression and whom he agreed to put up in his home.[43] There were very close links with the Amicale générale des travailleurs algériens (AGTA — General Association of Algerian Workers), a pro-FLN[44] organisation which brought together Algerians who were members mainly of the CGT and less frequently of the CFTC. Henri Benoîts even offered to give training courses for the AGTA and took part in the drawing up of certain leaflets or 'reports'.

There were good relations between the Trotskyists and the FLN, and an FLN representative was invited to the clandestine Eleventh Congress of the PCI in December 1955.[45] Soon printing work was no longer limited to the FLN publications, and the Trotskyists provided proof of their know-how in providing forged papers, always useful for Algerian militants who were persecuted by the police and subjected to constant identity checks. The forged papers were printed abroad for security reasons and were sometimes manufactured on the basis of genuine papers which had been stolen or 'lost'.[46] Some FLN communiqués to the press, to embassies, parties and unions were likewise handled by the Trotskyists, who took on the job of getting them to those to whom they were addressed.

However, if repression affected the far left as early as 1955, to begin with it was not for clandestine activities. It was because its press expressed support for the Algerian revolution and publicly condemned repression. There were numerous police confiscations of publications[47] during the Algerian war. From 1955 to 1957, it was essentially the left and far-left press which was affected.[48]

The FCL was the first organisation affected, and numerous issues of its paper were confiscated or prosecuted. As early as June 1954, *Le Libertaire* was confiscated together with a poster, *Free Algeria*. R Caron and Richer, FCL militants, were charged and held in custody for some days.[49] In December 1954 and January 1955, two issues of the paper were prosecuted for endangering the external security of the state, and five militants were questioned by the criminal police — Georges Fontenis, Caron, Donnet, Robert Joulain and Philippe.[50] In June 1955 it was for issues 404, 408, 410, 411, 413, 421, 422, 423, 426, 427, 428 and 430 that the five editors were prosecuted, having been previously cited by the rogatory commission of judge Monzein.[51] The tenth issue of *Jeune révolutionnaire*, a publication aimed specifically at youth, and which dealt in particular with 'the attitude of the young revolutionary towards the army', was likewise prosecuted.[52]

Pierre Morain,[53] a libertarian activist from Roubaix, seems to have been the first French person in mainland France to have been sentenced for political activity in support of the Algerian revolution. On 22 June 1955, he was questioned by customs officials at Wattrelos while distributing leaflets for the Mouvement de lutte anticolonialiste (a committee set up by the FCL). The DST (Home Security Police) came for him at his workplace, he was questioned for a whole day, and released after being charged for endangering the internal security of the state.[54] He was defended in particular by Yves Dechezelles, the MNA's lawyer and a member of the New Left; he was tried alongside Algerian militants and sentenced to five months in jail.[55] On 23 September 1955, after an appeal by the Lille public prosecutor, who considered the sentence was too lenient, Pierre Morain appeared in court again.[56] He was accused of the direct or indirect reconstitution of a banned organisation (the MTLD) for two articles which had appeared in the May issue of *Le Libertaire*: 'Bonzes, Draw Your Own Conclusions' and 'On May Day in Lille Algerian Workers Showed French Workers the Way'. He was sentenced to a year in jail for having 'defended actions by Algerians on 1 May, actions with the intention of reconstituting the MTLD'[57] and for 'anti-national activity'. The severity of the sentence can doubtless be explained by the concern to set an example, but also had the aim of striking hard against any attempt by French militants to show solidarity with the Algerians.

The repression also affected the Lambertist PCI; on 29 June 1955 the primary schoolteacher Jeanine Maquart was arrested and questioned right through the night; and on 30 June the engineering worker Jean Gouttefengas was detained throughout the morning.[58] As early as 1 February 1955, an internal circular of the PCI advised militants about their 'attitude to the police'.[59] Such caution was justified as it was the organisations supporting Messali Hadj's MNA which were the first to be affected by the repression: doubtless this was due to the fact that to begin with state repression was directed against the Messalists, who were better known to the police.[60] The MNA, and hence the French organisations which were supporting it, seemed to be the main enemy. Messali Hadj was the historical pioneer of Algerian nationalism, and the authorities had not yet grasped the dominant position held by the FLN.

The New Left's support for militants who were prosecuted or jailed was total; it was political, with the voting of motions and resolutions of support by its branches,[61] but also material, notably with the involvement of Yves Dechezelles among Pierre Morain's defence lawyers. In 1955, the New Left distributed a leaflet, signed notably by Claude Bourdet, in favour of freedom of expression.[62] Apart from the New Left, André Marty,[63] a Paris deputy, a former leader of the International Brigades in Spain and a Resister, who had been expelled from the PCF in 1952, was alone in sending a letter of support to Pierre Morain in jail,[64] thus renewing the anarcho-syndicalist sympathies of his youth.[65] The FA, for its part, criticised the FCL for this reconciliation with the man it considered to be the 'Butcher of Albacete' for his activity during the Spanish Civil War;[66] this episode merely added one more reason for ill-feeling to the antagonisms between the two anarchist groups.

However, here it was a question of repression with respect to 'legal' activities, distribution of leaflets or free expression of opinion in articles, and not of clandestine activities of direct and concrete support, material and not just political, to the FLN or the MNA. The Frank PCI was the first organisation to be affected by repression for illegal and clandestine activity, and not simply a matter of free speech. For the Fourth International was still handling the printing of the nationalist organisation's paper and distribution of it to FLN addresses.

After the first period when the printing was done in France, a decision was taken to do the printing in Belgium to avoid repression because the print-shops made use of in France were not reliable. The desire for profit seemed to be the main motivation of the printers who were approached, and this scarcely inspired confidence on the part of revolutionary militants who suspected that their 'accomplices' in producing an issue would not hesitate to denounce them if they had the slightest trouble with the police. However, given the quantities of papers that were printed and in order not to attract attention, they were sent into France in small packets to various addresses and post-office boxes.[67]

But in April 1956 some of these packets were opened (accidentally or in the course of an investigation by customs officials) and intercepted. They were addressed to post-office boxes in the names of Simonne Minguet, of Raymond Bouvet, a PCI militant, and of Janine Weil, a former PCI member now in the New Left. The three militants were arrested and detained on 5 April: if Simonne Minguet and Raymond Bouvet were aware of their organisation's activities, it was a total surprise for Janine Weil, who was no longer a member of the PCI, but who had agreed to let her name still be used for the post-office box of the theoretical journal *Quatrième internationale*, which was now also being used to receive the FLN's paper. The PCI Political Bureau met and there was a stormy debate; part of the Political Bureau urged Pierre Frank to give himself up to the authorities, firstly in order to take political responsibility as leader of the PCI for political solidarity with the FLN, and secondly to ensure the release of Janine Weil, who had not been informed of how her post-office box was being used. Pierre Frank hesitated because even for a revolutionary the perspective of going to prison was not particularly appetising, and also because he feared the consequences for the organisation of supporting the FLN too conspicuously. He did not want his organisation to go back into clandestinity as during the war, or for it to be banned. But in the end he conformed to the majority decision of the Political Bureau.[68]

The Political Bureau of the PCI announced publicly that Pierre Frank 'will appear before the examining magistrate to take responsibility for one of these addresses which is that of the journal *Quatrième internationale*'.[69] Arrested on 12 April by the DST, he informed the examining magistrate Giraud that he was legally responsible for the post-office box in Janine Weil's name. He was released on 13 April after questioning, and arrested again on 16 April.[70]

On 12 April, the PCI organised a meeting at the Sociétés savantes hall[71] in the course of which the fate of the Trotskyist militants was linked to that of Claude Bourdet and Henri-Irénée Marrou,[72] who were being prosecuted for demoralising the army.[73] Motions were carried to be sent to Guy Mollet, the new Socialist Prime Minister, elected on the programme of the Republican Front,[74] to SFIO branches and to *La Vérité des travailleurs*. A petition in support of those jailed got signatures from CGT and Force ouvrière militants, from such personalities as Henri-Irénée Marrou, Edgar Morin,[75] Michel Leiris,[76] Francis

Jeanson,[77] Jean-Paul Sartre and André Mandouze, from such representatives of the New Left as Claude Bourdet and Gilles Martinet, and from former members of the PCI now in the New Left such as Yvan Craipeau and Laurent Schwartz. Pierre Lambert, the 'hostile brother', and Georges Fontenis of the FCL also signed. André Marty and François Mauriac[78] were approached but refused to sign.

There was broad support, much more so than that obtained by Pierre Morain and the other members of the FCL who were charged. The Trotskyists could count on more effective support from the New Left and its most influential leaders, particularly since there were many former Trotskyists in that milieu. But the fact that a woman who was a member of the New Left had been imprisoned doubtless also had an impact. Finally, attacks on freedom of speech had been stepped up and were affecting publications of the New Left.

Other prosecutions followed. After numerous confiscations of *La Vérité des travailleurs*, Pierre Frank and Jacques Privas (Grimblat), who were legally responsible for the paper, were prosecuted for endangering the external security of the state. A 'Coalition in Defence of Democratic Liberties' was set up and a fund was launched to support those accused. A letter was sent to the Executive Committee of the SFIO, ending with the words: 'You cannot fail in your duty of proletarian solidarity.'[79] The aim of the Trotskyists was to sharpen the contradictions of the party in power, and above all to confront its rank-and-file militants with the 'betrayals' of the leadership (the text of the letter was sent to SFIO branches and distributed among its members).

On 20 April at a public meeting in the salle des Horticulteurs in Paris,[80] the PCI recognised the failure of the attempt to create a unified coalition, but received the support of the New Left, of the CGT and the CFTC at Vernon, and of the Rhône district of the national union of primary teachers. At the May Day demonstration at Vincennes, 60 000 leaflets were distributed calling for the release of the four imprisoned militants. On 4 May, a 'Stop the War' meeting was organised at Suresnes.[81] Those taking part were Claude Bourdet, Jacques Privas for *La Vérité des travailleurs*, and militants from the CGT, FO, the SFIO (Salmon), the PCF (Lafourcade) and the New Left (Chazines). Such unity was surprising, and doubtless was largely made possible by the local context, all the more so since at the end of the meeting an Action Committee for Peace was set up which gave its support to the four prisoners. A statement was sent by the members of this committee, including the PCF, to the parliamentary groups, to the Prime Minister and to the Minister for the Armed Forces.[82]

The united mobilisation paid off. On 9 May, Raymond Bouvet, Pierre Frank, Simonne Minguet and Janine Weil were given a conditional discharge. The prosecution was dropped because the inconsistent evidence did not succeed in proving their collusion with the FLN.[83] However, Frank and Privas continued to be prosecuted for the articles which had appeared in *La Vérité des travailleurs*; later, they received suspended prison sentences of six months,[84] a much lighter sentence than the one on Pierre Morain.

How can we explain this different treatment? It could be said that the Trotskyists had appealed to public opinion in a more effective manner than the libertarians, for a number of reasons. First of all there was a different strategy: the Trotskyists had a different analysis of the place and role of the far left on the French political scene. They were very conscious of being in a minority, and they knew that, at least in the short term, their party was not destined to become a mass party. It was social democracy, above all the PCF, and to a lesser extent the New Left milieu, which were organising the working masses and the other radicalised layers (in particular the intellectuals) of society. If the PCI was a revolutionary vanguard, it was not destined to become the 'party of the proletariat' as long as the stranglehold of the Stalinist and social democratic 'bureaucracies' survived. So it was a question of upsetting this hegemony by starting from the contradictions existing within these organisations and addressing the rank and file to stress the 'betrayals' of the leadership. For that, 'entrist' work was an essential aspect, in order to undermine these organisations 'from within'.

In France, entrism was carried out within the PCF, the biggest mass party, but it was combined with work which appeared openly. It was in this independent framework that activity with other left organisations was fundamental, since it was vital not to be isolated, not to cut oneself off from the masses, but at the same time to make one's own demands and proposals known.

This strategy of the PCI can be explained by what Trotsky called the united front policy. The different parties of the working-class movement had to 'march separately but strike together' against a common enemy, fascism, or as was the case here, imperialism. A concern for unity and effectiveness was linked to this practical imperative for Trotskyist groups which had almost always been in the minority. Thus on 15 January 1956, an internal document of the PCI stated:

> Participation in the Popular Front committees being launched by the PCF is at the present time unquestionably the most realistic lever to propel the organisation of the masses and to favour the unleashing of struggles. [For the PCI this is a]... fundamental task for both [its] entrist forces and its independent forces.[85]

On the contrary, for an organisation like the FCL, the approach was rather to address other revolutionary forces in order to form a 'revolutionary' pole. Thus for his part on 15 March, Georges Fontenis proposed the establishment of a 'bulletin of encounter for revolutionaries'.[86]

Of course the political context had changed, since there was no longer any question of a 'Popular Front', but the two initiatives revealed quite distinct approaches, even if convergences were not ruled out. Of course the Trotskyists did not really hope for the creation of a possible 'Popular Front', about which they had no 'illusions', but they wanted to work with broader forces than those on which the FCL was concentrating. In the minds of the leaders of the latter organisation, it was destined to become the party of the working class and to draw together all the revolutionaries. This was an optimism which was not merely a matter of propaganda, and which led to the claim that despite the prosecutions *Le Libertaire* must become 'the great revolutionary paper'.[87] On the occasion of Pierre Morain's trial, the National Bureau of the FCL published the following statement:

> It is also because every day new workers are proud to join the real struggle for true communism, by joining the Fédération communiste libertaire, the party which is finally emerging, young, new and free from all contamination, out of the slime into which venal working-class leaders and parties have plunged the working-class movement. And because the FCL is called on to regroup around itself the great mass of workers and lead them to the social revolution, the exploiters are trying to nip it in the bud, to break it at the very outset, before, in their wretched minds, it becomes too late.

Moreover, apart from any strategic question, the Trotskyists could count on numerous forms of support. We can mention former militants, whether or not they still called themselves Trotskyists, who belonged to the New Left milieu and who retained sympathy, and even genuine political solidarity, with their former comrades; then there were intellectuals and journalists with whom Pierre Frank in particular had been able to establish links of mutual respect (for example, with Claude Bourdet); finally links between organisations, maintained in the unified committees. The FCL had not succeeded in getting such a broad mobilisation around it, with the exception of certain sections of the New Left milieu, or recognised but isolated personalities such as André Marty or the libertarian intellectual Daniel Guérin.[88] These difficulties cost it a heavy price: prison for Pierre Morain and substantial fines.

Though repression is always difficult to put up with, even for militants who know what they are risking and who are convinced of the justice of their struggle, it also — as compensation, so to speak — provides the opportunity for the victims themselves to use it politically. To begin with, repression is a proof that the activity of the militants concerned is really effective and represents a danger for the government. To be a victim of repression means being in the forefront of the struggle, and the organisations concerned can take advantage of it as a sort of negative seal of approval of their effectiveness.[89] From this attitude may follow the stance of 'martyr' of the revolutionary cause: this was clear in the affair of the conviction of Pierre Morain. In *Le Libertaire* there was a report of the trial which dripped with revolutionary lyricism:

> Oh! How wretched the Lille prosecutor must have felt, when he said to Morain, 'You are a contemptible individual', and how strong and powerful Morain felt! He could feel flowing in his veins the cheering warmth of his complete confidence in the revolution, of his unfailing faith in his cause, in the libertarian communist cause, that of all workers.[90]

The FA, which laid claim to an anti-capitalism at least as lethal as that of the FCL, did not support Algerian independence, and was relatively untouched by the repression, at least until 1957. Without wishing to underestimate the very real sufferings caused by the effects of the repression, or the real courage of those who put their beliefs into practice despite the dangers they incurred, we can simply observe how this repression itself could be used in the service of the 'revolutionary cause', and became an element of propaganda, especially in the case of the FCL.

The fact of being the victim of repression also enabled the far left to acquire or increase a certain amount of sympathy from public opinion, and to obtain support from outside its normal sphere of influence. *Le Libertaire*, for example, stepped up its appeals for solidarity,[91] which could be expressed in financial terms. Each week the names of donors were published in the paper. It was also important to address militants and even (especially for the PCI) the leaders of other left parties, and to seek political support.

The far left did not aim to seek repression or to provoke it deliberately. The primary objective remained support for the Algerian revolution, whether political or practical. This is demonstrated by Pierre Frank's hesitations about handing himself over for judgement, and his fears of seeing the organisation collapse into clandestinity. Here the context was very important: repression only affected a very small nucleus of French activists, and, of course, the Algerian militants, but as there was no widespread support, then it followed logically that there was no repression against the population in general, and hence no hope of radicalising the masses by a reaction to a repression which did not affect them.

However, repression in the broad sense, which affected Algerian militants, who faced torture in police stations on the mainland or in barracks in Algeria, and which affected French militants engaged in support activities, and the censorship which didn't concern only the far left press, raised a certain number of questions. For in fact since the end of the Second World War the various mainstream political parties had created the myth, partly issuing from the Resistance, of a democratic France whose citizens enjoyed equal rights, set up as a model in response to the Nazi totalitarianism which had just been defeated or the Stalinist totalitarianism which remained a threat. Now colonial policy was demonstrating the limits of French democracy: not only were the colonial peoples largely excluded from these rights, but even in metropolitan France the consensus about 'liberal democracy' revealed its limitations. The government did not hesitate to infringe freedom of expression by censoring newspapers, jailing French militants and torturing Algerian militants with methods worth of a dictatorship!

The far left had no difficulty in denouncing the contradictions and hypocrisies of the system: it was easy to show that as far as colonial policy was concerned democracy was only very relative and that it often stopped at the doors of police stations. The far left's propaganda was based on examples of repression and infringements of freedom in order to try and show that the French system was not a true democracy but a 'bourgeois' democracy, and that under these conditions the defence by various governments of the colonial and capitalist system, clad in a fictional and purely formal democracy, came before the respect of liberties. Sometimes the critique went even farther, and pointed to the danger of seeing a fascist regime established in France as the 'last resort of the bourgeoisie'.

So the alternative was simple: revolution or fascism.[92] If repression could be used politically by the far left and not simply suffered, this was above all because it made it possible to denounce the hypocrisies of a system which claimed to be democratic, but which used authoritarian methods to crush the Algerian revolution and those who supported it; the far left could also brandish the threat of a fascist coup which would reveal the oppressive 'true nature' of bourgeois class power against which workers were urged to be on their guard. At the beginning of the Algerian war such propaganda could have only a very limited impact because of the weakness of the far left, but also because public opinion did not show any massive rejection of the policy being applied in Algeria. Repression as it was denounced by a part of the New Left milieu (that which had the easiest access to public opinion through the channel of the press, such as Claude Bourdet for example), or by progressive Christians (Henri-Irénée Marrou), was seen as a failure of the system.

Outside of a restricted circle, the far-left militants were unable to impose their vision of repression and lack of democracy conceived of as integral parts of the capitalist system. Nonetheless the PCI — and to a lesser extent the FCL — managed to win support beyond the far left, which partially protected it against repression. It carried out joint campaigns against repression with the New Left. Joint work was far more difficult with the PCF, since its leadership remained totally resistant to any action in defence of the ultra-left 'provocateurs' or the Algerian nationalists, and with the vote of special powers to the Guy Mollet government, the gap got even wider.

On the strictly practical level, the Trotskyists drew lessons from what had happened, and they decided that henceforward the printing of FLN publications would be done in France because use of the postal service was not 'reliable'. It was no longer possible to use the services of printers whose reliability could not be confirmed and so it became necessary for them to set up their own print-shop, a job which Pierre Avot-Meyers would take on.[93] At the same time, the rules of clandestinity with respect to contacts with Algerians would be tightened up even more. Pierre Avot-Meyers was the only one to be fully aware of details concerning clandestine activities. He was in direct contact with Pablo for the International, and Pablo was in in contact with Algerian leaders in exile abroad. If the forging of identity papers continued to be done abroad, the FLN gave the Trotskyist network a certain sum of money to enable it to rent or buy premises for a print-shop.

For reasons of necessity and to avoid attracting too much attention, several premises were rented under the names of figureheads and put to use.[94] There were premises in the rue Saint-Denis, another at Suresnes, and later another at Malakoff. Therefore the equipment used had to be light and easily transportable. Duplicators were chosen. But militants also put their heads on the line. And this meant women comrades in particular who worked as secretaries and who did work on the side, typing stencils and copying documents for the FLN in their workplace unknown to the boss.[95] Militant activity, even on the far left, sometimes reproduced the sexual divisions of society.

There were problems when it was necessary to repair the machines. It was out of the question to ask maintenance workers to come into the clandestine premises, and so Pierre Avot-Meyers himself had to go and look for spare parts. Manufacturers who wanted addresses to send the bills to didn't understand the refusal of this strange customer to provide the information. Pierre Avot-Meyers sometimes claimed to be representing a travelling circus whose printing machine had broken down. When the decision was taken to forge a certain number of false identity papers on the spot, and no longer only abroad, he likewise went round exhibitions and second-hand dealers looking for a typewriter which had a font similar to the special one used by the Seine police to produce the new national identity card. He finally found an American typewriter with movable characters which anticipated word-processing systems.[96] The papers and publications were delivered to business premises or cafés which were FLN 'dropping off points'. One of these was a grocery in southern Paris belonging to the FLN, but it was Michel Fiant,[97] a member of the PCI, who was responsible for the management, a camouflage for activities which were more clandestine than the sale of beans![98]

But by 1956 the Trotskyists were no longer the only ones supporting the Algerian cause by clandestine activities. Other networks appeared which brought together Communists who had broken with their party, progressive Christians and humanists, and no longer just the far left. Moreover the political context, with the arrival in power of Guy Mollet, aroused hopes of negotiations which were swiftly disappointed; the vote for special powers by the PCF provoked anger and incomprehension on the part of many militants, while the use of conscripts to fight the war led to a certain amount of opposition. Now the time of dissent had come. Dissent in the traditional left parties, the SFIO and the PCF, whose policies were challenged by some of their members; the dissent of those who in solidarity with the Algerians departed from legality and joined the Trotskyists in illegal activity; the rapidly suppressed dissent of those who, reservists or conscripts, refused to go and fight in Algeria.

Notes

1. From an Arabic word meaning administrative region; the FLN divided its activities into six *wilayas* in Algeria; metropolitan France was sometimes known as the seventh *wilaya* [*RH*].
2. The Mouvement Uni de la Nouvelle Gauche: see summary of Chapter 1 above [*RH*].
3. Not only could far-left militants not rely on solidarity from the PCF, but they were sometimes the physical victims of certain undemocratic methods. Thus in *Le Libertaire*, no 437, 30 June 1955 (CIRA archives), there was an article entitled 'Long Live Workers' Anti-Fascist Unity' which reported: 'In our last issue we protested against the attack by fascist thugs on PCF militants at Gentilly. However, a few hours later these same militants saw fit to snatch material from our comrades who were flyposting. Now on Sunday 19 June, one of our militants from Paris 14 was giving out a leaflet at the Perneety metro station when three PCF members tried to stop him leafleting and struck this worker. What did the leaflet say? We are reproducing it here: it listed the prosecutions against us, explained why we were being prosecuted and expressed surprise that other working-class organisations were not showing any solidarity with the FCL, its members and the paper that is being prosecuted. So it was a leaflet appealing for unity that our comrade was giving out, a leaflet calling for the unity of the working class against fascist attacks, and was not particularly addressed to the PCF, which was not named a single time!'
4. Laurent Schwartz, *Un Mathématicien aux prises avec le siècle* (Paris, 1997).
5. *Archives d'espoir: 20 ans de PSU* (Paris, 1988).
6. Pierre Naville (1903-1993): surrealist then Trotskyist, involved in organising founding conference of Fourth International; subsequently sociologist, prolific author and member of PSU [*RH*].
7. Jean Rous (1908-1985): veteran Trotskyist since 1932; see his article 'Spain 1936-

39: The Murdered Revolution', *Revolutionary History*, Volume 4, no 1-2 [*RH*].
8. Roland Filiâtre (1900-1991): French Trotskyist active during Occupation in contacting German soldiers; deported [*RH*].
9. Laurent Schwartz (1915-2002): distinguished mathematician, Trotskyist 1937-47 and lifelong left activist [*RH*].
10. Claude Bourdet (1909-1996): left-wing journalist; active with Resistance newspaper *Combat* during German occupation; deported; later involved in founding *France-Observateur* [*RH*].
11. Gilles Martinet (1916-2006): left journalist, one of the founders of *France-Observateur*; later in PSU and subsequently Socialist Party [*RH*].
12. This committee was the first to react publicly after the events of November 1954: on 17 December the FCL and the Lambertist PCI were the first to organise a meeting at the salle Wagram in Paris, which was however banned (interview with Laurent Saddock, Paris, November 1999 ; *Le Libertaire*, 15 February 1955; copy of a leaflet given out at a meeting at the Vel' d'Hiv, CIRA archives).
13. Document Fo 278, BDIC archives at Nanterre.
14. Document Fo 278.
15. André Mandouze (1916-2006): Catholic academic and journalist; later rector of the University of Algiers, 1963-65 [*RH*].
16. Yves Dechezelles (1912–2007): leading figure in a left tendency in the SFIO after the Second World War; left the SFIO in 1947, was one of the founders of the New Left, and later a member of the PSU. He was one of the lawyers of Messali Hadj and the MNA. [See obituary in *Revolutionary History*, Volume 9, no 4 — *RH*.]
17. Marceau Pivert (1895-1958): leader of 'Revolutionary Left' in SFIO in 1930s, then of PSOP (see next note); returned to SFIO after the Second World War [*RH*].
18. In 1938 the left of the Socialist Party, led by Marceau Pivert and Daniel Guérin, broke with Léon Blum's party, taking with it the majority of some federations, such as the Seine, as well as the Socialist Youth. This led to the creation of the Parti socialiste ouvrier et paysan (Workers' and Peasants' Socialist Party), and a majority of the French Trotskyists, following Trotsky's advice, joined this new party, which did not survive the outbreak of the war.
19. Document Fo Rés 442, BDIC archives at Nanterre.
20. Document Fo Rés 137/…, BDIC archives at Nanterre.
21. Confédération française des travailleurs chrétiens, the Catholic trade union federation, which in 1964 broke its links to the Church and became the CFDT.
22. Document Fo Rés 569/4, BDIC archive at Nanterre.
23. Vélodrome d'Hiver, indoor stadium in Paris with cycle track, also used for large political meetings [*RH*].
24. Interview with Simonne Minguet and Pierre Avot-Meyers, 17 November 1999.
25. The Parti Ouvrier Internationaliste (POI) had existed in the 1930s and was reformed under that name in 1942. The Comité Communiste Internationaliste pour la construction de la IVe Internationale (CCI) was a tighter-knit, more theoretical group. The October group had evolved out of the prewar Abondanciste movement. In 1944, the POI, CCI and Octobre groups united to form the Parti Communiste Internationaliste (PCI). See I Birchall, 'With the Masses, Against the Stream', *Revolutionary History*, Volume 1, no 4 [*RH*].

26. Action socialiste et révolutionnaire (Socialist and Revolutionary Action): a left group emerging from the SFIO in which Yves Dechezelles played a leading role [*RH*].
27. Interview with Yvan Craipeau, 7 February 2000; Y Craipeau, *Mémoires d'un dinosaure trotskyste* (Paris, 1999).
28. Interview with Henri Benoîts, 7 February 2000, and interview with Simonne Minguet and Pierre Avot-Meyers, 17 November 2000.
29. Interview with Yvan Craipeau, 7 February 2000.
30. Document Fo 137 /..., BDIC archives at Nanterre.
31. Simonne Minguet (1920-2005): arts student during the Second World War, she became a member of a Trotskyist group. Working at the Caudron-Renault factory at the Liberation, she was a leader of the big strikes in 1947 and 1948. During the 1950s, she was one of the few women leaders in the Fourth International, and was involved in support for the FLN, which led to her being imprisoned for two months in 1956. A member of the International Secretariat of the Fourth International, she sided with Pablo and lived in Algeria after independence. She worked as a journalist for APS, the Algerian press agency. She was arrested in 1965 at the time of the Boumediène coup and sent back to France. A member of the Alliance marxiste révolutionnaire (AMR), she became an interpreter.
32. Simonne Minguet, *Mes années Caudron: une usine autogérée à la Libération* (Paris, 1997).
33. Interview with Simonne Minguet and Pierre Avot-Meyers, 17 November 1999; Craipeau, *Mémoires d'un dinosaur*, p 172.
34. Interview with Henri Benoîts, 7 February 2000; interview with Simonne Minguet and Pierre Avot-Meyers, 17 November 1999; interview with Gilbert Marquis, Paris, 8 February 2000.
35. Sherry Mangan (Patrice, 1904-1961): coming from a wealthy family in Boston, he was originally a poet and journalist, notably for *Fortune*, and joined the Trotskyist movement before the Second World War. His activity as an international journalist enabled him, during and after the war, to maintain connections between different Trotskyist groups. He became an English translator for the journal *Fourth International*, and also took advantage of his situation as a journalist to do jobs for the FLN in France. In particular in an isolated country house he roneoed FLN publications.
36. Interview with Simonne Minguet and Pierre Avot-Meyers, 17 November 1999; 'Sherry Mangan' (obituary), *Quatrième Internationale*, no 13, July 1961, p 9; private archives of Jean-Michel Krivine.
37. Pierre Avot-Meyers (Serge, 1930-2009): metal-worker, Trotskyist militant and CGT member, member of the PCI Political Bureau, he was involved in support for the FLN during the Algerian war. He then ran the Fourth International clandestine print-shop in Paris until it was discovered in 1960. He took refuge in Italy and then lived in Algeria after independence. He sided with Pablo in the dispute that divided the Fourth International in 1965 and was subsequently active in the TMRI (International Marxist Revolutionary Tendency). Arrested at the time of the Boumediène coup in 1965, he was sent back to France. He became a proof-reader until his retirement.

38. Mohammed Harbi (b 1933): a leader of the French Federation of the FLN, he was one of the few Marxist cadres in the nationalist organisation. He resigned his responsibilities following political disagreements in 1958. After independence he was a keen supporter, along with Pablo, of experiments with workers management. Imprisoned for six years following Boumediène s coup, he then lived in France. A lecturer in political science at the University of Paris 8, he is now retired.
39. Interview with Henri Benoîts, 7 February 2000; interview with Simonne Minguet and Pierre Avot-Meyers, 17 November 1999.
40. Interview with Mohamed Harbi, 25 April 2000.
41. Interview with Simonne Minguet and Pierre Avot-Meyers, 17 November 1999.
42. Interview with Henri Benoîts, 7 February 2000.
43. Letter from Henri Benoîts in 1979, in his private archives: 'When racial persecution in the métro was common practice, could a consistent internationalist refuse to carry the packet of illegal leaflets for which an Algerian comrade was responsible? Could he refuse to offer refuge to this same comrade if he was being hunted by the police?'
44. On 14 February 1956, Messali's followers set up the Union syndicale des travailleurs algériens (USTA — Trade Union of Algerian Workers); a few days later the FLN created the AGTA (Benjamin Stora, *Messali Hadj, pionnier du nationalisme algérien* (Paris, 1986), p 246).
45. The following resolution was adopted at this congress: 'The congress was particularly concerned to examine ways of helping the revolution in North Africa and more particularly the tasks of the youth as the layer most directly affected by the struggle against the counter-revolutionary war in North Africa.' (*La Vérité des travailleurs*, January 1956, quoted in *La question coloniale et la section française de la 4e Internationale*, document O Col 1615, BDIC archives at Nanterre)
46. Interview with Simonne Minguet and Pierre Avot-Meyers, 17 November 1999; interview with Gilbert Marquis, 8 February 2000.
47. Sixty newspaper were confiscated in metropolitan France from November 1954 to 13 May 1958, and 179 from 1 June 1958 to June 1962: figures quoted in article by Christophe Barthélémy in L Gervereau, J-P Rioux and B Stora (eds), *La France en guerre d'Algérie* (Paris, 1992), p 122.
48. Concerning confiscations and the procedure: see Barthélémy article cited in previous note: 'Confiscation could be either judicial (article 51 of the law of 1881) or administrative (article 10 of the code of criminal procedure which on 13 February 1960 became article 30), but during the Algerian war it was mainly administrative confiscations which were used. Prefects can confiscate a publication in case of emergency and if there are "crimes and offences against the internal or external security of the state". The procedure is the following: publishers, once their papers are printed, must take a copy to three officials who have the job of supervising the press, respectively under the authority of the Minister of the Interior, National Security and the Ministry of the Armed Forces. Any article considered to be contentious is notified to the Ministry of the Interior which decides on the ban and initiates action by the prefect of Paris for the national press, and the prefect of the region concerned for the local press. The journal is then confiscated on leaving the printers, at the distributors or even at the newsagents, and the publisher has to

produce a second issue with the place of the incriminated article left blank or with a replacement article. Financially newspapers are penalised by such confiscations, even without the cost of a possible fine. Even if the paper is not confiscated it can still be prosecuted, that is, legal action can be taken against the editors of the paper or against the authors of incriminated articles.'

49. *Le Libertaire*, 19 May 1955; there is an almost complete set of *Le Libertaire* from 1954 to 1958 in the CIRA archives; Georges Fontenis, *Changer le monde: histoire du mouvement communiste libertaire (1945-1997)* (Paris, 2000), p 119.
50. *Le Libertaire*, 19 May 1955, CIRA archives.
51. *Le Libertaire*, no 435, 16 June 1955, CIRA archives.
52. *Le Libertaire*, no 435, 16 June 1955.
53. Pierre Morain: libertarian worker militant, member of the FCL, sentenced in 1955 to a year in jail for his writings in *Le Libertaire* in support of the Algerian revolution. After the dissolution of the FCL, he was active for a time in the PCF and the CGT from which he was soon expelled, then after the Algerian war he was active in various anarchist and libertarian groups.
54. *Le Libertaire*, no 437, 30 June 1955, CIRA archives.
55. *Le Libertaire*, special issue replacing no 441, 3 August 1955, which had been confiscated, dated 4 August 1955, CIRA archives.
56. For what follows on Pierre Morain's trial: *Le Libertaire*, no 446, 29 September 1955, CIRA archives.
57. In the article 'Bonzes, Draw Your Own Conclusions!', *Le Libertaire*, 19 May 1955, Pierre Morain attacked the attitude of the CGT which had, on the occasion of the traditional May Day march, refused permission to speak to Algerian workers who had asked to do so. He defended against the 'splitters' of the CGT 'the democratic and working-class Mouvement National Algérien, which has at its head a former semi-skilled worker from Renault, a shoemaker's son, interned for many years: Messali Hadj'. He also wrote addressing the 'CGT bonzes', that is, its leadership: 'And we declare that once the liberation of Algeria has been won, the Algerian people will be much further forward on the road to achieving a classless society than the French people, if the latter remains under your influence!' The term 'bonze' is used in far-left terminology to refer to reformist or bureaucratic leaders of working-class parties or unions.
58. *Le Libertaire*, no 438, 7 July 1955, CIRA archives.
59. 'Political Note on Organisation', no 2, document Fo, BDIC archives at Nanterre.
60. Stora, *Messali Hadj*, p 239: 'Between 1954 and 1956, it was mainly the Messalists who were affected by repression. The overwhelming majority of them were on police files.'
61. For example in *Le Libertaire*, no 435, 16 June 1955, we find the following inset: 'The Versailles group of the New Left protests unanimously at the prosecution against MM Fontenis, Donnet and Joulin for their writings in opposition to the reactionary policy currently being followed in Algeria (resolution carried on 23 May 1955). The Group Bureau.' In *Le Libertaire*, no 439, 14 July 1955, another organisation from the New Left milieu offered its support: 'The Federation of the Paris Region of the Left Socialist Party expresses its opposition to the confiscations and prosecutions against publications which provide information

on the true situation in North Africa. It protests vigorously against the accusation of endangering state security against five members of the FCL on the occasion of articles on the Algerian question in several issues of *Le Libertaire*.' (CIRA archives) It is not clear what exactly this Left Socialist Party was, but it certainly belonged to the New Left milieu.
62. Document Fo Rés 425/12, BDIC archives at Nanterre.
63. André Marty (1886-1956): one of leaders of Black Sea mutiny 1919; leading member of PCF; expelled 1952 [*RH*].
64. *Le Libertaire*, no 439, 14 July 1955, CIRA archives.
65. Fontenis, *Changer le monde*, p 24.
66. Maurice Joyeux, *Sous les plis du drapeau noir, souvenirs d'un anarchiste* (Paris, 1988), p 151 ; Fontenis, *Changer le monde*, pp 122-23. In his memoirs Maurice Joyeux repeats the accusation that André Marty had led the repression against the Spanish anarchists; Georges Fontenis refutes these accusations against the International Brigades veteran and maintains that Marty 'did not hold a command position which would have enabled him to exercise repression, other than the dismissal of certain members of the Brigades'. According to Fontenis the title 'butcher of Albacete', far from having been coined by 'Spanish anarchists' as Joyeux claimed, had been 'bestowed by a fascist deputy in parliament and it was this insult which certain Spanish comrades had taken up and popularised in a very frivolous fashion'.
67. Interview with Simonne Minguet and Pierre Avot-Meyers, 17 November 1999.
68. Interview with Simonne Minguet and Pierre Avot-Meyers, 17 November 1999; interview with Michel Fiant 8 November 1999.
69. Document Fo Rés 291, BDIC archives at Nanterre.
70. Document Fo Rés 291, BDIC archives.
71. Document Fo Rés 291, BDIC archives.
72. Henri-Irénée Marrou (1904-1977): distinguished Catholic historian of late antiquity [*RH*].
73. On 31 March 1956, Claude Bourdet had been arrested and released within the day, then charged for articles in *France-Observateur* (H Hamon and P Rotman, *Les Porteurs de valises* (Paris, 1979), p 47). On 10 April, it was the turn of Henri-Irénée Marrou, a Catholic academic, to be visited by the DST for an article in *Le Monde* on 5 April 1956 entitled 'France, My Country', in which he denounced the use of torture by the army in Algeria.
74. An alliance of the SFIO with Mitterrand's UDSR, left Gaullists and Mendès-France's followers stitched up to fight the 1956 election [*RH*].
75. Edgar Morin (b 1921): philosopher and sociologist, expelled from PCF in 1951 [*RH*].
76. Michel Leiris (1901-1990): surrealist and ethnographer [*RH*].
77. Francis Jeanson (1922-2009): philosopher, author of books on Sartre, manager of *Les Temps modernes* [*RH*].
78. François Mauriac (1885-1970): French Catholic novelist, Nobel Prize 1952 [*RH*].
79. For the preceding information, see Document Fo Rés 291, BDIC archives.
80. Document Fo Rés 291, BDIC archives. The GBL (Bolshevik-Leninist Group) of Favre-Bleibtreu and Michel Lequenne and the Lambertist PCI complained of not

having been 'invited' to this meeting.
81. It is an indication of the extent of the repression that Pierre Avot-Meyers was arrested and held briefly at Suresnes for putting up posters about this meeting and calling for the release of the four imprisoned militants (interview with Simonne Minguet and Pierre Avot Meyers, 17 November 1999).
82. For all the preceding, see Document Fo Rés 291, BDIC archives.
83. Interview with Simonne Minguet and Pierre Avot Meyers, 17 November 1999; *La question coloniale et la section française de la 4ᵉ Internationale*, document O Col 1615, BDIC archives at Nanterre.
84. *La question coloniale et la section française de la 4ᵉ Internationale*.
85. Document Fo Rés 137/..., BDIC archives at Nanterre. In January 1956, when the elections had seen the brief victory of the Republican Front, the PCF — which was not in the electoral alliance — made repeated advances in order to take part in the government and tried to stir up the 'myth' of the Popular Front. On 23 January 1956, before the government was formed, Maurice Thorez affirmed this intention in a radio broadcast: 'We repeat once more that we are ready, following the elections, to come to an agreement with the Socialist Party and the other parties of the left in order to give the country the government it expects.' (Cited by Hamon and Rotman, *Les Porteurs de valises*, p 43) But on 30 January the Mollet government was formed, excluding the Communists.
86. Document Fo Rés 137/..., BDIC archives at Nanterre.
87. *Le Libertaire*, no 435, 16 June 1955, CIRA archives.
88. Daniel Guérin (1904-1988): philosopher, writer, journalist, this intellectual was for a time close to Trotsky. A member of Marceau Pivert's PSOP, but also of the left wing of the Socialist Party, he was active in the UGS and then the PSU during the Algerian war and defended both the MNA and the FLN. He signed the Manifesto of 121. Throughout his life he was close to libertarian communism and became a theoretician of workers' management. He also contributed by his writings to opening up the workers' movement to struggles against normalcy in sexuality.
89. Thus in *Le Libertaire* of 4 August 1955 (CIRA archives) the National Bureau of the FCL wrote: 'The bourgeoisie, by striking the FCL and only the FCL, has marked it out as its class enemy, and hence as the party of the workers.' The necessary conclusion is drawn some lines later: 'Join the FCL, which tomorrow will be the great revolutionary party of the workers!' But also in no 443 of 8 September 1955: 'Pierre Morain, in jail, does not complain about his fate: on the contrary, he is proud to have been attacked by the capitalist machine because for him that is an irrefutable proof that he has been fighting the true revolutionary fight, the true class struggle, which is terrifying Borgeaud and the other settler bosses.'
90. *Le Libertaire*, special issue, 4 August 1955, CIRA archives. Fontenis comments in his memoirs about the FCL: 'It was however wrong to let itself be overly influenced by a workerist and declamatory style favoured in large organisations.' (Fontenis, *Changer le monde*, p 138)
91. Thus we have in *Le Libertaire* (no 446, CIRA archives) under the heading 'Revolutionary Solidarity': 'Comrade, today you have heard that Pierre Morain has been sentenced to a year in jail. Do we need long theoretical explanations to tell you your duty? Of course not. Proletarian solidarity is expressed by the heart, not

by words. To help our comrade Pierre Morain and all the prisoners who are victims of colonialism. To run a solidarity campaign: contribute to the special appeal from 26 September to 1 October. Revolutionary solidarity with Pierre Morain!'
92. An FCL leaflet given out in February 1954, when a meeting by Tixier-Vignancourt had been permitted in Paris and there was a renewed outbreak of far-right violence, stated: 'Successive bourgeois governments, advancing towards dictatorship, tolerate these provocations, while they ban working-class demonstrations and anti-colonialist meetings...' (*Le Libertaire*, 15 February 1955, CIRA archives)
93. Interview with Pierre Avot-Meyers and Simonne Minguet, 17 November 1999.
94. Thus an old doctor, Dr Zakine, who had been a member of the Second International and then a young member of the PCF, and who had been banned from practising for having carried out clandestine abortions, agreed to rent commercial premises under a false name (interview with Pierre Avot-Meyers and Simonne Minguet, 17 November 1999).
95. Interview with Pierre Avot-Meyers and Simonne Minguet, 17 November 1999.
96. Interview with Pierre Avot-Meyers and Simonne Minguet, 17 November 1999.
97. Michel Fiant (1928-2007): PCI leader during the Algerian war, he guided Alain Krivine's activity inside the Union of Communist Students, notably at the time of the creation of the University Anti-Fascist Front. He sided with Pablo in 1965. He became one of the leaders of the Revolutionary Marxist Alliance (AMR), the French section of the TMRI. Later a member of the 'Alternatifs'.
98. Hamon and Rotman, *Les Porteurs de valises*, p 62.

Chapter V: SFIO, PCF: The 'Betrayals': From 'Peace in Algeria' to Pacification

The 'Republican Front' coalition which came to power in France in 1956 was composed of Socialists and Radicals — the inevitable axes of any government during the Fourth Republic — and had the parliamentary support of the PCF. Thus the left had a preponderant position in this government, all the more so because Guy Mollet, the main leader of the SFIO, was Prime Minister. Guy Mollet was elected on a programme advocating 'peace in Algeria', but after the 'day of tomatoes'[1] in Algiers, he adopted a repressive course: that of the 'pacification' of Algeria, with the tacit support of the PCF, which on 12 March voted for 'special powers'. Now it was possible to send conscripts and to extend the state of emergency to the whole of Algeria.

The situation may seem paradoxical: it was the left which was stepping up the repression, and implementing a colonialist policy, to the point where a Gaullist like General Catroux, considered too moderate by the 'extremists' in Algiers, was replaced by the socialist Lacoste.[2] But such a policy was not automatic for left-wing organisations, and it did not fail to cause confusion in the minds of many activists and even of certain leaders. How did the far left recognise the left's accession to power in a stance of total obstinacy with regard to the

Algerian situation? What strategy did it adopt in order to have an impact on the contradictions of the left in power? And what new difficulties emerged in the context of an isolation which was even greater in comparison with the two main organisations of the left?

First of all, it must be clearly understood that if repression was found necessary in Algeria, this was equally the case in France, though certainly to a lesser extent, for organisations supporting Algerian independence, and above all for Algerian militants. As far as the French organisations were concerned, prosecutions of the press and of militants continued. Pierre Frank, Simonne Minguet, Janine Weil and Raymond Bouvet were imprisoned under this government, and Pierre Frank and Jacques Privas had to appear in court because of articles in *La Vérité des travailleurs*. Their 'hostile brothers' in the other PCI were also prosecuted for a breach of state security: four contributors to *La Vérité* — Bloch, Stéphane Just, Pierre Lambert and Daniel Renard — were involved.[3] The same was the case with the libertarians.[4] The FCL had to pay a total of three million francs[5] in fines, and the very question as to whether *Le Libertaire* could continue appearing was openly raised in the pages of issue no 486 on 5 July; no 487 — which nonetheless contained an account of a solidarity meeting held at Aulnay-sous-Bois, in which a PCF deputy, René Bellanger, took part — was the last issue to be published.[6]

The FCL was in great difficulties and its very existence was in question. A meeting of the National Council was held on 5 July to take decisions made necessary by the situation: the publication of *Le Libertaire* was suspended until a hypothetical issue in September, and it was planned that a theoretical monthly which would deal with current events 'in depth', *Partisan*, would appear. The FCL did not dissolve and carried on.[7] These were the official decisions, but neither the September issue of *Le Libertaire* nor *Partisan* ever saw the light of day. It was well and truly the end of the FCL. At the National Council meeting two views of the FCL's future had appeared: on the one side were those who supported a limited publication of *Le Libertaire* and a restricted public presence, but an organisational continuity — Robert Joulin, Roger Caron and Vandendriesche. On the other side was the majority around Georges Fontenis, Pierre Morain, Michel Donnet, Gilbert Simon, Paul Philippe and Albert Caron, who advocated suspending publication of the paper and going into clandestinity.[8]

What did such clandestinity actually mean? To start with, objective factors necessitated this decision, which was the death sentence for an organisation that had been weakened too much to deal with the conditions of illegality: not merely the prosecution of numerous militants, but also the fines which ruined it despite solidarity subscriptions and despite the sale of an aeroplane which a few years earlier had been intended for a failed attack on Franco.[9]

It should be stressed that on 13 July 1956, a few days after the National Council, Fontenis, Joulin, Caron, Donnet, Multot, Simon and Philippe were arrested and questioned by the DST while their homes and the FCL premises were searched. Mulot, who owned a weapon, was imprisoned.[10] Thus the FCL militants had good reasons for wanting to evade justice and the police, and the organisation ran a major risk of being destroyed by the arrest and conviction of the main leaders. The latter, often young, and perhaps lacking the experience and perspective necessary in an emergency, advocated radical measures.

But 45 years later in his memoirs, Georges Fontenis admits that there were other motives besides the difficulties caused by the repression and speaks of the 'temptation of clandestinity' in a context where reservists were demonstrating and where some rebels were deserting. These were rare cases, but hasty generalisations were made. He also refers to a certain 'romanticism' and even 'adventurism' among the young,[11] and among the older ones there were 'memories of the Resistance'.[12] None of these factors encouraged cool and balanced reflection, and those whom Fontenis calls the 'activists' threw themselves enthusiastically into clandestinity, publishing a leaflet in the name of a secret organisation, Volonté du peuple (People's Will).[13] Such attitudes were consistent with the general orientation of the FCL since its foundation, and fitted the tone used in *Le Libertaire*, in which revolutionary mystique and triumphant proclamations went hand in hand.

However, this move into clandestinity was not put into effect by the whole organisation, which, from this point on, had difficulty in surviving, either in legality or in clandestinity, because the leadership was divided. Some of them spent the summer of 1956 preparing for clandestinity, but in the end they were mainly those being prosecuted, the rest continuing to live 'normally', but without being active other than in trade-union work, since the FCL no longer existed. Among those accused, Roger Caron, Robert Joulin and André Moine in particular complied with the judicial procedures affecting them and did not go into clandestinity, while ceasing all collective activity for Algerian independence.[14] Others, Georges Fontenis, Simon and Philippe, left their jobs and their homes to go into clandestinity and tried to maintain a solidarity 'network' with former FCL members.[15]

Repression had got the better of the FCL, for the organisation no longer existed as such, becoming a 'network' which existed after a fashion through the commitment and contact work done by the 'clandestine members'. The various groups, in Paris and the provinces, continued to pay subscriptions and contribute, and the clandestine leaders, helped sometimes by other militants, collected these sums to print leaflets and the paper *La Volonté du peuple*, sold spasmodically at factory gates and in Paris.[16] But it was only a temporary reprieve.

The clandestine activists lived in difficult conditions, far from their families in various hide-outs. Thus Fontenis spent the winter in a freezing one-room flat lent by the girl-friend of a militant who was not threatened by prosecution. Sleepless nights under a heap of blankets left him some bad memories!

Amid the factors which led to the disappearance of the FCL, we should stress the illusory hopes of the FCL in an imminent revolution, its lack of clarity in analysing the political situation, and excessive confidence in its capacity to take on the state. All these factors, combined with pitiless repression on the part of successive governments, got the better of a young organisation carried forward by revolutionary enthusiasm. But this period enabled it to unite its members in the struggle against colonialism and to find a legitimacy there.[17]

As an organisation, the FCL was indeed dead, even if the activity of the 'clandestine members' enabled it to perpetuate the fiction of an 'underground' existence for some months. There remained resolute individuals who were not affected by demoralisation and who formed a 'network' ready for political action. Some, such as Fontenis, still played a role during the Algerian war. But it was the end of the dream of a libertarian communist organisation capable of challenging the PCF for hegemony over the working class and becoming the 'revolutionary workers' party'. All the more so because, early in 1957, some of the militants who were still active, notably Pierre Morain, were arrested for an attack on the premises of Pierre Poujade's movement[18] in the fifteenth arrondissement of Paris. Fontenis himself was arrested by the DST during a visit to his family in July 1957.[19]

The Trotskyists of the two PCIs, which were more solid organisations, managed not to fall into the trap of clandestinity, which does not mean that they ruled out clandestine activity: the Fourth International network is the proof of that. But this network was reorganised, and caution was required. It was the same for the public presence: there was no question of throwing themselves into a process of ever more extravagant statements in the Trotskyist press and 'provoking' convictions, even if these precautions did not always succeed in avoiding confiscations and fines. In February 1957, a solidarity campaign was launched to defend *La Vérité*: on this occasion an internal circular recommended greater caution in articles.[20] To protect oneself from attack, the trick was to suggest what was meant, to bank on the reader's intelligence in reading between the lines. This caution, together with the policy of 'united front against repression' on the part of both PCIs, enabled them to avoid suffering the same fate as the FCL.

But Guy Mollet's government was not content with stepping up repression against limited militant circles, and it decided to send conscripts to Algeria. This decision affected tens of thousands of homes and it was much more unpopular.

In August 1955, Prime Minister Edgar Faure[21] had already proceeded to recall the age groups of 1954 (who were due to be discharged in November) and 1953,[22] which provoked numerous demonstrations by the reservists, who refused to go and fight: on 11 September 1955, soldiers refused to board trains bound for Algeria in the Gare de Lyon in Paris; civilians joined in: wives, families and friends of the reservists; the station was cordoned off. When they were finally forced to board the train, the rebels set off the alarm bells every 300 meters to stop it. They were finally sent to Algeria by plane. Throughout France there were similar actions: at Rouen in September 1955, there were violent clashes between the soldiers, supported by part of the population, and security police. At the same time the SFIO organised a meeting in Paris at the salle Wagram to protest at the sending of conscripts, while on 8 October at Rouen the PCF held a demonstration of support for the rebel soldiers.[23] Similar events took place at Nantes, Tours and Valence. In November, Edgar Faure announced the discharge of 57 000 reservists[24] and he was obliged to dissolve the National Assembly on 2 December 1955.

The far left had intended to play a significant role in the reservists' demonstrations. At least for the Trotskyists this was not an automatic position, since some might see in it a contradiction with the Leninist principle that Communists should participate in wars in order to play an active revolutionary role: but here it was a question of an imperialist war to suppress a colonial revolution and so the Bolshevik 'rule' of participation in wars did not apply.[25] At Nantes, the FCL and the PCI tried to make connections between the strikes of workers which were paralysing the city and the reservists' actions.[26]

In early October 1955, the left youth organisations tried to set up a Committee Against Sending Conscripts to Algeria. This brought together the Socialist Youth, the UJRF (French Union of Republican Youth, a PCF-controlled organisation), the libertarian and Trotskyist youth, the Youth Hostels, the New Left, the Socialist Students (in which Michel Rocard[27] played a leading role), the FO Youth (a fictitious organisation consisting only of Trotskyists)[28] and even the secular boy scouts. Such total unity of youth organisations on such a subject was pleasing to the far left, but, under pressure from Guy Mollet, the Socialist Youth withdrew from the collective,[29] soon to be followed by the UJRF which denounced the presence of 'Trotskyist and libertarian police elements'.[30] The committee tried to organise a meeting on 13 October at the Mutualité,[31] but this was banned, and there were clashes with the police.[32] This was the last act of this short-lived committee.

When, on 12 April 1956, the cabinet decided to call up reservists and to send conscripts to Algeria, the demonstrations of opposition by the reservists and those who supported them resumed, and trains were again obstructed: on 3

May at Lézignan, on 10 May at Saint-Aignant-des-Noyers in Loir-et-Cher, on 17 May at Le Mans, on 18 May at Grenoble. There were also actions in the ports, on 23 May at Antibes, on 24 May at Le Havre, on 28 May at Saint-Nazaire. Often there were violent confrontations, and local inhabitants, dockers and railway workers gave their support to actions in which were involved the New Left, the far left and also the PCF, despite the reluctance of its leadership when faced with these 'provocations'.[33] Thousands of people took part in these actions which concerned young people. But the government remained inflexible and the PCF had cold feet: apart from the far left no party called for refusal to join the army, and the reservists left for the war. The first pictures of conscripts killed or missing in action against the independence fighters led public opinion to direct its anger against the FLN 'killers'.[34] The far left was not able to develop this movement and to ensure its continuity. Its small size was of course the main cause of this powerlessness. But its divisions also had an impact: thus Michel Lequenne, a member of the GBL (Bolshevik-Leninist Group) which had been expelled from the Lambertist PCI sent a letter to both PCIs deploring the 'distressing sight of divisions', the 'pedantic tone' and the 'expressions of childishness and cliquishness' of both organisations at a meeting at Chatenay-Malabry to set up a committee of youth organisations against the use of conscripts.[35] However, where it already had some roots, the far left managed to derive a certain 'political advantage' from the discontent of the reservists, as is shown by the story of Louis Fontaine[36] and the Vernon Trotskyist cell.

The Vernon LRBA (Laboratory for Ballistic and Aerodynamic Research) factory had military management, but those who worked there were civilian workers, not under army discipline. They had seven different sets of conditions of service, with very few civil servants (about 60 out of a thousand employees), and were mainly state workers or state auxiliaries with less secure conditions.[37] The French workers worked alongside German engineers, technicians and workers from the Nazi rocket factory at Peenemünde (where the V2 rockets were developed), who had been taken over and employed by France at the end of the war, and who gave solid support to the management in the event of strikes or social conflicts.[38] However, this isolated factory in the Vernon forest was the scene of intense political activity.

Louis Fontaine was a worker in this factory at Vernon and was one of the reservists due to leave for Algeria. He was not very political, although he had joined the PCF at the age of 18 and left six months later when he found that the main activity to which he was assigned was selling *L'Humanité-Dimanche*. His year in Algeria led to a sudden awareness and 'politicised' him; he was revolted by the poverty afflicting the Algerian population and he understood that 'Algeria is not France', that it was not a French administrative district 'like any other';

colonial policy outraged him. Drafted to a transport unit, he maintained good relations with the Algerians he met, especially with the *harkis*,[39] of whom some were obviously infiltrated FLN agents.

When he returned to the mainland in 1957, he was ready to act politically to assist Algerian independence. He joined the PCI through contact with a Trotskyist aged about 40, Camille Januel, who worked and was politically active in the Vernon factory.[40] A Trotskyist since just before the Second World War, he had succeeded in 1940 in stirring up his regiment against the officers who were deserting,[41] and, as a prisoner in Germany, had established a clandestine German Trotskyist cell in the sector where he had been sent as a result of the STO.[42] As a draughtsman, he was transferred from Saint-Etienne to Vernon in 1952 or 1953 for disciplinary reasons. He was very rapidly acknowledged by the workers in the factory, because he led strikes in his capacity as a CGT delegate. He managed to get rid of the leader of the CGT branch, a PCF member who had misappropriated some of the union funds.[43] In a letter reporting his activity to Pierre Frank and to the Political Bureau, he explained that he had been elected general secretary of the union in the factory by 110 votes out of 115, in first place, ahead of the 'orthodox Stalinist' candidates put forward by the PCF. His influence was such that, while he didn't get all the votes to be delegate during a first vote by secret ballot, since the Stalinists had crossed out his name, he nonetheless was elected unanimously when there was a vote by show of hands, since nobody wanted to vote publicly against him for fear of being discredited in the eyes of the other workers.[44]

Camille Januel[45] succeeded in setting up a Trotskyist cell in the factory, not an easy job because of the fact that it was a military reservation and because of the systematic opposition from the PCF.[46] So Trotskyist activity was developed at Vernon, right inside the rocket factory; leaflets, copies of *La Vérité des travailleurs*, calls for desertion were stuck on the walls. The Trotskyists were active above all in the CGT union, and that was what enabled them to be recognised in the factory.[47] Camille Januel managed to recruit Roland Vacher,[48] a CFTC militant who went over to the CGT with about 20 of his colleagues,[49] and who very soon took on responsibilities in his new union, given that Camille Januel was confined to administrative isolation.[50] In 1957, 'Camille' sent a list of PCI members in the factory to the Political Bureau: there were eight. Two of them were milling machine operators: Jean Bocquet, 24, and Louis Fontaine, 24. Four were fitters: Claude Rialland, 24, Jack Houdet, 33, Marcel Girard, 26, and André Morin, 25. Finally one was a radio technician, Roland Vacher, 27.[51] The age of these new militants is very significant.[52] Some of them were certainly among Guy Mollet's unfortunate 'reservists' and, as with Louis Fontaine, it was the Algerian war which had led them to commit themselves to the far left.

Other were persuaded by trade-union activity to join the PCI. The local PCI cell continued to grow and before the Évian agreements had reached a total of around 20 militants between Rouen and Nantes, giving birth to the Seine Valley branch.[53]

Gilbert Marquis' account confirms this hypothesis about the role of the Algerian war in the recruitment to the PCI: a member of the PCI Political Bureau, an entrist in the PCF, in 1956 he was a member of the secretariat of the CGT departmental organisation for the Seine-et-Oise[54] thanks to this entry work. But that same year he was denounced as a Trotskyist and had to abandon his departmental role in the union[55] to go and work at Nord Aviation. He set up a PCI 'youth committee', and gave out leaflets against the special powers and the sending of conscripts. He thus managed to establish an active cell with seven or eight members: for example, identity cards were 'borrowed' in order to enable the manufacture of forged cards, leaflets were typed in the administrative centre, here too by women. Gilbert Marquis was even elected a staff delegate.[56]

What happened at Vernon and Nord Aviation is certainly significant, even if these are only two examples. Where the Trotskyists had some strength, they succeeded in recruiting — partly through their denunciation of the Algerian war — young workers, who had often been recalled to the army, and they had some real political space. Their trade-union activity gave them credibility and protection, and thus also provided a vehicle for integrating new members. The report of the Twelfth Congress of the PCI in December 1956 published in *Quatrième Internationale* notes with pleasure the fact that the organisation has doubled its membership in the course of the previous year.[57] To 'double its membership' for such a small organisation is an achievement which must be seen in relative terms. The claims made at a congress are not necessarily the most reliable. But the PCI had undeniably recruited in the course of 1956, and the 'special powers' doubtless contributed to this. The whole problem was that the Trotskyists did not have 'forces' everywhere: indeed the places where they had them were rather few and far between, and the far left could not provide a political outlet for the discontent of the reservists even if a few of them were recruited.

There remain speculations about the role of the PCF, which had far more extensive roots, and which might perhaps have provided such an outlet for the rebellious reservists. If this 'speculation' is part of the history, it is because it fed the resentment of numerous Communist militants and sympathisers, and sowed doubt in their minds: 'And suppose that the party was not following the correct line?' Questions about the direction taken by the Thorez leadership became more numerous, and as well as the problem of the special powers there was the publication, in 1956, of the Khrushchev 'Secret Speech' and the PCF's unconditional support for the Soviet intervention in Hungary that same year. Some members openly criticised the PCF's policies, and for the Trotskyists there was the question of a turn in the work aimed specifically at the PCF: had the time come to split off 'whole sections' of the PCF?

What Specific Work Aimed at the PCF?

The question of work specifically aimed at the PCF was posed in two ways: on the one hand, in the individual relationships that each Trotskyist could develop with Communist militants in his or her workplace or field of activity, in a union or in the networks of support for the FLN; on the other hand, in the conscious policy of the whole organisation towards 'critical' Communist militants.

Meanwhile, numerous Communists did not understand or did not accept their party's policy. The confusion crystallised around two points: the vote in favour of special powers, which summed up the PCF's Algerian policy, and the support for the Soviet intervention in Budapest. Individual militants were asking questions, while others were thinking of organising an opposition inside the party. The Trotskyists were active specifically with a view to organising the latter, which didn't prevent them working with the former. Moreover they managed to win over certain individuals who were disturbed by the PCF's attitude, despite their misgivings about Trotskyists. For militants who were used to following unconditionally the 'line' of a monolithic party, the slightest doubt about an aspect of the party's policy could very quickly lead to much broader questions and even to a complete break.

The case of Alain Krivine is significant in this respect: in 1957, at the age of 16, he was a pure product of the party apparatus. He was a member of Les Vaillants (the Brave Ones), a sort of Communist boy scouts, then of the Communist Youth (JC) which replaced the UJRF; as 'star seller' of *L'Avant-garde*, the JC paper, he was entitled to take part in the Sixth World Festival of Democratic Youth in the Soviet Union in July and August 1957. On a very ecumenical theme, Peace, the festival brought together thousands of young people from all countries.[58] Alain Krivine naïvely thought he was doing the right thing by organising a meeting with a youth delegation from the FLN. He had a double surprise: first of all the young Algerians sharply criticised the cautious policy of the PCF on Algeria; then the young French Communist leaders gave him a good telling off for his 'initiative'.

Alain Krivine returned to France disgusted and decided to act in favour of Algerian independence. He didn't know that two of his brothers, the elder Jean-Michel and his twin Hubert, were already Trotskyist militants. Alain told them of his experience, and Hubert, who belonged to an FLN support network, offered to introduce him to it. Alain accepted on condition that this network was not

'Trotskyist'. Hubert promised and introduced him to Michel Fiant, a member of the Political Bureau of the PCI.[59] Alain thus became a 'suitcase carrier' and hid in the trenches around the Fresnes prison to observe at what time the guards did their rounds so as to enable the planning of escapes for Algerians. He was also involved with networks of rebels who had evaded conscription into the army in Algeria. By doing so, he was disobeying the PCF, and risked immediate expulsion if he was discovered, but he only engaged in such activities because he was asking more and more questions about the party, until he took the final step at the end of the 1950s and accepted Hubert's proposal to meet Pierre Frank and then to join the PCI.[60]

Alain Krivine came to Trotskyism through being convinced by concrete activity on the question of solidarity with the Algerian revolution, and his break with the PCF was explained by 'emotional' reasons:[61] the PCF was mistaken on Hungary and on Algeria. The party required unconditional 'faith' and once trust was broken on two such fundamental points, everything else went very quickly. Nonetheless, the number of Communist militants persuaded to join the PCI by Trotskyist activity was small, but such people did exist. For example, it was because of the question of support for the FLN that the secretary of the CGT branch at Nord Aviation, by the name of Avice, became a member of the PCI.[62] Other PCF militants, if they didn't go over to Trotskyism, worked with Trotskyists in support activity for the FLN. Such was the case with Clara Benoîts. A PCF and CGT militant, wife of Henri Benoîts, who was a PCI member, she typed leaflets for the General Union of Algerian Workers (UGTA) and tried to defend the position of support for the FLN in her cell. She was also active in a committee of the Mouvement de la paix,[63] and during one of its meetings, interventions by Communist militants and by Clara Benoîts provoked the departure, in fury, of the national representative of the Movement, a PCF cadre.[64] But most of the PCF militants, even if they were critical, even if they also worked with the Trotskyists in support of the Algerian revolution, remained in the party. It was very difficult to take the final step and leave the PCF, and the perspective of joining a Trotskyist *groupuscule* did not arouse great enthusiasm. In fact, Pablo admitted in a document in 1958 that the period had not been 'as fruitful as we might have hoped'.

However, the Trotskyists analysed the sudden turns of the PCF and diagnosed a deep crisis which was of particular interest to them. In November 1956, Pierre Frank wrote that 'the crisis of Stalinism is now coming to paroxysm. It will come undone in a relatively short time, a very short time.'[65]

The Trotskyist movement was banking on a 'political revolution' which would lift the Stalinist handicap from the leadership of the working-class movement in the capitalist countries and which would enable the overthrow of the 'Stalinist bureaucracy' in the 'degenerated workers' states' in the East. Hence any crack in the various Communist parties was of the greatest interest to them: thus in France the task was to overthrow the hegemony of the PCF. In a preparatory text for the Fifth World Congress of the Fourth International,[66] which was adopted more or less verbatim by the congress in question,[67] it was said of 'the decline and fall of Stalinism in the Communist parties in the capitalist countries' that 'the oppositional tendencies which are crystallising within the Communist parties can be classified into two categories: a right opposition tendency and a left opposition tendency'.

The fate of the right-wing oppositional tendency was dealt with quickly. Thus speaking of the group around Pierre Hervé,[68] an intellectual who was critical of the PCF, Pierre Frank wrote that 'in the crisis of Stalinism, there is no shortage of rootless people who think it is enough to meet and discuss everything and nothing in order to end up by finding something'.[69] For the Trotskyists this tendency represented 'the logical outcome of the right-wing opportunism practised by major Communist parties during long periods of their existence', and revealed the great disadvantages of taking literally 'Khrushchev's chattering about different roads to socialism' and of following 'an evolution in the direction of social-democratisation'.[70] The only interest of such tendencies was to open up, 'after decades of bureaucratic stifling', 'a long period of reflection, discussion and exchange of ideas', which obviously could only be to the advantage of Trotskyism, especially for those who were practising entrism.[71] For this reason, the Trotskyists would still seek dialogue with these tendencies.

But the real issue, which took up the main part of the work of the Twelfth Congress,[72] concerned the left-wing oppositional tendencies within the PCF, characterised as desiring a 'return to Lenin' and a 'more determined and effective struggle [against the]… imperialist bourgeoisie'.[73] The tasks of the Fourth International were to enable these tendencies to 'declare themselves openly': in short it was the job of the entrist militants to try to form an internal opposition in the PCF by starting from the internal contradictions of the party on the Algerian question as well as on the questions of democracy within the party and in the Eastern bloc. If the Trotskyists diagnosed a crisis of Stalinism, they nonetheless thought that a left opposition to Stalinism should be built within the party: in fact, taking into account the 'general conjuncture' and the 'even more abysmal bankruptcy of social democracy', notably in France with the Algerian war, 'the Communist parties will continue to channel the majority, and above all the most combative section of the proletariat', hence 'the most healthy and left-wing tendencies will be inclined to remain within the PCF'.[74]

Concretely, how could this strategy be implemented in France? It was around journals internal to the PCF that the Trotskyists attempted to form an internal opposition. On the decision of the Political Bureau in 1956, the Trotskyist 'entrists' in the PCF launched a journal, *Tribune de discussion*, whose contributors were mainly members of the Political Bureau such as Denis Berger, but also Gilbert Marquis,[75] Michel Ravelli or Michel Fiant.[76] Félix Guattari,[77] a member of the PCI, Lucien Sebag[78] and Anne Giannini were also involved in the editing. Most of the editors of the journal were also members of the PCF, and it was Denis Berger[79] who coordinated the entrist activity.[80] The journal was duplicated and distributed by Trotskyist militants to Communist members who 'were likely to be interested', that is, who showed a certain critical spirit. Of course the entrists did not say that they had produced the journal; they pretended to know of it simply through articles they had read in it.

The journal enjoyed a certain degree of success, and the time came when the Trotskyists thought it had a sufficiently large audience to let others take over, so that this audience could really become that of an internal opposition in the PCF and the members would take it over. So they called a meeting of all the regular readers of the journal at Gilbert Marquis' home at Clamart. There was just one problem, but it was a big one. Which Trotskyist militant could represent the 'editorial board' of the journal when they were almost all known as PCF militants who were sympathisers with *Tribune de discussion*? They couldn't reveal that they were really the writers for fear of arousing distrust, and perhaps even of revealing their status as entrists! Only Michel Fiant, who was not known as a PCF member, was finally available to present the journal, in the editing of which he had, however, played little part. The entrist strategy presented a few disadvantages and required some acting skill. Michel Fiant explained that for various reasons — of professional activity, health, etc, — a new editorial team would have to be established and that the readers of the *Tribune de discussion* had been invited for this purpose.[81]

A small team was established with Communist militants from the eleventh arrondissement of Paris, notably Gérard Spitzer.[82] Meanwhile, a small group of Communist intellectuals around Victor Leduc,[83] Henri Lefebvre,[84] Anatole Kopp, Yves Cachin and François Châtelet[85] were considering the formation of a 'critical' group inside the PCF.[86] Caught unprepared by the launch and relative success of *Tribune de discussion*,[87] they decided in the autumn of 1956 to launch their own journal *L'Étincelle* (*Spark*), in particular because, unlike the editors of the *Tribune*, and with the exception of François Châtelet and Henri Lefebvre, they did not disapprove of the Soviet intervention in Hungary.[88] However, Denis Berger made contact with Yves Cachin and, after discussions, the two journals merged in April 1957, taking the title *L'Étincelle (Tribune de discussion)*. But this unification was short-lived, for Lucienne Abraham (Michèle Mestre),[89] a former member of the Fourth International,[90] denounced Denis Berger and the others as 'Trotskyists' in the autumn of 1957. Shocked, Victor Leduc and his friends withdrew from the venture: in any case, they firmly believed that after the Twentieth Congress of the Communist Party of the Soviet Union and the Khrushchev 'Secret Speech', de-Stalinisation was in progress. So forming an oppositional group was pointless, and in 1958 they merely launched a theoretical journal, *Voies Nouvelles* (*New Paths*), with no intentions of political organisation.[91]

But Gérard Spitzer, Roger Rey and other militants decided to carry on working with Denis Berger and Félix Guattari. In January 1958, they launched *La Voie communiste* (*The Communist Path*), financed by Félix Guattari who, thanks to his clinic, had certain funds at his disposal.[92] But if the audience was broader than the Trotskyist circle, Denis Berger was now in open conflict with the PCI. As a member of the Political Bureau, he was opposed to Gilbert Marquis and Pierre Frank on an essential point: he did not think they should confine themselves to pulling together a 'Communist opposition' solely inside the PCF. In fact, according to him there were many Communist militants who had left the PCF, and new layers that had been politicised and radicalised by the Algerian war were to be found outside its ranks. Thus the *Voie communiste* was to appear publicly, being sold on news-stands and addressed to PCF members but also to those outside the party.[93] Pierre Frank and Gilbert Marquis, in accordance with the orientation adopted at the Fifth World Congress, supported a strategy centred on the political struggle inside the PCF.[94] Early in 1958, Denis Berger withdrew from the Political Bureau and his activity in the PCI became less and less intense.[95] He no longer believed in the policy being pursued by the PCI and wanted to see an open, broad and public Communist opposition.

Thus the *Voie communiste* went beyond being a mere journal and became an organisation which grew and was beyond the control of the PCI. This meant a break with the strategy of the Fourth International. So the new movement brought together Trotskyists who had broken their organisational links such as Denis Berger and Michel Ravelli, dissident Communists such as Simon Blumenthal[96] and Gérard Spitzer, but also the libertarian intellectual Daniel Guérin and former members of the FCL. The latter had regrouped, once the period of clandestinity was over, in a group (Action communiste) of former FCL members, whose aim was 'the formation... of a party which would include the majority of revolutionary elements'.[97] During the summer of 1958, Fontenis, who had, after a spell in Fresnes prison, sorted out his legal problems, thanks to the defence by Yves Dechezelles, and who had been able to pay his numerous fines thanks to the solidarity of his comrades,[98] joined the *Voie communiste* team, together with many members of Action communiste, which was thereby dissolved.

Their new journal appeared in January 1958. The sub-heading 'Bulletin of the Communist Opposition, Continuing *l'Étincelle–Tribune de discussion* and the *Bulletin de l'opposition*' located the approach of this publication in a direct line of descent from the two previous journals.[99] Very soon the strongest bond holding the organisation together was the question of support for the Algerian revolution. Early in 1958, Denis Berger was introduced to an FLN official as a representative of the Communist opposition.[100] The contact was made through the mediation of Roger Rey, a former regular soldier, who had been cashiered in 1952 for sticking up posters against the arrival of General Ridgway,[101] and who had become a commercial engineer in a sugar refinery. Anne Giannini, Roger Rey and Denis Berger regularly met with Moussa Khebaïli, a leader of the French Federation of the FLN, and began to do jobs for the Algerians.[102] The group began to operate around activity assisting the FLN, while moving further and further away from the Fourth International. Denis Berger, who was summoned to come and 'explain himself' to the Political Bureau of the PCI in December 1958, was unable to attend because he had been arrested and questioned by the DST: his expulsion at this point was only a confirmation of the existing situation, for in effect he had left the organisation.[103] In December 1958, a special issue declared that '*La Voie communiste* has not and never will have any organisational connection with the Fourth International'. Of course a journal claiming to represent the opposition inside the PCF had to clear itself in advance of any accusation of 'Trotskyism' if it wanted to have any credibility, but nonetheless this statement had a certain whiff of a split about it: *La Voie communiste* was henceforth independent of its mother organisation, the Fourth International.

Guy Mollet's accession to power with the backing of the PCF thus opened a new period for the far left. Yet there was continuity in the repression, which hit the FCL so hard that it led to its disappearance; a continuity in the government's determination to settle the Algerian question by military means; a continuity in the struggle of those on the far left who had chosen to support Algerian independence. Such events as the sending of conscripts to Algeria or the voting of special powers by the PCF effectively opened a new political period characterised by the intensifying of the internal contradictions in the Socialist and Communist Parties. In these conditions the Trotskyists linked to the Fourth International were preoccupied with forming an internal opposition inside the PCF, while at the same time denouncing the 'betrayals' of the SFIO and PCF leaderships. This policy made it possible to win to Trotskyism, on the basis of real struggles against the sending of conscripts and in solidarity with the Algerian revolution, some individuals disgusted by the vote for special powers or the war in Algeria. But there was no lasting organised oppositional tendency within the PCF, and the venture of *La Voie communiste* even led to the departure of valuable militants who believed the time had come to organise a broad open Communist tendency outside the PCF: so a new experiment was set up, here too on the basis of concrete solidarity with Algerian militants. The influence of the Trotskyists, even if some had broken their links with their organisation, was however essential in everything that at this time was attempted to the left of the PCF.

Moreover, as the war continued, concrete solidarity with the Algerian revolution, which the Trotskyists had been the first to initiate, grew to an extent which went beyond the framework of the far left: the Trotskyist network was no longer the only one to exist, and Christian, humanist and Communist militants also created networks of solidarity or for those who refused to be conscripted.

Notes

1. This was 6 February 1956, when Mollet was pelted with vegetables by settlers in Algiers who feared he would make concessions to the FLN [*RH*].
2. Robert Lacoste (1898-1989): SFIO deputy, Resident Minister in Algeria 1956-58 [*RH*].
3. Numerous issues of this paper were confiscated. A letter dated 26 May 1956 in particular deplored the confiscation of five issues in seven weeks. No 411, which contained an interview with an ALN officer suffered the same fate, likewise no 412, and later nos 442, 443 and 445 (document Fo 278, BDIC archives at Nanterre).
4. Issues of *Le Libertaire* that were prosecuted were no 474, 12 April, no 482, 7 June (which however did not include any article about the situation in Algeria), no 484, 19 June, and no 485, 26 June (Georges Fontenis, *Changer le monde: histoire du mouvement communiste libertaire (1945-1997)* (Paris, 2000), p 133).
5. These were 'old francs' — around one thousand were equivalent to a pound sterling of the time [*RH*].
6. Fontenis, *Changer le monde*, p 133.
7. Fontenis, *Changer le monde*, p 133.
8. Fontenis, *Changer le monde*, pp 134-37.
9. Fontenis, *Changer le monde*, pp 85-88, 205-09. Fontenis tells how he was contacted in 1948 by Aureliano Cerrada, a leader of the Spanish anarchists engaged in clandestine struggle against the Spanish dictator. He asked the FA leader to buy a second-hand tourist plane in his name, since it was necessary to be a French citizen to make such a purchase. The plane was bought by Fontenis for the sum of 1.6 million old francs from money handed over by the Spanish comrades. It was intended that the plane should take off in France and fly to one of Franco's homes where it would drop bombs through a trap-door that had been made in the fuselage. But the operation failed, the plane managed to get back and land in France, and this old and badly maintained plane was sold by Fontenis for 300 000 old francs in February 1955, with the agreement of the Spanish anarchists who were the plane's real owners, in order to replenish the finances of the FCL and assist with the production of *Le Libertaire*.

10. Press release from the National Committee of the FCL, document Fo Rés 137/..., BDIC archives at Nanterre.
11. According to Fontenis the average age of leaders and activists was around 25! (Fontenis, *Changer le monde*, p 137)
12. Fontenis, *Changer le monde*, p 135.
13. Fontenis, *Changer le monde*, p 135.
14. Fontenis, *Changer le monde*, p 143.
15. Fontenis, *Changer le monde*, p 144.
16. Fontenis, *Changer le monde*, pp 144-45.
17. Fontenis, *Changer le monde*, p 136, writes : 'But it must be a law of human societies that the more a group commits itself on the road of intervention at any price, getting ever more militant (above all verbally) in proportion to its impotence and the consequent frustrations, the more it refuses to see reality and rushes forward suicidally in panic.'
18. Pierre Poujade (1920-2003): his right-wing small-traders' party won 52 seats in the 1956 elections. One of its deputies was Jean-Marie Le Pen [*RH*].
19. Fontenis, *Changer le monde*, p 146.
20. Document Fo 278, BDIC archives at Nanterre.
21. Edgar Faure (1908-1988): Radical politician, later Gaullist; Prime Minister in 1952 and 1955-56 [*RH*].
22. Jean-Charles Jauffret, 'L'armée française au combat, de 1954 à l'envoi du contingent', in L Gervereau, J-P Rioux and B Stora (eds), *La France en guerre d'Algérie* (Paris, 1992).
23. H Hamon and P Rotman, *Les Porteurs de valises* (Paris, 1979), pp 19-22.
24. Fontenis, *Changer le monde*, p 125.
25. Interview with Michel Fiant, 8 November 1999.
26. Fontenis, *Changer le monde*, p 124.
27. Hamon and Rotman, *Les Porteurs de valises*, p 41. [Michel Rocard (b 1930), leading figure in PSU; joined Socialist Party 1974, Prime Minister under Mitterrand 1988-91 — *RH*.]
28. Interview with Michel Lequenne, 18 November 1999.
29. Hamon and Rotman, *Les Porteurs de valises*, p 41.
30. *La Question coloniale et la section française de la 4ᵉ Internationale*.
31. A large hall in Paris 5 often used for public meetings [*RH*].
32. Hamon and Rotman, *Les Porteurs de valises*, p 41.
33. Hamon and Rotman, *Les Porteurs de valises*, pp 48-49.
34. Hamon and Rotman, *Les Porteurs de valises*, pp 50-51.
35. Document Fo rés 137/..., BDIC archives at Nanterre.
36. Interview with Louis Fontaine, Le Var, 3 February 2000; Louis Fontaine: milling-machine operator at the LRBA factory at Vernon; recalled to the army during the Algerian war, joined the PCI on his return. Became full-timer doing support work for the FLN. With Pierre Avot-Meyers he ran the clandestine print-shop, but he also had to go into exile when this was located by the DST. Went to Morocco and worked in the arms factory set up by the Fourth International for the FLN. Close to Pablo, he settled in Algeria after independence until Boumediène's coup in 1965. He then lived in France, worked as a printer with Gilbert Marquis, then became a

postman in Southern France. Now retired.
37. This category of state auxiliary, with less secure conditions, was created by Maurice Thorez after the Liberation when he was minister in charge of the civil service.
38. Interview with Roland Vacher, Paris, 24 April 2000.
39. Members of Muslim militia units set up by the French to fight the FLN [RH].
40. Interview with Louis Fontaine, 3 February 2000.
41. Interview with Gilbert Marquis, 8 February 2000.
42. Interview with Roland Vacher, 24 April 2000. [The STO — compulsory labour service — was the scheme whereby French workers were deported to work as forced labour in Germany during the Second World War — RH.]
43. Interview with Louis Fontaine, 3 February 2000; interview with Roland Vacher, 24 April 2000.
44. Letters from 'Camille', document Fo Rés 137/..., BDIC archives at Nanterre.
45. Camille Januel (1916-2000) : Trotskyist militant, industrial draughtsman; during the Algerian war he organised in his factory at Vernon a Trotskyist cell which was very successful. It soon spread to the whole of the Seine valley. As a result of personal problems, he dropped out of activity in the 1960s.
46. In a letter dated 10 October 1957, Camille Januel cites a PCF 'newsletter', *L'Unité*, given out in the factory, in which one paragraph, headed 'Reply to a Rag', after a PCI leaflet, is devoted to the Trotskyists: 'We must distrust their lies and their activity.'
47. Interview with Louis Fontaine, 3 February 2000; interview with Roland Vacher, 24 April 2000.
48. Roland Vacher: radio technician at the Vernon factory, he was originally a Christian militant (in the CFTC), the son of a Communist Resister, he then joined the PCI in the 1950s under the influence of Camille Januel and joined the CGT. He became a member of the Political Bureau of the PCI, was particularly concerned with the organisation Jeune Résistance, and was active in the PSU as a follower of Michel Lequenne, to whom he was very close. He dropped out of activity in the 1960s, but returned after 1968 and joined the Ligue Communiste (successor of the PCI). As an engineer at Alsthom, he organised strikes against factory closures. Now retired.
49. Januel managed to persuade the Christian trade unionist to leave the CFTC: he convinced him to join the CGT by arguing about 'the coming war' and the need to defend the USSR.
50. The management made Camille Januel work in a shooting tunnel; he was given difficult working hours, kept separated from other workers in the factory, and was not allowed to move around freely (interview with Roland Vacher, 24 April 2000).
51. Letter from 'Camille', document Fo Rés 137/..., BDIC archives at Nanterre. The Political Bureau of the PCI took a consistent interest in this workplace cell, one of the few in the organisation: they tracked its progress carefully, and even offered places on the Political Bureau, which Roland Vacher joined even though he was still a very young member of the organisation (interview with Roland Vacher, 24 April 2000).
52. For example Roland Vacher applied to join the PCI in a letter dated 12 November 1956 (document Fo Rés 137/..., BDIC archives at Nanterre).

53. Interview with Roland Vacher, 24 April 2000. The Seine Valley branch did not survive after the end of the Algerian war. The internal debates and disagreements in the PCI remained obscure for working-class militants who had been recruited on the basis of concrete trade-union and political militancy. Moreover Camille Januel, who had personal problems, dropped out of activity, while Roland Vacher, demoralised by divisions within the Political Bureau and also affected by personal problems, dropped out of the PCI for some years. The branch, which was based essentially on these two men, did not recover.
54. This *département* no longer exists.
55. He would be expelled from it in 1958 (interview with Gilbert Marquis, 8 February 2000).
56. Interview with Gilbert Marquis, 8 February 2000.
57. 'France, the 12th Congress of the PCI', *Quatrième Internationale*, Paris, March 1957, pp 97-98 (personal archives of Jean-Michel Krivine).
58. H Hamon and P Rotman, *Génération I: les années de rêve* (Paris, 1987), pp 13-39 ; interview with Alain Krivine, 19 November 1999.
59. Interview with Alain Krivine, 19 November 1999.
60. Hamon and Rotman, *Les Porteurs de valises*, pp 88-89, 140-42.
61. Interview with Alain Krivine, 19 November 1999.
62. Interview with Gilbert Marquis, 8 February 2000.
63. Peace Movement, at this time effectively controlled by the PCF [*RH*].
64. Interview with Henri and Clara Benoîts, 7 February 2000; interview with Henri and Clara Benoîts in *Expression immigré(e)s-français(es)*, October 1993.
65. Letter from P Frank, document Fo Rés 137/…, BDIC archives at Nanterre.
66. 'Decline and Fall of Stalinism', *Quatrième Internationale*, Paris, March 1957, pp 75-92 (personal archives of Jean-Michel Krivine).
67. For the congress documents see 'The Fifth Congress of the Fourth International', *Quatrième Internationale*, special issue, December 1957 (personal archives of Jean-Michel Krivine).
68. Pierre Hervé (1913-1993): leading PCF member, expelled 1956, later a Gaullist [*RH*].
69. Letter from Pierre Frank, document Fo Rés 137/…, BDIC archives at Nanterre.
70. 'Decline and Fall of Stalinism', *Quatrième Internationale*, March 1957, p 90.
71. 'Decline and Fall of Stalinism', *Quatrième Internationale*, March 1957, p 91.
72. 'France, 12th Congress of the PCI', *Quatrième Internationale*, Paris, March 1957, p 98 (personal archives of Jean-Michel Krivine): 'Of course the main part of the congress dealt with the crisis of Stalinism and above all its impact on the French labour movement, with the perspective of a political convergence between our movement and the tendencies and activists in the PCF who want a "return to Lenin".'
73. 'Decline and Fall of Stalinism', *Quatrième Internationale*, March 1957, p 91.
74. For these quotations see 'Decline and Fall of Stalinism', *Quatrième Internationale*, March 1957, p 91.
75. Gilbert Marquis (Lenoir): worker, became a Trotskyist in 1949, after taking part in the labour brigades of young volunteers in Yugoslavia, organised in part by the Fourth International and by Pablo, following the Stalin-Tito split. A CGT member,

he played an active role in solidarity with the FLN during the Algerian war and became close to Pablo. As a leader of the Alliance Marxiste-Révolutionnaire, French section of the TMRI, he remained until the end of Michel Raptis' life one of his close and faithful associates. Later one of the main figures in the review *Utopie Critique*.

76. Interview with Denis Berger, 18 November 2000; interview with Michel Fiant, 3 February 2000; interview with Gilbert Marquis, 8 February 2000.
77. Félix Guattari (1930-1992): philosopher, doctor and former Trotskyist militant. During the Algerian war he financed the paper *La Voie communiste* thanks to his clinic at La Borde.
78. Lucien Sebag (1934-1965): anthropologist; pupil of Lévi-Strauss, tried to reconcile Marxism and structuralism [*RH*].
79. Denis Berger (Pierre François): Fourth International militant till 1959, he was responsible for organising a left oppositional tendency inside the PCF, and left the PCI, because of political disagreements, to establish the Voie communiste group. He and his group were involved in assistance to the FLN and in particular attempted to organise the escape from prison of FLN leaders, as well as the successful escape of women militants from the Jeanson network. Lecturer in political science at the University of Paris 8, he is now retired.
80. Interview with Gilbert Marquis, 8 February 2000.
81. For everything concerning the meeting at Gilbert Marquis' home at Clamart, interview with Michel Fiant, 3 February 2000.
82. Gérard Spitzer (1927-1996): son of Hungarian Jewish refugees; joined Resistance at age 15; expelled from PCF for opposing Russian intervention in Hungary in 1956; jailed for 18 months for support for FLN [*RH*].
83. Victor Leduc (Valdemar Nechtschein, 1911-1993): Communist from 1934; Resister, after war edited *Action*; left PCF 1968, later in PSU [*RH*].
84. Henri Lefebvre (1901–29 June 1991): philosopher and sociologist; leading PCF philosopher in postwar period but expelled in 1958 [*RH*].
85. François Châtelet (1925–1985): historian of philosophy, author of works on Plato and Hegel [*RH*].
86. Interview with Denis Berger, 18 November 2000.
87. Interview with Michel Fiant, 3 February 2000.
88. Interview with Denis Berger, 18 November 1999.
89. Craipeau, *Mémoires d'un dinosaur* (Paris, 1999), p 359. [Michèle Mestre (Lucienne Abraham, 1916-1970): later developed openly Stalinist positions — *RH*.]
90. She was the PCI candidate in a parliamentary by-election in 1954 (document Fo Rés 137/..., BDIC archives at Nanterre); she was a member of the PCI Political Bureau in the early 1950s (interview with Gilbert Marquis, 8 February 2000) and she left the PCI in 1954 with Mathias Corvin (Craipeau, *Mémoires d'un dinosaure*, p 49).
91. Hamon and Rotman, *Les Porteurs de valises*, pp 108-09; interview with Denis Berger, 18 November 1999.
92. Interview with Gilbert Marquis, 8 February 2000; interview with Michel Fiant, 3 February 2000.
93. The 'Draft Manifesto of La Voie communiste', certainly drawn up in late 1957,

is explicit on the point (document Fo 100/1-5, BDIC archives at Nanterre): 'The Twentieth Congress of the CPSU opens a new period for the Communist movement throughout the world... It is vital that there should be an oppositional publication which can reach all Communists, including those who are no longer in the party or who find themselves expelled as a result of the leadership's policy... it is vital that there should be united action between the true opposition groups'; the aim was to 'enable an effective ripening of the crisis affecting the party'. The objective was thus the same as that of the PCI, and the differences were about the strategy to be adopted.

94. Interview with Denis Berger, 18 November 1999; interview with Michel Fiant, 3 February 2000; interview with Gilbert Marquis, 8 February 2000.
95. Interview with Gilbert Marquis, 8 February 2000; interview with Michel Fiant, 3 February 2000.
96. Simon Blumenthal (d 2009): lawyer, expelled from PCF [*RH*].
97. Fontenis, *Changer le monde*, pp 148-50.
98. Fontenis, *Changer le monde*, pp 146-48.
99. A collection of *La Voie communiste* is available at the BDIC, Nanterre, document Fo P 2452.
100. Interview with Gilbert Marquis, 8 February 2000.
101. On 28 May 1952, there was a large violent demonstration against General Matthew Ridgway, who had come to Paris to take the position of Supreme Allied Commander, Europe of NATO [*RH*].
102. Interview with Denis Berger, 18 November 1999.
103. Interview with Gilbert Marquis, 8 February 2000.

Chapter VI: The Days of the Networks

The continuation of the war in Algeria, the growing indignation of a section of public opinion, a minority certainly, but very active, the refusal of certain young men to be involved against their will in a war to which they were opposed — all this led to the formation of certain networks: for solidarity with Algerian militants or to encourage refusal of military service. Faced with the failures of the traditional left, which was committed to repression or was timorous in opposing it, the far left carried on developing its own networks. It produced its own analysis in Marxist terms of the evolution of the colonial revolution. The history of these networks is complex. How did they evolve in relation to the situation in France and in Algeria? How did they relate to other networks not directly inspired by the far left? What regroupments might activity in support of the FLN lead to? What new questionings of society might such activities lead to, and how was this analysed by the far left?

To begin with, some found themselves more and more marginalised by the way in which the war in Algeria developed. This was the case with the 'Lambertist' Trotskyists who supported Messali Hadj's MNA, which was supplanted by the FLN among emigrant workers in metropolitan France as well as in the resistance in Algeria. The methods used on both sides were very violent: assassination was standard practice, and numerous 'patriots' died from the bullets of their Algerian 'brothers'. Massacres took place in Algeria, as at Melouza in 1957, where more than 300 villagers were killed in a locality controlled by the MNA. Faced with the scale of the massacre, the FLN had to deny all responsibility and condemn the action, but it was clear who was to blame.[1] But the MNA was losing its grip, its influence was in decline, while rumours spread that it was being manipulated by the French police. Its credibility was definitively undermined by the 'Bellounis affair'. Mohammed Bellounis, leader of an MNA resistance grouping, and a lieutenant of Messali Hadj, in December 1957 went over to the French army, and died in July 1958 after a further turnabout, killed by the French army. In 1958, Messali Hadj discredited himself by an attitude to de Gaulle that was considered too conciliatory — he failed to condemn the latter's proposals for a 'peace of the brave' and for a referendum.

The Lambertists, however, continued for a very long time to support the old nationalist leader and his movement. A draft report in 1958[2] began by trying to explain his evolution: the 'liquidationist policy of the FLN leadership' and the 'terrorist repression by French imperialism' were held responsible. Then some criticisms were suggested: 'Messali Hadj and the MNA still have the chance to carry out a rectification, which could mean nothing other than a refusal to take part in French elections or a French referendum.'

Both illusions and the Lambertists' very special conception of solidarity with Algerian militants were blatantly obvious in the proposals in the text: 'Help the rectification of the MNA... We shall continue to struggle to prevent this collapse [of the MNA], which could only be hastened by a premature political condemnation by our party.' By such exclusive support for an organisation which became further discredited with each passing day and which was losing the positions it had held at the beginning of the war, this party was condemning itself to playing only a minor role in the subsequent events linked to the war in Algeria. This pro-MNA 'fetishism' side-lined the Lambertist tendency from solidarity with the Algerian revolution, and its militants no longer had any direct influence on the struggles going on in France in support of the Algerian people. This tendency remained, on the Algerian question, stuck to 'Bolshevik' principles which were given the status of dogma, and once the MNA had been dropped, it withdrew, apart from entry work in the Socialist Party and the freemasons, into three sectors: the trade unions, where it was involved in Force ouvrière; activity in the student milieu with the CLER[3] which would become the FER (Revolutionary Student Federation); and the Youth Hostels.[4]

The Frank tendency Trotskyists did not of course complain that their Lambertist rivals had ruled themselves out of activity, and it is true that on the question of the MNA, the Fourth International had been more prudent and clear-sighted. In January 1958, Jacques Privas analysed the situation of the two Algerian nationalist organisations:

> The truth is that the MNA has ceased to be an organisation which leads or organises the Algerian revolution, which it did not initiate... For us it is not a question of idealising the FLN, or of seeing it as the Bolshevik party. But it is a fundamental fact of the situation in North Africa and of the Revolution.[5]

The author, moreover, did not fail to criticise the position of the other PCI.[6]

The Trotskyists in the Fourth International took the colonial revolutions, and the Algerian revolution in particular, very seriously. The resolution on the colonial revolutions was an important part of the documents of the Fifth Congress.[7] The text adopted at the congress about the 'colonial revolution' declared in its preamble:

> The dominant fact in the development of the world revolution since the end of the Second World War is the progress of the colonial revolution which includes three quarters of the earth's population, and which is developing on all the continents which have been colonised.[8]

At the beginning of the congress a colonial commission was set up to deal with these questions.[9] Now, as Pierre Frank insisted in his report, the revolution in North Africa represented 'the forefront of the colonial revolution'.[10] Therefore the revolution in Algeria required from revolutionaries 'not only political support but also, as far as is possible, material support for the revolutionary struggle which is being carried on there'.[11] This phrase represented the theoretical recognition of the activity of the networks, and the 'material support' which was called for left no ambiguity about the kind of concrete support to be given. There were thus two aspects, political support and material support, and for the Fourth International, without any hesitation, these two activities were not to be separated. The documents of the Fifth Congress went further: the task of concrete support being carried out by the French section of the Fourth International made it possible, in the light of the policies of the PCF and the SFIO, to save 'the honour of the working class in face of the bloodbath of which the *Versaillais*[12] masters of the Palais-Bourbon[13] have made themselves guilty'.[14] By so doing, the PCI had made it possible 'proudly to raise the flag of Lenin': revolutionary lyricism was confined to the FCL, but was characteristic of a period which believed that the world revolution was imminent.

Pablo was the one concerned with colonial questions and more particularly with the networks of solidarity with the FLN. He left France, where his comings and goings were under surveillance by the internal security police and the DST, and settled in the Netherlands from 1958 and regularly met FLN leaders. He centralised Fourth International activities in relation to solidarity with the Algerian revolution: militants in the German, Dutch and Belgian sections in particular were drawn in.[15] The German Trotskyist Jakob Moneta, who was the representative at the West German Embassy in Paris of the powerful German trade-union confederation, the DGB, used the 'diplomatic bag' to transport FLN documents.[16] But Pablo, an intellectual who drew on action to develop theory, also contributed to the Fourth International's considerations on the colonial question. He was one of those who pushed for this question to be integrated into the priorities of the Fourth International and in particular insisted on practical action: it was a matter of 'educating in action more or less broad layers about the real meaning and implications of the alliance with the colonial peoples'. In addition, he insisted in an internal document: 'Our support for the present revolution cannot be merely episodic, verbal and accessory, but on the contrary must be constant, practical and one the essential axes of our activity.'[17] Pablo had high ambitions for the Fourth International, which he spelled out in the same text: 'The aspirations of at least one wing of the youth tend towards support for the colonial revolution: we must be the organisers of this tendency.'

Taking into account their analysis, the Trotskyists therefore involved themselves in sustained assistance to the FLN: their network grew stronger, and a second full-timer (Louis Fontaine) supported Pierre Avot-Meyers in his practical tasks. Both were concerned with printing and producing forged papers. Fourth International sections also gave their assistance: thus in 1958 Georg Jungclas,[18] a German Trotskyist militant, and a leading figure in the left wing of the German Social Democratic Party (SPD), tried to put FLN leaders in Germany in touch with the Falcons (SPD Youth) who were interested in concrete support to the Algerian revolution.[19] With his friends, Georg Jungclas obtained for the FLN a garage in Cologne intended to serve as a store for weapons in transit.[20] In Germany, Belgium and the Netherlands, Trotskyists were the driving force in broad regroupments in support of the FLN or to assist prisoners and refugees in the camps in Tunisia. These militants did not risk jail, but they could be the victims of the activities of the SDECE[21] (the French secret service) or of the clandestine organisation called the Red Hand.[22] Thus a Belgian teacher who was not a Trotskyist, Laperche, was killed because he was coordinating legal activity in support of the FLN. He received a parcel bomb: it took the form of a book by an opponent of the war in Algeria which had been hollowed out and filled with explosives. The day after this outrage, Pierre Avot-Meyers went to Belgium to see a Belgian Trotskyist, Pierre Legrève, who was also responsible for support activities, and found him in a state of great distress: he had just received a similar parcel containing the same book, but a day later because of the delays of the Belgian post. This delay saved his life, for he had become suspicious on recognising the same book that had been fatal the previous day for the teacher Laperche.

For the Fourth International militants, assistance to the FLN was not confined to their own organisation. Thus Henri Benoîts had the opportunity inside his own factory at Renault-Billancourt to assist nationalist militants who were threatened by the police. When the PCF voted for the special powers, the Algerian militants who were members of the PCF, after a stormy meeting with party leaders, decided to tear up their cards to join the FLN as a group. Lattad, an Algerian Communist militant and a union representative, came to see Henri and Clara Benoîts and told them: 'I have good news for you, we've united all the Algerians and we've formed the FLN at Renault.'[23] From this moment on, Henri Benoîts did jobs for the FLN in his factory, but he did them as an individual and not in the framework of the PCI.

Sometimes the support was collective and involved the whole factory: known Algerian militants did not sleep at home for fear of being located by the police. The only way to arrest them was to do it at their workplace. But it was difficult to do this at the end of the working day: a factory such as Renault had 35 000 to 40 000 workers and several exits. So the police picked up 'suspects' as they were leaving the factory for reasons connected to their duties, with the backing of the security staff, and then arrested them. Early in 1958, Abdelgahni Ben Nacef, the CGT representative for the foundries, was thus summoned to the personnel office. A foreman from the foundry and a CFTC delegate warned him that in fact the police were waiting for him. He informed Ziani, the forge representative, who called a stoppage in the workshops. French and Algerians alike stopped work. The security staff were booed and had run away while Ben Nacef hid in the factory. A solidarity chain was then formed to get the FLN militant out and enable him to go into hiding, but also to get his belongings from his locker and his pay.[24]

It is true that as far as direct assistance to the FLN was concerned, by 1956 the far left was no longer alone in engaging in such illegal activities. Other broader networks had taken up the baton. The best known and probably the most important was the Jeanson network.[25] The philosopher, a disciple of Jean-Paul Sartre and managing editor of *Les Temps Modernes*, had in 1955 published with his wife Colette *L'Algérie hors la loi*, an analysis of the Algerian national movement which caused a scandal in colonial circles. In 1956, Francis Jeanson began to do 'jobs' for the FLN, and organised a proper network in 1957. Omar Boudaoud, leader of the FLN's French Federation demanded, for security reasons, the most complete clandestinity and a 'serious' network, that is, one divided into separate cells. Jeanson and those who like him became 'suitcase carriers' were mainly occupied collecting, counting and taking abroad the significant sums of money raised, voluntarily or forcibly, by the FLN from migrant workers in metropolitan France. All the sums collected by FLN 'taxmen' were centralised in the Paris region: it was French people who took on the job of transporting and counting the sums collected and then transporting the famous suitcases of money across the frontiers.

The Jeanson network brought together individuals from very diverse origins: the members of the network did not have a coherent body of theory, and their common denominator was the desire to struggle, for very different reasons, against colonialism. Some did it out of Christian humanism, such as the priest Robert Davezies or the seminary student Jacques Berthelet, others out of fidelity to the 'humanist' values of the left, others again from a Marxist commitment: among these many were dissidents from the PCF, such as Etienne Bolo or Jean-Louis Hurst. They had not joined a left opposition within the party, as the Trotskyists had hoped, but had gone into the networks as individuals and not into a political organisation of a party type. Others belonged to New Left circles, to the UGS, such as the actor Jacques Charby.[26] Some had evaded conscription and lived clandestinely. Most had begun by doing small jobs, often in the framework of a circle of friends round the Jeanson couple, and then had become committed to the point where they left their jobs, their homes and their families to devote themselves to clandestine support for the FLN. Jeanson's network included many members of the intellectual professions, teachers such as Hélène Cuénat, journalists such as Jacques Vignes, and people from show business such as Jean-Marie Boeglin or Cécile Marion.

This network turned out to be very efficient in everything that concerned the FLN's money, but also in organising the visits of FLN leaders from one country to another by diverting the attention of the customs and the police, in printing leaflets, in providing hiding places in 'safe' flats put at the disposal of the FLN and the networks, and in organising the production of forged papers. However, the members of Jeanson's network did not confine themselves to helping the FLN and 'safeguarding Franco-Algerian friendship', but they also wanted to be politically active in France, 'awakening' the French left and reminding it of its anti-colonialist 'duty'.[27] The network had a monthly budget allocated by the FLN, which was administered by Francis Jeanson personally: this sum enabled a full-timer's wage to be paid to those who spent all their time working for the network and also made it possible to pay the expenses incurred by the various activities of the network.

Another network was set up by the Egyptian Communist militant Henri Curiel,[28] a 'professional revolutionary' who had been living in France since being expelled from Egypt by King Farouk in 1950. He was put in contact with Francis Jeanson in the autumn of 1957,[29] and organised on the fringes of the Jeanson network a support group for the FLN consisting of his faithful supporters, Egyptian Jewish Communists who had been exiled at the same time as himself. While Francis Jeanson disagreed with the 'orthodox Communist' orientation of the struggle carried out by Henri Curiel, he recognised his qualities as an efficient organiser: the two networks were very much complementary in their activity, even if a powerful rivalry emerged between the two men.

To make up for the clandestine character of his network and in order to try and address opinion more broadly, Jeanson decided in September 1958 to launch an anti-colonialist bulletin *Vérités pour*,[30] a clandestine publication initiated and edited by Jeanson and his friends, while Curiel found a sympathetic print-shop. The papers were sent to sympathisers, to left-wing personalities, to trade unionists and journalists. Up to 5000 copies were distributed, even though it did not appear regularly. Intellectuals such as Sartre and Vercors,[31] a Resister and author of *Le Silence de la mer*, were interviewed in *Vérités pour* and openly supported assistance to the FLN.[32]

The police took a very close interest in this network which was so influential and which was made up of militants with little experience of clandestinity and who were sometimes careless. Moreover the leaders of the FLN French Federation were regularly located, followed and then arrested: under torture, inflicted in French police stations, some Algerian militants cracked and confessed the addresses of their French 'hosts'. Many militants from the network were arrested early in 1960, for example Hélène Cuénat and Jacques Charby, but the main leaders of the network, such as Francis Jeanson, Cécile Marion and Jacques Vignes, evaded the DST.[33] Francis Jeanson even permitted himself the luxury of organising a clandestine press conference in the middle of Paris on 15 April 1960 in the course of which he insisted that, contrary to government statements, the network was far from being dismantled, and replied to his detractors who accused him of acting according to a logic that was 'emotional' and even 'romantic' rather than political.[34] But the game was up for the philosopher; he was too closely watched to continue directing the network. Henri Curiel took over, with the strong support of the FLN.

Another minority trend which had a certain influence, even if it did not become a mass movement, was that of the 'deserters'. Pablo had said that 'the aspirations of at least one wing of the youth tend towards supporting the colonial revolution'. Certainly the aspirations of a section of the youth tended to make them refuse to go to Algeria, as was shown by the demonstrations by the reservists. But if there were many of them who pulled the alarm cords on trains or who 'went against their will', there were only a few who went so far as avoiding conscription or desertion. The case of Alban Liechti, a young gardener and PCF militant who refused to be called up and on 19 November 1956 was sentenced to two years in prison without, in the short term, getting any support from his party, was not designed to encourage them.[35] But it was not just a straight alternative between taking up arms or going to jail. Some went abroad in order to carry on activity against the war, which was more than a simple refusal to fight. Networks were set up to look after young men who wanted to cross the border and enabled them to take up residence, usually in Switzerland. Those who decided to go into exile like this probably numbered less than 500.[36]

A set of initials and an organisation appeared: JR, Jeune Résistance (Young Resistance),[37] and a certain number of militants, often deserters themselves, such as Jean-Louis Hurst or Louis Orhant, who belonged to the Jeanson network, took charge of these systems and encouraged desertion through leaflets distributed at demonstrations. Jeanson and Curiel took an interest in the organisation, and Curiel pushed for establishing a rigorously structured organisation on the fringes of the Jeanson network, for security reasons, but also to ensure a certain political control. The Trotskyists, beginning with a group in Bordeaux, involved themselves in Jeune Résistance: Michel Fiant met some of the leading activists in the network on behalf of the PCI and Alain Krivine became a member.[38] Roland Vacher, together with a deserter, organised clandestine meetings of JR, and organised food and lodging for this deserter who had the job of recruiting other draft refusers.[39]

The JR leaflets were calls to desert: the point was to remove doubts which might make prospective deserters hesitate. A duplicated leaflet by the organisation claimed:

> In almost all foreign countries the draft refuser is guaranteed to find: organised comrades..., foreign friends who will help him to find a job, somewhere to live or the chance to continue his studies... Crossing the border is no problem.[40]

But it was still difficult to make contact with the organisation. The same leaflet explained that JR 'has many friends in all walks of life', that 'by feeling your way you can find JR', and as if to prove the validity of this method, at the top and bottom of the leaflet were two lines reading 'copy this leaflet', 'copy this leaflet'.

In these conditions JR, which had some 800 members at the peak of its activity,[41] had great difficulty in becoming a very broad organisation. The account of the first clandestine congress of JR in a Belgian paper in 1960[42] explained this point: 'There is a mass movement. But nobody has supported us.' There was great bitterness against the 'failure of all the parties, of all the movements which we had a right to count on'. A delegate at the congress who was interviewed in the same article characterised the movement as 'a refusal which is a break with the established order, the laws, society'. Such a definition could not fail to arouse the keenest interest on the part of the far left and especially of the Trotskyists, even if for JR there was no question of giving aid to the FLN; its aim was rather to organise 'and extend beyond French borders the BERGA — Bureaux d'entraide aux résistants à la guerre d'Algérie — offices of mutual aid for resisters to the war in Algeria'. However, in some places the movement was only an 'empty shell', mere graffiti on the walls put there by a few militants who were ensuring a public manifestation 'which made up for their numerical weakness'.[43] But one of their propaganda weapons consisted in making themselves feared by letting the 'enemy' believe in the existence of a number of militants that was much larger than the reality.

As well as the Trotskyist network, the Jeanson and Curiel networks and the Jeune Résistance network, the Voie communiste network also took part in activities of support for the FLN. Something over a hundred militants from different positions, from libertarians (Daniel Guérin, Georges Fontenis) to dissident Communists (Simon Blumenthal), via the 'Trotskyist' Denis Berger, took part in the movement, and the review which bore its name was pluralist. The public political activity involving militants went alongside a clandestine activity to which a small core devoted themselves: Gérard Spitzer, Roger Rey, Gérard Lorne, Anne Giannini and Denis Berger, who had to be particularly discreet after he was summoned to the DST in December 1958.[44] In 'Balance Sheet of a Political Current', drafted in June 1965, Denis Berger, under the pseudonym of Pierre François, claimed that 'assistance to the FLN became the centre of most comrades' activity', certainly of those who were most active.

What did the movement really represent? The balance sheet document already quoted specifies that:

> The militants who came together at this time almost all belonged to a clearly defined category: young people, mainly intellectuals, who, through support activities or desertion, had *personally* experienced the disgraceful betrayal of the Algerian revolution by the PCF.

But the journal sold on news-stands nonetheless had a certain influence, all the more so because it was of good quality, since the coming together of various currents limited the temptations to dogmatism from which militant writing at this time suffered. The struggle for Algerian independence which united the movement figured prominently in the issues of the journal.[45] The *Voie communiste* network gave practical assistance to the FLN and in particular took part in preparing escapes from prison of Algerian militants or French suitcase carriers.[46] On 28 September 1959, one of the leading activists in *La Voie communiste*, Gérard Spitzer, was arrested and accused of being an FLN agent, while another militant, Gérard Lorne, at whose home sums of money belonging to the FLN had been found, had fled.[47] A solidarity campaign was immediately launched, while Spitzer went on hunger strike to demand political status. A defence committee for Gérard Spitzer was set up by November 1959, while Gilles Martinet, Yves Dechezelles and Laurent Schwartz expressed their solidarity. The trial of Gérard Spitzer and then the trials of various members of the Jeanson network made it possible to popularise the activities of the suitcase carriers amongst the general public.

The activity of the networks was increasingly obstructed by police investigations. Besides the arrests in the Jeanson and Curiel networks, and the arrest of some of the leaders of Jeune Résistance,[48] the Trotskyists themselves, who formed the most 'secure' network, came under investigation. First of all, Henri Benoîts was being watched by the DST: he was accustomed to giving accommodation in his flat to Algerian militants being sought by the police. Early in 1958, his concierge told him that the police had been asking about him. From this point on he was no longer involved with contacts with the Algerians dealing with relations with the press, and he was 'transferred' to solidarity with prisoners, a 'legal' activity which was less exposed, though this did not prevent him from being questioned by the DST in 1959.[49]

The members of the Trotskyist network were also sometimes guilty of 'beginners'' carelessness. While transporting stencils which had to be destroyed (because FLN documents were typed on them), a bag was left on the pavement outside a baker's shop. It was absolutely necessary to recover it because it also contained PCI material which would provide evidence of the support given by the Trotskyists. Simonne Minguet, already being watched by the police after her arrest in 1956, volunteered to try and recover the bag. At the baker's shop she was told that it had been taken to the police station: she went there in a state of great agitation. Fortunately it had not been opened, and the policeman returned it to her with a condescending comment: 'Oh, you absent-minded young ladies.'[50]

The trial in September 1960 of six Algerians and 18 French people linked to the Jeanson network was an opportunity for the accused and their lawyers, including Jacques Vergès[51] and Roland Dumas,[52] to use the court as a political platform to denounce the attitude of France in Algeria. But the trial took on much greater dimensions above all because of the Manifesto of the 121, signed by some of the most prestigious intellectuals and artists.[53] The text was a 'statement on the right to refuse to support the Algerian war', signed originally by 121 personalities, and soon by almost 400, among whom were

Jean-Paul Sartre, Simone Signoret, Pierre Boulez, Michel Butor, Françoise Sagan, Pierre Vidal-Naquet, Madeleine Rebérioux, Laurent Schwartz, Vercors and Jean-Pierre Vernant. The text declared that it was 'justified to refuse to take arms against the Algerian people…, and the actions of French people were justified who considered it their duty to give help and protection to Algerians oppressed in the name of the French people', and asserted that 'the cause of the Algerian people, which is making a decisive contribution to destroying the French colonial system, is the cause of all free men'. It was a statement of explicit support to the suitcase carriers who were on trial. The text was not published in France, but provoked an outcry and various responses, notably a petition by right-wing intellectuals, signed in particular by Rémy, Jean Dutourd, Marshal Juin and Jules Romains, which lambasted the 'scandalous statements… of a fifth column' which was prepared to attack 'the West'. The PCF and the SFIO also condemned the statement. State employees who signed the Manifesto of the 121 were immediately penalised and dismissed; in addition artists and journalists were sacked from French radio and television, and actors did not get jobs in state theatres. There were, however, no judicial proceedings.

The far left had some representatives among the signatories (Daniel Guérin, then Simonne Minguet and Michel Lequenne, who had not been among the original 121, added their names to the list). The far left could only welcome this open appeal to flout legality and the authority of the state on the part of the most prestigious and popular intellectuals and artists in the country. The Frank tendency of the PCI reproduced and distributed the text of the Manifesto of the 121, in particular at factory gates. It sometimes met strong-arm tactics from PCF militants. From 1955, when the far left was almost alone in organising support for the FLN to the Manifesto in 1960, which proclaimed the legitimacy of such clandestine activity, there had been enormous progress.

The political line-up on the left had changed, for all parties were obliged to take a position in relation to this act, this manifesto of disobedience. It was an ideal opportunity above all for the Trotskyists to leave everyone without a leg to stand on, to insist on everybody's contradictions, and to try to put forward the most radical slogans. Moreover, the far left was no longer isolated in the illegality of the networks, and the policy of support for Algerian independence, which had caused legal problems for the Trotskyists and the disappearance of the libertarian communist organisation, here found 'recognition' from the most illustrious élites of the Nation, even if it cannot be said that far left propaganda had convinced the militants in the networks.

Despite this favourable 'subversive' climate of opinion, the far left did not offer an outlet for the aspirations of the militants in the networks, and those of the intellectuals who had signed the Manifesto, although their aspirations resembled so closely the struggles that the far left had fought. It was too much in a minority, not accessible enough, too set in its ways for some, and it did not succeed in becoming a pole for restructuring the left. It was a different milieu, that of the New Left, which seemed to represent the aspirations of those who challenged the Algerian war, and it was the New Left which benefitted from the crisis in the SFIO and to a lesser extent from the attitude of the PCF. The New Left constituted, on the left, the most important new element for the decade, but it was heterogeneous. A certain far left, that of the 'old timers' or the 'entrists' played an essential role in it. The far left was thus called upon to take up a position in relation to this milieu whose development was directly linked to the Algerian war; but the relations were very different from those with the PCF. In what conditions was the pole of the New Left built, which would lead in 1960 to the birth of the PSU (United Socialist Party)? What was the role of the far left in its emergence and creation? What was the attitude of the far left in relation to this new pole in the concrete conditions of the Algerian war?

Notes

1. Benjamin Stora, *Messali Hadj, pionnier du nationalisme algérien* (Paris, 1986), p 263.
2. Document Fo 278, BDIC archives at Nanterre.
3. Comité de liaison des étudiants révolutionnaires (Liaison Committee of Revolutionary Students), set up by the Lambertists [*RH*].
4. Interview with Michel Fiant, 8 November 1999; interview with Michel Lequenne, 18 November 1999; Y Craipeau, *Le Mouvement trotskiste en France* (Paris, 1971), p 204.
5. 'What is the Situation with the MNA?', *Quatrième Internationale*, Paris, January 1958, p 29.
6. Pierre Frank's report to the Fifth Congress on the colonial question specifies, as far as support for the FLN is concerned, that the Fourth International's position is 'not a copy of that of the Lambert group, replacing one organisation with another', but that it involves supporting 'the Algerian revolution as it actually is, with the leadership it actually has' ('The Fifth Congress of the Fourth International', *Quatrième Internationale*, special issue, December 1957, p 56, personal archives of Jean-Michel Krivine).
7. *Quatrième Internationale*, December 1957, p 56.
8. *Quatrième Internationale*, December 1957, p 39.
9. *Quatrième Internationale*, December 1957, p 57.
10. *Quatrième Internationale*, December 1957, pp 53, 56: Pierre Frank particularly stressed this idea of 'the forefront of the colonial revolution', as he returned to it twice in his report and emphasised that it was a major aspect of the analysis.
11. *Quatrième Internationale*, December 1957, p 53.
12. A reference to the Versailles troops who massacred supporters of the Paris Commune in May 1871, taken as representative of counter-revolutionary violence [*RH*].

13. The seat of the French National Assembly [*RH*].
14. 'Manifesto of the Fifth World Congress of the Fourth International to the Workers and Peoples of the Whole World', *Quatrième Internationale*, December 1957, pp 5-12.
15. Interview with Simonne Minguet and Pierre Avot-Meyers, 17 November 1999.
16. Interview with Mohammed Harbi, 25 April 2000.
17. Internal document by Pablo, document GFo Rés 106, BDIC archives at Nanterre.
18. Georg Jungclas 1902-1975: German Trotskyist leader, militant on the left wing of the German Social Democratic Party; he organised support networks for the FLN in his country.
19. Ali Haroun, *La 7ᵉ wilaya, la guerre du FLN en France 1954-1962* (Paris, 1986). Ali Haroun was one of the leaders of the FLN's French Federation.
20. Haroun, *La 7ᵉ wilaya*, pp 212-13.
21. Service de Documentation Extérieure et de Contre-Espionnage [*RH*].
22. A settler terrorist group active since before 1954 [*RH*].
23. Interview with Henri and Clara Benoîts, 7 February 2000; interview with H and C Benoîts in *Expression immigré(e)s-français(es)*, October 1993 and April 1994.
24. Interviews as in previous note; letter from Henri Benoîts dated 16 November 1992 (personal archives of Henri Benoîts).
25. For all information on the Jeanson network, see H Hamon and P Rotman, *Les Porteurs de valises* (Paris, 1979).
26. Jacques Charby (1929-2006): son of syndicalist militant; stage and film actor; jailed 1960 for activity with Jeanson network; escaped and went to Tunisia where he worked with Fanon; returned to France after 1966 amnesty [*RH*].
27. Extract from a letter from Francis Jeanson to Jean-Paul Sartre published in *Les Temps modernes*, May 1960, reproduced in Hamon and Rotman, *Les Porteurs de valises*, p 59.
28. Henri Curiel (13 September 1914–4 May 1978): Egyptian Communist, forced to emigrate 1950; came to France, where active in support for FLN; assassinated in Paris in 1978 by a far-right group [*RH*].
29. Hamon and Rotman, *Les Porteurs de valises*, p 94.
30. For some extracts see Section IV below [*RH*].
31. Pseudonym of Jean Bruller (1902–1991): novelist, active in Resistance and one of founders of clandestine Éditions de minuit [*RH*].
32. Hamon and Rotman, *Les Porteurs de valises*, pp 155-59; Jeanson's interview with Vercors was published in April 1959; that with Sartre in no 9, June 1959.
33. Hamon and Rotman, *Les Porteurs de valises*, pp 180-96.
34. Hamon and Rotman, *Les Porteurs de valises*, pp 208-13.
35. Hamon and Rotman, *Les Porteurs de valises*, p 55. The support campaigns only began 14 months after his arrest, following an article in *L'Humanité* of 30 September.
36. Hamon and Rotman, *Les Porteurs de valises*, pp 216-17; interview with Michel Fiant, 8 November 1999.
37. This acronym naturally has no connection the present-day Jeune Résistance, which brings together some of the most violent far right grouplets, in particular the Groupe Union Défense and the national-revolutionary milieu.

38. Interview with Michel Fiant, 8 November 1999; interview with Alain Krivine, 19 November 1999.
39. Interview with Roland Vacher, 24 April 2000.
40. Document 4o 72 Rés, BDIC archives at Nanterre. Jean-Louis Hurst, writing under the pseudonym Maurienne in *Le Déserteur* (Paris, 1960) states: 'The problem with prison is that you only act once... we must preserve our freedom of action, and only exile enables us to do that.'
41. Interview with Alain Krivine, 19 November 1999.
42. Report of the first congress of Jeune Résistance, *Coexistence*, Brussels, special issue 73-75, September-December 1960.
43. Interview with Michel Fiant, 8 November 1999.
44. Interview with Denis Berger, 18 November 1999; interview with Gilbert Marquis, 8 February 2000.
45. Interview with Denis Berger, 18 November 1999; Georges Fontenis, *Changer le monde: histoire du mouvement communiste libertaire (1945-1997)* (Paris, 2000), pp 150-52. The various issues of *La Voie communiste* can be consulted at the BDIC at Nanterre: document Fo P 2452.
46. Among other things, the *Voie communiste* militants planned two escapes for the five FLN 'ministers' imprisoned in France; but both attempts failed because of 'deliberate' blunders by Ben Bella; they organised the escape of other FLN leaders or militants such as Bensalem, and of five young women belonging to the Jeanson network from the La Roquette prison. About these escapes, see Hamon and Rotman, *Les Porteurs de valises*, pp 340-51, 362-64; interview with Denis Berger, 18 November 1999; on the escape of the Algerian 'ministers' (Théodore plan), see Haroun, *La 7ᵉ wilaya*, pp 281-87.
47. *La Voie communiste*, no 6, 7 October 1959, document Fo P 2452, BDIC archives at Nanterre.
48. Interview with Michel Fiant, 8 November 1999.
49. Interview with Henri Benoîts, 7 February 2000.
50. Interview with Simonne Minguet and Pierre Avot-Meyers, 17 November 1999.
51. Jacques Vergès (b 1925): lawyer, defended many Algerian nationalists, jailed for pro-independence activities; later took other controversial cases, for example defending Klaus Barbie and Tariq Aziz [*RH*].
52. Roland Dumas (b 1922): lawyer, member of UDSR, joined Mitterrand's Socialist Party, twice Foreign Minister under Mitterrand [*RH*].
53. On this text and the reactions to it, see Jean-François Sirinelli, 'Les intellectuels français dans la bataille', in L Gervereau, J-P Rioux and B Stora (eds), *La France en guerre d'Algérie* (Paris, 1992), pp 106-13; Hamon and Rotman, *Les Porteurs de valises*, pp 307-21.

Chapter VII: The New Left

The Algerian war saw a restructuring of the French left, leading to the establishment in 1960 of the Parti Socialiste Unifié (PSU). This derived in part from the development, from 1954 onwards, of the Nouvelle Gauche (New Left). This was a very heterogeneous movement, and it was possible for a number of former Trotskyists, including Yvan Craipeau and Pierre Naville, to play a role within it.

The New Left was often seen as being petit-bourgeois, and Craipeau tried to strengthen its working-class base by developing links with the Mouvement de Libération du Peuple (MLP — People's Liberation Movement), an organisation of Christian workers. Craipeau also organised the stewarding of one of the first anti-war meetings in 1955, when 50 stewards armed with iron bars, assisted by Algerians attending the meeting, fought off 300 far-right activists who came to disrupt the event. On the basis of a document drafted by Craipeau, the MLP joined the New Left to form the Union de la Gauche Socialiste (UGS — Union of the Socialist Left) in 1957. But Craipeau insisted on refusing membership to former PCF members Auguste Lecoeur and Pierre Hervé with the formulation: 'The UGS welcomes all communists who are no longer Stalinists, but not Stalinists who are no longer communists.'

But unlike the PCI, Craipeau thought it more important to orient to the SFIO than to the PCF. Algeria had created a crisis in the SFIO. Craipeau persuaded the leader of the SFIO Youth, Michel Rocard, to move towards a split. Mollet's backing for de Gaulle in 1958 led to a section of the SFIO splitting to form the Parti Socialiste Autonome (PSA — Autonomous Socialist Party).

There were now discussions between the UGS and PSA about the possibility of a merger. However, there were considerable divergences; the PSA included former ministers, while some of the UGS leaders considered themselves revolutionaries. Some wanted to form a 'Labour'-style party, while others advocated a 'true socialist party'.

In April 1960, the PSU was founded by a fusion of the UGS and the PSA; the statutes, which Pierre Naville helped to draft, made it a broad organisation which included even the followers of Mendès-France. The one victory of the far left was to refuse admission to François Mitterrand. The new party had 30 000 members.

UGS students had been active in UNEF (the French national students' union), supporting the left-wing minority which in 1957 became the majority.

But the PSU was deeply divided over strategy in relation to Algeria. Former SFIO members in particular were very hostile to the solidarity networks with the FLN, arguing for a negotiated solution. Yet many individual PSU members were involved in the networks. Some PSU leaders argued that supporters of the solidarity networks should be excluded from the party. But Henri Benoîts, who had been told by the PCI to join the PSU because it would make it harder for the police to arrest him, became secretary of the Renault PSU branch and persuaded the majority of his branch to back Algerian independence and to support the networks. Craipeau thought that if the party supported the networks it would lead to its marginalisation; he personally sheltered FLN militants on the run and helped deserters cross into Switzerland, but he argued against the party taking a position one way or the other.

About 20 PSU members signed the Manifesto of 121, though this was not the party position. Meanwhile the PSU concentrated on organising militant demonstrations. On 27 October 1960, UNEF called an anti-war demonstration, which the PCF denounced as a 'provocation'. The PSU played an active part; when the demonstrators were attacked by the police, a former minister, Tanguy-Prigent, was seriously injured, and Mitterrand was slightly hurt. When a demonstration called for 1 November 1961 was banned, the PSU went ahead with the action. Their members assembled in cinema queues, and then formed a march, laid a wreath where two Algerians had been killed by police, and dispersed before the police could intervene.

Unfortunately the far left was unable to take the lead in the growing militancy against the war. The PCI was too small and was mainly oriented on the PCF, whereas in fact the PSU was the place where a newly-radicalised left was developing. Michel Lequennne and his friends had rejoined the PCI, and were told to do entry work in the Communist Party, but they deliberately sabotaged their application for membership so that they would be rejected and have no alternative but to join the PSU.

Thus the impact of both the PCI and the former Trotskyists in the PSU was limited, but they did make a certain impression.

Chapter VIII: In the Service of the FLN?

Revolutionaries gave critical support to the FLN, and often criticism disappeared in face of support. Yet the FLN's treatment of the MNA, and its record in power, showed it to be far from democratic. Both the PCI and *La Voie communiste* had illusions both about the socialist potential of the FLN and the possibility of the French far left influencing sections of the FLN. FLN leaders adopted a Marxist language to win support from the French left, but took good care that French leftists should not influence their cadres. (Thus when Henri Curiel was in jail with FLN prisoners, the FLN was very concerned that the classes he was running for the Algerians touched on Marxism and agrarian reform, and kept him under close surveillance.)

In the Fourth International, Michel Pablo argued strongly that the colonial revolution was at the centre of the world revolution. Pablo (along with Mandel, Frank and Maitan) was one of the four dominant figures in the Europe-based International Secretariat. Of these four Pablo, both an intellectual and a formidable organiser, was the most enthusiastic about support for the FLN, had close relations with the FLN leaders, and had high hopes of influencing the movement and recruiting supporters.

Pablo proposed to the FLN that he should set up an arms factory in Morocco to make weapons which the FLN was having difficulty in obtaining. The factory was operational from 1959, disguised as a marmalade factory, with equipment from Eastern Europe, and was staffed by skilled workers, Algerians in the majority, but also foreign workers, Trotskyists and others, from several countries including some British. Some of those involved in running the print-shop for the FLN had to leave France to avoid arrest, and Louis Fontaine, formerly of the Vernon factory, went to work in the arms factory.

Politically the work with the arms factory went further than other forms of solidarity, since the weapons being made would be used against French soldiers. But this meant that there was a danger that the Fourth International would appear as merely an auxiliary organisation of the FLN. It was difficult to maintain critical distance when involved in such activities, but as Pattieu puts it, 'for the Trotskyists it was not a time for critical distance, and action had the priority'.

The FLN also proposed to Pablo that he should produce forged French money for the FLN. The aim was to finance the FLN, but also, more implausibly, to try to destabilise the French economy. Some of the FLN, notably Mohammed Harbi, were opposed to the scheme, but Pablo agreed to go ahead. For reasons of clandestinity, Pablo did not inform the rest of the Fourth International leadership about this activity, only referring to it allusively to Mandel. He worked with Salomon Santen, a leader of the Fourth International in the Netherlands, and they approached a libertarian printer, Albertus Oeldrich, with a long record of left-wing activity. The equipment was operational by November 1959, and paper was obtained early the following year; but one of the two workers taken on by Oeldrich was a police informer. In June 1960 the police raided the secret print-shop and Pablo and Santen were questioned. Oeldrich cracked and confessed everything.

Pablo and Santen went on trial in June 1961. Although Frank and Maitan thought Pablo's actions had been adventurist, the Fourth International decided to wage a major campaign in support of Pablo and Santen, who admitted solidarity with the Algerian revolution, but denied forgery — something made easier by the fact that no forged notes had as yet been produced. Pablo and Santen received support from Sartre, André Breton, Claude Bourdet and many others on the French left, and internationally from Salvador Allende, Michael Foot and Isaac Deutscher. Politically the trial was thus a success, as the defendants managed to turn it into a platform for attacking French colonialism. Pablo and Santen got 15 months in jail, quite a light sentence in view of the charges.

But when the trial was over, Mandel, Frank and Maitan took advantage of Pablo's absence to reassert their control over the Fourth International's apparatus. In an internal letter circulated in September 1962, Mandel wrote that it was dangerous to 'abandon the leadership of the International to a single "thinker" surrounded by "dynamic" elements who merely carried out his orders'.

Chapter IX: Facing Fascism?

When de Gaulle seized power in 1958, many of those involved in solidarity activity with Algeria thought that this was opening the way to fascism. Pierre Frank argued that the Gaullist regime was not fascist but 'Bonapartist', but that there were fascist elements in the army and that the situation would oblige the French bourgeoisie to turn to ever more brutal solutions. After the failure of the generals' putsch in April 1961, the supporters of French Algeria formed the Organisation Armée Secrète (OAS — Secret Army Organisation) which adopted terror tactics in Algeria; it began a bombing campaign in metropolitan France, and among many others Pierre Frank's flat was bombed.

Deep divisions were emerging with the Union des Étudiants Communistes (UEC — Union of Communist Students). There was discontent about the PCF's refusal to support the UNEF demonstration in October 1960. Alain Krivine helped to develop the left opposition within the UEC, and this led to the formation of the Front Universitaire Antifasciste (FUA — University Anti-Fascist Front).

The Trotskyists had a real influence on the FUA, whose main activity was organising self-defence groups with the aim of defending the Latin Quarter against OAS supporters who were distributing literature and attacking left-wing militants. The FUA attacked right-wing paper-sellers, defended the Maspero left-wing bookshop, and prevented a 'French Algeria' public meeting from being held. The FUA also cooperated with the Groupes d'action et de résistance (GAR — Action and Resistance Groups) organised by the PSU. The PCF was reluctant to participate in anti-fascist activity, but pressure from the base obliged it to call a demonstration on 8 February 1962, which ended with eight demonstrators being killed by police at the Charonne metro station.

The FUA thus inaugurated a style of 'military' anti-fascism which survived in the student milieu until the 1970s, with physical confrontations between far-left and far-right students. And the young members of the PCI in the UEC had succeeded in doing what the PCI's entry work in the PCF had failed to do, that is, to create a left opposition current within the Communist student movement. The crisis in the UEC continued until 1965 when the oppositionists, some of whom became leaders during the events of 1968, were expelled. The Trotskyists had thus played their part in the regroupment of the left which took place as a result of the Algerian war.

Chapter X: *Pieds-rouges*[1]

The achievement of Algerian independence opened a new period in which the far left had to move from clandestinity to open political support, while the FLN was now confronted with the problems of power.

The Fourth International hailed Algerian independence as 'one of the greatest revolutionary victories since the end of the Second World War'.[2]

In the course of 1963, the Fourth International attempted to organise technical, cultural, financial and humanitarian aid to the new state. Sections of the Fourth International were urged to put pressure on Communist parties to persuade the USSR and the workers' states to organise economic aid for revolutionary Algeria. Jean-Michel Krivine, who remained an entrist in the PCF, and others organised medical training in Algeria.

The Trotskyists saw three main currents in independent Algeria: a socialist left, a Bourguibist right (that is, one that would go in the same direction as Bourguiba's[3] Tunisia), and a wavering opportunist centre. Therefore their aim was to encourage the socialist left. Pablo and Mandel urged Algeria to follow the Cuban example: 'Independence from imperialism, solving the agrarian problem, industrialisation, elimination of unemployment and illiteracy, liberation of women.' In order to achieve this the FLN would have to become 'a democratic revolutionary socialist party' with a 'political and socialism programme that is better expressed and more clearly defined'.[4]

Hence the Fourth International had great enthusiasm for the potential development of the Algerian revolution, expecting the masses to carry the leadership along with them. Already in 1960, the Fourth International had expressed the view that 'Algeria has the chance to go well beyond Cuba and Guinea and to give an irresistible impulse to socialist revolution throughout the Maghreb'.[5] Algerian President Ben Bella listened to Pablo's proposals for workers' self-management.

A different perspective was put forward in a discussion document signed 'Driss'.[6] This argued that the FLN was merely a 'conglomeration of factions united only by the anti-colonial struggle' and a 'bureaucratic-administrative apparatus, solely concerned with the military control of the masses'. Its 'pseudo-Marxist, pseudo-revolutionary language' was to be explained by 'the struggle in a world context where "socialist" terminology was widespread'. The FLN had 'never at any time put its "revolutionary" programme into practice', and a 'socialist outcome for the revolution was absolutely ruled out in the short term'.

Driss' analysis made little impression on the Fourth International, which in January 1963 affirmed that:

> This process could end with the establishment of an Algerian workers' state, based on an alliance between the urban and rural proletariat and the poor peasants, and led by a revolutionary Marxist tendency.[7]

Meanwhile *La Voie communiste* was supporting Mohammed Boudiaf, who had broken with Ben Bella.

Pablo became one of Ben Bella's advisers, and several of his supporters also settled in Algeria. Some supporters of the Mandel–Frank tendency also settled in Algeria. At the 1963 reunification congress of the Fourth International, Pablo found himself in a small minority. He advocated moving the centre of the Fourth International to Algiers. Pablo was criticised for factionalism and breach of discipline, and Mandel took over as secretary of the International.

In 1965, Mandel, Frank and Maitan imposed unacceptable conditions on Pablo and excluded him from the International. He subsequently formed the International Marxist Revolutionary Tendency (TMRI). But Boumediène's coup in 1965 led to the arrest and then expulsion from Algeria of Pablo's supporters. Some were even tortured in a manner similar to that used by the French army and police against FLN militants.

The period after Algerian independence saw further changes on the far left. *La Voie communiste* disintegrated once it no longer had the focus of the Algerian war; some of its members became pro-Cuban or Maoist. Some of the FCL anarchists also became Maoists, and it was only in the 1970s that French anarchism became reorganised. From 1965, the Vietnam committees became a significant political force in the universities. The expulsion of the left opposition from the UEC led to the formation in 1966 of the Jeunesse Communiste Révolutionnaire (JCR — Revolutionary Communist Youth), which would play a very active role in 1968. Meanwhile the PSU had established itself as part of the political line-up, and Trotskyists and ex-Trotskyists exercised an important influence within it.

Notes

1. Red Feet, that is, those who settled in independent Algeria; a term formed by analogy with *pieds-noirs* (black feet), European settlers in Algeria [*RH*].
2. *Quatrième Internationale*, July 1962.
3. Habib Bourguiba (1903-2000): President of Tunisia, 1957-87 [*RH*].
4. Letter from Pablo to the FLN, written in jail, *Quatrième Internationale*, November 1961.
5. *Quatrième Internationale*, July 1960.
6. 'Report by Comrade Driss, Balance-Sheet and Perspectives of the Algerian Revolution', international discussion document dated 10 October 1962, document Fo Rés 442, BDIC archives at Nanterre. Driss was certainly a pseudonym, and the author's identity is unknown. [The full text of this document is reproduced in the French edition of Pattieu's book, pp 234-49 — *RH*.]
7. 'January 1963 Resolution on the Current Phase of the Algerian Revolution', document Fo Rés 442, BDIC archives at Nanterre.

Chapter XI: Conclusion

The far-left groups had different responses to the Algerian war. Those which understood its importance and were able to analyse the impact in France of this national liberation struggle took part in a genuine mass movement and played a real role. The choice of fighting against colonialism was a difficult and brave one, calculated to provoke incomprehension from a large number of French people for whom 'Algeria was France', and exposed these minority groups to repression; the FCL did not survive.

This struggle which was carried out by part of the far left — the Lambertist PCI, the Frank tendency PCI linked to the Fourth International, and the FCL — brought them in particular into opposition to the 'traditional' parties of the left, the SFIO and the PCF, even if some members of those parties were to be found in the support networks or campaigning against the war.

The choice to assist the FLN by the Frank tendency PCI, the Fourth International and the *Voie Communiste* group was not automatic, given their historic links with Messali Hadj, founder of the MNA. But this decision was guided as much by principles of struggle against colonialism as by the pragmatic wish to back the organisation, namely the FLN, which was effectively leading the Algerian revolution. These militants were not the only ones to accept the constraints of clandestinity and the risks of arrest, in order to take part in a struggle based on their beliefs: the members of the Jeanson and Curiel networks were also in the front line in this struggle. The groups which did not support the demands for Algerian independence, such as the FA and *Voix ouvrière*, or which did not abandon soon enough exclusive support for the MNA, such as the Lambertist PCI, found themselves excluded from an essential political and social struggle.

In fact, going beyond the Algerian war, the far left succeeded in creating a space to the left of the PCF on an anti-colonialist basis. Opposition to the Algerian war, in all the forms it took on, from networks of support for the FLN to the struggles of the draft refusers and deserters and including the anti-fascist activity against the OAS, the demonstrations and the petitions by intellectuals, made possible, for the first time in a long period, the expression of a critical current outside the PCF. Even if the far left, and in particular the Fourth International Trotskyists, did not manage to give a permanent structure to an internal opposition within the PCF, it nonetheless built an area of influence in its student organisation, the UEC, by developing a left current on the question of anti-fascism with the creation of the FUA. It was from this left opposition inside the UEC that not only some of the main leaders of May 1968 emerged, but also some important actors on the political and trade-union scene today.

The far left during the Algerian war was thus able to be in step with some of the aspirations of the youth which was inexorably beginning to escape from the grip of the PCF, which faced competition on its left; this was particularly clear during the events of May 1968.

But these successes for the far left had a corollary, in the form of a certain number of illusions which had a political price. In the first place, these illusions concerned the PCF and its capacity to evolve, to accept the existence of an internal opposition. The Trotskyists above all overestimated the ability of a minority group to play a leading role in this internal opposition. Except for a few people, this overestimation of the PCF went hand in hand with a blindness towards the new role that the PSU was destined to play as the bearer of new aspirations and as capable of forming a political expression for the struggle against the Algerian war.

But above all hopes were placed in the FLN and in the possibilities of a true socialist revolution.

To analyse these disappointed hopes, the best thing is to refer to what represents one of the most lucid balance sheets of the activity of the far-left groups, drawn up by one of the actors in this story. This is the report by Denis Berger (Pierre François) concerning the *Voie communiste*.[1] The conclusions of this document can be applied equally to the Fourth International and even, as far as relations with the FLN are concerned, to the groups, such as the Lambertist PCI and the FCL, which backed the MNA.

Denis Berger observes: 'We let ourselves be deluded by the Marxist demagogy of the FLN's French Federation.'

The French militants did not correctly evaluate the fact that the adoption of a discourse with some Marxist overtones by numerous leaders of the FLN, in the context of the Cold War, and when the Algerians knew that in Europe they could count only on the camp of the left, did not mean endorsement of the project of social and political revolution which they were defending, but rather was a response to the immediate strategic imperatives of the struggle against French colonialism. The *Voie Communiste* leader stresses, likewise, the 'excessive trust in the automatic nature of the way in which a national democratic revolution would grow over into a socialist revolution'. This fault was also shared by both PCIs and the FCL. The Fourth International, and above all Pablo, followed this logic to its conclusion, which led them to give critical but consistent support to the Ben Bella regime. It is hard to say whether this 'growing over' was a foolhardy theory or whether putting it into effect would have been possible, and there is no point in giving retrospective lessons in realism. Nonetheless, it should be noted that the evaluation of the dynamic of the Algerian revolution involved an overestimate, especially on the part of the Fourth International.

This attitude does not only apply to Algeria, and it can be compared to the analysis of the Cuban revolution: if it permits openness to the new problematics posed by the colonial peoples, it constantly leads to an idealisation of models of revolution in the Third World. Minority groups such as the Trotskyists can be led to place great hopes in such revolutionary phenomena, all the more so because in certain Third World countries they have a mass influence.

As far as the analysis of the Gaullist regime is concerned, Denis Berger admits that he had attributed an 'excessive importance to the possibility of a fascist *coup d'état* against de Gaulle'. Such analyses were based on a real threat from the OAS, but underestimated de Gaulle's ability to stabilise the regime he had established. However, paradoxically it was this overestimation of the danger which enabled the Trotskyists to set up the FUA, and to succeed in doing in the UEC what they had not been able to achieve in the PCF.

However that may be, the Algerian war enabled a part of the far left, composed of various elements, from oppositional Communists to Trotskyists and libertarians, to engain formative experiences, which however bore within themselves the illusions of the following years.

Internationalism was a fundamental principle for this far left which was occupying the territory abandoned by the PCF. Those who committed themselves to the FLN were the forerunners of those who fought in the guerrilla struggles of South America. The other side of the coin of this commitment was a certain idealisation of colonial revolutions, without however reaching the level of the revolutionary romanticism of the 1960s.

For the first time in many years, the far left instigated actions that connected directly with a development of society, in this case decolonisation, and this struggle, both social and political, produced an echo which was not negligible, especially among the young. However, this led to a certain overestimation of the possibility of outflanking the large organisations of the left.

Initiatives such as the Manifesto of 121 had some influence on French society, and its signatories, who were among the most eminent personalities of the intellectual and cultural worlds, gave moral endorsement to activity which challenged the foundations of authority and order.

The *Voie Communiste* group scarcely survived after the Algerian war, but it provides an example of a non-dogmatic regroupment around a high-quality journal, and therefore enabled exchanges between revolutionary militants coming from different political directions.

But all the same, division won out over unity, in a far left which did not succeed in coming together: ideological divisions took precedence over anti-capitalist and anti-colonialist convergences. A cliquish attitude dominated, incomprehensible to anyone who did not know the ins and outs of persistent grudges, based on differing analysis and practices. The Algerian war, far from bringing together these practices and analyses, merely added new grounds for disagreement and ill-feeling.

A far left was about to be born, whose youthful qualities and defects were the enthusiasms, the successes and the errors of the future.

An age was coming to an end, and the fragments of debate and the echoes of struggle of far-left militants committed to fighting for Algerian independence may seem very remote from us.

Today the word 'revolution' no longer arouses fear, and for some it produces a smile, while the images of Lenin, Gandhi, Che Guevara and Marx are used to promote Internet Service Providers.

An historical period which began with the October Revolution in Russia ended with the fall of the Berlin Wall. Far-left militants were the actors of this century, who contributed to forming our own age, and their illusions, their hopes, their struggles, their victories, their failures, are all questions addressed to us. The end of ideology and the end of history have recently been announced, but they change nothing fundamental in the world we live in, which is a continuation of the one against which they fought.

Note
1. Berger Denis/François Pierre, '*La Voie communiste*, bilan d'un courant politique', document Fo 1001-5, BDIC archives at Nanterre.

Additional Material: The Far Left

In general Pattieu's account focuses on the wing of French Trotskyism headed by Pierre Frank, and takes a somewhat negative view of other currents of French Trotskyism. We are therefore complementing Pattieu's narrative with some material on the other two main Trotskyist currents, that led by Pierre Lambert and Voix ouvrière, as well as the Trotskyist-derived Socialisme ou Barbarie.

The Lambert Current

For the Lambert current we are presenting two articles in which Lambert speaks in his own words, and a note on the Committee for the Liberation of Messali Hadj, in which Lambert's organisation played a major role.

Pierre Lambert
Let the Algerian People Speak: Part V — Independence by Stages and the Constituent Assembly[1]

In our previous article we failed to mention another category of critics. Certain comrades who in private express their agreement with the political orientation of the Mouvement National Algérien, consider that they should not mention this in public. Their method of arguing is specious.

These comrades assert that it is a purely Algerian matter and that it is not for us to interfere in the internal problems of our Algerian friends.

If by 'neutrality' these comrades want to express the opinion that the duty of the French people is to defend unconditionally, especially with respect to repression, the struggle of the Algerian people and of its fighters, then that is an elementary truth.

It will be a cause of shame for the main political organisations, and above all for the leadership of the French Communist Party, to have refused to defend the 'Messalists' because of the political disagreements they have with the MNA. It will be a cause of shame for *L'Humanité* to have remained silent about the tortures suffered by Mustapha Ben Mohammed because he is a leader of the MNA.

For our part we have always defended and we shall continue to defend any Algerian who is a victim of imperialist repression, whatever his political positions may be.

But political 'non-interventionism' is unthinkable. For revolutionary militants there is a choice. To be present in the camp of revolution. In the camp of those who express politically the needs and objectives of the revolution.

Did we not take a position in favour of the camp of the insurgents in Barcelona in May 1937, the camp of the revolutionary militants of the POUM and the FAI against the Stalinists?[2]

So if we adopted the position of our 'critics', we should have to condemn the formal, clear, precise position taken in May 1937.

* * *

For the French revolutionary proletariat the historic importance of the Algerian Revolution is comparable to that of the Russian Revolution of 1917. Likewise in the Russian Revolution there were various formations claiming to represent the revolution. Only the Bolshevik Party of Lenin and Trotsky expressed the political objectives of the Revolution.

Today, in a new historic situation, which takes different forms, the MNA clearly represents anti-imperialist objectives. The comrades who criticise us agree with this latter judgement. Can they remain neutral? It is obviously impossible to take seriously the following line of argument which is often put against us: 'But we know who is in control of the resistance struggle, how far Messali has been outdistanced, we must be cautious, etc.'

We are not in the confidence of the gods and even if we were, it would not occur to us to reveal such secrets. To this false problem of 'information', we reply with the only valid question: Why has the Algerian people taken up arms? In other words, by what political strategy and tactics can the armed struggle achieve success?

Are the strategy and tactics developed either by the FLN or by the MNA appropriate to the anti-imperialist aims pursued by the people? And thereby to the revolutionary objectives of the French proletariat?

Such are the problems on which we have to take a position. To this end, we shall quote various public documents sent to *La Vérité* by the Secretariat of the FLN.

* * *

In a leaflet entitled 'Warning' received in October 1955 we read, after a very violent attack against both the person of Messali Hadj and the MNA:[3]

> But their machinations — the machinations of the Messalists — are systematically thwarted, as is shown by the interview with our brother Ouamrane[4] published by a Parisian weekly which has wisely chosen to get its

information first-hand.

What does Ouamrane say in the interview with Robert Barrat published by *France-Observateur* on 15 July 1955?[5]

> We have spoken of the principle of the right to independence. We are realists: independence must be achieved by stages and democratically.

The FLN has an absolute right to advocate independence by stages. But then does it have a right to make charges against Bourguiba and 'bourguibism', which are practising this policy in Tunisia?

And above all how is it possible to assert that 'independence by stages' represents the aspiration of the Algerian people?

Not long ago, at the time of 1946 elections, the overwhelming majority of Algerians, in voting for the candidates of the MTLD, clearly showed their determination not to accept the deception contained in such a formula. The overwhelming opposition to the 1947 'Statute'[6] is likewise a proof.

In any case, this point of view, in conformity with the ideas developed by the 'centralists' in 1954, represents the position of the FLN. But it is going beyond the bounds of democracy to state in a declaration issued in the name of the Secretariat of the FLN:

> To achieve these ends the FLN is putting forward an honourable platform for discussion with the French authorities: The opening of negotiations with the authorised representatives of the Algerian people.

Thus the policy of 'independence by stages' quite naturally means that the leaders of the FLN adopt the 'theory of authorised representatives', without the Algerian people being called upon to appoint these 'representatives' in advance in the course of free elections. We have shown in our previous articles how this policy led only to the prefabrication of representatives. We only need to observe the efforts of Soustelle[7] to understand that on this road the FLN will be overtaken. The statements against the elections of 2 January by Ben Salem, Farès[8] and others, if they express the people's fear, also have the meaning of a governmental operation aiming to restore the fortunes of the 'yes-men', with a view to making them into authorised representatives.

In France, moreover, the protagonists of this policy such as Gilles Martinet, J Daniel,[9] the Mendesists, etc… give, let us remember, a particular content to the theory of independence by stages: their 'realism' leads them to advocate the 'provisional' (of course) retention during a 'first stage' (of course) of the double electoral college.[10]

French revolutionaries must not deny the FLN its right to develop such a policy. But in the name of what democratic principle can it then assert that the policy of independence by stages and of authorised representatives represents the 'lucid and realistic policy which the people prefers' (from the leaflet quoted above)???

Notes
1. From *La Vérité*, 16 December 1955.
2. A reference to the anti-Stalinist Workers Party of Marxist Unification and the Iberian Anarchist Federation [*RH*].
3. The use of personal attacks by which the FLN's policy of opposing Messali is expressed is to be deplored. But that is indeed a question in which we do not have to interfere.
4. Amar Ouamrane (b 1919): PPA member, sentenced to death in 1945, then amnestied; joined FLN, commander of *wilaya* IV, and various other military functions; supported Ben Bella in 1962, then retired from political life [*RH*].
5. Barrat was a Catholic anti-colonialist journalist; this was the first interview with FLN leaders to appear in the French press. Following its publication *France-Observateur* was seized and Barrat was arrested. See M Evans, *Algeria: France's Undeclared War* (Oxford, 2012), p 142 [*RH*].
6. Compromise reform measures opposed by both nationalists and settlers [*RH*].
7. Jacques Soustelle (1912-1990): Governor General of Algeria in 1955–56, removed by Mollet. Served as minister in de Gaulle's governments from 1958, but broke with de Gaulle in 1960 and joined OAS [*RH*].
8. Abderrahmane Farès (1911-1991): member of first constituent assembly 1946 ; joined FLN, came to Paris 1956 to organise French Federation; 1962 president of Provisional Algerian Executive, but critical of Ben Bella and retired from political life [*RH*].
9. Jean Daniel (b 1920): left-wing journalist, later editor of *Le Nouvel Observateur* [*RH*].
10. The 1947 Statute set up an Algerian Assembly, elected by two electoral colleges each electing 60 members; the first represented 460 000 Europeans plus 58 000 assimilated Muslims; the second 1.4 million unassimilated Muslims — a blatant imbalance. See Evans, *Algeria*, p 102 [*RH*].

Pierre Lambert
Silence Becomes Complicity[1]

The four bullets shot through Abdallah Filali[2] have aroused strong feelings. Together with our friend Jean Cassou,[3] we have launched a first appeal published in this issue.

It is of some value to point this out since, in the coming weeks, we shall have to draw precise conclusions from this fact. Jean Cassou has personally sent a letter to the editors of those dailies and weeklies which have more or less declared themselves in favour of a peaceful solution to the Algerian problem, asking them to associate themselves, in whatever form they choose, with the protest for which he has taken the initiative. At present this appeal is being very widely distributed in all milieux and in particular will be sent to the leaders of the MNA and the FLN and to the people who support the latter movement. It will thus be possible to clearly establish responsibilities and complicities. It is obvious that, whatever point of view one has as to the solution of the Algerian problem, those who gave the orders to shoot down Ahmed Semmache,[4] Hocine Maroc,[5] Abdallah Filali and other militants, must be condemned. At the very least silence would be equivalent to complicity. Among other things, let us wait and see what position *L'Humanité* will take.

* * *

Contrary to what the right-wing press would like us to believe, these attacks are not a 'settling of scores', but rather the assertion of a policy which, from whatever angle we examine it, is contrary to the aims of the liberation of the Algerian people, a policy which only helps colonialism and its repressive forces. Nearly two years ago in a series of articles — for which we were prosecuted and convicted — we asked the question: what is the FLN? Today it is possible to reply more precisely to this question; and the reply will enable us to understand better the reason for the violent attacks against the leaders of the USTA.[6]

The facts that we are going to list are more than clues:

*   At the recent 'Cairo Congress' Ben Bella was given a purely honorary post. If the imprisonment of a leader obviously prevents him from playing an effective part in the leadership, the 'honorary' status takes on the character of a disavowal and a removal.

*   The rapid rise of Ferhat Abbas,[7] who, together with Yazid,[8] seem to be more and more the key figures in the FLN, may not mean the total take-over of the FLN by the former President of the UDMA,[9] but it shows in any case the leading role played by this spoilt child of the liberal milieu of colonialism — who, abroad, has become a hard-liner… in words!

*   We should compare the information reported in early September: during his meeting in Switzerland with Ferhat Abbas, Bourguiba is said to have advised the latter to take into consideration the outline law,[10] after the UN session.[11]

*   The contradictory statements by Yazid in New York about dropping the 'prerequisites for independence' express the internal contradictions of the FLN, but nonetheless prepare the way for a line which does not yet dare express itself openly. The recent statement to *Paris-Presse* by Bourguiba's minister, Bahi Ladgham, stating that the FLN no longer considers recognition of independence as a prerequisite for negotiations with France, confirms this new orientation.

In this respect, one cannot help noting how catastrophic these prerequisites have been, for they allowed colonialism to shelter behind the so-called intransigence of the FLN in order to make its preparations for total war. The prerequisites, the eight-day strike in January 1957, the random attacks, the all-out strike by students — all these things had the most dramatic consequences for the Algerian people.

* * *

But throughout this reorientation by the group currently leading the FLN, implying the abandonment of a whole series of previous positions, there remains despite everything a common denominator with yesterday's positions: the determination to monopolise the negotiations at all costs, for in a situation where a political solution to the Algerian problem is already here and now a certainty, the likes of Ferhat Abbas and Yazid understand perfectly well the danger which the policy of the MNA, based on principles, represents for them. Thus the — illegitimate — demand for a monopoly in the negotiations, accompanied by the dropping of the — wholly verbal — intransigence of the previous period, leads quite naturally to ordering the odious attacks on MNA militants and on the leaders of the USTA.

In concluding, let us repeat: this analysis, to which we shall return, expresses the particular point of view of our party: but the condemnations of the attacks should be unanimous in the working-class and democratic movements.

Notes
1. From *La Vérité*, 17 October 1957.
2. Abdallah Filali (1913-1957): came to France in 1934; 1936 elected to leadership of ENA; co-founder of PPA with Messali in 1937; major leader of PPA, jailed in 1939-43; organised PPA clandestinely; 1945 sentenced to death *in absentia*; leading organiser of MTLD; became Messali's chief spokesperson, involved in founding MNA; took part in negotiations with FLN; jailed by French in 1955-57; reorganised USTA; killed by FLN in 1957, a fatal blow to the MNA [*RH*].
3. Jean Cassou (1897-1986): writer, member of Resistance, Chief of Conservation at the national museums and peace movement activist [*RH*].
4. Ahmed Semmache: metal-worker, head of Paris region of USTA, killed by FLN in 1957 [*RH*].
5. Hocine Maroc (1930-1957): came to France in 1954; metal-worker, in CGT; organised USTA in factory; killed by FLN in 1957 [*RH*].
6. The MNA's trade-union organisation [*RH*].
7. Ferhat Abbas (1899-1985): politically active from 1924; elected to Algerian Assembly in 1948; described himself as 'moderate nationalist', joined FLN in 1955; President of GPRA in 1958-61; after independence President of Constituent Assembly; resigned in protest at excessive role of FLN; put under house arrest;

retired from political life after 1965 [RH].
8. M'Hammed Yazid (1923-2003): joined PPA in 1942; MTLD organiser in France — jailed for two years in 1948; joined FLN, became FLN delegate to UN; Information Minister in GPRA. After 1965 Ambassador to Beirut, responsible for contacts with Palestinian organisations [RH].
9. Union Démocratique du Manifeste Algérien (Democratic Union of the Algerian Manifesto), a middle-class reformist organisation established by Ferhat Abbas in 1946 [RH].
10. In September 1957, the French government proposed a *loi-cadre* (outline law) which would keep Algeria French but give more powers to the local population. See M Evans, *Algeria: France's Undeclared War* (Oxford, 2012), pp 222-23 [RH].
11. In February 1957, the UN debated Algeria, but following French manoeuvring passed a platitudinous resolution urging a just and peaceful solution. See Evans, *Algeria*, pp 192-98 [RH].

* * *

Ian Birchall
A Note on the Committee for the Release of Messali Hadj and the Victims of Repression

The Comité pour la Libération de Messali Hadj et des Victimes de la Répression was formed in 1954, when Messali Hadj was put under house arrest. Between November 1954 and April 1957, it produced 11 issues of a *Bulletin d'Information* (the first was duplicated, all the rest printed), containing news of the imprisonment of Messali and of repression in Algeria, including executions and death sentences. There are reports of meetings held and of support from trade-union organisations. If the attendance figures cited are accurate, the Committee clearly made a certain impact.

The Committee was animated by the Lambert tendency, and Lambert himself wrote several article for the *Bulletin*, but it clearly had a considerably broader base of support among trade-union activists and well-known intellectuals.

An article in the first issue of the *Bulletin*, dated 27 November 1954, describes the initial activities of the Committee:

> On 3 October, activists from all the trade-union organisations, CGT, FO, CFTC and independent unions and well-known personalities, launched an appeal for the immediate release of Messali Hadj. Very rapidly more than a hundred militants holding positions at various levels backed their action.
>
> On 15 October, there was a first meeting of Renault workers at the Place Nationale at Billancourt: they made a formal protest against the worsening of the conditions under which Messali Hadj, leader of the Mouvement National Algérien, has been deported.

Events speeded up after the explosion of 1 November 1954. The Algerian people fell victim to terror. Hundreds and thousands of militants of the national movement were arrested and tortured. Messali Hadj saw his conditions of deportation worsened yet again. He was confined to a hotel room at Sables d'Olonne[1] and his lawyers Yves Dechezelles and Pierre Stibbe[2] had a tough struggle to get to communicate with him. He was not allowed any contact with the population or with his friends. The leader of the national movement was under close surveillance, guarded by a large number of police inspectors and by helmeted CRS [riot police] on a war footing. Messali's children, Janina (aged 16) and Ali (aged 24) were under surveillance at all times. Messrs Mitterrand and Mendès-France can feel proud.

But on 3 November, the powerful and united independent Fédération de l'Éducation Nationale, with the authority of its 220 000 members, made its protest. Since then numerous other unions and working-class militants have associated themselves with the Committee for the Release of Messali Hadj and the Victims of Repression. An outline of the activity of the Committee will give an idea of the work it is doing.

On 13 November at Nantes, after a report on the situation by Maître Yves Dechezelles, a delegation led by Hébert, General Secretary of the FO departmental union for the Loire Inférieure, and including Georges Nouvel, a metal-worker and CGT delegate, André Cardinal, a primary teacher from the autonomous FEN, and Georges Fasa, a member of the committee of the local FO union at Nantes, went to Sables d'Olonne to meet Messali Hadj.

On orders from M Mitterrand, the police refused any contact between the delegation and the leader of the national movement. [...]

The Nantes local committee for the release of Messali Hadj has called for 23 November a meeting at which the speakers will be:

* Leblanc, on behalf of the independent FEN.
* Fasa, on behalf of the FO departmental union.
* Rousselot, on behalf of the CGT departmental union.
* And Maître Pierre Stibbe, lawyer at the Paris Bar.

A meeting is being planned very soon in Paris with Laurent Schwartz, professor at the Sorbonne, Jean Cassou, writer, and Maître Yves Dechezelles, lawyer at the Paris Bar.

In the provinces the Committee has made contact with trade-union organisations and militants in order to organise meetings in the following towns: Lyon, Saint-Etienne, Clermont-Ferrand.

The Committee's aim is to hold in Paris, on 16 January 1955, an assembly of Committees for the Release of Messali Hadj and the Victims of Repression.

In addition the Committee has published three documents which are attached to this *Bulletin*:

1. An appeal for the release of Messali Hadj.
2. Statement by Messali Hadj about the events in Algeria.
3. Report on the Messali case.

Originating from an active protest by militants in the French labour movement, the Committee calls on all those who believe that the honour of the French people is at stake in the monstrous military operations decreed by the rulers of this country to associate themselves with its activity:

Join the Committee!
Support its Action!
Subscribe!

The April 1955 issue contained a list of members of the Bureau elected by the first conference of the committee. As well as names already mentioned, this included Marceau Pivert, Jean Rous and Daniel Guérin. The same issue contained a letter from the novelist Albert Camus expressing support and offering to intervene any time 'it is a matter of releasing Arab militants or protecting them from police repression'. A further list of supporters in the issue of March-April 1957 included the surrealist poet André Breton.

The June 1955 *Bulletin* contained a report of a meeting attended by 400 Paris workers which passed a resolution:

* Protesting against the legal action taken against working-class organisations (PCI, FCL).[3]
* Protesting against the confiscation of working-class newspapers (*Le Libertaire, La Vérité, L'Humanité, Alger Républicain*).
* Protesting against the charges just made against comrades Donnet and Fontenis (FCL militants).
* Calling on workers to demand an end to these anti-democratic measures.

The June 1955 issue reported two other meetings:

> On 21 April, the Committee for the Release of Messali Hadj and the Victims of Repression held a meeting in the public hall at Lourches, a mining centre in the Nord. More than 400 workers had responded to the Committee's call…
>
> Five hundred workers crowded into the Gaillard Hall in Clermont-Ferrand on 13 May for a meeting called by the Mouvement de Libération du Peuple… [they heard] an extensive report by Pierre Stibbe on the situation in Algeria.

Notes
1. A small seaside resort on the west coast of France [*RH*].
2. Pierre Stibbe (1912-1967): lawyer, Pivertist before 1939, later in the UGS and a founder-member of the PSU in 1960 [*RH*].
3. See Pattieu, Chapter IV above [*RH*].

Voix Ouvrière and the Algerian War

Pattieu says very little about the Voix ouvrière tendency. This omission is largely justified, since VO played little part in solidarity activity. In the autobiographical interviews published under the title *La Véritable Histoire De Lutte Ouvrière* (Denoël, Paris, 2003), Robert Barcia, a leading figure in VO, was asked if the group had given 'logistic support' to the Algerian struggle for independence. He responded: 'In Marseille, we had contacts in the Algerian milieu. We didn't really provide logistic support, but we hid Algerians for a few days.'

He added:

> For our part, we were at that time the only political organisation to distribute workplace bulletins at the factory gates in support of the Algerian people's struggle for emancipation. We criticised certain reactionary characteristics of the FLN but we supported it all the same. It was not for us to choose what leaders the Algerian people would adopt. (pp 188, 192)

VO did produce regular propaganda on the Algerian question, distributed to workers, including Algerian workers, through paper sales and regular factory bulletins. To illustrate this, we are translating two articles from *Lutte de Classe*, a fortnightly paper which was sold in factories on the alternate week to the workplace bulletins.

We shall be putting on our website two further articles from *Lutte ouvrière*, the political successor of *Voix ouvrière*, showing the tendency's particular perspective on the Algerian struggle.

Tail-Ending[1]

The Évian negotiations are continuing without any visible progress. The official commentators, made cautious by previous twists and turns, and expecting to see them broken off any day, are pleased that they are continuing at all.

It now seems obvious that Algeria, which is moving irresistibly towards political independence, will emerge from these negotiations more or less in partnership with France, giving the word 'partnership' the meaning it has in 'partnership of capital and labour'. A number of points which seem secondary in relation to independence itself, such as the status of Europeans, the pre-referendum period, the question of the Sahara, the continuing presence of the

French army, etc, will in fact determine the greater or lesser dependence of the future 'sovereign' Algerian state in relation to France and the world imperialist market.

In this respect it should be noted that if the independence which Algeria will get is due to the devotion and courage of the FLN militants and to the commitment and enormous sacrifices of the Algerian proletariat and people, unfortunately the latter have not been able to create a political leadership worthy of them. The FLN leaders are constantly outdistanced, even panicked, by the initiatives of the French government. The most recent example is the unilateral truce. It is quite clear that the French military is not taking any risks by observing such a truce. But it is also clear that this puts the French government in a favourable light in relation to French, international and even perhaps Algerian opinion, which it certainly does not deserve. The FLN leaders were 'surprised' by this initiative which everyone had been discussing for weeks.

But it is the job of leaders to foresee. One of the delegates went so far as to ask a journalist whether he could give them an idea about it: 'We knew it was being discussed', they said, 'but we didn't think de Gaulle would do it.' That sums up the difference. For its part, the French bourgeoisie has men who are up to the situation. The Algerian people has not yet found them.

However, those really responsible for this state of affairs are to be found much more on this side of the Mediterranean than the other. All the more so because we don't know what leaders those fighting would pick if they had the possibility of choosing.

We, for our part, are not occupied by an enormous army. We are able to know and judge our leaders. We are able to choose and name them by means other than rhythmical clapping in Ivry or Saint-Denis.[2]

But what do we see? The political organisations of the working class and the trade unions are not doing anything, at Évian or elsewhere, in order to enable the Algerian people not to have to face the French bourgeoisie on its own. Far from intervening, they call off or limit trade-union action which could mobilise millions of metropolitan workers 'in order not to disrupt the Évian talks', that is, so as not to weaken de Gaulle's position in face of the FLN representatives.

It is certain that the latter accommodate to de Gaulle's manoeuvres or don't know how to reply to them because they are not revolutionary leaders determined to overthrow the social order existing in Algeria and elsewhere, and they do not go beyond the ambitions and aspirations of the Algerian petty bourgeoisie and intelligentsia. But it is even more certain that the leaders of the French left are playing de Gaulle's game and do nothing but tail him, because their sole role and function is to be the last barrier between the bourgeoisie and the proletariat, whether it be French or Algerian.

Notes
1. From *Lutte de Classe*, no 15, 30 May 1961.
2. Bastions of the PCF in the Paris suburbs, and locations of the PCF Congresses in 1959 and 1961 [*RH*].

Once There Was a Party...[1]

One of the main excuses used by the PCF to justify its lack of activity about the war in Algeria to its members and supporters is the claim that repression would force it into virtual illegality and that eventually it would be totally prevented from expressing itself.

To understand the full hypocrisy of this 'explanation', we only need look at the struggles which the young Communist Party (French Section of the Communist International) was able to put up, and in particular at its activity during the occupation of the Ruhr by the French army in 1923 (the PCF was just two years old).

In the autumn of that year, revolutionaries throughout the world had their eyes turned towards Germany, which was then going through an economic and social crisis which would culminate in the Communist insurrection in Hamburg on 25 October and the attempted Nazi putsch in Munich on 9 November.

It was certainly not the first crisis to affect Germany in the period after the end of the World War, but this one developed in the very specific context of the Ruhr occupation, and never did the facts show so clearly how the fates of different proletariats were linked across frontiers.

The origins of the crisis went back to the Treaty of Versailles. Defeated Germany had been crushed economically, stripped of its colonies and some of its provinces, and condemned to pay enormous 'reparations' to the victorious powers, principally France and Belgium, on whose territory the war had been fought.

But the economic situation in which the Treaty placed Germany made it quite incapable of paying its debts, all the more so because the German bourgeoisie intended to make the full burden of the requirement fall on the shoulders of the proletariat, and the only effective measure it took to get out of the difficulties in which it found itself was to launch an all-out struggle against the eight-hour day.

It was not only in Germany that capitalism was going on the offensive. After the revolutionary crisis that spread across Europe in the very first years after the war, capitalism had stabilised itself and had begun fighting to win back the gains it had had to surrender to the working class. France for its part was governed by a right-wing National Assembly, where the majority belonged to the Bloc National;[2] the level of strikes had been falling since 1920, the date of the great railway strike; and in the months just before the Ruhr Occupation, the French government did not hesitate to tell the army to shoot on strikers in Le Havre.

It was in the context of the decline of the revolutionary movement that the occupation of the Ruhr took place. On the pretext that Germany was unable to pay its reparations, the Poincaré government took the decision to reclaim its security and have the coal basin occupied by the French army, which was joined by Belgian troops. In fact for French imperialism it was an excellent pretext to carry out to its advantage the unification of the Lorraine iron mines and the Ruhr coalfields, something which had always tempted the two rival bourgeoisies.

Germany, effectively disarmed by the Treaty of Versailles, did not have the capacity for armed resistance to the French plan, and the Cuno government could do no more than proclaim 'passive resistance', but, despite that, there was no mistaking the fact that it was a new episode of the imperialist war.

But since the tragic days of July and August 1914, which saw the collapse of the Second International, there had been the Russian Revolution and the birth of the Comintern. In 1923, the different national sections of the Comintern, especially the French and German, were to show that although young and inexperienced, they were worth much more than the old social democracy. However, they were already showing certain dangerous symptoms which prefigured their future degeneration, and the action by the French and German parties was in some sense their swansong.

Even before the French troops entered the Ruhr on 11 January, the representatives of the French, British, Belgian, Italian, Czech and Dutch Communist Parties and the CGTU[3] had met on 6 January at Essen to determine the policy to be implemented. It was not merely a question of struggling against the occupation of the Ruhr; the 'war against imperialist war' which the conference decided on was to be carried out in the perspective of socialist revolution: 'We shall make the Rhine the graveyard of European capitalism.'

The French section of the Communist International had to take on one of the most difficult tasks, since it was the army of its national imperialism which was occupying the Ruhr; the major part of its activity was directed towards anti-militarist work, that is, a necessarily clandestine activity, to which the young party was not accustomed.

In 1923, the PCF was far from having the numerical strength it has nowadays.[4] A permanent crisis of revolutionary growth had been manifested in a constant reduction in numbers since the Tours Congress.[5] It had only about 60 000 members at the beginning of the year, and it would have scarcely more than 45 000 by December.

But this relative numerical weakness was not the main obstacle to its efforts.

In fact social-democratic habits and organisational methods had remained in force after 1920, and they rapidly revealed their pernicious influence.

The problems facing the PCF were new and vast, but if the party lacked political training and experience, its members lacked neither enthusiasm nor revolutionary zeal, and in a few months they achieved an enormous amount.

Since it was above all a matter of work in the army, the Communist Youth had a major role to play. They carried it out all the better because they had been won over to the ideas of the left tendency, whose authority in the adult party was much more open to challenge.

The first task to be carried out was to enlighten the masses as to what the occupation of the Ruhr meant, and to fight against chauvinist propaganda. While the PCF was organising in France, with greater or lesser success, rallies and meetings, the Young Communists, in collaboration with their German comrades, turned to the French soldiers from the very first day. Thousands of leaflets and posters declared: 'German workers are your brothers', 'Fraternise with the German workers', 'Do not shoot on German workers.'

Within a few months a whole range of publications aimed at the occupying troops was created and developed. A 'special soldiers' edition' of *L'Humanité*, illegal and appearing weekly, was born and a few months later even appeared twice weekly. The print-run of *La Caserne* [*The Barracks*], the Young Communist monthly aimed at soldiers, was doubled, so that it could be widely distributed in the Ruhr.

The colonial troops were not forgotten. To begin with, there were just leaflets and appeals in Arabic explaining: 'You are here to loot and rob on behalf of the same French imperialists who murder and rob you at home.' But leaflets were not enough, and a few months later appeared the *Caserne coloniale* [*Colonial Barracks*], a monthly publication in Arabic.

In parallel with this propaganda work, it was necessary to carry out organisational work of capital importance. Thus far contacts between young Communists in the army were very loose. What was necessary was to strengthen these contacts, and to build a centralised organisation based on cells in the various regiments.

Of course the French bourgeoisie did not stand by and watch this attempt to undermine its gangster policies. The two representatives of the PCF and the CGTU at the Essen conference, Cachin and Monmousseau, were arrested; Cachin's parliamentary immunity was lifted, and they were charged with endangering state security. In the Ruhr itself, the repression was more severe. About a hundred German Young Communists and some 15 French soldiers were arrested. The Mainz trial in June 1924 would sentence 37 militants to a total of 133 years in jail.

But despite the repression the activity bore fruit. Soldiers were among the first to subscribe in support of the German Communist press, which was in difficulties. Insubordination was manifested in every form: soldiers refused to pull down Communist stickers, walked out of official celebrations on 14 July, attended German trade-union festivals and sang the *Internationale*, and even demonstrated on the streets with German workers. In numerous cases, soldiers refused to shoot on workers, and Moroccan troops, who were then regarded as an unthinking tool of repression, refused to open fire at Neustadt.

With the rising revolutionary wave, by the autumn anti-militarist activity had taken on a capital importance. It was not simply a matter of making propaganda against the occupation of the Ruhr, it was also necessary to win the occupation army to a standpoint of benevolent neutrality towards the revolution, and to win over the most advanced sections to support it. And it is probable that if the German revolution had developed, it would have been difficult for the bourgeoisie to use the French army as an instrument of repression.

During these few months in 1923, the French Communist militants made a considerable achievement, and wrote the only glorious page in the history of the French Communist Party. But 1925 marked the great turning-point. If the policy of the PCF symbolises all that was positive in the Communist Party and the zeal and devotion of its members, the failure of the German revolution, called off at the last moment by the Communist International, marked the time of bureaucratic degeneration, in face of which the various sections of the International were not sufficiently armed ideologically to be able to resist.

Today the PCF has nothing to say about Germany except to talk of the dangers of German militarism in a style comparable to the statements of the social chauvinists of 1914 and 1923. A reminder of what the French section of the International — of which it is now no more than the tomb — was able to do 38 years ago is the most terrible indictment which can be made against a party which now finds itself in conditions that are much more favourable than those of the SFIC in 1923, and which boasts ten times as many members and five million electors, and benefits from the struggle waged by the FLN both in Algeria and in mainland France; yet during over seven years that there has been fighting in Algeria, it has proposed nothing but petition campaigns and a delegation to Évian, and even voted for 'special powers'.

Notes
1. From *Lutte de Classe*, no 27, 15 November 1961.
2. A coalition of right-wing parties which ruled France from 1919 to 1924 [RH].
3. *Confédération générale du travail unitaire*: a split from the CGT in 1922, in which the PCF was active [RH].
4. Official PCF figures for membership cards distributed — which probably

substantially overstate actual membership — were 506 250 in 1954 and 407 000 in 1961 [*RH*].

5. The PCF was founded at the Tours Congress in December 1920 [*RH*].

Ian Birchall
Socialisme ou Barbarie and the Algerian War

In his book Pattieu refers only very briefly to Socialisme ou Barbarie (SouB), and dismisses it as 'more oriented to theoretical debate than to practical activity'. While it is indeed true that SouB played little part in solidarity activity, its role during the war and its analysis of the situation deserve some attention.

SouB came into existence at the beginning of 1949, when a small group of PCI members broke with their party. Their main difference was on the 'Russian question'; they rejected any notion that Russia should be defended, and argued that it was a new form of bureaucratic society; later they defined it as 'bureaucratic capitalism'. The leading figures were Cornelius Castoriadis (also known as Pierre Chaulieu, Paul Cardan and Jean-Marc Coudray) and Claude Lefort. Initially SouB had little more than a dozen members, and until its dissolution in 1967 it never had more than 87 adherents. Yet it succeeded in publishing a well-produced if sometimes irregular magazine, and it was one of the few revolutionary groupings which made a systematic attempt to analyse the changed nature of the post-1945 world.[1]

SouB was initially slow to respond to the war. Some members took part in the Committee of Struggle Against Colonialist Repression, set up by Daniel Guérin in December 1954, but it was only in 1956 that SouB published its first article on the Algerian situation.[2] And only in 1958 did it devote an editorial, written by Claude Lefort, to the question. This argued that during the conscript revolts popular opposition could have made the continuation of the war impossible. But at a point when 'everything was still possible' the PCF came to the aid of the Mollet government. However, it was not simply the PCF's betrayal that explained the failure of the working class to intervene: it was necessary to recognise that 'the proletariat itself has been contaminated by the climate of colonial war'.

SouB argued that revolutionaries must give unconditional support to independence for Algeria; this went beyond the Leninist position of 'revolutionary defeatism', which, it claimed, implied 'deliberate ignorance of the aims and conduct of the "enemy"'. SouB also rejected 'permanent revolution', noting that many independence struggles had ended up with bourgeois or bureaucratic rule. Hence it took the position of supporting 'the cause of the exploited in struggle', but rejected any support for 'organisations as such'. It rejected support for both the 'conciliatory positions' of the MNA and the FLN's use of terrorism and liquidation of its rivals.[3]

SouB's analysis thus implied a rejection of any concrete support for the FLN, and this position was confirmed by an internal debate in 1960 (though for security reasons the discussion was minuted as being on the 'agricultural question').[4]

SouB demarcated itself very sharply from the mainstream of the left which invoked French 'national interest' and defence of the Republic. Castoriadis wrote a savage article in which he imagined left journalist Claude Bourdet and rebel general Massu singing the *Marseillaise* in chorus.[5]

At the end of 1960, SouB attempted to relate to the growing student opposition to the war by setting up 'action groups', notably in Paris and Caen, which drew in PSU members and others. But these did not last long, and succeeded neither in becoming effective united front bodies nor in recruiting to SouB. SouB suffered little from the general repression which affected the left, the only exception being three members in Caen who were charged with endangering the internal security of the state for distributing a leaflet.[6]

After the police massacre of Algerians in October 1961, *Pouvoir Ouvrier* made a stinging attack on the French left for abandoning the Algerians;[7] but of course SouB itself was far too small to initiate any activity. SouB reported that when a demonstration was eventually called, the CGT called for support — but when *Pouvoir Ouvrier* activists gave out leaflets about the demonstration at the Chausson factory at Gennevilliers, they were confronted by PCF members and called provocateurs.

But the SouB members who made the most interesting and perceptive analyses of the Algerian question were Daniel Mothé and Jean-François Lyotard. Mothé was a milling-machine operator at Renault Billancourt who had joined SouB in 1952.[8] In an internal debate he had opposed working inside the trade unions, but he had a group of young workers, some of them PCF supporters, around him.[9] He wrote a number of articles about factory life; two of these in particular dealt with the impact of the Algerian war.[10]

In the first article, dated in the summer of 1956, Mothé reported on the impact of the recall of reservists to fight in Algeria. This became a concrete issue when a worker from his workshop received a telephone call telling him he had been recalled:

> What was to be done to keep J with us, or at least to demonstrate our indignation and our solidarity. 'What is to be done?' suddenly became everyone's main preoccupation.

But the immediate response was a sense of impotence:

As for us, what could we do, the 150 in the shop? A hundred and fifty to oppose a governmental decision, to oppose a government supported by all the deputies — including the Communists — 150 in face of an edifice of laws, a constitution, a police, an army and a nation of over forty million inhabitants…[11]

Mothé's response was to draw up a statement in conjunction with other workers; he then tried to get other workers to sign it. The statement was a direct attack on the strategy of the PCF; nonetheless some PCF members signed, while others refused:

Without condemning small exemplary actions, we believe that to stop the war in Algeria we must launch general coordinated actions. Ending the war in Algeria cannot be left in the hands of the government. It must be obliged to act. That is why we condemn the method of action which consists of sending petitions to these very traitors, of continuing to trust them, of bursting into tears because they are taking away young men to get them massacred. It is not by tearful petitions but by forceful actions that we shall say to the government:

No, you don't have the confidence of the workers!

No, we don't believe you any longer.

You have betrayed us… Well! We shall fight against you because you are the henchmen of the colonialists and the gravediggers of youth!

We must address all workers throughout France for an appeal and propose to them a general stoppage of work against the war, against the recall of the reservists. Strikes of struggle, not petitions of confidence.[12]

When Mothé and his friends attended a meeting about the war, the Communists spread rumours that they had behaved disruptively, making a noise to interrupt speakers. Subsequently the CGT issued a leaflet saying that they had had to admit 'Trotskyist elements' into the Committee for a Cease-Fire in Algeria because the other unions (FO and CFTC) had insisted on it, but warning workers that the Trotskyists 'by launching adventurist slogans, always contribute to the weakening of the struggle and the divisions among workers'. When there was a demonstration outside the factory, the Communists chanted 'negotiate' and 'Peace in Algeria', while Mothé and his friends shouted 'No soldiers for Algeria'.[13]

In a second article, roughly a year later, Mothé attempted to assess why action against the war had not been more successful. He was critical of the mainstream left, but also saw part of the problem in the positions of the Algerian organisations:

Moreover, whether it is the FLN and the MNA on the one side, or the French unions and 'left' parties on the other, nobody is trying to give this struggle a proletarian character.

The North African organisations pose the problems solely on the nationalist level: the Algerian nation free and sovereign. They stand on the ground of international jurisdiction, appeal to the UN, to the great powers and to the Arab world. Apart from independence, there is no social demand. The French proletariat, which does not believe in its government and which is somewhat distrustful of its political and trade-union leaders, carries over this distrust and opposition onto the political and military leaders of the Algerian movement. In general it does not believe that the North African proletariat will be emancipated by national independence. When the MNA defends the Eisenhower plan,[14] when the FLN is backed by Nasser, the French worker is distrustful. Neither the FLN nor the MNA ever addresses the French proletariat.[15]

Mothé also reported some interesting observations about the young workers who returned to the factory after having done military service as reservists in Algeria. Few had changed their attitudes radically as a result of what they had experienced:

> Very few have bad memories. The reservist's resentment tends to be directed against the army. Often one of them told me bitterly that he was forbidden to shoot, or that he had to account for the number of bullets allocated to him. He would conclude: 'We didn't have the right to defend ourselves.' [...]
>
> Except for a few Communist militants, there was never any sign of proletarian solidarity between the reservists and the North Africans. However, it would be wrong to think that because a worker has put on a uniform, he has lost all the reactions which characterised him in the factory. The reservist behaved like a soldier towards the North Africans, but he often behaved like a worker towards his officers. He carried in his pack the same contempt he has for those responsible for oppressing him in civilian life. He reacted against army discipline, but as this discipline also limited his power as an occupier, he often had a tendency to tar them all with the same brush, the North Africans and the High Command. [...]
>
> Even the most gullible didn't believe in 'pacification'; as for patriotism, they were totally without it. [...]
>
> Yet not one reservist expressed the slightest solidarity with the Europeans in North Africa. First of all, the proletarian's reaction excludes any sympathy with the privileged layers; then the occupying soldier's reaction goes to the logical conclusion: Algeria is hostile territory, and its inhabitants, all its

inhabitants, are the enemy.[16]

Mothé's conclusion was pessimistic. A year earlier there had been the possibility of effective action, but this had been lost, and now workers were relapsing into apathy:

> Nonetheless, the workers were ready to act. At Renault a substantial number of workers were prepared to struggle to prevent workmates from their shop being called up. But the possibilities which undoubtedly existed at that time were undermined, sabotaged and finally crushed by the attitude of the 'left' organisations.

And he concluded:

> A few months ago people were saying: 'We must do something' and even 'We won't go.' Now they're saying: 'Wait till it's over.'[17]

SouB's most substantial contribution to analysis of the Algerian revolution came from Jean-François Lyotard — now best known as a post-modernist philosopher. From 1950 to 1952, Lyotard was a *lycée* teacher in Algeria and was influenced by another teacher, Pierre Souyri. On his return, Lyotard became a teacher in the Sarthe area in North-West France; in 1954 both he and Souyri joined SouB. Since he was geographically isolated from the organisation, he was given the job of becoming SouB's expert on Algeria.[18]

He wrote a series of 12 articles between 1956 and 1963, initially under the pseudonym François Laborde, and later in his own name. These have been collected in book form.[19] Lyotard's analysis of the class nature of the FLN has been commended by Mohammed Harbi, formerly a leading FLN activist and now a well-known historian.[20]

Lyotard was one of the more Leninist members of SouB (he went with Pouvoir Ouvrier in the 1963 split). But he later noted that his work on Algeria had obliged him to rethink the whole question of the Marxist theory of class.[21] And despite the fact that his theoretical work was sharply critical of the FLN, Lyotard belonged to the minority in SouB which argued in favour of concrete support for the FLN. Many years later he revealed that he had been actively involved in the Henri Curiel support network, something of which his organisation was unaware at the time.[22] Such a combination of practical solidarity and lucid analysis was very rare on the French far left.

Lyotard's first article, 'The Situation in North Africa',[23] appeared early in 1956. It began by noting that the events in North Africa marked a 'new phase in the decomposition of French imperialism'. After 1945, the French bourgeoisie had been incapable of preserving its colonial empire. 'The imperialist political apparatus has *cracked up* in the three countries of the Maghreb since 1954, and it has *given way* in Tunisia and Morocco.'

He pointed to the very high level of exploitation in Algeria; 'The average Algerian industrial wage is one third of the minimum industrial wage in metropolitan France', and peasants were even worse off. Such a rate of exploitation provided 'unbeatable profits'.

And this led on to the central question of why the national liberation struggle should be supported:

> In reality, there is no alternative to exploitation other than socialism; in reality, the national-democratic struggle of the North African people contains within itself the premises of a new form of exploitation. But for all that we should not underestimate the subjective and objective content of its aim. Subjectively, it expresses the maximum potential consciousness of a proletariat crushed by material and moral terror; it crystallises the meaning of a rediscovered dignity. Objectively, the winning of national 'independence' will force the settlers to step back, to abandon the terrorist apparatus which was necessary for super-exploitation; it thus creates a revolutionary situation characterised by the sharing of power, economic to the settlers, political to the 'nationalists'; and within this situation the question of property will eventually have to be posed.
>
> Therefore in metropolitan France we cannot but support this struggle in all its extreme consequences. Contrary to the whole of the 'left', our concern is in no way to preserve the 'French presence in the Maghreb'. We are unconditionally against all imperialism, including French imperialism. We are unconditionally opposed to the continuation of terror.

Lyotard, apparently writing before the PCF had backed 'special powers', already saw the position of the Stalinists as being 'objectively that of a "very enlightened" bourgeoisie'. Firstly, this was because Stalinism was very weak in Algeria and its only hope of extending its influence was to maintain links with metropolitan France. And secondly:

> At present the possibilities for American imperialism in an 'independent' North Africa are much greater than those of the Russian bureaucracy. By keeping the French bourgeoisie there, in one way or another, the PCF is keeping open the future action of Stalinist imperialism, of which we already have a prefiguration today in the Middle East.

Lyotard's conclusion was more cautious than that of other currents on the French left, recognising the potential of the liberation struggle, but also its probable limits:

In North Africa, like everywhere else but even more so, we must take on the task of rigorous ideological clarification. To recognise the potential revolutionary scope of a struggle for independence is necessary. But we must also be able to denounce the objectives of the nationalist leaderships which, under the cover of this struggle, are tending to impose the dominant indigenous strata as new exploiters who, in order to achieve this position, will inevitably join one of the imperialist blocs, the American or the Russian. Finally we must understand and explain that the only solutions, which none of the forces in struggle are prepared to put into practice, are class solutions — the very first of these being the direct take-over of the land by the peasants.

In another piece written at the end of that year, 'The North African Bourgeoisie',[24] Lyotard broached a subject which he would develop further, the 'old question of the Permanent Revolution'. He argued that it was a 'false problem' to try to apply Trotsky's analysis to Morocco:

The Moroccan proletariat is absolutely not in a position to build its own dictatorship. It is numerous, certainly, but the evaluation of revolutionary forces is not a question of mere book-keeping, and that is not the essential thing. The essential thing is that it does not possess a clear understanding of its own objectives and means. This working class is not socialist and has not yet produced a vanguard.

In another article from 1957, Lyotard set out to analyse the nature of the FLN. He saw it as giving the peasant masses a leadership originating in the petty-bourgeoisie:

These elements bring with them their own particular psychology: 'rationalism', a taste for organisation, a certainty that cadres are important, a tendency towards centralism on the one hand and on the other to populism, a sincere devotion to the cause of the impoverished masses, an authentic sense of sharing their suffering.

As for centralism, it originates in the very conditions of the struggle. The Front was originally a military body; the subordination of all its activity to support for the ALN and the guerrilla fighters implied the necessity for a single omnipotent leadership. For over two years this leadership has not been under the control of the masses; on the contrary, the masses are receiving the imprint of its propaganda and its action.

Now this *single, centralised* apparatus is driven by the logic of development to root itself more and more solidly in the countryside and the towns, and to control the whole of Muslim society more and more tightly. It is now tending to take the administration of the country into its hands. That means that *the FLN is now already preparing itself for the role of being the managing stratum in Algerian society and that it is working objectively to blur the lines between present organisation and the future state.*

It is still too soon to know whether, once the conflict is over, the apparatus will be incorporated and abolished in a 'democratic' type of state, or whether on the other hand it will swallow up the state in order eventually to establish a further example of the 'strong regimes' which are being produced by young nations liberated politically from the rule of colonialism. In any case, the question is already posed in practice.

Later that year, in a piece entitled 'The Accounts of the "Loyal Manager"',[25] Lyotard took on the question as to why the French working class had been so passive in its acceptance of the war; to some extent he was giving a more theoretical analysis of the factors noted by Mothé in the article quoted above:

> The working class has not fought energetically against the Algerian war: anaesthetised by bourgeois propaganda, held back in its initial impulse against the call-up of reservists by the reformist organisations which were 'tailed' by the CGT and PCF who were pursuing their manoeuvre of unity with the Socialist Party, victim of a carefully maintained mistrust of workers living a different kind of life to its own, the French working class understood the Algerian war in the only way that remained to it, in immediate practice, in its impact on prices, wages and speed-up of work. It is certainly not prepared to struggle to put an end to this war as long as the war remains in its present state; it is probable that it would start to struggle energetically if two or three hundred thousand more troops were sent; but it is certain that it will show its true combativity if the government touches wages, directly or otherwise.

In 1958, Lyotard returned to the class analysis of the war and the inadequacy of the theory of Permanent Revolution in an article entitled 'Revealing the Algerian Contradictions'.[26] This argued that the key to the present situation lay in the '*burying* of class antagonisms in colonial society':

> This interpretation does not mean that we should abandon the concept of class on the pretext that there are no classes in Algeria. [...] But we have to show how and why a bourgeois leadership [the FLN] is capable of successfully mobilising all classes of Algerians in the struggle for independence, that means showing that the significance of this objective is capable of temporarily masking class objectives in the consciousness of Algerian workers, and showing why this nationalist ideology has been able to acquire such power.

He made a brief critique of the Lambertist PCI, which he accused of applying the theory of Permanent Revolution mechanically and thus seeing the MNA as the instrument of proletarian revolution; 'the Permanent Revolution schema is absolutely inapplicable to North Africa'. He cited a resolution from the 1953 Second Congress of the MTLD to show that it did not have a socialist programme:

> Certainly the MTLD was not, and the MNA is not, Algerian Bolshevism, quite simply because there cannot be Algerian Bolshevism in the present conditions of industrial development.

At the end of 1959, Lyotard further developed his analysis of the FLN in an article called 'The Social Content of the Algerian Struggle'.[27] This began by noting the 'relative weakness of the role played by the Algerian bourgeoisie in the national movement' and examining the implications of this:

> If the revolutionary situation which has been going on for five years has not yet ended up in the way that could have been reasonably predicted, namely a sharing of power and profit between imperialism and a leading Algerian stratum, it was first of all because imperialism has failed to get its Algerian fraction back under its control, but above all because Algerian social reality could not provide it with negotiating partners who would be the representatives of a class whose interests could both serve as a pole for all Algerian classes and prove themselves to be immediately compatible with those of imperialism.

He then went on to analyse the way that the FLN had developed:

> The Algerian national fight could only develop in the form of guerrilla resistance struggles. These contain within themselves both the revolutionary meaning of the struggle and its social significance. Its revolutionary meaning, because the men who join the resistance consciously and virtually geographically abandon their traditional society to take arms against it. [...] Since Algerian society offered no legal possibility for its transformation, it was necessary to go outside the law to change it. [...] The present cadres of the FLN are for the most part elements from the middle classes, which means that the resistance is the point of convergence between the Jacobin bourgeoisie and the peasants.

His conclusion was pessimistic:

> The process going on within a revolutionary situation that is five years old is that of the formation of a new class, and all the factors which make up this

situation mean that this class will necessarily be a bureaucracy.

As the end of the war approached, Lyotard wrote an article called 'Algeria, Seven Years On',[28] in which he saw his analysis of the FLN being confirmed:

> ... the consolidation of the apparatus intended to manage the masses during the next stage, that of the construction of the new Algerian society, must be undertaken without delay and given equal importance to the struggle for national liberation. [...] By strengthening the apparatus, the Algerian leaders are seeking [even if they are not aware of it] to channel the living forces of the future society for as long as the liberation struggle enables them to demand and to get almost unconditional support; this will undoubtedly be less easy when the next stage comes. Thus even before imperialism has relaxed its grip, the class struggle in independent Algeria is being prefigured.

Lyotard wrote one more article on Algeria, a year after independence, entitled 'Evacuated Algeria'.[29] While many on the far left were enthusing about Ben Bella's regime and the development of 'workers' control', Lyotard presented a far bleaker picture:

> They expected a revolution; what they got was a country that had broken down. In the political vacuum that followed independence, the FLN leadership split into fragments. Joy that the war was over and the effervescence of liberation wilted, the masses became inactive. When they intervened, it was only to show the leaders that they had had enough of their quarrels. [...] There was no leader because there was no leadership.

Hence for Lyotard socialism was not on the agenda: the 'inability of the workers to create their own political organisation and ideology shows that the problem confronting colonial Algeria was not that of socialism. The alternatives were not: proletarian or free — but colonial or independent Algeria.' As he argued:

> The problem facing the country is not that of socialism. The word is used by the leaders, but the spirit of socialism does not move the masses, and it cannot, because the present crisis does not result from the inability of capitalism to assure the development of the country. [...] On the contrary, it results from the fact that capitalism itself, that is, a positive domination by man over his elementary needs — to work, to eat, not to die of cold or of disease — has not been developed. [...]
> The fact is that development and socialism are not the same thing.

The conclusion still looked to socialism as the only solution to Algeria's problems, but was able to evoke it only in a vague and remote fashion:

Algeria still does not belong to those who live there, and they still have the task of conquering it. It may be shaken by crises — famine, unemployment, poverty, despair will produce them. But none of them will be decisive, and give an answer to *the* crisis from which Algeria is suffering until one social class, or a strongly organised and rooted fraction of society, constructs and makes everyone accept a model of new relationships.

SouB and Lyotard were not always right in their analyses and predictions. But in SouB's approach there was a genuine attempt to apply a Marxist approach without merely repeating abstract formulae. SouB showed implacable opposition to French imperialism without falling into illusions about the motives and potentials of Algerian nationalism. For that its contribution deserves to be taken seriously.

Notes

1. On SouB, see Philippe Gottraux, *'Socialisme ou Barbarie'* (Lausanne, 1997); the best account in English is Marcel van der Linden, 'Socialisme ou Barbarie: A French Revolutionary Group, 1949-1965', *Left History*, Volume 5, no 1 (1997) (http://www.left-dis.nl/uk/lindsob.htm); see also the obituary of Claude Lefort in this issue.
2. Gottraux, *'Socialisme ou Barbarie'*, p 81.
3. 'French Proletariat and Algerian Nationalism', *SouB*, no 24 (May-June 1958).
4. Gottraux, *'Socialisme ou Barbarie'*, p 115.
5. P Chaulieu, 'Perspectives of the French Crisis', *SouB*, no 24 (July-August 1958).
6. Gottraux, *'Socialisme ou Barbarie'*, p 114.
7. *Pouvoir Ouvrier*, no 33 (October 1961), cited in Gottraux, *'Socialisme ou Barbarie'*, p 113. *Pouvoir Ouvrier* was the monthly paper of the SouB grouping; in 1963 *PO* split and became a separate group, including among others Jean-François Lyotard.
8. On Mothé, see also I Birchall, 'Nineteen Fifty-Six and the French Left', *Revolutionary History*, Volume 9, no 3, pp 166-68.
9. Van der Linden, 'Socialisme ou Barbarie'; Gottraux, *'Socialisme ou Barbarie'*, p 82.
10. 'May 1956 at Renault', *SouB*, no 19 (July-September 1956), and 'French Workers and North Africans', *SouB*, no 21 (March-May 1957). These were republished without significant changes in D Mothé, *Journal d'un ouvrier* (Paris, 1959). They are quoted here from the book version.
11. Mothé, *Journal d'un ouvrier*, p 47.
12. Mothé, *Journal d'un ouvrier*, p 53.
13. Mothé, *Journal d'un ouvrier*, pp 67, 76, 79.
14. This refers to the Eisenhower Declaration of March 1957, which looked to replace the role of the old colonial powers in the Middle East by the USA in alliance with moderate and anti-Communist nationalists.
15. Mothé, *Journal d'un ouvrier*, pp 101-02.
16. Mothé, *Journal d'un ouvrier*, pp 103-06.

17. Mothé, *Journal d'un ouvrier*, pp 108, 111.
18. Gottraux, *'Socialisme ou Barbarie'*, pp 72-73.
19. J-F Lyotard, *La Guerre des Algériens* (Paris, 1989); most but not all of these were translated in J-F Lyotard, *Political Writings* (London, 1993).
20. M Harbi, *Le FLN: Mirage et Réalité* (Paris, 1980), p 116.
21. J-F Lyotard and P Vidal-Naquet, 'Parler encore de la guerre d'Algérie', *Libération*, 9 November 1989.
22. Gottraux, *'Socialisme ou Barbarie'*, pp 116-17; Lyotard and Vidal-Naquet, 'Parler encore de la guerre d'Algérie'.
23. *SouB*, no 18 (January-March 1956); Lyotard, *La Guerre des Algériens*, pp 41-50.
24. *SouB*, no 20 (December 1956-February 1957); Lyotard, *La Guerre des Algériens*, pp 53-62.
25. *SouB*, no 22 (July-September 1957); Lyotard, *La Guerre des Algériens*, pp 79-86.
26. *SouB*, no 24 (May-June 1958); Lyotard, *La Guerre des Algériens*, pp 89-108.
27. *SouB*, no 29 (December 1959-February 1960); Lyotard, *La Guerre des Algériens*, pp 121-63.
28. *SouB*, no 33 (December 1961-February 1962); Lyotard, *La Guerre des Algériens*, pp 225-32.
29. *SouB*, no 34 (March-May 1963); Lyotard, *La Guerre des Algériens*, pp 235-83. An abbreviated translation of this article was published in *International Socialism*, no 13, Summer 1963, and is available at http://www.marxists.org/history/etol/newspape/isj/1963/no013/lyotard.htm.

Aspects of the War

The Algerian War Seen from Renault-Billancourt

This interview, conducted by Ramon Gomez, was originally published in *Expression Immigré(e)s-Français(e)s*, no 74, October 1993, and no 76, April 1994, and we are extremely grateful to Henri and Clara Benoîts for permission to translate it. During the period of the war Henri was a member of the Trotskyist PCI, while Clara was a member of the Communist Party.

* * *

On a late January afternoon, after a demonstration, we met Clara, Henri and a few other comrades. The closure of the Renault-Billancourt factory on the Île Seguin had just been announced. While there was a lot of talk about French working-class memories, it seemed to me we were tending to forget that Billancourt had also been a 'fortress' of foreign workers, in particular Algerians. Among other things, everyone remembers the film *Élise ou la vraie vie*.[1]

So, over a drink, we began the discussion. Was it true, in November 1954, that when Algeria caught a cold, Billancourt sneezed?

I had a tape-recorder with me, and that was the origin of this interview for *Expression Immigré(e)s-Français(e)s*.

One further detail. Clara and Henri Benoîts, who have long been militants in the ASTI[2] at Issy-les-Moulineaux, were also workers and CGT militants at the Renault Billancourt factory. Between 1954 and 1962, they were alongside the Algerian people fighting for its independence.

By appealing to their memory for a picture of the contribution to this struggle made by Algerian workers, and more broadly by immigrant workers, at Renault, of their relations with French workers, of their discussions with trade-union militants and the French left, we can, thanks to them, supply some precious fragments of the history of immigrants in this country.

Ramon Gomez

* * *

In 1954, Billancourt brought together the great majority of Renault employees (about 36 000). The factory at Flins was just beginning (about 2000)… 80 per cent of the staff consisted of male and female manual workers. The women, about 3000 of them, were mainly concentrated in the upholstery section and the small presses.

The North Africans, Algerians being the most numerous, were mainly concentrated in the foundries and on the assembly lines. Preponderant in terms of numbers, the Algerians were also the main force in the trade unions, holding numerous positions as elected workers' delegates and on the factory committee,[3] above all in the CGT. Some were nationalist militants, others Communists.

EIF: What was the impact in France of the launching of the insurrection on 1 November 1954 in Algeria?

Henri: It's difficult to answer that, especially on the level of the average Algerian worker. The media, which were chauvinistic and hostile, had very little grip on emigrant workers who had long been inoculated against official propaganda. The 1945 massacres at Sétif and Guelma, among other things, were still in their minds. So they knew what they could rely on.

However, the split in the Mouvement pour le triomphe des libertés démocratiques (MTLD), the main nationalist movement from 1953 which was divided between supporters of the Central Committee (centralists) and Messalists (from the symbolic name of Messali Hadj), caused a certain degree of confusion and did not contribute to total harmony.

On the other hand, for the Algerians who were known as militants, who were CGT delegates and close to the PCF or members of it, there was some confusion caused by the characterisation of 1 November 1954 as a danger of provocation or as 'recourse to individual actions liable to play into the hands of the colonialists, even if they weren't fomented by them'.[4] The synthesis at this time was symbolised by Ben Daoud. A CGT delegate in the foundries, he was very popular in his section, and indispensable. Already in 1952, he, in his personal capacity but mentioning his membership of the MTLD, had signed, along with others including myself, the strike call for 12 February at Renault. This strike hit the headlines with barricades being set up around the factory and the resulting repression. The Algerian workers knew what they were doing on that occasion. Ben Daoud was very highly thought of, and I had great respect for him. He had the qualities of a man who could relate to the masses.

Moreover the CGT leadership, knowing him to be sympathetic to the 'centralists' at the time of the 1953 split, considered him to be an excellent intermediary between the Communist Algerian CGT delegates and the nationalists, of whom they were completely ignorant and very distrustful. He was a member of the CGT Renault delegation both to the congress of the metalworkers' federation and to the confederal congress in 1955. As everyone knows, a delegation is supposed to be representative of the composition of the staff. So he played the role of the token immigrant, just as Clara in that same delegation was the symbolic representative of the non-manual workers, of women and in addition of youth. Moreover, Ben Daoud was arrested some time after the confederal congress in 1955 and before the FLN was organised in the factory. He was deported to Algeria and interned until the end of the war.

The Algerian trade unionists can be represented, among others, by Lattad, a delegate on the factory committee, and Ziani, a delegate from the forges. They were PCF members and Ziani was even a member of the Renault branch committee. Trained in the CGT tradition, they had a strong sense of class, and normally showed a certain caution, if not distrust, towards their 'nationalist' compatriots. They were listened to by the party and the union, but precisely as a result of this allegiance, they were not trusted by the Algerian emigrant workers, who were very much under the influence of the MTLD, which was the successor of the Parti Populaire Algérien (PPA), which had been dissolved by the French government in 1939.

The nationalists considered themselves as an integral part of the French working class, and so took part in its trade-union movement, but they were undoubtedly primarily concerned with the question of national independence and anti-colonialism, for they knew from experience how important these were to their people.

The expectation, so to speak, about 1 November was encouraged by the fact that the call for insurrection by the FLN was signed by militants who in the past had belonged to different tendencies of the MTLD, but who had been trained in the Special Organisation (OS), the clandestine wing of the MTLD formed back in 1947 to prepare the armed insurrection.

Confusion reigned in Algeria and among the emigrants. Who was leading the armed struggle? Messalists, centralists or activists of the CRUA and FLN? All had belonged to the MTLD which the government immediately dissolved on 5 November 1954. Since the split in 1953 there had been fights between Messalists and centralists at the organisation's premises, in market-places where the nationalist press was sold and in hostels inhabited by the Algerian community. New alignments were developing at the grassroots...

Remember that Krim Belkacem had been fighting a guerrilla struggle in Kabylia... since 1947. It was in this situation that the 'activists' — bringing together indiscriminately 'veterans' from the short-lived Comité Révolutionnaire pour l'Unité et l'Action (CRUA) which united centralists and 'activists' between the end of March and the end of July 1954, from the so-called 'group of twenty-two', formerly of the OS, from the external delegacy of the MTLD in Cairo, and from the Kabylia *wilaya* (which was however part of the Messalist tendency) — launched the insurrection.

As you know the declaration of 1 November was signed in the name of the FLN with the nine 'historic' figures known for a long time for belonging to the

PPA–MTLD, but above all to the OS. There were confrontations and polemics over a long period. The MNA (Messalist) was formed in December 1954, abandoning the label of the MTLD, which had been dissolved. Structuring around the FLN would take time. The 'centralists' joined it in July 1955. The Union Démocratique du Manifeste Algérien (UDMA) of Ferhat Abbas, which was still legal, did likewise in January 1956, although like the Communists they had participated in the cantonal elections of April 1955 which were boycotted by the nationalists. And also the Ulema[5] in February 1956.

On 16 February, the Messalists set up the Union des Syndicats des Travailleurs Algériens,[6] with its main base… in France. The FLN responded by founding, on 24 February, the Union Générale des Travailleurs Algériens (UGTA).[7] The French trade-union bodies maintained their departmental unions… since Algeria was part of France. It was only in August 1956 that the FLN held its first congress, in the Soummam valley, and created a National Council of the Algerian Revolution (CNRA). The Provisional Government of the Algerian Republic (GPRA) was only established in September 1958. But meanwhile a lot was going on. Abbane Ramdane, organiser of the Soummam congress, one of the main leaders of the CNRA who supported the primacy of the internal organisation over the external,[8] was assassinated in December 1957 (an internal settling of scores in the FLN, not yet fully explained). One of his comrades, Larbi Ben M'Hidi, was murdered by the French in March 1957. The Algerian Communist Party formed a short-lived guerrilla organisation in March 1956… before its survivors merged with the FLN.

In conditions of clandestinity, where information was manipulated as always, it is easy to understand the general confusion in public opinion. The French, in general, understood nothing. The far-left fringe, which had a tradition of solidarity with the struggles of colonial peoples, was itself asking questions. One part (nowadays commonly known as 'Lambertists'), as a result of longstanding contacts with emigrant militants from the MTLD, supported the MNA, which it presented as the expression of proletarian consciousness, since the emigrants were essentially working-class and that was where the nationalist movement had been born as a Communist initiative in the years after the October Revolution. This was nothing but a strict application of old schemas, without any concrete analysis of a concrete situation.

Finally, the control of emigrant workers in centres, hostels and cafés was traditionally taken care of by the MTLD apparatus, and the constant advance of the FLN shook the structure in France. It became inevitable that there would be a transfer of power. This happened as a result of numerous attacks, carried out clandestinely, since neither organisation existed legally. The high point of these confrontations was reached in November 1957.

The French police and army obviously played on these divisions. In Algeria, to counter the FLN, the French army even made an agreement with one of the leaders of the MNA guerrilla forces (Bellounis), which lasted till July 1958 when it was broken and Bellounis was assassinated. In France the MNA slowly disintegrated, partly because a certain number of its leaders went over to the FLN. By the end of 1958 it can be said that also in France the FLN was hegemonic among emigrants.

EIF: I suppose that at the start the MNA had networks, organisations, among the Renault workers?

Henri: Probably, but as far as I was concerned I never encountered them as such. There were people who were sympathetic to Messali, but from there to committing yourself as an MNA supporter, that was a lot more complicated. In general there was not the same sort of confrontation within the factory. Between the Messalists, the centralists and in particular the OS there were differences which I only learned about long after because they didn't appear publicly while the MTLD was still legal. In my view, the only decisive point in this period was the voting of special powers to Guy Mollet, in March 1956, which the whole of the French left and the right together supported on this occasion. At this point the Algerians realised that they belonged to a community facing a hostile French population. The PCF voted for special powers. The Algerian Communist militants (delegates to the factory committee or workers' delegates such as Lattad and Ziani) tore up their cards, asserted their Algerian identity, resumed contact with the nationalist militants and helped to organise the FLN at Renault by bringing together three components: former Messalists, centralists and Algerian Communists. Until then in the CGT there were internal tensions, political divergences, which of course is normal, but the main argument was always for creating unity against the enemy. When they formed the FLN, Lattad came to see us saying: 'I've got some good news to tell you, we've united all the Algerians and we've organised the FLN at Renault.'

He confided in me about this because we were already involved on the political level, in support work for the FLN. At this time I was known as a militant of the Parti communiste internationaliste (Fourth International), and our organisation had taken part in support for the FLN from the beginning. We gave priority to the real movement, where the revolution was unfolding, and not to abstract schemas. We thought the importance of the struggle in Algeria was the main thing, and that we should decide what to do on the basis of what was happening in Algeria. What would happen among immigrants would be the result of relations of forces which would be established or determined in Algeria itself.

Clara: As far as the special powers were concerned, since we've reached that period: it was a very tough time to live through, not only for me, but for all the PCF militants, especially the young ones... I should say that already in 1955, among the monthly-paid staff in building A, we had formed a committee for peace in Algeria which had some support. We produced several issues of a bulletin. This committee for peace in Algeria, which included Communists, had been formed after we collected signatures on the basis of a statement, and we succeeded in getting signatures from CFTC members and even two CGC[9] delegates. It was quite a broad committee with regular meetings of a good 20 people including half a dozen from the PCF, which wasn't taking part as an organisation. And we were criticised for this at a higher level. But since the committee existed, they couldn't stop us attending. This committee never took an anti-Communist position. We didn't distinguish between political organisations, and we invited all the organisations which existed at Renault without distinction (from the Socialist Party to the far-left groupings).

To the PCF we seemed to be a competitor to the Mouvement de la Paix, and we were criticised somewhat without being banned, because there were some forceful characters from our cell on the committee. On demos for peace in Algeria at this time we were criticised for shouting slogans which were not quite orthodox, like 'independence for Algeria'. That was frowned on.

Just before the vote for special powers our committee for peace in Algeria met and it was decided to send delegations to all the parliamentary groups and to organise petitions. Henri was part of the delegation which met the Communist group at the National Assembly, which told him that they wouldn't vote for the war. So we were reassured.

So when the special powers were agreed, the ground collapsed under the feet of all the Communist militants. There were young men from the PCF who were about to leave for the army. I was a delegate at this time, so I used my rights as a delegate and ran to the factory committee where Viviane Halimi worked; she came from Algeria and her husband, Léon Feix,[10] was in charge of the colonial section of the PCF Political Bureau. There were several young people with me, we were in Viviane's office, she was extremely embarrassed, she was justifying herself: 'We had to preserve unity...' All the same, you don't make peace by declaring war, by sending soldiers over there. The young men said: 'If we're sent over there, what are you going to do about it? We're going to take arms against the Algerians, come on, it's not possible.' It was even worse for a young Communist of Algerian origin in the factory who was called up and decided to refuse and went off to join the FLN.

There were also speeches at the factory gates on the Place Nationale, I wouldn't say there was a confrontation, but there were big arguments, most of the people present, including fathers whose sons were due to be recalled to fight in Algeria, voiced their disagreement.

Henri: At this point the Algerian militants took their distance from the French organisations; they organised the FLN in the factory but stayed in the unions, still considering themselves as 'an integral part of the working class'. Under their own momentum, without forming a rival union organisation, they set up the AGTA (Association of Algerian Workers), bringing together members of all the trade-union confederations. This was essentially at Renault. There was Maoui from the CFTC, and the large contingent of those holding elected positions, as staff representatives and on the factory committee, and Algerians from the CGT.

Clara: They got into contact with us, told us the good news, they were getting organised to ensure the homogeneity of the Algerian community. You said we were involved in support activity. Above all this was support outside the factory. Of course there were a few little implications, but on the individual level. For example, when an Algerian comrade thought that the cops were going to his home, he gave me his keys so I could go and remove some compromising packets... Odd jobs like that on the personal level. Otherwise we didn't work particularly with the FLN at Renault.

Henri: Officially, because of the work I had undertaken outside in support of the FLN, I was not supposed to do several jobs at the same time, but given personal links and the fact that I was close to people in the union context, that caused a problem.

So it was necessary to maintain contact on the level of everyday activity and then a certain coordination of work with the Algerian comrades, and there was also assistance for the AGTA. Training courses in the CFTC premises in which I was asked to put a lot of emphasis on the idea of class, and the struggle for independence. I had very precise instructions: not only to talk about trade unionism, about the primacy of the working class, but also to say that we were not only fighting for a flag but also for the content of this independence with a social character.

And then there was also the production of leaflets for the AGTA...

Inside the union there were many discussions and disagreements. The first appearance of the FLN, it is interesting to note, was the eight-day strike by the FLN in 1956. Thus, having scarcely come into existence, the FLN at Renault had the job of organising a strike by Algerians in response to the FLN's call for an eight-day strike in Algeria. And the strike took place at Renault, in sections where the Algerians, or more broadly North Africans, were in a majority. It was essentially Algerians, but there were also Moroccans and Tunisians. All my experience was of a high degree of solidarity between them. Everywhere that there was a big majority of North Africans, the strike, especially in the foundries, was effective. In the foundries, they made speeches. It was on this occasion that I met Ben Nacef, a CGT delegate and one of the organisers of this strike.

The FLN organised this eight-day strike at Renault with the slogan: 'Solidarity with the strike call in our homeland, we are taking part in the struggle being fought over there.' There was solidarity in the foundries and also on the Île Seguin, but in a less spectacular fashion because in the foundries there were more or less 90 per cent North African workers.

EIF: But how did this strike affect the French workers?

Henri: This FLN strike call also revealed a gap between French workers and Algerian workers. On the trade-union level, a movement of this sort, I mean political, brought about tactical problems. That is, militants, I'm thinking of delegates who had a CGT label but at the same time were FLN, making speeches in the foundries to call for a strike, that produced tensions…

The union didn't condemn it, it put up with it, but as always it tried to make the militants whom it could influence understand that this was helping to widen the gulf between the Algerians and French people. I don't know what they were able to do tactically. But in any case the matter was already settled.

EIF: Was there any special repression by the company management against the militants?

Henri: No, I don't remember any special repression. I would remember it, but they were all more or less known, they had a union label, a union protection and perhaps also at that time the management hesitated to provoke fresh incidents by disciplining people who after all were representative of those around them. Perhaps there was a compromise. And we'll see later on that the policy of the Renault Company was quite intelligent.

EIF: After 1956, did things become a bit clearer overall? The whole French political mainstream was committed to maintaining the Algerian territory as part of the national community. The Algerians were aware of the national fact, of the reality of who was leading the action, the on-going struggle, and among the French who took account of this national fact, there was also a process of clarification.

Henri: It was a minority (not a silent one) or a vanguard, call it what you like, but people who thought that the struggle was a just one, and that we should support Algerian independence and those who can achieve it. I must observe, they were people who had a communist spirit; personally I identify with the communist tradition, Trotskyism and proletarian internationalism. So I didn't have any problem, either individual or organisational.

Clara: To add to that, it should be said that among the PCF Communists, including those in the cells, that seemed pretty obvious. In our peace committee, it was agreed. I remember a public meeting when an official of the Mouvement de la Paix was horrified by what we were saying — we were referring to the inevitable independence of Algeria and our obligatory solidarity. Suddenly he stood up and said: 'But I can't hear anyone here talking about French interests, you're talking about something quite different and we are for peace in Algeria.' The Communist militants who were present said: 'If that coincides with French interests, all the better, but we aren't here to defend French interests, we're here to defend justice...', and he replied that it was not in the interests of France to make war in Algeria, and that was what we should argue. But we said no, it wasn't the only interest, even if it was an interest among others. The idea of independence was accepted by the most militant Communists. There was no opposition. The representative of the Mouvement de la Paix left the room in a rage. He was called Langignon if I remember rightly.

EIF: You said, there was a layer of individuals who committed themselves alongside the Algerians fighting for their independence. It wasn't simply all those with a communist spirit, there were also Christians...

Henri: Yes, they were acting in the name of a deep moral conviction, whether communists or Christians, all quite independent from tactical considerations. That started off in 1956, with important publications inside the company by our committee, *Vérité Liberté, Témoignages et documents*. We sold *La Question*,[11] *La Gangrène*,[12] all these little things published on the fringes of clandestinity and sometimes confiscated.

EIF: In 1956 networks were created that were not yet very unified or welded together?

Henri: The network I belonged was that of the Fourth International, and later, among intellectuals, there would be other networks, Francis Jeanson's in particular and also Curiel's. Moreover, at Renault, one chap would be arrested later on. He was a member of the Curiel network, and he was imprisoned until the end of the war. There was no unification of the networks. Each of us had our own relations with the FLN.

EIF: Between 1956 and 1958, did any events make a particular impression on you?

Henri: One of the first consequences of the formation of the AGTA was the arrest of the administrative secretary of the CGT union for being in possession of AGTA leaflets. She was imprisoned and meanwhile, as she was a member of the Communist Party and the CGT, a Communist leaflet stated publicly that the PCF, being in favour of mass struggle, condemned individual forms of struggle and ruled them out. Obviously the screws had to be tightened again in the CGT. In the course of a meeting of the executive committee of the general union, a committee of which we were both members on the basis of our union branch, noting what was characterised as this first breach of the principle of mass action, a call was issued by the secretariat for those who were giving individual assistance to the FLN to resign their positions.

On the executive committee, at least four of us were thus targeted, Eugène Tribout, Clara, myself and Raymond Leroy who was not in the PCF. We kept quiet, and it was the Algerians on the executive committee (Aït Aïssa, Bel Kaïd and others) who were furious and intervened in our support, and there was an epic confrontation. The Algerians threatened to leave the union if any disciplinary measures were taken against us. I think other comrades, independently of us, also supported the Algerian comrades. You must remember that at this time there were frequent police checks conducted on a racial basis in the streets and the underground stations. Somebody walking along with a packet, if they had an Algerian face, was more likely to be stopped. It was so easy to ask a bloke or a woman from your shop: 'Take this, I'm in danger of being caught.' This was probably the sort of assistance which French people, more numerous than is often thought, offered.

Ladlani, who was in charge of the FLN French Federation at the time, told us recently (October 1991) that if anyone had tried to make a serious calculation of the number of acts of solidarity by French people with their Algerian workmates, there would probably be several thousands. There are actions which cannot be measured but which still show that racism had not become universal.

We were convinced that we were on the right road. At a certain level of discussion and participation, we had the feeling, despite a general, artificial, exaggerated propaganda, that the great mass of people, said to be apathetic, were open to being convinced.

EIF: But there was still something of a hardening of attitudes in the working-class organisations. They hadn't yet understood, but they were going to understand. Slowly time went by, 1956, 1957 and there was also a hardening on the other side. How did that affect people?

Henri: For the great mass of Algerians, independently organised, ultimately they didn't give a toss about French organisations. They were oriented towards independence. But for the delegates, the political militants, trade unionists holding positions, those who had a foot in both camps, that was where problems arose. For their specific problems, they needed to be by themselves, to meet as militants of different union organisations, in addition to general trade-union action. Alongside the French workers they were defending the general interests of the working class. But for their own specific problems, they didn't need French observers. Within the trade-union committees where there were immigrants and French people they couldn't say everything and they couldn't bring along militants from other trade-union organisations to discuss the activity of the AGTA, for example, and all the more so, the FLN.

EIF: But there were official inter-union meetings of Algerian committees?

Henri: The AGTA brought together trade unionists from the CFTC and above all the CGT. The predominant position of the CGT had historical roots. Of course there was the problem of premises, and they are necessary for meetings. The AGTA was known, but it was a semi-clandestine organisation, expressing itself through leaflets and through Algerian delegates. The French organisations were aware of its existence and its links with the struggle of the Algerian people in France and over there.

There were refusals to let rooms, including at the Bourse du travail.[13] We made approaches at all levels, even at the level of the confederal bureau of the CGT, to ask for the possibility of hiring rooms. The refusal didn't spring from a repressive spirit, but mainly from the fear of seeming responsible for clandestine activity. It was a legalistic reflex.

Clara: Perhaps we should qualify this at least as far as militants were concerned. This rule was not always applied in certain circumstances, even by people from the PCF and the CGT. To show that, I'd point out that when Algerians believed to be members of the FLN were asked to leave their work and go to the factory gate, supposedly for a personal reason, but in fact so that they could be handed over to the police, then there was a display of concrete solidarity to protect them. Early in 1958 a foundry delegate, Ben Nacef, to whom this happened, immediately understood what was going on.

Henri: Indeed, the case of Abdelghani Ben Nacef posed an extremely important problem and was also an example of a certain atmosphere. Security staff came into the workshop and his foreman came to ask him to go to the office. He understood that the presence of factory security staff asking him to go with them to the personnel office was not normal. He refused to follow them. He thought 'they're trying to arrest me', and he went to find Ziani who was the forge delegate in the next workshop. Immediately the workers in the forge stopped work, booed the security staff and said: 'Clear out of the factory, no security in our workshop.' What is important, is that at this time in the forges the great majority of the workers were French, skilled workers, sometimes ranked as management because their pay was sometimes more than double. They were a labour 'aristocracy', but with a pronounced sense of class. More than 90 per cent of them voted for the CGT. The Algerian workers from the foundries and the mainly French workers from the forges united to drive out the security and Ghani hid in the factory…

What happened next is also interesting: Ziani came to tell me that 'the cops have come to arrest Ben Nacef, we must get him out'. It was payday. We had to get his clothes by breaking into his locker. This was done by Michel Eloy, the CGT delegate in the foundries, supported by Claude Poperen, the general secretary of the CGT.[14] The clothes were left at the factory committee office, and meanwhile, taking advantage of the lunch-break, I got him out of the factory and left him in Billancourt. We collected his pay by another Algerian borrowing Ghani's identity and I handed over everything (pay and clothes) to him. He then became clandestine. This example enables us to measure the enormous potential for solidarity which existed, and which, spontaneous to begin with, offered the possibility for a much greater solidarity in support of the Algerian people… if the French labour movement had been willing.

Another significant episode. At the next CGT congress, at the end of 1958 I think, Raymond Husse, another delegate from the forges and a Communist, spoke at the congress. He was a bloke who perhaps wasn't a top-class speaker, but he was a decent honest person. He spoke saying: 'Comrades, we shouldn't only be against the Algerian war just because it's expensive and French people are risking their lives; but even if it wasn't expensive, I should find that disgusting…' When he came down from the platform he leaned over to me and said 'What do you think?', and I said, 'Very good, Raymond.' Somebody near the platform heard this brief exchange. I was immediately suspected of having 'inspired' this intervention, which in fact was spontaneous. My candidacy for the executive committee, although it had been put forward by my union branch, was challenged in the special committee at the conference. All the pressure of the Algerians was necessary to keep me on the list, but at the congress my nomination was accompanied by 'a reprimand for an activity which, if it continued, could take on a factional character', according to a time-honoured formula. The Algerian comrades told me: 'We don't give a toss about reprimands, the important thing is that we got you elected.'

EIF: Was May 1958 an important date at Billancourt?

Henri: In 1958 there was of course the *coup d'état* by the generals in Algiers. That gave rise to some interesting discussions. Could fascism develop? Was de Gaulle's arrival in power something that was preparing us for pre-fascism? After the capitulation by Parliament on 1 June, the CGT and the PCF organised a counter-demonstration against the presentation of the new constitution on 4 September in the place de la République. There were confrontations in the neighbourhood of the square, and people got beaten up. From Renault there were a certain number of wounded, including some with bullets…

***

EIF: Algerians in France are very sceptical about information appearing in the media. What sort of information was distributed among the Algerians?

Henri: We typed and duplicated leaflets for the FLN and the AGTA. For the FLN it was above all press releases about what was happening in Algeria, various forms of information about the activity of the National Liberation Army.

These leaflets and appeals from the FLN were handed over in instalments to shops and businesses run by Algerians, who distributed them to their customers in the area.

Support for the paper *El Moudjahid*[15] outside the factory mainly came from the Algerian community, while *Résistance Algérienne* was addressed to French people, saying that this was a colonial war: 'You think you're fighting for France, but it's against a people which is struggling for its independence, you are defending the interests of the colonialists, etc...' A theme which the AGTA repeated quite consistently in 1960-61, and in the course of which they recalled the struggle of the French people against the occupation of the Ruhr...,[16] all of which is the history of the French working-class movement. It also recalled the strikes by Algerian dockers in Algiers who refused to unload weapons throughout the Indochina war; no warship could load arms in Algiers for the Indochina war, because the Algerian dockers refused to do so out of solidarity.

EIF: All round the Company, as the years went by, did police checks and surveillance get more intensive? After all there is a large Algerian workers' centre at Billancourt.

Clara: From 1954 on there were regular police checks and arrests, especially in the metro. In the districts round the actual factory, no.

EIF: There must have been mornings when workers were not present at their place in the factory?

Clara: Of course.

EIF: Did the Company management take disciplinary measures when a worker was absent because he had been stopped, interrogated, arrested, or held in police custody? Did they take him back?

Henri: They were taken back. Some were arrested and reinstated. But there were some who were deported or held captive in France, and some who were released after three or four days and came back. There were also checks, people held for 24 hours, in general militants who were known but they couldn't find anything to charge them with.

During our last visit to Algeria, Ziani told us he had been arrested and held for a few days. He had demanded to write a letter to the Company saying he didn't want to lose his job, and he came back to work.

But something else that should be noted, on one occasion we were warned that within the factory a head of department asked the foreman, as one of his duties, to enable the arrest of an Algerian. We intervened with the general personnel department through the intermediary of Lucente, who was a CFTC official and a PSU member, who contacted Clees, who at the time was industrial relations manager. The latter replied that unfortunately he couldn't oppose a state intervention, but that the Company was not an auxiliary of the police and he advised us to warn the person in question ourselves so that he could make arrangements to deal with the situation. All this doubtless after having consulted Dreyfus.[17] They couldn't go against the French police, but they didn't agree with collaborating with it inside the factory.

EIF: So we get to 1961. Had anything happened in the meantime with regard to the Company?

Henri: In late 1959 there was a strengthening of FLN support networks. I had had some problems with the DST and I had to cut off my contacts with the FLN. My activity was oriented towards solidarity. Within the factory I gave assistance to the AGTA comrades. More generally I was involved in setting up an assistance network to get 50 francs[18] from the FLN to those held in camps and prisons. For that we needed networks and people to do the work. We had to spend our weekends filling in money orders in the names of real and fictitious senders.

It was much easier to approach comrades on the level of humanitarian assistance. We could help people in prison, enlarge the circle of people who wanted to do something to help, and that didn't look like political or ideological assistance. For this we set up a prisoners' aid committee at Renault. The FLN told me to send the 50 francs without distinction to all the French prisoners. We thought it wasn't right that the FLN should pay. This solidarity should also be taken on by the French. This prisoners' aid committee was chaired by Robert Lucente. All this action was extended outside the factory.

EIF: How did you follow the evolution of the situation in Algeria?

Clara: Through the press and information from the FLN comrades. We still had *Vérité et Liberté, Témoignage et Documents.* Other committees for peace in Algeria continued to intervene episodically on significant events.

EIF: As far as political activity was concerned, when you sold papers, you sold them at Barbès,[19] etc, you didn't sell them in the factory?

Henri: We distributed *Vérité et Liberté, Témoignages et Documents* to interested people, in the factory and to people around us, but not on the street, not openly.

EIF: Were there minority working-class factions who intervened at the factory gates distributing leaflets about the Algerian war and supporting the demand for independence for the Algerian people?

Henri: Two or three organisations sometimes leafleted against the war. Apart from the Fourth International, the far-left groups had the same reservations as the PCF because supporting nationalists, and Muslims into the bargain, posed some problems for them. These groups were much smaller than nowadays.

There were no stoppages apart from those against the OAS and the massive strike which followed the Charonne massacre. The demos for peace in Algeria took place in the evening after work and more and more people came as the end of the war got closer.

EIF: Apart from the October 1961 demo, did the FLN French Federation organise other public initiatives?

Henri: No. It organised this demonstration in the first place to protest against the imposition of a curfew decided by the head of the Paris police, which forbade Algerians, although at the time they were 'French Muslims',[20] to go out between 8.30pm and 6.30am. This blanket ban was in contradiction with the official view that the FLN was a minority within the Algerian community. Perhaps also because the FLN, at a certain stage of its activity, had decided to broaden the struggle in solidarity with what was going on in Algeria and to show how representative it was. Moreover, you must also bear in mind that there were also racists in the police stations. Many Algerians had grounds for complaint about what went on there. There was also growing discontent among Algerian comrades who were saying that something should be done about it. There had always been settling of scores between the MNA and the FLN, but there were probably also murders of Algerians by the police, which were attributed to one or the other camp in order to stir up the divisions. It's a very difficult area to be clear about. Not all the Algerian deaths resulted from settling of scores, but at the same time there were, especially in 1961, Algerian commando actions against people considered to be torturers. Were these always well targeted? You have to judge according to the local situation. Imagine a policeman standing on guard outside a police-station who is machine-gunned. Was he really the person responsible for torture? I don't know. In the end, theoretically, every case should be taken on its merits, and mistakes could always happen. But there are questions to be asked about the appropriateness of the FLN French Federation's demonstration, and about the violence of the government measures, which breached the most elementary rights such as the right to move around between 8.30pm and 6.30am and about the violence of the repression. But we were at the end of 1961, and the die was cast…

In the Renault Company, Dreyfus had discreetly asked to make contact with FLN militants in the factory even before the end of the war. The Dreyfus–FLN interview, arranged by a member of the board of directors, took place. What was said, I don't know, but Dreyfus was already convinced that independence was inevitable and that the Company had to find a place in a potential market!

To come back to the curfew measures, they concerned Algerians who were not recognised as such, French Muslims. Now the only way to check them, was not only by identity card, it was by the colour of their face. It meant introducing a police mechanism into the checks, with all the excesses that that could entail.

The FLN, put in this position, pushed its own militants to do something. It was convinced that the struggle had made progress, but that it was nonetheless necessary to prove this, following the example of what had happened in Algiers in December 1960.[21] The FLN was in a position to mobilise and assert its authority over the Algerian immigrants. It chose to do so on 17 October 1961. My personal opinion is that, on the one hand, the French Federation was not dissociating itself from the struggle in Algeria, but at the same time it wanted to assert the existence of a French Federation (the seventh *wilaya*) and prove that it was representative not only to the French authorities but also within the national movement.

The FLN French Federation called for a controlled peaceful demonstration: not even a pin, not a knife. There is good reason to believe that the leaders knew there was a danger things could turn nasty. Several comrades from the factory, including ourselves, were approached to be observers. Our instructions were not to do anything under any circumstances, not to intervene and whatever happened not to do anything but observe. I seem to recall that this request came from a comrade in the factory who was directly linked to the coordinators of the FLN French Federation. However, I don't think the Federation had ever imagined that things could reach such a level of brutality and such a scale. Omar Boudaoud,[22] former leader of the FLN in France, confirmed this at the symposium in October 1991.

EIF: In the following days there was a black-out on information?

Clara: There was information available in *Franc-Tireur* and *France-Soir*. There were spontaneous things. At Billancourt, Algerians who had been on the demonstration perhaps did not come back. I think the FLN had decided not to expose its cadres who had only done the preparatory organisational work. After the demonstration there were no disappearances of very well-known militants from the company. But there were disappearances, no doubt about it. The next week in *L'Express*, at the time edited by Jean Cau,[23] Oumar Ouadj, a leading figure in the AGTA, made a series of revelations about the atrocities of 17 October 1961. There was a call for a demonstration the next day. But the French, the militants, didn't realise the scale of the massacre. Even those like us who were on the spot didn't realise what could have happened.

EIF: When did you begin to have an idea of the number of dead?

Clara: In the following days there was an issue of *Témoignages et documents* and a speech by Claude Bourdet at the Paris Municipal Council. There was also a call for a demonstration at Billancourt outside the town hall. Unfortunately it was not a very well-attended demonstration.

Throughout the Algerian war, the CGT had a more cautious attitude compared to the PCF. After all there was the WFTU,[24] the balance of forces on an international level and the pressure from the Algerians. If you analyse carefully all the CGT press releases, they were much less focussed on the question of tactics or national strategy than those from the PCF.

At that symposium in October 1991 at the Sorbonne, Omar Badouad, who at that time was living in Brussels, told us that immediately after 17 December 1961 he had been very disappointed by the behaviour of the French Communist Party, but that it had resumed contact with the FLN on this occasion. According to him, the PCF had sent a delegation to Brussels to ask for the organisation of a joint demonstration of Algerian women and French women. From 18 October onwards, Algerian women had in fact started making approaches to find their husbands who had disappeared. On the basis of this the PCF judged that it was right to formulate a proposal. But the FLN French Federation did not want to let it off the hook for its past behaviour by giving it such a mark of approval.

EIF: For some months there had been contacts, negotiations had taken place, there were discussions of the date, when independence would take effect, etc. What would happen between October 1961 and February 1962? Why did the demonstration that emerged from these negotiations end up at Charonne?[25]

Henri: There had been informal contacts between the FLN and the government. They had broken down from time to time and the discussion had gone on for nearly two years. In the end it was necessary to bring them to a conclusion. When the agreements were signed, there were many questions about the future of Algeria. The ambiguity of the positions of the French left was then revealed on the question of such independence, for example around the battle for the Sahara and its oil. They could put up with the loss of territory and the disappearance of colonial rule, but could they agree at the same time to lose the drillings at Hassi Messaoud,[26] the result of French technology? Could we not separate Algeria from the Sahara in order to keep it? The Algerians considered that the Sahara was an integral part of Algerian territory. The French bourgeoisie, for its part, was obviously more divided, and one faction wanted to resist to the very end, by if necessary conceding the shores of the Mediterranean but not the oil and gas of the Sahara which were said to be the fruit of 'our genius' and 'our investments' in a desert, etc. At this point the French organisations had a rather soft position. Remember that in France, and in Algeria which was part of it, the unions were organised in departmental[27] unions. When independence had been won, could these departmental unions continue to consider themselves to be affiliated to a foreign centre? This was where the PCF and the CGT showed their greatest ability to adapt to new situations because they understood straightaway that the FLN had won. So they supported independence for Algeria, including the Sahara. The CGT dissolved its departmental unions. To begin with they formed the Union Générale des Syndicats Algériens (UGSA) to try to make their departmental structures permanent, something that the CFTC and FO could not do so easily and which in fact I think they didn't do at all. Of course independence settled the question since the UGTA became the only trade-union centre. As for the Messalist USTA, it disappeared for want of people able to fight.

The acceptance of the idea of independence for Algeria would still raise reservations. By the end, the left had been won for the idea of peace, cease-fire and an end to the war. It was on this basis and against the OAS (the die-hards) that the demonstrations were organised, including that at Charonne in February 1962.

EIF: In October 1961 everything seemed to be settled, it was a question of days. Why did it take on a brutal, repressive character?

Henri: But we've forgotten to talk about the OAS, formed in February 1961. There was the generals' putsch in April 1961. They were waging total war. They wanted to drain the blood from Algeria so that it would be uninhabitable when independence came. Their aim was to destroy and at the same time to terrorise people who were making concessions. There was the attempt to kill General de Gaulle at Petit Clamart, and also a whole series of attacks on well-known figures and bombs planted at people's homes. Permanent blackmail. It is important to note that at this point the PCF was wondering about the risks of France going fascist. They had even made contacts with the FLN to try and coordinate activities against the fascist threat represented by the OAS. So there was all this side of things. In France, 'Peace in Algeria' had become 'struggle against OAS terrorism', with this sort of national unity which was being achieved. And there were stoppages against the generals' putsch. The moderate wing of the French unions joined in, and even some of the management in the Company stopped work at the time of the generals' putsch in Algeria. At this time there was the whole pressure of the state apparatus, Michel Debré,[28] and the appeal to the people to stop paratroops landing. There was a strike called at Renault, large but not massive. Most of the support came from the workshops, some of the offices and even some management. The traditional left was joined by Gaullists or people who were fundamentally hostile to the OAS terrorism.

The OAS bombs produced blunders (victims other than the well-known people aimed at). A whole range of people could be mobilised by this issue.

EIF: In the February demo, were the eight dead a blunder, the result of fascist elements in the police?

Henri: The cops were violent and no doubt some of them were developing towards fascism. You have to read Einaudi's book[29] about what was represented by the SGP (General Union of the Police and Uniformed Staff), the language used and reported in the union debates and in the police stations. And there were false rumours spread on 17 October 1961, for example that dozens of police had been killed by Algerians. Police chief Papon did not issue any denial. The racist savagery got out of hand.

EIF: Did not the dead of Charonne let the French political organisations off the hook for what happened in October 1961?

Henri: This is the notorious debate brought up in October 1991. Some people said that there was an attempt to remove 17 October 1961 from the picture. It would be better to centre the debate on the historic responsibilities of society (governments, parties, unions, etc…) and their manipulations of the French people.

Notes

1. *Elise or Real Life* (Michel Drach, 1970). For the novel on which it was based, see the appendix on fiction below [*RH*].
2. Association de Solidarité avec les Travailleur-euse-s Immigré-e-s — Association of Solidarity with Immigrant Workers [*RH*].
3. Factory committees were established by postwar law in all French workplaces with more than 50 workers [*RH*].
4. *L'Humanité*, 9 November 1954 [*RH*].
5. A body of Muslim scholars [*RH*].
6. Association of Unions of Algerian Workers [*RH*].
7. General Association of Algerian Workers [*RH*].
8. The Cairo-based leadership of the FLN [*RH*].
9. Confédération Générale des Cadres, union for management grades [*RH*].
10. Léon Feix (1908-1974): PCF member from 1925; Central Committee 1950-74, Political Bureau 1956-61, deputy 1962-74 [*RH*].
11. A 1958 book by Communist Henri Alleg, describing his experience of being tortured by paratroops; banned by French government [*RH*].
12. Book published in 1959, describing torture of Algerian prisoners, and promptly banned [*RH*].

13. Labour exchange run by the trade unions [*RH*].
14. Claude Poperen (b 1931): CGT secretary at Renault, PCF member, later on Central Committee and Political Bureau of PCF; left PCF 1991 [*RH*].
15. FLN newspaper (for a time Fanon was part of the editorial collective); after independence became state newspaper [*RH*].
16. In 1923 France invaded the Ruhr in response to Germany's failure to pay reparations. The PCF mounted a vigorous opposition [*RH*].
17. Pierre Dreyfus (1907-1994): managing director of Renault 1955-75; Industry Minister under Mitterrand 1981-82 [*RH*].
18. Presumably old francs: equivalent to around 10 shillings (50p) sterling at the time [*RH*].
19. The area round the Barbès-Rochechouart metro station, which had a substantial Algerian population [*RH*].
20. The 1947 Statute of Algeria granted Algerian men full citizenship in mainland France, but they were officially called French-Algerian Muslims, an ethnic designation that was widely resented [*RH*].
21. When de Gaulle visited Algeria, there were massive nationalist demonstrations [*RH*].
22. Omar Boudaoud (b 1924): joined FLN at its foundation; member of CNRA bureau prior to independence; elected deputy 1964, but retired from politics after Boumediène's coup [*RH*].
23. Jean Cau (1925-1993): writer, Sartre's secretary, but then moved sharply to the right [*RH*].
24. World Federation of Trade Unions: Communist-led international body to which the CGT was affiliated [*RH*].
25. On 8 February 1962, an anti-OAS demonstration was attacked at the Charonne metro station, leading to the death of nine demonstrators [*RH*].
26. The largest oil field in Algeria [*RH*].
27. *Départements* are the basic administrative divisions in France; Algeria, being an integral part of France, was divided by the 1956 reorganisation into 12 *départements* [*RH*].
28. Michel Debré (1912-1996): de Gaulle's Prime Minister 1959-62 [*RH*].
29. Jean-Luc Einaudi, *La bataille de Paris* (Paris, 1991) [*RH*].

* * *

La Vérité des Travailleurs, Save the Reservists of the Gare de Lyon From Military Justice[1]

Evidence of the potential for mass resistance among conscripts is given in these letters from soldiers published in the PCI paper.

* * *

Letters from Demonstrators at the Gare de Lyon[2]

On Saturday we learnt that we were being sent to North Africa, and at the same time that we would be confined to barracks until our departure on Sunday at

10.00am.

At the Gare de Lyon there were between six and seven hundred of us due to leave by the 2.00pm train for Marseille. But we got out of the train and demonstrated on the platform against being sent to North Africa and demanding to go home.

Reinforcements of security police arrived, and there were some scuffles with them. In the end we were taken in police vans to the Reuilly barracks where we were put into coaches for Villacoublay.

On Monday at 10.00am, we were put onto aeroplanes for Oran with riot police to guard us.

In Oran we were greeted by the police. They had truncheons, submachine-guns and dogs to keep us overnight in the sheds where we were confined.

From there we were broken up and sent in different directions by plane, obviously to ensure that we should not remain together.

* * *

A little before 2 pm, I came onto the platform and a large number of our mates were in the coaches. The Air Force police were there.

The lads resisted. There were shouts of abuse from all sides. The train couldn't leave.

We were taken to the Reuilly barracks in police vans. We were surrounded by security police. There was a General there; he wanted to address us, but he didn't push the point.

We were taken in coaches to Villacoublay. We were followed by vans full of security police.

Shouts echoed out every time we passed a place where there was a crowd. At Villacoublay we were put into huts, which were of course under guard. On Monday morning we took the plane, but what a reception at Oran. As soon as the plane had landed, we were surrounded by Air Force police with submachine-guns in their hands and truncheons.

We were put into huts with only straw to sleep on. There were 600 of us and only one tap to wash at. For drinking water there was a tank open to the sun. We stayed like that for two days.

When we went to eat we were accompanied by police. These are the facts. Unfortunately about ten of our mates are in prison for an unspecified time.

The Struggle in Brittany

One more thing demonstrates the great combativity of the lads; it's the struggle against the recall of reservists.

The Struggle of the Soldiers Against the War in North Africa

So ask the young reservists who were taken on board the naval troop-ship *Vire* at Brest, and who slashed the canvas covers of the vans taking them to the quay, whether they are not ready to fight; so ask those who were put onto the troopship *Laita* and who entered the Brest arsenal, holding their sailors' caps at arm's length and singing the *Internationale*, whether they are not ready to fight, and those who were put in groups of twenty on board naval planes at the Lanvéoc-Poulmic base and who, before leaving, literally ransacked their living quarters and put in hospital a naval cop who wanted to make them get on the plane too quickly; so ask the naval officers in Cherbourg why they don't dare go out into the town when they know that groups of reservists are wandering around there. They are all ready to fight, but not against the North African workers.

The reservists, in defiance of all traditions, are keeping the uniforms distributed to them and go around in them; tall men in uniforms that are too small and short men in uniforms that are huge...

On the question of support for the North African revolution, we must also regret the total absence of revolutionary politics on the part of the workers' organisations. Doubtless some committees have been set up to campaign against sending young men to North Africa, but they confine themselves to collecting signatures and demanding a policy of class collaboration, or else they protest against the use of young French workers in Algeria and Morocco, but in the name of the 'Spirit of Geneva'.[3] The proletarian internationalism, which is so dear to the working class, is totally absent from the propaganda of the PCF, the SFIO and the CGT. Nothing is said about support for the colonial revolution. Remember the campaign against the war in Morocco in 1925?

Letter from a Camp

In our camp there is a pretty large proportion of students. They are the ones who gripe the most. The workers too, but they are somewhat paralysed by the lack of guidance from the unions and the parties. Everybody is sickened for all sorts of reasons, but which all lead to the same conclusion. The students have interrupted their studies. Nobody worried if lads were married, if they had jobs. There are some dramatic situations.

The atmosphere is indescribable. The lads just want some action. All discussions come back to the war: 'They shouldn't think they can go on getting us smashed to pieces for seven years like in Indochina! And on top of that they'll have to give in in the end.' And it was the least conscious who were saying this. Many of them understood what was meant by 'Algeria four French *départements*'.[4]

Rumours are circulating. Sentries are said to have been attacked, so guards have been doubled and tripled. This hasn't stopped lads from taking a few days 'holiday'. The officers can't terrorise us, for they feel isolated amid the hostility. Among the officers quite a few served in Indochina. They give us big speeches about 'the French Union',[5] 'Our mission in North Africa', etc. But it falls flat. They make vague suggestions that we shall be demobilised in three months, but nobody believes it.

All the work is done slowly and with bad will. Above all there are demonstrations at meal times. Adjutants have been shouted at. As a result we were denied leave. But afterwards it was explained to us that this was not a punishment but the 'withdrawal of goodwill'.

But you out there, what the fuck are you doing?

Well Done the Young Soldiers

The first 'incident' involving soldiers in opposition to the Algerian war was the magnificent demonstration by reservists at the Gare de Lyon, which will go down in the history of the French working-class movement. Six hundred young soldiers, defying the military machine, not intimidated either by threats or by the carbines of the mobile police, refused to go and kill and be killed for the profit of the capitalists.

They have revived one of the most glorious traditions of the international revolutionary working-class movement. They have shaken the whole French working class, which its leaders are trying to lull with fine phrases about the 'national interest', with petitions and the most criminal passivity.

Since then there have been soldiers' demonstrations all over the place, carefully hushed up by the press which mentions them only when it is impossible not to.

We are observing the massive entry into struggle of the whole working-class youth. Disgusted by the banality of the 'national politics' of the Socialist and Communist Parties, by their lack of revolutionary vigour, it has abandoned the youth organisations. But, by its action against the recall of reservists, against colonialist war, it has shown that it has lost nothing of its fighting spirit and its readiness for sacrifice. It is prepared to organise in order to fight and win what is worth winning: the overthrow of its exploiters. By its action it is showing the way to the whole working class.

The working class must be aware that the youth today are in the forefront of the fight against the employers and the government.

That they will be subjected to the uncontrolled authority of the officers, cops and judges, that there will be an attempt to break them by unconstrained repression. We must support them by all means possible, and not allow them to even get the impression that the military apparatus has succeeded in cutting them off from their class.

In every factory a soldiers' support committee must be organised. Funds of the 'sou du soldat'⁶ sort must provide material support for them and their families. Correspondence must be organised (while taking care not to put the soldier at risk of repression). The information they send should be widely distributed to the whole press.

Everywhere strikers should add to their own demands the recall of the young soldiers from North Africa and the immediate cessation of hostilities.

Demonstrations should be organised for the release of soldiers imprisoned for their struggle against being sent to North Africa!

The main workers' organisations must organise meetings and demonstrations against the colonial war,⁷ and they should not merely shed tears but act — and the working-class youth will strike the hardest blows against the oppressor.

The war against the peoples of North Africa is at the same time a war against French workers! The first victims are the youngest. We must all stand alongside them!

Release the prisoners!
Withdraw the troops from North Africa!
Down with colonial war!

Notes

1. From *La Vérité des Travailleurs*, October 1955.
2. The main Paris railway station for southbound travel. There was a major revolt there by conscripts refusing to board trains on 11 September 1955 [*RH*].
3. A reference to the largely unproductive Geneva East-West summit conference in July 1955, a major theme in PCF propaganda [*RH*].
4. When Algeria became an integral part of French territory in 1848, it was divided into three *départements*. A reorganisation in 1955 increased this to four [*RH*].
5. 'Union française' was the new name given by the Fourth Republic to the French Empire [*RH*].
6. Before 1914, the French trade unions organised a special fund to keep soldiers in contact with the labour movement and make anti-militarist propaganda [*RH*].
7. At the time of writing not a single meeting or demonstration had been held by the PCF, the Socialist Party or the unions against the war in North Africa and the recall of the young soldiers.

Discussions in *Vérités Pour*

The following two articles are from *Vérités Pour*, the clandestine bulletin produced by the Jeanson network, and are examples of the debate on the far left about attitudes to military service, and in particular criticisms of the PCF's position, which was that soldiers should not refuse conscription or desert.

A Reminder of Principles[1]

Over the last few months public opinion has become aware that there exists in France a vast movement of desertion, that there are several thousand who have refused conscription or deserted…

Unfortunately the reaction of the official Left has been one of withdrawal, of defensiveness and fear: the whole spectrum of the 'left' press from *L'Express*[2] to *L'Humanité* has unanimously repudiated desertion, thus insulting the brave young activists of all tendencies who had refused to confine themselves to the epistolary or verbal ideal that was being proposed to them. Gilles Martinet 'cannot approve of them'; J-J Servan-Schreiber[3] pities them and their 'mentors'; finally, in the daily paper of the working class,[4] Etienne Fajon challenges anyone to name a single Communist who approves of or encourages desertion.

Of all these official disavowals, of all these climb-downs, the last is the most serious: the article which we are publishing below is written by a Communist militant. In reading it nobody can doubt the commitment of its author, or his knowledge of Marxism and how he puts it into practice.

* * *

The Algerian war has posed new problems which have caused great confusion in many minds. The young people, those most directly involved, above all because of the military service which they are compelled to do, have not found in the positions taken up by the left-wing political parties answers which can satisfy them. For those who do not accept this war and want to struggle effectively to put an end to it, it may be useful to recall some elementary principles which seem to have been forgotten by those who ought to have defended them.

1: For the Algerian people it is a *national* war to win *independence*; it is a *just* war. For the French government it is an imperialist war which aims to preserve colonial oppression, hence it is a *reactionary* war, absolutely unjust, which no higher principle can justify. Lenin declared unambiguously: 'National wars *against* the imperialist powers are […] *progressive* and *revolutionary*.'[5]

2: When a government is involved in a reactionary war, the duty of conscious workers is to adopt without hesitation a *defeatist* position:

> A revolutionary class cannot but wish for the defeat of its government in a reactionary war.[6]
>
> The reason why the chauvinists […] repudiate the defeat 'slogan' is that *this slogan alone* implies a consistent call for revolutionary action against one's own government in wartime. Without such action, millions of ultra-revolutionary phrases such as a war against 'the war and the conditions, etc' are not worth a brass farthing.[7]

Wartime revolutionary action against one's own government indubitably means, not only desiring its defeat, but really facilitating such a defeat.[8]

All these statements were written by Lenin between 1914 and 1916.

3: Already before the First World War the socialist parties had denounced as a crime the fact of shooting on workers from other countries. Jaurès, cited by Lenin, stated: 'We shall not go to war against our brothers, we shall not shoot on them.' And Lenin added: 'the workers will regard [...] as criminal any shooting each other down for the profit of the capitalists.'[9]

4: Lenin rightly considered that action against war must be mass action, for only such action could endanger the bourgeoisie engaged in a reactionary war: that is why he considered, during the 1914-18 war, that refusal of military service was a utopia, 'the miserable and cowardly dream of an unarmed struggle'.[10] This position was correct in the Great War between imperialist powers; individual refusals to respond to mobilisation would not be understood and their only effect was the useless sacrifice of vanguard elements. In these particular circumstances, the appropriate slogan was to go into the army to take arms and to prepare the transformation of the imperialist war into a civil war. Lenin was solely concerned to find the effective slogan in a particular situation. For the French Communist Party to take this slogan of Lenin's out of its historical context is a distortion.

In the particular case of the Algerian war, the refusal by reservists and conscripts to obey the call-up in 1955 was in process of becoming a popular slogan capable of involving the mass of soldiers, and of being supported by demonstrations of workers and peasants. By refusing to support and encourage this movement, by voting full powers to Guy Mollet, the French Communist Party failed to help the Algerian people and abandoned revolutionary action ('not worth a brass farthing').

From this time on it was inevitable that a narrower movement should orient itself towards forms of clandestine action to try and find the means for practical activity against the war. Even if this action remains the province of a small minority, because of the dereliction of duty by the traditional left parties, it has taken on an exemplary value which deserves to be unreservedly honoured.

5: On the national question, the left parties have chattered a great deal about the existence and content of the Algerian nation, but they have turned their backs on the constant teachings of the international socialist movement. It is the oppressed nation which alone has the right to define itself, to recognise the elements which compose it, to reject or accept those whom it considers aliens, to denounce its enemies. This point has also been stressed by Lenin when he recalled that:

Socialists must [...] demand the unconditional and immediate liberation of the colonies without compensation — and this demand in its political expression signifies nothing else than the recognition of the right to self-determination.[11]

6: Finally we must not forget that the Algerian war, by the corruption it has brought about and developed, has endangered all the democratic liberties which the people won in the course of long struggles. The *de facto* acceptance of the Algerian war, the refusal to support all forms of struggle against this war, have left the field open for fascist adventures by which we might have hoped not to be threatened.

Whatever happens next, and we as much as anyone hope for a rapid return to peace, it will still remain necessary to examine in a brutally frank manner the mistakes that have been made and to draw useful lessons for the future from them.

Notes

1. From *Vérités Pour*, no 17, 26 July 1960.
2. *L'Express*, weekly magazine which in 1950s supported Mendès-France and opposed the Algerian war [*RH*].
3. Jean-Jacques Servan-Schreiber (1924-2006): founder of *L'Express*; served in Algeria and wrote a book denouncing army brutality; later a Radical Party politician [*RH*].
4. That is, *L'Humanité*, the PCF daily [*RH*].
5. VI Lenin, 'The Junius Pamphlet' (1916), *Collected Works*, Volume 22 (Moscow, 1960), p 312.
6. VI Lenin, 'Socialism and War' (1915), *Collected Works*, Volume 21 (Moscow, 1960), p 315.
7. VI Lenin, 'The Defeat of One's Own Government in the Imperialist War' (1915), *Collected Works*, Volume 21, p 276.
8. VI Lenin, 'The Defeat of One's Own Government in the Imperialist War' (1915), *Collected Works*, Volume 21, p 275.
9. VI Lenin, 'The Collapse of the Second International' (1915), *Collected Works*, Volume 21, p 213, citing the Basel Manifesto of 1912.
10. VI Lenin, 'The Position and Tasks of the Socialist International' (1914), *Collected Works*, Volume 21, p 40.
11. VI Lenin, 'The Socialist Revolution and the Right of Nations to Self-Determination' (1916), *Collected Works*, Volume 22, p 151.

***

Bernard Randon
The Great Refusal[1]

The author of the following lines is a reservist from 1955-56. In a long analysis of which we can publish only the conclusion, he studies the different forms of refusal which the Algerian war has provoked among young people since 1954: collective demonstrations, individual refusal followed by imprisonment, refusal leading to exile or a clandestine existence in France. After the announcement of the arrest of some members of the Jeune Résistance network, which according to *France-Soir* got 1800 young French draft refusers out of the country, we think that an important phenomenon is occurring among French youth, on which the following text sheds some light.

***

The absence of a revolutionary refusal movement deeply rooted in the French masses explains the failure of the reservists' movement. This also explains the failure of the prisoners' movement, which it likewise aborted by narrowing its audience and limiting its scope.

Dozens of refusals to serve recorded since 1956 are not, for the most part, either conscientious objections ('conscientious refusal', as Domenach[2] called it), nor individualist stances (purely individual). Which means that those refusing do not refuse all wars *in the same way* (otherwise they would not fail to condemn the armed revolt of 1954 and the war of the Mujahideen, and none of those whom I am speaking about does so). This means, moreover, that the salvation of their soul or the cleanness of their hands is not the main motivation for their actions (you don't get rid of collective sins so easily, and one is not exempted from responsibility for national errors because one prefers jail to the armies of the republic).

At the least and to begin with, those who refuse want to bear witness. Bear witness to what? To the morally, politically and rationally intolerable nature of the Algerian war.

And their testimony aims to be *effective*. They are not merely the distillate of disgust, the vanguard of shame. The refusal to serve must serve the Refusal, the Great Refusal of injustice and unreason.

Otherwise, if they did not want to be witnesses, and witnesses who are listened to, followed, defended and approved, and if they were not offering themselves as living examples, raised up as symbols of the refusal of war, why would these young men come to sacrifice their youth before the unthinking judges of the courts? As soldiers, why would they sacrifice their freedom? There are other ways of not making war.

They are sacrificing their freedom, our fine twenty-year-old prisoners, so that we can have names, faces, heroes, so that we can have slogans, so that we don't have excuses.

It cannot be doubted that the prisoners' movement, considered in this context, has the meaning: arm the masses and force our hand.

To force the hand of the bleating liberal advocates of peace in Algeria, to compel the unconscious citizens, the hesitant militants, the recalcitrant leaders, to go beyond the stage of obsessive respect for legality, and of the drowsy, sometimes sleep-inducing agitation which for years has taken the place of struggle against war.

These young people remember the campaign in favour of Henri Martin,[3] incomparably more powerful than the one they have benefited from (they who are the many, who are the conscripts). They grew up at a time when so many walls proclaimed the name of the petty officer in giant letters that these illustrious witnesses could scarcely imagine that today we should rather tend to *apologise for* them, that we should ask for indulgence and comprehension from their judges, and that as a result of seeing them as *exceptional*, we should end up presenting them as effectively exhibitionists, hypersensitive and a bit abnormal.

They could not imagine that, being both useful and embarrassing at the same time, they would serve as a front rather than as banners, mainly as an excuse for their own side and not much of a weapon against the enemy.

The heroism of the Refusers is squandered capital: think of that. The Refuser 'refuses to fight an opponent whose cause seems to him to be just and to use against him methods of war which he considers to be vile' (Pierre-Henri Simon[4] about Jean Le Meur, *Le Monde*, 30 December 1959). The Refuser is in prison. Who, among the citizens of this responsible country, will agree to take the risk of going there, for the same reasons? Who will agree to say that the act of the Refuser is a form, deliberately assumed by an individual, of the refusal to take an attitude, a particular, extreme case of non-cooperation to be generalised, a concrete and dramatic example of insubordination to be spread? Who is willing to distribute in France, and in the army in Algeria through accessible channels (families, soldiers on leave, conscripts, Algerian population…) the ideas and slogans which advocate and organise an active challenge to the war?

Ask these questions and reply to them…

And then. I recall the words which a character in André Chamson's[5] novel addresses to Roux, the bandit who was a deserter in 1914:

> All the men on earth, when they were told to go and fight, should have gone up together onto the mountains of their countries; then perhaps, the Lord

would have come and sat down amongst them... But you are alone on your mountain... (*Roux the Bandit*, pp 115-16)

But you are alone on your mountain Alban Liechti.[6]

The Insubordinates

No, you are no longer alone. For coming after the failure of the movement of the reservists, that of the movement of the prisoners, a lesson learnt through experience by hundreds and hundreds of thousands of young people, has produced an enormous advance.

The movement of the insubordinates — that is the name that suits best — today reaches the very bottom of the problem and takes things from the starting-point. It is trying to promote in France the revolutionary movement of refusal, the existence of which the previous initiatives assumed in order to succeed.

For youth cannot wait for the birth of the organisation, and for the important people who could speak the truth about the war to make their minds up. It cannot wait till France has found its Henry Thoreau, the American hero of taxation refusal.[7]

Youth cannot put its trust in anyone but itself, and the best among them must themselves make propaganda for their refusal.

The task ahead of these young resisters is enormous. But undoubtedly they will awaken consciences, undoubtedly they will find support, undoubtedly they will strengthen hopes and encourage trends which are more numerous than is believed by those who eternally pontificate about the chauvinism of the masses.

The new revolutionary wave is thus taking on a new dynamic. Acting on the internal environment, basing itself on Europe against antiquated France, answering on our behalf in face of the world and the Third World, will the movement succeed in making the French people aware? What better means, in any case, to do so than asking them to help young people, their young people, to refuse dishonour, than to ask them to feed them, hide them, protect them by silence and support them in words?

The army and the far right, as we know, are very concerned with the state of mind of the home front and the education of the metropolitan population. The young revolutionaries are equally concerned with these things. If the repressive control by the *pieds-noirs* and the army were countered by democratic, civilian control, which would catch on better with the French masses, which would crush the other in the long run? And if in France enduring networks of refusal were set up, do you think that the army in Algeria would not be affected by it?

A physical haemorrhage to start with. Wars that have been too long and too unjust have experienced that. In the last years of the Napoleonic wars, the marshes, forests and mountains were full of draft refusers and deserters. In many *départements* the proportion of those refusing to serve was as high as one third, despite an over-staffed army at home and the prosecution of families.

And then a moral haemorrhage; I mean desertion of body and soul by the soldiers in Algeria, under the impact of their *moralisation*, as they are taken over by a prestigious vanguard, by the possibility given to their consciousness and their actions to escape from the conditioning of the dirty war.

'It isn't the job of the conscripts', people say, 'it's the job of the intellectuals and politicians, of the French people, to take on the responsibility of struggling for peace in Algeria.' Five years of war have taught the best of the soldiers in the army a different truth. They have had enough of making war. They have had enough of trusting.

And it may well be that the French people will soon also have had enough.

The conjuncture is favourable for the Draft Refusers. Who is not aware of the problem of the 'lean years' with a low birth-rate? It will be posed in 1961 most sharply. Hence the limitation of deferments, the possibility of further recalls of reservists. France has 1.1 million men in the armed services.

Among the people, and especially the peasantry, there is a growing weariness which will not continue to accept the situation. The length of military service is a scandal experienced for 27 months by young people who have put up with too much. Here are objective conditions that are scarcely spoken about and which cannot be overstated.

May the effort for an internationalist renewal be embodied, may the perspectives for a united and fraternal Europe be clarified thereby, and may they propose to the French people a greatness appropriate to their own time; conviction and determination will grow, though today they seem fragile.

A terrible failure, difficult new beginnings, the work of a generation? Yes, doubtless. The generation of Dien Bien Phu, whose first task is to lead the living France, won over for the human future, to meet on the mountain top the companions of the Great Refusal.

Notes
1. From *Vérités Pour*, no 15, 24 March 1960.
2. Jean-Marie Domenach (1922–1997): left Catholic writer, from 1957 editor of *Esprit* [*RH*].
3. Henri Martin (b 1927): Communist sailor, jailed 1950-53 for distributing propaganda hostile to the Indochina War. A major campaign was launched for his release [*RH*].
4. Pierre-Henri Simon (1903-1972): well-known writer [*RH*].
5. André Chamson (1900-1983): novelist. His novel *Roux le bandit* (1925), set in his

native Cévennes mountains, told of a peasant who refused to join the army in 1914 [*RH*].
6. Alban Liechti: PCF member imprisoned for refusing to fight in Algeria; the PCF were very slow to organise a campaign in his support [*RH*].
7. Henry David Thoreau (1817-1862): American writer and advocate of civil disobedience [*RH*].

* * *

Ian Birchall
A Note on the MNA

A major problem for those who sought to organise solidarity with the struggle for Algerian independence was that, in the earlier stage of the war, the movement for national independence was deeply divided, with a vicious struggle between the FLN (National Liberation Front) and the MNA (Algerian National Movement). At the time some outrageous claims and slanders were made and repeated by the supporters of both sides. With the perspective offered by hindsight it may be possible to examine the issues at stake more calmly.

The origins of the Algerian national movement are to be found in the 1920s, when the ENA (North African Star) was founded. Its key leader was Messali Hadj, a young Algerian factory worker and member of the Communist Party. The ENA was founded with the encouragement of the PCF, but very rapidly the PCF became distrustful of the movement's independence and began to criticise it sharply. In the 1930s, Messali and his followers worked with the left wing of the SFIO led by Marceau Pivert. Meanwhile the Stalinist attacks became more vicious; in 1937 a leader of the Algerian Communist Party called him an 'agent of Franco and Mussolini'.[1] The ENA was banned by the Popular Front government in 1937, but was reborn as the PPA, later, with the MTLD (Movement for the Triumph of Democratic Liberties) as its legal wing, Messali himself spent much of his time in jail or under house arrest.

By the early 1950s, Messali was a veteran leader of the movement, greatly admired both in Algeria and among Algerian workers in France. He was a man of great dedication and integrity, and was very popular. But he also had critics in his own ranks. Through no fault of his own Messali had spent little time in Algeria (except when jailed during the Second World War) since he came to Paris in 1923. As Ferhat Abbas — a moderate who later joined the FLN — put it many years later: 'Messali saw Algeria through the Parisian atmosphere and the laws which protected civil liberties in France. I saw it in the context of the *douar* where I was born.'[2]

He is also said to have had an authoritarian style; even when under house arrest in France, he endeavoured to keep control, telephoning orders every day.

Mohammed Harbi, a follower of Messali's who went over to the FLN, notes that among the Algerian people Messali was the object 'of a collective fervour which was not free of religiosity', but also recalls that he was shocked when Messali 'demanded full powers in order to "rectify the party"'.[3]

This led to a major dispute with the so-called 'centralists', who felt his dictatorial style was an obstacle to the organisation.[4] He succeeded in defeating them at a congress in Belgium in 1954. But meanwhile a secret grouping was developing which became the CRUA (Revolutionary Committee of Unity and Action) and then the FLN, and which launched the insurrection on 1 November 1954.

The situation immediately after the rising was complex. Daniel Guérin, a veteran anti-colonialist and a long-time personal friend of Messali's, telephoned him shortly after 1 November 1954. Messali was surprised and confused; he had not believed the CRUA militants, though they were his own followers, capable of such audacity, and he saw the action as a challenge to his own personal role.[5] Any action that Messali's organisation had been planning had been pre-empted by the action of the new-born FLN. Messali, who had always advocated political rather than military action,[6] was clearly critical of the tactics adopted by the FLN, but at the same time he could not condemn what was obviously a very popular action; however, he refused an invitation to escape to Cairo and join the FLN.[7] The FLN's rapid growth after 1 November 1954 reflected the fact that there was still deep anger after the massacres at Sétif and Guelma in 1945, and increasing impatience at the French government's failure to introduce any significant reforms. By late 1955, the FLN was already the majority movement in Algeria, with MNA members flocking to join the rival organisation.[8]

Many Algerians, especially those working in France, initially thought that it was Messali and his organisation which had initiated the struggle. So too did the French state. In the first months of the war it was Messali's supporters who bore the brunt of the repression, since they were the ones on the French police files, while the younger generation of FLN militants were still unknown. The MTLD was immediately banned, and Messali's organisation reformed itself under the name of the MNA.

What was the essential difference between the two organisations? Despite claims by some of the MNA's more enthusiastic supporters that it was in some sense a potentially socialist organisation, there was no significant programmatic distinction between the two nationalist organisations. As Benjamin Stora puts it in his biography of Messali Hadj:

> There would never be a clear-cut difference in programme between the FLN and the MNA. Their violent rivalry did not concern questions relating to the

place and role of the bourgeoisie, petty-bourgeoisie and proletariat in the revolutionary process.[9]

Daniel Guérin, whose sympathies were with the MNA, agrees with this point.[10] As Stora points out, ever since the 1930s Messali had seen the Algerian 'people' as a whole, rather than particular classes, as the force that would win independence.[11] But while Messali justified military action in Algeria, he still stressed the need for friendship with the French 'people', and opposed terror tactics in metropolitan France:

> It is undeniable that today the French people understands that Algeria has only turned to insurrection after having despaired of French colonialism. That is why it is vital to continue struggling in this way without resorting to terrorism and adventures on metropolitan soil. The French people is our friend and in these circumstances our duty is to inform it of our sufferings and our aspirations in order to win its sympathy and to prepare friendly relations with it for the future.[12]

The fundamental division was on the question of organisation. As Benjamin Stora has explained:

> The FLN was not a patriotic front of the Vietnamese type, which brought together parties and organisations united on the basis of a programme and retaining their organic independence. The appeal of 1 November required the disappearance of all former parties and adherence to the FLN on an individual basis.[13]

It presented itself as a unitary organisation embodying the unity of the Algerian people. It was therefore open to recruit individuals from a wide range of political positions, but it was unwilling to make alliances with other organisations. In terms of programme the two organisations had very similar demands — cease-fire, recognition of self-determination, release of prisoners, etc. Both were essentially nationalist and referred to social reform only in the vaguest terms. The one crucial difference, summarised in a contemporary journal, was as follows:

> The FLN demands a homogenous provisional government, appointed by itself, in order to negotiate, and does not envisage immediate elections.
>
> The MNA demands in the first place [immediately after the cease-fire] the election of a Constituent Assembly which will appoint the Algerian government.[14]

It would be wrong to see this purely as a power struggle, though undoubtedly the FLN contained a lot of ambitious young men already looking to their role in an independent Algeria, while Messali seems to have been concerned about his status as 'historic' leader of Algerian nationalism. As Mohammed Harbi puts it: 'Not being the bearer of a project different from that of the FLN, Messali could only hope to play a role in the future by preserving his past image.'[15]

But there was also a genuine argument about the most effective way to achieve Algerian independence.

In March 1955, there was a meeting in Algiers between the MNA and the FLN. (Messali himself, under house arrest in France, could not attend.) The FLN proposed that the MNA should dissolve and that its members should join the FLN as individuals. The MNA refused.[16] Ben Bella later told French journalist Gilles Martinet:

> An association of movements [what Messali Hadj demands] would present for us enormous dangers, for the French government would be able to play one against the other. That is why we are ready to welcome Messali to the FLN, but not to compromise with the MNA.[17]

As the armed struggle developed the National Liberation Army was formed, and initially the MNA participated in this, leading the guerrilla struggle in a number of areas.[18] But very soon the rivalry between the two organisations took a much nastier turn. Both sides came to see the other as an obstacle, and it was no surprise that the antagonism between the FLN and the MNA soon spilled over into physical violence.

It is very difficult to establish who started the violence. Some sources allege that the first attacks came from the MNA,[19] and since it was initially the larger and more established organisation, this would not be wholly implausible. An internal bulletin of the MNA as early as February 1955 described the FLN as 'saboteurs' and 'opportunists', using 'police spy methods' for their 'criminal task'.[20] Soon both sides were involved in the 'settling of scores' which took place throughout the years 1955-58. FLN leader Abbane Ramdane declared that all MNA supporters should be 'shot without a trial'.[21] (Abbane himself was killed in 1957 in a power struggle between various FLN leaders.)

The most horrific incident came in 1957, when the FLN massacred the inhabitants of a small MNA-supporting village in the Mélouza region. Some 300 inhabitants were butchered and mutilated. So shameful was the FLN's conduct that the organisation denied any responsibility and blamed it on the French army, though all the evidence is that the FLN were responsible. The FLN thus handed a major propaganda victory to the French, who compared the FLN atrocities to those committed by the Nazis in occupied France.[22]

The conflict spread rapidly to mainland France, where the MNA had extensive support. The quarter of a million Algerian workers in France were important for the FLN, who collected, voluntarily or otherwise, their financial contributions. It is estimated that some 4000 people were killed in mainland France in the armed struggle between the two factions, and perhaps 6000 more in Algeria.[23] While MNA supporters make much of the FLN attacks, both sides were guilty of murder — and both pleaded self-defence. Most of the leading MNA figures were well known because of their past in the movement, and the FLN tended to use individual assassinations. The MNA, on the other hand, were more likely to attack FLN meetings or cafés frequented by FLN supporters and kill as many as possible at random. And both sides made use of criminal elements who were often provocateurs paid by the French state.[24] The FLN planned to kill Messali himself.[25] Messali was deeply shaken by the murder in 1957 of Embarek Filali, one of his closest allies since the 1930s.[26]

In 1957, attempts were made to organise mediation, and Messali's supporters accepted a truce beginning on 1 September 1957, but the FLN refused to go along with this.[27] As late as 1959, President Bourguiba of Tunisia urged Messali to support the FLN, but the veteran leader refused.[28]

It is doubtless true, as Henri Benoîts suggests, that the French police encouraged the feud between the rival organisations[29] — it certainly served French interests. But the main cause was undoubtedly the political rivalry between the two organisations. And in the course of the struggle many accusations were made that one side or the other was serving French interests. Thus it was alleged by the FLN and its supporters that the French governor general in Algeria, Soustelle, had said that the MNA was his 'last card'. Daniel Guérin investigated this and found it to be false.[30]

Most damaging for the MNA was the Bellounis affair. Bellounis was an MNA military leader; after the Mélouza massacre, and threatened with destruction by the FLN, he made an agreement with the French to fight against the FLN, while still identifying politically with the MNA.[31] (Later he broke with the French and was killed fighting against them.) Though this was widely used to discredit the MNA, Messali and the MNA did not dissociate themselves from Bellounis. (Daniel Guérin repeatedly requested Messali to disavow Bellounis, but without success.[32]) This was a single instance and did not show the MNA to be pro-French. But it caused considerable disarray among Messali's supporters.

The FLN was far from homogenous, and the strategy towards the MNA was not universally agreed. Doubtless some assassinations were decided on by local leaders who may have gone further than their leaders would have wished. Mohamed Harbi, one of the main FLN organisers in mainland France, records that: 'This conflict undermined our relations with those French people, then a very small minority, who took the risk of supporting our struggle, but did not understand this fratricidal struggle between Messali, the old fighter, and the FLN.'[33]

When Ben Bella was informed of the assassination of one of the MNA's most senior trade-union activists, Ahmed Bekhat, he commented savagely: 'It's idiotic! There aren't two militants like Bekhat in the FLN!'[34] It is certainly true that the feud led to the deaths of a number of experienced trade unionists who could have played an important role in developing the working-class movement in an independent Algeria. Some FLN leaders may not have been too sorry about that.

In 1956, the MNA set up the USTA (Association of Algerian Workers Unions) because it felt the Algerian workers' cause was not getting sufficient support from the Communist-controlled CGT. This had its main base among Algerian workers in mainland France. It took up basic trade-union questions as well as support for independence. At its first congress in 1957 it claimed between 50 000 and 100 000 members, though these figures have been questioned by those who believe it was never more than a front for the MNA.

In response the FLN created the UGTA (General Union of Algerian Workers), but in metropolitan France it urged its supporters to stay in the French unions, while forming a 'friendly society' of Algerian workers. More seriously, the FLN embarked on a systematic programme of assassination of USTA leaders, which greatly weakened the USTA and the MNA.[35]

Remorselessly the FLN grew at the MNA's expense, with more and more MNA militants going over to the FLN. The FLN had clearly won the support of a significant section of the Algerian population by its willingness to fight immediately. The MNA, however, had suffered the main burden of repression in the early years of the war, when the French authorities still believed Messali to be responsible for the insurrection. Moreover, the FLN gave the impression of being more effective, since it was better armed, thanks to its contacts in Egypt, Tunisia and elsewhere. Later it got support from both Russia and the USA as it came to be recognised as the only legitimate representative of the Algerian people.[36] The FLN's critics accused it of being too dependent on Nasser's Egypt, but it is clear that it did not depend solely on external backing. That was the mistake made by Guy Mollet, when he thought he could crush the FLN by the invasion of Egypt in 1956. The FLN undoubtedly had a widespread popular base in Algeria.

The MNA retained its base in metropolitan France rather longer, but here too it was eventually eradicated, partly by terror, partly by the fact that the FLN was becoming obviously the main organiser of resistance. Only in the Lille area and Belgium did it survive till the end of the war,[37] perhaps for geographical reasons or because of its relation to the labour movement in those areas.

By the time de Gaulle came to power in 1958, the MNA had become an impotent minority. This doubtless accounts for Messali's response to de Gaulle. He seemed to think that de Gaulle's shifting position would offer him the possibility of breaking out of his isolation. In 1959, he was released from house arrest. In 1960, he looked forward to a French Community bringing together France's former African colonies which would be 'a new type of Commonwealth' in which Algeria would enjoy 'friendly relations and cooperation with the French Republic'.[38]

Decline and demoralisation led to splits, and one group of former MNA members, the FAAD (Algerian Democratic Action Front), actually made an agreement with the OAS in 1961. However, Messali and the mainstream of the MNA clearly dissociated themselves from this, and Messali began a rather belated purge of his organisation.[39]

During the last stages of the negotiations, de Gaulle at one stage threatened to break off negotiations with the FLN and talk to the MNA instead. But this was clearly just a negotiating manoeuvre and nothing came of it. Clearly peace could only be negotiated with the FLN, since they controlled the resistance. The MNA played no part in the Évian agreements which ended the war, and was excluded from playing any role in the July 1962 referendum in Algeria.[40] It had become an historical irrelevance.

Nonetheless, the existence of the MNA had caused serious problems for the far left; in a situation of open armed conflict those engaged in solidarity work had to make a choice. Michel Lequenne and others then in the Lambert organisation argued that the French Trotskyists should try to work for reconciliation between the FLN and the MNA.[41] It was a worthy aspiration, but clearly stood no chance of making an impact.

Both the FLN and the MNA found the support of the French far left very useful, and in their dealings with French leftists they often used a Marxist rhetoric which had very little relation to their actual programme or practice. This point was made by Mohamed Harbi, who had been responsible for FLN contacts with the French left, in an interview with Sylvain Pattieu.[42] Likewise an article by an unnamed MNA militant in *La Commune* argued that the French left was paternalist and that it was necessary to determine 'which of the Algerian nationalist movements is making the revolution of 1789 and which is making that of October'[43] — an argument clearly aimed at the French left. Both Pablo and Lambert seem to have suffered a certain number of illusions as a result.

Pattieu explains the fact that different sections of the far left supported different nationalist organisations in part by the prior contacts that had existed.[44] There was undoubtedly some truth in this. In the early period of the war, the Lambert group did some valuable work in campaigning for the release of Messali Hadj and other political prisoners.⁴⁵ Yves Dechezelles, Messali's lawyer, was close to the Lambertists though never a member.⁴⁶ The claim of FLN leader Abbane Ramdane that 'all the MNA literature is drafted by Trotskyists'⁴⁷ was doubtless an overstatement designed to curry favour with the PCF, but it probably reflected a certain reality (and must certainly have been flattering to Lambert).

Relations between the Lambert and Frank tendencies of French Trotskyism were not exactly good after the bitter 1952 split, but the situation was inflamed by the FLN–MNA dispute. Polemic does not always produce the best analysis, and Lambert was certainly guilty of exaggeration when he compared the MNA to the Bolshevik party and Messali himself to Lenin.⁴⁸

By 1958-59, Lambert was coming to realise that he had made a mistake, and the MNA was dropped. The reasons for this are not wholly clear. Benjamin Stora, a distinguished historian of the war who was formerly a Lambertist fulltimer⁴⁹ and knew Lambert well, was told by Lambert that it was because of Messali's favourable attitude to de Gaulle, but later he became convinced that the real reason was the MNA's declining support while the FLN was on the way to winning the war.⁵⁰ In 2002, Jean-Jacques Marie, the Lambert group's most prestigious historian, publicly acknowledged that support for the MNA had been a mistake.⁵¹

But support for the MNA should not be seen as a peculiarly Lambertist deviation. The MNA got support from a broader current of leftists, especially when leading members of the MNA were assassinated by the FLN. When Filali was killed in 1957, a protest statement was signed by Marceau Pivert, surrealist poets André Breton and Benjamin Péret, and prominent left intellectuals such as Maurice Nadeau, Laurent Schwartz, Michel Leiris, Colette Audry and Edgar Morin.⁵² (Breton, Leiris, Nadeau, Schwartz and others would go on to sign the Manifesto of 121, so they could hardly be accused of siding with French imperialism.) Daniel Guérin, a veteran campaigner for colonial independence, was close to Messali personally, though he took a position of impartiality between the two factions and urged 'their reconciliation and fusion into a single fighting body which will lead the Algerian people to victory'.⁵³ He was critical of the Lambertists' attempt to monopolise support for the MNA, accusing them of being 'paternalist' and 'more Messalist than Messali'.⁵⁴ Another longstanding leftist who backed the MNA and the USTA was veteran revolutionary syndicalist Pierre Monatte, of the pre-1914 *Vie ouvrière* and then the *Révolution prolétarienne*.⁵⁵

The dispute was also taken up by the international left. The Fourth International had split in 1953 and the two Internationals aligned with their French sections. In Britain the MNA was backed by both the Healy group (which became the Socialist Labour League in 1959) and the Socialist Review Group.

In 1956, the Healy group published a pamphlet by Messali Hadj with an introduction by Peter James (perhaps a pseudonym for Healy himself).[56] Messali's text, dated November 1955, was an indictment of French colonialism and as such is largely unexceptionable. But the MNA was presented as being the direct continuation of the ENA, without any reference to the 1954 split — indeed, the FLN was not mentioned at all in either text or introduction. Messali actually stated that: 'This rising movement since the recovery of the MNA gave birth to the Algerian revolution of 1 November 1954.' As a result the pamphlet gave the impression to an uninformed reader that the struggle in Algeria was being led by the MNA. Whether this was the result of ignorance on the part of the Healyites or deliberate distortion is hard to say.

In 1958, Michael Banda wrote a substantial piece on Algeria for *Labour Review*.[57] This was sharply critical of the FLN — 'this new constellation of patriots and charlatans' — while its assessment of the MNA was cautious but very positive:

> Whereas the FLN in its social composition and its programme is predominantly petty bourgeois, the MNA, because of its overwhelming proletarian composition and its long traditions of struggle, is, though not a socialist party, the *precursor* of a revolutionary socialist party of the future. It is difficult to predict when such a party will arise. That will depend on how soon a strong Marxist movement can be created in France and on how the war progresses.

The Socialist Review Group was at least equally enthusiastic about the MNA.[58] In 1957-58, *Socialist Review* published two extensive articles on Algeria by André Giacometti. Giacometti was the pseudonym of Dan Gallin,[59] who was linked to the Shachtmanite Independent Socialist League in the USA.

But while the analysis was Giacometti's, its pro-MNA stance was enthusiastically endorsed by *Socialist Review*. Editorial introductions (doubtless written by the editor Michael Kidron) contrasted the 'anti-socialist, anti-working-class' FLN to the MNA, which deserved the support of all socialists, and sneered at the FLN's supporters who 'are occasionally seen in the vicinity of the socialist fight'.

Giacometti's case was that, whereas it was correct to support any anti-imperialist movement in the absence of a working-class leadership, in Algeria this was not the case, as 'the struggle for national liberation does not have to depend on bourgeois leaders'. He stressed the MNA's history, and its support among 'the Algerian industrial workers in France'. He condemned the FLN's use of terror, arguing that: 'The FLN is fighting a bourgeois battle with totalitarian means, while the MNA is fighting a socialist battle with democratic means.'

Giacometti put great stress on the support which the FLN was allegedly getting from the PCF,[60] and he dismissed the Fourth International as a 'comical outfit'. He even argued that Bellounis' betrayal was understandable, if not justified, since the FLN's terror meant that in some areas 'collaboration with the FLN could be a worse fate than collaboration with the French'.[61] Giacometti at least had the merit of consistency. As late as 1960, he published a substantial two-part article in which he defended the politics of the MNA and continued to condemn the FLN.[62]

Even with 50 years retrospect it is hard to be completely detached about the arguments. The central argument for backing the FLN, made at the time, and which seems confirmed by the events of 1962, is that it was the FLN which was the main leader and organiser of the struggle against French rule[63] and which successfully carried through the struggle for independence. There is certainly some validity to this, and those who carried suitcases for the FLN can feel that they contributed to a just and legitimate outcome. Whatever reservations there may be about particular tactics, the intransigence of the Algerian settlers and the unprincipled cowardice of much of the mainstream French left make it clear that only an unyielding violent struggle could have won independence.

But this must be immediately qualified by the fact that the sad history of Algeria since 1962 shows the limits of the FLN's achievement. The FLN was a bureaucratic organisation from the outset, and some credit should go to those who pointed this out while the war was still on (see the article on *Socialisme ou Barbarie* in Section III above). The supporters of the MNA were often perceptive in their critique of the FLN, whatever their illusions in the 'socialist' nature of the MNA. Thus Yves Dechezelles was not far from the truth when he wrote in 1957: 'It is not impossible that a new Algerian bourgeoisie will be rapidly formed on the spoils of the colonial bourgeoisie.'[64]

In particular, the FLN's insistence on having a monopoly of the liberation struggle, even at the price of the physical elimination of its rivals, created a bitter conflict leading to the unnecessary deaths of a large number of activists, and those who backed the FLN are open to criticism for having acquiesced so willingly in this process.

Those who defended the MNA against the FLN's murderous attacks were undoubtedly justified. However, claims that the MNA were socialists, let alone Bolsheviks, seem naïve. If the MNA's base was more proletarian than the FLN's, it was mainly among workers in metropolitan France, who faced somewhat different problems than those in Algeria. There was nothing explicitly socialist about the MNA, and those who claimed that there was were victims of rather similar illusions to those that Pablo had in the FLN. Messali, a former Communist with a long history of connections with the French left, may well have been personally a socialist, but he made it clear that independence came first, socialism later. As he put it: 'While struggling to win its freedom, [the MNA]... is determined *after having done so* [my emphasis — IB] to join its efforts to those of all the democrats to go as far as possible on the road towards socialism...'[65]

Controversy remains about the issues, and old passions die hard. One of the best-known French historians of the war, Benjamin Stora, has written a largely sympathetic biography of Messali Hadj[66] (on which I have drawn in this account). But Jacques Simon, a historian and formerly with the USTA, has denounced Stora's work as 'stuffed with errors, lacking both science and conscience'.[67] The last word had undoubtedly not been said.

Yet in Algeria there are some signs of reconciliation. Today the airport at Tlemcen, Messali's birthplace, is called the 'Messali El Hadj Airport'. The veteran leader's enormous contribution to the cause of Algerian independence, whatever his later vacillations, has thus been recognised.

Notes

1. B Stora, *Messali Hadj (1898-1974)* (Paris, 1986), p 169.
2. Stora, *Messali Hadj*, p 105. A *douar* was a camp or tent village.
3. M Harbi, *Une Vie debout* (Paris, 2001), pp 113, 118.
4. M Evans, *Algeria: France's Undeclared War* (Oxford, 2012), p 109.
5. D Guérin, *Quand l'Algérie s'insurgeait* (Claix, 1979), p 55.
6. B Stora, *La Gangrène et l'oubli* (Paris, 1991), p 140.
7. Stora, *Messali Hadj*, p 232.
8. Evans, *Algeria*, p 141.
9. Stora, *Messali Hadj*, p 235.
10. Guérin, *Quand l'Algérie s'insurgeait*, p 58.
11. Stora, *Messali Hadj*, p 235.
12. Undated [1956-57] note from Messali to MNA cadres, cited in Stora, *Messali Hadj*, p 244.
13. Stora, *La Gangrène et l'oubli*, p 150.
14. *Interafrique Presse*, 29 September 1956, cited in N Sidi Moussa and J Simon, *Le MNA: Le Mouvement National Algérien (1954-1956)* (Paris, 2008), p 212.
15. Harbi, *Une Vie debout*, p 210.
16. J Simon, *Biographes de Messali Hadj* (Paris, 2009), p 100.
17. *France-Observateur* 14 December 1957; cited by Michael Banda, 'Marxism and the Algerian Revolution', *Labour Review*, Volume 3, no 2, March-April 1958, p 42.
18. Guérin, *Quand l'Algérie s'insurgeait*, p 85.
19. B Stora, 'La Gauche et les Minorités Anticoloniales Françaises devant les Divisions du Nationalisme Algérien (1954-1958)', in J-P Rioux (ed), *La Guerre d'Algérie et les Français* (Paris, 1990), pp 75-76.
20. Cited Sidi Moussa and Simon, *Le MNA*, pp 61-62.
21. Evans, *Algeria*, p 129.
22. Evans, *Algeria*, pp 216-17.

23. Evans, *Algeria*, p 217; Stora, *La Gangrène et l'oubli*, pp 143-44.
24. Guérin, *Quand l'Algérie s'insurgeait*, pp 120-21.
25. Stora, *La Gangrène et l'oubli*, p 142.
26. Stora, *Messali Hadj*, p 266.
27. Harbi, *Une Vie debout*, p 212.
28. Stora, *La Gangrène et l'oubli*, pp 155-56.
29. See interview with Henri and Clara Benoîts above.
30. Stora, *La Gangrène et l'oubli*, p 154; Guérin, *Quand l'Algérie s'insurgeait*, pp 80-81.
31. Stora, *Messali Hadj*, p 267.
32. Guérin, *Quand l'Algérie s'insurgeait*, pp 87-90.
33. Harbi, *Une Vie debout*, p 183. Harbi, who played an important role in developing the FLN's French Federation's relation with the French left, was one of the few FLN leaders to have some knowledge of Marxism. He had been taught at school by Pierre Souyri who later became a leading figure in *Socialisme ou Barbarie*.
34. Stora, *Messali Hadj*, p 265.
35. Guérin, *Quand l'Algérie s'insurgeait*, pp 116-18; Stora, *Messali Hadj*, p 246.
36. Stora, *Messali Hadj*, pp 239-40.
37. Guérin, *Quand l'Algérie s'insurgeait*, p 118.
38. Simon, *Biographes de Messali Hadj*, p 93.
39. Stora, *Messali Hadj*, p 279; Guérin, *Quand l'Algérie s'insurgeait*, pp 172-73.
40. Evans, *Algeria*, pp 300, 317.
41. M Lequenne, *Le Trotskisme: Une Histoire sans fard* (Paris, 2005), p 291; see also interview with Lequenne in K Landais, *Passions militantes et rigueur historienne (1)* (Cabrières d'Aigues, 2006), pp 342-43.
42. S Pattieu, *Les Camarades des frères* (Paris, 2002), p 172.
43. *La Commune*, no 3, June 1957, pp 6-7. *La Commune* had a broad range of contributors but was clearly under Lambertist influence — the managing editor was Pierre Broué.
44. See Pattieu, *The Comrades of the Brothers*, Chapter 3, above.
45. See 'Note on the Committee for the Release of Messali Hadj and the Victims of Repression' in Section III above.
46. See obituary in *Revolutionary History*, Volume 9, no 4.
47. *France-Observateur* September 1955, cited by Simon, *Biographes de Messali Hadj*, p 102.
48. See P Lambert, 'Let the Algerian People Speak: Part V', *La Vérité*, 16 December 1955, in Section III above.
49. See his autobiography, *La Dernière génération d'octobre* (Paris, 2003).
50. B Stora, *Les Guerres sans fin* (Paris, 2008), p 61.
51. J-J Marie *Le Trotskysme et les trotskystes* (Paris, 2002), p 125.
52. Guérin, *Quand l'Algérie s'insurgeait*, p 122; *La Vérité*, 17 October 1957.
53. Guérin, *Quand l'Algérie s'insurgeait*, p 82.
54. Guérin, *Quand l'Algérie s'insurgeait*, p 81.
55. C Chambelland, *Pierre Monatte, une autre voix syndicaliste* (Paris, 1999), pp 185-86.
56. Messali Hadj, *The Algerian Revolution* (London, April 1956). Thanks to Harry Ratner for providing a copy of this rare pamphlet.

57. Michael Banda, 'Marxism and the Algerian Revolution', *Labour Review*, Volume 3, no 2, March-April 1958, pp 37-44.
58. The claim by Jim Higgins, *More Years for the Locust* (London, 1997), pp 48-49, that 'both Healy's and Cliff's groups looked a little silly when Messali Hadj was found to have been a longstanding French agent' has absolutely no foundation, but it doubtless reflects the kind of slander that was flung around in the factional atmosphere of the time.
59. Later General Secretary of the International Union of Food, Agricultural, Hotel, Restaurant, Catering, Tobacco and Allied Workers Associations. See also http://www.globallabour.info/en/archives/the_giacometti_file/.
60. Giacometti's claims of PCF support for the FLN seem to be exaggerated. In fact, the PCF scrupulously avoided any declaration of support for the FLN. Giacometti's case seems to be based on the fact that the USSR supported Nasser and Nasser supported the FLN. In fact, explicit support for the FLN came from PCF dissidents and from independent leftists such as Francis Jeanson (whom Giacometti dismisses, rather unfairly, as a 'fellow traveller'). Where Giacometti is right is that the PCF had long been opposed to Messali Hadj and gave no support to the MNA in its dispute with the FLN.
61. A Giacometti, 'The History of the Algerian Revolution', *Socialist Review*, Mid-April 1958; A Giacometti, 'The Politics of the Algerian Revolution', *Socialist Review*, May Day 1958.
62. A Giacometti, 'The Algerian Revolution: Actors and Motives', *Clarion*, nos 11 and 12, January and February 1960. (*Clarion* was the journal of the National Association of Labour Student Organisations.) This was also published as a pamphlet by the Young Peoples Socialist League in the USA.
63. See J Privas, 'Où en est le MNA?', *Quatrième Internationale*, January 1958.
64. Y Dechezelles, 'La Gauche Française et les divisions de la Résistance Algérienne', *La Commune*, no 3, June 1957, p 5.
65. Messali Hadj, *The Algerian Revolution*, p 11.
66. B Stora, *Messali Hadj* (1898-1974) (Paris, 1986).
67. Simon, *Biographes de Messali Hadj*, p 200.

* * *

Ian Birchall
Mitterrand's War

One of the most appalling aspects of the Algerian war was the way in which the main traditional organisations of the working class abandoned any pretensions to internationalism. It was Guy Mollet, leader of the SFIO, who was responsible for the escalation of the war in 1956, while the PCF, aiming to revive a 'Popular Front', backed Mollet's introduction of 'special powers'.

What has been less discussed is the role of François Mitterrand, later French President from 1981 to 1995. After Algerian independence neither Mitterrand himself, nor his supporters (some of them former leftists),[1] had any interest in raking over his role during the war. A recent book by historian Benjamin Stora and political journalist François Malye,[2] based on the testimony of contemporaries and previously unused documentation, has revealed a clearer picture.

* * *

When Mitterrand was elected President in 1981, one of the first acts of the new government was to abolish capital punishment. But in the 1950s, Mitterrand's attitude to the death penalty had been rather different.

The general election of January 1956 brought to power a coalition government headed by Guy Mollet. Under the multi-party system of the Fourth Republic, most governments lasted a few months at best, but Mollet's lasted some 16 months, the key period of the escalation of the war. Mollet's second-in-command was Pierre Mendès-France, and François Mitterrand was the Garde des Sceaux (Keeper of the Seals), or Minister of Justice. In terms of cabinet protocol, he was the third most senior minister.

Mitterrand was only 39, but was already a veteran, having served in 10 previous governments. He was not a member of the SFIO, but was leader of the small UDSR (*Union démocratique et socialiste de la Résistance*: Democratic and Socialist Union of the Resistance), which gave him a bargaining position in the complex manoeuvring between parties.

On Algeria, as on so many things, Mitterrand's position was ambiguous. He had a record of liberal positions on colonial policy, and had favoured independence for Tunisia and Morocco. But Algeria was different. One of his closest friends, Georges Dayan, lived in Algeria, and he had spent many holidays there. At the outbreak of the insurrection in 1954, he had declared that negotiation with the rebels was inconceivable. He wanted to see social reforms in Algeria, which meant that many settlers regarded him as an irresponsible liberal. But he was also totally committed to keeping Algeria French.

Above all Mitterrand was an ambitious man. He had real hopes of succeeding Mollet as Prime Minister within a short time. And for Mitterrand nothing — certainly not humanitarian considerations and not even the long-term interests of French imperialism — outweighed the interests of his career.

Mitterrand had already resigned from the Laniel government over the question of Morocco. He was well aware that another resignation could be fatally damaging to his reputation.

The Mollet government saw a number of key stages in the escalation of the war.

*   The vote of 'special powers', which enabled government by decree, transferred substantial powers to the resident minister, Robert Lacoste, and replaced civilian courts by military courts. (Having trained as a lawyer, Mitterrand doubtless knew that the special powers violated the Constitution, but he accepted them.)

* The kidnapping of Ben Bella and other FLN leaders. (Mitterrand's immediate reaction was to say 'Well done!', and although he later realised that the illegal action had harmful consequences, he did not oppose the cabinet decision that the prisoners should not be freed.)
* The sending of an extra 200 000 troops to Algeria. (Mendès-France resigned from the government; Mitterrand said little but did not oppose the decision.)
* The Anglo-French invasion of Egypt (Mitterrand is recorded as having told the cabinet: 'Nasser must be liquidated. It's a duel to the death.')
* The 'Battle of Algiers' in which General Massu was given full powers to crush the FLN's organisation in the capital city. (Mitterrand was in regular telephone contact with Algiers at this time and must have been familiar with the illegal methods, especially torture, being used by Massu.)

In each case Mitterrand publicly supported his government's policy, sometimes with enthusiasm beyond that required by ministerial solidarity. While he seems to have had reservations on some points, he remained silent. In a press interview after the government had collapsed, he insisted that he approved the main lines of government policy in 'restoring order' in Algeria and in ensuring that Algeria remained French.

He was clearly to the right of the policy of his own very moderate party, the UDSR, which at its 1956 congress voted unanimously for a federal solution in Algeria. Only in March 1957, just two months before the fall of the government, did Mitterrand address a private letter to Mollet rather timidly expressing reservations about what was being done in Algeria.

Much of what was going on in Algeria was out of the government's control. The army effectively took the law into its own hands. Many Algerian prisoners were simply killed without any judicial process. (This often took the form of the notorious *corvée de bois*, when prisoners were sent in a party to collect wood, then shot 'trying to escape'.) There was a simple logic to this. If all prisoners had been tried, even with a much abbreviated procedure, the court system would have collapsed under the sheer numbers. And since officially there was no 'war', they could not be prisoners of war. Army officers and politicians — including Mitterrand — understood this well and tacitly accepted it. The use of torture was also systematic, not just the result of a few individuals going too far.

Just how much Mitterrand knew is difficult to assess, but it seems clear that he had a very good idea of what was happening. He was far better informed about Algeria than most of his fellow-ministers, including Mollet, and kept in regular contacts with informants. When, in 1956, the lawyer Gisèle Halimi came to tell him that her clients were being tortured, Mitterrand accused her of exaggerating.

Mitterrand appointed as the *procureur général* (equivalent of Attorney General) in Algiers Jean Reliquet. Reliquet seems to have been an honest liberal who respected legal procedures. But in the Algerian situation he was effectively powerless. For a time the resident minister, Lacoste, refused to meet him. He was effectively ignored by the army authorities.

This is the context of the executions, a matter for which Mitterrand had special responsibility. In the course of the war there were 222 executions,[3] of which the first 45 took place under the Mollet government. The Algiers executioner, Fernand Meyssonnier, hardly a bleeding heart, compared the wave of executions to the Terror of the 1790s.

In terms of the total casualties of the war[4] this was a small figure, but the political implications of the use of capital punishment were significant. The French government steadfastly refused to recognise that there was a war,[5] hence the whole movement for national independence was criminalised. Lacoste even denied the existence of the FLN, saying it was merely a gang of hooligans and a myth created by Parisian lawyers. Those prisoners lucky enough to get a trial were effectively treated not as combatants but as criminals. (The German occupiers, as many could remember, had taken a similar attitude to the French Resistance.) In some cases prisoners were not allowed to see their lawyers.

For the FLN the guillotine, rather than shooting, was seen as an expression of contempt. They would have preferred to face death from a firing squad, standing up, than suffer the indignity of beheading.

For the defenders of French rule, capital punishment had another significance. Everyone knew that sooner or later, one way or the other, the war would end — and that doubtless combatants would be amnestied. So execution seemed to be the only effective punishment.

Some of the FLN militants executed were guilty of killing policemen or civilians, and hence were 'murderers' in the light of the legal fiction that there was not a war going on. But some were executed for more minor offences. Mohamed Belkhiria threw a grenade from which the explosive charge had been removed into a bar in Constantine. Nobody was killed or injured, but he was sentenced to death — with Mitterrand's approval.

When the Mollet government came to power in 1956, 253 death sentences had been passed on Algerian nationalists (163 in absentia), but none had as yet been executed; there were 90 prisoners on death row. A cabinet decision had to be taken on whether the executions should be carried out. There is no formal minute, but an unofficial record kept by one of the ministers shows that

Mitterrand voted in favour.

Decisions on clemency were taken by the President of the Republic, René Coty, after consideration by the 12 members of the Conseil supérieur de la magistrature (higher council of the magistracy). Coty was an old man (74), often tired, who on one occasion confused two separate cases. Another member of the committee, a lawyer, slept through sessions and voted for death sentences in his sleep. So Mitterrand's influence, as vice-chair of the committee, was extremely important.

Mitterrand backed measures to speed up the execution process, so that in one month, February 1957, there were 17 executions in Algeria (only in two cases did Mitterrand oppose the sentence). He shortened the period allowed for appeals for clemency. Thus the procedures used in Algiers contrasted sharply with those used in criminal cases. February 1957 also saw the guillotining in Paris of Émile Buisson, a gangster and serial killer. His execution took place three full years after his arrest, and he had had time to get numerous psychiatric reports in support of his appeal.

Mitterrand thus established himself as a hard-liner on the question of capital punishment. Of the 45 executions carried out during his period in office, he opposed clemency in at least 32 cases. The incomplete records that exist show that he voted for clemency less often than Lacoste, the resident minister in Algiers, who was generally seen as defending the position of the most right-wing European settlers and army officers.

The argument was not simply about humanitarian considerations. The FLN had started out as a very small organisation. It was French repression which pushed large sections of the Algerian population into the arms of the FLN. The executions gave the FLN martyrs, and led to the FLN taking reprisals by launching a wave of violent attacks in Algiers, whereas originally the war had been mainly confined to the countryside. After the first executions the FLN issued orders to its supporters to shoot down any European male aged between 18 and 54. This in turn provoked settlers into forming racist lynch mobs and further polarising the situation.

One of the cases that drew most attention was that of Fernand Iveton, the only European civilian to be executed in the course of the war. Iveton, a member of the Algerian Communist Party, belonged to the wing of the party that wished to engage in active solidarity with the Algerian revolution. He therefore decided to plant a small bomb in his workplace, the Algiers gasworks. It was timed to explode at a time when it would have damaged property, but when no people would have been around to be injured; it was simply a symbolic gesture. In fact the bomb was discovered before it exploded.

Iveton was arrested, tortured and sentenced to death. The prospect of any significant number of settlers siding with the FLN was a very alarming one and it was felt necessary to act decisively. And the fact that Iveton was a Communist made it easier to denounce Communist influence on the FLN in the fiercely anti-Communist atmosphere following the Russian invasion of Hungary.

The trial took place within weeks of Iveton's arrest. On 6 February 1957, an appeal for mercy was heard by the Conseil supérieur de la magistrature. His lawyers had had only a few weeks to prepare a case; in an hour and a half 21 appeals were dealt with. Mitterrand voted to reject the appeal.[6]

Generally it was only rank-and-file activists who were tried and executed. More senior figures faced death without trial. In February 1957, French forces captured Larbi Ben M'Hidi, one of the original six founders of the FLN. Army leaders were determined that Ben M'Hidi should not have the opportunity of using a public trial as an international platform. Eight days later *commandant* Paul Aussaresses (who admitted this in his memoirs 40 years later) and his men hanged Ben M'Hidi and presented it as a suicide. When Mitterrand's office sought more information, the army told them that since it was a suicide there was nothing more to say. How much Mitterrand knew is hard to establish; certainly the Minister of Justice was completely powerless to prevent such acts by the army. And of course there could be no question of resignation, or even of making it into a major incident.

When the Mollet government collapsed in 1957 because of internal divisions and tensions caused by the war, it was replaced by a government under Bourgès–Manoury, a hardliner on Algeria and a major rival of Mitterrand. Mitterrand was not in his cabinet, and he never again held governmental office until he was elected President in 1981.

With nowhere else to go, Mitterrand moved to the left. When in 1960 the PSU (*Parti Socialiste Unifié*: Unified Socialist Party) was formed by members of the SFIO left who had broken with their party over its Algerian policy and support for de Gaulle. Mitterrand applied for membership. Three times he applied and three times he was refused. His record in office was undoubtedly a major factor here.

The SFIO, weakened by Algeria and the general strike of 1968, was on the road to collapse. It was Mitterrand, never a member of the SFIO, who managed to rebuild the new Socialist Party on the ruins, drawing in many who had been in the PSU, and who made an alliance with the PCF which was his stepping-stone to power. That his conduct during the Algerian war did not come back to haunt him, that he was able to create his own myths and ensure that much of the past remained hidden, is testament to his guile — but not to his integrity.

Notes

1. Michel Rocard, later Mitterrand's Prime Minister (1988-1991), recalled that he had once called Mitterrand a murderer at a public meeting.
2. François Malye and Benjamin Stora, *François Mitterrand et la guerre d'Algérie* (Calmann-Lévy, Paris, 2010).
3. Compare a total of 767 collaborators executed at the end of the Second World War.
4. Of necessity figures for war deaths remain uncertain and contested, but a reasonable estimate would be between three quarters of a million and a million dead, the great majority on the Algerian side.
5. Only in 1999 did the French government officially recognise that the war had been a 'war'.
6. There is a full account of the Iveton case in Jean-Luc Einaudi, *Pour l'exemple: l'affaire Iveton* (L'Harmattan, Paris, 1987).

Solidarity in Europe

Although the heart of solidarity action with Algeria was in France, there was also significant activity in many other countries. Solidarity committees were active in Austria, Belgium, Denmark, East and West Germany, Great Britain, Italy, Norway and Switzerland. To represent this we are publishing two items, a study by Fritz Keller of action in Austria encouraging desertion from the French Foreign Legion, and an account by John Plant of the Labour MP John Baird, who was heavily involved in support work.

Fritz Keller
Solidarity Action in Austria

The following is a chapter from Fritz Keller's doctoral thesis, and is reproduced by kind permission of the author, a member of our International Advisory Board. A book based on the thesis has now been published: Fritz Keller, *Gelebter Internationalismus: Österreichs Linke und der algerische Widerstand (1958-1963)* (Promedia Verlag, Vienna, 2010). The translation is edited and slightly cut, and most of the footnotes have been omitted.[1]

* * *

By the time of the Algerian war, Winfried Müller already had a life of adventures behind him. Winfried was born in 1926 in Dortmund in a conservative monarchist home. His father, who was of Jewish descent, disappeared during the Nazi period. His relatives sent the adolescent boy to foster parents in annexed Innsbruck for his own safety. In the winter of 1942-43, the 16-year-old secondary-schoolboy was arrested by the local Gestapo for anti-Nazi slogans and monarchist activity in the town. The security service made him join the German armed forces, in the naval artillery on the Eastern front. In the chaos of the German retreat he succeeded in going over to the Red Army. There he was allocated to the Free German National Committee, a committee of prisoners supporting Stalin against Hitler based on the remnants of the Sixth Army which had been smashed at Stalingrad. The initiative had come from old German Communist Party cadres, including Walter Ulbricht, Rudolf Herrnstadt and Wolfgang Leonhard.[2] Together with them, Communist poets such as Willi Bredel, Erich Weinert and Johannes R Becher had rather unsuccessfully attempted to persuade German front-line troops to desert, using leaflets and radio broadcasts.

Like members of the 'Ulbricht Group', he accompanied the fighting Red Army to Germany and was sent — after a short stay in Austria — to Wiesbaden, where he was supposed to build a local group of the Free German Youth. In 1947, he received a grant to study social sciences at the Karl Marx University in Berlin-Klein-Machnow. In 1949, he completed his studies with a teaching certificate for higher education. But in the same year he was briefly arrested on charges of 'Titoism', stripped of all the privileges resulting from his studies, and finally expelled to West Germany.

At first he made a living selling goods for the blind. In search of a future he went to Berlin, which at the time was a centre for all real and aspirant spies. Almost inevitably he fell into the hands of anti-Communist groups who were recruiting refugees from the Soviet Occupied Zone for Eastern bureaux and fighting groups.

He had acquired a new identity as Michael Müller-Samson. But unlike many others he had always attempted to keep clear of the dubious milieu of the intelligence services. An important step was his marriage in 1953, together with his efforts to be published regularly as a journalist. Still in the pay of questionable employers, he had therefore in 1954 in Paris made contacts, first with the MNA, then with the FLN. (He had won the confidence of the FLN when, during a police raid in the metro, he had taken 'suspicious' material from one of their couriers and thus saved him from arrest.) Around 1955, Winfried Müller began persuading members of the Foreign Legion to desert in rough dives and similar places. He also organised a spectacular escape of seven members of the French Army to West Germany.

Since he had also been concealing and transporting weapons, he had to leave the French capital very rapidly and go to North Africa, where under the name 'Si Mustapha' he joined the military wing of the FLN which was working out of Morocco. When in the West Algerian mountains near Tlemcen some German legionnaires had fallen into the hands of the insurgents, he learned from them that dissatisfaction in the Foreign Legion had grown even more. Remembering his activity with the Red Army, he resolved systematically to undermine the 30 000 to 40 000 legionnaires, mostly German or Spanish, stationed in Algeria, through desertion and weakening of morale. By the next day he had offered to meet the commander of the West Algerian military district (*Wilaya* 5), Abdel Khemais Dakhlaoui Boussouf. Two legionnaires who had deserted became his evidence. He was successful and his plan was accepted.

To begin with the FLN only organised safe passages. This meant being escorted by combat troops across the frontier into Morocco, although that had imposed a heavy burden on the guerrilla forces. Then it was necessary to smuggle them across the country which was still occupied by French troops — requiring hiding-places, transport and food — to Spanish Morocco.[3] There the FLN had agreed with the police that the ex-soldiers would be handed over to them. Of course this meant for legionnaires from countries that did not have diplomatic representatives in Spanish Morocco, or whose representatives were unwilling to commit themselves financially, that they would first be held in jail for months and then finally handed over to the French. This fate had befallen above all Belgians, soldiers from the Eastern bloc and Austrian deserters. A revolt by legionnaires in the jail at Nador had particularly impressed Winfried Müller with the fate of such persons. For the deserters who had broken out of prison had appeared in the FLN office and had declared: 'You brought us out of Algeria and treated us well — why must we now live as prisoners under such conditions?'

Thus originated a plan for a repatriation service for members of the Foreign Legion as a regular department of the National Liberation Army (ALN), the military wing of the FLN. It was inspired by a similar arrangement made by the Vietminh. The premises for the office, which had its own letter-head, telephone and rubber-stamp and issued its own communiqués, was in Apartado 243 in Tetouan, the former premises of the Spanish protectorate government.

Si Mustapha became a Muslim, was promoted to be an officer (in the end a major) in the Liberation Army and embarked on a major psychological war of attrition against the Legion. First of all, he infiltrated its second pioneer regiment and its second infantry regiment in Morocco, which France had just agreed to make independent under Sultan Mohammed V.

The population was informed by the FLN of the importance of their action for the independence struggle. Everywhere that off-duty legionnaires went, street traders and shoe-shine boys thrust leaflets into their hands, calling on them to desert. Within a few weeks numerous Germans in the streets of Fes, Berguent, Meknes and Oujda simply 'got lost'. They had understood for themselves that those who wore the 'white cap' had, in accordance with the Legion command 'march or die', a less than 50 per cent chance of survival. Sometimes Si Mustapha and a few stalwart Algerians helped them with their thought process when they enticed drunken mercenaries with 'Come along, comrades!', then knocked them out, tied them up and carried them out of Morocco into the Spanish enclave at Tetouan. As soon as the legionnaires regained consciousness, Si Mustapha presented them with an application form for the issue of papers for the return journey to their German home. Müller allowed himself a few other 'little jokes', for example he even brazenly went to reconnoitre inside the French officers' club. The Legion quickly moved out of Morocco. Eventually even the rifles of the sentries outside the barracks were secured by chains in case they were taken away by deserters. But even at the farewell parades numerous legionnaires disappeared, not wanting to miss their last chance to desert.

Si Mustapha spent 1957 and 1958 in Western Europe constantly looking for supporters for the FLN. The moral line of argument for the necessity of solidarity work in West Germany was presented in the editorial of the journal *Freies Algerien* (*Free Algeria*), published by a working group of Friends of Algeria:

> The Foreign Legion is one of the key sections of the French Army fighting in Algeria. About 80 per cent of the legionnaires are Germans, who in the confusion of the war and the postwar period came off the rails socially. The Algerian people should not be allowed to get the impression that these legionnaires represent the German point of view in the Algerian war. It is the job of all progressive people in the Federal Republic to make up for the capital crime of the German legionnaires by open solidarity with the liberation movement.

Foreign supporters were at this time particularly necessary. For the erection of gigantic fortifications (known as the *ligne Morice*) along the Moroccan (c 1600km) and Tunisian (c 600km) frontiers, made of barbed wire, minefields and electrified fences, was making the penetration of ALN troops into Algeria more difficult. Moreover, the so-called 'Battle of Algiers' had ended with a defeat for the independence movement. At the same time, making contact with mercenaries in Algeria was becoming increasingly difficult. The Legion authorities put a price of 15 000 francs[4] per head on the capture of deserters. Deserters — claimed the French in their counter-propaganda — would be tortured by members of the repatriation service, who were said to be Soviet agents, in order that they could collect material which would be useful in urging other legionnaires to desert. As the Legion — so a further piece of disinformation claimed — was subject to the NATO Supreme Command, Germans would have to reckon with a court-martial after their illegal return to the Federal Republic. Increasingly helicopters were being used in the search for deserters. Anyone who deserted with his weapon (and very few went without) was punished inhumanely if caught, or else was 'shot while trying to escape'. In a few Legion bases execution was carried out in front of the assembled troops as a deterrent, although such a procedure was forbidden even by French military law, since the deserting mercenaries had not sworn an oath to the flag, but had merely broken a contract of service. With each new attempt at desertion the officers imposed collective punishments such as the cancellation of leave for the whole unit. Moreover, Algerian civilians who assisted deserters were repeatedly betrayed by

French agents posing as deserting legionnaires; they were then often killed after terrible tortures.

Already in 1955 Winfried Müller had got to know Reimar Holzinger[5] on the occasion of a visit to his foster parents during a political event in Innsbruck. Holzinger (born in 1923) came from a 'red' railway family in Villach, Carinthia, and also had an eventful life behind him. He had got away from Southern Russia because of illness and then served in the army with a barrage balloon unit in Hamburg, and then was active in various places in France (Saint-Nazaire, Orange, Toulouse) and finally in Bordeaux. During the retreat in autumn 1944 he was taken prisoner, but immediately volunteered to serve with the Resistance against the Nazi troops. His first task was to accost, in a German uniform, German soldiers who were retreating on their own or in small groups, and to persuade them to surrender by pointing out to them: 'Watch out! Behind those bushes there's a whole company of French troops — give yourselves up!' But suddenly, contrary to all expectation a well-organised German unit appeared on the road. Holzinger had to join them whether he liked it or not, but deserted again at the first opportunity. After various adventures he found his way to the Resistance troops again, and at first he was temporarily arrested. After he had demolished all grounds for suspicion, he was invited to commit himself as a volunteer in the French army for the 'duration of the war', which he did.

When the war was over, he procured, from an Austrian wearing the uniform of a French major whom he had met by accident, regular documentation of his discharge from the French army. He was now determined to go over to Italy, adopting the principle: 'So what can they do to me? They can only throw me out again!' So he boarded the train for Italy, but got off again at Embrun before the border town of Briançon. With the assistance of a ramblers' map the passionate mountaineer made his way by hunters' paths and small Alpine passes illegally into the Po valley, where he reported to the authorities. He was briefly arrested once again and eventually put into a camp for displaced persons in Turin. He then hitchhiked via Milan, Verona, Bolzano and Franzensfeste and finally reached the frontier town of Niederdorf, from where a British military jeep took him directly to the front door of his parents in Villach.

Having been lucky enough to get home, Holzinger joined the Socialist Youth Movement (SJÖ) and already in in 1946 he was elected to the Federal Executive. After he had completed his studies at the Graz Technical University, he got a job with the management of the Austrian railways in Vienna. Then in 1955 the competent official was sent to Innsbruck to work on the rebuilding of the railway station. During his vacation he had travelled with a colleague, using an international free ticket and hitchhiking, round the Mediterranean (Switzerland, France, Spain, Morocco, Algeria, Tunisia and Italy). This plan was somewhat obstructed by the authorities in Franco's Spain, who did not want to give a visa to the free-thinking Holzinger.

The key points of this journey had been planned: visits to friends, to a railway worker's family in Paris who had helped him when he went over to the Resistance, and to the members of a Moroccan youth delegation, whom he had looked after in Gmunden when he was an official of the SJÖ. He also wanted to climb the 4165-metre-high Mount Tubkal near Agadir.

To begin with Reimar Holzinger was mistrustful of the politically homeless Winfried Müller[6] with his seemingly adventurous plans. But the two remained in correspondence. Müller kept stressing the urgency of his concerns, since legionnaires from Morocco who had deserted were held for months in jails in Spanish Morocco and then handed over to the French. The obstacles to cooperation were removed by an accident. When he was sharing a train journey from Cologne to Bonn with Hans-Jürgen Wischnewski,[7] the future West German Socialist politician suddenly came across Wolfgang Leonhard, who was on the same train, and introduced him to Reimar Holzinger. The latter took advantage of the situation and asked about Winfried Müller; he was told: 'He's someone you can trust!' After the initial distrust had been thus removed, Holzinger met Peter Strasser[8] in Vienna, in order to coordinate his activity with the Socialist Party (SPÖ).

The theme of their exchange of opinions was as follows: 'Even if our French fraternal party is showing a lack of solidarity and behaving chauvinistically, we must steer in the opposite direction.' On this basis Müller and Holzinger then discussed with Walter Hacker and Peter Strasser in Vienna, to where the railway employee had been transferred back, about the possibility of joint activities. In the meantime, the FLN in West Germany had brought the Algerians living there under its influence. In the Tunisian Embassy a semi-legal representation of the Algerian government in exile had been set up, consisting of Khemais Dakhlaoui Keramane (known as 'Malek') and the later Minister of Religious Affairs Mouloud Kassim (in reality Mouloud Nait Belkacem).

Working together with Karl Blecha,[9] who was then a Socialist Party student organiser, Holzinger put his activities on behalf of Austrian deserters on a strictly legal basis from the very beginning. The SPÖ Secretary of State or Federal Minister for Foreign Affairs Bruno Kreisky,[10] who was responsible for matters concerning legionnaires, and his close collaborator Rudolf Kirchschläger[11] therefore had to be involved in the project. The Young Socialists had positive expectations in Kreisky, who already from 1952 had given training courses for the Socialist students about foreign policy (Karl Blecha and Peter Jankowitsch were among those who attended), and later had given lectures to SJÖ assemblies with the title 'Socialist politics lead to world peace'.

The hopes were fulfilled with the following arrangement. When an Austrian legionnaire deserted, the repatriation service informed the Austrian representatives in Madrid, who arranged transport by ferry from Barcelona to Genoa, from where he made his way home (this route was chosen in order to avoid travelling through French territory). At the same time Winfried Müller had to drum it into the deserters' heads that they had been 'shanghaied' through deception into joining the Legion; if necessary he told them how to invent a suitable story. Kreisky and Kirchschläger thus liberalised the interpretation of citizens' rights, by making the obligation dependent on subjective circumstances. For until then in Austria people automatically lost their citizenship if they 'voluntarily entered the public service or military service of a foreign state'. The only exceptions were people who on joining the Legion were not adults and therefore were not in a position to sign a valid statement of commitment. (In practice this meant that those returning home had to repay the expenses of repatriation, and then like any immigrant foreigner had to have a regular residence for at least 10 consecutive years in the territory of the Austrian Republic in order to get their citizenship back.)

Henceforth with the agreement of the Embassy the Foreign Ministry was supposed to accept the following official justification: 'In order to give legionnaires of Austrian origin who have been discharged or who have deserted the possibility of taking part in the process of identification[12] and present personal reasons which could be cited against loss of citizenship, the Austrian authorities abroad' were supposed to 'be empowered at any time to issue to these persons travel documents restricted to certain times and places to enable their return to Austria.' To avoid bureaucratic difficulties, a leading official of the state police, Karl Reidinger, was likewise involved, who in problem cases approved official assistance in the form of the then police inspector Zwettler.

Together with Karl Tambornino — then an official of the Socialist secondary-school students' organisation — Holzinger produced the *Bulletin of the FLN and ALN Repatriation Service*. He contributed articles of two to three pages. In terms of content there was both general information and reports on concrete activities and appeals for support. Tambornino typed the text onto stencils and duplicated the material in small numbers on a hand-operated machine in the secretariat of the Association of Socialist Secondary School Students. The *Bulletin*, of which no copies survive, was addressed exclusively to a limited list of addresses, including two FPÖ[13] deputies. Holzinger also reported on the activities of his network in letters to Winfried Müller in Morocco. As he distrusted the postal service there, he sent all his letters without indication of sender. But his letters always ended with the formula: 'With cordial greetings, Si Abderahman.' He thus created his own *nom de guerre*.

The team around Si Abderahman worked effectively in the case of at least four Austrians, of whom the 85-year-old Holzinger still has a precise memory today:

1: A legionnaire from Vorarlberg, with whom the trade-union youth paper *Der Jugendliche Arbeiter* published an extensive interview. Here he described how he got a rough whispered message in Arab French: 'Tomorrow, on the Moroccan border, freedom for you!' He believed it, and in the evening after the parade in the barracks yard, he put his training clothes on over his uniform, attached his water-bottle and climbed over the wall to freedom. The simple Algerian peasants didn't ask too many questions, gave him food and drink and dressed him in an Algerian hooded cloak and directed him to a section of the Liberation Army, who guided him through the wire entanglements and brought him to the frontier. (And that, despite the fact that in Algeria the Foreign Legion had, as in the Middle Ages, 'carte blanche' to pillage anything: houses, money, clothes, jewellery and women.) Finally he was driven at breakneck speed to Tetouan, stopping off at a hotel by the sea.

2: A mercenary from Vöcklabruck called Franz Walchshofer, whose fortunes were used by Holzinger in *Der jugendliche Arbeiter* as an illustration for propaganda purposes, with the theme: 'The gate to freedom was opened for all who were willing and able to take the risk in order to get away from the inhumane system of the Legion.' In a statement made in the presence of several journalists and published in the *Arbeiterzeitung*, Walchshofer confirmed what those who knew the French war machine had long suspected:

> Towards the end of my training I was taken with 12 comrades to Sidi bel Abbès to get special instruction. There we were due to participate in an eight-month course, which was kept strictly secret. The programme included various forms of sporting training, the making and use of explosives, and parachute training. We were promised double pay and promotion. It was said that these special forces might be used in France or Morocco. We had to sign a declaration that we would not say anything about the course.

There were also deserters from Neufeld in Burgenland and Pöggstall in Lower Austria.

Four other mercenaries from Austria, with whom Holzinger says he didn't deal, appeared in press reports:

1: The FLN paper *El Moudjahid* reported in a French-language issue under the headline 'The True Face of the Foreign Legion' about the desertion and return home of Leopold Schriel from Judenburg in Styria, in which the facsimile of a postcard from the legionnaire to his former comrades was supposed to prove publicly the truth of the report. (In this connection Blecha remembers the story of a deserter from Styria, which was told to him in 1958 in Tunis by the head of the FLN's press service Ahmed Boumendjel; he thinks he passed on the information about this man to the Foreign Ministry in Vienna.)

2: Another article in the FLN central organ appeared under the headline 'In Austria and Germany: The Foreign Legion is Denounced'. It reported the experiences of two deserters during their escape. An Austrian called Günter Hellmund was deceived by the officers of his unit who held a ceremonial burial and told him that Peter Ohren, who had already deserted, had been murdered by the Algerians. In fact, as Hellmund himself could establish, he had arrived safe and sound in West Germany.

3: Holzinger himself reported in *Der Jugendliche Arbeiter* that:

An Austrian fled with eight others from his unit's night quarters in the Ain Sefra mountains. In a ravine they were shot down with machine guns and other weapons by a squad sent after them by the Legion, even though they were unarmed. He was the only one who managed to climb up a rock face and escape over the mountains. He was pursued by aeroplanes using rockets and phosphorus grenades. Algerian soldiers found him totally exhausted amid rubble, and took him over the border.

4: Hans Lebensorger from Olberndorf near Stegersbach in Burgenland made his own sensation in the press on his return. Not only had he fled to the Vietminh, 'because members of the Legion were practising such brutalities that I, not being French, could not accept'; he had then spent years in North Vietnam, first in an internment camp, and then later as a building worker and an interpreter. It seemed even more sensational to the media that nobody in the family of this 'black sheep', who still faced a prison sentence in Austria, would pay his return fare from Moscow to Vienna (his transfer from Hanoi to Moscow had been arranged by President Ho Chi Minh personally).

An attempt by the Young Socialists to give these deserters, numbering four to at the most eight, a kind of social 'aftercare' was a total failure, as their ways of life soon proved to be totally different. Despite everything, the deserters went to a pub frequented by former legionnaires at 22 Koppstrasse in the Ottakring district of Vienna. And a considerable number of them were once again liable for punishment. (To this day there is still a veterans' association supported by the French Embassy with the name 'Association of Former French Legionnaires in Austria'.)

Before the beginning of the activities of the Müller-Holzinger team, a German export-import merchant called Wilhelm Schulz-Lesum who was commercially active in Tetouan acted as the representative of the German Embassy in Madrid dealing with the evacuation of legionnaires who had deserted from Northern

Morocco. For this activity the West German President Theodor Heuss awarded him the Federal distinguished service medal. As there were a relatively large number of Austrians among the German-speaking deserters handed over by the Moroccan authorities, and since there was nobody there to deal with them, Wilhelm Schulz-Lesum took charge of them. He clothed them at his own expense, made arrangements by telegraph with the Austrian Embassy in Madrid, and provided them with a ticket to Madrid and an advance to cover travel expenses. The expenses could only be refunded after receipt of appropriate approval from Vienna, which meant weeks later. He never expected to get postal and telegraph expenses or any compensation for his own personal efforts. The young Austrians, who had been handed over to the Spanish police by the Moroccans as being 'without papers', were saved by Engineer Wilhelm Schulz-Lesum's action from the painful process of being moved from one Spanish jail to another until they were eventually handed over to the Austrian Embassy in Madrid. For these activities Wilhelm Schulz-Lesum also received in Austria on 2 April 1958 the gold medal of the Austrian Republic.

At the same time and partly in agreement with Schulz-Lesum, FLN activity developed various locations for repatriation.

* In Tetouan, that is, on the western border of Algeria — there was a repatriation office under the direction of Si El Hocine. In a propaganda pamphlet openly published by this repatriation office with the title *German Legionnaire! This Concerns **You**!*, alongside German, Dutch, Belgian, Portuguese and Spanish deserters, former legionnaires from Austria were listed by name and with pictures. For some of these deserters there are documents available in the archives of the Austrian republic about their hearings before the security authorities. Leopold Hager reported to the police command that the escape to Spanish Morocco, where he was handed over to the German representatives, in civilian clothes, organised by the Arabs, had lasted five days.

Adolf Nigl was even more explicit. Together with two other men from West Germany he had deserted from the barracks in Sidi bel Abbès and had set out on foot for the Moroccan border. With assistance from members of the Algerian underground movement they were taken to Tetouan, where the German consul gave them tickets for Madrid. In Madrid at the Austrian consulate he was given an Austrian passport.

Both former legionnaires stated that they had gone by boat from Barcelona to Genoa, and had then travelled to the frontier crossing at Arnoldstein, where the border authorities, having been informed in advance, were awaiting the arrival of the destitute travellers and they were given resources to continue their journey.

* According to the rather vague data given by Si Mustapha in an article for

Der Spiegel, 'some hundreds' of legionnaires of all nationalities were sent home by the FLN across the eastern border of Algeria with Tunisia and Libya.

Like the organisational structures, the number of deserters who actually returned home is unclear. At a press conference in September 1959, Si Mustapha himself said he knew of a total of 27 Austrian deserters, and a year later he wrote in *Freies Algerien* that he knew about 29 Austrian deserters — exclusively over the western Algerian border with Morocco. Both figures must be seen as the product of psychological warfare, for in a 'curriculum vitae' drawn up in 1991 the head of the repatriation service referred rather to 'around 10 Austrians', which according to current research is probably a realistic figure.

What do these activities of the repatriation service mean in relation to the total number of Austrians recruited by the Foreign Legion? Again the data are not available to give a precise answer to this question. If we make the last available total number of Austrian legionnaires from 1958, namely 232, the basis of calculation and relate it to the between four and a maximum of eight documentable cases of repatriation by Holzinger in the years 1959-62, there is a proportion of desertion of 1.7 or 3.4 per cent. With Si Mustapha's 1991 claim of '10 Austrians', the proportion of desertions rises to 4.3 per cent.

As well as with Austrians Holzinger was also concerned with the repatriation of Hungarian legionnaires. This is how it came about. Already the first Hungarian deserter, who had gone over to the FLN, was the underage Sándor Zsovinecz, who explained to Si Mustapha why his comrades would try anything to escape from the nightmare of the Foreign Legion. While official France was still staging spectacular solidarity events with the Hungarian 'Freedom Fighters', behind the scenes an almost perfect apparatus had been set up to oblige every refugee coming from Hungary to join the Foreign Legion. At first Zsovinecz and his 159 compatriots had been promised contracts for jobs in France. Scarcely were they in the refugee camp when the situation appeared quite different. Hungarian members of the Foreign Legion had first of all tempted the exiles with a deceptive idyllic picture of military life, in order to encourage the Magyars, who found themselves without work or accommodation, to sign up. Because that didn't work, they were sent off to a coal-mine in Northern France, where they had to toil under forced labour conditions for disgracefully low wages, from which their travelling expenses and the costs of accommodation and clothing were deducted. And even here Hungarian mercenaries were sent after them, who promised them higher wages and better living conditions in return for signing up for the Legion. But still the refugees hesitated. Finally the physically unsettled men could no longer resist the enticements of their 'compatriots' who travelled by taxi, waved banknotes about and offered cigarettes, meals and brandy. On 9 January 1957, Sándor Zsovinecz and 16 others signed up. In Marseille they met other Hungarians who had suffered the same fate. An attempted revolt was crushed by the military police. Only now did the Hungarians realise what the destination of their journey was — Algeria. They embarked at the end of January. When they arrived in Oran they demanded a meeting with the commander of their unit and protested against the war which they were being forced to fight in. This simply led to them being labelled as 'Communists' and ill-treated. Subsequently they were transferred to the training camp at Sidi bel Abbès and allocated to strenuous excavation work. All attempts by the Magyars to get discharged by writing requests to the International Red Cross were frustrated by the postal censorship and the French military intelligence.

The ball got rolling when eight Hungarians were able to escape from the Legion in July 1957. Si Mustapha had ensured that their fate was known throughout the world, while M'Hammed Yazid, the FLN observer at the UNO, presented the 19-year-old Sándor Zsovinecz's evidence to the international press. The impact in America and internationally was scarcely flattering for a great nation like France, though the Defence Minister declared that the statement of a single deserter was a particular case to be treated with caution.

This positive press coverage did not, however, solve the real problem of the Hungarian legionnaires who — as Zsovinecz announced — had likewise deserted. Suddenly all round the world no state wanted to accept them. Now the 'Freedom Fighters' were merely burdensome foreigners without papers. Deeply disillusioned with the West, embittered and hopeless, the deserters were even prepared to go 'home' to Communist Hungary. But what would await them in János Kádár's state? Si Mustapha asked Holzinger in Vienna to sound out this matter. So, accredited with full authority by the Algerians, he went to the Hungarian Embassy. After some bureaucratic toing and froing he was told that he would have to go to Budapest and make contact with one of the editorial staff of the Communist central organ *Népszabadság*. In fact this go-between enabled discussions, in an environment safe from surveillance, with some legionnaires who had already gone 'home' off their own bat. Walking in a park the returned soldiers reported unanimously: 'They questioned me thoroughly and then asked: "Where did you work? Go back there!"' On the basis of these researches between 10 and 15 legionnaires applied for Hungarian passports, again from the Embassy in Madrid, which they received without difficulty. And the difficulties after their return remained within the framework of what was promised to Holzinger.[14]

During and as a result of the repatriation efforts made by Si Abderahman on behalf of the Hungarian legionnaires, the number of those actively involved in Algerian solidarity work spread to the 'sophisticated part of the SPÖ cadre'. Directly involved with the repatriation project were Erwin Lanc and Ernst

Nedwed from the SJÖ, Helmut Braun from the Austrian Trade-Union Youth and Karl Blecha of the Association of Socialist Secondary School Students — for they all selected comrades in their areas who would steer the repatriations along structured paths and increase the numbers of deserters. How did the young women undermine fighting morale? Embittered with drill, defence and endlessly mounting watch in sun-drenched mountain wildernesses, sickened by looting, burning, torture, rape and theft under the label of 'pacification', tired of endless drinking bouts in various low dives, scared to death of depression, the legionnaires' ailment, which ended up with suicide or running amok, many mercenaries sought contact with the female gender in Austrian illustrated magazines. The preferred medium for this purpose was clearly the *Neue Illustrierte Wochenschau*.

This weekly magazine could be subscribed to at any post office in France, Italy, the Saarland and West Germany. In the magazine's own publicity material there was explicit mention of 'correspondence in foreign languages', and reference was made to 'marriage correspondence', both male and female, from Afghanistan, Australia, Denmark, Canada, New Zealand, Switzerland, Swede, the USA and West Germany. The Vienna weekly enjoyed great popularity, and certainly former legionnaires refer to this publication, which, it should be noted, gave a picture of events relating to Algeria which was favourable to the colonial power.

The selected female comrades answered adverts in this and similar publications. The correspondence began with harmless introductions, which had to be as individual as possible according to sender and appearance, in order not to arouse any suspicions on the part of the officers and the informers in the Foreign Legion. Once a certain relationship of trust had been established, then the female correspondents began to move gradually away from the purely personal level. To begin with, they enquired what had really motivated them to join the Foreign Legion. If the replies implied dissatisfaction with the present situation, then the female comrades expressed cautious doubts about the value of joining up for the glory of France. If the correspondent agreed, which happened quite often, for 'most legionnaires' were literally 'disheartened' after the debacle of Dien Bien Phu, the practical consequences were brought up. Since the Austrian correspondents were always kept informed by Si Abderahman and his friends about the present state of troop movements in Algeria, they could give 'their' legionnaire precise information as to when, where and how he could safely surrender. All he needed to do was to shout 'Long live Algeria' in Arabic. This was the code for being accompanied to the border, then escorted through the closely observed barbed wire fence, which was about a metre high, to safety, which meant, until they were transported back home, accommodation in a seaside hotel, 25 pesetas spending money per day, full maintenance and civilian clothes, a packet of cigarettes per day and free accommodation or invitations to the homes of Moroccan and Spanish families (and also discreet observation by representatives of Winfried Müller, who was very concerned about the infiltration of provocateurs).

With this correspondence device, the female comrades enticed 142 legionnaires of various nationalities into a correspondence, of which about eight previously mentioned Austrians took up the concrete offer of desertion with Holzinger's assistance. In West Germany, a similar project emerged in 1960 in the milieu around Klaus Vack, who was active in the young nature-lovers and as a trade-union secretary. Coordination with the Austrian activists was dealt with by the then federal president of the German Young Socialists, Hans–Jürgen Wischnewski, who was given by journalists the nickname 'Ben Wisch'. (In the two countries the repatriation service brought home, according to their own claims, which should be accepted with caution, by 22 December 1962, a total of 4111 legionnaires, including 2783 Germans, 137 Hungarians and one Korean.)

Indirectly involved with these repatriations in Austria was Peter Strasser, who as a deputy in the National Assembly asked a parliamentary question of the Minister of the Interior, Oskar Helmer. He asked for information about what measures the Austrian authorities were taking to prevent recruitment for the Foreign Legion in Austrian territory, and whether it was true that the recruiters were developing a particularly intensive activity in the camps for Hungarian refugees. He further asked to know what measures were being taken to bring Austrian legionnaires back home. In his reply the Minister of the Interior referred to an information campaign in the refugee camps which urged that recruiters for the legion should be immediately reported to the security authorities or to the camp administration. But when such reports had been made the recruiters had already made themselves scarce. According to Helmer, only diplomatic interventions were possible on behalf of underage Austrian nationals serving with the Legion. But such steps had generally been unsuccessful, since according to the French authorities' regulations about legal enlistment, it was enough for someone applying to join the Legion, if he did not possess a birth certificate or reference, to make a declaration that he was at least 18 years old.

Walter Hacker, editor-in-chief of *Neues Österreich*, wrote a front-page article in which he exposed the recruitment methods of the Foreign Legion, especially the shanghaiing of underage youths. Joseph Riedler, a member of the editorial staff of the *Arbeiterzeitung*, who had made contact with the FLN during the opposition to the World Youth Festival in Vienna in 1959,[15] wrote in the paper a full-page article against the Foreign Legion. In both cases, the wide circulation of the papers ensured more extensive publicity than the publications of the Young Socialists on the question. A widely distributed readership was confronted with information such as: 'Within three months half the Fourth Regiment of the Legion has deserted', or with facts such as the recruitment of Hungarian refugees, which was extremely embarrassing for the French military. For her specific audience, Eva Priester, of the editorial staff of the Austrian Communist Party's central organ *Volksstimme*, reported on the fortunes of the legionnaire Rupert Neumaier, who had been recruited by the French in Vienna, was a parachutist in Indochina, imprisoned by the Vietminh, then went back to the Legion in Algeria, from there to East Germany, and ended up in the shelter for the homeless in Meldemannstrasse in Vienna.

Especially in the case of the Hungarian refugees who had been forced into the Legion, Holzinger tried to get objective reports in papers that would not be considered to be on the left. He sent detailed documentation, with names, dates and sources to the editorial staff. But in vain.

Yet despite everything the French military had to treat the repatriation teams as serious opponents. 'We are faced [...] with a truly large-scale operation, which has been cleverly set up and run by the FLN, supported by Moroccan elements', wrote Colonel Lennuyeux about the repatriation service.

What a demoralising effect Si Mustapha & Co had produced is shown dramatically by the case of two French deserters, who after their training as parachutists were supposed to be sent to Algeria. They used their final leave to escape to Austria. After both of them had presented themselves as tourists and then run out of money, they sought refuge in the men's hostel in Wurlitzergasse in Vienna, and were reported to the aliens branch of the police as destitute foreigners. They were held on remand to be sent back home, but the Austrian authorities decided — as in the case of the legionnaire deserters whom Holzinger had been looking after — that they should be given a suspended ban on residing in the country. After their application for asylum had been refused, since they had not fled from France for political reasons, they were released from custody and looked for employment.

According to internal Legion documents there were recorded, between 1 November 1954 and 31 December 1962, 3400 deserters on Algerian territory. In effect 10 per cent of the mercenary troops had deserted. It remains undecided how far FLN propaganda and the support of the repatriation service was actually a determining factor in these desertions. To a significant extent the legionnaires, already demoralised by the defeat at Dien Bien Phu in 1954, 'had simply had enough of a war being fought with brutality on both sides'. 'Pictures of villages burnt by napalm, of bodies mutilated by grenades, the many victims — it was no longer an adventure. Here death ruled every day, every second.' And, as the author of a 'factual account' further notes, 'many sought salvation through desertion'.[16]

However that may be, Winfried Müller, alias Si Mustapha, could rightly conclude in a bulletin written on the occasion of the end of the fighting:

> Since the Foreign Legion had to carry out the most difficult, dangerous and horrific actions, here some thousand men were helped to freedom, and at the same time significant damage was inflicted on the French war machine.

This balance-sheet of results was also noted with growing attention by the 'Red Hand', a secret organisation, which specialised in terror against the FLN in close cooperation with the intelligence service and other security services. Behind the name worthy of an operetta was an obscure collection of hired killers, scattered desperadoes, obdurate anti-Semites fighting against Arabs as well as Jews, and diehard partisans of French Algeria. On two occasions, Si Mustapha was attacked with parcel bombs in revenge for his subversive activity. A house used by the repatriation service in Meknes was attacked and blown up. The teacher and FLN repatriation liaison man in Belgium, Pierre Legrève, narrowly escaped a packet with a lethal load, and Georges Laperche, a history teacher in Liège, was torn to pieces by a book bomb.[17] Bombings and arson attacks by the 'Red Hand' were everyday occurrences in German towns. When a list of people in the Red Hand's sights fell into the hands of the FLN, including 'an engineer in Vienna', Si Abderahman also saw himself as in great danger. Before starting his motor scooter, he always checked it, especially underneath. Holzinger only accepted packets through the post if he was informed in advance by letter that they had been sent. Bruno Kreisky urgently advised Blecha and Holzinger against travelling to France; according to information from the Foreign Ministry their names were said to be included in a list, jokingly known by the French passport authorities as the 'telephone book', in which all the 'undesirable' foreigners were named.

Notes
1. See also the biographical sketch of Dr Heinrich Schüller (1901-1962) by Fritz Keller in *Revolutionary History*, Volume 8, no 1, pp 114-17. Schüller was a veteran Trotskyist and anti-Nazi activist, who was involved in solidarity with the FLN, and who spent his last years working in an FLN hospital in Tunisia.
2. Wolfgang Leonhard (b 1921) went with his mother to the Soviet Union in 1935. He was active in the National Committee for a Free Germany, then held a leading position at the Socialist Unity Party's Karl Marx Academy in East Germany. In 1949, he escaped from East Germany because of opposition to Stalinism and went to Yugoslavia. From 1950, he lived in West Germany as an internationally-recognised expert on problems of the Soviet Union and international communism.

3. The Spanish protectorate of Morocco was under Spanish colonial rule until 1956, when Spain surrendered the territory to the newly-independent Morocco, formerly French Morocco [RH].
4. Around £15 sterling of the time [RH].
5. Sources include nine interviews with Reimar Holzinger between 2006 and 2009.
6. According to statements by his wife in the biographical film by Erika Fehse (*Si Mustapha Müller — Kurze Zeit des Ruhms*, Calypso-Film, 1992), Müller played an important part in the founding of the short-lived 'Titoist' Independent Workers Party in Worms on 24 March 1951.
7. Hans-Jürgen Wischnewski (1922-2005): German Social Democrat politician. In *And Red Is the Colour of Our Flag*, Oskar Hippe maintains 'He was introduced to me as a Trotskyist.'
8. Peter Strasser (1917-1962) was the former President of the International Socialist Youth Movement. At the time of the meeting, he was a prominent deputy from the party's left wing, responsible for foreign affairs.
9. Sources include three interviews with Karl Blecha between 1998 and 2009.
10. Bruno Kreisky (1911-1990): lawyer and politician (Austrian Socialist Party). Active in the Socialist Youth from 1926; imprisoned on political grounds in 1935-36 and 1938; 1938-45 in exile in Sweden; 1946-49 diplomat in Stockholm; 1951-53 political adviser to Federal President Theodor Körner; 1967-83 Federal President of the Socialist Party; 1976-89 Vice-President of the Socialist International; 1953-59 Undersecretary in the Austrian Chancellery; 1956-83 deputy in the Austrian parliament; 1959-66 Foreign Minister; 1970-83 Federal Chancellor.
11. Rudolf Kirchschläger (1915-2000): in 1958 envoy and Minister with full powers, in 1962 Deputy General Secretary of the Federal Ministry for Foreign Affairs. From 1974 to 1986 he was Austrian President (head of state).
12. With reference to their citizenship with the appropriate office of the provincial government.
13. Freiheitliche Partei Österreichs, Freedom Party of Austria: at that time a liberal party [RH].
14. After the collapse of the 'Communist' regimes Holzinger again contacted the person he had discussed with and was assured that the agreements they had made were fully adhered to.
15. The pro-Moscow Seventh World Festival of Youth for Peace and Friendship was held in Vienna in July-August 1959. The CIA and the International Union of Socialist Youth organised a counter-festival. See Fritz Keller, 'Trotskyism in Austria', *Revolutionary History*, Volume 8, no 1, pp 110-11 [RH].
16. Quotation from Horst Schluckner, *Abenteuer Fremdenlegion — Der Kampf der Fremdenlegionäre in Vietnam und Algerien (Tatsachenerzählung)* (Leipzig, 2004), p 95.
17. See Section 2, Pattieu, Chapter VI above [RH].

JJ Plant

John Baird: A British MP Who Supported the Algerian Revolution

Support from the British working-class movement for the Algerian revolution was not powerful, but neither was it lacking entirely in honour. The name most strongly associated with solidarity with the Algerians is that of the Labour MP John Baird. It is not yet possible to provide a full picture of Baird's political life, and there are good reasons, as I hope this note shows, why aspects of his life might generate reticence in some quarters. Nonetheless, Baird gave overgenerously of his time and energy to the Algerian revolutionary cause, and it seems no more than appropriate in this issue of *Revolutionary History* to record what we have been able to learn so far.

This note will focus on Baird's work in support of the Algerian revolution, and necessarily with his connections with the Trotskyist movements. His friend and Parliamentary colleague William Warbey described him as wearing himself out in support of every worthwhile cause, and here we cannot deal with his involvements with the Aldermaston marches, Cuba, the USSR and China, nor with his contributions to the left-wing press such as *Tribune* and *The Week*.

During the period in which he was active in support of the Algerian revolution, it is now possible to be confident that Baird was a Trotskyist, an active supporter and almost certainly a formal member of an organisation that described itself as the Fourth International (setting aside all the well-documented disputes about the claims to this title). Baird's revolutionary credentials have been fleetingly mentioned in print by John Callaghan,[1] Pierre Frank[2] and Professor McIlroy,[3] and a few supporting recollections have been acquired from comrades Mildred Gordon and Ken Weller.[4]

The founders of *Revolutionary History*, Al Richardson and Sam Bornstein, made no mention of Baird in their volumes on the history of Trotskyism in Britain. Al Richardson's reluctance to discuss on the record what he knew about 'entrism' in the Labour Party is well known among his surviving friends. A little less comprehensible in our present state of knowledge is the silence on Ted Grant's part,[5] who, as this note will try to make clear, had close knowledge of Baird and his activity. Grant was to become the leader of the tendency which was to succeed in placing three of its members in Parliament for the Labour Party, and it would be of immense strategic interest to understand what, if anything, Grant and his tendency were to learn from the experience of having an MP in their tendency, and how what they learned was applied subsequently. Of great interest, but as yet unknowable.

The basic biographical data available derive from obituaries. Those accessible are so similar that it is reasonable to consider that they all derive from *The Times* and the *Wolverhampton Express and Star*, 22 March 1965.

Baird was born in 1906 in Glasgow. His father was a coal-miner and his mother ran a small shop. He seems to have had one sister. He was to describe himself as 'not terribly bright' at school, which he left aged 14. His first employment was in a horticultural nursery, where he acquired a lifelong love of plants and flowers. He was then to follow his father into mining, but, finding this an unsatisfactory occupation, became a postman, and thereafter went through a series of jobs before finding an apprenticeship as a dental technician, a job which sparked in him a lifelong interest. He combined study with work, and won a scholarship to Glasgow University, where he graduated in 1923. He was to retain his licence to practice as a dentist for the rest of his life, and as an MP was often to raise concerns about the dental services available before and within the National Health Service.

His first exposure to political activity was in Glasgow University, where he joined the Liberal Party and became the Chairman of the Glasgow League of Young Liberals, and also the editor of the journal *Scots Radical*. He was always seen as being to the left of the Liberal Party, and nobody was surprised when he switched allegiance to the Labour Party in 1931.

The published obituaries refer to his contesting a Parliamentary election in Cheltenham for the Labour Party before the Second World War, but it has not been possible to verify this from the information available from Cheltenham library. Certainly he never contested a General Election in that town, but he may have been considered by some of its war parties as their potential candidate.

On the outbreak of the Second World War, Baird joined the Army Dental Corps, and eventually rose to the rank of Captain, with which title he was addressed when he entered Parliament. He did not speak much in Parliament of his military experience, but was occasionally forceful in asserting his knowledge of what happened in courts martial and to traumatised soldiers, on whose behalf he was an early campaigner.

In the first postwar General Election, in July 1945, he ran as the Labour candidate in Wolverhampton East, defeating the sitting Liberal MP Sir Geoffrey Mander[6] with a majority of over 6000 votes. His constituents were much concerned about demobilisation, and related issues such as being allowed to know where their family members still on active service were. Very soon after election he spent several hours in Wolverhampton market talking to families of servicemen and collecting their questions. This met with approving notice in the local press.

One of his early proposals in Parliament was for an amnesty for servicemen imprisoned for refusing to obey orders in battle. He drew on his wartime experience as a medical observer at courts martial, but predictably he won little support. He made his mark quickly and had spoken more than a dozen times before many other new MPs had made their traditionally anodyne 'maiden speeches'.

Baird's relationship with the leadership of his constituency party was far from easy. The Wolverhampton Labour Party had established a central structure covering the two constituencies. During 1948, as political activity resumed after the war, Baird was selected as the candidate for the North-East Wolverhampton constituency, and HD Hughes[7] for the South-East. The Central Party faced significant financial problems as the normal run of fundraising activities and affiliation fees had not operated during the war, and they needed to prepare, in short order, for a General Election campaign. They appointed a full-time, paid agent and started to reopen party premises. A dispute arose between the two MPs and the Central Party over financial contributions (of £50 per year) that the Central Party considered had been promised when the candidates were selected. Minutes of the Central Party Executive evidence the frustration and anger of the party leaders at what they saw as broken promises and prevarication. The wretched business dragged on for a year and certainly created an embittered view of Baird among several leading members, and it was not to reach its culmination until he was eventually not re-selected as the candidate. The Executive considered no political reports during this period, and never discussed the performance of either of its MPs.

No more pacific was his relationship with the professional heads of the dentistry profession. The British Dental Association was not the monopoly representative of the profession that it was to become, but was compelled to collaborate with the Incorporated Dental Society and the Public Dental Services Association to try to form a response to the establishment of the National Health Service. Without enquiring into Baird's politics, following his election they had decided to sponsor him financially in the expectation of his support in Parliament. The bulk of the dental profession favoured a scheme in which they would, in effect, continue to function as independent practitioners, paid by the patients at the time of service, on a scale they would be free to set. The patients should have recourse to 'grant in aid' from the government for all or part of the cost of the service received. Naturally this proposal had no appeal for Baird, and he spoke against it in public and in Parliament. The profession was outraged, but Baird had done nothing deceptive. He had described himself during his election campaign as a 'co-op dentist', which should have been clear enough. In June 1947, he wrote to the *British Dental Journal* terminating the sponsorship arrangement and accusing the three professional organisations of conducting a 'political campaign' against him, describing him as not a fit person to represent the profession in Parliament. Voices had also been raised in his constituency to the effect that he was spending too much time on dental matters and not enough on the constituency. The conflict between the dental profession and Aneurin Bevan about the basis on which NHS dentistry was to be conducted rumbled on into 1948. In February, Baird spoke in Parliament in support of Bevan, urging him not to compromise over grant-in-aid, and suggesting that the BDA did not have the support of its membership that it claimed. In this he proved right, as less than a third of the members contributed to a fighting fund set up by the BDA under the slogan 'Stay Out of the Service'.[8]

In 1956, Baird perpetrated what seems to have been a major political blunder. After visiting Hungary, he stated that the uprising was, as the Russians were claiming, a counter-revolution, and that reports in the British press of mass arrests were false. The press of the official Hungarian Stalinist party published an article from Baird to the effect that the uprising was a counter-revolution which had to be opposed. Somebody in the Labour Party apparatus saw fit to have the statement translated into English and it survives in the archives at the Working-Class History Museum. While this seems a very strange position for a Trotskyist to have taken, it was not unique. Bob Pitt's investigation of the Pablo-influenced St Pancras group led by John Lawrence[9] reveals that within the CPGB they considered their role to be that of strengthening the Communist Party's line against the Hungarian uprising. It is possible therefore that Baird's and Lawrence's positions had some shared origin in Pablo-influenced circles.

He was to redeem himself in June 1958 by protesting against the execution of Imre Nagy.[10] The statement, and the change in Baird's stance, is worth quoting as evidence of the impact on the left in Britain of the anti-Stalinist uprisings:

> We signatories of this message are Labour Members of Parliament who have always looked, and still look, with sympathy and a genuine attempt to understand the difficulties and special problems of Central and Eastern European countries following what they believe to be the road towards Socialism best suited to their social and historical conditions.
>
> Even when understanding was difficult, none of us has ever joined in the chorus of condemnation in which the enemies of all Socialism have indulged.
>
> For that reason we desire, in all sincerity and with regret, to express our horror at the execution of Nagy, Maléter and their two colleagues after a secret trial.
>
> To indict them before the world only after their death, thus denying them

any chance to be heard in their defence, we think contrary to all civilised standards.

To execute Nagy in breach of the safe-conduct on which he left asylum, and Maléter, arrested at a peace negotiation to which he had been invited, we think a recession to medieval barbarism.

We believe that the time will soon come when this deed will be remembered and compared with those in whose name it was committed, with the shame already felt at crimes committed in a period we had hoped was forever past.

Not sparkling language perhaps, and carefully avoiding any mention of the Soviet Union and its role, but a clear recognition that the development towards socialism was being endangered by the methods of the leaders of the Eastern European states. Not the language that Trotskyists were using in their attempts to understand what was happening, but far from the language of submission to the Stalinists.

Also in 1958, with Fenner Brockway, he introduced an unsuccessful bill in Parliament to make racial discrimination in public institutions illegal. This did not endear him to sections of his constituency where it was common for working-men's clubs to operate a colour bar.

The origins of solidarity action in Britain for the Algerian revolution appear to have been in 1957, when the Algerian Red Crescent sent a representative to London to investigate whether it would be possible to obtain some aid for the refugees massing on the borders with Tunisia and Morocco.[11] France had refused recognition to the Red Crescent, and the British government showed reluctance to upset the French by drawing attention to the refugee issue. The first responses therefore came from non-governmental humanitarian organisations — OXFAM, Save the Children and the Red Cross. A British Committee for the Algerian Refugees was formed to coordinate the work. No evidence has come to hand thus far of any significant support from trade-union or socialist organisations, nor indeed that the Red Crescent had any expectation of a response from organised labour.

The FLN established an initially tenuous presence, led by Mohamed Kellou in London under cover of supporting Algerian students. The police monitored their activities constantly and applied pressure to Algerian students to concentrate on their studies and not to be involved with revolutionaries. In 1958, the FLN made its first breakthrough and was able to present its case at a meeting in the Palace of Westminster. The first fruit of this was that three MPs, Baird, Stan Awbery[12] and Anthony Wedgwood Benn, visited Tunisia in June 1959 to see the problem of the refugee masses at first hand. Baird's visit was cut short, when members of his constituency party complained publicly about his absence during a crisis over the closure of locomotive works in the town.[13] He had evidently seen enough, however. Both he and Awbery became involved in active support for the Algerian revolution, while Wedgwood Benn attempted to press in Parliament for the government to act to bring the fighting to an end.

Baird launched the newsletter *Free Algeria* with its first issue on 15 April 1960, carrying the subtitle 'Published by British Friends of the Algerian Revolution'. It appeared approximately monthly until June 1962, initially in eight pages and later expanding to 12. It was always professionally laid out and printed, and most issues included photographs. I have not found any information on the volume of sales achieved.

Ken Tarbuck, in his autobiography,[14] describes working on *Free Algeria*:

> There was another publication which I became involved in at the time. A committee supporting the Algerian fight for liberation had been set up in London, one of the main supporters being the Labour MP John Baird, who had been a long-time Trotskyist sympathiser. This committee produced a small information bulletin, and I — along with Brian Biggins[15] — became involved in the production work. During this time the Algerian FLN were setting up arms production factories in Morocco and Tunisia, and were in urgent need of skilled engineering workers to assist in this project. From Nottingham we were able to recruit several tool-makers and other skilled workers who were willing to go abroad and assist in this project. This had to be done in a clandestine manner since it was strictly speaking illegal to render such aid to 'rebels' operating against a 'friendly' power, that is, France. To achieve our ends we had to use a number of subterfuges.

The first issue set out the newsletter's position, which was to remain consistent over its life. Awbery wrote a general introduction to the Algerian revolution, and Michael Foot sent a welcoming message. Baird's first editorial contrasted the widespread outrage about the violent, indeed lethal, repression of blacks in South Africa with the lack of media coverage of the war and the huge refugee crisis in Algeria. He declared support for the FLN and called for their victory. An anonymous article criticised Messali Hadj and the MNA, accusing them of murdering FLN members, and pointing to the need to combat supporters of the MNA on the British left. There were short articles on the development of support on mainland Europe, a theme which was to be carried in most issues. (The solidarity work among German students driven forward by Georg Jungclas[16] for the 'official' Fourth International was never mentioned. Nor was the French state's attempts to suppress the Trotskyist paper *La Vérité* that had begun in 1956. This paper, and its associated political current, supported the MNA.)

The second issue carried a lead article from Brockway, and a welcoming letter from Wedgwood Benn. The editorial and two articles dealt with the prospects for uniting independence struggles across Africa and the economic conditions for independence. A protest meeting in Central Hall Westminster was announced for 24 June, at which Baird, Wedgwood Benn and others would speak.

Baird continued to press Labour MPs into some literary (at least) support for the Algerian revolution. Thus we see Stephen Swingler contributing a very short statement to Volume 1, no 3, likewise John Stonehouse to Volume 1, no 4, and Ian Mikardo contributing a supportive letter to Volume 1, no 4. But this line of development seems to have reached its plateau. Zilliacus seems to have avoided the temptation to commit himself in writing to *Free Algeria*. Baird's best supporters, Awbery and Wedgwood Benn, did not appear in print for *Free Algeria* any more. Swingler contributed a book review to Volume 1, no 10 (April 1961), but no more. It is likely that Baird was sailing closer to the wind than his colleagues were prepared to go. It was rumoured that he was involved in gun-running for the FLN, though no evidence has emerged that he did more than raise and smuggle money.

In the August 1960 issue there first appears the name of Gertrude Elias, though it seems likely she wrote an article on Jews in Algeria serialised over the two preceding issues. She was soon to become Deputy Editor, and later published articles in a number of left-wing journals, including *Race and Class*. The following issue was targeted at the Labour Party conference and called not only for donations from Labour Party branches and trade unions, but also for action through the Socialist International to bring pressure on the French Socialist Party to abandon its pro-imperialist line.

In November 1960 there appeared *Bulletin*, no 1 (no others have been found) of the Raptis–Santen Defence Committee, with an address at 374 Grays Inn Road, London — where many left-wing organisations have found a roof. Baird is named as the International Defence Committee President. The membership of this committee is not revealed, nor is the name of the Secretary who wrote the introductory statement calling on labour-movement organisations to send protests against the arrests to the Dutch Ambassador in London.

The *Bulletin* includes a statement of protest signed by three MPs — Baird, Zilliacus and Julius Silverman, and also Ian Mikardo as a member of the National Executive Committee of the Labour Party. It also includes biographical sketches of Pablo/Raptis and Sal Santen, referring explicitly to their roles in the Fourth International. There is a summary of international protests against the arrests, including Baird's unsuccessful attempt to visit the prisoners and to send in books for them. An article describes the circumstances of the arrests and detention. At this point, the Defence Committee was expecting the trial to take place in December 1960. The whole tone of the *Bulletin* was much more 'Trotskyist' than that of *Free Algeria* at the same time, but even here there are no ideas advanced beyond that of national independence. The future role and status of the working class in liberated Algeria is not discussed.

It was not until the January 1961 issue of *Free Algeria* that any mention was made of 'two European socialists' awaiting trial in Amsterdam, with an appeal for defence funds. The two are not named, though clearly Raptis and Santen are meant, and nothing is said about the allegations against them. The same issue lists a schedule of public meetings to be addressed by Baird and Kellou.

The following issue was much delayed, and Baird pleads the pressure of Parliamentary work on the issue of NHS dentistry and the financial basis for it. The issue consists largely of photographs and statements reprinted from official FLN sources, and indicates indirectly how far it was a one-man operation on Baird's part.

In the April 1961 issue (Volume 1, no 10), a letter from Camberwell Trades Council appears, naming Raptis and Santen for the first time in the publication, and demanding full rights of legal defence for them.

In May 1961, as the Évian talks began, Volume 1, no 11 sets out a position of 'Positive Realism' in an unsigned article which explicitly subordinated all other political, social and economic questions to the national liberation question. The same issue reports horrific war crimes by French troops and for the first time raises the possibility of a 'Nuremburg for Algeria', and sets itself against the French proposals for partition which would have left substantial natural resources under French control.

In Volume 1, no 12 (June 1961), there is a small note on page 8 about a 'Political Trial in Holland', which clearly refers to the arrest and trail of Pablo/Raptis and Santen but does not use their names. The next issue, Volume 2, no 1 (July/August 1961) has two paragraphs, no more, on the same matter, but again not naming the two 'European Socialists' accused. It states that Baird and Zilliacus had flown to Holland to appear as character witnesses, but that the accused had been sentenced to 15 months' imprisonment. Given that they had undergone pre-trial detention of 14 months, this was a minimal punishment, the practical effect of which was to be a short imprisonment. Two other MPs, Swingler and Will Griffiths, had flown to Holland, but had not been allowed to give evidence because they had not been able to prove personal knowledge of the accused.[17] The lead story expresses for the first time Baird's enthusiasm for 'Arab Unity' on his return from a trip to Iraq.

At this point the correspondence between Baird and Jimmy Deane[18] appears to confirm Baird's status as a Trotskyist. Deane wrote to Baird on 3 July 1961, sending some money and stating that 'John Smith' would be in contact to provide additional money collected. A letter from Baird to Deane on 11 July states that Baird had paid for Zilliacus' flight and would not be charging it against the rather small sums collected by the campaign in the Labour Party. Deane wrote to Baird on the same date, with criticisms of the lack of energy that the Fourth International people had applied to the Algerian issue and particularly the defence of Raptis and Santen. Deane wrote again to Baird on 19 August, criticising some (unnamed) members of the Fourth International group and indicating that 'a number of us are looking forward to discussions with you and possibly other leading comrades on these and other questions'. This difficult vocabulary seems to point to the incipient tensions between the 'official' Fourth International of Pablo and Mandel (and in particular their main UK supporters in the 'Nottingham Group' — Jordan, Coates and Tarbuck) and the Grant–Deane group for whom the scars of the 'Lee Affair' had never scabbed over. Baird's letter to Deane of 24 November refers to 'antagonism between Ted and Jordan'. Letters in 1962 deal with Deane's organising speaking opportunities for Baird in Liverpool and Hackney. They also discuss the possibility of Baird recruiting support from MPs for a petition on the rehabilitation of Trotsky. Germain (Mandel) had raised this possibility with Deane. It is clear from all this that Deane, as a leading Trotskyist, was treating Baird as a fellow member.

On 18 September 1961, the news broke of the events following the release from Dutch prison of Pablo/Raptis. During his imprisonment his passport had expired and his freedom of travel was consequently impaired. The Greek embassy in Holland was prepared to issue a visa for travel to Greece but to no other destination. Nobody was under any illusion about the kind of welcome that the Greek regime would have prepared for its prodigal son. A rescue plan was developed, the details of which remain unknown. What is clear from the press reports of the time is that 'a group of socialists', which included Baird and his wife, contrived to obtain two Moroccan passports for Raptis and his wife via an (un-named) 'West European capital city'. These documents, once obtained, had to be delivered to the Raptis couple. Mrs Kirrie Baird undertook the mission, acknowledging that she was less well-known than John Baird and therefore more likely to succeed. By whatever route, she got the documents through to Raptis and his wife, describing it to reporters as 'really quite an adventure'.[19] The Raptis couple were able to fly to London where they stayed in the Baird family flat. It has not yet been possible to ascertain who else was involved in facilitating this escape from probable torture and not-unlikely death. Nor do we know at this point who, if any, among the UK Trotskyists was able to meet Raptis during his brief stay in London. Flights were purchased for the Raptis couple from London Heathrow to Tangiers, where they would be safe, at least for the time being. The actual flight time was tense, since if the plane were forced down by technical problems into Spain or Portugal, or some parts of North Africa, an unfriendly (at the least) greeting might have been expected. The Bairds were at pains to praise the UK immigration authorities in the press for their fairness in handling the Raptis case, and there are occasional traces in the documents of some reciprocation of this goodwill in the handling of Baird's immigration cases.

The September issue of *Free Algeria* reports briefly that Raptis was safe in North Africa. However, the main business was to report the deposition of Abbas and the installation of the leadership of Benkhedda. Baird seems to be unclear about what position to adopt, and his front-page piece approves the new leader's 'Marxist background' which is 'not necessarily Communist'. Believing that an FLN victory is in sight, he cannot for ever evade all the questions of programme. He believes that 'land reform, the Maghreb and the development of the Sahara will give the government a programme'.

Free Algeria, Volume 2, no 3 (October/November 1961), finds Baird obliged to go further. It carries a four-page article in the form of an open letter to the FLN from Raptis on the way forward for a victorious Algerian revolution. Baird introduces him as 'the well-known Trotskyist' — the first time any reference to Trotskyism was made in *Free Algeria*. Raptis stresses the importance of the military and material power of the workers' states in the global revolutionary process. He boosts the example of Cuba, and explains that in the hour of victory Algeria will have to choose between the roads of (Bourghibist) Tunisia and (Fidelist) Cuba, that is between seeking accommodation with imperialism or overthrowing it. He urges the FLN to transform itself into a political party with a socialist programme.

This finds a response in the following issue, where an article from Benkhedda describes a journey through Latin America, and the inspiration given by the Cuban revolution. The Bairds describe their impressions of three weeks in Morocco close to the border. The February 1962 issue returns to the theme of warning against emergent bureaucratic tendencies within successful national revolutions. Diplomatically, Baird expresses certainty that Algeria will avoid such problems.

The following issue of *Free Algeria*, Volume 2, no 6 (June 1962), was to be the last. The war was over and the FLN was formalising the position of the Provisional Government. *Free Algeria*'s front page offered 'in all humility' certain fundamental principles; these were avoiding the danger of bureaucracy, a planned economy on the basis of socialism, clarity of programme and philosophy. This was underpinned by a report from Raptis on the economic principles the new government should follow — most importantly raising the living standards of the rural/agricultural majority, based on redistribution of land to the workers, the provision of credit and the encouragement of cooperative production. There is also an unsigned article, 'The Next Phase in Algeria', which has much of the style of the RSL (possibly Grant himself) about it, bristling with quoted statistics while determined to locate the issues in an international economic context.

But Baird's editorial is titled 'In Memoriam' and faces up to the fact that the role of *Free Algeria* has ended with the war. He reports that a new 'Algeria Committee' has been established, which has not invited his support or participation, and which appeared to have the support of the FLN and the Provisional Government. He offered his continued support to the revolution, and his efforts to the work of the new committee. He urged the Algerian revolution to listen to Raptis and Franz Fanon. It was a sad, wistful end to an admirable period of devoted struggle, and Baird did not seem to get even a polite letter of thanks from the incoming government.

The question of Baird's alcoholism cannot be evaded. It was a powerful weapon in the hands of his political opponents, and may have been used very early against him when elements in the dentistry profession described him as unfit to represent them. Alcoholism is a problem that rarely receives sympathetic treatment; the sufferer is usually considered self-indulgent, weak and contemptible — undeserving of solidarity. Pierre Frank refers tactfully to a life-long illness. Memoirists from other tendencies trend between the ungenerous and the aggressive.

Denis Freney is not atypical, describing his meeting with Pablo in 1962 and learning about his pro-FLN activity:

> Some comrades... had acted as couriers, carrying millions of francs out of France which had been collected among the Algerian migrant workers.
>
> One of them had been a left-wing British Labour Party MP, John Baird. He was old ex-Trotskyist who had willingly agreed to work for Michel's ring of FLN supporters. But unfortunately he was also an alcoholic. One night in Paris, after he had collected many thousands of francs to smuggle to London, he drank himself into a stupor in his hotel room. The next morning, the money was gone. Somehow Baird and Michel managed to raise enough to replace it.[20]

No more charitable was John Charlton, describing the work of the CND group at King's College Newcastle in 1960:

> Because of our large membership we got lots of money from the students union so could afford to get speakers up from London, including Konni Zilliacus, Michael Foot, Frank Allaun, and on one occasion, an apparently

drunken Labour MP, an ex-dentist, who had a son at King's. He successfully alienated the thankfully small audience.²¹

The speaker is identified as Baird in a footnote.

When Baird acquired this sickness is one of the things we don't know. It is possible that he was already a victim when he first entered Parliament. There is a record in *Hansard* that might indicate Baird being drunk in the House at a very early stage.

John McKie (1898-1958), the member for Galloway, had won his seat as an Independent Conservative, having been deselected by his party in 1945 and defeating the official Conservative candidate. On election he had declared his affiliation to an organisation called the Right Club, whose declared aim was 'to clear the Conservative Party of Jewish influence'. Despite this, the Conservative whip had been restored to him in March 1948. He was present in the House, late in the evening of 28 November, when Baird raised the question of amnesty for soldiers imprisoned for refusal to obey orders under fire, which was described as 'desertion' though most of the soldiers affected had not deserted the ranks, just finding it impossible in the prevailing conditions to advance towards the enemy. Baird had just begun his presentation when McKie intervened with a point of order, asking the Deputy-Speaker if it were in order for a member to remark of another: 'Put him out, he is drunk.' The Deputy-Speaker claimed not to have heard the remark, but another Conservative insisted the comment had been made, by none other than DN Pritt,²² who was then required by the Deputy-Speaker to withdraw the comment, which he did. The passage in *Hansard* is too opaque to be completely certain that Pritt was accusing Baird of being drunk, and that ultra-right Tories were waiting late into the night to pounce on what they would have seen as a difference among the left, but it seems the most probable explanation of the incident, and Baird resumed his theme with renewed combativity and coherence. He made his case, basing it on his knowledge of many courts martial to which, as a dental professional, he had been required to attend in the capacity of medical observer, 'proper' doctors being in short supply. But it was a case for the record only, and the House closed its business for the day leaving the distressed soldiers imprisoned.

In the early 1960s, Baird's health was suffering increasingly seriously and he began to spend time in hospital. In February 1962, the North-East Wolverhampton Constituency Labour Party, having jumped through all the procedural hoops set for it by the party rules, decided by 'a large majority' not to re-adopt Baird as its candidate for the next General Election. The local press of the time was unable to persuade any members of the party to specify any criticisms of Baird. Baird identified three bases of criticism — his illness, his resolute opposition to the colour bar (he accused some local Labour councillors of failing to oppose racist attitudes in the constituency), and the time he spent on international affairs. The Labour Party's National Executive did not use its right to intervene in the reselection process, and Baird's base of support within the constituency party was insufficient to maintain his position. (There was, somewhat perversely, a tactical gain for the left in the Labour Party out of the affair. The NEC's recognition of the right of a constituency to de-select a sitting MP was later to be valuable in the struggles to de-select right-wing MPs such as Reg Prentice.)

John Baird died in March 1963 in the Royal Free Hospital, London. Whatever the imperfections of his political strategy, he had devoted most of his life to the socialist cause, and upheld the banner of the Algerian revolution when it was most needed.

* * *

I acknowledge gratefully the assistance of the librarians at Wolverhampton and Cheltenham local authority libraries, at the Modern Records Centre at Warwick University, the IISG and the British Dental Association. Ian Birchall drew upon his prodigious memory to excavate useful extracts and quotations. Alun Morgan pointed my attention to the archives of the Socialist Party deposited at Warwick that provide the most convincing documentation, in the form of Baird's correspondence with Jimmy Deane, of the former's allegiance to a Fourth Internationalist organisation. Fritz Keller's thesis provided valuable European context. All errors, inaccuracies and misconceptions remain mine undiminished. We will try to put supporting documents for this note on the *Revolutionary History* website.

Notes

1. John Callaghan, *The Far Left in British Politics* (Blackwell, Oxford, 1987), p 192: 'Amazingly, since no one noticed the fact, the RSL also had the assistance of the Labour MP for Wolverhampton North-East, John Baird, who must be counted as the first Trotskyist MP.'
2. Pierre Frank, *The Long March of the Trotskyists* (available at http://www.marxists.org/history/etol/writers/frank/works/march/ch10.htm): 'John Baird, Labour Party MP, who was always on our side.'
3. John McIlroy, 'The Revolutionary Odyssey of John Lawrence', *Revolutionary History*, Volume 9, no 2.
4. Ken Weller recalled Baird intervening in a meeting called by the Healy movement, of which he (Weller) was a member at the time, and being identified to him as a supporter of the Grant tendency.
5. Ted Grant, *History of British Trotskyism* (Wellred, London, 2002 and online).
6. Geoffrey Mander (1882-1962) was a significant industrialist in Wolverhampton. First elected for Wolverhampton East in 1929, he held the seat until defeated by

Baird. It was among the last urban constituencies held by the Liberal Party. He was widely regarded as a radical among the Liberals, and was a prominent opponent of the appeasement of the emerging Fascist leaders in Europe and was one of the first industrialists to introduce the 40-hour week. He drew the logical conclusion from his defeat and joined the Labour Party in 1948 and served the party on Staffordshire County Council. He had offered to finance the purchase for the nation of William Morris' Red House, and donated his family home, Wightwick Manor, and his substantial art collection to the National Trust in 1937.

7. Hughes was defeated by Enoch Powell in 1950
8. This episode is summarised in JFL Wood BDS, 'The Battle Over the Health Service: Bevan and the BDA', Part 1, *Dental Practice*, 21 June 1984.
9. Bob Pitt, 'Red Flag Over St Pancras', a series in four parts beginning in *What Next?*, no 7, 1997, http://www.whatnextjournal.co.uk/Pages/Back/Issues.html.
10. The other MPs who signed the statement were Stephen Swingler, Julius and Sydney Silverman, Emrys Hughes and Konni Zilliacus.
11. Fritz Keller, *Solidarität der österreichischen Linken mit der algerischen Widerstandsbewegung* (University of Amsterdam, 2010); and in book form, Fritz Keller, *Gelebter Internationalismus: Österreichs Linke und der algerische Widerstand (1958-1963)* (Promedia Verlag, Vienna, 2010).
12. Stanley Stephen Awbery (1888-1969), Labour MP for Bristol Central from 1945 to 1964. He persistently put down questions in Parliament about the plight of refugees from the fighting in Algeria.
13. *Wolverhampton Express and Star*, 4 June 1959.
14. Available at http://www.revolutionaryhistory.co.uk/ken-tarbuck/autobiography-of-ken-tarbuck-to-1964.html
15. Biggins was earlier a member of the Glasgow-based Left Fraction. As a conscript he was stationed near Nottingham where he became a regular visitor to the bookshop operated by Pat Jordan, and he subsequently joined the RSL. Traces of his history can be found in articles in *Revolutionary History*.
16. A translation of Ernest Mandel's obituary for Georg Jungclas will be available in the near future on the *Revolutionary History* website.
17. *Wolverhampton Express and Star*, 22 June 1961.
18. Deane is acknowledged by Grant as a leading member of the RSL in the 1950s and early 1960s (*History of British Trotskyism*, p 298).
19. 'Real Life Adventure for Mrs Baird', *Wolverhampton Express and Star*, 18 September 1961.
20. Denis Freney, *A Map of Days* (William Heinemann Australia, Port Melbourne, 1991), p 155.
21. John Charlton, *Don't You Hear the H-Bomb's Thunder?* (North East Labour History and Merlin, London, 2009).
22. The MP for Hammersmith North and a notorious fellow-traveller of Stalinism.

Past and Future

The internationalism shown by the far left during the Algerian War was part of a long tradition. To put this period into context we give, firstly, documents from the debate among North African Communists in the early years of the Comintern, and secondly an account of how the radicalisation produced by the Algerian War fed into the mass struggles of May-June 1968.

The eighth condition of affiliation to the Comintern required Communist parties to take a firm anti-colonialist position. But when the newly-formed PCF set up sections in Algeria and Tunisia, they were largely dominated by settlers. Hence the resolution reproduced below, carried by the Second North African Interfederal Communist Conference, which denied that the indigenous Algerian population was capable of emancipating itself. The resolution produced two stinging replies, from Hadjali Abdelkader and Robert Louzon, also reproduced here. The resolution was discussed at the Fourth Congress of the Comintern in November-December 1922, and condemned by Tahar Boudengha, delegate from Tunisia, and by Safarov and Trotsky. See J Riddell (ed), *Toward the United Front: Proceedings of the Fourth Congress of the Communist International, 1922* (Leiden & Boston, 2012), pp 701-03, 719-20, 1000-01. See also LD Trotsky, 'Resolution on the French Question' (2 December 1922), *The First Five Years of the Communist International*, Volume 2 (London, 1974), pp 275-90.

Report to the Second North African Interfederal Communist Conference on 24 September 1922, Adopted Unanimously[1]

The Algerian Point of View

The colonial question is characterised by absolute and inevitable lack of unity.

In Egypt, in Tripolitania, in Syria, in Tunisia, in Algeria, in Morocco, in the Sudan, in Senegal, in Madagascar, in Indochina, in the East and West Indies, etc, the question is posed in totally different conditions, because there are oppressed people who are already now ready for sovereignty and others who are not; there are peoples in guardianship who are now already capable of governing themselves and others who are not yet so; and if Communist duty requires us to give freedom to the former, it requires us even more imperiously not to abandon the latter to their wretched fate; it strongly requires us to serve them as humane and impartial mentors.

So the Communist Party could not have a *single position* on the colonial question.

Now the only precise text which lays down the attitude of the Communist Party with regard to the colonies is that of the eighth condition for affiliation to the Communist International, which puts it as follows:

> A particularly marked and clear attitude on the question of the colonies and oppressed nations is necessary on the part of the Communist Parties of those countries whose bourgeoisies are in possession of colonies and oppress other nations. Every party that wishes to belong to the Communist International has the obligation of exposing the dodges of its 'own' imperialists in the colonies, of supporting every liberation movement in the colonies not only in words but in deeds, of demanding that their imperialist compatriots should be thrown out of the colonies, of cultivating in the hearts of the workers in their own country a truly fraternal relationship to the working population in the colonies and to the oppressed nations, and of carrying out systematic propaganda among their own country's troops against any oppression of colonial peoples.

This text has the defect of being too general, and of being applied indiscriminately to all colonies and oppressed states, without taking into account their specific conditions and the means of action available to the party in each of them, and not indicating an order for the accomplishment of the various tasks it lays down.

In fact, it seems to us that there is no necessary synchronisation of these actions and that they depend essentially on the state of the colonial milieu, on the strength of the party's organisation and on its influence both on the masses and on the dominant bourgeoisie.

As far as Algeria is concerned, if there is an immediate possibility of 'cultivating in the hearts of the workers in their own country a truly fraternal relationship to the working population in the colonies', if there is an immediate possibility of 'exposing the dodges of its "own" imperialists', if there is at present almost a possibility of 'carrying out systematic propaganda among their own country's troops against any oppression of colonial peoples', the same does not hold true for 'supporting every liberation movement' and the demand for the expulsion from the colonies of the national imperialists.

We must adapt tactics to the conditions of the situation, of the social and intellectual development of individuals and take account, in our propaganda, of the psychology of the masses to be reached.

The failure to recognise these necessities can cause serious disappointments, and Algeria has experienced some of these.

The action carried out hitherto by the Executive and by the Communist press does not seem to us to have been opportune and inspired by a proper understanding of all the factors of the problem; hence we have a bounden duty to criticise the policy followed, to point out the errors and gaps in it, since we are well placed to do so.

It is also up to us to provide the party with the information it lacks on the specific situation in our region, and to propose to it the methods which should be used in order to avoid false starts and mistakes which might have serious consequences.

The Algerian Native Mentality

A: The Native Élite: The influence of education has not succeeded in eradicating a profoundly rooted hereditary nationalism among the educated Muslims.

It is in the governing assemblies[2] that we can judge the men formed in this way. Any careful study of their political action rapidly reveals minds that are imprecise, lacking in energy, constantly swayed between their nationalist impulse and fear of reprisals from the administration.

They are thus obliged to conceal this nationalism by exaggerated protestations of loyalty and French patriotism.

They go so far, in order to benefit from personal advantages (paid positions and honours) as to block the legitimate aspirations of their proletarian fellow believers.

In this frame of mind, the intellectual élite expects a great deal from the party's Parisian Arabophilia, while considering the Communist militants in Algeria as very tainted.

Conclusion: The Arab bourgeoisie, by its origins, by the systematic education it receives, by its customs, by its interests as a ruling class, cannot be an ally for us.

Native nationalism in Algeria appears to us to take the same form as other nationalisms.

B: The Masses: Their Ignorance: In the first place, what characterises the native masses is their ignorance. This is above all the main obstacle to their emancipation.

This ignorance is systematically maintained, in the first place by the native leaders, whether administrative or religious, who base their prestige and their influence on this lack of education in the masses; then, and above all, by the government, which, according to the bourgeois method, allows the élite which will serve it to develop, while it is content to maintain workers in a state of ignorance which serves capitalist interests.

* **Fatalism and Fanaticism**: Fatalism and religious fanaticism, which are well developed in the Muslim proletariat, can be mainly explained (leaving aside hereditary tendencies) by the influence of the *marabouts* and the religious brotherhoods on masses who are totally ignorant and entranced with the supernatural.

Fatalism, which has the result of suppressing any individual effort, and religious fanaticism, which is opposed to the assimilation of the race, raise a formidable obstacle to propaganda among the natives.

* **Feminism**: The idea of equality for women and their emancipation, which are one of the essential bases of communism, are not even accepted in principle by the educated natives and even less so by the proletarian class, for whom women are slaves, often of less value than any animal.

The Arab woman herself refuses to grasp the humiliation of her condition. Even among the very few educated native women, there has never been an attempt to create a movement for emancipation as in Turkey, Egypt or even Tunisia.

In the deliberative assemblies, the native representatives are passionate opponents of education for girls. At the General Council of Oran, in 1920, at the Municipal Council of Tlemcen, in 1921, they opposed the setting up of primary schools for native girls.

* **Social Conditions of the Natives: Emergency Laws**: It is not useful to develop this question here. It has been the subject of major parliamentary debates and it was drawn to the attention of public opinion in 1913 by the League for the Rights of Man.[3]

There is a generally recognised fact: this legislation establishes the absolute power of administrators of mixed communes[4] over five million natives. This emergency regime, firmly established, holds the proletarian mass within such narrow limits that it is impossible for it to attempt any action aiming at independence.

* **Conscription**: From the theoretical point of view we should oppose this measure, which obliges the dispossessed victims to defend their oppressors militarily.

But from the military point of view conscription has the following results:
1. To cause deep discontent among the recruited natives and their families.
2. To make them hostile to the government which imposes on them the discipline of the barracks.
3. To open their minds to observation through travel and residence in towns.

In short, in the present state of affairs, we have reached the paradox that it is military service which is the best means of awakening a critical spirit in the native masses.

However, with the purpose of preventing the bourgeois government from recruiting in its colonies an imperial army intended to drown in blood any movement for liberation in the metropolis, the Communist Party has the duty of opposing native conscription; it will thereby show the natives that it is concerned about their most cherished demands and will thus win their sympathies.

* **Trade Unionism**: Algeria is developed only as far as agriculture is concerned, and Communist cells exist thus far only in the main towns.

The result is that native unions are pretty much non-existent. There is no agricultural trade union, although the labour force in agriculture is almost entirely native.

This is one of the most important aspects of the question. In fact, how can we reach all these workers scattered over properties often extending for thousands of hectares, when even the Europeans in the inland centres are totally ignorant not only of the most elementary socialist theories, but also of the most mild form of trade unionism?

Only in the main ports of Algeria does there exist a native workers' union; that of the dockers. These trade unionists, whom we have often seen in action in the course of numerous dockers' strikes, possess real qualities: highly developed discipline, great ability to stand up to physical hardships, which allows the native strikers to 'hold out' with very limited financial resources. This union is moreover the only one through which it is possible to reach native workers.

The influence possessed by a very small minority of Europeans over the native majority within this union proves the importance of mixed trade unionism (Europeans and natives).

Notes

1. From *Bulletin communiste*, 7 December 1922.
2. That is, the departmental and local councils, on which Muslim representatives were in a minority and appointed by the French authorities. Only a tiny minority of Muslims had French citizenship [*RH*].
3. Human rights organisation, founded in 1898 at the time of the Dreyfus affair [*RH*].
4. *Communes mixtes*: districts with a large Muslim majority, but run by a French administrator [*RH*].

* * *

Communism and the Colonial Question[1]

A second article developed the practical implications of the above analysis.

* * *

The emancipation of the native populations of Algeria can result only from the revolution in France.

The uncultured masses, held in semi-slavery for centuries, fanatical and fatalistic, patient, resigned, submissive, imbued with religious prejudices, cannot at present conceive of their liberation: they merely aspire to an improved condition which they believe can be achieved by reforms and by acquiring certain political rights.

Even if we suppose that they overcame their apathy and united their forces which are so divided, and attempted a liberation movement, this would immediately be drowned in blood, for the bourgeois imperialist forces are much larger and better organised than the potential Algerian forces (scarcely four million individuals without weapons or ammunition, without tools and without technicians).

The immediate aim of Communists in Algeria is therefore not to support or arouse such a problematic movement which would be doomed to failure, but to employ all means to win the sympathy of the native masses, so as to prevent them being enrolled *en bloc* in the counter-revolutionary troops when the revolution is launched in France.

To achieve this result there is no need, at the present time, to make open Communist propaganda in the rural Arab areas; there is no need for our press to carry calls for revolt, nor for us to distribute leaflets in Arabic as some recommend.

The publication of the 'Appeal by the Communist International for the Liberation of Algeria and Tunisia' was a mistake, and this is proved by the fact that this appeal was reproduced in the bourgeois colonial press in order to discredit us in the eyes of public opinion, an aim which was partially achieved, *whereas this appeal made no impact on the masses whom we wanted to reach.*

Direct Communist propaganda aimed at the Algerian natives *in the rural areas* is *at present* useless and dangerous.

It is useless because these natives have not yet reached an intellectual and moral level which would enable them to acquire Communist ideas. It is useless because these masses, entirely imbued with religious fanaticism, only believe their *marabouts*; in order for us to influence them we should need influential Arab Communists, whom we have not yet begun to train.

It is dangerous because it would certainly lead the bourgeoisie to launch a major repressive onslaught, which would certainly be successful, all the more so because the native masses, feeble and corrupt, would not hesitate to inform on and sacrifice their best members.

It is dangerous because, done without prior preparation of the European proletariat, which is deeply imbued with prejudices against the natives, it would alienate the sympathies of this proletariat and would lead to the desertion of our supporters. [...] [The article ended with a set of resolutions summing up the practical conclusions.]

1. The French Communist Party, understanding the importance of the revolutionary role of the colonies, will try to develop the groupings already existing in North Africa; it will make every effort to intensify its propaganda and will take on the small burden of nominating a permanent delegate and of periodically sending militants from metropolitan France.

2. The Communist Party will take a position on all questions which interest the native population; it will defend the demands of this population in its press and in the parliamentary arena, but it will not publish in the press aimed at the public at large doctrinal articles about colonial matters and calls for revolt.

3. Communist militants in Algeria will apply themselves to spreading the ideas of trade unionism among native workers and will endeavour to struggle against racial conflicts by showing that the only thing that matters is the international front of the oppressed proletariat against the international front of capitalist oppression.

4. The Colonial Study Group will keep in permanent contact with the colonial federations in order to study questions that concern them, and will always ask their opinion before embarking on any action in their sphere of concern.

Notes
1. From *Bulletin communiste*, 14 December 1922.

* * *

Hadjali Abdelkader
Colonial Action[1]

Despite the eighth condition for affiliation, despite the resolution of the Second Congress of the Comintern, despite the repeated demands of the Comintern Executive, the colonial question seems — alas! — to have been dropped from the preoccupations of the French party.

I should like to interest the readers of the *Bulletin communiste* in this important question which takes up so much space in the thought of the most eminent of the Russian comrades, from Lenin, Trotsky and Zinoviev to Safarov[2] who has just drawn up a draft thesis on the Eastern question and the colonies in general.[3]

There is an obvious danger in leaving the native proletariat of the colonies under the influence of the bourgeoisie and at the disposal of militarism and imperialism, without preparing it to refuse to let itself be recruited to come and smash the revolution if the case should arise.

Believe me, comrades, you must realise that any indifference in this respect is a mortal danger for the revolution in such countries as France, Britain and Italy.

You must realise that in all the colonies the native workers, thanks to the Russian Revolution, are awakening and beginning to rally round and to seek their way forward so as to break their chains.

You must realise, finally, that the colonial bourgeoisie is by no means unaware of this movement and that it is doing all it can to lay hands on these embryonic groups and channel them for its own benefit.

Of course, in order to do this, it puts on a mask of benevolent democracy towards them: it devotes itself above all to establishing a barrier between these native workers and Communism which will be difficult to surmount if you don't set about it in time.

So what are we doing? We should be the first to take the leadership of these groups.

Believe me, comrades, the native workers are more open to our propaganda and our ideas than to those of outdated democracy; that comes from their experience. They haven't forgotten the lying promises made to them by the bourgeois groupings during the war for the rule of law and civilisation in order to send them to the slaughter.

If you really want to make the revolution, you must not only undertake to maintain the neutralisation of the native proletarians, not only win their sympathy, but, by methodical and truly Communist propaganda, prepare yourselves a revolutionary guard from among them, in case the need arises.

You can do that, all the more so because all the natives, from the intellectuals to the most primitive, know that the Russian Revolution has liberated many peoples who were under the yoke of Tsarism.

Some of you refrain from dealing with the colonial question, under the pretext that you are not familiar with the life and way of thinking of the natives of the colonies. Now I am not aware that there is a special Communist doctrine for the colonies.

People will reply that from the tactical point of view it is not the same thing; I shall be told that it is necessary to find an appropriate tactic according to the degree of development in each colony. I'm glad to agree with that. So what are we asking for?

1. That the party should lay down a general line of conduct for its militants

and federations in the colonies.

2. That it should assign to them, *in precise fashion*, the aim to be achieved; to make propaganda and to recruit among the natives and, in order to achieve this to adopt as a platform the immediate demands of the natives, namely: suppression of the *Code de l'indigénat*;[4] the rights of French citizenship for all; abolition of the repressive courts; equality before the law; abolition of the arbitrary administrative measures which impose on the mass of native peasants and workers all sorts of forced labour and constraints which are unworthy of civilisation, etc, etc. The results will soon be visible.

According to our comrades in Algeria, propaganda and recruitment among the natives are very dangerous things. For the time being, I do not want to comment on this way of looking at things. I am simply submitting this fact for the consideration of metropolitan militants.

It is time that Communism should no longer be restricted to a few scattered Europeans in the colonies while we ignore millions of native proletarians who are reaching out to us.

Hadjali
Fifth Section

Notes

1. From *Bulletin communiste*, 14 December 1922. Hadjali Abdelkader (1883-1957) was a French citizen from 1911, and was married to a French woman. A travelling salesman, he was wounded in the First World War, and set up in business as an ironmonger. He was a member of the SFIO and a founder member of the PCF, and was involved with *Le Paria* (a journal for colonial activists, edited by the young Ho Chi Minh), the anti-militarist paper *La Caserne* and the Union intercoloniale. A parliamentary candidate in 1924, he narrowly failed to be elected. He recruited Messali Hadj to the PCF. He was the first President of Etoile Nord-Africaine. He was a member of the PCF Central Committee in 1926, while a practising Muslim. He was expelled in the early 1930s for standing in a municipal election without permission, and became a supporter of Ferhat Abbas [RH].
2. Georgi Safarov (1891-1942): Bolshevik from 1908; held responsibilities for Far East in Comintern; arrested and exiled 1934 [RH].
3. The 'Theses on the Eastern Question' are published in J Riddell (ed), *Toward the United Front: Proceedings of the Fourth Congress of the Communist International, 1922* (Leiden & Boston, 2012), pp 1180-90; Safarov's speech to the Fourth Congress appears on pp 719-22 [RH].
4. The *Code de l'Indigénat* was the set of laws applying to the native inhabitants of the French empire, most of whom did not have citizenship; it was designed to protect colonial authority and crush any revolt or insubordination [RH].

* * *

Robert Louzon
A Disgrace[1]

In a recent issue, the *Bulletin communiste* published a report on the colonial question presented at an Interfederal Congress for North Africa and, it appears, approved unanimously by the delegates at this Congress.

This report is a disgrace for the so-called Communist who drew it up and for those who voted for it without, I hope, having read it carefully,

If the Communist Party failed to make a vigorous protest against this report it would be, according to the apt expression of the Congress of the Communist International, siding with the defenders of slavery.

The key point of the report is the declared intention to *maintain the colonised peoples under the yoke of the colonising nations.*

In the opening lines it is already stated: 'There are oppressed peoples who are already now ready for sovereignty and others *who are not.*' And since the rest of the report shows clearly that for its author the natives of Algeria fall into the second category, that of peoples who are not 'ready for sovereignty', who must be maintained 'in guardianship', the practical conclusion is that the French capitalist bourgeoisie must continue to rule over the native masses of North Africa and to impose on them its 'guardianship' — if necessary with machine-guns — if they attempt to rebel.

This is the most shameless justification for the present state of affairs, it is the most unmistakeable condemnation made of the attempts by the native inhabitants of all the colonised countries, in Algeria as well as elsewhere, to free themselves from the yoke that Western capitalism has imposed on them; it is a proclamation of the right, for the bourgeoisie in industrial countries, to carry out 'primitive accumulation' by expropriation of agricultural peoples not yet subjected to capitalist rule.

Moreover, all this is concealed under the same hypocritical phraseology as is always used by the bourgeoisie to cover up the material interests which motivate it. It is 'in order to serve as humane and impartial mentors to the colonised peoples' that it imposes itself on them. This can be read in all the official speeches… and in the report of a Communist Congress!

Having posited the right to dominate, they have to try to justify it. The author of the report in Algiers applies himself to this task by transcribing the terrible commonplaces which make up the habitual arguments of café conversations among the most backward elements of the European bourgeoisie in Algeria. He does so without noticing that what he says of the natives applies just as much to the French.

The native masses, he says, are ignorant. For certain regions, Kabylia for example, that is untrue. For others it is correct.

But are the French masses well-informed? How many French people knew how to read when universal suffrage was introduced? In 1789 or even in 1848 there were scarcely more French people who knew how to read than today there are Arabs able to do so: does therefore the author of the report consider that as a result the French people was not then ready for 'sovereignty' and that it should have remained subjected to the 'guardianship' of a monarch or a foreign people?

Even today, according to a senator, M Roustan, 'out of 437 000 French conscripts 150 000 had received a totally inadequate education'. Is the author of the report going to advise that the French people be put in 'guardianship' by the German people, whose educational level is much higher?

Then the report points to 'influence of the *marabouts* and the religious brotherhoods' on the minds of the natives. Would people in Algeria be unaware of the influence of priests and monks on the minds of most French people? Would they be unaware that the number of pilgrims to Lourdes and other places are counted in hundreds of thousands every year? Would they not have noticed that during the war the number of French soldiers who did not wear some sort of amulet and who, when they were wounded, refused the chaplains' practice of exorcism, was very small?

Equality between men and women does not exist among the natives. That is true. But does it exist in France? Neither in civil rights nor in political rights is there equality between French men and French women.[2]

Finally! The supreme argument! According to the author of the report the best proof that Algerian natives need 'guardianship' is that native agricultural workers are not unionised! But does the author know many trade unionists among the European agricultural workers in Algeria, and even in France, does he think that the Federation of Agricultural Labourers has a very high membership?

* * *

But above all, how is it that the delegates at the Algiers Congress did not remember that France has been in Algeria for nearly a century? And so how did they fail to understand that if after a century of 'guardianship' the natives are still in the backward state in which they depict them, it is because 'guardianship' is a tool of domination, and not a tool of progress. Prolonging the guardianship will merely prolong the state of ignorance and fanaticism that is described. In order to develop, a people needs to be free from subjection. The necessary but not sufficient condition for a people to progress is independence. To keep natives in a state of servitude is a certain means of preserving the soul of a slave.

As for the accusation of nationalism which the report makes against those natives who are struggling for the political emancipation of their race, it is based on a shamelessly specious argument. It is a specious argument to see all nationalisms as equal. There is no equivalence between the nationalism of an oppressor people whose nationalism consists in oppressing another people, and the nationalism of an oppressed people whose nationalism aims simply to get rid of the oppressor people. There is no equivalence between the nationalism of the English who want to go on ruling Ireland, and the nationalism of the Irish who want to rule themselves. In the first case, nationalism means *imperialism*, in the second it means *independence*.

Anyone who, in order to justify his own people's imperialism, denounces as nationalist the will for independence of the people it is oppressing is guilty of disgusting hypocrisy.

Let us be clear!

A Communist must have a Communist mentality, not an 'Algerian mentality'. He must not believe himself superior to the native because he wears a hat instead of a fez, or because he calls on the name of Jesus rather than that of Allah. He must realise that compared to the native he is a 'privileged' person whose privilege in the last analysis is based only on the power of bayonets, that his situation as a French citizen puts him in the same position as an 'exploiter' as his boss occupies in relation to him, and that should encourage him to a great deal of modesty. Above all, it should prevent him from using, in order to combat the natives' efforts for political emancipation, the same argument of 'ignorance' and 'incapability' as those which are used daily by the bourgeoisie to resist his own efforts for social emancipation.

Communism is the struggle for the emancipation of workers, of *all* workers, not for putting some of them under 'guardianship' by a foreign proletariat or a foreign capitalism. Communism has nothing in common with a politics which is only concerned with winning higher pay and privileges for *French* officials in North Africa, who are proud of wearing detachable collars and having been to school.

Notes

1. From *Bulletin communiste*, 4 January 1923. The article carried an editorial footnote reading: 'The article against which our comrade Robert Louzon protests with legitimate vehemence appeared in the *Bulletin communiste* during the short period when the *BC* was in the hands of the centrists.' This was a reference to the Centre tendency in the PCF, led by Cachin and Frossard, which opposed the Left, which included Rosmer and Souvarine. Robert Louzon (1882-1976) was associated with the syndicalist *Vie ouvrière* from its outset. He went to Tunisia to farm in 1913; and after fighting in the First World War returned to Tunisia in 1919, joined

the SFIO and became a founder member of the PCF. In 1921, he was involved with launching an Arabic Communist daily paper, which was promptly banned. In 1922, he was jailed for six months for publishing Communist publications in Arabic. Expelled from Tunisia, he worked on *L'Humanité*, but resigned from the PCF when Rosmer and Monatte were expelled in 1924. In 1925, he helped to found *Révolution prolétarienne*, with which he remained associated for the rest of his life. In 1937, he fought in Spain at the age of 54 [*RH*].

2. In 1919, the French National Assembly agreed to give equal voting rights to women, but this was delayed for three years by the Senate, and then rejected. Female suffrage was included in the Vichy Constitution which was never implemented, and it was only in 1945 that French women got the vote. Muslim women in Algeria did not have the vote till 1958 [*RH*].

* * *

Manus McGrogan
From the Algerian War to May 1968 and After:
The Roles of Left Radicals and Their Press

To conclude this collection we are publishing an article by Manus McGrogan, based on his doctoral research, showing the continuities between the isolated opposition to the Algerian War and the mass movement that erupted in May 1968.

* * *

This concluding piece is a contribution to the history of resistance to the Algerian War, highlighting the connections between movements of the 1950s and early 1960s, with groups of militants active following the mass upheaval of May 1968 in Paris. It is drawn from my thesis/work on the Mao-libertarian paper *Tout!* and the radical left press in France at the dawn of the 1970s. One aspect of this work examined how the Algerian War, ending in 1962, shaped the outlook of younger militants, breaking them from orthodox left allegiances — principally to the Parti Communiste Français (PCF) — and impelling them towards a new-style *gauchisme,* or leftism, of the 1960s and 1970s, often dubbed the '68 years' in a bid to situate May within the wider temporality of radical left movements.[1]

This rupture can be traced to underground publications such as *Vérité-Liberté* and *Voie Communiste* during the war, laying a path after Algerian independence for subversive reviews such as *Révolution (Africaine)*, and influencing the dissident Communist student monthly *Clarté*; publications that were, according to academics Philippe Artières and Michelle Zancarini-Fournel, the 'theoretical laboratories of May '68'.[2] By 1966, young Trotskyists and Maoists, freshly excised from the 'parent' Communist Party, were active in building resistance to the Vietnam War, in a period of anti-colonial, or Third Worldist outlooks on the French left. The cumulative experiences of a new, student-based radicalism would eventually converge in *Action*, the unitary paper forged in the heat of the street battles of May-June 1968.

Following the seismic events of that year, new groups and papers of different political hues sprang up, seeking to apply, as they saw it, the lessons of the May events. Some of these — mainly those of the Marxist left — also carried the memories, analyses and debates relating to anti-colonial struggles, including that of the Algerian War, at a time when mainstream, conservative France, as embodied by the paternalist de Gaulle, the supine official media, and indeed the traditional left opposition, had buried this shameful episode of the country's very recent past.

My approach is based mainly on a reading of the original papers; also, crucially, on an oral history that seeks to fill the detail of past experience and reveal motivations. Interviewees were necessarily limited to militants who would ultimately create newly-energised revolutionary publications in the wake of 1968. Nonetheless, their testimony highlights an important continuity of left radicalism that ran through from the 1950s to the 1970s, shaped by Algeria and anti-colonialism, boosted by May '68 and informed by the new militancy of the early 1970s, particularly that of immigrant worker movements.

The Algerian War, Clandestine Press and Growth of *Gauchisme*

The question of immigration was the flip side of an anti-imperialist coin for the French revolutionary left in May '68 and after. Put simply, racism and resistance at home were seen as a reflection of colonialism and national liberation struggles abroad. May's Beaux-Arts poster *Français-immigrés unis*, alongside a plethora of multilingual information posters and leaflets, illustrated the understanding in radical left circles of the divisive cancer of racism, and an attempt to reach out to different, multicultural sections of the working class. Indeed, the themes of racism and borders were recurrent during the May-June events, as evidenced during the events in the chauvinist comments directed at student leader Daniel Cohn-Bendit by the government press and, notoriously on the left, by the PCF's Georges Marchais.[3] This accompanied the expulsion of foreign students in a government-instigated hysteria over outside agitators. Similarly, immigrant workers who struck, occupied and demonstrated during the events did so under the threat of ejection from French territory.[4]

Solidarity with immigrant workers flowed naturally from the politics of a layer of '68ers' who had been active in the 1950s and 1960s. Among them were

Maoists Jean-Paul Dollé and Jean-Paul Ribes. Dollé's initial dissidence flowed from his shock and anger following reports in mainstream liberal papers such as *L'Express*, *France Observateur* and *Témoignage Chrétien* in the late 1950s of the brutal torture of Algerians by the French army. From 1960, he read *Les Temps Modernes*, inspired by the work of philosopher Jean-Paul Sartre and encouraged by the journal's outspoken support for the Algerian nationalist Front de Libération Nationale (FLN). Moreover, it was the publication of the Sartre-led *Manifeste des 121*, in September 1960, a declaration by high-profile intellectuals writers and artists against the war and in support of army deserters, in the small journal *Vérité-Liberté*, that appealed most to Dollé:

> The *Manifeste des 121* was decisive for me. The impact was enormous, it gave me heart… Sartre was really well-known, and there were others: people I trusted, intellectual authorities. At the time there was nothing for the young people who were interested in Algeria, no protection. No party would help us, we were alone. The only ones who helped us were 'the intellectuals', so this movement of the 121 was like a breath of fresh air. I felt we were no longer alone. It had an enormous mobilising effect, a tremendous impact on youth morale.[5]

Indeed, the intervention of anti-war left intellectuals, in particular Sartre, in the public domain, would set a precedent for the far left's turn to prominent intellectuals and personalities in the early 1970s. Sartre assumed the nominal directorship of the Maoist *La Cause du Peuple* and *Tout!* and the semi-Trotskyist *Révolution* in this later period. The 1960 manifesto further provided a model for the *Manifeste des 343* of 1971, a cornerstone of the modern women's liberation movement.[6] The intellectuals' stance, fortified by their political and moral standing in the country, thus constituted a protective barrier against the state's censorial intentions throughout the '68 years.

The impact of the *Manifeste* was decisive. Dollé subsequently came into close contact with a secret support network for the FLN. He denotes the declaration as a turning point in not just his own, but a general political orientation, a rupture with the parliamentary left, the birth of a radical left, *gauchisme*:

> [*Le Manifeste*]… had prepared us for an anti-institutional position, as it was an act of transgression. We had a right to insubordination… and that's a big word. It demolished what was seen as legitimate. I think it was central to what happened next, in other words the establishment of a libertarian, almost insurrectional culture. It led to what we know as the *gauchistes*; we were more or less born then. We could do things outside of the left parties, we could have a radical anti-politician position. I held the Socialist Party in contempt,

because of Algeria. And the PCF was still Stalinist, they did nothing for peace in Algeria… they didn't have a clear position on decolonisation.[7]

This early *gauchiste* culture was circumscribed by the state's banning of critical or pro-FLN publications, foremost of which was Henri Alleg's *La Question*, instilling a clandestine atmosphere in the anti-war movement. However, as the historian of French resistance to the Algerian War, Martin Evans, argues, 'suppression of this nature quickly became a dynamic element in the growth of opposition'.[8] Journalist Jean-Paul Ribes, then a student and supporter of Algerian independence, later a contributor to pro-immigrant and counter-cultural magazines, confirms this analysis. He recalls his time as a *porteur de valise* — a carrier of suitcases containing FLN documents and/or money — and as a seller of banned newspapers:

> *Vérités-Pour* was created by a little group of anti-colonialists. One of those responsible was a very committed Christian called Robert Barrat… he asked for our help to sell this clandestine paper… I was a *porteur de valise*, carried a valise of banned papers. People came to see our little team, asking: 'Have you got the latest issue of…?' We were sellers of papers that had been suppressed. The security was poor but it was an essential part of our political education… At the same time, we carried out the missions given to us, we got people into the networks.[9]

Papers and bulletins such as *Vérités-Pour, Témoignages et Documents* and *La Voie Communiste* grew from the late 1950s, combining political critique with news reports, and providing an informational milieu for both *porteurs de valise* and open anti-war activists. Indeed, Simon Blumenthal of the dissident communist *Voie Communiste* group, prolonged an underground activity at his print-shop, producing the papers of numerous *gauchiste* groups after 1968, notably *La Cause du Peuple* and *Vive la Révolution*. Similarly, the radical bookshop *La Joie de Lire*, situated in the middle of the Latin Quarter and run by François Maspero, was a hub of leftist literature and activity during the Algerian War. Indeed, Maspero Editions published the classic anti-colonial text *The Wretched of the Earth* by Frantz Fanon (with a preface by Sartre) in 1961, as well as other anti-war material that would incur state bans. Maspero's became the leftist bookshop *par excellence*, providing a wealth of radical literature and meeting place for myriad French and international activists before, during and after 1968.

Underground papers and seditious manifestoes were the literary appendages of a growing anti-Algerian War street movement. A Young Communist in the late 1950s, and later leader of and presidential candidate for the Trotskyist Ligue Communiste in 1969, Alain Krivine joined the Jeune Résistance network in 1959.

In fact it was the work of the Trotskyists within Jeune Résistance in subverting the French army's war effort that drew Krivine in. He helped to organise safe passage to Switzerland for army deserters, and distributed leaflets to soldiers on trains bound for Marseille, where the army's embarkation for Algeria took place. Like Dollé, Krivine today sees the rebellion around Algeria as seminal to forthcoming movements:

> So those were the very beginnings of what would later be called the far left... it brought together several hundred young people. It was an awakening for me. At the same time, I was still officially a member of the Communist Students; but the leadership didn't know about my clandestine activity.[10]

October 1960 saw the anti-war movement break into the open when some 15 000 demonstrated against the war in Paris. A genuinely popular movement had emerged in resistance to the war, centred on the student union UNEF following its campaign against student conscription. This overt opposition, with a new repertoire of street-fighting tactics, foreshadowed the creation of the Front Universitaire Antifasciste (FUA), which existed to counter the threat of the far-right Organisation de l'Armée Secrète (OAS) and its hangers-on, following the April 1961 generals' putsch in Algiers. It was the FUA, with the Comité Anti-colonialiste, that organised a protest over the massacre of hundreds of Algerians by the Paris police on 17 October 1961.[11] Comprised of Trotskyists, members of the Parti Socialiste Unifié, Young Communists, Christians and others on the student left, the FUA employed a rhetoric and propaganda that were openly revolutionary, its aim physically to confront, and ideologically to defeat the young fascists and militarists who had also emerged in the wake of the OAS. According to Krivine, the front could regularly mobilise large numbers against open fascist activity in Paris:

> Several hundred of us would meet in the courtyard of the Sorbonne to discuss what to do; we had people riding round town on scooters, and as soon as we got word that pro-OAS or other leaflets were being given out, we'd go down there and — boom! — we smashed it up; we cleaned up the Latin Quarter.[12]

Krivine again speaks of the Communist Party leadership's distance from the street radicalism, via the notion that they 'supported us, without supporting it, and still somehow supported it', an ambivalence that would fuel his own and many other *gauchiste* ruptures from the PCF in the months and years to come.

Third Worldism, *Clarté* and the Break from the PCF

The itineraries of Krivine, Ribes, Dollé and the 'left of the left' would diverge following Algerian Independence. Some rejected Soviet Communism, dubbing it 'revisionism' and moved closer to the Chinese model; Dollé speaks of the Chinese '25-point letter' returning to a revolutionary position.[13] Others like Krivine gravitated towards Trotskyism, the expression of a more open anti-Stalinism. The fight against colonialism, then imperialism, attracted some to Cuba and support for the new Castro regime. Dollé was one of a number who moved to Algeria for a period following independence — part of a wave of young leftists and pro-Algerian French sympathisers sometimes dubbed *pieds rouges*, an ironic take on *pieds noirs*, to offer their services to the newly-liberated country.[14] In Algiers, Dollé collaborated on the Third Worldist paper *Révolution Africaine* with the 'pro-Chinese' lawyer Jacques Vergès and the anarchist cartoonist Siné; the latter had helped transport FLN members clandestinely prior to independence, and was a regular visitor to Algeria in subsequent years,[15] designing the logos and artwork for the Algerian petrochemical industry, Sonatrach, in 1967.

One of the ideological battlegrounds for these realignments was at the Communist student (UEC) paper *Clarté*, in the early 1960s; *Clarté* can be seen as a forerunner of *Action* and the radical press of the early 1970s, for its revolution in journalistic form and content. The then editor, Jean Schalit, describes a growing internal divergence with PCF conservatism over the Algerian War:

> The PCF had very conservative positions on the war. They said: 'You can't shock people.' They were [even] quite colonialist. Their slogan at the time was 'Peace in Algeria', whereas we were starting to think and reason for Algerian independence. The Algerians wanted their independence and the French party said: 'No, the slogan is too vanguardist, we can't be too *gauchiste*, we have to have peace in Algeria.' So there was already some discord. Then, gradually, we saw that as an independent organisation, we could think for ourselves… We were more open to the world, we'd become the biggest paper in the Latin Quarter. Everyone read us.[16]

Schalit, later editor of May '68's 'paper of the movement', *Action*, takes credit for training a generation of journalists, citing future *Libération* editor Serge July and *Actuel* writers Michel-Antoine Burnier and Bernard Kouchner as active members of the editorial team at *Clarté*. These were the so-called *italiens*, admirers of the Partito Comunista Italiano (PCI), initially the strongest oppositional current in the UEC before the Trotskyist Jeunesses Communistes Révolutionnaires (JCR) and the Maoist Union des Jeunesses Communistes Marxistes-Léninistes (UJC(ml)) took shape and the internal opposition was ultimately expelled from the parent organisation in 1965-66.

Clarté's 'openness' encompassed cultural questions, including travel, jazz, literature, theatre and, particularly, film. The journal championed the New

Wave of French cinema and carried regular contributions by the latest directors including Jean-Luc Godard, Claude Chabrol and François Truffaut. There was space for discussion of delicate social and personal matters, issues like sexuality, with unprecedented articles such as 'Is it Good to Flirt?', cutting through the period's (and the party's) moral and sexual conservatism. Furthermore, Schalit transformed *Clarté* from a standard black-and-white information sheet into a colourful graphic magazine. This was partly achieved by approaching famous painters, who agreed to donate pieces of artwork in solidarity; the paintings would grace the cover of *Clarté*, and the further sale of each piece would raise the necessary money to pay for a colour paper. Thus Schalit obtained covers for the journal from, amongst others, Fernand Léger, Pablo Picasso, Georges Braque and Marc Chagall.

Clarté would also publish the sketches of Siné, probably the foremost anti-war cartoonist of the Algerian War period. His work then included, amongst others, the parachutists' torture of Algerian militants, provocative cartoons alternately published and rejected by *L'Express* and other mainstream publications. In 1962, following Algeria's declaration of independence, Siné quit *L'Express* and launched *Siné Massacre*, a journal of caustic caricature attacking de Gaulle, the returning Franco-Algerian *pieds noirs*, the OAS, racism and French colonialism. These thematic sketches would resurface in another impromptu Siné-led publication, *L'Enragé*, during May '68. The government's prosecution of the artist, for each of the nine issues of *Siné Massacre*, underlined an authoritarian intolerance of dissent, particularly with regards to the impugning of the President and the figureheads of the French army, a provocative dissident practice that would endure well into the 1970s.[17]

Vietnam and May '68

Although there are few direct references to Algeria and the war in the radical literature, the leaflets, posters, papers, pamphlets, etc, of the May-June events of 1968, the intervening period had seen the growth of a more widespread militant opposition to the Vietnam War, again centred on the student movement, again employing street-fighting tactics (increasingly, besides the far right, with the police) and again, through its open support for the Vietnamese NLF, in contradistinction to the mild anti-war stance of the parliamentary left, especially the PCF, who reprised their earlier Algerian slogan with 'Peace in Vietnam'. May '68's student movement was imbued with the anti-imperialist language and action reflexes inherited from the resistance to French colonialism in Algeria.

Indeed it was the leftist 'commando' attack on a Paris American Express office, symbolic of American imperialism, in early 1968, that prompted the arrests of student activists, leading to the student occupation at the University of Nanterre and the creation of the 22 March movement. As is now commonly agreed among historians, Nanterre provided the spark (the students referred to themselves as 'the detonator') for the mass explosion of May, which saw student riots and a generalised strike of up to 10 million workers paralyse the country and almost topple de Gaulle.[18]

Rushed out by Schalit within days of the first street-fighting, his paper *Action* encapsulated the spirit of the street movement and occupations. Among Schalit's strongest collaborators were Siné and Dollé, supplying caricatures and articles respectively, while groups like Krivine's Jeunesses Communistes Révolutionnaires sold *Action* alongside their own publications. Its reports reflected the resurgent revolutionary left's internationalism and continued support for Third World national liberation struggles, in particular Vietnam. Furthermore, as the unofficial 'paper of the movement', it brought together writers, artists and activists from across the socialist and anarchist spectrums and so reflected a variety of views whilst retaining a clear revolutionary outlook. Alongside the posters of the Beaux-Arts, *Action* advertised, documented and helped build the unfolding movement of action committees and occupations. The paper simultaneously railed against a dictatorial de Gaulle and a rampantly violent police force, recalling the brutality of the colonial era and its repercussions in metropolitan France. References to past instances of police brutality were commonplace in the output of May '68, but did not necessarily elaborate on relevant wider questions, such as the Algerian War. Not until the early 1970s, in the context both of domestic workers' movements and Middle Eastern struggles, were the links to France's colonial past made more explicit.

New Immigrant Movements and *Le Paria*

Radical left outlooks on the development of immigrant struggles were rooted in the recognition of immigrant workers' involvement in 1968's general strike. In the 1970 film *On vous parle de Flins* (*We're Speaking of Flins*), Algerian writer Kateb Yacine explains:

> Immigrant workers were up front in the May '68 demonstrations. They acted spontaneously because they were the most exploited, and were most interested in the revolutionary explosion. But there was no way of organising them. They didn't have their own organisations in the French workers' movement.[19]

Furthermore, immigrants lacked a voice in the press. Not until 1970, with a number of scandals relating to the exploitation and death of immigrants, did the dailies begin seriously to address the issue. One instance was the Aubervilliers hostel fire, in which six African workers died through asphyxiation. The desperate living conditions of migrant workers received a hitherto unseen level of media coverage following the tragedy, prompting Prime Minister Jacques Chaban-Delmas to visit, then commit himself to erase the vast *bidonvilles* (shanty towns) of French cities.[20] On the other hand, the far left sought to build out of the angry protests against racism, sections — principally Maoist — prioritising the largely non-unionised, 'overexploited', yet growing immigrant workforce. By 1970, this was estimated at three million strong, with 650 000 believed to be living in the sprawling *bidonvilles*.[21]

The first paper to emerge which exclusively addressed these questions was the *gauchiste Le Paria*. Named after the 1922 Communist publication of Ho Chi Minh, then an immigrant in Paris, *Le Paria* sought to promote discussion, exchange experiences, and 'analyse the concrete forms imperialism takes in France'.[22] Then a Maoist sympathiser and contributor to *Le Paria*, Jean-Paul Ribes explains:

> How did *Le Paria* come about? It was a mix of the heritage of internationalist solidarity we showed in the 1960s by organising support networks during the Algerian war; Third Worldism, solidarity with peoples who wanted to free themselves… and the May '68 aspect saying we'll no longer tolerate any kind of exploitation, we're fighting back. It was no accident that the group came together in memory of 17 October… and chose as its name the title that Ho Chi Minh gave to his paper when he was in Paris.[23]

In referencing the massacre of 17 October 1961 as a factor in eventual Algerian independence, *Le Paria* dwelt on the heroic aspect of mass Algerian protests in defiance of the French authorities, rather than the scandalous tragedy and cover-up the event ought to represent.[24] A Maoist-influenced approach was further evidenced in *Le Paria*'s conduct of investigations in the run-down *foyers* and *bidonvilles*, and the paper's habitual denunciation of the PCF.[25] However, Ribes indicates that the spirit of *Le Paria* was to go beyond a Maoist theorisation of the role of immigrant workers, to get closer to real immigrants' lives.[26] A libertarian link could be deduced from the prominent anarchist Daniel Guérin's directorship of the paper, and its affinity with *Défense Active*, an anti-repression group linked to the 22 March movement of 1968, its bulletin at the service of struggling immigrants.

Despite its low profile and small circulation of 500 to 1000, *Le Paria* ran off 150 000 copies of supplements in January 1970 in response to the Aubervilliers deaths and the resulting occupation of the headquarters of the French employers' federation in Paris. Here, the paper made copious use of the protestors' banner and graffiti slogans — 'Down with slave-drivers, the bosses are killers' — in French, Spanish and Arabic to drive home its approval of the direct action.

A February issue focused on the exploitation of immigrants in housing and related a successful campaign of African workers against the extortions and deprivations of the Ivry *foyer*. Another headline insisted on *Le Paria*'s mission: 'To Expose the Class Enemy of all French and Immigrant Workers: The Imperialist Bourgeoisie'.[27] Much of the discussion was taken up with how to overcome specific workplace divisions between French and foreign workers, denouncing the mechanisms by which the police and employers controlled the situation and the movements of immigrants.[28]

New Arab Struggles in France: Palestine and the Mouvement des Travailleurs Arabes

Maoists and Trotskyists were active in the setting up of *Comités Palestine* in the wake of Black September 1970, along with a number of Arab students in Paris. A first action involved the defence of a PLO delegate who had come to speak at the Parisian faculty of Censier, against a commando-style attack by the Zionist group Beta, and cited as another example of 1968 leftists' street-fighting prowess.[29] Militants of the Sartre-backed Gauche Prolétarienne (GP) combined with some Arab workers on the issue of Palestine and together pushed for an action outside the Chausson factory in Gennevilliers, where the immigrant presence was strong. This was among the first steps taken by young Arab militants in the direction of immigrant self-organisation, built through leafleting at the factory gates as much as in the *foyers*, hotels and cafés frequented by Arab workers. By February 1971, a pro-Palestinian public meeting at the Mutualité would attract hundreds of immigrant workers. Former Tunisian student Saïd Bouziri explains:

> It was a real breakthrough because for the first time a majority of foreign workers had come together to lend their support for an external cause (the 'Palestinian revolution') and at the same time express their involvement in struggles to improve working and living conditions here in France.[30]

The Black September-initiated committees gave way to *Comités Palestine* in April, part-modelled on the pre-1968 Vietnam committees and built through some of the older Algerian support networks animated by a Maoist stalwart, Gilbert Mury.

The 1970-71 *Comités Palestine* were an important catalyst for immigrant organisation.[31] As one of the organisers, Tunisian Saïd Bouziri, felt an affinity for the loose Maoist spontaneist drive for autonomy, the language of new identity movements that sprang up in the early 1970s:

> It was the idea of autonomy and the movements... For me, leaders had to

come from the movements, for the youth..., gays too... This is what allowed us to dissolve the Palestinian support committees, to create groups to go to the masses.[32]

One of a number of immigrant GP Maoist sympathisers, Bouziri co-founded the Mouvement des Travailleurs Arabes (MTA) in 1972, bringing together Arab immigrants involved in disparate anti-racist campaigns. As a first, symbolic protest over the murder of Maghrebi worker Mohammed Diab in a police station in December 1972, the MTA marched through the Paris boulevards to the Rex cinema where the police massacre of Algerians had taken place on 17 October 1961. The terrible events of that day were instrumentalised by the MTA as part of its mobilising repertoire, in a context of increasing attacks on Arab and in particular Algerian workers in France in the early 1970s — a situation that ultimately led the Boumediène regime in Algiers to halt emigration to France.

Appearing for the first time in 1973, the Arabic-French-language paper of the MTA, *La Voix des Travailleurs Arabes*, also known as *Al Assifa*, called for the establishment of 'popular writing committees' to provide the news it needed. An October issue highlighted the convergence of immigrant themes following a spate of vicious racist attacks that occurred in Marseille:

> This paper comes to the workers at an important time, when Arab workers are rising up *en masse* though strikes and demonstrations in self-defence. At a time when the racists and fascists want to take away their right to express their hopes and concerns, that's why it's so important for Arab workers to have their own paper.[33]

Bouziri speaks of the 'very spontaneous' movement in Paris that rose in segue with the Marseille strike. The MTA acted as an informational network, then an organising forum to pull out immigrant workers in construction sites and 'hundreds of factories' including the bastion of Citroën, in the capital.[34] *La Voix* was unequivocal on the independence of immigrant action: 'We've been able to lead a movement ourselves, without a shepherd.'[35]

Other immigrant papers incorporated resistance to the oppression of immigrants into their native oppositional polemics. These included the Tunisian *El Amel Tounsi*, *Al-Jaliya* of Moroccan nationalists, the Portuguese anti-colonial *Camarada,* and Grenoble's *O Alarme*, all of varying print quality and often mimeographed and stapled. The paucity of immigrant means spelt a temporary existence for most of these bulletins, and therefore a need for bilingual leaflets and posters to generate rapid support for particular campaigns.

Conclusion

It is fitting that in the fiftieth year of Algerian Independence we should celebrate the role played by the French far left in that struggle. Indeed, as I have tried to show, it was a two-way relationship: Algerians fighting for national liberation inspired new political currents in metropolitan France and so helped shape the events of 1968. Furthermore, it is not simply because we can re-establish the connections between the Algerian War with movements against the Vietnam War, May 1968 and beyond, that this article has been written, but because there is a persistent urgency to restore radical and revolutionary history against the wall of silence, suppression and distortion of memory imposed by the Establishment.

Lest we forget, the French state only recognised the battle for Algeria as a war in 1999, having formerly denoting it only as 'the events…'. Debates over the role of the French army in the torture of both Algerian activists and civilians, resurfaced around 2000 with the publication of interviews with ex-FLN militant Louisette Ilghariz, and the candid, disgracefully unapologetic admissions of French generals Aussaresses, Bigeard and Massu. It appears that a renewed attempt by some French intellectuals to force the French state into recognition of its role in torture has come to nothing.[36] Meanwhile, despite coming to public attention during the trial of the war criminal and subsequent Paris police prefect Maurice Papon, the massacre of 17 October 1961 has receded again from the public domain, kept alive only in the publications and memorials of Algerians and the French radical and libertarian left, despite recent authoritative studies on the subject by historians such as Jean-Luc Einaudi, Pierre Vidal-Naquet, James House and Neil MacMaster.

Former President Jacques Chirac's botched attempts in 2005 to have the 'positive legacy' of French colonialism taught in schools highlight the continuing arrogance and mendacity of the state in its reconstruction of the past, and the continuing, spiteful trampling on the memory of the Algerian War. It reminds us of the work that we must continue to carry out to restore the true history and legacy of this struggle for national liberation.

Sources

Papers
Action
Al-Assifa (*La Voix des Travailleurs Arabes*)
La Cause du Peuple
Clarté
Le Paria

Tout!
Vérité-Liberté

Interviews

Saïd Bouziri, Paris, 27 November 2008
Jean-Paul Dollé, Paris, 22 December 2008
Jean-Paul Ribes, Maule, 5 October 2007
Alain Krivine, *France Culture*, 15 December 2011
Jean Schalit, Paris, 10 February 2008
Siné, Paris, 24 January 2008
Michel Wlassikoff, Paris, 2 April 2009

Notes

1. See for instance Geneviève Dreyfus-Armand *et al*, *Les Années 68: Le temps de la contestation* (second edition, Complexe, Paris, 2008).
2. Philippe Artières and Michele Zancarini-Fournel, *68: une histoire collective* (La Découverte, Paris, 2008), p 76.
3. The PCF leader decried Cohn-Bendit as a German anarchist in *L'Humanité* (6 May 1968), which was widely seen as anti-Semitic among intellectuals, students and in the burgeoning street movement.
4. See Peter Fysh and Jim Wolfreys, *The Politics of Racism in France* (Macmillan, London, 1998). The authors draw on research to conclude that 250 foreign workers were expelled for their part in the events of May-June 1968 (p 33).
5. Jean-Paul Dollé, interview, Paris, 22 December 2008.
6. *Le Manifeste des 343* listed women, some high-profile, who had had abortions, the practice then illegal in France. Some of the activists who helped compile it also contributed to *Tout!*.
7. Dollé, interview, 22 December 2008.
8. Martin Evans, *The Memory of Resistance: French Opposition to the Algerian War (1954-1962)* (Berg, Oxford, 1997), p 144.
9. Jean-Paul Ribes, interview, Maule, 5 October 2007.
10. Alain Krivine, interview, *France Culture*, 15 December 2011, www.franceculture.fr/player/reecouter?play=4357775.
11. 'Massacre d'Algériens à Paris: Pourquoi une si longue indifférence?', http://www.alternativelibertaire.org/spip.php?article4471.
12. Krivine, interview, *France Culture*, 15 December 2011. Indeed Krivine talks more generally of mobilising thousands.
13. Dollé, interview, 22 December 2008. For the 25-point letter, see Christophe Bourseiller, *Les Maoïstes: la folle histoire des gardes rouges français* (Points, Paris, 2008), p 45. This was the Chinese Communist Party's declaration of opposition to Khrushchev's policy of peaceful coexistence with the West, which was seen as the abandonment of the legacy of Marx, Lenin and Stalin.
14. The soubriquet for the Franco-Algerian (white European) colonists who had decamped *en masse* to mainland France following independence.
15. Siné, interview, Paris, 24 January 2008.
16. Jean Schalit, interview, Paris, 10 February 2008.

17. Siné, interview, 24 January 2008.
18. For an effective summary of the students movement's build-up to May, see Chapter 5 of Chris Harman, *The Fire Last Time: 1968 and After* (Bookmarks, London, 1988).
19. Kateb Yacine in Guy Devart, *On vous parle de Flins* (Slon-Iskra, 1970).
20. See the Institut National de l'Audiovisuel (INA) clip of Chaban's statement: http://www.ina.fr/economie-et-societe/environnement-et-urbanisme/video/CAF89001601/monsieur-jacques-chaban-delmas-visite-les-bidonvilles.fr.html. It was not until 1977 that the last shanty towns 'disappeared'; immigrant workers were relocated in high rises or reconstructed *foyers*, hostels or dorms.
21. Fysh and Wolfreys, *The Politics of Racism in France*, p 36.
22. *Le Paria*, no 1, December 1969, p 1.
23. Ribes, interview, 12 January 2008.
24. See the authoritative work on the killings in J House and N MacMaster, *Paris 1961* (OUP, Oxford, 2006)
25. Additionally, *Le Paria* was printed at Simon Blumenthal's NPP. The young French Maoists took their cue from the Chairman's precept that 'he who has not investigated has not the right to speak'.
26. Ribes, interview, 12 January 2008.
27. *Le Paria*, no 3, 1 May 1970, p 1.
28. 'A bas la gangrène des SAT!', *Le Paria*, no 3, 1 May 1970, p 6. Two examples are given: the Fonds d'Action Sociale (FAS) and the Service d'Assistance Technique (SAT), both created in the 1950s, to regulate Algerian workers and, in the case of the SAT, round up FLN supporters among them.
29. Michel Wlassikoff, interview, Paris, 2 April 2009.
30. S Bouziri, 'Itineraire d'un militant dans l'immigration', *Migrance*, no 25, September-October 2005, p 37.
31. Rabah Aïssaoui, 'Le Mouvement des travailleurs arabes: un bref profil', *Migrance*, no 25, third trimester, 2005, p 12.
32. Saïd Bouziri, interview, Paris, 25 November 2008.
33. 'Grève générale des travailleurs arabes contre le racisme', *La Voix des Travailleurs Arabes*, October 1973, p 4, www.generiques.org, http://odysseo.org/img-viewer/FRGNQ_P0051_1973_001_S/viewer.html.
34. Bouziri, interview, 27 November 2008.
35. 'Grève générale des travailleurs arabes contre le racisme', *La Voix des Travailleurs Arabes*, October 1973, p 4.
36. *L'appel des douze*, a statement issued by 12 intellectuals in 2000, not unlike that of the 121 intellectuals issued almost 40 years earlier, and signed by some of the same anti-war intellectuals who drew up that manifesto.

Bibliography

Some Further Reading

For English readers, the best general account and analysis of the war is Martin Evans, *Algeria: France's Undeclared War* (Oxford UP, 2012). Alistair Horne, *A Savage War of Peace: Algeria 1954-1962* (Macmillan, 1977) has a lot of factual material but little political analysis.

For a history of Algeria from 1830 through to 2007, putting the independence war in context, see Martin Evans and John Phillips, *Algeria: Anger of the Dispossessed* (Yale UP, 2007). Benjamin Stora (see below) is one of the best-known historians of the war, but his only book available in English is *Algeria 1830-2000* (Cornell UP, 2004), a good brief account and analysis; about one-third of its 231 pages are devoted to the war for independence. There is a valuable account of French rule in Algeria and the origins of the nationalist movement in Roger Murray and Tom Wengraf, 'The Algerian Revolution — 1', *New Left Review*, I/22, December 1963. Unfortunately, the second part never appeared.

On solidarity with the Algerian struggle, the most interesting account is Martin Evans, *The Memory of Resistance* (Berg, 1997). This is a work of oral history, and contains accounts of interviews with Michel Raptis (Pablo), Georges Mattéi, Francis Jeanson, Gérard Spitzer and over 40 other activists. David Porter, *Eyes to the South: French Anarchists and Algeria* (AK Press, 2011) has a substantial section on anarchist attitudes to the war of independence.

There are biographies of both Francis Jeanson and Henri Curiel, who played a major role in organising support networks. Marie-Pierre Ulloa, *Francis Jeanson: A Dissident Intellectual from the French Resistance to the Algerian War* (Stanford UP, 2008) covers the many aspects of Jeanson's life. However, Gilles Perrault, *A Man Apart: The Life of Henri Curiel* (Zed Books, 1987), is only the first half of the French original, *Un Homme à Part* (Barrault, 1984). The promised second part, which would have covered his activity in support of the FLN, apparently never appeared. Simone de Beauvoir, *Force of Circumstance* (Penguin, 1968) covers the Algerian conflict from the point of view of the milieu around *Les Temps modernes*, which opposed the war from the very start. There is a useful short account of the 1956 conscript rebellions by Martin Evans in *Socialist Worker*, 27 May 2006.

Henri Alleg's *The Question* (John Calder, 1958; reissued University of

Nebraska Press, 2006) describes his torture at the hands of French paratroops. When the French edition was published in 1958, it was confiscated by the police, the first time this had been done for political reasons in France since the eighteenth century. An article about the book by Sartre (published with it in the English editions) was also seized.

The Marxists Internet Archive has a valuable selection of texts in English at http://www.marxists.org/history/algeria/index.htm, 'History of Algerian Independence'. These include 'Ouradour-sur-Glane in Algeria', from *Ohé Partisans!* on the 1945 massacres, FLN statements and texts by Messali Hadj, articles from *La Vérité des Travailleurs*, *The Arab Revolution* by Pablo, Alain Krivine's reminiscences of his support activity, and the text and list of signatures of the Manifesto of 121. *Socialist History*, no 39 (2011) is devoted to the Algerian war and contains an interview with Henri Alleg, dealing with, among other things, the role of the Algerian Communist Party.

On the PCF, Danièle Joly, *The French Communist Party and the Algerian War* (Macmillan, 1991) gives a critical and well-documented account of the party's role. Left critiques of the PCF, especially from *La Voie communiste*, are quoted sympathetically, and the text refers to interviews with Denis Berger, Alain Krivine, Laurent Schwartz, Gérard Spitzer and others. Irwin M Wall, 'The French Communists and the Algerian War', *Journal of Contemporary History*, Volume 12, no 3 (July 1977) is a brave but unconvincing attempt to defend the PCF line.

The writings of Frantz Fanon are essential to an understanding of the Algerian Revolution. In relation to solidarity action, of particular interest is the essay 'Algeria's European Minority' in *Studies in a Dying Colonialism* (Earthscan, 1989), in which he discusses those settlers who gave practical support to the FLN. For a Marxist analysis of Fanon, see the forthcoming Leo Zeilig, *Frantz Fanon: The Militant Philosopher of Third World Revolution* (IB Tauris, 2013). The *Journal of Pan African Studies*, Volume 4, no 7 is a special issue devoted to Fanon (available online at http://www.jpanafrican.com/vol4no7.htm)

Jim House and Neil MacMaster, *Paris 1961: Algerians, State Terror And Memory* (Oxford UP, 2006) deals with the 17 October massacre, and contains references to an interview with Clara and Henri Benoîts. Peter Fysh and Jim Wolfreys, *The Politics of Racism in France* (Palgrave, 2003) discusses the origins of contemporary French racism in the Algerian conflict; and Daniel A Gordon, *Immigrants and Intellectuals* (Merlin, 2012, reviewed in this issue) looks at immigrants in the two decades after the war.

* * *

There is a huge literature in French on the Algerian war. Benjamin Stora, *Le*

Dictionnaire des livres de la guerre d'Algérie (L'Harmattan, 1996) lists 2130 titles of books dealing directly or indirectly with the Algerian war.

The classic study of French solidarity with the liberation struggle is Hervé Hamon and Patrick Rotman, *Les porteurs de valises: la résistance française à la guerre d'Algérie* (Albin Michel, 1979). *Génération* (two volumes, Éditions du Seuil, 1987, 1988) by the same authors traces the fortunes of some of those radicalised by Algeria through 1968 and into the following decade. Jacques Charby, *Les Porteurs d'espoir* (La Découverte, 2004) is a collection of testimonies by individuals involved in solidarity work, including Francis Jeanson, Denis Berger, Alain Krivine, Gérard Spitzer and Henri and Clara Benoîts. Daniel Guérin, *Quand l'Algérie s'insurgeait* (La Pensée sauvage, 1979) is the personal account by a veteran anti-colonialist, who was in close contact with Messali Hadj and other leading figures. M-Ali Haroun, *La 7e Wilaya: la guerre du FLN en France 1954-1962* (Éditions du Seuil, 1986) describes the FLN's activity in metropolitan France. Benjamin Stora, 'La Gauche et les minorités anticoloniales devant les divisions du nationalisme algérien', in J-P Rioux (ed), *La Guerre d'Algérie et les français* (Fayard, 1990) discusses the French far left's responses to the FLN–MNA conflict. On the Trotskyists, see the Ligue Communiste educational pamphlet, *La question coloniale et la section française de la IVe Internationale* (François Maspero, 1973). *Résister à la Guerre d'Algérie: Par les textes de l'époque* (Les Petits Matins, 2012) is a collection of documents — manifestos, newspaper articles, letters and songs — from the opposition to the war.

One of the best-known and most prolific French historians of the Algerian war is Benjamin Stora. Among other works may be mentioned *La Gangrène et l'Oubli* (La Découverte, 1991), on the memory — and suppression of memory — of the war, his biography *Messali Hadj (1898-1974)* (L'Harmattan, 1986; revised edition Hachette, 2004), and his *Dictionnaire biographique de militants nationalistes algériens: ENA, PPA, MTLD (1926-1954)* (L'Harmattan, 1985) which provides brief biographical sketches of the militants who built the Algerian nationalist movement. Stora's autobiography, *La dernière génération d'octobre* (Stock, 2003) describes his own political evolution, from his childhood in Algeria to his years as a Lambertist full-timer.

Mohammed Harbi, *Le FLN: Mirage et réalité* (Éditions JA, 1980) provides a critical account of the FLN based on Harbi's own experience as an FLN organiser in the earlier part of the war. The first volume of his autobiography *Une Vie debout* (La Découverte, 2001) describes his activities in the 1954-58 period, making contact with the French left — Pablo, Guérin and others — on behalf of the FLN.

Jacob Moneta, *Le PCF et la Question coloniale 1920-1965* (François Maspero,

1971), by a veteran Trotskyist actively involved in solidarity work, puts the PCF's stance on Algeria in the context of its changing line over the decades. Jean-Luc Einaudi, *Pour l'exemple, l'affaire Fernand Iveton* (L'Harmattan, 1986) tells of an Algerian settler Communist who was executed for supporting the FLN. Paulette Péju, *Ratonnades à Paris* (François Maspero, 1961; reissued La Découverte, 2000) is an account of the 17 October 1961 massacre; the original edition was confiscated by the police at the publishers.

Other relevant works are mentioned in the footnotes to this issue.

Finally, for those able to read German, Christophe Kalter, *Die Entdeckung der Dritten Welt* (Campus Verlag, 2011) provides a very interesting account of the impact of the Algerian war on the development of 'Third Worldism' on the French left, with detailed studies of the review *Partisans* and of the PSU. It is to be hoped that this book will eventually appear in English.

IHB

A Note on Some Novels Dealing with the War

Not surprisingly, the dramatic events of the Algerian War have inspired many imaginative works. The following are a few novels of interest in relation to the theme of French support for the independence struggle; the many works describing the war from the Algerian point of view are not covered.

The main treatment of the Algerian war in English fiction is in the trilogy of novels by Alan Sillitoe, *The Death of William Posters* (WH Allen, 1965), *A Tree on Fire* (Macmillan, 1967) and *The Flame of Life* (WH Allen, 1974). Sillitoe had first made his reputation with his depiction of working-class alienation in *Saturday Night and Sunday Morning* (1958).

One of the two main characters in the trilogy is Frank Dawley, a factory worker and trade-union militant. In *The Death of William Posters* he meets an American called Shelley Jones who is supplying arms to the FLN, and agrees to be his co-driver in a lorry taking weapons into Algeria. In *A Tree on Fire* Dawley joins the FLN and stays to fight in order to 'help a country labouring under barbarous torments and oppression'. 'He had wanted to fight so that those considered the exploited and downtrodden could stand up to the so-called master races of Europe.' He achieves satisfaction participating in the collective struggle: 'He was again united with the only part of the world that mattered. It was a similar experience, certainly as real and perhaps more valuable, to when he was first set on a machine in the factory fifteen years ago.' Yet his politics remain vague; when asked by an Algerian if he is a Communist, he simply responds: 'I might be.'

In *The Flame of Life* Dawley has returned to England, but the memories and implications of his time in Algeria remain with him. He notes the paradox of his actions: 'I joined up with a guerrilla army which, when it's got the country it's fighting for, will begin building the same industrial society which I was forced to escape from.' Yet he retains the hope (this seems to be set around 1963) that Algeria will develop towards socialism.

Perhaps the best-known French novel set in the context of the Algerian war is Claire Etcherelli, *Élise ou la vraie vie* (Denoël, 1967), translated as *Elise or the Real Life* (Deutsch, 1970). Élise is a young woman from Bordeaux who, in the late 1950s, comes to Paris and takes a job on the production line of a car factory. There she meets and falls in love with an Algerian, Arezki. Although there are some Communist characters, there is not much in the novel that is explicitly political. What the book does is to evoke vividly the atmosphere of Paris in the period of the Algerian war, in particular the deep racism which penetrated French society and the permanent menacing presence of the police. It is also one of the relatively few novels that focuses on working-class experience — the workplace, housing, poverty.

Georges Mattéi, *La Guerre des gusses* (Balland, 1982) is one of the most remarkable novels dealing with the war. Mattéi (1934-2000) had been a Trotskyist as a young man. In 1956, he was called up as a reservist to fight in Algeria. He was appalled by his experiences, especially the use of torture. On his return to France he became a 'suitcase carrier' for the FLN. The '*gusses*' of the novel's title are the conscripts and reservists sent to fight in Algeria. The book begins with the attempted revolt by conscripts. There are vivid descriptions of the brutality of the war, and satirical portrayals of the army officers. One soldier, Nonosse, goes over to the FLN. The book ends with the police massacre in Paris on 17 October 1961.

François Maspero, *Le Figuier* (Éditions du Seuil, 1988) is a mixture of autobiography and fiction, drawing heavily on Maspero's own experiences as a left-wing publisher and bookshop owner. It vividly recreates the atmosphere and events of the period. The narrator's bookshop begins to promote the Algerian struggle, leading to police raids and attacks. When the shop is attacked by the far right, left-wing activists stay overnight to defend it. They publish pro-FLN material, some of which seized by police. But the FLN is not romanticised; some material is published under threat from the FLN. The group around the narrator are also involved with the Manifesto of 121 and the October 1961 massacre. The fortunes of various characters link the Algerian struggle back to the Spanish Civil War and forward to revolutionary struggles in Latin America in the late 1960s.

Claude Faux, *Le Réseau* (Julliard, 1960) is the story of a woman doctor who is arrested and questioned, then imprisoned for activity in support of the FLN. Other members of the network are also questioned, and there are flashbacks to the group's activity. There is little plot and much discussion of personal motivation and the political context. Faux was Sartre's secretary and husband of lawyer Gisèle Halimi, who defended MNA militants. Published in the year of the Manifesto of 121 and the Jeanson trial, the book was clearly a contribution to the current debate about support for the FLN.

Heidi Seray, *La Trahison* (Favre, 1984) gives a rather negative portrayal of solidarity activity. It is the story of Yasmina, a young Swiss woman of partly Turkish descent, who goes to Paris in the 1950s and 'carries suitcases' for the FLN, but soon develops reservations about the FLN's authoritarian methods and about the manipulative attitude of FLN men towards women. One FLN activist is shown as using prostitutes to locate MNA members so they can be murdered.

Léo Malet, *Les Eaux troubles de Javel* (Robert Laffont, 1957) is something of a disappointment. Before the Second World War, Malet (1909-1996), an anarchist singer, became a surrealist and briefly a Trotskyist. (It was he who identified the headless corpse of Rudolf Klement, probably murdered by the GPU.) He then turned to writing novels about Nestor Burma, a cynical but good-hearted private detective. In this book Burma is investigating the murder of a Citroën worker, who had many North African contacts, and this brings Burma into contact with the FLN. But there are few political insights. Burma is no racist, but he speaks the colloquial language of the day which contains many racist epithets. He is contemptuous of the FLN, telling them: 'I don't give a fuck for your political activities. If you want be beaten with a different club, that's up to you.' The plot involves a European businessman supplying arms to the FLN, but this is shown to have solely financial, not political motives. There is a depiction of a violent clash between the FLN and a rival group, presumably the MNA, but they are not identified and there is no discussion of the political issues, dismissed by Burma as 'political rivalry and the whole blessed stupidity'.

Roger Ikor, *Les Murmures de la guerre* (Albin Michel, 1961) is the story of Ludovic Fenns, a reservist on active service in Algeria. He comes from an anti-militarist family, and appears to be some sort of utopian socialist. He is taken on to the staff of a reputedly left-wing, 'republican' colonel. When he is confronted with the reality of torture, he finds himself confronted by moral dilemmas which the author leaves unresolved.

Finally, as an indication that France's colonial history is still a living issue, the 2011 Goncourt Prize was awarded to Alexis Jenni, *L'Art français de la guerre* (Gallimard, 2011). This large, 630-page novel traces the story of the soldier Victorien Salagnon through 20 years of warfare, from the Resistance to Indochina and then Algeria. The brutality of French colonialism is starkly depicted, although its opponents are not romanticised. The episodes of

Salagnon's military life alternate with another narrative, set in the 1990s, in which Salagnon teaches a young man to paint. Though Jenni denies any overt political intentions, he constantly links France's colonial past with present-day racism. As Salagnon remarks, observing a police operation in a quarter inhabited by people of North African descent: 'They have as much force as we had, and it won't do them any good either… They'll experience failure, just as we experienced failure, the same bitter, heart-breaking failure.' Hopefully this powerful novel will be translated into English.

IHB

Work in Progress

CERMTRI's Digital Library

CERMTRI's digital library, created in April 2011, has expanded and now includes:

* The entire journal *Bulletin Communiste*, the organ of the Committee of the Third International and later of the Parti Communiste (SFIC), for the years 1920 to 1933.
* The newspaper *La Vérité*, including a part of the year 1929 (the year of its creation) and the full run of 1952 to 1961.
* From *Les Cahiers du mouvement ouvrier*, the summary and the 'Chroniques des falsifications' of numbers 17 to 51, as well as articles on the October Revolution.

These publications represent a total of 600 documents, containing almost 7400 pages. The documents of the digital library are presented year by year. This material is available at http://www.bibnumcermtri.fr or via CERMTRI's main site http://www.trotsky.com.fr.

The comrades at CERMTRI have also devoted two recent issues of their series *Les Cahiers du CERMTRI* to South Africa. They draw on material by the late Baruch Hirson, a member of the Editorial Board of *Revolutionary History*, and draw attention to his remarkable life story.

* * *

The Marxist Internet Archive and John Maclean

Considerable improvements have been made in the John Maclean archive on the Marxist Internet Archive: http://www.marxists.org/archive/maclean/index.htm. Although no praise can be too great for his daughter, Nan Milton, who published the first collection of the work of this most important Marxist leader, *In the Rapids of Revolution* (Allison & Busby, 1978), considerations of space and expense meant that this was by no means a 'complete' works. Quite a number of articles were cut, though this is always made clear in the text, where there are ellipses showing that something is missing. Efforts have been made to have as complete a selection of Maclean's articles from *Justice* as possible, though work must continue with other publications, and help would be much appreciated.

In her biography *John Maclean* (Pluto Press, 1973), p 57, Milton wrote 'During the summer of 1911 Maclean began to write the regular "Scottish Notes" in

Justice, using the pseudonym *Gael*.' In fact the first one was on 11 November, although there is one earlier column under the same pseudonym on 6 May 1911 entitled 'News from the North'. The last 'Scottish Notes' was published on 30 July 1914, just before the outbreak of war. Apart from an occasional letter of protest, after this Maclean wrote only one more article for *Justice*, on 6 August 1914, entitled 'The Coal Crisis'. Though a considerable amount of material, nearly a thousand words a week, these 'Scottish Notes' do not seem to be referred to elsewhere much, if at all, but provide a clear look at Maclean's politics in the very important period of working-class history from 1911 to 1914 when he does not otherwise appear to have written a great deal. Maclean's views on trade-union struggle, electoral tactics, the role of women (he is very hostile to suffragette ladies, very supportive of self-activity in trade-union struggles), housing, landowners and his role in the British Socialist Party are all important aspects of his opinions found here. One thing that I have not seen discussed is that to a non-expert, as the transcriber is, it seems that this column must have played an important role in organising and building up the Scottish section of the BSP. It would be good to have a study in depth and greater historical expertise applied to these and other questions.

There do appear to be lots of typos by the transcriber, but a good many of them, if not the vast majority, of malapropisms, etc, occurred in *Justice* itself. The only one about which Maclean publicly complained in the following week was using 'Lancashire' for 'Lanarkshire', which in the context of the coal-mining struggle does rather change the political meaning, but there were many others. With enormous self-restraint the transcriber did not change them to what he thought Maclean must have meant. Quite often the photocopied text was pretty bad, and the scan was a mess. It did need a lot of work, and many punctuation errors in particular may have slipped through.

Perhaps even more important have been the efforts made as regards *Vanguard*, where a complete index for the journal http://www.marxists.org/history/international/social-democracy/vanguard.htm is now available on the MIA for 1915 and 1920. The National Library of Scotland apparently has the only approximately full set in the world. It has been done from the issues there by Allan Armstrong, to whom the Marxist Internet Archive is very grateful. In addition, every article for 1915 available in the NLS, most dealing with the vitally important revolt on Clydeside, can now be read on the MIA. Eventually 1920 will follow. The copies of *Vanguard* in the NLS seems to be the personal collections of Maclean via Nan Milton, plus Harry McShane's, while there are none in any other copyright libraries.

There may be somewhere a copy of both the first issue and the eleventh, probably in different depositaries. Alas, all the fifth issue (January 1916) were seized by the police and destroyed. The MIA would be most interested to learn where copies of any of these missing issues are. They are probably not catalogued as such, but simply listed as various or miscellaneous in personal collections somewhere.

Ted Crawford

The Complete Works of Marx and Engels

When the Institutes for Marxism-Leninism in Moscow and Berlin (GDR) began planning the new *Marx-Engels-Gesamtausgabe* (complete edition) (*MEGA*) in the 1960s, it was decided that the volumes should include all the manuscripts and other types of written material left behind by Karl Marx and Friedrich Engels. Most of the manuscripts are held by the International Institute for Social History in Amsterdam and the former Institute for Marxism-Leninism (now the RGASPI) in Moscow. This was made possible by the work carried out by DB Riazanov in the 1920s, who had obtained the permission of the German Social Democratic Party (SPD), with whom the archives of Marx and Engels was lodged, to photocopy the available manuscripts. The bulk of the manuscripts had been left to the SPD in 1895, when Engels died. Furthermore, Riazanov instigated a thorough search for unknown material, for example, letters. In this he succeeded extremely well, and today about a third of the papers left by Marx and Engels are in Moscow (partly as photocopies), some of which have disappeared from the original holdings.

Furthermore the editorial principles which Riazanov developed are important: to publish everything in full, in the language of the original, including relevant comments and notes on the historical situation in which the texts were originally written. In the second half of the 1930s, work on the first *MEGA* was discontinued. Only 13 volumes and some additional volumes of this first *MEGA* were published.

The New MEGA or MEGA^2

What was a new feature for the second version was that not only the letters from Marx and Engels would be published, but also those sent *to* them, as well as some supplementary material which could provide new insights into the political and personal life of Marx and Engels. The editors sought to establish cooperation with other (including Western) scholars who were active in this field, and so published two sampler volumes in which they exemplified their intentions and called for a discussion of these principles. This invitation was as open as it could be in the years immediately following the end of the Cold War, and openness gradually became more pronounced as the volumes were published.

The *Gesamtausgabe* (*MEGA^2*) has been published from 1975 onwards, but this edition is still a long way from being completed as only about 60 out of the 114 volumes planned had been published by the end of 2011. The *Gesamtausgabe* contains, in the original languages, *all* the material left behind by the two men (also works which were not published or reprinted for some reason or another), including the author's handwritten corrections; there are no 'silent corrections' of spelling or other errors. Each document is accompanied by a textual history which indicates where the original manuscript is located, and the context in which it was written. 'In the original language' means that the texts published are not only in German, but in all the other languages used by Marx and Engels, which means that 60 per cent are in German, 30 per cent in English, five per cent in French and the remaining five per cent in various other languages, including translated texts which were authorised by them. The introductions, the explanatory notes and the indexes — names, subjects, periodicals and literature mentioned in the letters or texts, archives and literature used by the editors — are very extensive. This material is in German.

The *MEGA* is a scholarly edition at a very high academic level — it entails an exact processing of the manuscripts, a precise description of their genesis, and full annotation. The form chosen, together with the principle of publishing every part of the material, means that this edition will consist of very comprehensive volumes and that it will not be completed for another 30 years. It goes without saying that the problem of procuring funding is partly due to the political tenor of the texts.

A New Beginning after 1990

After the breakdown of the GDR and the Soviet Union, a new publisher had to be found, viz, the Internationale Marx-Engels Stiftung (IMES, the International Marx-Engels Foundation), located in Amsterdam, at the International Institute of Social History (IISG), whereas the secretary of the IMES for the latter years had been working out of Berlin.

The early 1990s saw the publication of a number of volumes that were so near completion that they could only be published in accordance with the old guidelines (however, without the introductions). An international conference was organised to discuss new guidelines for future volumes, and these were adopted in 1993. The five years between 1993 and 1998 were spent adapting the new editorial guidelines and the work done up till 1998 to the new realities, also in connection with the technological possibilities developed at the time. Not until 1998 was a new volume published, and the years since then have seen the publication of one or two volumes every year. Thus, publication proceeds at a slow pace, but it does proceed.

The edition is subdivided into four sections. The first contains all works, articles and dissertations, 19 out of 32 volumes have been published, work on eight volumes is in progress, five are in abeyance; the second section, *Capital* and preparatory studies were completed in 2011; the third, correspondence, is planned to consist of 35 volumes of which 12 have been published, another seven are under preparation; and the fourth, excerpts from books written by other authors, notes, marginalia, and other types of material — in this section 11 volumes have been published, 17 of the remaining 21 volumes are currently in progress. The finished edition will provide an extraordinary extension of the material available, as so many of the manuscripts have never been published before. This goes especially for the second section with the voluminous studies Marx carried out for *Capital*. About half of the 10 000 letters to Marx and Engels have not been published as yet. Most of the excerpts, etc, in the fourth section have not been published at all, so all in all there are some surprises ahead, and the discussion of 'what Marx really meant' may reach new heights.

Commentaries and registers sometimes take up more space than the texts themselves. The commentaries and explanations provided mean that especially the volumes of the first and third section of *MEGA*, that is, the political texts and the correspondence, constitute very central contributions to the understanding of the development of the labour movement between the 1840s and 1895. In future, it will not be possible to write about the history of the labour movement without taking these volumes into consideration.

One of the registers in the letter volumes is a list of non-located letters written by Marx and Engels. The correspondence makes clear that the letters have been written, but apparently not been preserved by the recipient. As the registers now stand, they can be used to trace missing letters; actually several letters by both Marx and Engels have been found over recent years.

Political Journalism

For a long time, Marx worked exclusively as a journalist and editor of the *Rheinische Zeitung*, the *Deutsche Brüsseler Zeitung*, and the *Neue Rheinische Zeitung*, and he and Engels contributed to a number of other papers, such as the labour newspapers *The People's Paper* and *Das Volk*, the democratic paper *Neue Oder-Zeitung* (*NOZ*), and several others of which the *New York Tribune* is the most important. This means that a great deal of the two authors' writings consist of newspaper articles, such as, for example, *The Eighteenth Brumaire of Louis Bonaparte*, which was intended for the weekly magazine *Die Revolution*, published in New York.

To some extent this work has been overshadowed by *Capital*, but new research has shown that the result of the journalistic work is not without interest for the subsequent evolution of their theoretical works: it is obvious that Marx has recycled material from that period in those manuscripts that have been published in the second section of *MEGA²*. The material is also extremely relevant for the development of the political aspects of Marxism. It is, but not only for this reason, important to clarify the journalistic work, which means accurately to establish where Marx and Engels might have written which articles, as they were often published anonymously. However, intensive research efforts have led to the discovery of several new texts, and others have been clarified.

Internationalisation of World History

It is easy to see that essential elements of Marxism were only developed through journalistic work. Marx's journalism was very much concerned with the economic implications of the political and military events taking place at the time. However, these articles also reveal other lines of thought.

Volumes 10 to 14 of the first section, volumes 3 to 7 of the third section and volumes 7 to 9 of the fourth section (covering 1849-51), make it possible to assess Marx and Engels' development from the end of the 1848 revolutions until the mid-1850s. Until now it has not been possible to follow developments with the same degree of precision.

In the recently published volumes (I/30 to I/32) all of Engels' articles from the period after Marx' death are published. They shed new and coordinated light upon Engels' understanding, not only of theoretical problems, but especially in respect of his ability to apply his theoretical cognition to concrete and current problems, that is, the problems arising out of the new historical situation after the emergence of mass movements of workers in Germany and Great Britain in 1889 and the foundation of the new International in the same year. This in itself puts paid to any doubts existing concerning his Marxist stance or dialectical ability.

Continuing Research

As mentioned, the second section was completed in 2011. Several volumes in sections one, three and four are under preparation, and there is hope that the sections will have come so far by 2015 to encourage a decision to complete the edition. It is a significant factor in this publication odyssey that in order to promote scholarly internationalisation and to pre-empt any country from monopolising this work, groups of researchers in several countries, for example, Denmark, Germany, Italy, Japan, the Netherlands, Russia and the USA, are now deeply involved in the project. *The edition faces a problem insofar as many of the collaborators of the earlier volumes have retired or are about to do so. As so many volumes — especially in the third section (the correspondence) — have been edited by the Moscow work groups and the collections in the RGASPI in Moscow are immense, an enormous amount of detailed knowledge is to be found in Moscow. Unfortunately, only one work group is still active, which means that much of this important collective insight of vital importance to the edition is in imminent danger of disappearing.*

Since 1991, a yearbook, *Beiträge zur Marx-Engels-Forschung Neue Folge*, has been published by the *Argument* publishing house in Berlin/Hamburg without direct ties to *MEGA²* (www.marxforschung.de). The articles published in the *Beiträge* are mostly in German, but some are in English. The yearbook is only the latest in a long series of periodicals published by authors and editors who are connected with *MEGA*. It is a periodical of great interest in respect of *MEGA* and its history.

Almost parallel with *MEGA²*, an English-language 'works edition' *Karl Marx/Frederick Engels: Collected Works (MECW)* was begun. This 50-volume edition was completed in 2005. Currently the *MECW* is the most complete works edition; here the 'Manuscript 1861-1863' is published in English on the basis of the corresponding *MEGA²* volumes, so most of the writings of Marx and Engels are available in English. The texts discovered in connections with the research for *MEGA²* have not all been included as yet. It would require a supplementary volume (or volumes) to have them published in English and a decision on this question is obviously yet to be taken. The German 'works edition' now consists of 43 volumes, more are under preparation, and several volumes have been published in new versions, including the new results developed by the work on *MEGA*. This also applies to the Italian and Chinese 'works editions' — the results of the new complete edition, *MEGA²*, are transferred to more usable editions, so that many more can benefit from this work.

The Marx-Engels Foundation has gone on-line with some volumes of the second section. The original material is to be found in the original-language versions, as is, of course, the case for the printed material. What is now available in digital form can be found at http://telota.bbaw.de/mega/. For the time being, introductions are only available in German. Further texts for online publication are in preparation.

Gerd Callesen

Obituaries

Robert J Alexander (1918-2010)

Robert Alexander will probably be best known to readers of this journal as the author of the compendious *International Trotskyism 1929-1985: A Documented Analysis of the Movement* (1991). We reviewed that work at some length, and it is not necessary to repeat any of those comments here. While a work of global scope is never going to satisfy the requirements of scholars familiar with specific localities, Alexander's book has become widely used as a result of his permitting the online use of much of it via Google Books and the Marxists Internet Archive.

Alexander was born on 26 November 1918 in Canton, Ohio, the son of a junior academic. He graduated from high school in 1936. While still in school, in 1934, faced with the Great Depression, he joined the Young People's Socialist League. On leaving school he made a trip to Spain, where he acquired an enmity towards Franco and his movement, as well as a lifelong interest in Spain and via Spain in Latin America. He studied at Columbia University, graduating in 1940 and taking a Masters in 1941. He was an active organiser for the YPSL at Columbia, and for its parent body the Socialist Party of America. In this connection he met Jay Lovestone, and worked with him on many occasions later, through Lovestone's Free Trade Union Committee and later the AFL-CIO International Department.

Alexander was drafted into the US Air Force and in that service spent two years in Britain beginning in 1942. Here he acquired the habit, which was to form a foundation of his research method, of interviewing people at every level of society, to obtain first-hand knowledge of their attitudes and aspirations. Out of this experience came an unpublished book, *A Yank's Eye View of Britain*, and a pamphlet *What Do You Know About British Labor?*, written jointly with David Shub and featuring an introductory contribution by Clement Atlee.

Returning to the USA on demobilisation, he found a grant that allowed him a year in South America, researching for his PhD on labour relations in Chile, receiving his Doctorate in 1950. While engaged in this work, he became an Assistant Professor at Rutgers, and was promoted to Associate Professor in 1956, and Professor in 1961. He resumed active work in the SPA, and served on its Executive Council from 1957 to 1966.

He wrote prolifically on Latin America, assembling encyclopaedic information on the labour movements in almost every country. Although his books were often cited by cold warriors, his own politics were not corrupted by the privileges of study and travel, nor by contact with think-tanks and policy makers. He remained opposed to US support for dictatorships across Latin America, and espoused the alleviation of poverty and the extension of democracy as barriers to what he thought of as 'communism' (which we would call Stalinism). As well as his international history of Trotskyism, he published comparable international studies on Maoism and Lovestoneism.

Robert J Alexander died on 27 April 2010, not a revolutionary but an historian and researcher of principle and talent.
Bridget St Ruth

* * *

Robert Barcia (Hardy) (1928-2008)

Despite its creation of the largest open assembly for left-wing groups in France, and its repeated attempts at unification, the Lutte Ouvrière current is not gifted at winning friends among other left-wing groups, and less so, of course, among the friends of the ruling class. But that alone is insufficient to excuse the petty quake of *schadenfreude*, and of curiosity crossing the frontier of prurience, that trembled the cut-price seismometers of the French press and bloggers when news of the death of Robert Hardy became public. That a propaganda group should contrive such a PR blunder is obviously deeply contradictory. I am prepared to accept that the motivation for reticence was honourable and dignified, if grotesquely miscalculated. Barcia/Hardy merits a tombstone commensurate with his dedication to the revolutionary cause.

The main source for this note is *La Véritable Histoire de Lutte Ouvrière*, a series of interviews with Barcia/Hardy conducted by the French journalist Christophe Bourseiller (Éditions Denoël, 2009). There have been *Véritables Histoires* before. It is a title that bespeaks a high polemical style. The first and best was of the First International. It was with no little chutzpah that a *Véritable Histoire* was dedicated to two or three dozen hobbyists in revolutionary polemic who were pleased to designate themselves the Situationist International. Lutte Ouvrière deserves to be taken seriously as a current within the revolutionary movement. Numerically it eclipses the situationists, and far exceeds the First International. (Though of course the First International was not greatly concerned with statistics of individual membership.) Perhaps there is something to be learned from such differences.

Barcia was born on 22 July 1928 in Paris. His father was of Spanish origin, a supporter of the Socialist Party but with anarchist sympathies. He moved to France under economic pressures and after 1917 developed strongly communist ideas, but as an exile subject to deportation did not join the PCF. Barcia's mother was a factory worker, later a market trader, who encouraged him to read from an early age. One of Barcia's early memories was of his mother, anxiously watching the retreating French army for a glimpse of her brothers as they abandoned Paris.

At the age of 15, in 1943, Barcia had his first political experiences. While gathering among other teenagers in a Paris square, he encountered youth opposed to the German occupation. He was persuaded to support the distribution of 'Gaullist' literature by conspiratorial means, to discover that the cell he had joined was in fact part of the PCF, which occasionally distributed its own literature under Gaullist cover. The details of this secret work are very interesting, and Barcia recalls them in great detail in the interviews. His political and organisational thinking was deeply marked by this experience. He was imprisoned as a result of this work, and in prison he was able to associate more openly with PCF prisoners. One of the prisoners' acts of resistance was to create a large portrait of Stalin, based on their recollections of illustrations in party literature. Their pride was punctured when a guard enquired of them why they as Communists should have taken such trouble to create a portrait of Laval.

The time in prison was, however, dedicated mainly to political study. He read the *Communist Manifesto* and was expected to make a handwritten copy of it to be passed to other prisoners. Following the release of masses of resistants, he resumed work with the PCF, where with great tact and caution he was exposed to Left Oppositionist ideas by Mathieu Bucholtz, operating under the *nom de guerre* 'Pamp', and first read the oppositionist organ *La Lutte de Classe*. Shortly after the 'liberation' of Paris, Bucholtz was murdered by PCF members and his body was later found floating in the Seine. He was not the only victim of such treatment. Pierre Bois, another long-term leader of the Lutte Ouvrière current, and his brother Jean, were seized by Stalinists and were lucky to escape. It was only at this stage that Barcia came to understand that he was a sympathiser of the 'Barta Group' among the Trotskyists.

Chapters in the Bourseiller book give a sketch of Barta and his early history. It is regrettable that this material is not yet available in English. Barta (David Korner) was born in Romania in 1914. In 1936, he appears in the history of the 'official' French Trotskyist organisation, the Parti Ouvrier Internationaliste, and in 1938 he supported the minority that followed Trotsky's recommendation to enter the PSOP. In September 1939, Daladier ordered the dissolution of Communist and Trotskyist organisations. Barta separated himself from the POI, initially over an organisational squabble but soon enough opposing the conception advanced by Marcel Hic that the German occupation of France called for a cross-class alliance against the occupying enemy, just as it would have in a colonial country.

Barta managed to hold a small group (no more than a dozen strong even at the time of the 'liberation') of militants around him, and following the expansion of the German occupation in October 1942 was able to engage Michel Pablo (Raptis) to deliver a course of lectures. Barta's reflections led him to the conclusion that it had been the petit-bourgeois social composition of Trotskyism in France that had prevented the penetration of Trotsky's ideas into the proletariat in the country. He set about the task of creating a new Bolshevik organisation of a proletarian social character. Such an organisation naturally required its own body of theory, and Barta did not shrink from the task of writing it in the duplicated *La Lutte de Classe*. The survival of this tiny group was a remarkable achievement in itself. Barcia, the youngest was only 17; Bois was 22, and Barta himself no more than 31. Its enemies in the PCF held powerful positions in government, supporting De Gaulle, and had the benefit of very large numbers, many of them armed, across the country. They were capable of breaking up attempts at public meetings by the Parti Communiste Internationaliste PCI (as the official Trotskyist section now named itself), which was much more numerous than the Barta group.

In 1944, the group changed its name from Lutte de Classe (the name of its duplicated bulletin) to Union Communiste, while asserting themselves to be Fourth Internationalists. The bulletin remained illegal after the 'liberation' because the group refused to sign a declaration that its activity during the occupation had been patriotic. According to Hardy, the PCI had no such scruples. Hardy managed to organise a couple of cells of young workers in factories, operating through factory bulletins circulated from hand to hand, and factory gate sales which were often prevented by violence from the Stalinists.

This method found its greatest success in the Renault strike in 1947. Pierre Bois had managed to join the workforce, where a few UC members were already working. The group focussed on supporting his progress towards an unofficial leadership role. The strike triggered such widespread support among the working class across France that the Stalinist and Socialist parties were obliged grudgingly to use their apparatus to channel solidarity donations on a huge scale. The UC made some recruits out of the strike among experienced industrial militants. They faced a serious problem when a large group of the Renault workers wanted to break away from the PCF-controlled CGT. Barta and Bois were hesitant about such a move, but after a discussion with Pierre Monatte, the veteran revolutionary syndicalist, concluded they would have to go with the wish of the active workers and an independent union was set up; it achieved a degree of influence, though never enough to challenge the large union federations. Hardy was elected into one of its leading positions, and jointly edited the regular factory bulletin.

Hardy resigned from the UC in 1948; '*par lassitude*' was his own comment. Hardy's education had been interrupted by the political events in which he had begun to participate at such an early age. He resumed study during the 18 months of 'lassitude', acquiring the skills of a kind of medical salesman (*visiteur médical*) and a taste for the pleasures of the Latin Quarter. As a result he did not take a direct part in the crisis of the UC, which found itself unable to sustain the intensity of trade-union work required by the independent union, at the same time as producing the theoretical and political writing that been regularly published before the strike. In Hardy's account of the events, Barta took certain decisions on behalf of the UC without discussion, and clashed with Bois. He accused Bois of breaching discipline and proposed the dissolution of the organisation. A split was inevitable, and soon took place. Barta and his partner Irène soon ceased any political activity. It appears that Barta drew pessimistic conclusions from the experience of the Renault strike; particularly that the UC had failed to recruit and win influence sufficiently while testing its theory and method. Hardy returned from his 'lassitude' to support the group still adhering around Bois. Attempts to draw Barta back into the work did not succeed, and the reply quoted by Hardy has a distinct petulance about it.

The split was not amicable. There were disputes over debts and assets. But the Bois group were determined to resurrect their organisation, and under the name Groupe Révolutionnaire Communiste, began publishing a bulletin. Barcia was one of the editors, and he rapidly moved into a position of joint leadership with Bois. The objective of the time was to retain the relationships between the core group, reduced to a dozen, and the periphery developed during the Renault strike. Pierre Frank attempted to recruit the GRC into the PCI, but there were no takers. Barcia won over a few young workers from the Socialist and Stalinist parties and the slow, molecular growth seemed to resume. Barcia, however, fell victim to TB late in 1950, and was under medical care for the following two years. He continued to discuss politics with fellow patients at every opportunity. One of them, exasperated, had shouted: 'So Stalin is not a communist. Tito is not a communist. Nor Mao. Nor Thorez. That leaves only you!' After the publication of Khrushchev's 'Secret Speech', this person, by then a history teacher, wrote to Barcia: 'It must have been hard to have been right all alone for so long!' (During this period, Bois struggled on inside the Renault factory, reinforced at one point by a group of dissident PCF members.)

After discharge from medical care Barcia was in difficult conditions. TB was regarded as a disqualification from work, and he had only a few months' experience of employment over four years earlier. He managed to get work again as a *visiteur médical*, but after a few months the TB returned, incapacitating him for a further six months. By 1954, the group had recruited a few youth from the PCF, SFIO and Hashomer Hatzair. The *Socialisme ou Barbarie* group offered joint production of a bulletin, which appeared as *Tribune Ouvrière*. The political line of this publication was explicitly state capitalist in its view of the Stalinist states. This hardened the line against the PCF. They were able to resume production of factory bulletins in a number of places, at first called *Tribune Ouvrière*, but after separating from SouB in 1956 it was called *Voix Ouvrière*. During the revolutionary struggle for Algerian independence, the factory bulletins were uncompromising in their support for the FLN. This organic growth generated pressures towards a formal structure, which was eventually to be adopted fully in 1960. Hardy devoted as much of his time as possible to writing and editing the literature of the group, usually anonymously, but he came to be recognised as to all intents and purposes the joint leader with Bois.

It was also in 1960 that the group reclaimed the name *Lutte de Classe*. In reply to Barcia's correspondence, Irène had written: '*Un drapeau abandonée appartient à celui qui le ramasse.*' In common with much of the left in France, VO saw in De Gaulle's accession to power, and the creation of the RPF, the threat of dictatorship. An alliance was established with the Lambert current, which endured for several years, based around VO's methods of factory propaganda and penetration. The USFI group led by Pierre Frank chose not to participate. VO sought to take part in the 1966 conference convened by Gerry Healy to 'reconstruct' the Fourth International, and Barcia was among the half-a-dozen VO delegates (which necessitated his resignation from his post as *visiteur médical*). The disgraceful treatment of the delegation from the Spartacist League has been much written of. The same disrespect was shown to VO, which naturally ended any collaboration with the Lambertistes.

Barcia had drawn up a training programme for *visiteurs médicals* on the basis of his professional experience, and used this as the basis of a business that would provide him with the means of subsistence and some funding and facilities to the organisation. But the complications of this venture absorbed time and energy that he was reluctant to contribute. When the events of 1968 exploded, he was ready to turn his back on the business.

VO had not developed any specific student organisation and consequently had a limited purchase on the 'student revolution', while in no way failing to recognise and applaud the courage and commitment of the students on the barricades. In May, VO signed a joint declaration with the PCI led by Frank, the Pablo group and Alain Krivine's JCR, and subsequently Barcia was to propose (unsuccessfully) a unification. Along with other groups, VO was proscribed in June 1968, to which it responded by dissolving itself and eventually reconstituting itself under the name Lutte Ouvrière, after a period in which the regional groups operated with a great deal of autonomy.

In the aftermath of the events of 1968, although LO gained supporters, it did so much less than did the official USFI section. This was a consequence of the proletarian focus that UC/VO/LO had dedicatedly followed. Much of the USFI's recruitment came from student and teachers' unions, where VO had made no interventions even when it had recruited students. The integration of the new elements was slow and careful, and many of the 'spontaneists' drifted away as their enthusiasm waned.

In 1971, LO inaugurated its famous Fête (in which *Revolutionary History* endeavours to participate in each year) where left organisations are welcomed to debate and sell their literature, and to share in holiday fun. This was intended, in part at least, to rebut the widespread accusations of secrecy thrown at LO. Overall, this marked a time when LO felt it had the resources to turn towards presenting its politics to the masses, as an extension of its strategy, and not as a substitute for it.

By 1973, LO had the capacity to intervene into national elections, in a campaign led by Arlette Larguiller, which gave them some access to radio and TV. At the same time, they were able to expand the number of factory bulletins. In 1978, at great financial cost to the organisation, they were able to make an appearance in every constituency. The following year in a novel initiative they set up committees of public-transport users, to contest the decline of services. And in 1981 they set up an independent FM radio channel. In 1982, there began a campaign aimed at the recruitment of the most senior of school students, and this brought in a valuable addition of human resources. LO continued to intervene in national elections, making great use of the propaganda opportunities they allowed, and utilising Larguiller's growing presentational skills in the mass media. The group followed the same strategic principles that could be traced back to its earliest days — factory-based interventions and tight focus on proletarian recruitment.

Bourseiller and Hardy devote a little space in their book to LO's persistent approaches to the rival Trotskyist tendencies (including the Moreno/MAS current outside France) for unification, which have borne no fruit, and only a little space to the establishment of an international organisation (which they do not regard as an 'International'), the Union Communiste Internationaliste in 1994.

Pierre Bois was to separate himself from the group after a dispute over electoral tactics, and he died in 2005. Hardy and Larguiller came to be regarded as the leadership of the group, though Hardy rarely accepted any public visibility. He continued selflessly to dedicate his time to the literary and organisational aspects of the life of the organisation until his death.

Bridget St Ruth

Jean-René Chauvin (1918-2011)

'At five in the morning, as always, the reveille was sounded by a hammer-strike on the rail by the staff quarters.' So begins *A Day in the Life of Ivan Denisovich*, which made the name of Alexander Solzhenitsyn. When I read these words in 1963, the prolonged *diiing* pierced through me, from my eardrums to the pit of my stomach. I had been there. Twenty years previously in the winter of 1943-44, I slept one metre from that rail, on the top bunk by the always-open window on the corner of what was then Block 1 of the Loiblpass North Camp. Every morning, also at five o'clock, the 'anti-social' black-triangled *Lagerältester* Rudi would come to strike the piece of rail hanging on the side of the barracks, almost at the height of my ear. By habit — and in such privileged circumstances nothing comes so easily as habit — I had already woken up before the hammer-strike, hearing his steps in the snow through the window.

Thus Jean-René Chauvin introduces the tenth chapter of his autobiographical *Un trotskiste dans l'enfer nazi* (*A Trotskyist in Nazi Hell*), a testimony to the struggle for revolution against both Stalinism and fascist tyranny.[1] The last survivor of the generation which upheld the Fourth Internationalist banner during the Second World War, Chauvin experienced the Nazi jackboot at first hand, imprisoned at the Buchenwald, Mauthausen and Auschwitz concentration camps. While he was certainly not the only Parti Ouvrier Internationaliste member to suffer such a fate — Buchenwald survivor David Rousset rose to much greater notoriety with his *L'Univers Concentrationnaire*, introducing the term 'Gulag' into French — Chauvin's memoir is notable for its effort to integrate the author's own experience of the camps into a wider internationalist politics. Chauvin explored not only his experience in the Nazi *Lager* and the analogy with Stalinism, but equally the internment of Spanish Republican refugees in democratic France and the British Empire's camps in South Africa. Anti-fascism could not just mean supporting the Western Allies and their surrogates. Indeed, while Chauvin managed to escape the fate of a Pietro Tresso or a Mathieu Buchholz — murdered by Stalinist maquis fighters — he saw with his own eyes the potentially lethal threat that Communist Party cadre represented to Trotskyists amidst the turmoil of the war.

Neither fear of repression nor the Allies' democratic appeal served to dissuade Chauvin and his comrades of the need to defend an internationalist standpoint. On the contrary, the POI produced propaganda for German troops calling for working-class fraternity across borders, most notably in the newspaper *Arbeiter und Soldat* (*Worker and Soldier*). This perilous activity registered a grim balance-sheet, occasioning the deaths of dozens of German and French comrades when the soldiers' organisation was cracked by the Gestapo in October 1943. Dozens more fell into police custody or were sent to the camps, where they continued to keep the revolutionary flame alive.[2] It may seem strange, then, that so many POI cadre devoted themselves so wholeheartedly to such dangerous work at the height of Nazi repression, only then to lessen their activity after the war was over. But this can be explained by the great hopes of the early Trotskyist movement that the war would bring capitalism to the brink: thus even small but well-organised groups could have a decisive impact in directing the inevitable strikes and mutinies. This apparent lesson of the conclusions of the First World War disappointed in 1944-45, it was only natural to question the real likelihood of imminent revolutionary change and the nature of political organisation.

Early Political Formation

However, even if Chauvin was particularly notable for his experience of the camps, the arduous war years were just part of three-quarters of a century of activism as a Trotskyist. This was a lifelong struggle, notably marked by non-sectarianism, a commitment to the unity of the radical left, and with that a certain independence of minds.

Even from a very young age he was strongly politicised. This was in part thanks to his father René, an MP for the SFIO and personal secretary to Jules Guesde, leader of that party's 'intransigent' opposition to participation in bourgeois governments. René Chauvin left the SFIO soon before Guesde capitulated and joined René Viviani's War Cabinet in August 1914. Although an opponent of the SFIO's gradual assimilation into bourgeois political life, René Chauvin had little time for the Communist Party (PCF) born in the wake of the First World War, alienated by its 'Bolshevik hardness'.

Nor would his son Jean-René, a child of November 1918, ever display particular attraction to that party. Having read Leon Trotsky's *My Life* — 'a book I read as you would swallow down strong liquor'[3] — and witnessed the monstrous spectacle of the Moscow Trials as a teenager, he was put off the pro-Moscow PCF. Rather, his first political involvement was in the Jeunesses Socialistes, the autonomous youth wing of the SFIO. As a 15-year-old, the junior Chauvin attended his first protest, the mighty Paris demonstration of working-class unity against fascism on 12 February 1934. This march came in response to the far-right riots of 6 February, which brought down Édouard Daladier's liberal government: and this at a time when the PCF was still spreading word of the 'social-fascism' of the SFIO.[4] The fascist threat was soaring, just one year after Hitler's coming to power in Germany: nonetheless, Chauvin reckoned he was the only boy from his *lycée* to skive a day off school to attend the counter-protest.

But the clearly-growing strength of the fascist 'anti-establishment' demanded a sea change in the French left's whole outlook. Indeed, after 6 February, the PCF soon abandoned the lunatic 'Third Period' theory that the real threat to workers came from the 'social-fascist' SFIO, and a degree of working-class unity was achieved. However, the new strategy quickly developed into something quite different, the cross-class People's Front of all forces opposed to fascism.[5] When the People's Front entered government in 1936, a young Chauvin soon realised that 'cross-class' unity was in fact anti-working-class and no means to fight fascism, as evidenced by SFIO Prime Minister Léon Blum's apathetic stance to the crushing of the Spanish Republic. As a Madrid government of noticeably similar composition to that in Paris was besieged by Franco and his accomplices Mussolini and Hitler, Blum waved the white flag of non-intervention. Chauvin was repulsed by this attitude.

Indeed, it was in support of a comrade who had gone to fight in Spain that Chauvin first spoke at a Jeunesses Socialistes meeting, leading to his selection as a member of the Gironde regional leadership of the SFIO youth. This was in fact after the point at which the Trotskyists' Groupe Bolchévique-Léniniste had borne significant influence in the Jeunesses Socialistes leadership, with figures such as Yvan Craipeau, Jean Rous and Fred Zeller having left in the wake of the 1935 expulsions, and Chauvin was drawn to Marceau Pivert's centrist Gauche révolutionnaire. However, Chauvin was already in contact with Pierre Naville and quickly left the social democracy in favour of the country's largest Trotskyist formation, the Parti Ouvrier Internationaliste (POI). Like Trotsky, Chauvin favoured the POI's merger with the centrist PSOP (created after the Gauche Révolutionnaire was expelled from the SFIO in 1938), but in January 1939 the POI decided it would not follow this course of action, with individual members being allowed to join if they so wished.

The Camps

Chauvin and his former Jeunesses Socialistes comrades in Bordeaux thus formed a local PSOP section, although their conduct was perhaps more daring than the centrist party's general demeanour might suggest. After the announcement of the Hitler–Stalin Pact, the Bordeaux PSOP youth headed to the ship-building yards with thousands of anti-war leaflets, the first sentence being Trotsky's 'Stalinism is the mortal enemy of communism'.[6] Two days later Chauvin and his comrades were picked up at home and charged with 'provocation of soldiers to sedition, anarchist goings-on and propaganda of foreign inspiration'. The trial was a farce, and Chauvin was sentenced to two years' imprisonment... however, given the chaos of the French war effort, he was in fact passed from barracks to barracks, with officers completely unable to decide what to do with him.⁷ This did at least spare him from any front-line service, although he remained prisoner even after the June 1940 armistice, and he was not released until October 1941.

The first efforts to build a Resistance movement within France were already underway, in particular given the growth of PCF involvement following the Nazi attack on the Soviet Union. The PSOP had collapsed under the pressures of war, while the POI⁸ had quite different perspectives from the Stalinists and the French-nationalist Resistance. It sought not to promote the Allied cause, the French nation or vague notions of democracy, but rather to use the crisis to promote independent and internationalist working-class politics. This was a difficult task both politically and practically, given the extreme repression and the fact that the group had only three or four hundred members, with no experience of underground work.⁹ Chauvin himself was too well-known in Bordeaux for clandestine activism, so he headed for Paris, the nerve-centre of the POI's operations and its newspaper, *La Vérité*. He was charged with the party's ties to groups outside the capital and, from August 1942, contacts with German refugees. The idea behind this latter project was to disseminate revolutionary propaganda amongst the German troops and encourage revolutionary sentiment in Germany, a strategy quite at odds with the PCF's 'Everyone kill a Kraut' chauvinism. This would later lead to the production of *Arbeiter und Soldat*, a newspaper for the Wehrmacht rank-and-file.¹⁰

However, Chauvin never had the chance fully to participate in this work. Having once been arrested and managed to escape police custody through a window, he was arrested for good by the French police on 15 February 1943. In what was a terrible year for the POI, seeing dozens of its members captured, tortured and murdered in a string of Gestapo attacks, Chauvin too was lost to the organisation. He did not return to its ranks until after the war was over. He was taken first to the Compiègne transit camp, then to forced labour at Mauthausen, Auschwitz and Buchenwald. Unaware of what was really happening in the world around him, unaware if and when he would ever be released, he lived through two years of dizzying terror. However, moral courage (and no small degree of physical strength) meant he would outlive the thousand-year Reich.

While it would be remiss of me simply to précis an account of camp life so thrillingly detailed in *Un trotskiste dans l'enfer nazi*, linking his own hardship to that of so many other camp prisoners worldwide, one particular aspect deserves particular mention: the twin threat posed by Nazis and Stalinists. Within the underworld of the camps, the etiquette and rules imposed by prisoners on each other, the overriding Stalinist policy was to anathemise and boycott Trotskyists, who were accused of all sorts of complicity in fascism. Sometimes, however, this went a step further, not least the murders of Pietro Tresso, Jean

Reboul, Abraham Sadek and Pierre Salini by the Camp Wodli *maquis* after their liberation from the Puy-en-Velay prison camp. Chauvin came under similar threat at Buchenwald as two Stalinists threatened to 'break the neck' of this 'Hitlero-Trotskyist'. When the blows started landing, Chauvin's rugby and boxing experience served him well, however, and another pair of Communists intervened to break up the fight.

The end of the war meant Chauvin was at liberty, although *La Vérité* was refused a licence to appear legally and thus maintained a degree of semi-illegality.[11] Upon his return from Buchenwald in June 1945, Chauvin wrote a letter to *Sud-Ouest*, *La France* and the PCF's *La Gironde Populaire*, also signed by another five former Mauthausen detainees, calling for freedom of the press. These newspapers all printed the letter, but, dismissing Chauvin's experience, *La Gironde Populaire* replied the next day with an attack on 'Hitlero-Trotskyists who collaborated with the Nazi occupation'. Chauvin successfully sued for libel, but Bayet's decision stood: *La Vérité* was not authorised until April 1946. This only came some 18 months after Liberation, during which time six Trotskyists were arrested for their illegal propaganda.

Postwar Activity

The Trotskyist movement was not in good shape coming out of the war period, its hopes of revolutionary outcomes to the Resistance disappointed. The year of 1944 saw the POI merge with two of the other three Trotskyist groups, the *Octobre* group and the CCI led by Pierre Frank and Marcel Bleibtreu, thus forming the Parti Communiste Internationaliste (PCI). In 1946, Yvan Craipeau became the party's General Secretary, leading a 'broad' faction including Chauvin (who became Secretary) and such other long-standing POI leaders as Albert Demazière and Roland Filiâtre. As well as doubting the Fourth International's belief as to the 'degenerated workers' state' in Russia, the tendency did not accept the assertion that capitalism would not recover from the war: if anything, the potentially revolutionary moment of the late war years had been and gone. Indeed, given the lack of growth of Trotskyist forces, Chauvin, like Craipeau, believed the POI should have done more to try and participate in the maquis, even while repudiating Stalinist and Gaullist politics. This was in contrast with the line of the CCI, which was essentially blind to the existence of any national question in France, and when the former CCI leadership took charge of the PCI in 1947, the organisation as a whole adopted similarly unreal perspectives. Whereas the 'broad' tendency had worked to influence the Jeunesses Socialistes (expelled from the SFIO for supporting the Renault strike), the post-1947 leadership proclaimed the imminence of capitalist collapse and thus the need for organisational 'tightness'.

This dismayed many of the more serious militants, and most of the 'broad' tendency left: Chauvin himself was expelled. This aggravated the already-existing crisis in the PCI, which also saw a break to the left in the form of *Socialisme ou Barbarie*: indeed by 1952 the PCI had shrunk to about one-quarter of its 1947 size. However, the task of regrouping the anti-Stalinist left beyond the PCI proved a challenging one. Chauvin joined the Rassemblement Démocratique Révolutionnaire (RDR) led by David Rousset, Georges Altman and Jean-Paul Sartre, which promised a sizeable alternative to the PCF. Former prominent POI figures such as Pierre Naville and Fred Zeller also took this step. However, the RDR lacked political cohesion and struggled to carve out an independent space between the SFIO and PCF as the Cold War got colder: this 'third force' soon collapsed. Chauvin's visit to Tito's Yugoslavia in 1948 — and total disappointment with what he found there — similarly attested to the difficulties in finding any significant alternative force which could challenge Stalinism from the left.

The splinters of the RDR did have something of a continuity across the 1950s, from the Nouvelle Gauche to the Parti Socialiste Autonome, the Union de la Gauche Socialiste and finally the Parti Socialiste Unifié, a party of some 10 000 by 1968. The New Left was not quite at one with his own politics, which were more specifically Trotskyist: however, he was somewhat of an independent-minded figure, not valorising any particular organisation as the sole incarnation of revolutionary spirit. One gesture of anti-sectarianism displays this in particular: when almost the entire far left was banned in June 1968 following May's general strike, and the groups were thus forced to reconstitute themselves, he agreed to be registered as legally liable for Lutte Ouvrière, even though never associated with that tendency as such. Instead he turned from the PSU to the Ligue Communiste. This organisation was itself banned for a second time after a violent clash with the fascist Ordre Nouveau (in fact an episode of particular merit in its curious student-Guevarist turn), and, after the group's reconstitution as the Ligue Communiste Révolutionnaire in 1973, Chauvin became a leading figure in its Tendance 3, which advocated more of a commitment to unity in action with reformist forces.

Chauvin enjoyed several periods in and out of the LCR, continuing to advocate an essentially similar perspective to that for which he had argued in the debate in the POI in 1939 on unity with the PSOP: revolutionary, yes, but not standing aloof from reformists. For instance, in a 2001 article for *Carré rouge*[12] he argued for a 'States-General' of the left, drawing explicit parallels with the formation of the POUM. In this sense he was sticking to his life-long original conceptions rather than developing new ideas, although the idea of the groups one day overcoming their divisions (and that, not just advocated as one sect looking to swallow up the others) was certainly a worthwhile perspective.

Aside from his involvement in the organised left, Chauvin's activity was strongly influenced by his time in the camps. As early as 1946 he participated in a meeting of Trotskyist camp survivors; he was not afraid to speak out against the Stalinist gulags even when the Cold War dominated French political life; and well into old age he spoke at schools about his experience of the totalitarian nightmare. This also informed his 2006 book, *Un trotskiste dans l'enfer nazi*, his only published volume. In 2002, he was the subject of a film, whose title bore witness to his critical-thinking spirit: *Jean-René Chauvin, trotskyste indépendant*.

Jean-René Chauvin was the last of the generation who upheld the revolutionary message in the Second World War, a lifelong revolutionist and a man of great wit, courage and activist experience. His loss is a loss to all those who wish to understand the vivacity and critical-minded spirit of the early Trotskyist movement, its heroic struggle to survive in occupied France and its darkest period of repression. Sadly, the united radical left he always fought for, lived and breathed, remains a work yet to be accomplished. He died on 27 February 2011, aged 93.

David Broder

Notes

1. See the review by Ian Birchall in *Revolutionary History*, Volume 9, no 4.
2. See the April 1945 'Declaration of the International Communists of Buchenwald', written by the Austrian Trotskyists Ernst Federn and Karl Fischer, the POI's own Marcel Beaufrère and the Belgian Florent Galloy. Available at < http://www.marxists.org/history/etol/document/fi/1938-1949/ww/1945-buchenwald.htm >.
3. Jean-René Chauvin, *Un trotskiste dans l'enfer nazi* (Syllepse, Paris, 2006), p 60.
4. 'The Parti communiste will never tolerate a policy of over-arching entente, the politics of retreat and abdication before the social-fascists.' (Maurice Thorez, *L'Humanité*, 8 March 1934)
5. In 1939, Maurice Thorez even suggested this front could be extended to include those 'patriotic' Croix de Feu fascists willing to fight German Nazism.
6. Chauvin, *Un trotskiste dans l'enfer nazi*, p 65.
7. Humorously recounted in ibid, pp 66-73.
8. To be precise, in the early wartime period the group took the name Comités pour la IVe Internationale; from April 1942 Comités de la IVe Internationale; and then POI again from June 1943, a name I will use throughout for simplicity's sake.
9. Yvan Craipeau, *Contre vents et marées* (Savelli, Paris, 1977), p 93.
10. In English: < www.marxists.org/history/etol/newspape/soldat/index.htm >, originally in *Workers Liberty*, 3/20, June 2008.
11. In *La Libération Confisquée* (Savelli, Paris, 1978), Yvan Craipeau also attributes some of the responsibility for this to the POI itself, given its failure to participate in the various parties' take-overs of printing presses which coincided with the Liberation of Paris.

12. 'Un texte de Jean-René Chauvin', *Carré Rouge*, no 18, Summer 2001, available at < http://www.carre-rouge.org/Numeros/N18/69.pdf >.

* * *

Martin Conway Cook

Martin was a founder of *Chartist* in 1970 and his untimely death marks the end of an era — he being the last of the founders left on the Editorial Board and Management Board of the journal on which he served continuously for 40 years, rarely missing a meeting.

Martin died on his fifty-ninth birthday. He was an only child and went to school in Dulwich Hamlet Primary, south London, passing his 11-plus and going on to Wilson's grammar school. From an early age MCC (as he often signed himself) showed a prodigious intelligence, usually coming in the top two or three — but also his radical and socialist convictions. He helped form the Independent Pupil's Union, then joined the Schools Action Union in 1968. At 16 he joined Gerry Healy's Socialist Labour League Young Socialists, but was soon disenchanted and left to join the Labour Party Young Socialists.

During this time he met other refugees from the Trotskyist movement and joined the Revolutionary Communist League which by 1972 had morphed into Socialist Charter with its monthly paper *Chartist*.

From Wilsons he went to the University of Kent, gaining a first-class BA in History and Politics, then a Masters in the history of the postwar French left. His writings on the 1968 student/worker Paris revolt have a particularly contemporary ring as students and workers take to the streets against Sarkozy.

Martin was a man of many different parts. A man of huge integrity, selfless, committed, principled — a revolutionary traditionalist and passionate about his causes.

Martin was a self-confessed anorak when it came to train-spotting. He could identify an engine and track gauge from a hundred paces. This love of old trains took him off on countless adventures in China, India, Russia and Europe — particularly the old Eastern bloc, where he was able to observe steam beyond its Western sell-by date.

I have an abiding memory of standing on the platform of Halesworth station in Suffolk five years ago waiting for a steam engine to pass through the station on a special Sunday nostalgia run. As the train arrived there he was, flat cap on head and a glass of Adnams to his side. We chatted briefly and then he disappeared off in clouds of steam.

And there's a link to another abiding passion: CAMRA and Real Ale. Martin could name every ale and the site of the brewery throughout the land. Whether at a Labour Party Conference — and we were religious attenders through the

1970s and 1980s — or an Editorial Board meeting, we had to adjourn to a real ale pub for drinks.

Martin was also an expert on medieval history. There wasn't a year that passed when he wasn't signed up to some evening class in an aspect of the history of buildings: Romanesque architecture in the thirteenth-fourteenth century or gothic cathedrals in middle Europe. Again Martin's memory for building styles and locations was legendary. I'd name a village and he'd quote chapter and verse the Pevsner description of the church, declaring a Saxon round tower here or a Jacobean brick house there.

It was through his Morley College evening classes that he met Jennie Howells, who was to be his love and companion for over 20 years. Travelling together on historical tours and to their beloved coastal retreat at Deal had been one of Martin's greatest pleasures over the last decade. Jennie had been a rock of support during his brave ordeal against brain cancer, being at his bedside on a daily basis for the last few months of his life.

A love of buildings combined with his mathematical mind led him into the world of demographic planning, first at the GLC and then after abolition to Southwark council with a brief sojourn at the Strategic London Planning Authority. He was meticulous, conscientious and thorough in his work (I'd often ring him well after 6.00pm where I'd be sure to catch him to talk about an article or a meeting).

Martin was also a great fan of rock music and particularly that issuing from the American West Coast and his obituary of Jerry Garcia of the Grateful Dead is memorable (*Chartist*, no 156, September-October 1995). He had a punk rock band Blyth Power playing at his fiftieth birthday party on the top floor of Guy's Hospital, where he was later to be nursed after his unsuccessful operations.

Martin was also a committed trade unionist. A NALGO/Unison activist all his working life, he was a shop steward and represented many fellow white-collar workers; striking against Thatcherite cuts or demonstrating against some ill-conceived Tory measure when necessary. He was proud to hold a union card.

Above all he was an active socialist and a good comrade. Politicised at an early age, he had always stood up for the dispossessed and disadvantaged. No follower of hackneyed slogans or half-baked theories, he was always able to sniff out shallow thinking, sectarianism or opportunism. His *Myth of Orthodox Trotskyism*, written in 1975, remains a classic critique of ossified manifestations of the Fourth International. It helped many of us along the path to a more enlightened, humanist socialism. While he remained a Marxist in much of his thinking, he was always open to new ideas, and was a democratic, if slightly conservative, with a small 'c', socialist.

We disagreed at times on Ireland. Whilst he supported British withdrawal he championed the rights of the Protestant working class and felt their needs were often overlooked.

His commitment to democracy saw him become a founder member of Labour Reform and its treasurer. He fought tenaciously to rescue the Labour Party from the centralism and top-down élitism of the Blair years. He was passionate in his defence of public services, advocating a democratic state against the capitalist corporations. His contribution to *New Maps for the Nineties* (1990) was a powerful advocacy of class politics in an age when much of the left had lost its way. He argued vigorously against the Blairite neo-liberal, pro-market politics of New Labour. His pluralism meant he also was a regular attender of South London Fabians and an early member of the Labour Coordinating Committee and Labour Committee on Palestine. His sequel contribution to *Beyond Blair* (2006) again reveals a penetrating mind providing wide-ranging analysis of the New Labour years in a global context. His conclusions that the socialist critique of both late capitalism and old Leninist and Fabian technocratic top-down approaches had been vindicated, but that alternatives remain marginalised awaiting the rise of Latin American-style popular mass movements, remains a valid assessment.

Perhaps MCC's greatest talent was his writing. We have calculated that he contributed an article to almost every issue of *Chartist* — whether the early monthly or from 1978 the bimonthly, including the short-lived international journal where he penned articles on such varied topics as sexual politics to the Portuguese revolution — where he joined many of us on the streets of Lisbon to support the revolutionary workers, soldiers and farmworkers in their successful overthrow of the dying fascist Salazar regime in 1975.

From the early 1990s, he started the Growser column which we insisted on naming Cook's Column. Here his droll humour was given full rein. I rarely edited the content, but spent issue after issue deleting full-stops from abbreviations. He was a stickler for correct grammar, Orwellian in his precision of language. He was also Orwellian in his passion for preserving certain traditions, for a particular Englishness. Whilst an anti-imperialist he was also with the Anglo-Saxons against the Norman conquest.

Martin was a walking Wikipedia. Indispensable when putting *Chartist* together, a meticulous proof-reader, he always knew the right date, the right person and the right spelling. He was a passionate European. He taught himself Dutch, enjoyed German and French. He knew and followed the politics and left movements in most European states, often bemoaning the lack of political rigour, theory and radicalism of the British left. But equally he followed the socialist and labour movement on the other side of the pond making valuable political connections which *Chartist* still maintains.

He could always be relied upon to turn up at a meeting, demonstration, rally or conference, usually with an armful of magazines to sell. In discussions he'd always be ready to make a pithy but measured intervention running down a list of points to make his case or demolish an opponent's argument with forensic skill.

He kept up his love of learning, gaining a further Masters last year. He kept up his active political involvement until the last few months of his life — his last articles being on the rise of Die Linke in Germany, which gave him great heart. He kept up his witty one-liners until he could barely speak. He kept up his conviction in socialism, internationalism and a better, more egalitarian world to the end.

Mike Davis
Editor, *Chartist*

John Plant, obituaries editor for *Revolutionary History*, adds: I knew and worked with Martin Cook for more than a decade in the GLC branch of NALGO before Thatcher abolished the GLC, and remained intermittently in contact with him thereafter, through correspondence, e-mail and occasional meetings at beer festivals. In NALGO he was, as noted by Mike Davis, exceptionally diligent — I don't think he missed a single meeting while I chaired the branch Executive — and always contributed productively and thoughtfully to our discussions. His pamphlet *The Myth of Orthodox Trotskyism* deserves a place still in the reading of those who want to understand the history of the Fourth Internationals. Some of its insights would recur in the vigorous contributions to debate by the co-founder of *Revolutionary History*, Al Richardson, also a founder of the RCL–Chartist. Al would recall, with a typical mixture of exasperation and affection, a trip into Poland armed with what was then illegal Trotskyist material, when Martin's exuberant pursuit of steam locomotives seemed enough to attract the attention of the authorities. Although now overtaken by a huge volume of academic material in French, Martin's MA on the history of the left in France was for many years the only reliable source in English on the origins of the competing Trotskyist (and Maoist) currents in France.

* * *

Robert V Daniels (1926-2010)

It is rather saddening to note how little obituary writing has been done for Robert V Daniels. His 1960 book *The Conscience of the Revolution: Communist Opposition in Soviet Russia* was far ahead of its time in providing a picture of the many currents and shades of opinion that went to make up the Bolshevik party before, during and after the October 1917 Revolution. It was the book version of his doctoral thesis on Trotsky, Zinoviev and the Left Opposition. One of his supervisors was Merle Fainsod, whose 1958 book *Smolensk under Soviet Rule* was among the first to show how important was access to primary sources in the presentation of Soviet Russian history. Much of what Daniels then wrote could not have been improved upon until the opening of the many archives in the post-Gorbachev era.

As an *ingénu* in the Trotskyist movement I had internalised the 'Punch and Judy' history of the revolution led by Lenin, its destruction under Stalin, and the tragic failure of Trotsky to rescue it. Reading Daniels' book was like having the light turned on. It revealed a world of independent actors, thinking and fighting for themselves, coming together and separating in complex movements and waves. It remains today one of the most important sources of evidence against those who would foist upon the world a picture of 'totalitarianism' that began in the head of the youthful Ulyanov, horrified at the execution of his older brother, and grew steadily and destructively into Stalin's state of terror overflowing the Russian state boundaries.

His *A Documentary History of Communism* was also a great stimulus to self-directed study, thanks in great part to its appearance in a cheap two-volume paperback edition, especially after the Moscow-subsidised volumes of Marx and Lenin became harder to lay hands on. Here an aspirant heretic could find enough source material to begin to ask questions. Even today, with the enormous resources of the internet, I often turn first to the *Documentary History* for a quick picture of the context of key documents.

Most of his academic career was spent at the University of Vermont, in the course of which he produced major textbooks on aspects of the communist movement and the Russian state. After his retirement in 1988 he continued to respond to the collapse of the Stalinist regime with new books, and was widely honoured among academics in his field. He also wrote numerous articles for such liberal journals as *Dissent* and *The Nation*. He served on the Vermont State Senate for the Democratic Party from 1973 to 1982. He died on 28 March 2010.

JJ Plant

* * *

Sitanshu Das (1926-2010)

Sitanshu Das, a prominent journalist and author of several studies on Indian nationalism, died on 20 November 2010 in New Delhi at the age of 84. His last book, *Subhas: A Political Biography* (2000), went through three reprints in less than two years. He also led *The Hindustan Times* on-line project on Bose. A Trotskyist in his youth, Sitanshu described himself as a nationalist who was never accepted by either the Stalinist left or the fundamentalist Hindu right.

Sitanshu Mohan Das was born in Sylhet, now part of Bangla Desh. His father, an academic administrator who had resigned his position in solidarity with the Congress Non-Cooperation Movement in 1921, taught him to revere the nationalist leaders, particularly Swami Vivekananda, who advocated service to the poor for the regeneration of India. While still a schoolboy, he joined the Bengal Students Congress. In 1941, in his first year at Calcutta University, he took an active role in the Bengal Students Federation and came into contact with a small group of Trotskyists, known as the Bolshevik-Leninist Party of India (BLPI), who were actively supporting the anti-imperialist struggle.

With the police breathing down his neck, Sitanshu went to Jamalpur in Bihar, where his elder brother was living. During the 'Quit India' upsurge in 1942, he issued leaflets in the name of the BLPI urging the people to revolt. He was arrested and jailed for two years in horrific Bihar jails.

Released in 1944, he returned to Calcutta and joined the BLPI. To shield his identify from the police, he used a pen name, 'Nazeem' (in Urdu, 'one who organises'). He attended the first all-India conference of the BLPI, held clandestinely in Madras in 1944. An energetic activist on the student front in Calcutta, he was elected a delegate to the next party conference in 1947. However, in 1948 he parted company with the Trotskyists on friendly terms, having decided in his heart that he was truly a nationalist, not an internationalist socialist, of which the Trotskyists were the purest variety.

In the 1950s, he became a journalist, writing for the Press Trust of India. He was the Karachi correspondent for the *Times of India* in the early 1960s. In 1962, he moved to London to become the West European correspondent for the *Indian Express*. During his tenure in London, he appeared on BBC television and radio as an expert on South Asian politics, and he was President of the Indian Journalists Association. He went to the London School of Economics, where he studied Transport Economics and embraced the mellow Fabian Socialist ideas of that institution. He was on the editorial boards of two Fabian Socialist journals, *Venture* and *Third World*. After his return to India, he held a senior position in the Indian Express chain of newspapers, including as editor of *The Times of India, Tribune Trust, Patriot* and *Link*. He also was Professor of Journalism at the Indian Institute of Mass Communication.

I first met Sitanshu in New Delhi in 1974, when I was just starting my research into the history of the Indian Trotskyist movement. I renewed contact in 2003. He was planning to begin an ambitious book on the future of the nation-states of South and Central Asia, but declining health forced him into retirement. He suffered a brain haemorrhage on 17 November 2010 and then cardiac arrest three days later. His wife and two sons, Shubhranshu and Amitanshu, survive him.

Charles Wesley Ervin

Will Fancy

The death of Will Fancy last year at the age of 76 severs another link with the early days of the Socialist Review Group and later the International Socialists, led by Tony Cliff. Will was one the relatively small number of recruits who joined the SRG in the 1950s from the Labour League of Youth. Indeed by the time the IS began its great phase of expansion in the later 1960s, Will was already regarded as something of a veteran, not only because of his experience in the Labour youth movement, but because he won a reputation as a respected militant in the anti-war movement (he served a time in prison for sitting in front of a warplane with Bertrand Russell and other Committee of 100 activists).

Will was born into a working-class family in south London, but, very unusually for the 1950s, he won a scholarship to attend Exeter University. It was only during the 1960s that significant numbers of working-class students in higher education became a serious force on the revolutionary left. In the following years Will became one of the best-known and highly-thought-of militants in NALGO (later Unison). In 1972 he was elected to the Executive of the union with the support of the NALGO Action Group, one of the best-organised rank-and-file movements of the period.

In March 1974, Will Fancy chaired the first ever national rank-and-file trade union conference — initiated by the International Socialists, but drawing on a wide spectrum of support from shop stewards and other militants with a range of different affiliations on the left across the country. Always known for his dry and caustic wit, Will found himself pilloried in the *Daily Mail* as 'the most dangerous man in Britain', but he always added 'well I was for that week anyway'.

I first met Will on the editorial board of *Rebel*, a paper launched by the SRG/IS for Young Socialists in the very early 1960s and edited by Gus (now Lord) MacDonald. He always impressed his comrades by his calm and rational manner of debating even contentious issues — a quality not universally present on the left. He had little time for rhetorical left sectarians, but his cool and analytical style was always very effective in the internal debates in the IS and the wider labour movement.

His sense of humour never let him down. The late Jim Higgins used to recall that on one occasion when Will was the secretary of an SR branch in south-east London, he responded to irritating and repeated requests from national headquarters about whether a particular individual was a reliable member, replying: 'X does not pay dues, does not attend meetings, does not sell the paper — but he can in every other respect be considered an exemplary member.'

In later years Will drifted apart from the Socialist Workers Party (as the IS had become), and had major differences with the SWP over its opposition to

full-time elected trade union officials. Although his later years were plagued with illness, he remained a committed socialist and was active in the Socialist and Environment Resources Association, producing its monthly bulletin. He also found time to pursue his interest in ancient societies such as that in Papua New Guinea. He leaves his partner, Julie, his brother and sisters, three children, 11 grandchildren and a great-grandson.
John Palmer

* * *

Georges Fontenis[1]

Georges Fontenis, one of the last figures of the anarchist movement from the period 1940-50, died in Tours on 9 August 2010 in his ninetieth year. He will remain in the memory of the labour movement as a tireless fighter for libertarian communism, an important supporter of the Algerian struggle for independence, a trade unionist in the tendency l'École émancipée, an animator of May 68 in Tours and a pillar of the Libre-Pensée in Indre-et-Loire. Until his last days he was an adherent of Alternative libertaire.

Born into a modest working-class family in Lilas, Georges Fontenis was propelled into anarchist activism by the events of June 1936 and his enthusiasm for the Spanish Revolution. A clandestine member of the CGT under the occupation, this young teacher in Paris became, after the Liberation, one of the most prominent activists of the Fédération anarchiste (FA). In 1946 he was elected General Secretary of that organisation, a hub of resistance to the hegemony of the Stalinists in the labour movement of the time.

Very close to the Spanish CNT-FAI in exile, Georges Fontenis was in 1946-50 a promoter of the French CNT (CNT-F), which presented itself as an alternative to the Stalinised CGT and the Atlanticist CGT-FO. After the collapse of the CNT-F in 1950, he joined the Fédération de l'Éducation nationale (FEN) and was active in its revolutionary syndicalist trend, l'École émancipée.

Georges Fontenis became one of the protagonists of the libertarian communist tendency in the struggles that tore apart the leadership of the anarchist organisation in 1951-53, and resulted in the transformation of the FA into the Fédération communiste libertaire (FCL) following the defeat of the individualist tendency. The tendency he helped to organise was called l'Organisation Pensée Bataille. Its aim was to transform the FA into an effective revolutionary organisation capable of providing leadership to the class. He won himself a 'sulphurous' reputation in the heat of the factional struggle. He explained himself in his memoirs, first published in 1990. Republished in 2008 by Editions Alternative libertaire as *Changer le monde: histoire du mouvement communiste libertaire (1945-1997)*, these memoirs are of prime importance for historians of anarchism, but also as a political appraisal of this period, not without self-criticism.

At the outbreak of the Algerian insurgency in 1954, the FCL engaged in support for the independence movement and Georges Fontenis put together, with his comrades, one of the very first networks of 'suitcase carriers'. This was not a covert action, however, but open propaganda which resulted in the FCL being dismantled by the forces of law enforcement. Arrested by the Direction de la Surveillance du Territoire after several months on the run, Georges Fontenis spent nearly a year in prison and was proscribed from working in the national education service in the Paris region. This period has been described in a documentary of 2001, *Une résistance oubliée (1954-1957), des libertaires dans la guerre d'Algérie*.

After his release, Georges Fontenis settled in the area of Tours, which he would never leave. The FCL having been destroyed, he continued his work among the networks supporting Algerian independence.

He was again called to play a role in May-June 1968, being one of the leaders of the Comité d'action révolutionnaire in Tours. In the aftermath, he tried to revive a Mouvement communiste libertaire, strongly tinged with councilism, but was unsuccessful. He would later join in 1980 the Union des travailleurs communistes libertaires, and subsequently Alternative libertaire.

The life of Georges Fontenis has for decades been linked to the labour movement and its libertarian current. He shared its progress, setbacks and passionate struggles. As a political activist, he could draw lessons from failures without giving in to discouragement. But the itinerary of Georges Fontenis was also a personal journey. Shaped by anarchism, he wanted to transform it in depth. For this he was strongly criticised by some, whilst others viewed him in France and elsewhere as a reference point. Does his record, for all that, form a totality, to be accepted or rejected *en bloc*? Not at all. But Alternative libertaire and beyond that, the International Libertarian Communist current know that they owe him a debt, and for this reason we honour a man who now belongs to history.

The activists who worked with him in his struggles will keep the memory of a warm, jovial comrade, gifted with humour and great insight. This was the image he left in the documentary which was dedicated to him in 2008, *Georges Fontenis, parcours libertaire*.

Note
1. Adapted from *Alternative libertaire*, 10 August 2010.

Francisco Gomez Palomo (1917-2008)[1]

On 23 January 2008 Comrade Francisco Gomez Palomo of the POUM died, a victim of cardiac arrest, aged 90 years, in Paris, where he lived since 1939.

Born in Madrid on 7 September 1917, his political activities began at the age of 15, in 1932, as a militant among the youth of the Izquierda Radical Socialista (Radical Socialist Left), and a member of the Local Committee in Madrid. In mid-1933 he joined the Communist Youth where he campaigned until early 1935 when, in disagreement with the 'new line' of the Communist Party, he broke away along with a group of comrades in Madrid, to join the Izquierda Comunista (Communist Left), and later the POUM. He belonged to the Union of Insurance Workers in the UGT from 1933. His first arrest came in 1935, in connection with a workers' demonstration wishing farewell to the new recruits, in the depth of the 'bienio negro' (the period of reaction, 1934-36)

As a POUM militant, he was a member of the Committee of the Madrid section, working in the administrative secretariat. He was a delegate to the Madrid section of the POUM military conference, held on 18-19 January 1937. He was arrested on 16 June 1937 in Barcelona, where he went as a delegate from the JCI to the POUM Congress scheduled for 19 June, and was sent to the Model Prison in Barcelona.

He was initially indicted in the POUM trial. Released in 1938, he returned to Barcelona and finally managed to move to France before the arrival of Franco's troops. There he was interned in the Argelés camp and finally managed to reach Paris.

In France he campaigned in the French Trotskyist movement (in the same cell as Castoriadis, later to found Socialism ou Barbarie). In the Union Internationale Ouvrière (the product of a splinter of the Partido Comunista Internacionalista) he fought alongside Edgar Petsch, Sania Gotanbert, Lambert Dornier, Sophie Moen, Benjamin Péret, Augustine Rodriguez, Jaime Fernandez and G Munis.

In the 1960s, he participated very closely in the May 1968 events, as he lived in St-Germain-des-Prés.

After abandoning political activity, he nonetheless retained until his last days his social and critical commitment to the cause of freedom and equality and human emancipation.

Note

1. From notes on the Nin Foundation website, based on information from the book *Experiencias de la revolución española* by Ignacio Iglesias, an obituary in the magazine *Etcetera*, and an e-mail from Rosa Muñoz Garrido, a family member.

Hoàng Don Tri (1916-2011)[1]

Hoàng Don Tri died on 21 July 2011 at the age of 95. An engineer from the Ecole Centrale and an advanced mathematician, he became an aeronautical engineer at SFENA (Société Française d'Equipments pour la Navigation Aérienne)[2] where he was one of the leaders in the fields of automatic piloting and blind landing.[3] But parallel to this activity in scientific technique, he was throughout his life a militant, Trotskyist leader and theoretician. His older brother had been one before him,[4] and he was a pupil of Ta Thu Thau (a member of the International Left Opposition and founder of the Vietnamese Trotskyist movement who survived, though half paralysed, the years of the Second World War in the terrible French camp of Poulo Condor, only to be shot on the orders of Ho Chi Minh). Tri was already a Trotskyist when he came to study in France.

During the Second World War, with his student friend Claude Bernard (known in the Trotskyist movement under the pseudonym Raoul), he became a member of the Comité Communiste Internationaliste (CCI). With him he recruited a small group of Vietnamese students, and he managed to get in touch with his compatriots interned in camps who had been forcibly recruited in Vietnam to replace workers in France who had been conscripted to the forces. The German occupation of France resulted in the Vietnamese workers being imprisoned as forced labourers. Tri wrote a report on their situation, which he sent to the Red Cross in Geneva. But he managed at the same time to make contacts in the camps and to send in Trotskyist anti-colonial propaganda which won over a large number of prisoners at a time when the Communist Party, according to its policy of a patriotic united front — the '*union sacrée patriotique*' — was limited to anti-fascism.

After the Liberation this political work enabled him to form a significant and solid Vietnamese Trotskyist group which brought critical support to the long war against France, and then against the United States. In 1947, he and Marguerite Bonnet published *Mouvements nationaux et lutte de classes au Viet-Nam* under the pseudonyms Ahn-Van and Jacqueline Roussel (issued by the Fourth International), a little book that deserves republication. The group expressed itself in particular in a newspaper, *La Lutte* (*Tranh Dau*), which had one edition in France and another in Vietnam, and whose distribution was extensive. But the group in France was faring badly at the end of the war, with the victory of the Viet Minh concealing the Stalinist nature of the new regime. The attempt to return to Vietnam ended in the repression of all those who could not hide their Trotskyism. It was only late in the day that Tri and those who remained in France had taken notice of their denunciation of the bureaucratisation of the Communist Party of Vietnam and of the degeneration with which we are familiar.

Although he had suffered from French racism, Tri loved France for its great revolutionary traditions and high culture even to the point of joining a society for the defence of the French language and of the francophone tradition.[5] He never ceased in the struggle for the freedom of his country, and succeeded in getting some publications into Vietnam that received a certain, if limited, response.[6] Until a few years ago he was still writing texts on struggle and history, and had to leave behind many unpublished writings, which he passed on for eventual publication to the writer of this obituary, his friend since early 1944.

Michel Lequenne

Notes
1. From *Inprecor*, no 575-576, juillet-septembre 2011.
2. An aeronautical supply company set up by the French state, now privatised as part of the Thales group.
3. A Google search reveals something of his scientific achievements, which are outside our scope here. At the end of his scientific career he wrote about 'artificial intelligence', stating that it was the opposite of 'natural stupidity'. After retirement he began to learn Japanese and went everywhere with a little notebook in which he wrote new words and their equivalents in French, Vietnamese and English.
4. See http://www.revolutionaryhistory.co.uk/allobits/khoi.html for our obituary of his brother.
5. It may have been his resolute opposition to the growth of 'Franglais' that earned him the affectionate nickname 'One Two Three [Tri — sic]'.
6. Although in a French TV documentary in 2008 he said: 'I do not advise my children to become Trotskyists like me; you have to give everything, even your life, and get back nothing but blows and insults.'

* * *

Edmond Kovacs (1924-2010)[1]

Edmond Kovacs, probably better known by his nom-de-guerre in the Socialist Workers Party of Ted Edwards, was a life-long active socialist. At the age of 10 his father was active in the Schutzbund uprising against the proto-fascist Dollfuss regime in 1934; the young Edmond earned his first revolutionary recognition as a volunteer messenger at the front line. At 16 his family emigrated to the United States, where after high school he joined the army, enrolling in the famed Tenth Mountain Division, ski troops who underwent lengthy training in the Rocky Mountains before being despatched to Italy in the last days of the war, in early 1945. Edmond took part in the assault on Riva Ridge, a 1500-foot vertical assault on a heavily-fortified German position in which the ski troops used their mountaineering skills to ensure the element of surprise, attacking from positions the Germans had considered to be impossible. (An interesting account of this operation can be read at http://www.10thmtndivassoc.org/

Hampton.pdf.)

It surprised many to learn that such a vigorous war hero had taken a full share in underground fraternisation with German soldiers and prisoners. In fact he had close family members in the German army.

Back in the United States he joined the Socialist Workers Party. Trained as a chemist, he worked in the aircraft industry in Southern California until he was blacklisted during the McCarthy witch-hunt. At that point his father taught him watch-making, and thereafter he made his living running a small jewellery shop. Under his party name for many years he hosted a weekly radio broadcast and was a frequent speaker at party forums. He taught at the New Left College in Los Angeles and contributed regularly to the *International Socialist Review*, notably in the long discussion on the nature of the East European states. A crack-shot and an athlete, on several occasions over the years he defended himself from armed gunmen who tried to rob his store, once defending his mother who was in the store at the time.

The last of these episodes took place in 1983 when three anti-Castro Cubans entered his store in Glendale. Two of them drew pistols while a third began to pull a shotgun from under his coat. Already facing two drawn guns, Edmond grabbed his own gun and shot it out with the robbers, killing one, wounding another, and holding the man with the shotgun until police arrived. The SWP, then in the early stages of its planned break from the Fourth International, was looking for grounds to expel older members who were unlikely to agree to its still unstated new policy. Edmond was the first victim, of what was to become the Jack Barnes purge, being put on trial in Los Angeles and expelled from the party over a sudden sympathy for the robbers.

He followed the same route as many of the best in the SWP, as a founding member of Socialist Action, and later of Solidarity, in which he was still active at the time of his death. In 2000 he spoke at a conference on the history of Trotskyism in the USA that was organised by Paul LeBlanc, making a presentation on Murray and Myra Tanner Weiss. It was very much an insider's account. He explained how after standing down from the leadership, James P Cannon became concerned with the 'routinism' of the new Farrell Dobbs leadership and persuaded the Weisses to move to New York to liven things up. When they did not succeed, he sent Carl Feingold on the same mission. It was Feingold's achievement to recruit Jack Barnes and the Carleton College group that were eventually to destroy what remained of Trotskyism in the SWP.

In late 2009 his breathing became difficult and eventually a large cancerous growth was found in his throat. He lapsed into a coma from which he did not awaken. A small number of his friends gathered at his bedside this morning, and when his doctors confirmed that his situation was hopeless his breathing tube was withdrawn and he died. A fighter to the end, they saw that his heart continued to beat for 10 minutes after he had stopped breathing.

Note
1.   Drawn upon notes by Leslie Evans, Mike Alewitz and Louis Proyect.

* * *

Claude Lefort (1924-2010)

Claude Lefort, who died in October 2010, was a distinguished French academic, author of numerous books on political theory. But in his earlier years he played a significant role in the development of the French revolutionary left.

Lefort first became politically active as a school student during the German Occupation. One of his teachers was the existentialist philosopher Maurice Merleau-Ponty, who asked him if he had read Trotsky. When Lefort replied 'No', Merleau-Ponty told him that if he read Trotsky, he would become a Trotskyist. Lefort joined the CCI (Comité Communiste Internationaliste — which in 1944 merged with two other groups to form the Parti Communiste Internationaliste — PCI) and organised a clandestine Trotskyist group in his *lycée*.

At the Liberation he continued with his activity in the PCI. But he remained close to Merleau-Ponty, who encouraged him to write for *Les Temps modernes*, a new intellectual journal launched by Merleau-Ponty and Jean-Paul Sartre. This enabled Lefort to reach a wider audience than he could have got through the Trotskyist press. In 1947 he debated with the Vietnamese philosopher Tran Duc Thao on the war in Indochina, deploying a combination of existentialism and the theory of permanent revolution to make a critique of Stalinist strategy.

But already Lefort was becoming dissatisfied with orthodox Trotskyism, which did not seem to him to fit the realities of the postwar world. He began to work closely with Cornelius Castoriadis (see obituary in *Revolutionary History*, Volume 7, no 2), a Greek exile and also a member of the PCI.

In 1948 Lefort published a major article in *Les Temps modernes* entitled 'The Contradiction of Trotsky' (http://libcom.org/library/contradiction-trotsky-claude-lefort). Here he was sharply critical of Trotsky's tactics in opposing Stalin and argued that it was a central weakness of Trotsky that he failed to see that Russia had become 'a system of exploitation'. For this he was roundly denounced by Pierre Frank in *La Vérité* for having run away from the revolutionary struggle. The PCI had just lost half its members in a disastrous and unnecessary split, but the leadership — soon to fly apart — saw no solution but insisting on the orthodoxy.

Lefort and Castoriadis saw no point in remaining in the PCI, and early in 1949 split to form *Socialisme ou Barbarie* (*SouB*), a group which always remained small (never more than a hundred members), but which produced one of the few journals of the French left in this period which made a consistent attempt to analyse a changing world. (For a full history of *SouB* see Marcel van der Linden's article at http://www.left-dis.nl/uk/lindsob.htm.) *SouB* was critical of the PCI on a number of substantial points — the analysis of Russia, the attitude to Yugoslavia and the changing nature of imperialism — and dismissed the PCI as merely 'a revolving door for activists constantly joining then leaving'.

But from the very outset there were divergences between Lefort and Castoriadis. The latter had a long background in political organisations, going back to the Communist Youth in Athens. Although he rejected the 'Leninism' of the PCI, he still believed in the necessity of forming a revolutionary organisation. Lefort was increasingly sceptical about the need for a party, arguing that the only way in which the proletariat could develop its power was through autonomous forms of organisation. Lefort dropped out of *SouB* in the early 1950s, but soon rejoined. But the final break came in 1958. The crisis caused by de Gaulle's return to power led to *SouB* making some small but significant gains in recruiting new members. Castoriadis still had the perspective of building a revolutionary organisation. Lefort dissented; while recognising the need for coordination and the exchange of experiences, he denied that a party was necessary, and with other *SouB* members left to form Informations et Liaisons Ouvrières (ILO), which changed its name in 1960 to Informations et Correspondance Ouvrières (ICO) and survived until the early 1970s. But Lefort, seeing the contradiction of an organisation which did not aspire to be an organisation, left in 1960, and was never again a member of any political group.

In 1960 Lefort and Merleau-Ponty refused to support the Manifesto of 121, which supported those who refused to fight in Algeria, and initiated a 'softer' statement calling for a negotiated peace. Lefort was sympathetic to the mass strike of 1968, and, together with Castoriadis and Edgar Morin, published a book of essays on the events. But while being enthusiastic about mass action he was hostile to all forms of organisation: 'if in the future revolutionary struggles develop, it will be by the initiative of improvised agitators, indifferent to the orders of unions... and on the margins of political parties, great and small.'

The major shift came in the 1970s, when Lefort championed Solzhenitsyn. And in 1981 he published an article arguing that Mitterrand's alliance with the Communist Party (PCF) would open the door to the 'expansion of totalitarianism under the flag of Communism'. Not only was this a surrender to outdated Cold War clichés, it was politically inept; Mitterrand had the Communist Party stitched up, and the PCF's entry into government in 1981 was the start of the party's irreversible decline.

Lefort had now broken all links with Marxism and the left, and went on to pursue a successful career. But in the late 1940s he, like CLR James, Raya

Dunayevskaya and Tony Cliff, was one of a small group of Marxists arguing that it was necessary fundamentally to rethink old ideas in face of a rapidly changing world. For that he should not be forgotten.

Ian Birchall

* * *

Moshe Lewin (1921-2010)

The distinguished historian of the Soviet Union, Moshe Lewin, died in Paris at the age of 88, in August 2010.

He was born in 1921 in what was then Wilno, Poland, now Vilnius, capital of Lithuania. His mother was Russian and his father a Polish Jew who became head of the Wilno circus after beginning his career as an acrobat. Both Lewin's parents disappeared in 1939 during the extermination of the Jews of this city. Lewin himself, aged 20, escaped by jumping aboard a truck leaving Soviet Lithuania ahead of the approach of the Nazi army. From this early encounter he naturally acquired a deep respect for the people of the Soviet Union, which was not, however, to cloud his insightful and critical assessment of their state.

He worked first on a collective farm, then as a blast furnace operator before enlisting in the Soviet army in 1943, where he was selected for officer training. He did not see active service. He returned to Poland after the war and lived for a time in Paris before emigrating to Israel in 1951 prompted by the 'Labour Zionism' of his youth. There he worked as a kibbutznik and later as a journalist before undertaking a university course and graduating in 1961. He won a scholarship to the Sorbonne, Paris, where he researched the collectivisation of Soviet agriculture for his PhD. He was then employed for a year as a Director of Studies at the École Pratique des hautes études (later to become EHESS).

His thesis was transformed into his first book *Russian Peasants and Soviet Power: A Study of Collectivization.* His *Lenin's Last Struggle* also appeared in 1968 in English. Together these books dissented from the prevalent view of the Soviet Union as an unchanging, totalitarian state, emphasising how and where choices were made and alternatives lost.

In 1967 he became a Senior Fellow at Columbia University, and from 1968 to 1978 a Research Professor at Birmingham University (England). During this period he wrote *Political Undercurrents in Soviet Economic Debates: From Bukharin to the Modern Reformers* which further developed the view that Stalinism was not the inevitable outcome of 1917. His promotion (together with that by Stephen Cohen) of Bukharin's vision as against Stalin's appeared prescient when Gorbachev rehabilitated Bukharin, but such optimism was shown to be transient.

His next move was back to the USA where he took a professorship at the

University of Pennsylvania until retiring in 1995. During this phase he was able to access Soviet archives opened to 'Western' academics under the Gorbachev thaw. In a further series of books, *The Making of the Soviet System*, *The Gorbachev Phenomenon*, *Russia—USSR—Russia* and *The Soviet Century* he continued to trace and analyse the changes in Russia following Gorbachev.

Corula Star

* * *

Bess Lomax Hawes (1921-2009)[1]

Bess Lomax Hawes, a folklorist, teacher and singer who helped write 'MTA', an enduring folk ditty about an unfortunate subway commuter that became a hit for the Kingston Trio in 1959, died on 27 November 2009 in Portland, Oregon. She was 88 and lived in Portland. Her death was announced by her daughter Naomi Bishop.

As the youngest child of the song collector John A Lomax, and a sister of the folklorist and ethnomusicologist Alan Lomax, Ms Hawes was part of the premier family of American folk scholarship. She assisted her father in his research and had a distinguished career of her own, teaching anthropology and directing the folk arts programme at the National Endowment for the Arts. In the 1940s, she performed alongside Pete Seeger and Woody Guthrie in the Almanac Singers, and she later taught the rudiments of folk guitar to generations of musicians.

Yet she is perhaps most famous for a song she considered mere electoral propaganda for hire. While living in Boston in 1949, Ms Hawes and a fellow 'leftist folkie', Jacqueline Steiner, were asked to write campaign songs for the Progressive Party's mayoral candidate in Boston, Walter A O'Brien Jr. Ms Hawes and Ms Steiner seized on O'Brien's call to roll back a subway fare increase by the Massachusetts Transit Authority. They borrowed the tunes from two old folk songs, 'The Ship That Never Returned', written in 1865 by Henry Clay Work, and 'Wreck of the Old 97', and wrote new lyrics about a hapless commuter named Charlie who rides the train endlessly because he can't pay the nickel exit fare. 'Charlie's wife goes down to the Scollay [pronounced Scully] Square Station every day at quarter past two', the song goes, 'And through the open window she hands Charlie a sandwich as the train comes rumblin' through.'

In the 1940s, the MTA fare-schedule was very complicated — at one time, the booklet that explained it was nine pages long (reminiscent of the tricksy fare structures deployed after the piratisation of the railways in Britain). Fare increases were implemented by means of an 'exit fare'. Rather than modify all the turnstiles for the new rate, they just collected the extra money when leaving the train.

'MTA' was one of seven songs written for O'Brien's campaign, each one emphasising a key point of his platform, reform of the fare system and rolling back a recent increase was one of them. One recording was made of each song, and they were broadcast from a sound truck that drove around the streets of Boston. This earned O'Brien a $10 fine for disturbing the peace.

O'Brien lost the election. He moved back to his home state of Maine in 1957, and became a school librarian and a bookstore owner. He died in July 1998.

In 1957, a singer named Will Holt recorded the story of Charlie as a pop song for Coral Records after hearing an impromptu performance of the tune in a San Francisco coffee house by a former member of the group. The record company was astounded by a deluge of protests from Boston because the song made a hero out of a local 'radical'. During the McCarthy era of the 1950s, the Progressive Party had become conflated with the Communist Party, and, since O'Brien was a Progressive, he was (falsely) labelled a Communist. Holt's record was hastily withdrawn from sale and airplay. When the clean-cut Kingston Trio recorded it two years later, they substituted a fictitious name, George O'Brien, and the song went to No 15 in the pop chart.

The San Francisco singer whose performance in a coffeehouse inspired Will Holt's recording goes by the name 'Specs' and he owns a tavern in San Francisco. He learned that a theatre company was interested in the song and a friend warned him to copyright it before they got their hands on it. He told the two writers about what had happened and they were so grateful about him saving it from being copyrighted by someone else that they cut him in one-third for publishing royalties. When the Kingston Trio made their big hit with it in 1959, the money really started rolling in and to this day when the odd cheque shows up, people in the tavern Specs owns find themselves with a 'drink on the house' sitting in front of them.

'MTA', sometimes called 'Charlie on the MTA', has subsequently been particularly revered in Boston, where in 2004 the Massachusetts Bay Transportation Authority (as the MTA had become) announced the introduction of the automated CharlieCard.

Bess Brown Lomax was born on 21 January 1921 in Austin, Texas, and joined the family business at a young age. As a teenager she aided her father and brother in transcribing field recordings for their book *Our Singing Country* (1941), and her duties sometimes brought her to the front lines. In her 2008 memoir, *Sing It Pretty*, she recalled being led into the depths of Angola state penitentiary in Louisiana to transcribe an inmate's song because her father lacked recording equipment. 'Folkloring in those days was a family affair', she wrote.

In 1941, she graduated from Bryn Mawr College with a degree in sociology and moved to New York, where she worked in the Office of War Information and performed with the Almanac Singers, often repurposing old tunes with topical protest lyrics. She married one of her bandmates, Baldwin Hawes (known as Butch), in 1942, and in Boston in the late 1940s she began to teach guitar to large groups. By 1952, she and her growing family had relocated to Southern California, where she continued to teach guitar and also joined the anthropology faculty at San Fernando Valley State College, now called California State University, Northridge.

After working on the Smithsonian Institution's Festival of American Folklife in 1975 and 1976, she joined the National Endowment for the Arts, where she established the National Heritage Fellowships and a state folklorist programme. She retired in 1992, and a year later was awarded the National Medal of the Arts by President Bill Clinton. In 2000, the endowment established the Bess Lomax Hawes Award, which recognises scholars and arts advocates.

In addition to her daughter Naomi, of Portland, she is survived by a son, Nicholas Hawes, also of Portland; another daughter, Corey Denos of Bellingham, Washington; six grandchildren; and two great-grandchildren.

Charlie on the MTA

Let me tell you the story
Of a man named Charlie
On a tragic and fateful day
He put ten cents in his pocket,
Kissed his wife and family
Went to ride on the MTA

Charlie handed in his dime
At the Kendall Square Station
And he changed for Jamaica Plain,
When he got there the conductor told him,
'One more nickel.'
Charlie could not get off that train.

Chorus:
Did he ever return?
No he never returned
And his fate is still unlearn'd
He may ride forever
'neath the streets of Boston
He's the man who never returned.

Now all night long
Charlie rides through the tunnels
Charlie rides through the station

Saying, 'What will become of me?'
Crying 'How can I afford to see
My sister in Chelsea
Or my cousin in Roxbury?'

Charlie's wife goes down
To the Scollay Square station
Every day at quarter past two
And through the open window
She hands Charlie a sandwich
As the train comes rumblin' through.

'I can't help', said the conductor,
'I'm just working for a living,
But I sure agree with you.'
'For the nickels and the dimes
you'll be spending in Boston
You'd be better off in Timbuktu.'

As his train rolled on
underneath Greater Boston
Charlie looked around and sighed:
'Well, I'm sore and disgusted
And I'm absolutely busted;
I guess this is my last long ride.'

Now you citizens of Boston,
Don't you think it's a scandal
That the people have to pay and pay
Vote for Walter A O'Brien
Fight the fare increase!
Get poor Charlie off the MTA.

Notes

1. Based on an obituary by Ben Sisarion in the *New York Times*, 1 December 2009 posted by Louis Proyect to marxism@lists.econ.utah.edu, and a 2008 article by Peter Dreier and Jim Vrabel in the journal *Dissent*.

Bongani Mkhungo (1953-2009)[1]

The story of comrade Bongani (his formal name Bonginkosi E Mkhungo) is that of an extraordinarily brave man, dedicated to the cause of socialism and the victory of the South African masses. His story epitomises that of the South African working class, on its long march to self-emancipation. His life was always about the struggle, in the first case against apartheid, which he understood had to be transformed into the fight for socialism, and then against the side-lining of that latter fight in the interests of a developing black bourgeoisie. He understood very clearly that the derailment of the struggle for socialism in South Africa opened the door for further brutal exploitation of the black masses.

His father was the among first generation to leave the land to work in domestic service in Durban to acquire the pass which would enable him to live in the city and find work in a factory. He worked for 10 years for the British Tyre and Rubber Company (Dunlop) — one of the many British-owned corporations in South Africa which profited by using the savagery of apartheid to super-exploit their black employees. When he fell ill, the factory sent him home to die — his family could not afford hospital treatment. Bongani left school to become a breadwinner, eventually at the same BTR factory where his father had worked.

His father's life, and his own, illustrated the remarkably swift, savage transformation by capitalism of a rural peasantry into a layer of brutally exploited urban workers. This led to their radicalisation and transformation into the powerful, organised, class-conscious trade union movement which made South Africa 'ungovernable' and was instrumental in the smashing of the apartheid system. When the Boer businessmen saw their profits leaking away as the trade unions stood up for workers' rights, they knew they had to change the way South Africa was governed, or risk losing everything.

During the 1970s and 1980s Bongani assisted at the birth of the South African trade unions. He witnessed the first unorganised expressions of resistance — the Coronation Brick Factory strike in 1973 when the workers marched through the streets shouting the same Zulu war cries used in the Zulu wars against the European settlers who stole their land. He helped organise the strike for trade union recognition in BTR, led the strike, and was integral to the subsequent series of strikes for trade union recognition in the 1970s in Durban.

The union he helped found and build was the Metal and Allied Workers Union (MAWU) which became the National Union of Metalworkers of South Africa (NUMSA), and joined with 11 other unions to form the Federation of South African Trade Unions (FOSATU) in 1979, which went on to become the Congress of South African Trade Unions (COSATU) in 1986. As MAWU and the other new unions came into being, the stewards met regularly to discuss how they could take forward all aspects of their struggle. Because of the apartheid-imposed curfew, the only time they could meet and talk was overnight, on the way home from work. As the world opened up to them as a result of their new organisations, one of the main topics they discussed was socialism.

Bongani played a leading role in ensuring that MAWU from the outset was the most consciously socialist element in FOSATU, as shown by the following resolution adopted by the union in 1983, declaring that the union will:

> ... develop amongst metal workers in particular, and the organised working class and its allies in general, a coherent understanding that the demands of the Freedom Charter, and all other demands of the workers, can only be realised in the lives of the working-class masses through the practical leadership of the industrial working class in the struggle for the establishment of a socialist society where workers' control of government and industry will be enforced in the practice of a liberated South Africa.

Workers in NUMSA, including Bongani, fought for the Workers Charter — against the ANC's Freedom Charter. The Workers Charter maintained that in order to achieve a just society, South Africa needed to evolve further from the overturn of apartheid and the winning of universal franchise to socialism:

> In order to ensure that victory in the national liberation struggle is not hijacked by a new exploiting class, of whatever colour... we see the winning of such a non-racial democracy as part of a continuous process of creating conditions for the building of a socialist society which will be in the interests of all our people; a society free of all exploitation of person by person which alone can complete the liberation objectives in all spheres of social life.

Bongani was among the workers who drew up the Charter and understood the central role of their class in the fight for liberation and for socialism:

> We are the most vital social constituent of the broad liberation movement in which we play a part both as individuals and through our trade unions and political organisations. We stand ready to work together with all other classes and groups genuinely committed to a non-racial democracy, at the same time safeguarding our class independence and our right to propagandise and mobilise for a socialist future.

The Workers Charter demanded:

> The commanding heights of the economy shall be placed under the ownership and overall control of the state acting on behalf of the people. Such control shall not be exercised in an over-centralised or commandist way and must involve active participation in the planning and running of the enterprises by

workers at the point of production and through their trade unions.

The aims of the Workers Charter are still very far from being met. When apartheid fell, 90 per cent of land was owned by the white élite, and 10 per cent by black people. Fourteen years later, just four per cent more land has been acquired by black South Africans. And in the cities the most unequal distribution of wealth in the world is to be found. While unemployment stands at (officially) 23 per cent, there is a huge crisis in health, especially the continuing spread of HIV/Aids; decent housing, education and other public services are out of reach for millions, prices of food, power and water are going through the roof, and violent crime is rampant.

Bongani was associated with the International Committee of the Fourth International led by Gerry Healy. Under these auspices he visited London and Merseyside in the 1980s, building up links of solidarity between COSATU and British workers. Many British friends and comrades he met during that stage sent messages to his funeral. When the ICFI disintegrated he continued to ally himself with the Workers International tendency.

Bongani's life story dramatically illustrates how the ANC, with the South African Communist Party (SACP), supplanted the South African workers in the leadership of that powerful uprising, with the result that a black middle class was added to the white ruling class, equally determined to exploit the South African masses in order to maintain their own privileges.

The ANC leaders acted out of the conviction that theirs was the way forward for South Africa — that there was no socialist path. They quickly jettisoned those elements of their own Freedom Charter that spoke of redistribution of wealth and land. They went on to become a privileged élite allied with the old apartheid bosses to continue the same exploitation of the black masses — this time with black exploiters as well as white. The SACP also acted out of ideological convictions, handed down from the old Soviet Union: the two-stage theory, which said: 'First we must have "democracy" which puts a black middle class in power, and then much, much later, we don't know when, we will fight for socialism and the rule of the masses.'

During the 1980s Bongani was centrally involved in the campaign to defend Moses Mayekiso — at that time also very much a part of the struggle between the forces for socialism, and those for the creation of a black middle class to help exploit the workers. Mayekiso, an official of NUMSA, was detained by the apartheid regime in 1985 and charged with treason in 1987. NUMSA elected him National Secretary, and appealed to the international trade union movement for a campaign to release him. This was supported by the bulk of the international labour movement — but opposed by the ANC and the SACP.

Since then, Mayekiso, like too many others, has joined the ruling élite. Such people gained personal benefit and advantage from the self-sacrificing struggle of thousands of ordinary people, and acquired prominent positions in the new South Africa. Bongani himself on many occasions was offered the chance to reject his socialist principles and join the exploiting élite. Each and every time he refused. During this time, from 1985 onwards, while the masses were fighting — and dying — to overthrow apartheid, and finding their way towards the conviction that socialism was the only path to social justice, the ANC leaders started negotiating with representatives of the apartheid regime behind their backs.

The period of savage violence in the townships between the UDF and Inkatha supporters also taking place at this time was used to divide and demoralise the workers. It was not the ungovernability of the townships that frightened big business profiting from apartheid so badly, but the demand for a socialist society emanating from an influential current within the trade unions.

The ANC and SACP seized the moment to take control of workers' organisations. Key to this process was the merger of FOSATU with the non-FOSATU unions, and the discussion on whether to adopt the ANC's Freedom Charter or the Workers Charter as the expression of the workers' independent voice. Cyril Ramaphosa, then leader of the National Union of Mineworkers of South Africa used the numerical strength of his union to oppose the adoption of the Workers Charter. Bongani explained that workers were persuaded that in the interests of unity (with the background of terrible divisive violence), that a committee would be set up to merge the two Charters.

It never was set up, and the workers' demand for socialism and that their victory over apartheid should not simply result in the addition of an extra layer of black oppressors was sunk. The defeat of the Workers Charter reflected the side-lining of those like Bongani who had fought for socialism in the workers' movement. The leadership of COSATU agreed to the tripartite alliance with the ANC and the SACP, which went on to subordinate the interests of the working class to those of a rising black middle class.

In the 1990s Bongani participated in South Africa and the UK in the campaign to publicise the ANC's torture and murder of its own young militants in its camps during the so-called mutinies in Angola in the 1980s. It was during this time that he and other socialists were increasingly singled out for persecution. He was sacked by BTR, and when he leafleted a big ANC gathering in Durban about socialism he was physically attacked by ANC members.

He moved to the UK and worked with the Transport and General Workers Union for a while, but when he made clear that he was a socialist and did not support the ANC, he was sent back to South Africa with the promise of a job in the South African TGWU. This job never came about, and he was asked to carry out extremely dangerous conciliation work between the warring factions in the townships.

He could see no other way of making a life and living for his family but returning to the UK, where he worked as an 'illegal' agency worker, suffering dreadful abuse and exploitation. His greatest frustration was that he couldn't organise a trade union for his fellow workers, whom he saw suffering the same oppression as himself. While he was in the UK, despite ill-health and lack of money, he worked on building the workers' party that South Africa needs above all — a party embedded within the working class, and expressing the independent interests of that class.

In 2009 he decided to return to South Africa and work to build that party in the place he knew best, in the way he knew best. As he returned he was more certain than ever that the goal for his class was socialism, and he set out once again to fight for it. Now his friends and comrades in the UK are shocked and saddened to hear of his sudden and untimely death after a short illness.

Bongani was a remarkable individual — he understood the importance of socialism for the working class so clearly, and he held to that principle unswervingly, with enormous dedication and courage. He was sustained in his socialist conviction by the continuing struggle of the ordinary people of South Africa. His death is a huge loss to the workers' movement both in South Africa and internationally. We extend our condolences to his family and comrades. *Hamba kahle, qabane* (Go well, comrade).

Note

1. Based on material in *Socialist Studies*, January 2010.

***

Jakob Moneta (1914-2012)

Jakob Moneta, who died aged 97 in March 2012, lived a remarkable life marked by consistent commitment to revolutionary principles.

He was born in Błażowa (now in Poland) to Jewish parents. One of his earliest memories was of an anti-Semitic pogrom in which his mother and father were physically assaulted. The family moved to Cologne in Germany, but there was no escape from anti-Semitism. He recalled as a young man the constant violence on the streets, but also the heated debates between different currents on the left. One young Nazi argued that war was the solution to unemployment: he got the prompt answer: 'Hang yourself and there'll be one less.'

Not surprisingly he became involved in Zionist politics. But in 1931 some of the Social Democratic Party (SPD) left, including much of the youth movement, split to form the SAP (Socialist Workers Party of Germany) and Moneta joined this. He was introduced to the writings of Trotsky by Hans Mayer, later a distinguished literary scholar.

His socialist politics did not please his parents — his father was a small businessman — and when Hitler came to power he did not follow them to Cuba, but instead went to Palestine, where he arrived with just one English pound in his pocket. He became a member of a kibbutz, where one of his comrades was Rudolf Segall (see obituary in *Revolutionary History*, Volume 9, no 3).

In many ways, the kibbutz was a positive experience. Later he would recall:

> If I were asked the basis of my unshakeable confidence that human beings can free themselves from greed, love of money, competitiveness, selfishness and subservience… If I were asked about the deep roots of my belief that human beings can shape their own lives without external compulsion as free and equal members of a collective, then I would reply that this was demonstrated to me by my experience of the practice of the kibbutz in those days.

But the Arab revolt of 1936-39 made him aware of the real nature of Zionism. He wanted to stay on the kibbutz as an anti-Zionist, but he was excluded. He found employment elsewhere, and became a founding member of the only trade union in Palestine which united Jewish, Muslim and Christian workers.

In 1939, he was arrested, and imprisoned for over two years without any form of trial. He later described the prison conditions and the brutality of the British authorities, commenting that he had learnt that democratic imperialism fighting to preserve its empire was just as bad as fascism trying to conquer a new one.

One of those he met in prison — and still vividly remembered 65 years later — was Ygal Gluckstein (Tony Cliff). But he also had long conversations with the future military and political leader Moshe Dayan. He used the time to learn languages (eventually he would know around 10 languages) and to run a 'prison university'. Finally he was released following the intervention of British lawyer (and later Labour MP) Hartley Shawcross.

He stayed in Palestine for a little time after the war, but was very unhappy as he saw the process leading to the formation of the Zionist state. As he commented later: 'Now it was the Jews who were running the pogroms.' (And he knew what a pogrom was.)

He returned to Europe in 1948 and after a short period in Belgium and France returned to Germany. Here he got a job on the pro-SPD *Rheinische Zeitung*, for which Marx used to write. But he soon fell out with the proprietor — one reason was that he commissioned too many articles from Ernest Mandel. He also joined the German section of the Fourth International, of which he remained a member until his death. In accordance with the Fourth International's strategy of 'entrism', he joined the SPD.

From 1953 to 1962, he was attaché for social affairs at the West German Embassy in Paris. His diplomatic privileges put him in a position to do clandestine work on behalf of the FLN during the Algerian war.

Then he returned to Germany and for 16 years was editor of *Metall*, the monthly newspaper of the German metal workers' union. Its circulation grew to 2.2 million, and he pioneered editions in other languages in order to draw immigrant workers into the trade-union movement. One of the writers he encouraged was Günter Wallraff, the well-known undercover investigative journalist, who published articles about working conditions in German factories. He visited Chile two months after the 1973 coup and met trade unionists. He also organised in 1976 the concert by East German dissident singer Wolf Bierman which led to the latter being exiled from East Germany.

After the fall of the Berlin Wall, Moneta was expelled from the SPD after over 30 years membership. In 1991, he joined the PDS (Democratic Socialist Party, the former East German Communist Party). Until the age of 80 he a was member of its Executive Committee.

Moneta was also a copious writer of books, pamphlets and articles. While in the SPD he wrote for Fourth International publications under a pseudonym. He wrote a regular monthly column in the *Sozialistische Zeitung* until after his ninetieth birthday.

One of his books, inspired by his work in support of the FLN, was a history of the French Communist Party's changing position on the colonial question, illustrating with selected documents and a commentary the party's changing line from the internationalism of its earliest years, through the Rif war, the Popular Front and the postwar participation in government. This was originally published in German, and even before it appeared in French it provoked an angry denunciation by the Communist Party historian Jean Suret-Canale in the *Cahiers de l'Institut Maurice Thorez*.

I interviewed Moneta in Frankfurt in 2005, just after his ninetieth birthday. Though frail in body, he still had a vivid memory of people and experiences from 65 years earlier in Palestine. As he once put it, looking back on the horrors of the age he had lived through: 'Someone who was not murdered in the concentration camps, not killed in the gas chambers, and did not die in imperialist wars, has no right to give up the struggle for socialism.'

A fascinating autobiographical sketch (unfortunately not in English) is available at http://www.tlaxcala-int.org/article.asp?reference=6999 (German) and http://www.tlaxcala-int.org/article.asp?reference=7000 (French).

Ian Birchall

Hugo Gonzales Moscoso (1922-2010)

Hugo Gonzales Moscoso was born on 27 April 1922 in Monteagudo, Bolivia. His parents were from wealthy landowning and farming families. His father, a lawyer, died, leaving his widow with three children, of whom Hugo Gonzalez was the youngest. When his mother remarried, he spent much of his time being cared for by working people and peasants, and it was to this experience that he ascribed his greater sympathy for them than for the wealthy class into which he was born. After primary and secondary education, he took a degree in law and social policy.

In the fifth year of secondary school he was exposed to philosophical ideas and to Marxism by the intellectuals Ernesto Ayala and Peñaranda Agar. His response was to join the Partido Obrero Revolucionario (POR). The POR had been formed in exile in 1935, and had affiliated itself with the Trotskyist movement. With the ceasefire in the Chaco War (for control of territory disputed with Paraguay) in 1938, the revolutionary leaders were able to return to Bolivia. Bolivia appeared to have lost the war, allowing Paraguay control over most of the disputed lands (though it later became apparent that the lands retained by Bolivia were rich in natural gas and petroleum and those won by Paraguay had none), which led to widespread disaffection among the 'Chaco generation' with the élites previously ruling Bolivia. As well as the growth of the POR, the other main symptom of this disaffection was the formation and growth of the Movimiento Nacionalista Revolucionario (MNR).

Among Moscoso's earliest political activities was to act in a radio show protesting against the assassination of Trotsky. After graduating, he worked as a civil and labour lawyer, but dedicated most of his time to party work, soon joining the leadership of the POR, and he took part in the general strike that was violently crushed by the oligarchic 'Rosca' regime. With other leaders he was arrested, tortured and interned. A collective hunger strike forced the Rosca to exile them to Chile. He took part in the Third World Congress of the Fourth International in 1951, before returning illegally to Bolivia to reorganise the POR.

In the revolutionary events of early 1952, Moscoso and comrades of the POR took leading roles in the seizure of military barracks. The military surrendered, but the MNR established itself as the new government and failed to deliver on the workers' and peasants' expectations, though it had to begin some land reform and nationalisation of mines. The POR's slogan (and strategy) was to transform the national revolution into the proletarian revolution. The POR supported the formation of the Central Obrera Boliviana (COB) — a new federation of trade unions. Moscoso was elected to the leadership of the COB representing workers of Santa Cruz. However, the MNR succeeded in removing many of the POR leaders from positions in the COB.

A strategic discussion on whether to continue working alongside the MNR whilst continuing to press for the workers' demands, or to break from it, turned into a factional dispute. Guillermo Lora's faction supported the line of staying in to support the left wing of the MNR, Moscoso's that of independent work. When a group of Lora's supporters took the logical step of dissolving themselves into the MNR, Moscoso's faction acquired a majority in the POR and was supported by the Fourth International. Lora's faction split away and claimed the name POR for themselves. Moscoso's faction eventually came to be called POR-Combate.

The POR-C was subject to vigorous repression, and for the most part its leaders were exiled again, in Chile and Argentina. They were still recognised as the section of the Fourth International, by now led by Ernest Mandel, and through those connections were strongly influenced by Castro and Guevara. When Guevara launched a guerrilla campaign inside Bolivia, the POR-C gave it their support, calling for action by the workers and peasants especially in the cities. Moscoso sent a group of supporters to Cuba for military training, and pursued alliances with the guerrillas. The military proved too powerful for anything the left could put together, and by 1970 the threat was overcome. In the somewhat softer conditions that arose under Torres, Moscoso and many others on the left managed to create a Popular Assembly, which again took the country into a crisis that could be solved either by the workers or the military taking power. The Trotskyists fought alongside the workers against the Banzer coup but were heavily defeated, many of them being forced to take refuge in embassies. Moscoso went to Allende's Chile to organise the exiles into a united front. The Pinochet coup put an end to this work, and forced many of the exiles to take refuge in embassies, from which they were eventually rescued after great diplomatic efforts. He went to Brussels and worked with the Fourth International before returning to Chile in preparation for going underground in Bolivia again in 1978. He was yet again captured and tortured before an international campaign won his next exile to Sweden. When some elements of democracy in Bolivia were restored he made his final return. He worked again to organise workers and peasants in preparation for the 2005 election, giving critical support to Evo Morales' MAS, and supporting the new constitution that flowed from it.

He died on 10 January 2010. The history of Trotskyism in Bolivia, and of the Fourth International, contain many decisions to debate, but what cannot be debated is the courage and self-sacrifice of Hugo Gonzalez Moscoso.

Bridget St Ruth

William W Norton (1925-2010)

The adventurous life of William Norton typifies a certain admirable current in American socialism — practical, courageous and committed, based on independent learning and thinking.

William Wallace Norton Jr was born on 24 September 1925, in Ogden, Utah. When the Depression hit, he and his parents moved to California, settling in El Monte, where he attended high school and became a student body president. A journalism teacher there encouraged his interest in writing. In his senior year, he conceived a child out of wedlock and was thrown out of school, along with his soon-to-be-wife, Betty Conklin. (They later divorced.) Drafted into the Army, he saw combat in Europe during the Second World War, including taking part in the liberation of the Mauthausen camp. In a later interview he was to say of his war experience, under Patton's command:

> From various readings, I understood that fascism was paid and supported and came into being through capitalist financiers. It was the capitalist method of controlling an unruly social situation, as we later did in Chile, when General Pinochet was the wrong man to stop the socialist-oriented president that had been elected. So I was totally anti-fascist, and I was, what would you say, I was not only a dutiful soldier, but I was a volunteering kind of soldier. I was not opposed to the war in any way.

Exactly the kind of soldier whom the Trotskyist movement had wished to address through the Proletarian Military Policy.

After the war, he worked briefly as a reporter for an El Monte newspaper, but found small-town journalism unchallenging. Proud of his working-class roots, he switched to construction work. At 21, he joined the Communist Party and was an active member for five years.

He took work in the California State Park Service, at the same time striving to carve out for himself a career as a writer of short stories and plays. During this period he supported the third party presidential candidate Henry Wallace (the Communist Party's endorsement of Wallace cost him a great deal of support, but he never disavowed it), and as a consequence was summoned before the House Un-American Activities Committee and questioned. He forced from them the concession that he was not charged with any crime, but they repeatedly asked him to name people he had met during campaigning. His reply was:

> Well, I'm very pleased that Chairman Moulder and the House Un-American Activities Committee and the United States Government have declared that I have not violated any laws. I would be happy to write a 10 000 word analysis of what I have seen of the socialist and radical movement in the United States.

But as far as telling the names of individual people that I saw at the meetings, I'm just not gonna do that.

His support for Wallace and opposition to Truman grew out of his horror at the news that the USA had developed atomic weapons, while he was still with the occupying forces in the ruined cities of Germany. He was later to say of his joining the anti-war movement that it led him to become 'a red'.

Some of his scripts were turned into low-budget films, among them *The Farmer's Other Daughter* (1965), a bawdy comedy. His greatest success is generally thought to have been *The Scalphunters* (1968), the story of an escaped black slave far smarter than his persecutors. This was his breakthrough into a major career as a film scriptwriter.

With his second wife Ellie, he joined various support groups for left-wing movements in Central and Latin America, particularly Guatemala. Through those contacts he was asked to help buy weapons for the rebels, a task he happily undertook, travelling around country gun shows making discreet small purchases and meeting couriers for clandestine handovers. This activity later embraced the movements in Nicaragua and El Salvador.

While travelling in Ireland (his mother was of Irish stock), he and his wife met one of the hunger strikers and decide to support 'the Irish struggle for equal rights for people in Ireland and civil rights and housing'. They had witnessed the intimidation of families and communities by masked gangs of Loyalist thugs and decided to help resist it. They found the Irish National Liberation Army (INLA) to be the appropriate vehicle for them, because of its socialist orientation. Norton described the IRA as 'non-political, not wanting to get mixed up with socialism'. They planned to move to Belfast on Norton's retirement, but before that happened they were asked to go back to their role in weapons acquisition. A first venture, involving a camper van with a hidden consignment of firearms being shipped from the USA to Holland for the couple to use while on holiday, was successful. A second such trip, however, led to their being arrested and imprisoned in 1987

When released they went to live in Nicaragua. In the period of growing terrorism on the part of the contras, one night Norton shot dead one of them who was attempting to get into their house. After the victory of the contras they moved to Cuba. Norton was convinced that the FBI still wanted him for the gun-running adventure, but eventually smuggled himself back into the USA in 1990.

William Norton died of a heart aneurysm in Santa Barbara, California on 1 October 2010. His son, TV director Bill L Norton (credited with *Buffy the Vampire Slayer* and *Angel*) said that he died with very little money, having given

away most of what he had earned. His will provided for the scattering of his ashes in Northern Ireland.
Bridget St Ruth

* * *

Vinayak Purohit (1927-2009)

Dr Vinayak Purohit, the veteran Indian socialist intellectual, died in December 2009 in Pune at the age of 82. Vinayak had been involved in the left-wing movement since 1942, when at the age of 15 he joined an underground Trotskyist group fighting the British. In 1948 he went into the Socialist Party of India along with his Trotskyist comrades in what turned out to be a fruitless effort to steer that party to the left.

In 1956 Vinayak joined the new, militant Socialist Party that Dr Ram Manohar Lohia launched to revitalise the movement. In 1962 Vinayak played a key role in bringing an historic motion of no-confidence in the Nehru government to the vote in Parliament. After Lohia died in 1967, his Socialist Party disintegrated, leaving Vinayak adrift. He became an independent political journalist, well known for his biting attacks on just about every politician and party.

But Vinayak Purohit was not a man who lived by politics alone. He steeped himself in the rich culture of India. He became a music, drama, art, architecture and film critic. In mid-life he earned a PhD in art history. He also wrote plays, made a film, and designed an immense architectural monument, the *Gitai Mandir* in Wardha. He wrote fluently in English, Gujarati, Hindi and Marathi.

I interviewed Vinayak once, in 1974, when I was starting to research the history of the Trotskyist movement in India. I renewed contact with him in 2004, as I was finishing my book, *Tomorrow is Ours: The Trotskyist Movement in India and Ceylon, 1935-48*. His politics had changed dramatically (and in my opinion, for the worse). Having 'moved through Marxism and Trotskyism', as he put it, he evolved his own very nationalistic brand of what he called 'revolutionary democratic-socialism'.

In 2005 Vinayak published, in pamphlet format, the first chapter of what he envisioned to be an open-ended autobiography, which he aptly titled *A Life of Surfeit and Overflow*. He published two more chapters in 2006 and 2008. He died while preparing the fourth. Unless otherwise indicated, the quotes in this article are taken from these pamphlets.

Vinayak Purohit was born in Calcutta in 1927. His father, Kailashnath Jagannath Purohit, was a wealthy, London-educated Gujarati businessman who ran a successful auditing firm. He was a deeply cultured man whose interests ranged across history, literature, classical Indian music, art and politics. He was also a nationalist who surreptitiously contributed money to the clandestine

Bengali revolutionary groups who terrorised the British officialdom in those days.

A child of affluence, Vinayak grew up with servants in a bungalow on Ray Street in Bhowanipore, which then was a posh residential area of South Calcutta. A stone's throw away was the ancestral home of the nationalist leader Subhas Chandra Bose. Vinayak was privately schooled at Bhowanipore Gujarati Shala, which his parents had founded, and then at St Xavier's Collegiate School, a prestigious Jesuit institution. Driven by curiosity even as a boy, he read books from his father's vast library, including studies of the Irish, Turkish, Persian and Chinese nationalist movements and Trotsky's *History of the Russian Revolution*.

In 1938, after his father died prematurely, the family moved to Bombay. Vinayak attended a progressive Montessori school in Vile Parle from 1939 to 1942 and then entered Elphinstone College, which was like the Harvard of India.

In August 1942, as Japanese forces pushed through Burma, Gandhi called upon the Indian people to commence a non-violent mass struggle to force the British to 'quit India'. The panic-stricken British government arrested Gandhi and the top-echelon Congress leaders. Vinayak, who was then 15 years old, went to a protest demonstration in Shivaji Park. A policeman clubbed him and left him on the ground with a fractured skull. As he joked later, 'the hole in the skull allowed my brain scope for expansion'.

Vinayak threw himself into the tumult of the Quit India revolt. In December 1942, he was arrested for 'attempting to burn a policeman alive' while leading a torchlight procession.

As the protests subsided, Vinayak joined an underground cell of militants who were trying to keep the movement going. One of them recognised that this young hothead had real potential. He arranged for Vinayak to meet two Trotskyists, introduced as 'Comrade Rup Singh' and 'Comrade Dias'. Only later did he learn that they were actually Philip Gunawardena and Colvin R de Silva, the two main leaders of the Trotskyist party in Ceylon (the Lanka Sama Samaja Party) who had come up to India to help build a Trotskyist party, the Bolshevik-Leninist Party of India (BLPI).

Vinayak recalls being 'bowled over' by the articulate speech of the duo. They put their brainy 15-year-old recruit through a crash course in Marxism:

> The most memorable lesson that I learnt from Philip [Gunawardena] was his description of the comprador bourgeoisie as a 'squad of Tuppiahs'. This is the Sinhala term meaning the trained monkeys used by coconut growers to climb the tall trees and harvest the monthly crop of coconuts.

This contempt for the Indian élites who aped Western culture or enriched themselves as agents of the imperialists became one of his core values for the rest of his life.

The clandestine BLPI group in Bombay became his new family. He lived in one of the party's communal flats in Bombay with a half dozen or more other young comrades. That made him prey for the police, who were combing Bombay, looking for the Trotskyists. Before dawn on 15 July 1943, the police raided their hideout and he was jailed in the Worli detention camp.

After his release seven months later, on the basis of his youth, he went back into the underground to continue the struggle. He found shelter in the slums with members of the Forward Bloc (followers of Subhas Chandra Bose), who were very sympathetic to the Trotskyists. He continued to study: 'I remember that I had begun to read the *Encyclopaedia Britannica* in the Mumbai University Library from 1944 as though they were a set of novels, from cover to cover.'

In 1948 Vinayak joined the Socialist Party along with the rest of his Trotskyist comrades. The BLPI had made that decision only after a prolonged internal debate. Vinayak had been part of the faction in the BLPI that wanted to merge with the Congress Socialist Party. His rationale was that the BLPI, as a tiny party, new to the scene, would have better prospects as a Trotskyist ginger group within the Socialist Party, which had recently withdrawn from its mother organisation, the Indian National Congress, now the ruling party of independent India.

The Socialist Party assigned Vinayak, who was then 21 years old, to serve as secretary of one of their unions, the Bombay Press Employees Union. Though a novice to this kind of work, he learned quickly. As he recounted in his memoirs, he earned a reputation as 'a fighting firebrand'.

However, the entry into the Socialist Party didn't work out as he had expected. The Socialist leaders were too savvy to allow the Trotskyists to recruit to their own ginger group. No factional activity was allowed. As a result, the Trotskyists started to sink into the quicksand of the Socialist Party.

In 1952, after their humiliating rout in the general elections to the first Lok Sabha, the leadership of the Socialist Party decided, on their own, without calling a party conference, to merge with a breakaway group from the ruling Congress Party. Vinayak and his comrades opposed the merger, called a conference of dissidents, and tried to keep the rump Socialist Party going.

While the rump party had pockets of strength in Madras and a few other areas, Vinayak was isolated. In 1952 he 'retired hurt from politics' and moved back to Calcutta. One of his father's associates hired him as a clerk at the National Insurance Company. His health deteriorated. He described this period as 'my darkest days of political isolation and abject destitution'.

In 1956, Vinayak, eager to end his isolation, joined a new Socialist Party that had just been formed by Dr Ram Manohar Lohia, the veteran freedom fighter and old Socialist warhorse. In joining Lohia's party, Vinayak made a definitive break with the Marxist-Leninist-Trotskyist politics of his youth. Lohia was a radical nationalist who rejected Marxism as a White European ideology that was at best irrelevant to India. But he was a powerful orator, a charismatic personality and a creative thinker. He gathered around him a team of talented, ambitious socialists, including Vinayak.

Vinayak became a regular contributor to *Mankind*, the journal that Lohia launched in 1956, and through his new trade-union connections, resumed his support work in the powerful socialist trade unions in Bombay. By the 1960s, the Lohia Socialists (as they were then called) had become the main left opposition to what Vinayak regarded as the 'comprador' Nehru government. In 1962, the Socialists tried to topple the Congress government through a no-confidence motion in Parliament. Vinayak played an important, albeit behind-the-scenes role in mustering the support the Socialists needed in Parliament to get the motion on the floor for the vote.

All that came to an abrupt end when Lohia died prematurely in 1967. His Socialist Party quickly disintegrated. Once again, Vinayak was left isolated:

> I would occasionally feel and suffer acutely from this sense of separation and isolation, but on the other hand, I was so absorbed and was in such a headlong rush to develop all sorts of other capabilities and occupations that I hardly had the time to dwell on this loneliness.

Like his father, Vinayak was a connoisseur of the arts, especially Indian music. As in politics, so too in music, he was fanatical and a fast learner. In 1956 he became the North Indian Classical Music critic for the premier English-language newspaper in India, the *Times of India*.

In 1971 Vinayak entered the PhD programme at Bombay University, supporting himself by running a small advertising agency. Four years later he submitted his dissertation, *The Arts of Transitional India: Twentieth Century*, a 1600-page *tour de force* covering history, aesthetics and philosophy.

In 1971 he wrote his first play in Gujarati, *Steel Frame*, which was an indictment of the corrupt bureaucracy of independent India. (The title is a reference to the well-known phrase that was used to describe the civil service in British India.) He followed that with *Tribheto*, which took up the theme of the criminal bourgeois; *Amina ane Teno Zamano*, which deals with the criminalised politician; and *Byalis*, an extended parable of the Quit India movement. He wrote *Sociology of Art and Politics* (1989-92) and *Sociology of Indian Film* (1990).

Meanwhile, Vinayak was reading deeply in Indian history. He presented a series of papers at the annual sessions of the Indian History Congress from 1979 to 1982. These were provocative broadsides aimed at just about every school of thought — from the old British Imperial historians to the so-called Marxists (the Stalinists).

He started by attacking Marx and his thesis of the 'Asiatic Mode of Production'. Marx had recognised (in my opinion, correctly) that pre-colonial Indian society seemed to have little in common with the chaotic feudalism of Europe. In order to explain the relative stability of 'Asiatic society', he posited that these societies must have been based on self-sufficient villages where private property in land (and hence class differentiation and struggle) hadn't developed. Citing a huge body of historical evidence to the contrary, Vinayak argued that this hypothesis isn't tenable.

But that raises the following question. If pre-British India wasn't like feudal Europe, and if it wasn't an 'Oriental Despotism' based on an Asiatic Mode of Production, then what was it? Vinayak answered that question by *reversing the terms of the analogy*. In his view, the benchmarks for measuring historical progress were the great civilisations that flourished on the Asian landmass for several millennia, not the poor, backward societies of the peripheral western peninsula of Asia, now called Europe that arose much later. In other words, we shouldn't be asking if Asia had been feudal like Europe. We should be asking if Europe had been feudal like Asia.

Vinayak developed this seminal insight in the next three papers he presented to the Indian History Congress. In brief, he argued that India had evolved from a hunting–fishing–food-gathering society to a pastoral society in the period 7000BC to 4500BC; that the pastoral (or Vedic) society developed into a feudal society by 700BC; and that this feudal society went through four distinct stages prior to the arrival of the European colonialists:

> We had a feudal period which extended over 2500 years. Indian feudalism was the most prosperous, the richest in export surpluses, and the most powerful that the world had ever known. It was precisely because it was so overwhelmingly strong that capitalism could not win against such an adversary. Capitalism triumphed in Europe from the eleventh century onwards precisely because European feudalism was petty, divided, weak and poverty-stricken. The International Feudal Chain broke at its weakest link in Europe! (*Mankind*, May 1999)

On the basis of this line of thinking, Vinayak rejected Marxism as hopelessly Eurocentric. I think he threw the baby out with the bath water. His theory is intriguing and deserves further study. And if it turns out to have merit, then I see no reason why this interpretation couldn't replace the antiquated theory of the 'Asiatic Mode' and thereby *strengthen*, rather than invalidate, Marxism in its totality.

In an article in *Mankind* (October 1997) he wrote the following lines, which seem to me to be a fitting tribute to the man:

> I am an atheist. I do not believe in any god who is going to guide us. I am a humanist. I know that we must be guided by what is essentially human, that is within all of us. We are masters of our destiny. We can do that which is good for all of us. There are thousands of arguments — economic, political, sociological, biological, cultural — in favour of socialism. But the most overwhelming are the arguments based on ethics, morality, decency, fairness, justice, aesthetics and truth! This side of the question can never be lost sight of. The case for socialism is really very simple. It is a moral choice.

Vinayak made his choice at age 15 and he lived it to the end.
Charles Wesley Ervin

* * *

Corin Redgrave (1939-2010)

It is a cliché too easily broadcast, but it is nevertheless the case that Corin Redgrave's speech at the WRP's central premises in Clapham on 14 October 1985 will live in infamy — '*We are neither for or against corruption, we are for the socialist revolution*', he began. The faction of which he was a leading member had decided to tackle the charges of financial and sexual misconduct against the long-time party leader Gerry Healy head-on. Redgrave's opening was calculated to provoke outrage among many party members who, rightly of course, found the revelations shocking and repellent. Many victims of Healy's sexual malpractice were present, and in many cases their partners, spouses or other family members. The very last thing Healy's supporters wanted was a serious political discussion, in which there would have to be consideration of how a Trotskyist organisation had been transformed into its opposite (to use a phrase more Healyite than Trotskyist). How had it ceased to be a weapon of liberation and become a means of subjugation and exploitation of the revolutionaries themselves? Cliff Slaughter was later to say that the party had brought into itself all the qualities and methods of Stalinism. The most astounding thing about the meeting was that the pro-Healy faction actually won the vote against any disciplining of Healy. Redgrave's provocation had succeeded in baiting Healy's opponents into irrational fury, which naturally meant political incapability. It was a short-lived success, however, and it is to the credit of those who survived the experience of the 'Clapham Ragnarok' that Healy was eventually expelled and that some human and political dignity was preserved. The WRP and its

International were shattered beyond hope of repair, but many of the best of its militants found ways to go forward. Their opponents find opportunities to sneer; I find the determined political survival admirable. As to Redgrave, however dedicated and self-sacrificing he undoubtedly was, his role in defending the indefensible Healy was so contemptible that it inevitably colours any attempt at an obituary. *Caveat lector!*

Born on 16 July 1939 in London, he was christened Corin William (Corin after the character in Shakespeare's *As You Like It*, in which his father had scored an early success). His grandmother had vetoed William Corin, insisting that future schoolmates would mock the 'WC' initials. He spent most of his early years in Bromyard, near Worcester, growing up with sisters Vanessa and Lyn. Undoubtedly, as the *ad hominem* critics of the Redgraves insist, this upbringing had some idyllic aspects, but the Redgrave children were separated from their parents for long periods, as father Michael and his wife Rachel Kempson pursued their acting careers in London and elsewhere. One of his obituarists claimed that aged six he failed to recognise his father on stage. After a short and unhappy period in boarding school he went to Westminster School, where he won a scholarship to King's College Cambridge; there his love of drama was to shape the next, highly successful, stages of his career as an actor.

Physical separation was not the only component of a difficult relationship with his parents. Michael Redgrave was an active bisexual, conducting frequent affairs with well-known theatrical men. In the 1960s, the liberal view of such activities now prevalent in London did not apply. It is easy to speculate that Corin Redgrave might have found in Gerry Healy all the qualities that Michael Redgrave failed to provide a boy. However, Michael's bisexuality would seem to have been the route through which socialist ideas came into the family. Michael's first flirtation, when he was only 16, was with 25-year-old Oliver Baldwin, son of Prime Minister Stanley Baldwin. Oliver gave Michael an interest in left-wing politics, and he was to write: 'I could not politically call myself anything but a socialist.'[1]

Redgrave joined what was then the Socialist Labour League (SLL) in 1971, before it became the Workers Revolutionary Party (WRP) in 1973. He had been drawn into political activity by his sister Vanessa, who involved him in the Campaign for Nuclear Disarmament (CND). He was later to recruit her into the SLL. He devoted increasing amounts of his time to the WRP and became an important leading figure, always allied with Healy (as was Vanessa). Tim Wohlforth (in Bob Pitt's account of the life of Healy) describes being positively impressed by both of them for their seriousness and dedication to the work of the party. Both the Redgraves (and at the same time the *Sunday Times* journalist Alex Mitchell) were rapidly promoted into leading positions. By 1973, on the basis of about two years' experience in the movement, the two Redgraves represented the SLL at the conference of the International Committee (the fragment of the former Fourth International led by Healy and Lambert).

The Redgraves were influential in recruiting a wide layer of people from the worlds of theatre, film and TV, their contacts and influence supporting the status the SLL had begun to develop through longer-serving members such as Ken Loach and Jim Allen. Among the major names that became involved with the SLL at this stage were Roy Battersby, Trevor Griffiths, John Arden, Margaretta D'Arcy, David Mercer, John McGrath, Colin Welland, Neville Smith, Tom Kempinski, Troy Kennedy Martin, Tony Garnett, Kenith Trodd, Roger Smith, Tony Selby, Jack Shepherd, Frances de la Tour, Malcolm Tierney, David Calder and David Hargreaves.[2] A wider circle of star contacts was also utilised to raise funds and boost the influence of the SLL/WRP.

The significance of these contributors can easily be underestimated in the UK in the twenty-first century, where media trivialisation has effectively marginalised culture, and 'Britart' and 'Britpop' have actively supported the process. In the late 1960s and early 1970s, some elements of the arts were seen by the ruling class as a threat to social stability. This was the era of *The Wednesday Play* and *Play for Today*, when TV drama regularly sparked political debate in the mass population. This layer of left-wing intellectuals wielded an influence disproportionate to their numbers. The group of actors and actresses wrote and performed dramatic pieces for WRP rallies and meetings, on such historical topics as the Peasants' Revolt.

I met Corin Redgrave briefly when the WRP attempted to intervene into the struggle to deselect Reg Prentice MP as the sitting candidate for Newham North-East Constituency Labour Party. He attempted to recruit the constituency secretary, Tony Kelly (who knew all he needed to know about Healy from the wily veteran Trotskyist Sam Bornstein). He was accompanied by two adoring young female comrades, who were aghast that we failed to recognise him. Redgrave found his turn to be aghast when offered a toke on a comradely joint; he made his excuses and left. Vanessa had taken an active role in the WRP's election campaign in Newham North East. I remember her, megaphone in hand, shouting 'Nationalise the superstores!' — a worthy enough slogan (though superstores were thin on the ground in East Ham), but rendered laughable by the fact that she was shouting at the East Ham Co-op.

It is undoubtedly the case that Redgrave's acting career suffered during his time in the SLL/WRP. He claimed that he was 'blacklisted', and later 'rehabilitated'. It is unlikely that the management of the BBC would be so clumsy as to operate a formal blacklist, and some of the other actors and actresses who were attracted to the WRP (in large part because of the Redgraves' prominence and persuasiveness, but the much longer record of dedication by figures such as Ken Loach and Jim Allen should not be discounted) did not suffer comparable neglect. It seems more probable that leading right-wingers in Equity, the actors' union, would have used their influence against him, and also that the commitment of his time to the WRP made it difficult for him to promote himself adequately. His professional reputation was certainly damaged in 1974 when he attempted to evade his contractual obligation to go to Australia for filming; Edward Heath had called the General Election, and Redgrave's priority was clearly to take part in the WRP's campaign.

His first marriage, to model Dierdre Hamilton-Hill, which had produced two children, failed at about the same time, though they were not to be divorced until 1981. Hamilton-Hill provided some jaundiced recollections of the relationship. The family home was usually full of what she called 'itinerant Marxists', and Redgrave banned wine and French cuisine as 'bourgeois'.

To the media the most notorious aspect of his involvement with the WRP was the affair of the 'Red House', as they delighted in calling it. He played a major role in raising the money to purchase 'White Meadows', a large house in Derbyshire intended to be used as a WRP training centre, and the purchase was made in his name. Before there had been time for much training to be done, it became the centre of a scandal and state-provocation in September 1975. *The Observer* newspaper published a report that an actress, Irene Gorst, had arrived late for the very first training course at the centre, targeted at actors and actresses exclusively. She had been subjected to harsh interrogation as to the reasons for her lateness, and prevented from leaving. Some accounts indicate that Gorst was Redgrave's girlfriend at the time, and that she was late because she had gone to lunch with a previous boyfriend. In the paranoid political atmosphere that Healy had instilled in the WRP, it was obvious that somebody arriving late could only have been meeting his or her controller in the secret state. It seems that nobody considered that would be the very last thing any competent controller would have organised.

But the authorities had not failed to take an interest in 'White Meadows', and the Gorst affair was the pretext for a large armed raid on Saturday, 27 September 1975. While we must always be cautious about the most paranoid Healyite excesses, there are circumstances surrounding the raid that have to be taken due account of. In his memoirs *Staying Red: Why I Remain a Socialist*, Norman Harding, whom I have met and am prepared to consider a reliable witness, describes how he was working in London preparing the party's daily newspaper. Part of his routine was to go to Fleet Street to collect the very first copies of the Sunday newspapers. *The Observer* had an article describing the raid in some detail, even specifying the number of police involved, and stating that an arms cache had been discovered. *This had been printed hours before the raid actually took place.* The Gorst allegations had been in the hands of *The Observer* for two weeks and first appeared in this same article. Everything had been calculated to make front-page news on the first day of the Labour Party conference; the star turn at the conference was to be the deselected and defeated Reg Prentice, warning the party against 'extremist infiltration'. It subsequently emerged that the raid had been personally authorised by Home Secretary Roy Jenkins, who was to leave the Labour Party and co-found the SDP. By the time Harding was able to telephone to 'White Meadows', the real raid was beginning.

The BBC TV documentary *True Spies*, Episode 2, dealt with the raid. The following (edited only for readability) extract is from the transcript on the BBC website.

> **Commentary**: Special Branch recruited spies in every corner of the Far Left — each with their own number.
> **Tony Robinson**: Lancashire Police Special Branch, 1965-81. **Tony Robinson sync**: Starting off with 672 in the rails branch of Communist Party, industrial branch. Followed up with 735, Workers Revolutionary Party. Then I had 846 in the International Marxist Group, 919 Revolutionary Students Group, 10.77 in the Young Communist League, and Michael — Leyland Motors branch — Communist Party.
> **Commentary**: The splinter group to be seen in was the Workers Revolutionary Party — the WRP. This was revolution with glamour — the vanguard of writers, directors and stars. Vanessa Redgrave was its leading lady. But MI5 believed the WRP was involved in more than just theatre — much to the outrage of its party members.
> **Roy Battersby**: Workers' Revolutionary Party, 1968-80. **Battersby sync**: One has to say that we were legal, we were public, there were no secrets in what we thought. So in a sense you say well how does that make me a subversive. My politics are not about to bring down the state.
> **Commentary**: MI5 told one of its Special Branch handlers in the Midlands that it wanted intelligence on the WRP's educational centre in Derbyshire, known as the 'Red House'.
> **Dennis**: West Midlands Police Special Branch, 1977-98. **Dennis sync**: Let's see what's going on behind closed doors, is this just a left-wing, Trotskyist, revolutionary party spouting out all the information you'd expect them to spout, or is there a hidden agenda?
> **Commentary**: To find out, Dennis recruited an agent to spy on the WRP. MI5 paid him £500 a month — in cash, tax free.
> **Tom**: Special Branch Agent, 1977-87. **Tom sync**:

Interviewer: Did they talk revolution at the Red House?
Tom: They always talk about that, that was their main thing, revolution, that we need to change from this to that.
Vanessa actuality: This was the immediate necessity to prepare for the threatening catastrophe which threatens the working class.
Commentary: What was Vanessa Redgrave like?
Tom: Sometimes she can be very rude, and she would be outspoken. And many times it was say that we should get this government out. Workers Revolutionary Party should take over, and we can control the workers.
Commentary: There were suspicions that the Red House was more than just a talking shop and that armed revolution was being plotted behind closed doors. [*Pause*] Special Branch raided the premises, looking for evidence.
Battersby sync: They asked me what this door was and I said oh it's just an empty space, it's going to be for storage and stuff. And they then asked me could I get a stronger bulb for the light on the stairway and I went back into a bathroom and unscrewed a bulb, and by the time I came back out onto the stairs, looking down at this cupboard, they had the cupboard door opened and a Special Branch officer was leaning in, and he came out of the cupboard and went, 'Eh! Look what I've found!' And opened his hand and from the top of the stairs I could see that he had three 2.2 shells in his hand, and I said literally, 'Where are they supposed to have come from?' And he said, 'Are you suggesting we planted them?', and I said, 'I'm not suggesting anything. I'm just telling you that they didn't come from inside that cupboard.'

(Roy Battersby, the well-known TV producer, had been instructed by the WRP to leave London and oversee the construction work at the centre.)

The Redgraves sued *The Observer*, claiming the report had damaged their reputations. There are still some ex-WRP members who claim that the WRP won the case (although in her memoirs Vanessa Redgrave states that they lost). The jury was asked three specific questions. Here they are, with the jury's replies:

Are the words complained of defamatory of the plaintiffs? — Yes.
Are all the words complained of substantially true? — No.
If all the words complained of are not substantially true, do the words which are not true materially injure the reputation of the plaintiffs? — No.

The court awarded costs against the complainants, in the sum of £75 000, which was a massive blow to the WRP.

Of Irene Gorst, Google informs us little, and that little, if not much admirable, is not actually discrediting. She is recorded with a role in the film *Confessions of a Pop Performer* (1975) as a policewoman, 'Penelope', who interrupts the sexual antics in a store-room of the lead characters, after which she adjourns to the same store room with a policeman, there to pursue their own carnal ends. One of the less elevated internet filmographies has it that: 'Irene Gorst, as the cop, strips to her bra, garter and knickers.' To be specific about the singular of 'garter' shows attention to detail which we must consider proper and scholarly. *Confessions…* is listed in the *NY Times* filmography as her only entry. This is unfair. She is also entitled to credit (according to the British Film Institute) for her part as one of a group of 'bar dancers' in *Moon Zero Two* (1969), billed as 'The first moon western', as 'a dancer' in *Man at the Top: How To Make a Fortune* (1972), and as 'Carol' in two 1975 films *The Wackers: No Rest for the Wicked* and *The Wackers: Everybody's Doing It* (my recollection is that in the early 1970s 'wack' was slang for 'masturbate', which may assist readers in understanding the *double entendres* in the titles). She retained some connection with the theatre after the 'Red House' affair, as she was listed as one of those present at the 19 March 2009 memorial service to the distinguished actor Paul Scofield.

Redgrave stood as the WRP's candidate in the 1978 by-election in Lambeth Central, where he got 271 votes, putting him in sixth position. The far-right National Front got 1291.

Much of the activity of the Redgraves, Alex Mitchell and Healy in the following few years was to take place around Healy's astonishingly successful abandonment of all the principles of Trotskyism and his diplomatic engagement with a number of Middle Eastern leaderships. This entailed the party engaging in spying for these states, while at the same time accusing Healy's historical rivals in the (US) Socialist Workers Party of being spies in the service, simultaneously, of imperialism and Stalinism. Norman Harding has described how a secret opposition slowly and cautiously grew in response both to these developments and to the movement's isolation from the concerns of the working class.

The lid blew off at the end of June 1985. In a letter to the Political Committee, Aileen Jennings revealed the extent of Healy's sexual abuse of female members of the party. She also revealed that the party had attempted to deal with the same problem as early as 1964, when Healy had promised a Control Commission to cease such practices.

The story of the path from these revelations to Healy's eventual expulsion is too complex to deal with here. Bob Pitt's on-line history and Norman Harding's memoirs provide some of the material.

'Tom Burns', who wrote the report in the Spring 1988 issue of *Solidarity*, on the WRP's financial disaster and its political origins, was, I have recently learned, Adam Westoby. He mischievously appropriated the pseudonym previously used by Healy himself, and prior to that by Jock Haston. He managed to assemble deep knowledge of what was going on in the WRP, including collecting a full set of internal bulletins from the period in question. It is largely due to his work that we know as much as we do about the financial and political corruption that was to destroy the WRP and the International Committee. The Workers International League (Workers Action) was later to make the report available — the only one of the post-WRP fragments to do so, as far as I know. Ken Weller edited Westoby's report and checked to confirm what he could of the factual evidence before it appeared in *Solidarity*.

The same issue of *Solidarity* published sections of the report by the International Committee's commission of enquiry. Healy's opponents had ill-advisedly left him and his faction in control of the party centre for a period, during which large numbers of documents disappeared. The commission had to operate with such material as remained. Even this residue was devastating. It documented a process of political accommodation to non-proletarian forces, starting around 1976. Corin Redgrave was named as one of two signatories to a secret (even within the WRP leadership) agreement between the WRP and Libya. Part of this agreement was that the WRP would provide intelligence on 'Zionists'. Healy drafted a document for a speech that 'reconciled' the WRP's perspectives with those of Gaddafi's *Green Book*. By 1979, Healy and the Redgraves were meeting the royalty of several Arab states, while declining to make contact with leftists there. The proceeds of these visits financed the colour presses on which the daily *Newsline* was produced, and the network of 'Youth Training Centres'. By mid-1981, these relationships were cooling off, and the flow of Arab money was drying up, and it came to an end when the 1982 Israeli invasion of Lebanon decisively pushed the Arab bourgeoisie rightward.

There was also a relationship with Saddam Hussein's Iraq regime, which included filming a demonstration by Iraqi oppositionists in London, sold to the embassy for £1600 and duly receipted.

The commission proved that Healy had received well over a million pounds from overseas regimes, about half of it from Gaddafi's Libya, but other very large contributions came from the states of Kuwait, Qatar and Abu Dhabi. There was also evidence that substantial sums of cash were brought to the centre and never accounted for, so the total figure may have been very much larger. The Redgraves and Alex Mitchell were named as key figures in these dealings.

Both Redgraves displayed a fierce loyalty to Healy through this whole period and later, despite the evidence of political, financial and personal malpractice on a colossal scale. When Healy's position among the last of the WRP fragments that would tolerate his presence became untenable, they assisted him in founding a new group that called itself the Marxist Party. Corin Redgrave became

its General Secretary, and embarked, with Healy, on a whole new trajectory based on the discovery that Mikhail Gorbachev was in the process of achieving the restoration of the revolutionary movement in the Soviet Union and the overthrow of the Soviet bureaucracy. Again they showed a remarkable talent for making and manipulating important contacts, and took part in international conferences in Moscow. After Healy's death in 1989, inevitable crises shattered the Marxist Party. 'White Meadows', still held in Corin Redgrave's name, was sold. Corin began to turn his attention ever more seriously to reviving his acting career. With a small rump of supporters from the Marxist Party, he and Vanessa founded the Peace and Progress Party, which engaged in some human rights campaigns and token electoral activity. It still exists in the form of a website, which has yet to mention the death, on 6 April 2010, of its illustrious founder.
JJ Plant

Notes
1. Baldwin was a fascinating character. Engaged as he was in almost constant political but not personal conflict with his father, he may have been a significant model for Corin. Eton educated, and after a brave record in the First World War in Armenia, involving imprisonment by both Bolshevik and Turkish forces, he took to journalism. He described himself as a Marxist, and often held forth at Hyde Park Corner. After joining the Labour Party he won the Dudley constituency seat in 1929 at the second attempt. He was a critical back-bencher in the Ramsay MacDonald Labour government, and refused to follow MacDonald into the National Government. (He had a very brief association with Mosley's New Party, which lasted a whole day before he returned to Labour!) He lost his seat at the next election, and when he became a Peer on the death of his father, his political career was at an end. He was offered a diplomatic position in the Caribbean and caused a scandal by taking with him his (male) lover.
2. Thanks to World Socialist Website for this list.

* * *

Friederike Schlesak (Friedl) (1912-2011)

Friederike Schlesak, known to all her political friends and comrades as Friedl, was a determined political activist and revolutionary from Austria who died in May 2011, in her hundredth year of life. Friedl was known for her warm hospitality, especially towards young revolutionaries of the MRCI/LRCI Trotskyist current who visited Vienna for political discussions in the 1980s and 1990s.

Her life covered periods of great change: the Russian Revolution, two world wars, the turmoil of the interwar period and the rise of fascism, as well as the political changes in postwar Austria.

Born in February 1912, she was a child when her father was drafted into the army during the First World War. The effects of his experience left an indelible imprint on her life as well as his. Having worked as a coachman after moving to Vienna from the countryside, her father experienced the cruelty of that war so intensely that he came to the conviction that 'there can be no god'. This made him turn towards social democracy (the SDAP) where he became a union and party representative.

Friedl accompanied him to many meetings and was attracted by the political discussions, many provoked by the Russian revolution and its consequences. Throughout his life his main concern was that 'the workers must not be divided' — thus he opposed his daughter moving to the left of social democracy and, at a later stage, becoming a revolutionary.

Her mother originated from Czechia and worked as a maid until she gave birth to her four children. She also became a convinced social democrat, and Friedl experienced all the liveliness of political debates at home too.

The SDAP could have taken power during 1918-19, but it insisted it had to protect the masses from a revolution that would be doomed to failure. It argued that Austria — reduced to a small portion of its prewar size — was not economically viable as a socialist state, and that in any case the powerful Entente powers would not have allowed such a revolution. Otto Bauer, a leading social democrat, saw a dual role for the SDAP: using the revolutionary potential to gain power in communities, schools, factories, but obstructing any move towards revolution and civil war, which he equated with starvation, invasion and counter-revolution.

Austria moved from a monarchy to a republic, and in some places, particularly in 'Red Vienna', social democrats introduced measures — such as an impressive public housing programme, progressive changes in social and labour laws, parks being opened to the public, childcare facilities being built — that nourished reformist illusions of changing capitalism through parliamentary and municipal reform.

The SDAP's path of 'winning power by the ballot paper' did not impress the Austrian bourgeoisie. It rearmed its private armies, the Heimwehr and Frontkämpfer (Combatants), and already in 1923 workers were dying in bloody clashes with these forces. The SDAP leadership retreated step by step in the face of a bourgeois offensive.

The workers soon realised that demonstrations and marches were not sufficient to win change. Due to the pressure of the rank and file the SDAP finally founded the Republican Schutzbund, a paramilitary workers' group which supposedly would defend the workers' organisations.

In January 1927, an invalid and a child were murdered by the fascist Heimwehr, but in court their murderers were later acquitted. Demonstrations and strikes erupted spontaneously, the Palace of Justice — symbol of the hated class justice — was set on fire and the police fired shots into the angry crowd.

Friedl remembered how her father participated on that day:

> It was terrible! ... when my father heard that workers had gone on strike and were marching towards the Ring (the city centre), he was one of the first to join, even though he risked a lot working for a small company. My mother and I wanted to walk in too — information ran like wildfire, that there were demonstrations, shots... And behind the Volkstheater in the park, my father, they almost got him, mounted police shot fleeing workers. He was not caught, because he was well hidden in a bush. But they rode full speed into the people and shot unarmed workers...
>
> My mother and I did not get to the Palace of Justice... Everything was sealed off. And we stood in a doorway, a whole group of working-class women with children... Everybody was disgusted. We all saw it as an attack of the capitalists on us, workers, and the whole labour movement.

Friedl was at school at this time. Being a good student she had the privilege to continue into secondary school. It was a reactionary school, and the other students were rich compared to this worker's child. Giving private tuition, she earned a little money and got access to books. It introduced her to Vienna's cultural life, its richness in literature and poetry, and she was even invited to some plays in the theatre — a real treat for her, a passion that stayed with her all her life. During these years she was active in the SDAP's school-student organisation and local sports club.

In 1928, at the age of 16, she started training as a nursery teacher. She joined the SDAP and became an enthusiastic member. The party branch became her second home, she was able to read books on socialism and culture, and get involved with debates. After training she obtained work in a community childcare centre. She loved her work with children and the fact that it was organised by social democrats.

The events of 1927 showed that social democracy had little with which to protect the workers against the rise of reaction, except radical words. The bourgeoisie increasingly felt strong enough to go on the attack and clean up the 'revolutionary waste'. In 1933, parliament was liquidated and a dictatorship under Chancellor Dollfuss was instituted. The gains of the working class were taken back step-by-step: there were cuts in wages and social services, restrictions upon the right to strike. The Communist Party and the Trotskyists were the first to be made illegal, then the press was censored, organisations like the Schutzbund made illegal and weapons confiscated.

In February 1934, the fascist Heimwehr occupied Innsbruck and forced the dismissal of the local government. Alongside this, the central government started a broad attack: party premises were searched for weapons, representatives of the Schutzbund were imprisoned. Social democracy's reply was to negotiate, not to act. Thousands of Schutzbund members waited in vain for weapons, instructions and information. Part of the SDAP leadership fled the country; others had been arrested straight from the negotiating table.

At last when workers started an armed fight-back, it triggered off an unstructured, uncoordinated general strike and armed resistance. Friedl's later husband, Willi, went to the agreed meeting point of the Schutzbund, and she described what happened:

> They hid in the bus garage, but there was no battle. They hid for two days. A young one became impatient and crawled out of the cellar window. So they all got arrested, but they managed to hide the weapons in time and in the next days they were released, because they had no weapons and because there were no battles in this area due to the betrayal of the leaders.

With no leadership and growing demoralisation, the resistance and the general strike soon collapsed. The retreats and concessions of social democracy did not avert civil war, but left workers demoralised. It also opened the road for the victory of fascism.

In the summer of 1936, Friedl met Willi, her future husband in a nudist club, a meeting point of illegalised social democrats: 'We were both full of hate for our leaders, who betrayed us in 1934, who did not turn up, waited to be arrested, did not want to be drawn into anything.'

The Austro-fascist regime had a profound effect on every aspect of life. In her kindergarten Christian values now had to be taught. 'Our beautiful gym, we had to erect an altar to Mary… now we had to pray in the morning and we could not do sports because of the altar! This was somehow symbolic. Now they were ruling.' Female nursery teachers were obliged to be unmarried to keep their jobs, so she cohabited with Willi outside of marriage.

When the Nazis came to power in 1938, the law was changed and they married in time for their first child. Friedl gave up her work for her own children but carried on her other interests. Apart from culture, she was a dedicated sportswoman playing fistball and going skiing, swimming and hiking. Her abilities in knitting and sewing gave her the chance to earn some money, later doing it as a home-work trade. She kept contact with comrades and friends as much as she could during the years of illegality under fascist rule.

By the end of the Second World War, Willi was in captivity in Russia. There he met comrade Stadler, a leading member of the Trotskyist Frey group before the war. The disappointment with the politics of the SDAP, especially the experience of 1934, convinced Willi of the correctness of Stadler's politics. Not being Nazis, both were released from captivity and made their way back to Austria. Friedl was easily convinced to join the revolutionaries, and by December 1945 they were both members of the Kampfbund. However, Stadler soon left both Vienna and the organisation.

Austria at the time was dominated by hunger and deprivation and divided into four occupation zones by the occupying powers. Trotskyists were particularly in danger, since they were consciously repressed, especially by the Red Army. Vienna was heavily damaged by bombs, and the other comrades in the group had no flats of their own. Willi and Friedl soon became leading members. Their 33m² (355 sq ft) flat was not only a home to two adults and two children, but also a place for meetings and for printing the Kampfbund's paper, which was spread out to dry on the beds.

By 1948, the economy was expanding, but wages were so low that workers could not survive. Hunger struggles started — a strike wave in October 1950 had a revolutionary potential but was defeated; it was the last major strike for decades. With the long boom, concessions and promises were made to the trade unions, and the anger of the workers was dissipated.

Expecting a revolution after the war many on the Trotskyist left were confused and demoralised. Many groups and individuals capitulated to reformism, while others left the movement. The Kampfbund continued, but it remained illegal and an underground organisation. Sectarianism and lack of perspective were the result. After Frey's death the Kampfbund was in crisis, but it did not give up.

From 1954, political educationals had been organised for the Kampfbund members' children. First contacts were made outside the organisation at the beginning of the 1960s, particularly with students. The young people in the Kampfbund started rebelling against restrictions of underground work, and founded a semi-legal organisation at the fringes of the group. In the early 1970s, when the young members made contact with another group and wanted to found a new, legal organisation, a split with the Kampfbund was inevitable. Friedl and the Kampfbund majority joined the International Communist League (IKL) in 1975.

In the autumn of 1976, Willi, Friedl's husband, fell ill and Friedl was constantly by his side. For week after week she visited him in hospital, but his situation deteriorated. He died in January 1977 at the age of 69. An harmonious and productive marriage had come to an end.

In 1985, the IKL itself split and the Arbeiterstandpunkt was founded. It became part of a new international tendency, the Movement for a Revolutionary Communist International (MRCI). Friedl, now aged 73, was part of the new organisation, its Treasurer for some years and later its honorary President. She hosted many international guests from the other sections of the MRCI, and later LRCI, at her flat in Vienna. At the same time she continued to meet the remaining members of the Kampfbund and organised regular meetings in her flat.

In 1994, she moved into a flat in a pensioners' home and regained her vigour. Soon she was the floor representative at the home and gave support to others in a weaker position. She remained interested in politics and a supporter of the Gruppe für revolutionäre ArbeiterInnenpolitik.

Even when she moved into the home's nursing section, she had her daily keep-fit training. Only in the last five months of her life, when she was hardly mobile, did she lose the joy in life. In May 2011 at the age of 99 she faded away, surrounded by beloved friends and relations and without pain.

She created a huge 'family', into which all of her friends and comrades were included. She was a dedicated fighter and wonderful mother and grandmother to all of her 'children' worldwide. With her acuteness and her consistency, her courage and her cordiality, she will live on in our memories.

The comrades of the GRA

All quotations from Friedl are from *Marxismus*, no 10, December 1996, AGM or her Autobiographical Notes.

* * *

Irwin Silber (1925-2010)

Those parts of the London press that have marked the passing of Irwin Silber have concentrated almost exclusively on his role as an organiser and promoter of folk music. They have acknowledged the connection of this activity with left politics, but have largely ignored the breadth of Silber's life-long involvement in the left.

As with many others, the experience of childhood in the depression in New York was to form much of his motivation and attitude. Like so many others of a Jewish family, he turned to the Communist movement in early youth, undertaking his first campaign in school, demanding subsidised milk. At a children's camp organised by the Communist Party of the USA, he met Paul Robeson, who sang and played with the children. By the time he entered college he was already combining politics with traditional music and dance collected from the many European cultures in the locality.

In 1947, Silber, Pete Seeger and others formed an organisation called People's Songs, to 'Create, promote and distribute songs of labor and the American People', promoting Robeson, Woody Guthrie and Leadbelly. This organisation had formal membership, a regular newsletter and a structure of branches, and this concern with organisation was to mark Silber's politics forever. People's

Songs campaigned in support of the Progressive Party presidential candidate Henry Wallace. There was an immense anti-communist backlash following Wallace's defeat, and People's Songs collapsed under the pressure.

They regrouped to found the magazine *Sing Out!*, which still operates. Silber edited it from 1951 to 1967, contributing to the growth in popularity of folk and folk-based music, much of it having overt sentiment against war and racism. His regular column was titled 'Fan the Flames'. In 1963, he organised a boycott of a weekly show on the ABC channel which had blacklisted Seeger. Both Seeger and Silber had been hauled in front of the notorious House Un-American Activities Committee in the late 1950s, although Silber had parted company with the CPUSA about 1955. In 1964 he began his life-long partnership with Barbara Dane (his third wife), also a folk singer and political activist. In the same year he published his famous open letter to Bob Dylan (which he was to retract in 1968) criticising Dylan's development into introspective, rock-influenced amplified music.

In 1965, Dane broke the US embargo to perform in Cuba, which led to another theme in Silber's and Dane's political life together. They collaborated with the Cuban government to organise the 'First Protest Song Gathering' in 1967, and Dane's son by a previous relationship, the now well-known musician Pablo Menéndez, was to spend much of his life in Cuba.

In 1968, Silber left *Sing Out!* to become the Cultural Editor of the radical newspaper *The Guardian* and began to write on a wide range of political and social issues. He became the Executive Editor in 1972, and drew the paper towards the New Communist Movement (NCM — a congeries of Maoist and Maoist-influenced groups, most of which originated in student activism in the 1960s). With Dane he formed the recording label Paredon that specialised in songs and music from liberation movements around the world, but he was to be increasingly engaged in arguments about, and attempts to organise, a new revolutionary party.

In the spring of 1973, *The Guardian* organised a series of forums to which most of the NCM was invited, to discuss a range of questions, first of which was party building. Although well attended and participated in, there seemed to be little progress emerging from the forums. In March 1975, one of the NCM components, the October League, provoked a split by refusing to take part in the International Women's Day march because of the participation of the 'revisionist' CPUSA. A number of OL members left *The Guardian*, allowing Silber to develop a number of positions. Silber had already been developing differences with many of the NCM groups, over the question of black nationalism in the USA (he opposed a separate black state) and the role of China in Angola (where he preferred the supporting role of the USSR and Cuba). Now he became open in his criticism of the NCM's submissiveness towards China, and its sectarian dogmatism. By 1977, he had moved to a position of explicitly rejecting the Maoist 'three worlds' theory. *The Guardian* had up to then been content to be a paper that gave a platform to the NCM, it now began to consider the need for its own organisation. In 1977, it established a network of Guardian Clubs, which soon grew away from the paper. By 1979 the clubs renamed themselves as the National Network of Marxist-Leninist Clubs. Silber resigned from *The Guardian* and became the head of the new network.

He also functioned as the editor for the Line of March group, following the incorporation of the Clubs into that group. As Maoism continued to disintegrate in the USA and Western Europe, Line of March increasingly reconciled itself to the Soviet camp — particularly the Gorbachev 'reforms', and to the version of black politics embodied by Jesse Jackson. But nothing would prevent its continued decline, both in numbers and influence.

After the collapse of the Stalinist regimes in Russia and Eastern Europe, Silber made a visit to Russia to study at first hand. The result was his 1994 book *Socialism: What Went Wrong? An Inquiry into the Theoretical and Historical Roots of the Socialist Crisis* in which he concluded that the material conditions for socialist revolution had never existed in the twentieth century, and that consequently all revolutionary strategies had been mistaken. Walter Kendall reviewed the book approvingly in *Revolutionary History*, and concluded his review with a quotation:

> We need to get back to the idea that the real world is the only repository of truth; and that changing it depends on understanding it, not as something fixed in previous texts, but as a constantly developing living organism in all its complexity, possibilities, limitations and richness. Certainly it is hard to get used to the idea that the Socialist epoch, which many of us thought had dawned in 1917, has not yet arrived. But accepting that fact and learning from this false start in the attempt to develop an alternative to capitalism can be an important first step in regaining the ideological momentum that will help put the Socialist project back on history's agenda.

In his last years Silber fell victim to Alzheimer's disease, which was eroding his capacity to write and think as incisively as he had always done. Complications from the disease ended his life on 8 September 2010.

Bridget St Ruth

Mahendra Singh (1923-2010)

The veteran Indian Trotskyist Mahendra Singh passed away in June 2010. He had been actively involved with the Trotskyist movement for 50 years. Mahendra was notable not only for his tenacity and tenure in the movement. He also was truly a worker who became a professional revolutionary.

Mahendra was born in Khajurawha, a village near Jaunpur in what was then the United Provinces (now Uttar Pradesh). His parents were small-scale farmers. Sent to school in nearby Benares, he joined the local branch of the Youth League, the mass radical-nationalist student organisation that the charismatic Congress leader Subhas Bose had launched in the 1920s to mobilise youth to fight for unconditional independence. After finishing his eighth year in school, Mahendra went to Bombay to live with an uncle who was a textile worker. He lived on the Senapati Bapat Road. Still a teenager, Mahendra went to work in the mills and joined the Communist-led textile workers' union, the largest and most militant labour organisation in British India.

In 1940, Mahendra encountered a small group of Trotskyists led by a white South African, Murray Gow Purdy, who had come to India in 1936 on a personal mission to form an Indian section of Trotsky's International Left Opposition. Purdy was a controversial character, to say the least. On the one hand, he was one of the first Marxists, if not the first, to delve seriously into the complex question of caste and its role in class struggle. He concluded that the downtrodden, propertyless 'Untouchables' (Dalits) were the key to socialist revolution in India. On the other hand, Purdy also took positions that Trotsky himself would have characterised as ultra-left, such as rejecting the demand for a Constituent Assembly and glorifying violence as the *sine qua non* for revolution. In any case, Purdy was basically a rough-and-tough man of action who recruited young men who weren't afraid to face the Communist thugs in mill districts. Mahendra was their first true worker recruit.

Around this time the Purdy group came into contact with some of the Trotskyists in the leadership of the Lanka Sama Samaja Party of Ceylon. The LSSP was sending organisers up to India in an effort to unify the scattered Trotskyist groups in India. But when Purdy discovered that many of the LSSP leaders who were from wealthy families still lived 'bourgeois lifestyles', he became hostile and characterised the LSSP as a 'capitalist party'. And so when the LSSP succeeded in launching the Bolshevik-Leninist Party of India (BLPI) in May 1942, the Purdy group was left out. At that point, the Purdy group took the name Mazdoor (Workers) Trotskyist Party.

While both groups claimed to be Trotskyists, events soon revealed the significant differences between them. In August 1942, the 'Quit India' revolt erupted. Both the Mazdoor Trotskyists and the BLPI gave unconditional support to the Quit India struggle. However, the BLPI supported the struggle mostly at the level of propaganda, whereas the Mazdoor Trotskyists actually joined with Congress Socialists and other militants actively to fight the British. Mahendra returned to Jaunpur and joined a roaming group of militants who harassed the British authorities and sabotaged the roads and railway lines that carried troops to the trouble spots. After the police ambushed a number of these militants, Mahendra went back to Bombay to rejoin his comrades who were working in the underground. Purdy and some of his comrades actually carried out 'revolutionary expropriations' (that is, armed robberies) — like the Bolsheviks had done in the period after the 1905 revolution in Russia — to get money to finance the party. Purdy was arrested in 1944, but he escaped during his trial. Mahendra sheltered him in a hut on the outskirts of Bombay. The police eventually found them both in 1946, and Purdy was given a long prison sentence.

After the war, Mahendra moved back to the United Provinces and devoted himself full-time to building the party. In early 1947, he went to Kanpur, a major industrial centre and hotbed of labour militancy, to support the general strike of the textile and jute workers. By contrast, Jaunpur was a rural backwater with no industry. And so he was confined to work among the poor farmers and agricultural labourers. In 1948, he set up the Gavai Mazdoor Sangh (Village Workers Association), and he led militant struggles for land reform in Jaunpur, Pratapgarh, Sultanpur, Rai Barelli and Benares.

In 1948, the Congress Socialist Party left the Indian National Congress, which had become the ruling party in independent India. The BLPI — the official section of the Fourth International in India — decided to carry out an 'entry tactic' in the Socialist Party. The Mazdoor Trotskyists also debated whether or not to enter the new Socialist Party. Mahendra was adamantly opposed. He was committed to building the party, and he remained optimistic about the future. The Mazdoor Trotskyists decided to stay the course and denounced the BLPI for liquidating into the Socialist Party. Unfortunately, as Mahendra predicted, the Socialist Party won over the Trotskyists, rather than the other way around.

With the demise of the BLPI, the Mazdoor Trotskyists became the main, albeit *de facto*, representative of Trotskyism in India. Mahendra and his comrades took the initiative to regroup some of the small Trotskyist splinter groups. This is an important fact that needs to be emphasised. Despite the fact that Purdy himself was an adventurer, his followers matured and played a key, indeed critical, role in the slow, patient, hard work of rebuilding a Trotskyist party in India in the 1950s and 1960s. When others wanted to compromise and take shortcuts, Mahendra and his comrades fought hard internal struggles to preserve the independence of their Trotskyist party, no matter how isolated they had to be in that moment.

The issue of entrism once again reared its head after the defeat of the left in the 1952 general elections. Some Trotskyists wanted to join larger regroupments. Again, it was the Mazdoor Trotskyists, including Mahendra, who fought against what they characterised as defeatist moods and get-rich-quick schemes. Largely as a result of their struggle, the Revolutionary Workers Party of India (RWPI) was formed in 1958 as an explicitly Trotskyist party in full solidarity with the Fourth International. The top leadership positions in the RWPI, including the General Secretary and editor of the party newspaper, were held by former Mazdoor Trotskyists. Mahendra moved to Kanpur to carry out party work in the trade unions.

Sadly, this promising restart didn't last long. In 1959, the Bengal branch proposed that the RWPI merge with the Revolutionary Communist Party, a larger group that criticised Stalinism from a kind of Titoist perspective. Again, Mahendra and his old comrades fought hard against a liquidation of the RWPI into what they regarded as a centrist party at best. They couldn't carry the day. In 1960, the RWPI merged with the RCP, giving up key elements of the Trotskyist programme in the bargain. But that unprincipled merger fell apart after only two years when the two sides took opposing positions on the India-China border war; the Trotskyist section called for unconditional defence of People's China, while the old RCP majority caved in to the jingoism of the Nehru government. In 1965, the remnants of the former RWPI, including almost all the original Mazdoor Trotskyists, formed the Socialist Workers Party of India. Again, the Mazdoor Trotskyists held key leadership positions.

When I interviewed Mahendra Singh in 1974, he was living in Jaunpur and contributed articles to a new weekly Trotskyist paper in Hindi, *Mazdoor-Kisan Kranti* (*Worker-Peasant Revolution*). He survived on the Freedom Fighter's pension that the government of India awarded to those who had served time behind bars in British jails during the days of the independence struggle. He expressed bitter disappointment that some of the Trotskyists in India preferred the shortcuts of entrism and mergers to the long, hard road of patiently building up the party. He continued to be active in struggles of the local peasants.

In the 1990s, he developed health problems and he had to retire from active politics. Since he had never married, he had no family of his own. He lived with his younger brother, SN Singh, in Khajurawha.

With his passing, we have lost a rare living link to a long, rich history. Although Purdy was an adventurer, his recruits turned out to be some of the most effective, tenacious, unflinching Trotskyists. Were it not for Mahendra and his comrades, the continuity of the Trotskyist movement in India would probably not have survived the shipwreck of the BLPI. Mahendra Singh was truly a worker Bolshevik.

Charles Wesley Ervin

Wilebaldo Solano (1916-2010)

Wilebaldo Solano, honorary President of the Fundación Andreu Nin (Fundanin), died on 7 September 2010, at 13.30 in the Hospital Clinic of Barcelona, at the age of 94, following some months of illness. A ceremony of homage was held on 9 September, and he was buried in the cemetery of Sarriá. His 94 years encapsulate the story of the revolutionary movement in Spain — its countless (and as yet uncounted) tragedies and its incomparable resilience.

Approaching Solano's life as it were in reverse, coming to know of his work and to learn from his insights starting from the wealth that he contributed late in life in literary and historical work, I have discovered that, despite the personal modesty of his writings, there is a panoramic, heroic quality to his biography only subtly hinted at in his published materials. The struggle for 'historical memory' in Spain, the determination to prevent the loss of personal and political reflection on and recollection of the best and the worst times of the Spanish revolution, is one that strikes the deepest resonances with us in *Revolutionary History*. We strive to face the problems of 'deconscientisation' of our class (and they are not insignificant), but we do not have to face the problem of the suppression or marginalisation of the historical record. The comrades in and around Fundanin have had to struggle for the valuing and recording of the sufferings of an entire class, which 'modern', 'European' capital would wish to bury. For them, disinterment means not the discovery of neglected documents, but overcoming the physical and bureaucratic obstacles to honouring the negated dead. Wilebaldo Solano, after a long and most honourable life in the revolutionary movement, found in this late phase a fight worth fighting, a fight that makes history a worthy pursuit.

Born in Burgos on 7 July 1916, he finished high school at the Instituto Balmes (Barcelona). At the time of the fall of the Primo de Rivera dictatorship he was one of the organisers of the first group of high-school students and, later, one of the founders of the Federación Nacional de estudiantes in Catalonia. He studied medicine at the Autonomous University of Barcelona. In 1932 he joined the youth organisation of the Bloque Obrero y Campesino (BOC — Workers and Peasants Bloc) and contributed to setting up the Asociación de Estudiantes Revolucionarios de Barcelona. As a member of the Executive Committee of the Youth of the BOC, he began working as a journalist in 1934, on *Adelante* (*Forward*), the daily paper led by Joaquín Maurín. The surviving documents of the time show that he argued repeatedly that the crisis facing Spain was such that socialist revolution was the only solution available to the workers and peasants. He participated in the events of October 1934 as member of the Alianza Juvenil of Catalonia.

Most of his political life was dedicated to the POUM, which was founded in September 1935 with the merger of the BOC, directed by Maurín, and the Communist Left, led by Andreu Nin. From its inception the POUM was a very clear and distinctive party. Its revolutionary determination set it apart from the social democratic parties. Its opposition to Stalin's suppression of opposition and even democracy within the party that had achieved the first workers' revolution won it no friends among the 'official communist' parties of the Comintern. Its explicit criticisms of the Moscow trials of leading Bolsheviks drove additional nails into that coffin.

In early September 1935, Solano was elected General Secretary of the Juventud Comunista Ibérica (JCI) at a general conference held in Barcelona, after a stay in Valencia as a delegate of the Executive Committee of the POUM, where he had established the weekly paper *El Comunista*.

The POUM was clear, at the beginning of the Civil War, that the achievements of the revolutionaries should not be abandoned, and it placed itself on that ground alongside the CNT and the anarchists. During the revolution and the Civil War, Solano represented the JCI's Executive Committee and edited the weekly youth paper of the POUM, *Juventud Comunista*. In November 1936 his revolutionary prestige and quality was recognised at international level. He was elected, at a conference in Brussels, as Secretary General of the International Bureau of Revolutionary Socialist Youth, which included youth organisations from England, Germany, Italy, Sweden, Greece and other European countries.

The Stalinists, and in Catalonia the PSUC, finding it difficult to defeat the POUM in political argument, began the process of international slander, describing the POUM as being in the service of fascism. The POUM did not submit. Solano was one of the promoters of the Frente de la Juventud Revolucionaria (Revolutionary Youth Front), formed in February 1937 by the JCI, the Juventudes Libertarias and other youth groups. Friction within the Republican side exploded into fighting in May 1937.

The result is well known: the POUM was pilloried by the Stalinists as responsible for the events, and after the change of government, with the forced resignation of Largo Caballero and the appointment of Juan Negrín, they began a tough crackdown on the POUM, openly accusing them of being agents of Franco. Most of the Executive Committee of the POUM were arrested, and its Political Secretary, Andreu Nin, was kidnapped by the Soviet political police, and soon after murdered.

Solano escaped the Stalinist-police coup of 16 June 1937 against the POUM. With Molins i Fabrega, Gironella, Josep Rodes and Joan Farré Gassó he was a member of the second Executive Committee of the POUM. This body was established in intensely difficult conditions to build resistance to the repression of the POUM and to promote the international campaign for Andreu Nin and the other imprisoned leaders. During that period, Solano directed the weekly underground paper *Juventud Obrera*.

Solano was arrested in April 1938 and held in Barcelona State Prison (previously the convent of Deu y Mata) with the other leaders of the POUM (Andrade, Gorkin, David Rey, Gironella). He was due to be included, with Rodes, Farré and others, in the second trial of the POUM, which in the event did not take place because of the fall of Barcelona. Evacuated to the prison of Cadaqués with the other leaders of the POUM, he went to France in February 1939 as part of the great emigration of the revolutionaries, which numbered in all some 700 000. After a brief stay in the mass camps on the beaches of Southern France, he lived for a few months in Paris and Chartres, under house arrest, and was part of the Executive Committee of the POUM which tried to reorganise the party both in exile and in Spain, and to maintain relations with similar organisations in France, other European countries and America.

Detained in Montauban in February 1941, he was tried and sentenced to 20 years' hard labour by a Vichy French court in the service of the Nazis. He was released on 19 July 1944 after the assault on the fort of Eysses by a group of French Resistance fighters. He remained with the *maquis* who had released him until he could organise, with militants of the CNT and the POUM, a unit of Spanish guerrillas, the *Batallón Libertad*. He was granted demobilisation in April 1945 at his own request in order to devote himself to the reorganisation of the POUM and the publication of *La Batalla*.

In 1947, after a clandestine visit to Madrid and Catalonia, he was elected General Secretary of the POUM at a general party conference in Toulouse, with representatives from the illegal Spanish party and exile groups from France, North Africa and Latin America.

During his long exile in France, in addition to directing *La Batalla*, considered one of the best publications of the Spanish emigration, Solano founded and encouraged *Tribuna Socialista* in 1960, a magazine widely circulated in Spain in a time when resistance to the Franco dictatorship was gaining new hope. In addition, he participated in numerous international activities and in particular the creation of the Movement for the United Socialist States of Europe, one of the first organisations in Europe after the war, and the Congress of Peoples Against Imperialism, which included most of the national liberation movements of Africa and Asia. The POUM was at the forefront among these movements, enhancing its prestige in the anti-colonial movement.

Professionally, he worked at Agence France-Presse between 1953 and 1981, where he was Head of Features in Spanish. In 1975-76, during the crisis of the POUM, he opposed the dissolution of the party into the social democracy. He promoted *Tribuna Socialista* as the POUM's magazine and called for the regroupment of all the groups that were inspired by revolutionary Marxism. In the late 1960s and early 1970s, the home he shared with his companion Maria Theresa in Paris was a constant centre of attraction for exiles and for residents of Spain who kept up the clandestine struggle against Franco. And from there he continued to organise and provide resources to the movement. In one obituary notice, Boni Ortiz with evident pleasure recalled the gift of a 'Vietnamese copier' — a hand-operated screenprinter that was smuggled to Salamanca and operated secretly in the loft space of the Jesuits' university.

In the 1980s, he was one of the founders and leaders of the Andreu Nin Foundation, which set itself the objective of the complete rehabilitation of the prominent revolutionary and the clarification of the riddle of his death at the hands of the Stalinist intelligence services, at the same time as defending revolutionary Marxism and establishing a dialogue with all shades of the socialist and labour movement.

A prolific writer, he produced a biography of Nin, a history of the JCI and numerous essays on the POUM, the Spanish exile in France and the problems posed by the collapse of the USSR and the collapse of Stalinism, working intensely on such films as *Land and Liberty* (Ken Loach), *Operation Nikolai* (based on research in the Moscow archives on the murder of Nin) and *Esperanza como memoria* (Jorge Amat). He continued writing regularly for various newspapers in Spain and France. In late 1999 his book *El POUM en la historia. Andreu Nin y la revolución Española* (*The POUM in History: Andreu Nin and the Spanish Revolution*, Libros de la Catarata, 1999) appeared, and was to achieve considerable acclaim. It is still available from the Nin Foundation, and a French edition was also published. It is regrettable that no publisher has been able to produce an English edition.

The Andreu Nin Foundation's website hosts a large collection of Solano's texts, which represent a major resource for the study of the Spanish revolution, and also a selection of his writings on current issues and perspectives. We warmly recommend them to our readers.

The Nin Foundation had been screening a documentary called *Doblemente Olvidados* (*Twice Forgotten*), the cornerstone of which was a long interview with Solano made a couple of years ago. Despite his age, he was lucid, clear — vindicating the anti-capitalist and anti-Stalinist positions that he had represented in the POUM.

His death fell just a few days short of the seventy-fifth anniversary, on 29 September, of the founding of the POUM. One of the many obituaries in Spanish concluded: 'Always remember these words of Wilebaldo Solano: "The radical critique of the Stalinist experience and new trends of capitalism impose upon us the need for a powerful revival of the authentic values of socialism." He devoted his life to the defence of freedom and equality.'

JJ Plant

Ken Loach has kindly contributed the following: 'When we were making *Land and Freedom* it was great good fortune to meet Wilebaldo Solano. Andy Durgan, who was our principal advisor, told us of his long and principled career in revolutionary politics. Wilebaldo was not only helpful with information and guidance in interpreting the past, he was also a source of inspiration. It is through him and others like him that the idea of the transformation of society in the interests of working people has been kept alive. His life is a challenge to those who remain not to be faint-hearted in the struggle.'

* * *

Richard Stites (1931-2010)

Richard Stites made his first and probably largest impact with his 1978 book *The Women's Liberation Movement in Russia: Feminism, Nihilism and Bolshevism, 1860-1930*, opening up an area for study that had previously been almost inaccessible. He went on to write and edit a number of valuable books on popular culture in Russia, mostly in the revolutionary period. *Revolutionary Dreams: Utopian Vision and Experimental Life in the Russian Revolution* (1989) has been described as charting 'the wilder strains of political, artistic and social thought that briefly flourished immediately after the Bolshevik seizure of power'. I take a contrary view, and greatly enjoyed this presentation of the huge upwelling of creativity with which the revolution was greeted.

He started life in the rough and disreputable working-class area of Fishtown, in Philadelphia, which was avoided by all who could avoid it. He nearly died from scarlet fever while still at school. His father was a flamboyant gambler and bookmaker, and his mother abandoned the family when Richard was aged only three. An unverified tradition runs in his family of an ancestor who served in the Cromwellian army and witnessed the execution of Charles I. Both his older brothers served prison sentences, and one of them died of a knife wound that turned septic. With the support of an aunt, and a succession of school teachers, Richard was able to take full advantage of the educational opportunities available to him

Although he served as a Captain in the army reserves, he was never sent to Korea. A series of down-market jobs, including door-to-door salesman of vacuum cleaners, and waiter, were eventually succeeded by university studies at Pennsylvania (graduating in 1956) and later George Washington University (where he took his Masters in 1959). He was offered a teaching position at Lycoming College, Pennsylvania on condition that he specialised in Russian history. For that reason he studied at Harvard and his doctoral thesis on women under Tsardom was later to become his first major book.

He held a series of university posts and wrote and edited a number of books including *Bolshevik Culture* (1985), *Mass Culture in Soviet Russia* (1995), *Culture and Entertainment in Wartime Russia* (1995), *A History of Russia: Peoples, Legends, Events, Forces* (2004) and *Serfdom, Society and the Arts in Imperial Russia: The Pleasure and the Power* (2005). He also translated the three volumes of the history of the Russian Revolution by Pavel Miliukov, the leader of the 'Cadet' Party.

Numerous warm personal reminiscences have been provided at http://hrs3.net/stites/ from which much can be learned of his great qualities as a teacher and researcher, as also can some glimpses of his immersion in the life of Russia. 'Many years living and studying in Moscow and Leningrad', journalist Katrina vanden Heuvel wrote in *The Washington Post* in 1993, 'frequenting places where scholars are rarely found — sleazy nightclubs, movie houses, vaudeville theaters, pop concerts and workers' clubs — brought him face to face with the country's lower-depth realities.'

He had acquired a great love of Finland, and kept an apartment in Helsinki, where he was eventually to die and be buried, after a period fighting cancer. He became an expert on all things Finnish, including the concept of 'krapula', or hangover. Interviewed for a *Washington Post Magazine* article one morning in 2006 after a boisterous evening with colleagues, he admitted that he was in a state of krapula. 'There's a whole culture of krapula in this country', he said. 'You would never show up for work in the US and tell people about your hangover. In Finland, everyone understands.'

Corula Star

Reviews

Georg Adler, **Peter Hudis** and **Annelies Laschitza** (Eds), *The Letters of Rosa Luxemburg*, Verso, London/New York, 2011, pp 656, £26

This volume is a translation of the German selection *Herzlichst, Ihre Rosa*, edited by Adler and Laschitza and published by Karl Dietz Verlag (Berlin) in 1990, comprising 190 letters, supplemented by 40 more recently discovered ones included in *Gesammelte Briefe*, Volume 6 (Berlin, 1993), and is a pilot volume for a project to publish 14 volumes of *The Complete Works of Rosa Luxemburg*, including five volumes of letters, in collaboration with the Rosa Luxemburg Stiftung and Karl Dietz Verlag. Hudis, the general editor, in his brief introduction, informs us that all of Luxemburg's works previously published in English will be translated anew. Laschitza, the eminent Luxemburg scholar, and author of biographies of both her and Karl Liebknecht, provides a 28-page introductory essay detailing the efforts over the decades following Luxemburg's murder to get her letters into print.

The translator, George Shriver, explains his method of rendering Luxemburg's letters, mostly in Polish, sometimes in Russian, German or French, but often with words, phrases or whole passages in a variety of other languages, into English. They are apparently translated from the German editions due to the difficulty of consulting the originals. The translator chose to insert most of this 'foreign-language material' in square brackets in the text in order to impress the reader and show Luxemburg's capabilities and knowledge of the international labour movement. He has also, presumably where possible, translated her terms of affection for Jogiches, or left the original Polish terms, that are used, we are informed, by adults addressing children.

This method seems over-pedantic to me and often clutters the text with words or phrases that the reader will not understand anyway. In my opinion, it is preferable to insert the particular phrase or word in brackets only when an exact translation is impossible, or where there is doubt as to the sense. Luxemburg refers to Jogiches sometimes as 'my golden one' and 'Gold', the latter of which Shriver writes could be 'treasure'. Personally, I have no experience of words prefaced by 'golden' as terms of endearment, on the contrary 'golden balls' and suchlike referred to workers who sucked-up to the foreman and got the best jobs and overtime. 'Gold' just sounds awkward, so why not use 'treasure', a common term of affection in many European languages? Schatz (German) and skat(t) in Scandinavian tongues, that is, treasure, are rendered as 'darling' in English. In fact, the love letters are not my cup of tea, but presumably appeal to Nosey Parkers, or those women who read romance novels and agony-aunt columns.

There are further problems with the translation, some of the style, others of the sense, and a few relating to facts. Without being pedantic I give some examples. On page 171, 'Vorgehen' is procedure, not development; on page 174, Marx wrote 'Theorien der Mehrwert', not 'Mehrheit'; on page 218, 'Wetterleuchten' is summer lightning, 'Ist das nicht zum Heulen?' is 'Isn't that a damn shame?', and Luxemburg's exhaustion and sleep-deprivation could simply be due to 'insomnia caused by thoughts spinning around', or similar, rather than 'hangover of the psyche'. 'Heide im Winter' is surely 'Heath in the Winter', not 'heather' (p 318). A 'Pflichtmensch' is a dutiful person; why write 'a person with a strong sense of responsibility' (p 357)? 'Pferdekuren' is 'drastic remedies' (p 196). 'Quertreiberei' is 'intrigue' (p 326). A 'Kalfaktrice' is a female caretaker, not 'odd-job worker' (p 430). Why are the names of locations anglicised? The most ludicrous must be 'Friedrich Street'. Surely readers of this book will be familiar with Friedrichstrasse? Probably the most famous street in Berlin, appearing in countless spy novels and films, due to its S-Bahn station being the East-West border crossing, and the road crossing at Checkpoint Charlie.

The letter to the editors of *Social-Demokraten* in Denmark, first published by Gerd Callesen in *Årbog for Arbejderbevægelsens Historie* (Copenhagen, 1971), should be 'Annual' not 'Archive for the History of the Workers' Movement'. And *Het Volk*, described as a 'Social-Democratic paper in Stockholm' (pp 340, 342 and 573), would have sold poorly there, as it is Dutch. This might be an error from the German edition.

A number of prominent German social-democrats are described in the glossary as 'lathe-operators' where it should be 'turner'. The former is semi-skilled while the latter is a craftsman. As a fitter and turner in my youth, I, and other workmates, would have taken great offence at being called a lathe operator.

I had always thought that Verso was a London publisher, but it seems that it is now in New York, too. Not surprising then that the text is peppered with Americanisms. The 'gottens' and 'off ofs' will irritate many non-US readers coming from Luxemburg's pen; 'chickadee' (p 448) will raise a laugh for those of us who have seen WC Fields' films but puzzle others, as it is not used here, the equivalent being 'chuck(y)', which brings to mind characters in a certain Manchester TV series. 'On a high' (p 40), though, is modern patois linked to the drug-culture; 'elated' would be more appropriate. 'Oddball', too, is modern US slang, an 'oddity' or an 'original' would be more suitable. It seems that Verso has not bothered to check the translation approved by the American editors, and one wonders what other gems from relatively recent US slang will be foisted upon Luxemburg.

In the letter to Stefan Bratman-Brodowski (3 September 1918), one of those first published in *IWK* (September 1991), which we published in English in *Revolutionary History* (Summer 1996), along with the ones to Warski and to Lenin, on p 469, a sentence is missing. I have checked it against both our version, *IWK* and *Gesammelte Briefe*, Volume 6 (Berlin, 1993). Following '… completely silent', and before 'Neither he…', should be: 'Julek [Marchlewski] wrote to me that he is quite fully immersed in the question of food supplies, which is of course the most vital matter — in the short term.'

Another matter of concern is the attempt by Hudis to present Luxemburg as a feminist. In an interview in *Red Pepper*'s May-June 2011 edition, he claims that 'in a letter to Zetkin she writes how proud she is to call herself a feminist. It was to bring this dimension to attention that Kevin Anderson and myself included a collection of her writings on women in *The Rosa Luxemburg Reader* (New York, 2004).' Such a letter is not among the selection under review. In *The International Newsletter of Communist Studies Online*, Volume 14, no 27 (2008), the latter volume is reviewed by the renowned German Luxemburg scholar and researcher Ottokar Luban. He diplomatically remarks that, on the basis of a speech and three articles, 'the editors tend to thoroughly overestimate Luxemburg's role in this area'. That is, the feminist movement. In fact, both Luxemburg and Zetkin opposed the feminists of the time because it was a bourgeois movement representing a reactionary, privileged layer. The petty-bourgeois feminism of recent decades did not exist then. Readers can consult Luxemburg's 'The Proletarian Woman' in *Revolutionary History*, Volume 10, no 1 (2009).[1]

Having set out what I see as the negative features of this volume, I must point out the positive ones, too. One sees Luxemburg arrive in Berlin a nobody and quite quickly gain confidence and become an equal to all the SPD's leading lights, and, of course, she begins to challenge those who are clearly backsliding. Her political letters are priceless documents. Her letters from the various jails she inhabited during the 1914-18 war are also impressive, as she does not whinge about her own situation but writes to encourage her friends and comrades, such as Sophie Liebknecht, Karl's wife, and Luise Kautsky, Karl Kautsky's wife, and she expresses her concerns about Clara Zetkin's frail health. The letter in reply to Mathilde Wurm of 28 December 1916, is magnificent. Mathilde supports the positions of Spartacus but not openly, as her husband Emmanual is a centrist.

Luxemburg absolutely flays Mathilde for her hand-wringing, cowardice and so on, and likewise the 'heroes' of 'the swamp'. She analyses the personality of the type, but finishes by sending Mathilde a kiss, as 'you actually are an honourable, well-intentioned little girl', thus showing that she is still a friend regardless and handing her a lifeline. Luxemburg's personality is summed up in that letter: political solidity, plain-speaking and humanity.

At £26/US$40 for a 600-page hardback volume, in spite of the problems which I have pointed out, this book is worth every penny. Let us hope more rigour is applied to future volumes.

Mike Jones

Notes

1. In the same review, Luban finds it incomprehensible that a version of Luxemburg's 1918 criticism of Bolshevik policy in Russia has been utilised which omits the key second to last sentence. Following: 'In Russia the problem [of the realisation of socialism] could only be posed', should be: 'It could not be resolved in Russia, it can only be resolved internationally', but it is missing. See *Gesammelte Werke*, Volume 4 (Berlin, 1983), p 365.

Ross Bradshaw and others (compilers), *Remembering Colin Ward, 1924-2010*, Five Leaves Publications, Nottingham, 2011, pp 52, £5

So prolific and influential an author, speaker and activist was Colin Ward that this journal found no volunteer who felt able adequately to write his obituary. A note to promote this little memorial is the sad best we can provide. The compilers have assembled and edited contributions made by Ward's friends at his cremation and at a subsequent memorial meeting in Conway Hall.

For me, the keynote contribution is that from Stuart White, who recollects Ward's questioning whether anarchists made their ideas 'respectable' enough, that is, did they present them in such a way that they have to be taken seriously. White describes himself as a social-democrat, constantly challenged by Ward's questioning the need for state intervention into everyday life. 'Anarchy', in Ward's presentation of it, in the sense of voluntary cooperation and self-organisation, is an ignored but huge element of our lives, taking myriad forms ranging from Friendly Societies to Wikipedia. It is not an alternative to our present society; it is an essential part of it. The task of anarchists, in Ward's vision, is to expand it, to give it more opportunities and to promote its effectiveness.

During two main phases of my career, first in housing and later in education, I always found Ward's books and articles a great source of new ideas, challenges and insights, but always put forward in such a way that it was easy to consider them. He never wrote, as too many anarchists do, only for an audience of ultra-radicals and intent on excluding any reader who does not start from a point of agreement.

Born in 1924 into a middle-class family and the labour tradition, Ward left school at the age of 15 and worked in one of the many businesses that depended on the thriving air-raid shelter industry, before he joining an architectural practice in Ilford that specialised in the rehabilitation of municipal housing. Working next in the studio of the architect Sidney Caulfield, who had known William Morris and was very close to the Arts and Crafts Movement, he adopted the approach to urban planning and architecture that he held to for the rest of his career. In 1942, he first came into contact with anarchists. Called up in Glasgow, he attended the Mitchell Library and frequented Glasgow Green, a rendezvous for local libertarians, among them former miner Frank Leech, who made a big impression on the young Colin and encouraged him to establish links with the London magazine *War Commentary*, led by Vernon Richards and Marie-Louise Berneri. From these two bases — town planning and anarchism — Ward was to develop, from the 1950s, an original line of thought on such issues as housing, urban space, education and self-organisation of work, as evidenced in the early volumes of his prolific output, including *Anarchy in Action*, *Housing: An Anarchist Approach* and *The Child and the City*.

Around *Freedom* — which succeeded *War Commentary* — he came into contact with such talented colleagues as George Woodcock, Herbert Read, Alex Comfort, Geoffrey Ostergaard and Gerald Brenan. Biweekly initially, then weekly from 1951 despite the weakness of its resources, by the seriousness of its approach and its modern theme *Freedom* exerted a real influence on the critical British left. This publishing venture, which owed much to Vernon Richards, and to the too soon to disappear Marie-Louise Berneri — with whom Ward said he was 'like everyone else, in love' — was the arena in which his ideas could develop and broaden.

In his account of the early 1960s, Ward described how the rich experience of *Freedom* pushed him towards working on the monthly journal *Anarchy* — for which he would have preferred the title *Autonomy: A Journal of Anarchist Ideas*. For 10 years, Ward contributed prolifically, and under a number of pseudonyms.

Ward was always generous in giving recognition to his influences, foremost among them of course Kropotkin and his theory of Mutual Aid. But he did not share Kropotkin's historical optimism, once describing anarchy as 'a form of creative desperation'. Also important were Alexander Herzen for his critique of fanaticism, and Gustav Landauer. Later researchers and activists, including Paul Goodman, AS Neill and Lewis Mumford, counted heavily in his intellectual development. On another level, reading Camus, Orwell and political writings of Simone Weil sharpened his libertarian outlook. He admired Bookchin and

Chomsky, but did not consider himself a theorist, rather a practitioner of anarchism.

His contribution to modern anarchist thought was enriching. He promoted cooperation, shared ownership of space, self-help and self-organisation, as immediate practical improvements to human life. He questioned the efficacy of direct revolutionary subversion and worked to define a libertarian reformism or possibilism that would practically demonstrate the possibilities for change, and in the phrase of one of his reviewers, 'open here and there, windows on utopia'.

The indefatigable Five Leaves Press has kept many of Ward's books in print, for which they are entitled to our gratitude.

JJ Plant

Gerd Callesen and **Wolfgang Maderthaner** (eds), *Victor Adler–Friedrich Engels Briefwechsel, Dokumentation Verein für die Geschichte der Arbeiterbewegung*, 1-4/2009, Vienna, 2009, pp 147, €28

Gerd Callesen and **Wolfgang Maderthaner** (eds), *Victor Adler–Friedrich Engels Briefwechsel*, Akademie-Verlag, Berlin, 2011, pp 300, €99.80

In 1922, Friedrich Adler, who was at the time President of the International Working Union of Socialist Parties (the so-called 'Two-and-a-Half International'), published a comprehensive edition of articles, speeches and letters written by his father, Victor Adler, who had died on 11 November 1918.

In 1954, he resumed this editorial activity. By this time, his continued insistence on the Austro-Marxist line of thought had made him *persona non grata* within the postwar Austrian Social Democratic Party. As he was prevented from taking part in practical politics at home, he found the time and peace of mind in his exile in Switzerland to write his commentary on the 700 pages of correspondence between Victor Adler on the one hand and Karl Kautsky and August Bebel on the other. For reasons we don't know, a manuscript which he had also completed in respect of a new and expanded version of the correspondence between his father and Friedrich Engels was not published.

Publication of this material is envisaged in the context of the *Marx-Engels-Gesamtausgabe* (*MEGA*), but it remains uncertain when the relevant volumes (III/30 to III/35) will in fact be published. Now the Labour History Society (VGA) in Vienna has anticipated the planned publishing of this correspondence, and the VGA's volume has probably been issued to serve the legitimate interest of analysing and understanding the roots of the Austrian labour movement. However, when reading this volume, it soon becomes clear that a number of issues taken up by Adler and Engels in their correspondence from 1890 to 1895

will be of interest to non-Austrians:
* The relationship between industrial action and the general strike.
* The relationship between elections, election campaigning, parliamentarianism, May Day demonstrations and universal suffrage demonstrations on the one hand, and, on the other, violent revolutions and barricade fighting in the streets.
* The relationship between internal opposition within a Socialist party and open discussion.
* Rampant anti-Semitism, which Engels sees 'as a characteristic of a backward culture' (p 107).

Within the framework of this review, I shall deal only with the question of violence. Engels took up this issue in 1895 in his introduction to the new edition of Karl Marx's *The Class Struggles in France, 1848 to 1850*. In the original series of articles in the *Neue Rheinische Zeitung*, 'revolutions' are praised as 'the locomotives of history' (*MECW*, Volume 10, Part III). The position which Engels formulated in keeping with this immediately met with vehement opposition from the leadership of the German Social-Democratic Party (SPD). An all-too-revolutionary rhetoric, they argued, might lead the German Reichstag to adopt a bill, which had already been tabled in December 1894, to change the Constitution. Against this position, Engels maintained: 'My view is that you have nothing to gain by advocating complete abstention from force. Nobody would believe you…' (Letter to Richard Fischer, 8 March 1895, *MECW*, Volume 50, p 457) Nevertheless, Engels did take account of 'the apprehensive objections, inspired by the Subversion Bill, of our friends in Berlin' (Engels to Karl Kautsky, 25 March 1895, *MECW*, Volume 50, p 480), for instance, by allowing the passage in italics to be deleted in the following text:

> Does that mean that in the future street fighting will no longer play any role? Certainly not. It only means that the conditions since 1848 have become far more unfavourable for civilian fighters and far more favourable for the military. In future, street fighting can, therefore, be victorious only if this disadvantageous situation is compensated by other factors. *Accordingly, it will occur more seldom at the beginning of a great revolution than at its later stages, and will have to be undertaken with greater forces. These, however, may then well prefer, as in the whole great French Revolution or on 4 September and 31 October 1870 in Paris, the open attack to passive barricade tactics.* (F Engels, 'Introduction…', *MECW*, Volume 27, p 519)

Before the brochure which had been modified in this way came out, the SPD's central organ, *Vorwärts*, published a notification for bookshops with the title (in translation) 'How Revolutions Are Made Today'. Without any prior agreement with Engels, with this purpose in mind Wilhelm Liebknecht 'trimmed' the introduction once more 'in such a way as to present me as a peace-loving proponent of legality' (Engels to Karl Kautsky, 1 April 1895, *MECW*, Volume 50, p 486).

On the other hand, Engels did at the end of the day accept a compromise: the authorised text in the brochure was published in the theoretical organ of the SPD, *Die Neue Zeit* (nos 27 and 28, 1895). The regional press not only in Germany, but also in France, Bulgaria and North America, continued to run the version that he disliked (see the textual history to *Die Klassenkämpfe...* in *MEGA*^{2}, I/32, pp 1206, 1210-12).

The Viennese *Arbeiter Zeitung* of 7 April 1895 certainly did keep to the brochure text authorised by Engels (see *MEGA*^{2}, I/32, pp 330ff, and *MECW*, Volume 27, pp 509ff). However, in the edition published in Berlin in 2011 an introductory comment, which in all probability was penned by Victor Adler, under the title of 'Revolutionäre Taktik einst und jetzt' ('Revolutionary Tactics Then and Now'), Engels was once more quoted as being an unequivocal advocate 'of universal suffrage as one of the most useful emancipatory weapons...'. In the surviving correspondence between Engels and Victor Adler at that time, no attention was paid to these comments on his 'political testament' — what the two men did discuss prior to Engels' death on 5 August 1895 were the difficulties Adler had with reading Karl Marx's *Capital* (Engels to Adler, 16 March 1895, *MECW*, Volume 50, pp 468-70).

The thoroughly described attitude of Engels and his willingness to find a compromise in the controversy concerning the 'Introduction' confirms the thesis once advanced by Ernest Mandel to the effect that the proven fighter was no longer capable of realising that 'the tried and tested tactic [of establishing an alternative society by means of electoral successes] had in this new epoch [of intensified social conflicts] lost all justification'; from an organisational principle it was to be transformed into a death trap for the European working class ('Rosa Luxemburg and German Social Democracy', *Quatrième Internationale*, no 48, 1971, p 3).

Furthermore, the correspondence between Engels and Victor Adler supplies us with a great deal of material hinting that as the Nestor of the international labour movement grew older, his wish became the father of an optimistic assessment of developments.

* In 1885, he was still talking about the 'philistines' and 'educated know-alls' surrounding him (Engels to August Bebel, 22-24 June 1885, *MECW*, Volume 47, p 308).
* Five years later, he resignedly summarised the situation: 'I sowed dragons and I reaped flees.' (Engels to Lafargue, 27 August 1890, *MECW*, Volume

49, p 22)

* In 1894, he attributed to, of all people, Victor Adler, 'a highly significant historical mission':

> It is you who will constitute the vanguard of the European proletariat, and initiate the general offensive which we can only hope will not falter again before we achieve victory all along the line — and it is you yourself who will be leading that vanguard; so unless you go out into the country forthwith and thoroughly recoup your strength, you will be neglecting what is your foremost duty. And how serious that duty is becomes all the more apparent when you reflect that the only rivals whom you might have as a vanguard are the French. (Engels to Adler, 17 July 1894, *MECW*, Volume 50, p 324)

Adler, reminded of his duty in such a manner, replied somewhat hesitantly: 'I wish I could share the confidence that you have in the Austrian movement.' (Adler to Engels, 26 November 1893) In this judgement, the self-appointed 'Royal Councillor of the Revolution' who 'feared nothing more than a premature explosion' in the Danube Monarchy (Adler to Engels, 25 August 1892) was to be proven correct.

Fritz Keller

Richard B Day and **Daniel F Gaido** (eds), *Witnesses to Permanent Revolution: The Documentary Record*, Haymarket Books, Chicago, 2011, pp 682

> The revolutionary movement that is flaring up in Russia may become the most powerful means of overcoming the spirit of flabby philistinism and sober-minded politicking that is beginning to spread through our ranks; it may reignite the flame of commitment to struggle and passionate devotion to our great ideals. — K Kautsky, *The American Worker*, 1907 (page 64 of the volume)

The *Historical Materialism* book series has yet again done a great service to our movement. *Witnesses* is but one of several excellent *HM* publications of long-forgotten documents from our history.

It is difficult to do justice to the variety of complex historical and contemporary political questions that emerge from these fascinating texts. The volume is so full of eminently quotable passages that this author had a hard time deciding which quotes to include at the expense of others.

For all the criticisms I may have of Daniel Gaido and Richard Day's interpretive framework, it goes without saying that any serious Marxist should have this volume to hand. Gaido and Day have done a solid job of translating, editing and introducing these forgotten polemics, speeches and theoretical tracts into one weighty, yet easily readable, volume. It provides an English-speaking audience with a unique insight into the electric intellectual atmosphere of the Second International and its debates on revolutionary strategy. Some of its most influential leaders make an appearance — Rosa Luxemburg, Leon Trotsky, Alexander Parvus, Georgi Plekhanov, Franz Mehring and the 'papal' authority of Marxism at that time, Karl Kautsky.

The backdrop is the powder keg of the Tsarist 'prison-house of nations', the Russian empire in the early 1900s. It was a hated regime presiding over a majority peasant country with a small, concentrated working class using some of the most advanced technology imported from abroad. What was the nature of the coming Russian Revolution? Was it a 'bourgeois' revolution, or was it a 'socialist' one? Or, given the sheer political cowardice of the bourgeoisie and the fact that 'socialism' was impossible within the confines of Russia itself, was it a case of the Russian working class gaining hegemony over the peasantry and leading the democratic revolution to the end?

These questions, like permanent revolution itself, are often extremely difficult to pin down. Like many core concepts of our movement, permanent revolution is shrouded in historical mystery and subject to a multiplicity of interpretations and misunderstandings. This volume goes some way in overcoming some of them.

It is commonly held that permanent revolution originates with the precocious Marxist Leon Trotsky, and as such has furnished titles of a whole swathe of Trotskyist publications and groups. Indeed, the blurb of Pathfinder Press' reprint of Trotsky's essays on permanent revolution lauds the 'certain symmetry' of 'the two famous theories': Trotsky's permanent revolution and Einstein's theory of relativity.[1]

One strength of this volume is that it aims to provide slightly more context to Trotsky's writings. It does so through a 'rediscovery and elaboration of the concept of permanent revolution in the years 1903-07' (p xi). One of Day and Gaido's principal discoveries is that: 'Leon Trotsky, while certainly the most famous and brilliant proponent of permanent revolution, was by no means its sole author; indeed, several major contributions came from a number of other Marxists.' Some of these, such as David Ryazanov[2] 'have rarely been mentioned in this connection, while others — Karl Kautsky in particular — have often been regarded as pseudo-revolutionaries whose real commitment was always to parliamentary politics' (p xi). As they appositely put it:

> It is a remarkable irony that Karl Kautsky, who subsequently denounced

the Bolshevik Revolution and was famously condemned by both Lenin and Trotsky as a traitor and a renegade, in fact played a key role prior to 1905 in inspiring Russian Marxists. (p 60)

Further, he was 'the first West-European Marxist to employ the theory of permanent revolution in connection with events in the Russian Empire' (p 41). This is what makes the volume so important. It addresses a significant lacuna in the understanding of some of the finest aspects of the history of our class.

The authors state that 'the task of historians is to clarify great issues first, but the very act of doing so poses new questions' (p xii). For the purposes of this short review, I will zoom in on one new question that I hold to be far and away the most important posed by the volume: the disputed legacy of Karl Kautsky and, more generally, 'Second International Marxism'. For me, the historical misappropriation of this legacy has actually skewed our understanding of 'permanent revolution' — and many other things besides! — for far too long.

The common story goes that Second International Marxism was so imbued with fatalism, determinism, scholasticism and a disdain for the dialectic that it was of no use to any revolution at all, let alone the Russian Revolution. Oddly, this view represents a broad, cosy consensus from Cold War warriors in the academy through to modern-day Stalinists, many Trotskyists and even anarchists.

Day and Gaido hope that the publication of Kautsky's writings on the Russian Revolution will help 'to overcome the stereotypical and mistaken view of Kautsky as an apostle of quietism and a reformist cloaked in revolutionary phraseology' (p 569). They locate the near omnipotence of this conception of Kautsky in 'an over-generalisation drawn from Kautsky's anti-Bolshevik polemics after 1917' and in 'the ultra-leftist philosopher Karl Korsch in his reply to Kautsky's work *Die materialistische Geschichtsauffassung* [*The Materialist Conception of History* — BL] (1927)'.

Their argument is buttressed by one constantly overlooked fact: the notion that Kautsky had more in common with evolutionary Darwinism than revolutionary Marxism was one that Lenin *never* entertained. (The editors also say this is true of Trotsky, although I think here the matter is a little more complicated.) But it certainly was not a view held by other leading figures such as Clara Zetkin, who talks of Kautsky's 'fall from grace' in 1914.

But the reasoning offered differs. For Lenin, Kautsky scabbed because he shied away from the political project to which he had previously committed himself. For Korsch, and other similar thinkers, Kautsky scabbed because of the impoverished and vulgarised version of Marxist *philosophy* that had plagued him throughout his entire career. Lenin was fond of Kautsky's grasp of the dialectic. Korsch was not.

I agree that Karl Korsch is certainly one of the leading culprits of what Gaido himself deems the 'throw the baby out with the bathwater' school of historical interpretation.[3] Yet I do wonder if the wedge that was driven between the Bolsheviks and their origins in the 'Erfurt model' of German Social Democracy actually sets in slightly earlier. Perhaps it was a concomitant of the 'Bolshevisation' of the Communist parties and the rise of a new generation of thinkers, leaders and functionaries who did not go through the school of the Second International, and who thus (perfectly understandably) projected Kautsky's scabbing back onto his earlier writings.

Nonetheless, some of Korsch's conclusions simply become even more absurd in the hands of other leftist thinkers down the line. In his popular *The Politics of Combined and Uneven Development: The Theory of Permanent Revolution* (reprinted, also by Haymarket, in 2010), Michael Löwy boldly states that there is such an affinity between anti-Marxists and the 'evolutionist' Marxists of the Second International, that Karl Kautsky would agree with Karl Popper: '... according to Marxism, the proletarian revolution should have been the outcome of industrialisation, and not *vice versa*, and it should have come first in the highly industrialised countries, and only much later in Russia.' (p 1)[4]

Those such as Kautsky, then, are seen as holding a stagist mechanistic and thoroughly undialectical view of social development. As Löwy puts it:

> The theory of permanent revolution, first formulated by Leon Trotsky in 1905-06 [!], was *uniquely placed* [my emphasis — BL] to understand the politics of combined and uneven development in capitalism, and thus postulate the need for 'the uninterrupted transition from the democratic to the socialist revolution'. Uniquely, Trotsky understood this international 'totality' of the revolutionary process.

Yet this is simply not true. Kautsky, like all the writers in this volume, is clear about both the uneven development of Russian capitalism *and* that this can have implications for revolution in 'backward' Russia itself. Kautsky describes the peculiarities of capitalist development in Russia: 'The surplus-value produced in Russia will thus serve to increase his [the capitalist's — BL] influence in France, not in Russia.' Thus, unlike in the USA where the intelligentsia is corrupted by imperialist booty and the workers' movement is as weak as capitalist development is strong, 'nowhere is the number of theoretically-educated socialist agitators greater than in the land of the illiterates' (p 649) — that is, Russia. Or, to quote Kautsky's 1909 *Road to Power*, where he describes the interrelated revolutionary developments across the globe:

Today, the battles in the liberation struggle of labouring and exploited humanity are being fought not only at the Spree River and the Seine, but also at the Hudson and Mississippi, at the Neva and the Dardanelles, at the Ganges and the Hoangho.[5]

There was no social scale that ranged from countries ready for revolution to countries that weren't. There was a globally concurrent revolutionary process. A 'totality', if you will.

But so what? Kautsky may not have been as rotten as he is often made out to be. But why does it even matter? The problem is that views like Löwy's are the precondition of a second — and, in my opinion, equally ahistorical — view about Lenin and the Bolsheviks commonly held on the left, that is, that the strategy of revolution they had developed was junked in 1917 when they finally cast away the fetters of the old 'Second International Marxism'.

In a review in *International Socialism*, Esme Choonara sums up an all-too-familiar argument: 'But he [Lenin — BL] too accepted that there would need to be a "democratic revolution" before a socialist one. He rectified his position decisively in practice, if not explicitly in theory, in the 1917 revolution.'[6]

The material contained in this volume places this and similar views on extremely shaky ground. The volume makes it apparent (although not to the authors) that what was meant by 'permanent revolution' in the Second International debates was *not* the 'uninterrupted transition from democratic to socialist revolution' (that was Trotsky's unique *application* of the term permanent revolution), but an understanding of the democratic revolution being pushed constantly, uninterruptedly forwards against the bourgeoisie, maintaining revolutionary momentum to drive away any vestiges of Tsarist oppression, and introducing the far-reaching democratic reforms needed to take the class struggle to a higher level.[7]

A good summary of this approach comes from Lenin in October 1915: 'The task of the proletariat in Russia is to carry out the bourgeois-democratic revolution to the end, *in order* to ignite the socialist revolution in Europe.' There could be no socialism within the confines of Russia. But Lenin's idea, which was not unique to him, was that a provisional government, based on *majority* support, could drive forward the revolutionary process and initiate the very same era of global, internationally-related revolutions Kautsky describes above. This was neither a sanctification of the bourgeois order or of the 'historical role' of the bourgeoisie.

But this is often how Lenin's contribution to Marxism is portrayed. Before his alleged 'epistemological break' with Second International Marxism, his strategy is regarded as sowing illusions in the bourgeoisie, and as such was largely irrelevant to the actual course of the Russian Revolution itself.

Yet once more these documents speak for themselves. Neither Kautsky, Lenin, Luxemburg nor Trotsky held that the bourgeoisie would play any significant role in the struggle for democracy — it was too intimidated by the power of the burgeoning working class. As Kautsky himself put it, the further east you look, the more cowardly and duplicitous is the bourgeoisie.

Gaido and Day have provided us with ample explosive material to blow this idea of an 'epistemological break' in Lenin's thought out of the water. In addition, they have made available some of the key texts that moulded Lenin's outlook. (A good example is Kautsky's 'Prospects and Driving Forces of the Russian Revolution' — both Lenin and Trotsky wrote fawning prefaces for their Russian readers!) Yet the authors themselves have not broken with this basic approach.

In his excellent and extensive review of *Witnesses*,[8] Lars T Lih makes this point with typical clarity:

> In the traditional picture painted by writers in the Trotsky tradition, Trotsky stands alone in rejecting the fatalism and determinism of the Second International (Löwy, 2010). Day and Gaido do not really challenge this framework. All they do is shuffle the players, moving some writers from the 'fatalistic' slot over to the 'dialectical' slot. But someone is still needed to play the role of fatalist, and Plekhanov is picked to be the fall guy whose obtuseness sets off everybody else's brilliance.

Perhaps it is no surprise that this should be the case, given that such an interpretation of the Russian Revolution is dominant on today's far left. Yet in my opinion it is a view that is both historically and politically disarming. It throws overboard some of the central tenets of Bolshevism and the strategic lessons it assimilated from the 'revolutionary wing' of the Second International, not least on the question of republican democracy and the need for majority support. Indeed, today these fundamental tasks are often disdainfully described as sowing illusions in 'completing the bourgeois revolution' or engaging in some stagist (sic) Menshevik schema. This *is* to throw the baby out with the bathwater and embrace the KAPD line of Korsch, ditching the revolutionary aspects of Second International strategy.

Following the ignominious collapse of the Second International, Bolshevik leader Grigory Zinoviev was adamant:

> We are not *renouncing* the entire history of the Second International. We are not renouncing what was Marxist in it. ... In the last years of the Second International's existence, the opportunists and the 'centre' obtained

a majority over the Marxists. But in spite of everything, a revolutionary Marxist tendency always existed in the Second International. *And we are not renouncing its legacy for one minute.*[9]

Nor should we.

What is striking in reading the passages in *Witnesses* — and this is another blow to the 'big man' theory of history so beloved of Cold War warriors on both sides of the barricades — is the sheer wealth of ideas in this 'Marxist tendency of the Second International'. Our revolutionary tradition was not passed on by Lenin on tablets of stone, or invented by Trotsky in a laboratory. It was forged by the leaders of mass parties in the heat of open, fraternal and honest exchanges at an extremely high political level.

Given the truly astonishing neglect of so many important documents from our movement in the twentieth century, *Witnesses* is a significant contribution to our movement's efforts to re-emerge from the deep slumber of Stalinism and to re-articulate the Marxist political project.

These texts should not be limited to those who devote their time and energy to the history of the socialist movement. They are of burning, actual interest to our movement today, and can hopefully become — like Kautsky's *The American Worker*, which went through seven editions in Russia! — basic educational texts and reading materials for new militants and activists worldwide. In his review[10] of *Witnesses*, David North is right to point out the relevance of these debates to the tumultuous events unfolding in the Arab world. Our brothers and sisters struggling for democracy and working-class power will draw much inspiration from the ideas and innovations of these great Marxists. Kautsky's description of Russia in 1907 could have been a description of Egypt or Tunisia in 2012:

> The struggle that we now see beginning in Russia involves more than physically pitting force against force. The revolutionising of minds advances alongside the revolution of fists. The now-awakening strata of the people are being seized by a passionate thirst for knowledge and are attempting to clarify for themselves their historical tasks so that they might learn to resolve the most complex and difficult problems, rising above the small events of the daily struggle to survey the great historical goals that it serves. (p 64)

Lenin was right: how well Kautsky wrote when he was a Marxist.

Ben Lewis

Notes

1. LD Trotsky, *The Permanent Revolution and Results and Prospects* (Pathfinder, 1969).
2. While interesting, I do not ascribe the same importance to Ryazanov's critique of

the *Iskra* draft programme as the authors. Ryazanov's article shares some of the misconceptions about Lenin's supposed 'party of a new type' with the authors themselves. Perhaps Lars T Lih's *Lenin Rediscovered: 'What Is To Be Done' In Context* had not appeared by the time Gaido and Day were completing *Witnesses*, but it does seem a shame that they condemn Lenin, via Ryazanov, for the supposed 'narrowness' of his organisational concepts, which were markedly different from the Mensheviks, who 'hoped for a movement similar to that in Germany' (p 73). In light of Lih's research published on the same *HM* series, these all-too-familiar conclusions jar somewhat.

3. Interesting in this regard is Karl Kautsky's review of Korsch's *Marxism and Philosophy*. It is published in translation for the first time in the *Platypus review*, no 43, February 2012.

4. Against such a caricature of Kautsky's 'fatalism', it is worth quoting the man himself: 'The world is not so purposely organised as to lead always to the triumph of the revolution where it is essential for the interest of society. When we speak of the necessity of the proletariat's victory and of socialism following from it, we do not mean that victory is inevitable or even, as many of our critics think, that it will take place automatically and with fatalistic certainty even when the revolutionary class remains idle. Necessity must be understood here in the sense of the revolution being the only possibility of further development.' (p 223)

5. If only to underline the absurdity of Löwy's claim, it is worth pointing out that Kautsky still asserted this basic point in *1917*. While somewhat cryptically expressed in order to circumvent the prying eyes of the censor, he writes: '… the international interdependence of state life for the peoples of Europe has already made too much progress for such a tremendous event as the transformation of the tsarist empire into a democratic republic to occur without repercussions for the other states', including 'a tremendous upswing in the political power of the working classes in the entire capitalist realm' (K Kautsky, 'Prospects of the Russian Revolution', *Weekly Worker*, 14 January 2000).

6. Esme Choonara argues that the book 'overplays' Kautsky and his role. Yet just how the book does this remains Choonara's secret. The review is revealingly entitled 'Skipping Stages' (*International Socialism*, no 128, October 2010).

7. Pointing out, *contra* Day and Gaido, that Trotsky's conception of permanent revolution was different to that of the other authors who use the term does not in any way imply that Lenin then fully adopted this unique approach in April 1917. With his talk of 'steps towards socialism', Lenin adopted the view that, in light of the world situation, the peasants *could* adopt socialist measures, and thus a transition to socialist transformation on the back of majority support *was* possible. This was new, and reflected a convergence between his and Trotsky's views. Yet it is clear that Trotsky thought socialist measures were possible *without* the support of the peasantry. Thus without the internationally-connected revolution they were all expecting, there would be 'civil war with the peasantry'.

8. Lars T Lih, 'Democratic Revolution *in permanenz*', *Science and Society*, forthcoming, 2012. Lars' expertise on the Russian movement allows him to provide a much more solid interpretation of the issues at hand, and I would recommend that readers study *Witnesses* alongside this article.

9. John Riddell, *Lenin's Struggle for a Revolutionary International* (Pathfinder, 1984), p 105.
10. D North 'A Significant Contribution to an Understanding of Permanent Revolution' (http://www.wsws.org/articles/2010/apr2010/perm-a19.shtml).

Jean-Numa Ducange (Editor), **Karl Kautsky** and **Jean Jaurès**, *Le socialisme et la révolution française*, Demopolis, Paris 2010, pp 252, €21

Let us recall that at the Palais-Bourbon on 28 November 1940 the Nazi ideologue Alfred Rosenberg addressed a selected audience of civil, military and clerical reactionaries, assembled to hear their new master:

> The epoch of 1789 is reaching its end. It has been defeated on the battlefields of Flanders, Northern France and Lorraine; this epoch, which though rotting still wanted to determine the fate of Europe… Nineteen forty has witnessed an historic event comparable to that, which a thousand years ago, brought Christianity to the heart of Europe.

Alfred Rosenberg was a bit premature. One could even say that he shot himself in the foot. What followed showed that the burial of the French Revolution was premature. It has maintained — in admittedly very different economic and social conditions — a certain presence in a Europe in which, two centuries later, parasitical monarchies (including a grand-duchy) still exist, often linked to very European tax havens. Hence the interest of the book published by Demopolis.

In 1889, the year of the foundation of the Second International, Karl Kautsky published in German *The Class Struggles in France in 1789*. Despite becoming, after Engels' death in 1895, the universally recognised theoretician of Marxism, there fell on him the shadow of the person who, at the outbreak of the 1914 war, defended the massive rallying of the social democrats to the bourgeoisie and their state — arguing that the International could be effective only in peacetime but not in wartime (as if the fire brigade could only be useful in the absence of conflagrations…). But this should not diminish interest in his analysis of the French revolution, republished by Jean-Numa Ducange in *Le socialisme et la révolution française*.

A decade later, Jean Jaurès produced his monumental *Histoire Socialiste de la Révolution Française*. It is not comparable with Kautsky's analysis, neither in its length (more than 2000 pages as against a hundred), nor in the richness of its documentation, nor by its viewpoint and its vision. Jaurès attributes great importance to the actors in the revolution whom Kautsky ignores in favour of an analysis of economic and social mechanisms. Jaurès draws very vivid portraits of these actors — marked by his antipathies (Hébert, for example) or his sympathies (Robespierre, among others).

Kautsky's text is constructed like a manual — which does not at all lessen its interest because, after all, many manuals justify, or have justified, more ambitious volumes. In a series of chapters he presents an analytical vision of the principal social factors in the revolution: the absolute monarchy, the aristocracy and the clergy, the aristocracy of functionaries, the revolt of the privileged, the bourgeoisie, the intellectuals, the sans-culottes, the peasants, the foreigners... One must recognise in Kautsky a definite talent for drawing in a dozen pages a living analytical portrait of each of the social forces present. If Daniel Guérin had read Kautsky's 12 pages on the sans-culottes, he might perhaps have corrected his vision of a French revolution containing within it the germ of a proletarian revolution nipped in the bud by the bourgeoisie.

However, the mere recitation of the headings of the chapters shows that Kautsky has ignored the political forces and living actors of the French revolution: he does not deem it necessary to mention the actions of individuals, of the press which was very lively at the time, nor of the various groupings (Girondins, Montagnards, Feuillants, Jacobins, Cordeliers, etc). It is one of the great merits of Jaurès' *Histoire Socialiste de la Révolution Française* that it brings to life the actors without whom the revolution could not have been conceived.

Kautsky has a mechanistic conception of history which is brutally expressed in a paragraph which I must be forgiven for quoting at length. But this is necessary, so blinding is the clarity of this passage. Describing the rise and subsequent fall of the sans-culottes, he writes:

> Their decline, which started with the overthrow of Robespierre — on 9 Thermidor (27 July 1794), preceded by Hébert's fall, and which was confirmed on 4 Prairial (24 May 1795) — was described as the defeat of the revolution. As if an historic event, an event resulting from a chain of situations could 'fail'. One of the components of a whole enterprise, a *coup d'état*, a riot could fail, but not a whole sequence of operations. A revolution that fails is simply not a revolution. A revolution can no more fail than a storm. During a storm more than one ship will sink, and during a revolution more than one party will fail; but the sinking of a ship is not a failure for the storm and one must not attribute to the revolution what is no more than the aim of a party.

The actions of men evidently count for nothing in a storm. They can only suffer it. According to Kautsky, revolution is merely the outcome of a mechanical process of economic development and of the struggle of the social forces produced by this development.

Kautsky's work has 10 chapters all devoted to an analysis of social classes and layers... but none (with the very partial exception of 'The Revolt of the Privileged') on the actors and their actions. Kautsky judges it useless to study the actions of those active in the revolution! Of the revolutionary (or counter-revolutionary) press, the clubs, the popular societies, the sections — nothing! In the scientific study of a storm one does not pay much attention to the drowned fishermen…

It is a simplistic schematisation of Marxism. For Marx it is men themselves, and no others, who make history, even if they make it in economic, social and even political conditions and circumstances independent of their wills. Kautsky's Marxism is nothing more than a learned commentary on events, and it offers no guide to action. It is a cult of passivity, and it borders on fatalism.

Five years after the first edition of Kautsky's book, the youthful Lenin, speaking of other things, wrote in *Who the Friends of the People Are* that 'the whole of history is precisely made by the actions of people, who are undoubtedly active forces' which certainly do not arbitrarily determine the course of history. And Lenin, above anyone else, would insist on the necessity of organisation in order to act.

In his introduction Jaurès — closer to Lenin than to Kautsky — wrote: 'What we want to trace in their main lines are the progress and play of social forces since 1789.' Here he seems to follow the same path as Kautsky. But he stresses, 'let us not forget that Marx himself, often narrowly misinterpreted, never forgot that it was on men that economic forces acted', and that the transition from pre-history to history is marked by the fact that man ceases to be a simple blind and blinded object of history but becomes its subject. Jaurès re-establishes the status of the actors.

His lyricism which enables him to draw rich and vivid portraits sometimes impels him to assign to the French revolution a content beyond its essence. Thus he writes 'the revolution was socialist in its conception of property', which is evidently mistaken. It was only under pressure from the starving sans-culottes that the Montagnards temporarily limited the right of producers and traders to fix food prices (the Maximum).

In the same way, Jaurès pushes things a bit when in a passage, also reproduced in this volume, he evokes 'the revolutionary tradition of the French proletariat' and asserts, 'if it had allowed itself to be paralysed by pedantic formulas it could not have smashed the old world a century ago'. As Kautsky rightly emphasised:

> … the proletariat was still embryonic within the womb of the sans-culottes, a truly revolutionary heterogeneous mass, filled with intense hatred of the privileged, of the masters of corporations, the priests, the aristocrats, but also of the bourgeoisie… Despite this hatred and the brutal manner of its expression, these revolutionary elements were not socialist. The proletariat as a social class conscious of itself did not yet exist.

But Jaurès paints a picture of the dynamics of the revolution and of its contradictions which has lost nothing of its power.

Jaurès does not hide any of the difficulties raised by the revolution, in which he sees a barbaric way of putting an end to capitalism.

Though revolted by the Terror, he writes:

> When a great revolutionary country is struggling simultaneously against internal armed factions and against the world, when the least hesitation or the least mistake can compromise, perhaps for centuries, the fate of the new order, those who lead this immense enterprise do not have the time to rally the dissidents, convince their opponents… They fight to the death to create around themselves the immediate unanimity they need.

In order to organise the debate, both historical and political, between Jaurès and Kautsky, Jean-Numa Ducange has reproduced in his volume Jaurès' admirable introduction to his *Histoire Socialiste de la Révolution Française*, some articles by Jaurès on this question and a Jaurès–Kautsky polemic on 'socialist ministerialism' in connection with the struggle for the separation of church and state. The theoretical criticism that Kautsky makes of Jaurès' reformist politics seems pertinent, but Jaurès was to fight against the threatening world war to the end, to the extent of losing his life, while Kautsky was passively to accept the rallying of his party to German imperialism.

Even if the historical conditions have changed, this exchange, illuminated by the subsequent fate of both men, has lost nothing of its sharpness.

Let us add in passing that Jaurès' words quoted here allow us to appreciate the distance which separates him from the overwhelming majority of those who claim his mantle today and who would find it difficult to endorse these lines which open his article entitled 'French Socialism' reproduced in this volume: 'International socialism is of one piece; it has but one aim, which is to transform capitalist private property into collective property.' This is does not go down well with the sacrosanct European Union, which insists on the dismantling of all state monopolies and the general privatisation of public services which remain so only in name. Jaurès is actually very present in the sense that his official heirs are doing exactly the opposite of what he advocated.

Jean-Jacques Marie
Translated by Harry Ratner

William J Fishman, *The Insurrectionists*, Five Leaves Publications, Nottingham, 2009, pp 216, £9.99

Fishman's central thesis is that eighteenth-century France pioneered radical political methods and objectives, exemplified in Jacobinism, that finally evolved into its finished form in twentieth-century Russia as Leninism. The principal intermediary links between these two phases he identifies as Blanquism and Russian populism. What each shared was not only a vision of a new kind of society, more just and, after a period of preparatory dictatorship, more free, but the conviction that these goals could only be reached under the tutelage of a ruthless and tightly organised élite, drawn chiefly from the radicalised intelligentsia, who would not only make the revolution, but ensure afterwards that its goals were realised. Fishman skilfully traces this lineage, citing texts that render his argument difficult if not impossible to refute.

But along the way one encounters confusions that hinder his own case. For example, at the outset, we are told that the 'notion of an egalitarian society' emerged 'as a practical possibility' in the eighteenth century (p 3). Those familiar with Marx and Engels' critique of utopian socialism might come to a different conclusion. And indeed, on page 6 so does Fishman, asserting that 'Mirabeau, Danton and even Robespierre found it impossible to fulfil their obligation to the dispossessed'. No less perplexing is the designation of Robespierre, the apostle of terror and the 'surrender of the individual to the legislator', as the 'Messiah' of 'Jacobin Communism'. True, Lenin identified his own tendency with the hyper-centralism of Jacobinism, but never described Robespierre's regime as communist. Such a term surely pertains to a movement's socio-economic objectives, which above all require the abolition of the private ownership of the means of production. Even Marat, more radical in this respect than most Jacobins, only went so far as to demand that 'the fortune of the wealthiest be reduced' (p 23). As Fishman demonstrates in chapter two, only with Babeuf, after the fall of Robespierre, is there advanced a programme for the abolition rather than reform of a still infant capitalism, what he calls the 'point of take-off of modern Jacobin Communism' (p 31).

Chapter three introduces the central character in the story, Auguste Blanqui and, for the author, its hero. Fishman is at pains to prove that Blanqui has been maligned as little more than a failed exponent of the *coup d'état*. True, all his coups did fail. But, Fishman argues, Blanqui was also a theorist of substance, worthy of as much respect as Marx and Engels, while his insurrectionary techniques could and in fact did succeed given the necessary conditions — witness the Bolshevik overturn of November 1917. However, matters cannot be left there. As Fishman shows, Marx certainly respected Blanqui as a fearless fighter for the revolutionary cause. He nevertheless made some acute observations on the milieux in which the Blanquist current necessarily moved and recruited its army of professional revolutionaries. It is to be found in Volume 10 of the *Marx-Engels Collected Works*, being a review of two books by French police officials on aspects of the revolutionary events of 1848. The authors were both professional revolutionaries turned police informers and as such had much to say concerning the world inhabited by Blanqui and his co-conspirators. One, Lucien de la Hodde, like those he betrayed, saw 'in every revolution the work of a small coterie', while the other described in some detail what we would call the 'life-style' of this same coterie. It was comprised largely of former workers who now 'devoted their whole energy to the conspiracy and had their living from it'. This grouping, anticipating by a full half-century and more the Leninist cadre which would in time form the core of the emergent Stalinist apparatus, formed the 'intermediate stratum between the workers and their leaders'. Of necessarily limited economic means, they found themselves 'constantly obliged to dip into the cash-boxes of the conspiracy'. There is much more in the same vein, all describing a caste excluded by choice or circumstance from the normal processes of economic life whose sole means of support is the profession of revolutionary conspiracy. Given the success of the enterprise, it is not hard to see how the same cadre could (and in the Soviet Union did) aspire to a similar relationship with the vastly more richly endowed institutions of the new revolutionary power.

The second half of the book, chapters five to 10, deal with the Russian experience, and do it well. Beginning with the Jacobin-inspired Decembrists, through the various stages and trends of populism to the emergence and triumph of Bolshevism, Fishman traces a lineage of élitism challenged, tragically unsuccessfully, by those who took their guide from another tradition. This is an aspect unfortunately neglected by Fishman. Marx and Engels stoutly resisted attempts by Russian terrorists to subvert the First International (though Soviet historians would later praise them as forerunners of Bolshevism), while Trotsky, Martov, Luxemburg and Axelrod, to name but four, all attempted to resist Lenin's drive to 'Jacobinise' the Russian revolutionary movement, in the words of Rosa Luxemburg, to create a party which enforces the 'blind subordination, in the smallest detail, of all organs, to the party centre, which alone thinks, guides and decides for all'.

But for all its omissions and muddles, well worth a read.
Robin Blick

Pierre Frank, *The Long March of the Trotskyists*, Resistance Books, London, 2010, pp 202

This history was first published in *Quatrième Internationale* in 1969 and the first English translation by *Intercontinental Press* in 1972. An expanded edition was published in 1979 by Ink Links, London, with an introduction by Brian Grogan, National Secretary of the International Marxist Group, which was, at the time, the British section of the United Secretariat of the Fourth International (USFI).

This new issue can be downloaded from the internet by logging on to http://bit.ly/LongMarch. This site, in addition to the reissue of Frank's book, includes an appendix by Daniel Bensaïd taking the history from 1979 to 2007, a biographical sketch of Pierre Frank by Ernest Mandel, the key resolution 'Role and Tasks of the Fourth International' adopted by the 2010 World Congress, a statement by the Ligue Communiste Révolutionaire on its decision to dissolve itself into the Nouveau Parti Anticapitaliste in 2008, and a lecture given by Ernest Mandel on the Trotskyists and the Resistance in the Second World War to a school organised by the International Marxist Group in London in 1976.

The events covered in Frank's book and the accompanying documents stretching over nearly 90 years and encompassing the whole planet cover such a multitude of subjects that any review attempting to deal with all of them would be as long, or even longer than, the original book. So this reviewer will, I hope, be forgiven if he deals only with the most salient issues raised and passes over others.

Pierre Frank was born in Paris in 1905, the son of Russian parents who had emigrated to France. He joined the Communist Party in 1925, having already been involved during his studies as a chemical engineer in the foundation of the General Union of Technical Students in Industry, Commerce and Agriculture (UGETICA). In 1927 he was among the first in France to rally to the support of Trotsky's Left Opposition and helped launch the Trotskyist publication *La Vérité* and the first Trotskyist organisation in France, the Ligue Communiste, in 1930. In 1932 he went to Turkey to act as secretary to Trotsky, then in exile on Prinkipo. From then on, for the rest of his life he was in the leadership of the international Trotskyist movement, both in the International Left Opposition and then in the Fourth International, with the exception of a period of a few years from 1936 when he and Raymond Molinier broke away from the official French section, the Parti Ouvrier Internationaliste, to form the Parti Communiste Internationaliste.

A warrant for Frank's arrest was issued in 1939, and he was sentenced in absentia to several years in prison for activities against the state. He fled with Molinier to Belgium to avoid arrest and then to England, where he lived as an illegal immigrant until interned in the Isle of Man for most of the war. Back in France after the war, he was able to participate again in the leadership of the Fourth International. He was once again arrested for his work in solidarity with the Algerian National Liberation Front. He continued his work for the French section and the International until giving up all leadership responsibilities at the end of the 1970s. At the Eleventh World Congress of the Fourth International in 1979 he was elected consultative member of the International Executive Committee in recognition of his long service to the movement. He died in 1984 at the age of 79.

This reviewer had the opportunity to experience Pierre's humanity and intelligence at close quarters both in France in the PCI and then in England while harbouring him in illegality until his arrest.

Frank is at pains to establish the continuity of revolutionary Marxism from Marx and the First and Second Internationals to the Third, and reminds us that the Trotskyist movement was born within the Third International. *The Long March* sets out to give a general history of the Fourth International from 1938, but also to trace its origins in the conflict between the Trotskyist Left Opposition against the Stalinist ascendancy in the Soviet Union. The early chapters deal with the main questions on which the Bolshevik-Leninists (as the Trotskyist faction called itself) combated the Stalinists and Bukharinites in the USSR — the abandonment of the struggle for international revolution in favour of building socialism in one country and its effects on the politics of the Communist International and its parties on such issues as economic policy in the USSR, the attitude to British trade union leaders in the 1926 General Strike, and the subordination of the Chinese Communist Party in 1925-27 to the Kuomintang. This period ended with Trotsky's expulsion from the USSR in 1929.

Frank explains that though expelled from the Third International and its parties, the Trotskyists nevertheless still considered themselves as a faction of that International with the aim of winning it back to revolutionary policies. It was only after the victory of Nazism in Germany, made possible by the German Communist Party's ultra-left policy of 'social-fascism', treating the social democrats and not Hitler as the main enemy, and the refusal of the Stalinists to admit their responsibility for this defeat, that Trotsky declared that the Third International was beyond reform and declared the need to build a Fourth International. After four years of preparation it was officially constituted in 1938.

From 1929 till the formation of the Fourth International, the Trotskyist movement was reduced to small groups in various countries outside the mass social democratic and official communist parties and subject to virulent attacks both slanderous and physical from the Stalinists. Contact with the Russian Trotskyists, most of whom were now in prison and camps, was minimal. From 1929 the Trotskyists made constant efforts to regroup the various oppositional currents and organisations into a new revolutionary Marxist international tendency, and from 1933 onwards into a new, Fourth International. This involved attempts to work with such groups as the British Independent Labour

Party, the German SAP, the Dutch RSAP and ex-Communist Party people such as the Dutch Sneevliet, Victor Serge, and French syndicalists such as the Rosmers and others. Frank relates how most of these attempts came to nothing — even the very supportive Rosmers who gave Trotsky much assistance in exile refused to join the International. It has been mentioned by many writers, even those sympathetic to Trotsky, such as Isaac Deutscher, that one of the main reasons for this failure was Trotsky's dogmatism and inability to tolerate dissent, which was reflected in the general culture of the movement and unnecessarily repelled possible allies. Another obstacle was that Trotsky insisted on making agreement on the 'Russian question', Trotsky's disputes over policies in China in 1927 and the Anglo-Russian Committee of 1926 a condition for unity and more important than agreement over current policies between Trotskyists and others in a particular country. Another obstacle was the fact that many of those who joined the Trotskyists came from the Zinoviev wing and brought with them an ultra-leftist and dogmatic approach and proclivity for organisational solutions to problems.

Frank ignores these negative aspects and concentrates his fire on 'centrism'. In a section on the struggle against centrism he writes:

> This struggle was characterised by a denunciation of the policy of the London Bureau and centrist organisations such as the Spanish POUM, the English ILP, the German SAP and the Norwegian NAP… The struggle against centrism is one of the most difficult and yet essential tasks of revolutionary Marxists… Centrism needs more than theoretical denunciations in order to be fought efficiently… Centrist currents often go out to win large sections of the masses by offering short cuts, throwing overboard part of the revolutionary Marxist programme. Not to believe in short cuts, to defend the revolutionary Marxist programme as a whole, is regarded as evidence of 'sectarianism' by the centrists. But up to now no victorious revolution has travelled such a road.

Frank rejects the idea that a more patient, fraternal approach might have brought better results. He continues:

> It may perhaps be more tempting, in the light of the difficulties encountered by the Trotskyist movement, to set out on a seemingly shorter road with a lighter theoretical and political burden. But all those who have acted thus — and there have been many of them in half a century — have come to nothing.

Deutscher and other otherwise sympathetic historians of the movement have described the general atmosphere within the movement (which this reviewer also personally experienced), the exaggeration of political differences to justify personality conflicts, the attachment of labels to anyone who disagrees — 'centrist', 'revisionist', 'petty bourgeois deviationist' (uttered by someone with impeccable middle-class origins). Frank stresses the deep internationalist culture of the Trotskyist movement. Very desirable. However, it often expressed itself in the comrades of one national section (who have failed to achieve any successes at home) telling comrades in another country, about which they know little, how to accomplish *their* revolution.

Having failed to bring about a unification or international regroupment, however loose, with those closest to them — that is, the centrists mentioned by Frank — the Trotskyists went ahead anyway and formally set up the Fourth International at a secret conference in Paris in 1938 after an international conference in 1936 had failed to agree to this. There were still serious reservations among Trotskyists as to the wisdom of such a step; that it was necessary first to build viable parties in a number of countries. Frank dismisses these objections. He writes:

> ... the objection could again be heard that it was too early to announce the formation of the Fourth International, that such a decision would not be understood by the masses, etc — in short all the arguments that had led to the unfavourable decision in 1936... against the founding of the Fourth International, the considerable ebb of the working-class movement and the absence of Trotskyist organisations with a mass base were invoked as reasons. But what is to be done to transform circumstances in order that they should become favourable and create organisations with a mass base? It is impossible to renounce the programme and the organisation until the objective conditions are transformed in a favourable way. Indeed these objections only serve to conceal an opposition to the programme and a refusal to fight for it in extremely difficult conditions.

One important factor that Frank could have mentioned that made the foundation of the International so urgent in the minds of Trotsky and others was their overall perspective — their absolute conviction that capitalism was in terminal crisis (in its death agony), that the war would rapidly radicalise the masses and create revolutionary conditions which would enable the tiny Trotskyist groups to develop rapidly into mass parties capable of leading successful revolutions. Trotsky in a speech relayed by radio to a meeting of Trotskyists in New York in 1940, shortly before his assassination, declared that within a few short years the Fourth International would be leading millions.

We now know that though the war did create revolutionary situations, the

Trotskyists failed to build mass movements that could challenge the hegemony of the social democrats and Stalinists and that capitalism survived to enjoy a long postwar boom (and that today despite the repeated crises, environmental threats and wars of the last 30 years, the left is weaker and more fragmented than ever). Neither Frank nor Bensaïd in his appendix have tackled this problem because it would entail a radical re-examination of the basic premises on which Trotskyist ideology is founded.

The above criticism of the Trotskyist position should not, however, lead us to ignore the courage and devotion to the cause displayed by the Trotskyist cadres in the course of the war. Frank describes this period thus:

> The war brought considerable losses to our movement — first and foremost the assassination of Trotsky several weeks after he had written the Manifesto of the Emergency Conference (1940). There was a wholesale slaughter of our comrades in the European countries: in France, Marcel Hic and Pierre Tresso (Blasco), former member of the Political Bureau of the Italian CP; in Belgium, Leon Lesoil and Abram Leon; in Greece, Pouliopoulos; the German comrade Widelin — to cite only the names of a few leading comrades. But our dead in the Second World War can be counted by the hundreds. Our European sections, for the most part, were changed from top to bottom and their leaderships almost wholly replenished by youthful elements.

As both Frank and Mandel (in his appendix) report, the main political issue facing the Trotskyists was their relationship with and attitude towards the resistance movements that developed in the countries occupied by Nazi Germany. They had to steer a course between accommodating themselves to nationalism and an uncritical attitude to nationalist and bourgeois-led resistance groups on the one hand, and, on the other, a sectarian refusal to support genuine movements because these were influenced by nationalist ideas or were tied in some way with one of the warring camps. Of the two French groups, the POI and the CCI (before they fused in 1944), the former was guilty of the first error and the latter of the second before they arrived at a better, more balanced approach, which was to support and participate in all resistance against the occupying oppressor, even if led by non-revolutionary elements, and to work to replace them with a revolutionary leadership, transforming the resistance into a struggle to replace both the foreign and domestic oppressors by a workers' and peasants' government. This was a course which, Mandel points out, was carried out by the Yugoslav Communist Party, under Tito, even though in a bureaucratic and autocratic manner.

It is surprising and disappointing that Frank does not mention in his chapter on the war the anti-Nazi work carried out by the French Trotskyists in the

German occupying army with the publication of *Arbeiter und Soldat* and the building of anti-Nazi cells in the German army. (Although there is a mention in the list of Trotskyist martyrs at the end of the book of Martin Monat (Widelin), responsible for this work, who was arrested and killed by the Gestapo.) If the Trotskyists can be proud of anything it is of their work during the war and their upholding of the traditions on international working-class solidarity — not only in words but in deeds, paying with their lives.

The problem faced by the Trotskyists in Britain and the USA was how to reconcile responding to the spontaneous popular hatred of Nazism and (in Britain) the desire to oppose invasion with opposition to the imperialist war aims of the ruling class. There is no mention by Frank of how the attempt to do so led to the adoption of the Proletarian Military Policy nor of the problems of how to apply it in practice.

The last period of the war — from 1943 onward — and its immediate aftermath did see the revolutionary or pre-revolutionary situations which were predicted at the time of the foundation of the Fourth International, but the Trotskyists were nowhere able to establish mass parties — and, thanks partly to the collaborationist policies of the social democratic and Stalinist parties, capitalism survived to embark on a prolonged postwar boom which saw the introduction of welfare states and increased living standards. The Trotskyists remained marginal in the working-class movements (and remain so to this day). Only in Vietnam (formerly Indochina), Bolivia, Sri Lanka (Ceylon) and Argentina were they able for a time to establish any significant influence.

This was a complete refutation of the perspectives of the 1938 congress. Even when the signs of a recovery of capitalism from 1948 onward were visible, the Fourth International leadership, including Frank, continued to insist that the immediate alternatives were either revolution or military dictatorship. In a polemic with Ted Grant in 1947, Frank insisted: 'The development is towards socialism or, in the event of defeat, towards military dictatorship… the actual political regimes in Western Europe are above all regimes of transition.' These 'transitional' regimes have continued to exist — despite occasional crises — to this day.

How does Frank in *The Long March* deal with this major refutation of the International's basic ideology? He does not admit in so many words that the Fourth International and he were wrong, but admits that when the Second World Congress met in 1948 'the situation was in the process of developing in a totally unexpected direction. The few signs pointing to this development were still too weak at the time of the congress to permit a correct evaluation.' Frank ignores the fact that the British Revolutionary Communist Party majority was already challenging the Fourth International's economic perspectives of an imminent or even actual slump, and Felix Morrow's criticism of its analyses. Further on Frank writes: '... totally unexpected events occurred immediately after the Second Congress and for some years thereafter. Their results were unpredictable.' Surely Frank must have asked himself whether there was not something very wrong with the Marxism espoused by the International which claimed to be a science unveiling the objective laws which govern developments in human society. Did not this demand a critical re-examination of the basics of Marxism? Frank admits:

> Certain Marxist tenets seemed to [*only 'seemed to' — not 'were'!* — HR] to be placed in doubt by some aspects of the situation. As a result, a multiplicity of assessments and theories proclaiming the bankruptcy of Marxism appeared. Marxists could not answer these arguments with a pure and simple repetition of basic tenets, treating the latter as eternal truths... The primary task of the Fourth International was to place the basic teachings of revolutionary Marxism in juxtaposition with the new world picture, to redefine the situation, to re-evaluate perspectives and tasks.

Frank was not questioning the basic tenets or methodology of Marxism but merely their interpretation and application, as he makes clear several pages later:

> ... it was necessary to proceed to an examination of the situation with the help of revolutionary Marxism, to seek therein the key that would permit an explanation of this new situation, to see what adjustments, rectifications and enrichments had to be brought to revolutionary Marxism.

Frank remained a convinced Marxist to the end of his life; and the Trotskyists (all 57 varieties) continue to proclaim their Marxism.

But exactly what were these adjustments? The Fourth International still saw the overall picture as the continued development of world revolution, but in a more complex way and on several fronts at different tempos. The Chinese revolution, Frank writes, created a huge shift in the overall relationship of forces on an international scale to the advantage of socialism. It gave a tremendous impetus to the colonial revolution which spread from continent to continent: Vietnam, the Algerian revolution, Cuba, etc. Another front was the battle against Stalinism in the USSR and the satellite states, aided by the fact that the USSR was no longer isolated. On the other front, that of the developed capitalist nations of Europe, it was admitted that as a result of the prolonged boom and 'unparalleled prosperity, the European workers' movement... experienced stagnation and even a pronounced political decline'. However, this was seen as only a temporary delay in the advance of the revolution in Europe. Frank writes:

> There was a general agreement among economists — both bourgeois economists and those in the labour movement, Marxist or not — that following a postwar period of reactivation and reconstruction, a serious economic crisis would occur. Marxists, basing themselves more particularly on Lenin's concepts of imperialism, believed that the loss of colonies would contribute to the disintegration of the imperialist centres.

Another mistaken analysis.

The document on the colonial revolution presented by Frank to the Fifth World Congress in October 1957 stressed that it was the dominant feature of the postwar period; it had upset all the perspectives that had been made since the origin of the working-class movement, even those made after the October Revolution, because all the perspectives had been based on the victory of the revolution in the West before it could triumph in the East. The document pointed out that the colonial revolution could triumph only as a permanent revolution. Again harsh reality has not confirmed theory. In most of the former colonies national liberation has not been accompanied or followed by social revolution, unless regimes like Mugabe's can be described a socialist. Even in countries like Vietnam the 'socialist' regimes set up by the Communist parties are descending back into some form of capitalism.

As a result of the disappointment of hopes for revolution in Europe, the focus of Trotskyist activity became more and more directed to support for the movements of national liberation in the colonies and the Third World — Vietnam, Algeria, Cuba.

The French Trotskyists in particular were heavily involved in practical support for the Algerian national liberation movement. Two Trotskyist leaders, Pablo and Santen, were imprisoned for this work. There was also a move in the direction of getting involved in cross-class issues such as feminism, gender politics and other single-issue campaigns.

Another issue on which the Trotskyists had to decide their response was Yugoslavia's break with Stalin's Soviet Union. We have already seen how during the war the Yugoslav Communist Party, in defiance of Stalin, carried out the expropriation of the landlords and capitalists. Now Stalin's break with Tito was open, and this opened a new phase in the crisis of Stalinism. The Fourth International rushed to support Tito — in the opinion of some too uncritically. Here is how Frank describes its response:

As soon as the split became public knowledge, the leadership of the Fourth International understood that the international crisis of Stalinism would… be out in the open… that it was necessary to help the Yugoslavs resist the Stalinist attacks; and that the Yugoslav conflict would sooner or later have big repercussions — which should be utilised to build new revolutionary leaderships — inside the Communist parties and the workers' states. The Trotskyist organisations very quickly mobilised to help the Yugoslav revolution answer the torrent of slander emanating from Moscow and the Communist parties. Campaigns were launched in numerous countries. Leaflets, pamphlets, meetings were used in the fight against Stalinism. In several countries it was the Fourth International's organisations that initiated the youth brigades that went to Yugoslavia — brigades of inquiry, support and work in the service of the Yugoslav revolution. These brigades were relatively successful, with an enrolment of several thousand young people. For Stalinism, the Yugoslav affair was a wound that never healed. For a short period, the sections of the Fourth International, profiting from the Yugoslav crisis, became stronger. But this process was interrupted during 1950 when, at the beginning of the Korean war, the Yugoslav leadership — which until then had made progress in many areas of domestic policy (self-management, etc) and in its criticism of part of the Stalinist past — took a disgraceful position on the international scene. In the United Nations General Assembly, Yugoslavia voted for UN military intervention against North Korea. This position succeeded in alienating many of Yugoslav's defenders. The hopes of recruiting a larger revolutionary vanguard because of the Soviet–Yugoslav dispute were thus destroyed, until such time as the crisis of Stalinism would erupt again.

Alas, the following and final crises of Stalinism resulted in the restoration of capitalism throughout the Soviet bloc, and Yugoslavia, far from becoming a healthier workers' state, split up in a flurry of nationalist and ethnic massacres, presided over by former Stalinist rulers turned into warlords. Thankfully for Pierre Frank he died before he could witness these tragic outcomes.

A major setback for the movement was the split of 1953 which saw the American Socialist Workers Party, the Healy group in Britain (soon to become the Socialist Labour League and then the Workers Revolutionary Party) and the Lambert group in France (the Organisation Communiste Internationaliste) secede from the International to form the International Committee of the Fourth International.

This was preceded by splits in the French section and in the American SWP. In both cases the International's leadership, particularly the International's

Secretary, Pablo (Michael Raptis), was accused of factional interference. Frank writes that the document 'The Rise and Decline of Stalinism' written by Mandel in 1953 in preparation for the 1954 World Congress sparked the powder keg.

However, in the opinion of this reviewer, he fails to give an adequate account of either the basic differences in perspectives that divided the factions or the theoretical contribution of Pablo which drew the most bitter condemnation by the ICFI. As early as 1951 Pablo had begun to develop the concept of War–Revolution — of the coming war between the Soviet and capitalist blocs merging with world revolution. He argued that in the coming war, which was basically a conflict between socialism and capitalism, the Soviet Union, despite its degeneration and its Stalinist leadership, was in the socialist camp and that the duty of all Marxists was to support the Soviet Union against capitalist attack. This was a position accepted by the whole International. But Pablo went further. He argued that the Communist parties in the capitalist countries, the French, Italian, British, etc, would be compelled by the objective situation — by the fact that 'peaceful coexistence' was no longer possible — to develop revolutionary policies. (The case of Tito and the Yugoslav Communist Party being forced to become 'objectively revolutionary' in the course of the war was an example.) Several possibilities flowed from this. One was the possibility of centuries of 'deformed' workers' states following the overthrow of capitalism by these Communist parties and/or the victory of the Red Army. In these situations the Trotskyists would constitute a 'loyal opposition', pushing for truly Communist policies, workers' democracy etc. The immediate strategy that flowed from this perspective was that the small Trotskyist groups should enter the mass Communist parties 'sui generis', that is, as a long-term strategy. When Pablo and the International leadership tried to impose this policy on the French Trotskyists, the majority, led by Lambert, split away.

The Lambert group in France, the Healy grouping in Britain, the American SWP and small groups elsewhere formed the ICFI. They accused the 'Pabloites' of capitulating to Stalinism and denying the need to build revolutionary parties.

Although some Trotskyists such as John Lawrence in Britain and Michèle Mestre in France did liquidate their groups, abandoned Trotskyism and joined the Communist Party, the rest of the International, including Mandel and Frank, did not follow that path and continued to attempt to build the Fourth International. (Pablo did split away although that never stopped Healy and Lambert continuing to denounce the 'Pabloite' USFI.) By 1960 the SWP reunited with the USFI after it became clear that they were in basic agreement in their responses to Cuba, the Hungarian revolution of 1956 and the developments in the Soviet Union. This was followed in the 1970s by a split in the ICFI between the Healyites and Lambertists. Par for the course!

Frank's account, while not factually inaccurate, does not reveal to a full extent the organisational conflicts and manoeuvres, the clash of egos, and how differences were invented or magnified. For example, although both sides supported the Algerian revolution, they supported different wings into which the Algerian movement had split. The Healy group continued to support Messali Hadj's MNA, while the USFI supported to the FLN. One suspects that the membership of the Healy group and the supporters of the USFI who engaged in bitter disputes over this in British trade union and Labour Party meetings had little knowledge of what was actually happening in Algeria or had any first-hand knowledge of any MNA or FLN publications. (Nor, one suspects, did their leaders.) Positions were taken up for factional reasons irrespective of their merits.

To continue to deal in detail with all the discussions and events that *The Long March* and its appendices cover would make this review as long or longer than the book itself, so from here on one must restrict oneself to an overall summary rather than a blow-by-blow account.

The general thrust of the final chapters is of the onward march of the world revolution — almost unstoppable, despite setbacks and detours and defeats here and there — and the growth of the movement — again despite the odd disputes and splits, from which the International develops an even better understanding of revolutionary Marxism. The text is peppered with references to the onward march of the revolution and the growth of the Fourth International. Here are some extracts:

> ... the main documents adopted by this [1969] Congress were theses on the new rise of the world revolution... the Ligue Communiste, ten times larger and with immeasurably greater influence than the pre-May 1968 events... participants at the world congress reported progress practically everywhere... new blood... Most of the Fourth International's sections as well as the Socialist Workers Party in the USA, grew considerably in the period following the Ninth World Congress... 30 000 at a demonstration in Paris in May 1971 called by the FI... [etc].

Frank reports that the theses adopted by the Tenth World Congress (1974) 'confirmed and updated the general orientation defined by the preceding congress on the new upsurge of the world revolution since May 1968'. Writing in 1979, the year he wrote the final update of his book, Frank writes:

> Since the Tenth World Congress the advance of the Fourth International has experienced very few interruptions... In relation to the years which have

passed since its founding, the Fourth International has unquestionably made great progress.

Yet Frank is too honest and too intelligent to ignore the fact that the great hopes that accompanied the foundation of the Fourth International were not being fulfilled. Capitalism, despite crises, is still dominant in the advanced industrialised countries. In none of these have Trotskyists built mass parties and been anywhere near leading successful revolutions. Where they have exceptionally succeeded in winning substantial influence in the colonial and former colonial countries, they have either been physically exterminated by the Stalinists (Vietnam) or the mass party they have built up ended in a coalition with bourgeois parties and then disappeared from the scene (Ceylon/Sri Lanka).

Frank tries to explain this overall failure while still holding on to the basic tenets of Marxism and finding a justification for the Fourth International. He writes:

> We are the very first to regret the Fourth International's incapacity for so many years to mobilise and lead mass movements. Without denying the errors that have been committed, we think that these did not bear on the essential problems, so that even if these errors had been avoided, changes of a qualitative nature in the relationships between the Fourth International and the mass workers' movement would not have resulted. It is difficult to imagine that during 50 years, *had there been objective possibilities* for so doing, a team capable of solving the problem of a mass revolutionary Marxist leadership could not have been found — what with the numerous attempts that were made. None of the Fourth International's manifold critics have demonstrated how to do better — and none have done better.

A curious statement. Frank is saying that the objective conditions for the growth of mass revolutionary Marxist movements have not existed. It must follow therefore that the objective conditions for revolution have not existed. Frank, despite his repeated references to the advance of the revolution on a world scale, seems to be denying the whole basic Marxist perspective on which the Third and Fourth Internationals were founded. There has (not yet) been a terminal death agony of capitalism and the objective possibility of socialist revolution! Whatever the Fourth International did it could not succeed! Yet Frank asserts the historical justification for the Fourth International.

When one types in 'Trotskyist parties' on Google it comes up with 12 pages of names of Trotskyist 'Internationals' and their affiliates — over 20 internationals in all, not counting their national sections. A list that speaks for itself.

Yet one cannot end on a purely negative note. If the Fourth International has been a failure, it has been an honourable failure. Hundreds of Trotskyists have given their lives for the movement, have died in Stalin's gulags, in Nazi concentration camps and Gestapo torture cellars, have been 'disappeared' by the Argentine military, and have known prisons all over the world. Pierre Frank ends his book with a list of these martyrs.

Daniel Bensaïd's appendix takes the history up to 2007, but despite valiant efforts and occasional successes there is still no significant breakthrough.

Bensaïd ends his account with these words: 'One chapter has ended. A new one is just beginning. Filling the pages of this new chapter will require clarity, courage and a great deal of hurried patience.'

The world goes on; capitalism still creates poverty, unleashes devastating wars, threatens environmental catastrophes. And present and future generations will continue to fight for a better world. The journey to a desired destination is never straightforward. It includes detours, taking the wrong turnings, wandering off the path into swamps and finding the road again. All this is part of the journey and later generations are inspired by and learn from their predecessors. Whether to try to continue on the same road or find new paths is for those who read Pierre Frank's book to decide.

Harry Ratner

Daniel A Gordon, *Immigrants and Intellectuals*, Merlin Press, Pontypool, 2012, pp 348, £18.95

One of the most important aspects of 1968, and especially of the French general strike, was its internationalism. The French May was inspired by the Tet offensive in Vietnam and the defence of Daniel Cohn-Bendit — 'We are all German Jews' — remains unforgettable.

Yet the most concrete manifestation of internationalism — the role of immigrants, especially immigrant workers, in the struggle — is often neglected. As Daniel Gordon points out, the little booklet that Tony Cliff and I wrote on the events — based on extensive discussions with French activists — contains only one passing reference to immigrant workers. And we were typical.

So Gordon's new book, subtitled 'May '68 and the Rise of Anti-Racism in France', is to be welcomed. It covers the period from the end of the Algerian war to 1983, and is based on over 10 years' work, using both archival material and interviews and discussions with participants. The bibliography alone is a valuable research resource. Yet while the book is scholarly in the best sense of the term, it is not academic in the worst sense. It is clearly written, without jargon and full of detailed examples, and makes clear the author's passionate personal involvement in his material.

'Immigrants' are not an homogeneous mass. While racism and colonialism are central themes, Gordon also discusses the large numbers of European immigrants in France, notably from Spain and Portugal. There were immigrant workers, but also immigrant intellectuals and students. And not all immigrants responded to their situation in the same way. After all, Nicolas Sarkozy is of immigrant descent.

As for the intellectuals of the title, they are not mainly the celebrities, though Sartre, Foucault and Jean Genet gave honourable support to immigrant campaigns (Genet had his wrist broken by the police for his pains). But mainly Gordon is concerned with the students radicalised by the events of 1968 and their subsequent activity.

Contrary to the current fashion for rubbishing 1968, Gordon (born in 1975) sees the experience as basically positive. He notes Niall Ferguson's comment that 'the 1968 revolution was all about clothes' (which perhaps tells us all we need to know about Ferguson as an historian). Gordon's judgement is rather more balanced: 'We have seen the arrogance and the presumptuousness of the Left, but we have also seen the power of its commitment, solidarity, imagination and idealism.'

Of course the famous Beaux-Arts poster that declared 'French and Immigrant Workers United' was over-optimistic. One the one hand, students from relatively privileged backgrounds had little understanding of the realities of immigrant poverty and the conditions in the shanty towns. On the other, immigrants in struggle feared — sometimes with some justice — that political activists merely wanted to take over and manipulate their struggles. Yet he demonstrates that in 1968 'bonds were... forged between French and immigrant workers where they had previously been absent'. In the following year victories were won, and real solidarity between French and immigrant workers was visible.

But if Gordon is clearly sympathetic to the post-1968 left, he has no political axe to grind and attempts to give a balanced account of all currents of the French left. He recounts the vagaries of Maoist politics, ranging from physical attacks on town halls and luxury stores to setting up '*crèches sauvages*' (unofficial anti-racist childcare).

Likewise Trotskyists are given their fair share of credit, but some are also shown to be mechanical in their orthodoxy. Thus at a demonstration protesting at appalling housing conditions that led to a fire in an immigrant hostel which killed five African workers, a Trotskyist militant declared, 'But in truth, comrades, the main thing is not in the hostels, but in the factories', an illuminating insight which must have been of great help and consolation to the survivors. (This is quoted from the Ligue Communiste paper *Rouge*, but it is not clear if it was said by a member of the LC or one of its political rivals.)

Some of us might feel that Gordon is a little too generous towards the French Communist Party and the union it led, the CGT. But he shows that by the 1970s the party's Stalinism was beginning to crumble with an influx of new members. It did accommodate to racism at its base — but it also contained many genuine anti-racist militants.

Gordon traces the everyday racism and anti-racism in French society over two decades, and thus puts some of the more well-known events into context. He begins with the massacre of over a hundred unarmed Algerians by the French police on 17 October 1961. He is perhaps too harsh in questioning the testimony of Georges Mattéi and Jean-Luc Einaudi by calling them 'ultra-left' in writing off the French working class. Both made a valuable contribution to the struggle against racism and colonialism. But Gordon is right to point out that, contrary to some claims, the French left was not completely passive after the massacre; there were many short strikes and protests.

Likewise Gordon notes that Maoist Pierre Overney, murdered by a Renault security guard in 1972, was a Renault worker handing out leaflets protesting at the sacking of three of his colleagues, including one Tunisian and one Portuguese. And he points out that the attack by the Ligue Communiste on a meeting of the Ordre Nouveau in 1973 could be explained by the fact that this represented the moment of take-off for the French far right. Nothing, however, could justify the ultra-left lunacy of that particular episode.

Likewise the incident at Vitry-sur-Seine, where the Communist municipality ordered the bulldozing of an immigrant hostel (claiming that immigrants were being 'dumped' in Communist municipalities) is well known. But it is also true that a CGT member refused to drive the bulldozer.

Gordon gives us a balanced picture. Racism in France is very real and has a tenacious grip on sections of the working class. The decline of the French Communist Party has allowed the far right to grow. Yet he also gives evidence of a solid anti-racist current with very real potential. The die is not yet cast.

Gordon ends his account in 1983, which he sees as the end of post-1968 *gauchisme*. Racism survived and was indeed strengthened by the appalling record of the Mitterrand government. Immigrants and their descendants faced new problems and organised in new ways. Yet there was continuity between generations; old activists survived and brought their experience to new campaigns.

Hopefully there will be a sequel to this book, covering the last three decades. Nobody would be better qualified to write it than Daniel Gordon.

Ian Birchall

John Gorman, *Stratford: Another East End*, Five Leaves Publications, Nottingham, 2009, pp 23, £2.25

John Gorman deserves our gratitude as a documenter of the visual history of the labour movement in Britain, in his three best-known works, *Banner Bright*, *Images of Labour* and *To Build Jerusalem*. This pamphlet is a reprint of his contribution to a volume of essays honouring Professor William Fishman. It drew from his autobiographical work *Knocking Down Ginger*, which is sadly out of print. This odd title is the traditional East London name for the street game of knocking on doors and running away, now almost extinct as children no longer enjoy any street life. Even were the children inclined to leave their game consoles or tablets, neither parents nor cops would countenance street play, and it would be swiftly and sharply punished as anti-social behaviour.

Gorman's charming little work recounts his bringing up and childhood in Stratford E15, at that time a solidly proletarian area based around the railway workshops and depot, and the associated fruit and vegetable market. (Now of course its heart has been ripped out for the Olympic Games industry.) There had long been some industry around Stratford, as much of the legislation restricting 'obnoxious trades' (polluting chemical processes, as well as such activities as bone-boiling and the extraction of glue from animal carcases) applied only as far as the middle of the River Lea. Eastward into what was then the County of Essex was unregulated, and Gorman cites several legal cases. Many later to be prominent names in the chemical industries established themselves first in Bromley by Bow to evade regulation. And on the site now occupied by the West Ham Gas Works (which houses a most interesting but infrequently open museum of the gas industry) was Congreve's rocket factory, where Tipoo Sahib's innovations were adopted by the British military and the entrepreneurial Congreve.

But the 1847 building of the great railway works by George Hudson drew in and assembled an entirely new working-class population from all across England. In Gorman's telling of the story, the railway workers represented the best and most militant aspects of 'old unionism', emerging at the same time as the 'new unionism' of the gas workers, dockers and 'match-girls'. They set up their own clubs and institutes, regulated apprenticeships, and, after a couple of false starts, launched the Stratford Cooperative Society that eventually grew, together with other societies, into the mighty London Cooperative Society.

Gorman's account of his childhood is intimate and charming. His depiction of his father and his working life is noble. And he records details of life in the area that are not available elsewhere. Until *Knocking Down Ginger* is reprinted, this pamphlet remains a valuable source and a good read.

JJ Plant

Ernst Hanisch, *Der große Illusionist: Otto Bauer (1881-1938)*, Böhlau Verlag, Vienna, 2011, pp 478, €39

The history of the rump Austria during 1918-34, in the wake of the collapse of the Austro-Hungarian monarchy, was characterised by an armed struggle between the Social Democratic and the Christian Social camps for control over the state. The opposing poles in this conflict, which ended in the ousting of the labour movement and the establishment of a clerical-fascist regime entirely at the mercy of Benito Mussolini, were personified by, on the one hand, Otto Bauer, the leader of the Social Democratic Party (SPÖ) and the defender of parliamentary democracy, and, on the other, Ignaz Seipel (1876-1932), who paved the way for a corporate state dictatorship along the lines of the Pope's encyclical letter *Quadragesimo Anno*. Until now we have been presented with two scholarly biographies dealing with the Catholic moral theologian and politician with the cognomen 'Prelate without Mercy', whereas there was not a single comprehensive biographical study of the party leader and spokesman of Austro-Marxism. The present study, based on several years of research, attempts to remedy this situation.

This observation immediately raises the question of why no Social Democratic historian had taken on this task. Part of the answer is to be found in the fact that after 1945 the SPÖ leadership rejected Austro-Marxism, along with any other variety of Marxism, and acted according to the following motto: 'Praised be the name of the Lord — but are we grateful he is dead!' It is also in this light that we must see the voluminous edition of Otto Bauer's works, which did not follow scholarly principles. (The official peace settlement between Otto Bauer, who had shed this mortal coil, and the SPÖ leadership was not achieved until Alfred Gusenbauer, party leader at the time, wrote an article about him in the daily newspaper, the *Standard*, on 5 July 2008 on the occasion of the seventieth anniversary of his death.)

But why did Otto Leichter, who sympathised with Otto Bauer's ideas, produce a study which was far more a work of political science than a biography, *Otto Bauer. Tragödie oder Triumph* (*Otto Bauer: Tragedy or Triumph*, Vienna-Frankfurt-Zürich, 1970)? And why did Mark E Blum structure his *The Austro-Marxists, 1890-1918: A Psychobiographical Study* (Kentucky, 1985) as an anthology ending in 1918?

The answer can be easily guessed at. Precisely because they identified with him, neither Leichter nor Blum wanted to confront the remaining left-wingers in the SPÖ with the problematic stance of the party's leader *vis-à-vis* crucial episodes of the class struggle during the time of the First Republic. Thus, tribute should be paid to Hanisch for charting new territory, as, for the first time, he provides a detailed study of two situations in which Bauer was completely overtaxed, not just as a (verbal) revolutionary, but also as a crisis manager.

This shortcoming could be observed for the first time on 14 July 1927, when the outrage of the Viennese workers over the acquittal in court of three members of the Home Guard, a voluntary nationalistic organisation mainly consisting of war veterans, threatened to explode. In connection with a clash with some Social Democrats, they had killed a 40-year-old adult and an eight-year-old child. Bauer wrote a stirring article, 'Arbeitermörder' ('Murderer of Workers'), attacking the unfair verdict, in the Social Democratic daily, the *Arbeiterzeitung*, presumably with the intention of letting off steam in order to get this autonomous protest on the part of the rank and file back into the well-regulated demonstrations organised by the party. The convincing evidence presented in this biography leaves us in little doubt that during the following night when a delegation of Viennese electricity workers demanded that practical decisions be taken concerning the way forward, he asked his staff to deny his presence and stole out of the party central office through a back door. On the following day at one o'clock in the afternoon, dismayed demonstrators in fury set fire to the Palace of Justice, which they saw as a symbol of class justice.

The second time, during the period from March 1933 until the February Uprising of 1934, when the Austrian parliament had been put out of action, Bauer was visibly overtaxed. At first he tried to whitewash his own shortcomings by resorting to militaristic bluster against people in his own ranks: 'What do you do with people who, in the middle of a battle, speak in such a [sceptical — FK] manner? According to the old military service regulations they should have been mown down.' When the uncompromising reactionary government under Engelbert Dollfuss, Seipel's successor, confronted the Social Democrats with the same choice as the German SPD had been faced with by Hitler — to capitulate or to risk a hopeless military rebellion — all contemporary witnesses agree that he seemed to be paralysed by panic, incapable of taking any action, fearful even to the point of considering suicide. On 12 February, he agreed to the shutting down of the electricity supply as a signal to begin a general strike and an uprising, but on the very next day he left the tenement house in 'Red Vienna' that had been appointed the headquarters for the 'military command', and in a luxury motor-car borrowed from a banker and disguised as a swish foreign gentleman he left for Bratislava in Czechoslovakia. He replied in his declarations from his exile to the reproach that he had abandoned the members of the *Schutzbund*, the paramilitary organisation of the Social Democracy, to fight alone on the barricades, by referring to the impending risk of his being executed by a fascist military court.

In *My Life*, published in 1930 in New York, Trotsky portrays Otto Bauer as having 'represented the type that was furthest from that of the revolutionary'.

Hanisch shares this assessment. How should we understand the absence of any will on his part to seize power? Hanisch, whose family includes members who sympathised with Nazism, perceives himself as a 'liberal Catholic' (p 14) and obviously likes Bauer's disinclination to shed blood in the civil war as 'someone who is responsible to the mothers of the country', as Bauer put it in a speech to an assembly of shop stewards and other officials on 7 March 1933. Although one would have thought that a comparison virtually forces itself upon Bauer's biographer, he does not contrast this stance with the wholesale bloodshed of the Great War in which this dashing officer of the Imperial Austro-Hungarian Army, who won for himself the Military Cross Third Class, took such a mettlesome part.

It therefore seems useful to try to fill the gap in Hanisch's interpretation. Is this transition on the part of Otto Bauer from warhorse to pacifist perhaps the result of a process of political ripening? Or was Bauer simply not just an 'ingenious theoretician', but rather 'a man bearing all the ordinary human contradictions'? The present reviewer is inclined to favour the latter interpretation; however, he does think that in one essential factor Bauer's pattern of behaviour in the (civil) war years of 1914-18 and in 1934 remained a constant: throughout his life, in thought and emotion, he remained deeply attached to civil order. There is intellectual evidence of this as early as in 1907 when his book *Social Democracy and the Nationalities Question* was published. In defining the concept of Nation as a purely spiritual construction which only required cultural autonomy and could not legitimately make any territorial claims within the framework of the Monarchy for its realisation, he wanted to defuse the problem of the Habsburg state which Marx had bluntly described as 'filth' (letter to Engels, 27 July 1866). Bauer remained true to this deeply reformist stance in later years when it was the turn of the sword to speak and no longer the pen. Defending the Existing till blood flowed — yes! Questioning the state's monopoly of power — never! And more than that: a special characteristic of the civil order of Austria was a structural conservatism justified by the Habsburg restoration of Catholicism coupled with 'traditionalism' in the Weberian sense of the word. After the failed revolution of 1848, these factors gave rise to a state ideology because it became evident that in view of national conflicts any profound change in domestic or foreign policy would threaten the entire Austro-Hungarian power structure. This is expressed by the Austrian national poet, Franz Grillparzer, in his tragedy, which was completed in, of all years, 1848, through the lines spoken by the Habsburg Emperor Rudolph II: '... the awareness which when enacted, one way or another, lays the powder, which will thunderously blow this mine into the air.' Corresponding to these intentions, the Emperor Francis Joseph (ruler from 1848 to 1916) and his successor Charles (regent during 1916-18) only used the Diet as window-dressing in disguising their Emergency Ordinances which in actual fact constituted government policy.

However, precisely this Structural Conservatism and Traditionalism can be seen as the central pattern of thought in the Austro-Marxism of which Bauer was a significant co-creator. Orthodox Marxism is preserved as an academic school of thought without any revolutionary objective. There is absolutely no confrontation with the modern bourgeois world-view prevalent around the turn of the century (Positivism, Econometrics, Psychoanalysis, etc). However, when dealing with the past or the future, Bauer in brilliant academic studies demonstrates the inevitability of events, and his primary method for promoting the social revolution is to wait for it to take place. The essence of his Austro-Marxism is really fatalism, as Pierre Frank established in a biographical essay on Otto Bauer, 'A Representative Theoretician of Austro-Marxism', *International Socialist Review*, Volume 30, no 3, May-June 1969, pp 36-41. Even the Linz party programme of 1926 which Bauer assembled is characterised by this fundamentally defensive attitude: '... in the democratic republic, the class struggles between the bourgeoisie and the working class will be decided in the struggle between the two classes for the minds and hearts of the majority of the population.'

Thus, the struggle for the majority will be won and lost on the basis of the existing legal system. Once the majority has been won, democracy will not be quashed, and the rights of the right-wingers amongst the bourgeois minority will be upheld. If Bauer threatens the bourgeoisie with the 'Dictatorship of the Proletariat', he does so with a long list of legalistic provisos:

> If, however, the bourgeoisie were to oppose the radical social changes which the working class as the executor of state power is implementing, by means of an organised suppression of economic activity, by violent rebellion, by means of plotting with foreign counter-revolutionary powers, then the working class would be forced to quash the opposition of the bourgeoisie with the tools of dictatorship.

This concept is far removed from the model of a revolutionary vanguard seizing power by means of armed force. Workers' and soldiers' councils as an alternative system of government are not even discussed. As Trotsky had already pointed out in 1929 in his article 'The Austrian Crisis and Communism' (*The Militant*, New York, no 1/1930), the Social Democratic position could be described as follows:

> In this regard, as in many others, Social Democracy only repeats the history of liberalism, whose belated child it is. More than once in history, the liberals

helped feudal reaction triumph over the popular masses only to be liquidated by the reaction in turn.

Nevertheless, Hanisch interprets the Linz programme as having been 'conceptually defensive, yet having offensive consequences'. Because the programme proclaims the Social Democratic demand for absolute rule, it is 'more likely to have provoked civil war than to have prevented it'. With this thesis he follows in the footsteps of Norbert Leser, who can be categorised as a right-wing Social Democrat, who in his book *Zwischen Reformismus und Bolschewismus. Der Austro-Marxismus als Theorie und Praxis* (*Between Reformism and Bolshevism: Austro-Marxism in Theory and Practice*, Vienna, 1968) attempted to prove that Social Democracy must bear 'some of the blame' for the demolition of democracy in Austria. The present reviewer is of the opinion that the behaviour of the Social Democracy, willing as the party was to relinquish every demand, nay, even its own right to exist, particularly in the years 1933-34 — Otto Bauer's offer to accept the clerical-fascist corporative state! — will suffice to refute any such 'complicity' on the part of the victim.

Hanisch's interpretation of events, which the present reviewer does not share, would be legitimate if it were not based on significant gaps and bias in the choice of literature on which he draws. The extensive bibliography fails to mention the key studies by Blum and Frank quoted above. Josef Strasser and Anton Pannekoek — contemporary critics of Bauer's theory of nationalities — are not considered either; see *Die Arbeiter und die Nation mit einem Anhang: „Schriften zum Austro-Marxismus"* (*Workers and Nation with Annex: 'Austro-Marxist Writings'*, reprint Vienna, 1982); *Klasssenkampf und Nation* (*Class Struggle and Nation*, Reichenberg, 1912). Trotsky's article quoted above, 'The Austrian Crisis and Communism', has also been overlooked. The same is true of an article by August Thalheimer, the German Communist theoretician, 'Die Auflösung des Austromarxismus' ('The Dissolution of Austro-Marxism'), *Unter dem Banner des Marxismus*, 1925, pp 474-557 and 1928, pp 76-83. To be sure, Julius Braunthal's book *Auf der Suche nach dem Millenium* (*In Search of the Millennium*, Vienna, 1964) is listed in the bibliography, but the evidence included in it, according to which Victor Adler, the leader of the Social Democracy until 1918, failed to inform the striking workers about the contemporary uprising of the seamen of Cattaro (Bota Kotorska), thus unnecessarily prolonging the death struggle of the monarchy, is not mentioned in the text.

The collaboration between the Austrian Social Democracy and the Austro-Hungarian minister for foreign affairs, Count Ottokar Czernin, in connection with the Brest-Litovsk peace negotiations, amply documented by Roman Rosdolsky, see *Studien zur revolutionären Taktik* (*Studies on Revolutionary*

Tactics, Berlin, 1973), pp 19ff, is described by Hanisch — without mentioning his source — as totally unproblematic because he sees it — this can be deduced from his description of events — as Bauer's 'great contribution in having prevented a dictatorship by workers' and soldiers' councils in Austria' (pp 172-73). By contrast, the author does not discuss whether Bauer's policy led to the failure of the Bolshevik world revolutionary project and thus to the emergence of 'Socialism in One Country' under the aegis of Stalin. Nor are readers of his book told that according to research by Lajos Kerekes, *Abenddämmerung einer Demokratie. Mussolini, Gömbös und die Heimwehr* (*Twilight of a Democracy: Mussolini, Gömbös and the Home Guard*, Vienna, 1966), p 182, the disturbances of July 1927 had deliberately been provoked by Johannes Schober, the Vienna Chief of Police and later Chancellor, in order to prove the existence of 'a Bolshevik Peril'.

Similarly, the reader will fail to find any reference to the following standard works on the subject: Yvon Bourdet, *Max Adler: Démocratie et conseils ouvriers* (Paris, 1967); Yvon Bourdet, *Otto Bauer et la révolution* (Paris, 1968); Anson Rabinbach, *The Crisis of Austrian Socialism: From Red Vienna to Civil War 1927-1934* (Chicago, 1983); Detlev Albers, Josef Hindels, Lucio Lombardo-Radice, et al, *Otto Bauer und der „dritte Weg"* (*Otto Bauer and the 'Third Way'*, Frankfurt, 1979); Uli Schöler, *Otto Bauer — nein danke? Austromarxismusdiskussion und historische Standortbestimmung marxistischer Sozialdemokraten* (*Otto Bauer — No Thanks? The Austro-Marxism Discussion and Historical Locations of Marxist Social Democrats*, Berlin, 1984). Helmut Gruber's writings about cultural policy in Red Vienna, a subject of international discussions, are not even mentioned. Josef Hindels is only mentioned in connection with his, in many respects rather rosy, memoirs, *Erinnerungen eines linken Sozialisten* (Vienna, 1996). As regards Peter Goller, we do find a mention of an article written by him entitled 'Österreichische Staatsrechtswissenschaft um 1900' ('Austrian Scholarship on Constitutional Law around 1900'), but not his book, *Otto Bauer — Max Adler — Beiträge zur Geschichte des Austromarxismus (1904-1938)* (*Otto Bauer — Max Adler — Contributions to the History of Austro-Marxism (1904-1934)*, Vienna, 2008).

Thus, readers will find that most of their initial expectations will be dashed, even in respect of the preparation of source material.
Fritz Keller

Annelies Laschitza, *Die Liebknechts. Karl und Sophie*, Aufbau Verlagsgruppe, Berlin, 2007, pp 551

Until 1933, on 15 January, socialists and communists in Berlin remembered the two German revolutionaries Karl Liebknecht and Rosa Luxemburg by a mass visit to the Lichtenberg-Friedrichsfelde cemetery. Since 1925, there had been, moreover, commemorations for Lenin–Liebknecht–Luxemburg, mostly with talks which sought to sketch out their ideas and activity. After 1945 and to this day the two who were murdered on 15 January 1919 are remembered each year by the working people of Berlin. As different as they are in their ideas and their biographies, they belong to the great tradition of the communist movement. Their thought remains topical and will in every phase of the movement be interpreted anew and sometimes controversially. Annelies Laschitza has now presented us with a further biography of Karl Liebknecht, which relies on extensive material from public and private archives.

In the first three chapters, the significant family and the education of Karl is described. In spite of their limited means his family enabled him to study until he became established as a solicitor together with his elder brother Theodor, who untiringly supported him and his family and thereby made possible Karl's intensive political activity. It was unavoidable that the son of the co-founder of the Social Democratic Party (SPD) would grow up as a critical thinker in politics, even if in character he was not wholly equal to his father. After advice from Bebel, he wanted to remain financially and politically independent of the party apparatus. Instead, however, he also received, besides Theodor's help, considerable solidarity contributions from comrades both abroad and in Germany, as well as temporarily from his second wife's family who, for the most part, lived in Breslau am Dom, and who had been wealthy before the Russian Revolution.

Not only the earlier intimate relationship to his second wife Sofie (Ryss), but also his solidarity with the persecuted Russian social-democrats, some of whom emigrated to Germany after 1905, led him into solidarity work and strengthened his interest in political developments in Russia.

He soon came into opposition to the reformist bureaucracy of his party, which tried to take the youth organisation under its wing and to do so made use of the law on association, which forbad political activity among the youth, although nationalist and paramilitary youth organisations were permitted to conduct the 'education' of the working-class youth. Liebknecht preferred an independent, critical, anti-militarist, proletarian youth, and supported their political and organisational aspirations particularly intensively; and as a result he gained much trust among them.

Gradually his party comrades' confidence in him grew and he was obliged to stand for the Berlin City Council, then for the Prussian Diet, and finally for the Reichstag. In all of these bodies he was always well prepared regarding the subject matter, had pertinent criticism and proposals, and his sharpest criticism was for the policies of the imperial government. Apart from the youth question, the most important theme for him was the policy of German imperialism and militarism: passive rearmament (with its consequences of international collaboration and corruption and for the living standards of the working people), foreign policy, war preparations, and the ever more distinct danger of war. With his irrefutable facts he irritated his opponents, put them on the spot. He used the parliaments as a tribune, from which he appealed to the masses outside. He exposed armament scandals, and also demonstrated the collaboration of the arms industry with 'enemy' countries.

In order to stop his revelations, in 1907 he was charged with high treason. He saw this political persecution as another opportunity to enlighten and mobilise the working people. His courageous accusations in court showed his bravery, but of course could not prevent the class justice from passing sentence. He served his confinement in Glatz (Silesia). Family and friends visited him; he received gifts from friends and was able to undertake his work. Apart from his political work here he started his extensive philosophical studies, on which he produced many excerpts and notes.

On his return from confinement he immediately resumed his work — defending Russian comrades in Leipzig, speeches at mass meetings, criticism in the Prussian Diet. In spite of his complicated extra-marital love-life, he constantly provided for his family — for the maintenance and the education of his three children, whom he again and again, in affectionate letters from his confinement, urged to study and to take up further education. His 'family life' took second place only to his political tasks. At the congress of the Prussian SPD in Berlin in 1910, he submitted a programme of democratisation, with which he hoped to democratise the Prussian bastion of the empire. It primarily proposed a democratic voting system instead of the three-tier one. Rosa Luxemburg, who likewise pursued an intensive struggle and mobilised the masses over the voting system, found Liebknecht's proposals vague, perhaps too illusory as well. Could this state with its solidly-fixed bureaucracy become democratic merely through new laws? At this time there was as yet virtually no personal contact; Luxemburg was quietly critical regarding his parliamentary activities.

Evidence of his growing esteem was the invitation from the National Secretary of the Socialist Party of America to undertake an agitational tour, as his father had done 60 years previously. It began on 1 October 1910. His well-prepared lectures met with a good response from the listeners and in many newspapers. His criticism was directed against modern capitalism in the USA as much as against German conditions; reports from informers to the authorities back home, defamation in the reactionary press, bear witness to it. Naturally he used the journey for intensive observation of both the social relations and the beauty spots of the country. After more than two months abroad, he arrived back in

Berlin on 7 December 1910.

In 1912, following an intensive election campaign, he won the imperial constituency of Potsdam-Spandau-Osthavelland and now had the possibility to advance his accusations in the Reichstag. Soon the dominance of reformism — August Bebel had died in 1911 — showed itself very clearly within the parliamentary group. Liebknecht's insistence on upholding the old principles led to huge tensions over the bill for the military budget. On 4 August 1914, he stuck to discipline and, against his own conviction, voted for the war credits, which was a greater shock to his left-wing friends than the assent of the others in the group. After the German occupation of Belgium he went there to demonstrate against his government and to show his solidarity with the Belgian comrades. In December his was the only opposition vote. In 1915, others began to follow his example.

Liebknecht suffered the vilest abuse from his opponents, and not just from the bourgeois ones. He was even accused of insanity on account of his opposition to the madness of the imperialist war. Hermann Molkenbuhr, of the SPD Executive, remarked in his diary that he was 'not mentally normal'; the president of the Reichstag spoke of an 'obvious mental sickness'.

The critics within the SPD were excluded from the party and set up the Sozialistische Arbeitsgemeinschaft (Socialist Working Fellowship). Liebknecht was unable to carry out opposition work in parliament. On account of his being an active anti-militarist he was called up into a labour unit, 'unworthy' to bear German arms and unarmed he had to dig trenches close to the front. He helped found the Gruppe Internationale (later known as the Spartakusbund) and on 1 May he demonstrated on the Potsdamer Platz with the call: 'Down with the government! Down with the war!' Arrest and sentencing to two-and-a-half years' penal servitude followed, which he had to serve in Luckau until shortly before the end of the war. Again he used the time for studying and attempts to formulate his philosophical ideas in writing, but also concerned himself greatly over his family and the intellectual development of the children.

Liebknecht had never found the time systematically to set out his philosophical works in writing. He had wrestled with society's laws of motion. Their publication has involved difficulties both political and regarding comprehension. Annelies Laschitza has taken great pains to present them in an understandable form for the average reader. In some points Liebknecht nears Marxism; taken as a whole they remain a fragment that is not easily understood. However, the author states self-critically that she has 'judged arrogantly' those writings in a previous biography of Liebknecht.

Finally released from Luckau on 23 October 1918, he was enthusiastically received and he immediately threw himself into political activity, which the last two chapters deal with. The author sums up the period from October until his murder on 15 January 1919 precisely and impressively. The facts are well known. The close collaboration of the SPD leadership with that of the defeated army, its militant anti-communism and anti-Soviet attitude, the brutality of the SPD Minister of War Gustav Noske, the full political responsibility for the two murders on 15 January 1919 and the many to follow, the traces of blood of the German counter-revolution that later also swept along many of the strongest opponents of the revolution (such as Matthias Erzberger) is very clear.

Laschitza shows both the indecisiveness of the Independent Social Democratic Party (USPD) and the way in which it repudiated the revolutionaries on the grounds of their lack of clarity and their lack of a good organisation; only at the end of the year did they unite a few groups to form the German Communist Party (KPD). The German counter-revolution was once more organised, well-armed, instantly prepared ruthlessly to employ confused soldiers returning home against the 'enemy within', to hinder the revolution which could have meted out the historically-justified punishment for the crime of the imperialist war begun in 1914 — the removal of those responsible from power. The war-weary workers and soldiers were unable immediately to see through the sham socialist propaganda of the SPD.

The book is honest also in showing the differing evaluations of the actual situation and the great differences between Luxemburg and Liebknecht, between her and the hyper-active revolutionary, who to his great discredit was seduced into the belief that his solo activity could change the relationship of forces, who in his activity found no time for reflection or for conversation with his comrades. Laschitza also informs us about the debates among the leading Spartakists and the criticism of Karl's freelancing: 'Surrounded by pugnacious rejoicing masses, he orated himself into a revolutionary intoxication. The discrepancy between his effect and reality was not clear to him.' (p 429) Quite different the revolutionary Marxist Luxemburg, showing solidarity in spite of her misgivings and criticism, up until their tragic end, followed in turn into the grave by many other revolutionaries. The discreet criticism of Karl by no means prevented the loving and patient care for his wife Sofie (Sonja), who in her difficult situation was nevertheless helped in various ways.

The great revolutionary Karl Liebknecht was hardly a Marxist, but in those times there was tolerance among Marxists, as long as the socialist goal and the desire for revolution were held in common by the revolutionaries. With Stalinism it was wholly different: faithfulness to the line, no critical thought — those were the criteria. The earlier tolerance must surely be learnt once more.

In the last chapter Annelies Laschitza deals with the difficult lot of the Liebknecht family.

Her biography, critical and self-critical, splendidly researched over a considerable period, does justice to the great revolutionary and humanist. Thus both here and in the international labour movement he still lives at the side of Rosa Luxemburg.

The fates of the leading social-democrats of that period were wholly different. Friedrich Ebert was of course President of the Republic; soon his ungrateful cronies included him among the 'November criminals', and he complained in vain against this unjust insult. Gustav Noske reports in his memoirs that Minister of the Interior Hermann Göring assured him in 1933, 'one does not leave a man like you in the lurch'; he received his full pension as a previous lord lieutenant of the Prussian province of Hanover. Phillip Scheidemann fell out with his party and abandoned it while in exile.

Theodor Bergmann
Translated by Mike Jones

Deborah Lavin, *Bradlaugh Contra Marx: Radicalism and Socialism in the First International*, Socialist History Society, London, 2011, pp 86, £4.00

Deborah Lavin is a person of many talents. Poet and playwright, she is a member of the Freethought History Research Group and the Socialist History Society. She has now authored the twenty-eighth of the SHS's Occasional Publications.

This a fascinating glimpse into socialist and radical politics in the mid-nineteenth century. On the one hand there is Karl Marx, a Communist and political exile in London. On the other Charles Bradlaugh, who rose from humble origins to become the leading nineteenth-century advocate of Secularism and an MP for Northampton. Both were political giants. In his day Bradlaugh was far better known than Marx. Although the National Secular Society, which Bradlaugh founded in 1866, is still going, there is nothing of his prolific writings in print. Although the cheap editions of Marx produced in Moscow are no longer being printed, his work is still being published, and, in the light of the current economic crisis, his theories hotly debated.

The First International, albeit short-lived — it lasted less than a decade — was the first attempt by the working class to organise on an international scale. Marx joined almost by accident, being invited to join as a delegate from Germany by Victor Le Lubez, a French political exile and close friend of Bradlaugh who was an active Secularist both in Greenwich and nationally. Marx quickly became a leading figure in the International.

Ms Lavin is an undoubted protagonist of Marx and seeks to undermine Bradlaugh as an heroic figure. Indeed she rather over-eggs the pudding, and at times comes near to character assassination, if not defamation. She shows that Bradlaugh's role in the trial of himself and Annie Besant under the Obscene

Publications Act for publishing and distributing the birth control pamphlet *The Fruits of Philosophy* was far less heroic than has been depicted. Besant was related to the Liberal Lord Chancellor Lord Hatherley, and Ms Levin alleges that he used his influence to ensure that Mrs Besant and Bradlaugh were not imprisoned. On the other hand, Edward Truelove, a former Chartist and the International's printer, got four months for distributing the pamphlet.

Ms Lavin decries Bradlaugh's and Besants' neo-Malthusianism which sees the sole cause of working-class poverty as their being profligate in their reproduction. She accuses Besant of giving incorrect information in her birth-control pamphlet *The Population Question*. She does not mention Dan Chatterton, who, while working with the rather puritanical Malthusian League, advocated sex for pleasure.

Ms Lavin depicts Bradlaugh's role in the struggle over the oaths question — he wanted to affirm his loyalty to Victoria her heirs and her successors, rather than swear a religious oath — as more accidentally than deliberately heroic. Bradlaugh was a leading Republican, but Ms Lavin doesn't address the conflict between Bradlaugh and John De Morgan, a former member of the Cork Branch of the International, in the Republican movement of the 1870s.

Ms Lavin writes that Marx's daughter Laura says that Marx went to hear Bradlaugh speak in the 1850s, then seeing him as a muddleheaded Radical possibly capable of reforming himself, or of being reformed. In any event, Marx did his utmost to keep professional atheists out of the International, in particular the Holyoake brothers, who were opponents of Bradlaugh. Here I think he was wrong. George Holyoake was a pioneer cooperator, when he died nearly 400 cooperative societies subscribed to erect a building in his memory. He could have brought many cooperators and Secularists into the International.

Bradlaugh was a leading member of the Reform League, which had been formed in 1866 to advocate the extension of the franchise to more working-class males. It staged some of the most militant demonstrations since Chartist times. Ms Lavin compares these to the anti-Poll Tax demonstrations of the 1990s and more recent student demonstrations against rises in tuition fees. During one, demonstrators tore down the railings in Hyde Park and used them to defend themselves from police baton-charges. Ms Levin shows how the leaders of the Reform League were bought by the Liberals to mobilise newly-enfranchised workers behind Gladstone and keep independent working-class candidates out of the contest. Although initially opposed by the Liberals, Bradlaugh eventually became an official Liberal Party candidate.

The first International was riven with conflict between Marx's Communism, English trade unionists who in essence remained Liberals, followers of the French Anarchist Proudhon, and supporters of the Russian Anarchist Bakunin. All of these came together to support the Paris Commune of 1871, which was drowned in blood by the forces of reaction. Although Bradlaugh was a Freemason and the French masons supported the Commune, he opposed it. This led to a fierce clash between Marx and Bradlaugh in the pages of the *Eastern Post*.

Marx's first battle in the International was against the followers of the Italian nationalist Mazzini. Although Mazzini was religious, he had the support of Secularists, including Le Lubez and Bradlaugh. The supporters of Mazzini only left the International after Bradlaugh's application to join had been rejected.

Ms Lavin writes that Bradlaugh was strangely drawn to anyone opposed to Marx, including the French exile Felix Pyat, described by Marx as a fourth-rate author of melodramas.

The International was soon in a bad way, and by 1872 it was in effect dead. At its Hague conference its General Council was moved from London to New York. Bradlaugh now tried to form his own International. From 1877 this was mooted in Bradlaugh's weekly *The National Reformer*. Bradlaugh had wanted to call the new body the International Workingman's Association, the original name of the International, but it was decided to call it the International Labour Union. Among its supporters were the Reverend S Headlam, and the anti-socialist trade unionist Edith Simcox, one of the first female delegates to the TUC. The ILU began to slip out of Bradlaugh's control. It supported cotton workers striking against a pay cut, and, when George Howell attacked Marx, Harriet Law, who had been involved in the original International, offered Marx space to reply in her *Secular Chronicle*. Law and Hales, who had been involved in the original International, proposed a lecturing circuit to preach socialism, and Bradlaugh withdrew his support. After that the ILU faded out of existence.

Marx died in 1883, and the following year Henry Hyndman formed the Democratic Federation. He debated with Bradlaugh and many seem to think Bradlaugh won. But within months two of the triumvirate which led the NSS, Annie Besant and Edward Aveling, had become Socialists.

Ms Lavin has long been working on a biography of Aveling. If it is as good as this pamphlet it will be well worth the wait.
Terry Liddle

Dorian Lynskey, *33 Revolutions Per Minute: A History of Protest Songs,* Faber and Faber, London, 2010, pp 843, £17.99

There is a big market for writing about 'popular' music. When I see buyers lugging away three or four of the heavier music monthlies, I wonder how they will ever find time to read all the content. Have they mastered the skill of listening to the free CDs on the cover at the same time as reading the descriptive and historical articles?

And books about music are now often accompanied by their own playlists — only 36 pages in this volume — which this reader at least experiences much more as a guilt load than as an invitation to musical pleasure. If each line in the list represents a stereotypical 'two and a half minute single' (though in many cases the list refers to a key track from an album), then the list tots up to over 50 hours continuous listening. Can I really have read the book at my usual speed if I don't know all the music listed? Well be damned to all that — I won't spend my remaining years listening to music I don't enjoy (though I will often hazard a few hours trying something new, or retrying something old). And I will not turn listening to music into an obsessive-compulsive list ticking activity; no more will I turn my bird watching into 'twitching', nor my love of real ale into writing a logbook of tasting. I am pleased to learn from the playlists that Martha Reeves recorded an anti-Vietnam-War song that failed in the market because the radio stations refused it air-time. I will believe the list but I won't be able to spend time tracking down a copy. Well sung Martha, well researched Dorian. No sale ici.

I will even take the list-building seriously enough to criticise a little. The omission of Howling Wolf's 'Natchez Burning' from the chapters that discuss the (substantial) tributary flow of protest song originating in black songs against racism is, I feel, incomprehensible. (Captain Beefheart and the Magic Band performed it occasionally, but as far as I know, no official recording has ever been released. For those who have the time and diligence to seek it out, there is a performance of towering power on a bootleg recording of a concert in Finland.)

Although it was never a song, Duke Ellington's 'A Tone Parallel to Harlem' would, IMHO, have merited a mention in the same area. On the famous London recording, the Duke talks the audience through the composition before performing it for them. He mentions that they might catch the sound of the orchestra in their 'civil rights mode' at one point in the tone poem. And, may their gods and goblins forgive them, they snigger. It's there in digital data — inerasable. The London audience had not heard the Duke in more than a decade — yet they snigger at the idea that a black band leader who had to rent a train to ensure that his musicians had somewhere clean and decent to sleep after their work in many cities across the USA, whereas being black they were not allowed to eat or drink, much less sleep, in the hotels they performed at, might have some concern with 'civil rights'. Well if music could not teach them, Notting Hill, Brixton, Handsworth, New Cross and many other battlefields did, and there are good chapters in the book about how it happened, and how music became a potent weapon in the fight against fascism and racism at crucial times. Thus we might essay a theorem — music follows key events and does not lead them, but it thereafter can contribute to the development of a movement triggered by those key events.

In such a competitive market as that for music journalism, a fat, data-stuffed book like this is good value for money. You could easily spend more in a month on music magazines than this modest cover price. There are huge numbers of interesting anecdotes and front line reports here to dip into, to admire the courage and integrity that went into them. The author is a skilled and knowledgeable journalist who maintains an enjoyable pace through a lengthy volume.

I regretted the truncated historical and ethnic perspectives, but in such a field it is impossible to please everybody. 'Protest Songs Before 1900' are treated in just over two pages, and soldiers songs against two world wars somehow slip through the net. The songs of the Russian workers shot down on the orders of the aristos on 'Bloody Sunday' 1905 (recreated in Shostakovich's *1905 Symphony*) surely merit a sentence. And of Irish Republican rebel song, can silence be justified? Doubtless every reader would find similar quibbles. And that would be because music that expresses the desire for liberation, or protests against repression, is a much broader category than the one catalogued here. To test the limits of the protest song category, consider whether Lionel Bart's 'Fings Ain't What They Used To Be' ought not to have been included. Enough however of counting dancing angels, it is undeniable that music, popular song in particular, has contributed greatly to the support for revolutionary and radical causes since the Second World War, and this book is a not unworthy attempt to document that involvement.

Lynskey imposes a periodisation on his account; it would be difficult to write it otherwise. His first period begins and ends with black women. Billie Holiday's 'Strange Fruit' in 1939 forced awareness of racist lynching and burning onto an often unwilling, sometimes resistant jazz audience. This period ended with Nina Simone's 1964 'Mississippi Goddam', her response to the dynamiting of a bible study class for black children (her first response had been to try to manufacture a zip gun). Lynskey links the lyrics to the words of the heckler against Martin Luther King's speech at the end of the March on Washington — 'Fuck that dream, Martin! Now! Goddam it, now.' It was an end of patient protest and the beginning of expression of anger. The music had followed the mass mood on that journey, via Woody Guthrie, Pete Seeger and Bob Dylan (whose 'Masters of War' was a highpoint in the involvement of folk singers in the protest movements) and had contributed to its spread.

In the second period, 1965 to 1973, the Vietnam War became a central concern, opening with Country Joe and the Fish's 'I Feel Like I'm Fixin' to Die Rag'. The focus also shifted from the folk-based, usually acoustic, music to the higher energy of amplified rock. Dylan's self-transfiguration into the front man for a howlingly loud electric ensemble, sneering his way through a repertoire of dense dark poetry and never a 'come all ye' to be heard, was to generate its own wave of protest. Ewan MacColl, the Zhdanov of British folk music, is believed to have coordinated the attempts at heckling by members of the Young Communist League, against Dylan's British tour. 'Judas', they shouted, until their energy failed and the sheer volume of the amplified instruments prevailed. It summed up the change in the times clearly enough. Folkies could still be seen and heard on CND marches and the like, but increasingly the young marchers were thinking of the big gig at the end of the march as their music — listening, often paying, and not playing or singing. Jeff Nuttall spotted it in his memoir *Bomb Culture*. Other changes were in play too. Musicians expressing radical dissent found unsuspected strength in their relationships with their record companies. John Lennon was one of the most marked examples, acquiring the ability to support a range of causes on the platform of his ability to sell records and concert tickets, and taking the opportunity with vigour. Success in this arena required new artistic and management strategies — anger and compassion were still essential of course, but had to be organised, promoted and financed.

Drugs too came to have a cultural prominence that from today's vantage point can be seen as preposterous, but at the time it was not uncommon to hear conflated the right of oppressed people to self-determination and the right to unrestricted use of exotic intoxicants, or for that matter to unlimited sexual gratification. Country Joe and the Fish were, at the time of 'Fixin' to Die' known at least as much for their promotion and enjoyment of psychedelics as for their engagement with the anti-war movement. The forces of the state to some extent shared this perception of the revolutionary potential of the trinity of sex, drugs and music, though with opposite value signs attached to them. More Machiavellian policy makers might have calculated that the stoned and enervated Woodstock generation was a lesser evil than similar numbers stoning the police. Likewise, the spread of addiction through poor black urban areas had its drawbacks from the point of view of urban governance, but might have been preferable to the rapid spread of black militancy. Stevie Wonder's 'Living for the City' summed it up.

There were voices beginning to be heard during this period that warned against the superficiality of the revolutionary self-images being peddled and consumed. Important were The Last Poets, and Gil Scott-Heron, whose *The Revolution Will Not Be Televised* tried to point a way out of the contradictions of revolutionary rock and roll. The negative turn of mood among wealthy white musicians as the limits of the anti-war protest movement emerged was dramatically reflected by the band Jefferson Airplane, who turned away from the increasingly risky identification with ultra-radicalism and renamed themselves Jefferson Starship, to assemble a new Mayflower myth, in which they and their fan club would hijack the NASA programme and escape to a planet where they would be 'free'. Everybody's worst expectations flowered in Nixon's crushing election victory in 1972.

Lynskey's third period, 1973-77, is one where the focus shifts away from the metropolitan centres. Military and police power had defeated, if not broken, the anti-war movement in the USA. The charismatic singer/writer Phil Ochs, retreating with the dubious aid of drink and 'anti-depressants', journeyed to Chile with the activist Jerry Rubin. There they were to be blessed with reinvigoration through contact with the singer/writer Victor Jara, who was especially connected with the Allende movement. Lynskey's chapter on Jara and Allende is the most moving and sad in the book. Ochs found renewed strength following the hideous destruction of the aspirations of the workers and peasants by the military coup, but was personally unable to sustain it at the political level required by the events he faced. The deaths of Ochs and Jara marked a low point for humanity and the revolution, but their songs carried forward a message of determination, if not of optimism. We can note that the military victory of the Vietnamese Stalinists against the USA did not leave any legacy of inspiring song or poetry.

Jamaican music had been connected with the fight for independence and socialism from its earliest moments. The rebel slaves ('Maroons') had melded their multiple African identities using song and fighting techniques almost instinctively. The failure of Marxism to strike root in the soil of Jamaica and the Caribbean is a subject to be dealt with elsewhere. The 1972 election victory that brought the populist left-winger Michael Manley to power owed a lot to the support Manley won from reggae musicians (including Bob Marley), and the Rastafarian movement/religion. Max Romeo's song 'Let the Power Fall' was adopted as the PNP's anthem. Lynskey's chapter on the relationship of the music to the politics in the period up to the collapse of Manleyism under pressure of the US economic sanctions is, in my opinion, the best in the book. And the only one for which I will be assembling MP3s of the playlist. (Though Michael Smith, the greatest of the reggae poets, whose life was ended by thugs commanded by the cat's-paw of US imperialism, Seaga, is unjustly disregarded.)

Lynskey's Fourth period opens with 'White Riot' by The Clash. Punk's essential nihilism was always political in a very general sense, but The Clash sought to be a voice for the disaffected youth routinely in conflict with the state in the cities across Britain. Tom Robinson, Sham 69 and others shared the same ambition, but The Clash best reflected in their music the shifting mood as the punk wave peaked and waned. There was also a growing openness about right-wing attitudes by millionaire musicians such as David Bowie and Eric

Clapton, the former advocating a dictatorship, the latter espousing the cause of Powellism. Black musicians and writers, epitomised by Linton Kwesi Johnson, articulated the resentments generated by the 'sus' law and the routine use of stop and search to harass the black youth of the inner cities. This was the period that saw the rise of Rock Against Racism and its role (together of course with the Anti-Nazi League) in the transformation of the mass mood that marginalised what had been a resurgent far-right capable of mounting intimidating marches and demonstrations through areas with large black and Asian populations. The music was central to the mobilisations against the National Front in this period, and I think significantly it was around live performance more than what could get through the editorial policies of radio and TV. The music, and the movement of which it was part, went beyond the category 'protest', getting beyond passive disagreement and seizing the initiative. Lynskey's focus is on the music, and he does not adequately assess the extent to which the left was (or was not) able to build permanently out of this massive movement.

I find Lynskey's attempt to define a period covering 1989 to 2008 the least satisfactory. Perhaps we are all too close to the events (or absence of events) yet to see things with a clear shape. Some of the subjects of his chapters — Rage Against The Machine, Public Enemy, Manic Street Preachers — more than merit political consideration. But their output is not 'protest song'. Nobody sings 'BombTrack' to themselves while stuffing envelopes or waiting for the red LED in a call centre. (Perhaps an exception should be made for Steve Earle, whose solidly folk-based songs can actually be sung.)

In his Prologue, Lynskey seems to have resigned himself to the music and song having yet again been usurped and recouped by the state. He discusses Obama's inauguration speech, adapting Sam Cooke's 'A Change Is Gonna Come'. The song itself featured in the inauguration concert, where Pete Seeger and Bruce Springsteen duetted, and Stevie Wonder contributed his most anodyne material. Pete Townshend is now protecting his damaged hearing by restricting his public performances. We need him to blast out one last time 'Won't Get Fooled Again'! A whole sudden new generation of rioters in England and the USA should hear it.

JJ Plant

Merilyn Moos, *The Language of Silence*, Cressida Press in conjunction with Writersworld, Woodstock, Oxfordshire, 2010, pp 288, £9.99

Merilyn Moos' novel *The Language of Silence* is a fascinating study of political activism and everyday life over eight decades. The heroine, Anna Weilheimer (who, despite the disclaimer in the preface, has a marked resemblance to Merilyn herself) lives in London in the early twenty-first century. Her elderly mother is suffering from dementia and requires residential care. As she tries to deal with her mother's problems, Anna becomes more and more curious about her parents, refugees from Nazi Germany. The central core of the novel is Anna's slow and difficult attempt to dig out the truth about her parents' and grandparents' experiences and commitments in the 1930s.

And these discoveries help to explain why Anna's parents were so overprotective during her childhood, of which there is a powerful and poignant description. Judged by today's standards, most people in the 1940s and 1950s had repressive childhoods, but Anna's had its own very special horrors.

Anna has a son, Sam. While she is anxious not to make the same mistakes as her own parents, she cannot avoid friction, and the relationship is often difficult. Sam becomes a committed climate change activist. In some ways his life and preoccupations seem very remote from those of his grandparents; he is sceptical of the traditional tactics of the left. Yet there is also a powerful sense of the continuity of struggle; future historians may well note that climate change killed many more than the Holocaust. As I read the book, I was reminded of Victor Serge's prediction that the successful revolution will be made by those who are 'infinitely different from us, infinitely like us'.

This summary does not exhaust the complex range of themes covered in the novel. The personal and the political are constantly intertwined; as Anna notes, her very conception was a result of the battle of Stalingrad: 'If it had not been for the millions of Russians who gave their lives in 1942, pushing back the Nazi invaders, my parents would not have felt safe enough to have had a child.'

Anna's loathing of Nazi anti-Semitism is combined with, indeed seems to inspire, a committed anti-Zionism; visiting her mother in a Jewish care home, Anna announces in a loud voice that she is off to a 'Hands Off Lebanon' demonstration.

Questions of identity and oppression run through the book. It is now easy enough to sentimentalise refugees from Hitler, safely in the past. But Anna draws out the parallel with today's asylum seekers: meeting a Nigerian refugee she notes: 'At least there was some sympathy for left-wing intellectuals fleeing Nazism. For him, it's out of the frying pan into the fire.'

Anna is also a college lecturer and trade-union activist. There is disappointingly little about this in the book — hopefully Merilyn is planning a sequel. She notes, 'management was child's play compared to the feuding with members of the Communist Party and the Maoists'. Many will remember Merilyn as one of the main driving forces in the ATTI/NATFHE Rank and File organisation in the 1970s, where much of the left in NATFHE/UCU cut their political teeth. I still have vivid memories of being repeatedly telephoned at midnight to discuss amendments to Outer London Region standing orders. But probably few of us who knew Merilyn at that time realised the complexity of her political motivation. It is a salutary reminder that those who devote themselves to the necessary but burdensome minutiae of trade-union organisation generally do so because they have a broader political vision.

We can only regret that, unsurprisingly, such an interesting novel did not get the commercial sponsorship and promotion it deserved.
Ian Birchall

David North, *In Defense of Leon Trotsky*, Mehring Books, Oak Park, 2011, pp 194

Assessments of Robert Service's recent biography of Trotsky broke down roughly into two rival schools of thought. On the one hand, it received fulsome praise from those who agree with Service's damning verdict on Trotsky. Simon Sebag Montefiore considered it 'outstanding' and 'revelatory as the scholarly revision of an historical reputation'; whilst fellow historian John Gray thought it 'a powerfully demystifying biography of one of the most heavily mythologised figures of twentieth-century history'. The novelist Richard Harris confidently assured his readers that 'seldom has the pathology of the revolutionary type… been more mercilessly exposed than in this exemplary biography'. On the other hand, Trotskyists naturally wasted no time in laying into Service's work, and, perhaps carrying more weight as he is definitely no sympathiser of Trotsky, Bertrand Patenaude, author of *Trotsky: Downfall of a Revolutionary*, contributed a harsh review in the *American Historical Review* (June 2011).

The book under review here is a compilation of no less than four essays and speeches about Service's book by the leader of the US Social Equality Party (formerly Workers League), along with his review of two earlier and shorter biographies of Trotsky by Geoffrey Swain and Ian Thatcher, and two essays on Trotsky's place in history.

North does not mince his words when describing what he sees as 'an exercise in character assassination':

> The real purpose of Service's grotesque portrayal of Trotsky — which reverberates throughout the bourgeois press and will eventually be echoed in subsequent pseudo-historical works that dutifully cite Professor Service's 'authoritative' and 'magisterial' volume — is the concoction of an entirely new historical persona. All traces of the real Trotsky — as he was described and remembered by comrades and friends, and, above all, as found expression in his words and his deeds — are to be effaced, obliterated and replaced with something monstrous and grotesque that bears no resemblance to the real human being. The historical persona of the great revolutionary, political

genius, military leader and master of the written word is to be replaced with something abominable and contemptible. Trotsky, *à la* Service, as one of the political monsters of the twentieth century!

North, like many of the book's critical reviewers, points to the considerable number of factual mistakes in Service's biography, something which Sebag Montefiore, Gray and Harris all failed to notice, but which Patenaude numbered at 'more than four dozen'. Going beyond mere factual errors, North also asserts that Service has deliberately distorted texts, such as Trotsky's *My Life* in respect of his relationship with his first wife Alexandra Sokolovskaya, and Max Eastman's account of a conversation with Trotsky in 1920 about problems facing the revolutionary movement in the USA — which Patenaude calls 'an act of outright falsification' — in order to reinforce his unflattering personal and political picture of him.

North criticises Service for his dismissive attitude towards Trotsky as a thinker and writer, providing a host of citations:

> Always he [Trotsky] wrote whatever was in his head.
>
> [Trotsky]... made no claim to intellectual originality: he would have been ridiculed if he had tried.
>
> He refused to bother himself with research on most questions currently bothering the party's intellectual élite...
>
> Intellectually he flitted from topic to topic...
>
> He simply loved to be seated at a desk, fountain pen in hand, scribbling out the latest opus...
>
> His thought was a confused and confusing ragbag...
>
> He spent a lot of time in disputing, less of it in thinking... This involved an ultimate lack of seriousness as an intellectual.
>
> His articles were full of schematic projections, shaky reasoning and ill-considered slogans.

Now whilst some of these statements refer to specifics — for example that Trotsky 'made no claim to intellectual originality' was in respect of his writings on the course of Russian history — rather than generalities, anyone reasonably acquainted with Trotsky's writings cannot read these assertions without a sad shake of the head.

To compound this offhand dismissal of Trotsky's literary capabilities, Service curiously declares, as North is quick to point out, that 'it is as important to pinpoint what Trotsky was silent about as what he chose to speak or write about. His unuttered basic assumptions were integral to the amalgam of his life.' Now, whilst silence can be telling, variously signifying a studied indifference to the topic at hand, a cowardly reluctance to demur or a disdainful refusal to grace an unworthy question with an answer, and whilst sarcasm or irony can place an entirely different meaning upon what has literally been said or written, this emphasis on what Trotsky *didn't* say might have some resonance if our biographer had actually subjected Trotsky's voluminous works to any sort of detailed analysis, because, as North states:

> Service provides no examples of Trotsky's 'confused and confusing ragbag of ideas'. Service does not attempt to analyse, or even present an adequate summary of, a single work by Trotsky. Characterisations such as those cited above are dished up without any examination of, or citation from, the actual texts. Even the most significant concepts and ideas associated with Trotsky — such as the theory of permanent revolution and his analysis of the socio-economic foundations of the Soviet Union as a degenerated workers' state — are not explained.

Furthermore, North considers that Service also deals superficially with the background to Trotsky's writings, 'reduces the immense and complex drama of the revolutionary epoch in Russia to a series of vacuous tableaux', and:

> The coming to power of the Nazis in 1933, the eruption of the Spanish Civil War and the formation of the Popular Front in France are dealt with in a few desultory sentences. Even the Moscow Trials and the Terror merit little more than a page. Far more attention is given by Service to Trotsky's brief intimacy with Frida Kahlo!

North points to the peculiar manner in which Service's biography of Stalin goes out of its way to present its subject as an intellectual. One might add here that Service's *Stalin* has a solid six-page précis of 'Marxism and the National Question' (pp 96-101), a pedestrian work that would have long been forgotten had the author not come to subsequent prominence, whilst *none* of Trotsky's works gets anything like that.

North considers that not a little of Service's critique of Trotsky — as with those of Swain and Thatcher — follows that of Stalinism, and he is convinced that Service is trying to rehabilitate the reputation of Stalin. I feel that the intention is a little more subtle: that Service thinks that Trotsky's reputation as a thinker is overblown, whilst Stalin's has been overlooked, and that a better balance is required. But even without taking an uncritical view of Trotsky's theoretical works, and even with putting Stalin's in the best light, that is a hopeless task. When Riazanov gave a friendly warning to Stalin not to engage in theoretical encounters — 'Stop it Koba, don't make a fool of yourself. Everybody knows that theory is not exactly your field.' — he was not only putting himself firmly in Stalin's bad books, but was telling the truth.

One need not be sympathetic to Trotsky's ideas to produce a systematic analysis of them, as Baruch Knei-Paz's *The Social and Political Thought of Leon Trotsky* demonstrates, but irrespective of one's view of Trotsky, or of particular aspects of his works, any biographer of the man is surely obliged to take into serious consideration what he wrote about such key topics as the basis for a workers' revolution in Russia, the nature of Stalinism and the Soviet Union, the impact of the idea of 'socialism in one country' upon the Communist International, and the rise of fascism. North correctly points to this lacuna in the three books under review.

However, North strays beyond the bounds of fair criticism when dealing with Service's coverage of Trotsky's Jewish background. Now it is reasonable to ask why Service refers to the young Trotsky as 'Leiba', and also to ask why Thatcher refers collectively to Trotsky, Natalia Sedova and their two sons as 'the Bronsteins'. However:

> Service's continuous harping on Trotsky's religious background is obsessive, obnoxious, and, in its cumulative impact, ugly. He employs the suspect device of noting anti-Semitic attitudes and then proceeding to reinforce them.
>
> The use of anti-Semitism as a political weapon against Trotsky is so well known that it is impossible to believe that Service's incessant invocation of his subject's Jewish roots is innocent. Whatever Mr Service's personal attitude to what he refers to as 'the Jewish problem', he is all too obviously making an appeal precisely to anti-Semites for whom Trotsky's Jewish background is a major concern. It is fairly certain that the Russian-language edition of this biography will find favour within this reactionary constituency. One cannot help but suspect that Professor Service has taken this into consideration.

Although I feel that Service deals with this topic in a rather heavy-handed manner (compared to, say, Isaac Deutscher's treatment of it in his Trotsky trilogy and *The Non-Jewish Jew*), North is well out of order here. One of the regular writers for this journal studied under Service, and he told me that there are no grounds whatsoever to suspect him of harbouring anti-Jewish sentiments or of wishing to pander to the Russian anti-Semites. This, like some of North's other examples of finding conspiratorial designs on the part of the authors and their publishers — most notably the idea that 'the more politically thoughtful sections of the bourgeoisie' recognise and fear the 'danger' of 'a renewed interest in the life and work of Leon Trotsky' and that these books 'represent a sort of pre-emptive strike against the re-emergence of Trotskyist influence' — is typical of the political pedigree of North's party. Any group that still upholds

Gerry Healy's paranoid 'Security and the Fourth International' campaign will be bound to discover murky ulterior motives lurking all over the place, and North's ferreting about to unearth them here tends to undermine the validity of much of his general critique.

Trotsky played a huge role in the socialist movement of the first half of the twentieth century, and Marxists will always defend him against the superficial criticisms and inaccurate assertions that are to be found in the three books reviewed by North and elsewhere. It is, however, another matter to defend Trotsky uncritically. Trotsky's contributions to Marxist theory and practice will remain an inspiration to those who want to see a better world. He was one of the small number of socialists who kept the flame of human liberation alight when the bulk of the Second International threw their lot in with the slaughter of the First World War; he was amongst the tiny number of socialists who kept that flame alight when capitalism resorted to fascism and again to war and when Stalinism grew like a poisonous weed from the wreckage of the October Revolution. But Trotsky also played a negative role when he advocated and theoretically justified the militarisation of labour in the Soviet republic during 1920-21. He showed hesitation and confusion when faced with the rise of Stalinism, and undermined his later desire to build an anti-Stalinist Marxist movement through ill-tempered polemics and harmful excommunications. North fails even to mention these faults; he presents an all-too-shining image of Trotsky, and this gives ammunition to those who wish to denigrate him.

Cheney Longville

Joshua Rubenstein, *Leon Trotsky: A Revolutionary's Life*, Yale University Press, New Haven and London, 2011, pp 225

Just what the world needs, yet another biography of Leon Trotsky. True, if you're running a 'Jewish Lives' series 'dedicated to illuminating the range and depth of the Jewish experience', it's a bit hard to leave him out. And although Trotsky's biographers have addressed to varying degrees the Jewish dimension of his life, there has been only one full-length work on the topic, Joseph Nedava's *Trotsky and the Jews*, which appeared way back in 1971 and is almost unobtainable today.

Rubenstein dissociates himself from what he sees as Isaac Deutscher's 'too forgiving' and at times hagiographic trilogy and Robert Service's 'gratuitous criticism of Trotsky's character and personality' (pp 212-13), but he broadly concurs with the rejection of Trotsky's philosophy and life-work presented by Service and other liberal and social-democratic biographers of the man. Hence we get a condemnation of the Bolsheviks' overturn of the Provisional Government, the closing of the Constituent Assembly, the establishment of a

Communist political monopoly, and so on, and the usual homily that Trotsky ended up at the sharp end of the very state that he helped to create. Readers of *Revolutionary History* will be familiar with this, as they will be with the stock accounts of Lenin's *What Is To Be Done?*, the prediction of Bolshevik substitutionism in Trotsky's *Our Political Tasks*, and, to move on to later days, how Stalin outmanoeuvred Trotsky, stole much of his programme for the First Five-Year Plan, and finally had him assassinated. Rubenstein has a fluent writing style, but as an account of Trotsky's life, it adds little either factually or conceptually to the many biographies that have been published over the years.

Rubenstein points out that although Trotsky denied any causal connection between his Jewish origins and his political views and actions, the Jewish question impinged heavily upon his political life. Hence he describes his part in the fight against the Bund in 1903, his call during the 1905 revolution for the workers to repel pogrom gangs, his condemnation of official Jew-baiting when on trial in 1907, his angry commentary during the Beilis trial of 1913, and his poignant descriptions of beleaguered Romanian Jews in his coverage of the Balkan wars. Rubenstein then looks at how it impacted upon Trotsky after 1917, including his reluctance to be head of state lest it exacerbated anti-Semitism, the fraught days of the Civil War in which the White forces used the presence of Trotsky at the head of the Soviet regime as an important mobilising factor in their vicious pogroms that ravaged many areas of the former Russian Empire, then on to Trotsky's disgust at the use of anti-Semitism by Stalin in the fight against the Left Opposition and during the Moscow Trials, his continued refusal to endorse the Zionist project, and finally his ominous premonition of the fate of the Jews as the Second World War drew near.

On the one hand, Rubenstein claims that 'it is hard to sort out the motivations behind Trotsky's complex reaction to the Beilis trial' and his descriptions of Romanian Jews (and by implication the other times when he condemned anti-Semitism), whilst, on the other, he suggests some sort of subconscious forces were at work:

> Twice he mentioned feelings of disgust and nausea that overtook him when he contemplated their misery. Perhaps he did not think of himself as a Jew in the same way that they were Jews; he was a Marxist, a convinced internationalist, a man who resisted any narrow, parochial appeal in the name of a universal, political faith. But he had still been born and raised as a Jew. Perhaps the starkness of their lives touched something so deep inside his emotional life that he needed to vomit it out, to disgorge it before it compelled him to see himself in their faces. At moments like these, Leon Trotsky was a Jew in spite of himself. (p 67)

Elsewhere, Rubenstein seems to be perplexed by Trotsky's standpoint. After relating Trotsky's sharp critique of the Bund in 1903, he proceeds: 'But Trotsky was not indifferent to Jewish suffering.' (p 31) With one short word — the conjunction 'but' — Rubenstein creates a contradiction that did not exist: there was nothing contradictory in opposing the Bund's specific demands vis-à-vis the structure of the Russian Social Democratic Labour Party and being strongly opposed to the Tsarist regime's treatment of its Jewish subjects.

It is true that Trotsky's general attitude towards the plight of the Jews was considerably more vocal than that of many of his contemporaries. Jews were especially oppressed within the Russian Empire, liable to be attacked by pogrom gangs, subject to discriminatory legislation, and treated with suspicion by many of their fellow-countrymen. This he despised, and the Beilis trial — a particularly vile episode even by Tsarist Russian standards — brought forth his deep hatred of discrimination and bigotry. His anger here, and his subsequent feelings of disgust in respect of Stalin's use of anti-Semitism and his prediction of Hitler's Holocaust, was based not upon a recognition, conscious or otherwise, of his Jewish origins or a fear that he too could personally be a target, but upon the intimate connection between Tsarism and such uncivilised behaviour, and the continued existence and indeed revival of the latter in a supposedly socialist land or in a modern country such as Germany. It was not the result of any self-identification with Jews on his part, or a plea for any special treatment of Jews, but the recognition that Jews were the immediate and primary target of systematic state-run bigotry, be it in Tsarist Russia or Nazi Germany, or were being picked out as a scapegoat in an act of outrageous hypocrisy by an allegedly progressive regime, as in Stalin's Soviet Union.

That Trotsky drew little attention to his Jewish origins did not contradict his militant opposition to any acts of discrimination against Jews. His strong stand against anti-Semitism was not based upon any subconscious atavistic identification with the ethnic group into which he had been born. Rather, it was rooted in his socialist principles, to which he remained fully committed to the end.

Not surprisingly, Rubenstein's verdict upon Trotsky is negative. In rejecting Judaism for Marxism, he 'spurned one messianic religion' and 'adopted an alternative utopian faith — one that was secular and far more dangerous' (p 115). Rubenstein criticises Trotsky not merely for rejecting the tenets of liberal democracy once the Bolsheviks took power in 1917, but also for his stubborn adherence to his revolutionary principles after the rise of Stalinism. Although it is easy for Marxists to be dismissive of liberal criticisms of the disdain shown by the Bolsheviks for bourgeois democracy, on the grounds that the capitalist world has been notoriously inconsistent in its democratic credentials, Rubenstein cites an pertinent assessment of Trotsky by Victor Serge. Serge wrote that whilst the majority of the Left Opposition resisted Stalinist totalitarianism 'in the name of the democratic ideals expressed at the beginning of the revolution', some old Bolshevik leaders defended a 'doctrinal orthodoxy which, while not excluding a certain tendency towards democracy, was authoritarian through and through' (p 188). This is an important matter. Any socialist regime will almost certainly come under terrible pressures from within and abroad, and authoritarian measures might be necessary at some point or another. But Marxists must never forget that such a regime requires the maximum of democracy not only to thrive but indeed to survive in a recognisably socialist form.

Contrary to Rubenstein's assertion — and he is by no means the only one to assert this — Deutscher's trilogy is not hagiographic. It is sympathetic, but certainly not uncritical. Indeed, one of its strong points is that it describes how the Soviet regime became bureaucratised and how the Soviet Communist Party became transformed into a ruling élite, and how Trotsky both consciously opposed and inadvertently assisted those processes. Having read a large number of biographies of Trotsky, I remain firm in my opinion that, despite its age and its shortcomings, Deutscher's trilogy is still the best account of Trotsky's eventful life, and is the work that I would recommend to anyone wishing to learn about one of the last century's most controversial and, for Marxists, inspiring figures.
Paul Flewers

Victor Serge, *Retour à l'Ouest: Chroniques (juin 1936-mai 1940)*, Agone, Marseille, pp xxv + 372, €23

One of the delights of being a Victor Serge enthusiast is that there is always more. Serge wrote copiously, under his own name and various pseudonyms, for the scattered and obscure publications of the far left. Over 60 years after his death there are still discoveries to be made, still writings to be rediscovered.

Now Richard Greeman has prefaced, and Anthony Glinoer has edited, in unobtrusive but scrupulous fashion, articles written by Serge for *La Wallonie*, a Belgian trade-union-owned daily paper based in Liège with an extensive working-class readership. Serge had got out of Russia just before Stalin's purges turned truly murderous, and these articles represented part of his effort to reconnect with the left in Western Europe.

Each week he wrote around a thousand words on a particular topic of current or historical interest. In modern parlance he was a 'columnist', but he was far removed from the cocaine-addled mediocrities who write so much of our newspapers today (as Serge shows by quotation, the same species existed in the 1930s). Glinoer has selected 93 items out of a total of 203. It is hoped that some of the others will appear on the Agone website (See http://atheles.org/

agone/memoiressociales/retouralouest/).

The articles cover a wide range of subjects. Historical pieces range from the fall of Constantinople to a surprisingly balanced piece on Kronstadt, where Serge is critical of Lenin and Trotsky but examines the dilemmas in a way calculated not to bring comfort to polemicists on either side. He discusses current events from China to Tunisia, and contemporary French writers like Malraux and Saint-Exupéry. Even where Serge is wrong (as in his repeated predictions that the Second World War isn't going to happen), he is always perceptive.

Some commentators have tried to distinguish Serge's 'artistic' achievements (his novels) from his mere journalism. In my view this is misguided — the same qualities underlie the virtues of both forms of writing. In an interesting essay on his own book *Midnight in the Century* — which he calls a 'rigorously truthful novel' — Serge discusses the way in which the novel represents truth — differently from other forms of writing, but truth all the same.

Necessarily, however, the collection focuses on the central issues of these grim years, overshadowed by the parallel ascensions of Stalinism (the Moscow Trials) and fascism (the Spanish Civil War), two forms of what Serge was one of the first to call 'totalitarianism'. Serge felt deeply involved in both; he had been politically active in Spain before going to Russia in 1919, so he had a deep sense of identification with both Spanish workers and Russian victims of oppression.

A significant proportion of the pieces are obituaries. Serge had been in Russia from 1919 to 1922 and had known personally many of the key figures of that era of hope. Now all too many of them were falling victim to the rising repression. In Italy Gramsci was effectively murdered by Mussolini, while in Spain Andrés Nin was quite literally murdered by Stalinists. Symbolic of the age were the Mühsam couple: Erich was killed by the Nazis; his wife took refuge in Russia and was deported to Siberia.

And in Moscow were beginning the trials which would destroy so many Bolshevik militants who had been Serge's close comrades less than 20 years earlier. Serge insists that the defendants did not confess out of cowardice: 'I know them too well to have any doubt about it.' Hence he tries to explain why so many defendants confessed; to Serge it seemed like a final gesture of loyalty to the party for which they had sacrificed so much.

But if there is gloom enough in the subject-matter of these articles, what also comes through is Serge's irrepressible optimism. This is not the facile optimism of Stalinist cliché. Serge understood only too well the reality of defeat. In Russia a whole revolutionary generation was being destroyed, and Serge, who had for some years been a part of that generation, knew that the losses were irreparable.

In a few articles Serge discusses views of history, trying to put the struggles of the present in a longer historical perspective. He insists on the materialist view of history, on the fact that it is material forces, not ideas or great men, that make history. (Thus he argues that if Lenin had lived till 1937, he would have shared the fate of his comrades from 1917.) As he points out, 'history is not in a hurry, but all the same it is moving quickly'.

Hence his belief, right up to September 1939, that all-out war could be averted. The colossal destruction that such a war would entail was not in the interest of any ruling class, and the memory of 1914-18 was close enough for it to be a real warning.

Likewise Serge was very clear about the essential weakness of the fascist regimes. The terrible repression unleashed by Hitler and Mussolini was, in his view, precisely a recognition of the very real danger of proletarian revolution. The Western democracies tolerated fascism because working-class revival would be more dangerous. Likewise Stalin feared the fall of Nazism for it would 'shake… the very foundations of Russian totalitarianism'. Serge was of course quite right to point to the fragility of fascism; within just a few years Hitler and Mussolini would both be gone. Terrible as its effects were, fascism was only a very temporary means of preserving capitalism.

Serge also saw the weaknesses of Stalinism. Unlike the Stalinists, who hailed the achievements of the Russian economy, and the anti-Communists, who raised the spectre of everlasting totalitarianism, Serge pointed to the irrationalities and inefficiencies at the very heart of the Russian economy, showing the various devices used by factory managers to conform to impossible targets imposed from above. He linked this quite directly to the absence of workers' democracy.

There is much more in this volume than can be covered in a brief review. All lovers of Serge — and indeed all who appreciate good writing and perceptive analysis — will learn much from it. It is to be hoped that an English translation will appear soon.

Ian Birchall

Alan Thornett, *Militant Years: Car Workers' Struggles of the 60s and 70s*, Resistance Books, London, 2011, pp 392

Recently in a meeting to promote *Militant Years*, Alan Thornett aptly described his account of militant car worker struggles in Britain in the 1960s and 1970s in which he played a pivotal role as a leading shop steward at British Leyland's massive Cowley plant near Oxford, as a 'trade-union whodunit'. Of course the chalk outline at the crime scene was that of the powerful unofficial leadership that emerged on the shop floor in the postwar years. This seems an unlikely description for a book whose protagonists and subject matter include Cowley's TGWU 5/55 branch, the Ryder Report, the plant JSSC, the Assembly plant, the

Combine Committee, the National Industrial Relations Court, Measured Day Working and so on, but Thornett's book proves to be as compulsive as any fictional pot-boiler.

Historian Royden Harrison judged the extraordinary shop-floor revolt of 1969-74 that saw widespread mass civil disobedience and defiance of the law, and finally a second miners' strike in February 1974 that landed Heath's beleaguered Tory government 'on the rocks', to have far surpassed the 1910-14 Great Unrest (*The Independent Collier*, 1978, pp 7-8).

In our own conjuncture shaped by years of defeats and retreat, *Militant Years* is an arresting reminder of just how militant Britain's shop floor was. Yet even by the standards of an extraordinary period of struggle, Cowley was exceptional, and it is hard to think of any other comparably important or strategic workplace where the unofficial leadership had been won to Trotskyism. Car workers were in the *forefront* of the rising tide of industrial struggle, and the pitch attained by these struggles certainly stretched the limits of British trade unionism as it had developed hitherto, offering tantalising glimpses of the fraternisation of economics and politics. The other important feature of *Militant Years* is the careful recall of the hair-raising betrayals and sabotage wreaked by the union officials and the right in the course of the struggle. Clearly these prepared the ground for the far-reaching reversals of the Thatcher years.

If this were the only *raison d'être* for the appearance of *Militant Years*, then it would need no further justification, but, as many readers of *Revolutionary History* journal will know, Thornett has told this story before in two earlier books: *From Militancy To Marxism* (Harvester, 1987) whose arc was from the toehold the unions achieved thanks to the Second World War, through the two defeats of the 1950s that paradoxically spurred Cowley's stewards to organise more effectively, to the flowering of a talented young group of shop stewards initially led by the old saw Bob Fryer; and *Inside Cowley: Trade Union Struggle in the 1970s: Who Really Opened the Door to the Tory Onslaught?* (Porcupine Press, 1998) that picked up the story from the early 1970s to the chilly years of Thatcher.

Inevitably, having one volume to retell the story previously outlined in two means that detail is filtered out, and this clearly falls *more heavily* on the role of the Socialist Labour League/Workers Revolutionary Party at the plant (the Oxford branch barely appears at all) and the breakaway Workers Socialist League, founded by Thornett and his comrades after their expulsion from the WRP in November 1974 after criticising the WRP's decline into 'an ultra-left spiral' (p 128).

Instead we get a more straightforward account of the shop-floor struggle that occasionally conveys the impression that Trotskyist politics were less vital to the

Cowley stewards than perhaps Thornett believes. This new *emphasis* probably reflects our own period when the verities of Trotskyism in all of its varieties are more frequently met with indifference and scepticism by those recently politically awakened in, say, UK Uncut or the Occupy movement. Thornett has said that Militant Years was written with one eye on the slow re-emergence of the organised working class, and the book condenses the story of Cowley and the backdrop of industrial strife very well, and may be treated either as a companion to the two earlier books or a stand-alone volume.

In discussing the surprising renascence of Trotskyism in the industrial sphere from the 1960s onwards, John McIlroy observed that while most workers remained stubbornly loyal to labourism and the older Communist Party trade unionists travelled further to the right whilst nesting in the official trade-union structures, Trotskyism became a pole of attraction for a layer of young workers chafing at the restraints of the *affluent worker*, repelled by the prosaic Wilson governments of 1964-70 and radicalised by a growing global revolt. Though relatively marginal overall, Trotskyism was a growing force in certain parts of industry and in certain workplaces and lent a 'radical cutting edge' to shop-floor militancy, and nowhere was this potent combination more evident than the Cowley car plant. Committed to a vision of conflict as endemic and class struggle as transformative, Trotskyism and militant trade unionism were a potentially fertile combination (see John McIlroy, '"Always Outnumbered, Always Outgunned": The Trotskyists and the Trade Unions', in John McIlroy, Nina Fishman and Alan Campbell (eds), *The High Tide of British Trade Unionism*, 1999).

In terms of perspectives and industrial strategy, McIlroy registers the inevitable weaknesses accompanying Trotskyism's effervescence (even in what he argues was the refreshingly heterodox version of the International Socialists, whose rank-and-file strategy was tempered by revolutionary realism): the overly sunny evaluation of the balance of forces, the underestimation of the limits of shop stewards' power, the absence of a hard-headed analysis of the rhythms of the capitalist economy, the ups and downs of particular industries, the lack of an appreciation of the fragility of workers' power *within* capitalism, the downplaying of the system's resilience, and so on (McIlroy, p 260). Clearly, such an appraisal of Trotskyism's weaknesses is closely linked to the infirmities of aggressive trade unionism with which it sought to unite. Many of these arguments are implicitly addressed in *Militant Years*, with Thornett deftly underlining the key illustrative lesson that, despite conspicuous successes, militant trade unionism *could not ultimately stop the plant closures*.

But how was the shop-floor leadership of a major car plant won to Trotskyism in the first place? At Cowley, a talented group of young shop stewards initially guided by Bob Fryer (a left-wing working-class Hungarian Jew who escaped Nazi-occupied Europe and joined the British army) spearheaded the resistance to Barbara Castle's *In Place of Strife* (1969), the Industrial Relations Act, the 'colour bar' at BL and the introduction of Measured Day Work.

Thornett was entirely typical of the workers drawn in search of higher wages from the area surrounding Cowley. After working as a farm labourer, Thornett started at Cowley as a lorry driver in 1959, having recently voted Tory in the General Election (pp 1-2). This was year that Frank Horsman, a new breed of aggressive shop steward, was victimised by management (pp 9-12). Thornett was soon active in the union, and within months had joined the Young Communist League.

By the mid-1960s, near 100 per cent union shops had been won at Cowley. The plant averaged 300 stoppages a year, though most were short lived and sectional. During the 1966 general election, Cowley's shop stewards hit the headlines when they were baselessly accused of intimidating scabs in an incident quickly dubbed the 'Noose Trial' (pp 18-21). The unofficial shop-floor movement was widely accused of being the root cause of Britain's lack of economic competitiveness. Tory leader Edward Heath claimed the 'Noose Trial' typified irresponsible trade unionism. Heath lost the election, but the union officials launched an investigation and though the stewards were exonerated, a precedent was established, and the closer official attention of the next decade eventually hatched into a full-blown campaign to extirpate 'Trotskyism' from the plant, despite the fact that this campaign undermined resistance to the gathering employers' offensive (pp 23-24).

The year of 1966 was also the one in which the unofficial plant leadership, including Alan Thornett, joined Gerry Healy's Socialist Labour League, and though Fryer did not take this step he remained a close collaborator. The Cowley stewards clearly represented the SLL's greatest asset in the industrial sphere. In time this talented levy of stewards, with the exception of Tom White, would break with Healy as the SLL's *relative* sobriety mutated into the WRP's shrill sectarianism. Yet initially Healy, who took a great deal of interest in the plant, helped Thornett and his comrades raise their eyes to wider political horizons, capital's evolving strategies towards the shop floor, the role of the union officials and so on, a perspective largely absent from the Communist Party (p 24).

The most significant struggle at Cowley was probably the resistance to management's efforts to sweep away piecework and introduce Measured Day Work, based on a flat rate of pay with the work-rate established by time and motion study. The introduction of MDW was intended to undermine the basis of shop steward power as piecework allowed the stewards to negotiate the rate for the job on behalf of their workmates. A seven-week strike ended in defeat as a result of the defection of the union officials to management's side. Defeat saw the Deputy Convenor Reg Parson's break with the left. Damagingly, Parsons began collaborating with the union officials and BL management to nullify the left in the plant (pp 40-50).

As the 1970s unfolded, the right wing in the plant with the tacit official union backing they enjoyed trampled on the union rulebook and finally broke the bedrock TGWU 5/55 into two branches (5/55 and 5/293). Yet the left and the rank and file fought back against all the odds, and at the end of 1977 won the plant leadership in bitterly-contested TGWU elections (pp 235-40). Yet the victory proved to be pyrrhic. Nationally the union leaders had swung behind the Labour government's incomes policy. In 1975, BL was nationalised by the then Industry Secretary Tony Benn, but within months Benn was gone, sacked by Wilson and replaced by Eric Varley (pp 130-37). In 1976, another key struggle against 'participation' which aimed to incorporate the unions and side-line the militants, was lost when it was forced in with the help of the union officials of BL's 14 unions (pp 143-52).

The writing was on the wall. In 1977, Eric Varley recruited the ruthless South African businessman Michael Edwardes from the National Economic Board. Astonishingly Harold Wilson had originally appointed Edwardes to the NEB despite the South African's aversion to nationalisation. Edwardes was given *carte blanche* by Callaghan and Varley to restore BL to profitability and return it to the private sector (pp 247-53), and capacity and manning levels were cut with gusto, often with the connivance of the national officials of BL's trade unions (p 277). At the Kenilworth conference in February 1978, Edwardes gathered together 700 managers, national and local union officials and convenors in a gathering *unimaginable* before 'participation' was introduced, and in a speech lasting an hour announced that at least 12 000 jobs would have to go to ensure BL's survival. Then a vote of confidence was sprung on the gathering and *only five voted against* (all from Oxford). Derek 'Red Robbo' Robinson led the *enthusiastic* standing ovation for Edwardes (pp 250-53), but a year later Robinson was out, victimised by management as an emboldened Edwardes closed plant after plant.

Ominously, Edwardes' ruthless shedding of jobs at BL anticipated the mass shakeouts of labour in manufacturing during Thatcher's early years. Unsurprisingly, Edwardes, admired by Thatcher, stayed at the summit of BL until 1982 before leaving. That year was also the one in which Thornett, now a well-established national hate figure of the press, was finally victimised because he forgot to renew his HGV licence (p 341). Thornett's valuable book leaves the reader with a vivid appreciation of the real strengths of the militant trade unionism in Britain in the 1960s and 1970s, and something of its limits too.

Julian Alford

Paul Trewhela, *Inside Quatro: Uncovering the Exile History of the ANC and SWAPO*, Jacana Media (Pty) Ltd, South Africa, 2009, pp 242, £14.95

Paul Trewhela worked with the late Baruch Hirson, a valued member of the Editorial Board of *Revolutionary History*, to write, produce and distribute the small but highly influential journal *Searchlight South Africa* during the period of transition from the apartheid regime to the modernised capitalist regime overseen by the ANC. The radicalism and independence of this little journal earned it a prompt state ban in South Africa, as well as the admiration of independent-minded leftists who were fortunate enough to come across it. After Baruch's death, Paul and the tiny group that supported *SSA* did not feel able to continue publication. *Revolutionary History* collected Baruch's articles on the history of the left in South Africa and posted them on our website. But it has always been a disappointment to me that the full series of the journal was not available on the Internet. It is much to be welcomed then that this selection of Paul's important writings, much of it from *SSA*, is now available in print.

The theme of the collection is specifically the brutality of the internal regimes in the 'national liberation movements' that came to power in South Africa and Angola (the ANC and SWAPO) and more generally the ethical and political consequences of state power falling into the hands of such organisations. *Revolutionary History* supported from an early stage the exposure of this brutality, and made available relevant material on our website. We continue to be interested in the matter (see for example our obituary in this issue of Bongani Mkhungo). We are not alone in retaining such interest, but we are more alone than we would wish to be.

In his introduction, Paul acknowledges that one of the fractions emerging from the implosion of the Workers Revolutionary Party and its International Committee was almost unique in providing practical support for and contacts to the work of *SSA*. It was no accident that this was the case; the WRP derived its political heritage from opposition to Michel Pablo's fundamental revision of Trotskyism (subsequently to become the orthodoxy of the Pablo/Mandel tendency and its derivatives) — his teaching that Stalinism would and therefore should replace the working class as the engine of revolutionary change. While such a difference, dating back to the 1950s, is today often derided as irrelevant and obscure, it was a life-and-death matter for those who attempted to make the political revolution in the Buffer Zone of Eastern Europe, in Vietnam and China. (Trewhela does point out that Tariq Ali's *Black Dwarf* at an early stage helped to publicise the case against the ANC's prison-camp regime.) And it was no less a life-and-death matter for those who demanded that the overthrow of apartheid should lead to socialism, not to the restabilisation of capitalism with a black middle class.

Paul Trewhela no longer appears to sympathise with any of the Trotskyist currents. The realignment of his thinking and feeling arises from direct experience, and deserves to be quoted (Introduction, p viii):

> We were totally isolated, bar the single fraction of the Workers Revolutionary Party. At a joint meeting on South Africa held at the London School of Economics, at which *Searchlight South Africa* was one of three contributory groupings, I was told from the platform that I 'deserved a bullet' when I compared the ANC's prison camps with the IRA's bombing campaign of civilian targets. The systemic cruelty of this generality of the Trotskyist left in Britain was a great education to me, at that time, and afterwards, in the pernicious character of Marx's doctrine of the dictatorship of the proletariat, and the degree to which this 'progressive' advocacy of dictatorship among the British intelligentsia was a masked vehicle for personality disorders of all kinds.

A deplorable state of affairs, wherein one of the best defenders of the black workers of South Africa is threatened with murder (albeit a threat which the perpetrator had *at the time* no ability to carry out) by somebody who claimed to be a Marxist revolutionary. In the main text it is clarified that the perpetrator was a member of the Revolutionary Communist Party.[1] Those of us who have spent time in membership of any of the Trotskyist, Pabloite or State-Capitalist groups will be able to shudder at the thought of certain individuals being able to wield power (I once attended a dramatisation of *Animal Farm* in which Squealer had the voice, phrasing and body language of a leading member of my own organisation so accurately that I had to adjourn to the bar long before the interval; I could never convince myself, despite his protestations, that the amateur actor had not modelled himself on the Trotskyist I knew) — just as we would be able to find examples of self-sacrifice and dedication to admire and wonder at. But to sympathise with Paul is not the same thing as to share his conclusions about Marx.

The main value of Paul's book is his *evidence*. It begins with the eye-witness statement by the 'Nairobi Five' describing the mutiny of the ANC's armed force, *Umkhonto weSizwe* (MK), refusing to be used against the Angolan UNITA forces. Prominent ANC figures including Tambo and Hani attempted to regain control, but the mutineers, somewhat perversely, stood by the statements of ANC leader Joe Slovo about the importance of democracy in the struggle for national liberation, demanding that the ANC live up to their own fine words. In expounding their grievances they set out the first account of the suppression of internal democracy in the ANC and the ascendancy of its security section, which had created the long-secret Quatro prison, into which dissidents disappeared with horrible regularity. They hated the way the ANC was keeping them away from their objective — that of bringing military support to the struggling masses inside South Africa. In addition, they were becoming aware of the material privileges the ANC leadership bestowed upon itself, financed by solidarity donations around the world, and criminal activities in areas under their control (particularly smuggling).

The ANC responded with increased 'security' activity (which uncovered networks of previously unsuspected spies among the dissidents) and tightened military discipline in the camps. In Quatro they got busier with beatings, torture and murder. This was the basis on which the ANC took control over the mass of revolutionaries who wanted physically to destroy the apartheid state. It was a method that was to serve them well — they were able to demonstrate to imperialism that they could control the revolutionary forces that would otherwise inevitably succeed. The statement describes in detail the conditions suffered by the rebels inside Quatro. In a footnote the author points out that the 'Truth and Reconciliation Commission' eventually confirmed the reports of murders by ANC guards in Quatro. Further articles reprinted from *SSA* show how the evidence of the ANC's brutal regime was diligently assembled and published from a front room in North London by Trewhela, Hirson and a few others.

There are also accounts of individual murders inside South Africa that were the responsibility of the ANC — best known among these being by Winnie Mandela's amateur bodyguard, but others implicating more ANC leaders, including Zuma. (The ANC's London press office is still contending against Trewhela on this theme.)

Useful too is the article reminding us of the corruption and rottenness of the security elements in the ANC's London office, and the iron grip they retained over their black militants. These same people ordered anti-apartheid activists to discontinue their permanent picket of the SA embassy in London, and when this was refused, engineered the retraction of Russian funding for David Kitson's research at Ruskin College as a reprisal.

SSA was later to expose parallel horrors perpetrated by SWAPO against its own supporters. Especially obscene is that SWAPO's torture centre was officially named the 'Karl Marx Reception Centre'!

So this is a valuable book, bringing together most of the central documents from *SSA* on the appalling truth about the ANC and SWAPO. These are not pretty stories, but they have to be told and understood if the black working masses of Southern Africa are to reach the historic goals of their own liberation. Paul Trewhela's journalistic work continues — he remains a prolific and insightful writer on South Africa, and happily he has also become a successful painter. *Searchlight South Africa* was — and still is — a splendid example of the power of truth-telling. In whatever unpredictable way, at whatever unpredictable time, the fact that *SSA* recorded these stories and made them public will contribute to the ultimate success of the South African workers. For the many victims described, we can only express our sympathy and admiration.

JJ Plant

Note

1. One of the Editorial Board of this journal was present at this meeting, and confirms that the RCP speaker was citing Trotsky's phrase 'the British socialist who fails to support by all possible means the uprisings in Ireland, Egypt and India against the London plutocracy — such a socialist deserves to be branded with infamy, if not with a bullet'. It was not meant as a personal threat against the author, but was a rather juvenile example of quotation-mongering in a heated debate. As it was, our Editorial Board member called in his RCP branch for support for the *SSA* campaign, but was told that this campaign was not helpful to the struggle against apartheid.

Jürg Ulrich, *Kamenev: Der Gemäßigte Bolschewik. Das kollektive Denken im Umfeld Lenins*, VSA, Hamburg, 2006, pp 232, €19.80

Biographical studies of Bolsheviks have very much concentrated upon, to borrow the title of Bertram D Wolfe's book, 'the three who made a revolution': Lenin, Stalin and Trotsky (although, to draw upon the title of another study, Stalin would be more justly labelled as the man who almost missed the revolution). The shadows of these three men loom so heavily over Soviet history that it is inevitable that they will have always attracted the greatest attention from Western academic researchers. Moreover, because the overwhelming majority of these academics consider that the 'logic' of the October Revolution led inexorably to Stalinist dictatorship and ultimately to collapse, it was felt reasonable to pay little attention to that broad layer of revolutionaries without whom neither the revolution nor its result, the early Soviet republic, would have existed. This remained the case when considering the many of them who made an important contribution to the counter-revolution that Stalin personified, and who subsequently became its victims. Despite this, some biographical material on a few of them has appeared, most notably Bukharin, but also, through the works of Richard Day, Preobrazhensky. Another example is Karl Radek, not least because he constantly moved within the labour movements of different countries.

One of the most prominent Bolsheviks who has been largely overlooked or at least far too little considered is Lev Kamenev, despite the fact that until the mid-1920s he was one of the party's most important leaders. He chaired Politbureau sessions and was the first editor of Lenin's works. Following Lenin's death, he was complicit in the marginalisation of Trotsky; he then went into opposition to Stalin, but by late 1927 had forsaken oppositional activity. Even though after that date he was no longer engaged in any significant political activity, he was one of the main defendants in the first Moscow Trial, in 1936, and he was condemned to death and executed, followed in the ensuing months by his whole family: his wife, children, siblings and their next of kin. Jürg Ulrich has produced the first sizeable biography of Kamenev. Neither in English nor Russian do comparable works exist, though in the latter language there are at least a series of Lexicon articles and biographical essays.

Kamenev was born Lev Rozenfeld in 1883, into a family of Jewish railway workers in Moscow, and he thus belonged to the small group of socially better-off and largely 'Russified' Jews allowed to live outside the pale of settlement. The example best known to a broader public is surely that of the family of the author Ilya Ehrenburg. Recently, in his Trotsky biography, Robert Service has condemned the former for not feeling sufficiently Jewish. Kamenev described his ethnic origin in the Soviet Union, as was required in passports, as Jewish, whereas he had described himself as Russian to the tsarist police. It seems that when young he may have been baptised, though the appropriate 'stigma' of his origins may have always stuck to him, which surely was a motive for leading him into opposition to tsarist society. He seems to have been quite uninfluenced by Jewish culture, and there is no evidence that he spoke Yiddish and or had any contact with the Jewish (that is, Yiddish-speaking) labour movement. His field of political activity was to be the centre of the Russian Empire, above all its capital St Petersburg, or Siberian exile.

His time as a law student in Moscow from 1902 did not last long. He immediately immersed himself in the student movement and joined the Social Democrats. Thus began the usual trajectory of a Russian revolutionary from activity to imprisonment and exile. He soon distinguished himself by his agitational and organisational capabilities. As early as his first exile he came into contact with Lenin, and thereby almost immediately landed in the Bolshevik faction which was being formed in 1903. He took the party-name of Kamenev, which is derived from the Russian word for 'stone'.

The particulars of his rise in the Bolshevik faction can only be outlined here and are set out in detail by Ulrich, who shows that he very quickly made his mark, especially as a journalist. As a result of the repression and the decline of the socialist movement following the defeat of the 1905 revolution, in 1908 he was forced into exile abroad. As one of the important Bolshevik leaders, he was involved in vigorous polemics with the other currents of the social-democratic movement, in which he early on struck a very hard tone, which seems to Ulrich to anticipate his writings of the 1920s. Trotsky, whose brother-in-law he had ironically become — through marriage to Trotsky's sister Olga — would find himself on the receiving end of it. While Trotsky stood, as is known, some way from Bolshevism, he occasionally received financial help from his rather better-off brother-in-law. At times Kamenev was also the Bolshevik representative on *Pravda*, the newspaper edited by Trotsky in Vienna, until finally in 1912 the factions became independent parties. Only the new upturn in the Russian labour movement on the eve of the world war brought him back into Russia, where, as the brains behind the Bolshevik parliamentary group, he was in practice the leader of the party within the country. The outbreak of war led immediately to his imprisonment and exile in Siberia for 'life', from which the February Revolution freed him. Back in Petrograd, he was the party's real leader until Lenin's return in April.

Kamenev's attitude in the year of revolution is well known. He was one of the spokesmen of the Bolshevik party's right wing, which strove for collaboration with the other socialist parties and came out publicly against its independently seizing power. As events nevertheless created facts and Bolshevik rule was established in the winter of 1917-18, his membership of the party leadership was again uncontested, which showed itself in the fact that he usually chaired the sessions of the Politbureau. Ulrich follows him through the known stages of his activity in the Soviet Republic, which cannot be set out here. As Lenin's health dramatically declined, Kamenev, Zinoviev (with whose name he was now coupled even more than in 1917) and Stalin formed the Troika, which in 1923 prevented Trotsky from taking over the party leadership. The Troika collapsed in 1925, and Kamenev and Zinoviev allied with Trotsky in 1926 in the United Opposition, only to capitulate to Stalin in late 1927. Their hopes that Stalin in his 'left turn' would take up the demands of the Opposition were dashed. Kamenev called himself a 'political corpse', withdrew from activity and henceforth concentrated wholly on literary and historical works, producing, for example, such noteworthy items as a Pushkin edition and more fundamental studies of the nineteenth century.

In the use of the broad brush of historical-political analysis, Ulrich follows the well-known interpretation similar to that of Victor Serge, Trotsky and Isaac Deutscher. What makes this work interesting is that Ulrich describes in detail Kamenev's activities, of which little is known to the non-specialist. For instance, as the editor of the first edition of Lenin's works, through the compilation of the texts and his introduction and notes, he played a decisive part in the invention of 'Leninism', that is, the ideological cloak under which the Troika legitimised itself. Nevertheless, this first Lenin edition contrasted considerably with the subsequent ones compiled under Stalin, and as a result would soon vanish from the libraries.

Even though in the 1930s Kamenev no longer had any political role, he was simply by virtue of his historical career and his political-theoretical capabilities a potential challenger to Stalin, and if there was a really deep crisis in the party he was ready in the wings. From the end of 1934, following Kirov's murder, his removal became the highest priority of the Stalinist apparatus. Imprisoned immediately after the murder, he was at first accused, in two trials during 1935, of actively pulling the strings behind it, until the case for the prosecution for the first Moscow Trial, in August 1936, was concocted. He and Zinoviev were presented at the trial as the head of a 'Trotskyist' conspiracy. At this point Ulrich bases himself on the revelations of the Gorbachov era, in which were revealed for the first time how the falsification of 'evidence' and the extortion of the confessions were achieved.

For his extensive work Ulrich bases himself predominantly upon the new Russian secondary literature and the biographical material on the Bolsheviks murdered by Stalin that has been published since the end of the 1980s. He was unable to consult archive material which undoubtedly exists in a whole number of places, above all in the old party archive and surely in the intelligence service files of the time. The revelations he has collected originate from these Russian publications, and some are brought to non-Russian readers for the first time. A comprehensive work based on primary sources is therefore still needed, as this would undoubtedly be able to reveal even more details and wholly unknown aspects of Kamenev's life. After reading this book, one can raise some very interesting questions which need more precise explanations. One would be on how the Troika functioned; another would be on Kamenev's particular relationship with Zinoviev over the years, which is dealt with here all too briefly. Another important theme would be the creation of the myth of 'Leninism' and the precise role played in this by Kamenev's edition of Lenin's works, together with a comparison with later Stalinist editions. All this would have required a far more ambitious work than anything this author could afford to attempt.

Some academic historians will not be satisfied with this book. But as a political portrait that shows the various episodes of Kamenev's life and his evolution over the decades it fully succeeds. It makes Kamenev more widely known and shows why he was persecuted and killed by the Stalin dictatorship. It also clearly illustrates his weaknesses, which led him in the early 1920s, in the first phase of the establishment of Stalinism, to be one of the Troika and, from purely tactical considerations, to assist Stalin's ascendancy over the party, although the course of events must have become clear to him early on. In 1937, Trotsky characterised him as a propagandist with analytical competence and a reflective bent, but with a propensity for excessive caution. In the factional struggles in the party, this would lead to his doom.

Considered from these angles, this book is a most helpful addition to our appreciation of Kamenev and his times.

Reiner Tosstorff

Ben Watson, *Adorno for Revolutionaries*, Unkant Publishers for the Association of Musical Marxists, London, 2011, £10.99, pp 256

This book by Ben Watson (edited by Andy Wilson) includes a number of lectures given and essays written by him over the years on Theodor Adorno, philosopher and musicologist.

Adorno lived in Germany through the First World War; a war lost by Germany and followed by a bankrupt economy. There was the possibility of proletarian revolution, but instead Hitler and the Nazis took power. Adorno, exiled in America, took with him his Institute of Social Research, known as the Frankfurt School. This did not return to Germany until after the end of the Second World War.

Watson writes that Adorno refused to make intellectual or musical life a haven from these events, for his Marxism brought social ideas into every concept. He wanted to develop a theory which was materialist and historical and which refused the idea of abstract and eternal laws, for he saw musical taste as a political question.

During the early 1900s tonality in music broke down as secular subjects gave way to bourgeois buyers wanting more and more spectacular music. Music was for sale, a commodity from which profit would be made (similar to the arrival of abstraction in painting). Adorno attacked consumer society for its every conversion of quality into quantity. If everything is exchangeable, nothing has value in itself.

And yet, Watson writes, postmodernist cultural studies characterise Adorno as 'modernist and élitist'. This caricature arises from a profound ignorance of philosophy, for Adorno saw philosophy as not abstract but grounded in social conflict.

With the advent of the Beatles in the 1960s, opposition between popular and classical music became a key symbol of class difference, especially in Britain. The middle-class notion of pop music as the positive choice of the working class confuses consumption with production and conveniently ignores the role of capital. Sales charts are constructed in order to sell CDs, which are where the major profits are made. Watson writes that when sociology abandons aesthetic judgement and draws lessons about social identity from sales statistics, it is no longer pursuing social science, but is researching into business practice.

Adorno was keen to understand the effects of new technology on aesthetic matters. *Current of Music* was the title he gave to his various writings about radio. Watson writes about this under the title 'Three Years of Late Lunch on Resonance' — Resonance being the small Central London arts radio station on which he works as a volunteer.

Adorno was concerned with how much of the genuine force of Chamber or Symphonic music could appear when piped through a wooden box. However, he saw that modern composers could work with the new technology.

Watson criticises Heidegger's *Philosophy of Authenticity*, against which Adorno wrote *The Jargon of Authenticity* (published in 1967). Heidegger held that every human being is thrown into a world to which he or she must adjust. Such a human is fallen and inauthentic. To become authentic it involves accepting the world as it is. Adorno was scornful of Heidegger's philosophy with its Biblical overtones and support of the status quo. Heidegger, as Rector of Heidelberg University, welcomed Hitler's national revolution as the only way of preserving the élite against the communist mobilisation of the envious masses. And yet, Watson remarks, postmodern liberals, confident that working-class socialism can lead only to Stalinist tyranny, are forever flirting with Heidegger.

Watson writes that Adorno had nothing but good to say about fantasy. Fantasy can establish the relationship between objects which is the irrevocable source of all judgement. Should fantasy be driven out, judgement too, the real act of knowledge, is exorcised (Adorno, *Minima Moralia: Reflections from a Damaged Life*, London, 1974). The bourgeois revolution brought fantasy and fancy into disrepute. This was the era of hard facts, which Watson writes, went along with hard bargains and hard beds (as poked fun at by Charles Dickens in *Hard Times*). Adorno rejects the cosy middle-class view of fantasy and rebellion as 'a passing phase'. Watson quotes from Trotsky 'all conscious action begins with a mere idea (fantasy)'.

Watson looks at music in its historical perspective and quotes: 'Art, no less than science, is the fruit of a dialectical relationship of man and nature-labour.' The interest of the recording industry is to turn talent into purchasable commodities. With regard to jazz, it is necessary to understand the history of black people in the United States, and that history is incomprehensible without an understanding of the exigencies of capitalism. Recommended is John Kofsky, *Black Nationalism and the Revolution in Music* (New York, 1970), republished as *John Coltrane and the Jazz Revolution of the 1960s* (New York, 1998). Kofsky was a Marxist whose analysis benefited from an appreciation of leadership derived from Trotsky's *History of the Russian Revolution*. Also recommended is *Free Jazz Black Power* by Phillipa Corles and Jean-Louis Comolli (Paris, 1971). The historical materialism of these writers made sense of a music which had previously been mystified by various concepts of art.

Jazz grew up with the recording industry and was a result of capitalist enterprise at the lower end of the social scale. For its workers to encounter socialism and Marxism required the same hard school of exploitation as any other industry. Watson writes about the wave of militancy which swept the American working class following the San Francisco General Strike. The Communist Party (CPUSA) took advantage of this by working with Father Divine in Harlem and staging anti-segregation benefits by jazz musicians. Duke Ellington played benefits for the CPUSA and supported the campaign to save the Scottsboro boys in 1931. By 1938, the CPUSA had over 1000 black members in Harlem. However, in 1935 the Communist International had begun its attack on the musical curiosity and sexual license of jazz, in favour of 'folk values, untainted by bourgeois decadence'. (Hitler, of course, also used folk music to foster a sense of national identity.) Watson concludes that this lesson from black America is something every musician (and non-musician) must learn.

The 1950s was the period in which American capital reshaped Europe in its image. Communist Russia which had been an ally in the Second World War, was now seen as a totalitarian menace. The recent Jackson Pollock exhibition in New York and London served as a reminder of Cold War propaganda with its use of strategies derived from Dada and surrealism to underline the 'free' nature of market capitalism. For Stalin had incarcerated modern artists in psychiatric clinics, while the CIA encouraged bankers and tycoons to buy modern art. In this way postwar modern art became a badge of élitism. That is what concerns Adorno in these discourses. Watson writes that Adorno questions the notion that in a society based on inequality and exploitation, liberated music can serve a particular class.

Watson reviews a book on club cultures and music by Sarah Thornton. He writes that music remains the great unsaid protest at the spiritual poverty of capitalism, but, as Thornton discovers, it also remains a site of resistance to academic analysis. Certainly few academic writers have shown fluency in dealing with musical form. However, left activists have had persistent recourse to music. Apart from music deriving from black America, Rock Against Racism is one of the few left interventions in culture to bear fruit. Thornton defends popular culture, but seemingly does not understand how capitalism mediates it. In the name of research, Watson says, Thornton hung out in a few nightclubs in Glasgow and London and from her experiences in these, she draws her conclusions, giving observation the status of science. She appears to have no interest in the actual economics of club culture, the sexual mores or in the racial component of the music's genesis and image. Watson concludes that sociology designed to promote the sociologist is not a riveting read.

Under the heading 'Born to Die', Watson tells us of a contribution he made to the Conference of Critical Musicology, King's College London on 19 April 1996. His paper caused consternation and Watson was asked to leave the conference. Georgina Born was given the platform to denounce Watson's 'neanderthal Marxism' and 'sexism'. In writing about Born's *Rationalizing Culture* (IRCAM — Institut de Recherché et de Coordination Acoustique Musique, 1995.) Watson states that while Thornton uses sociology to give her statements academic gravitas, Born uses structural anthropology. Diagrams of her 'field' research slot into a variety of structures, the dominant schema being tripartite: modern, postmodern and popular. These diagrams, Watson says, substitute for attempts to understand what was actually being argued about at IRCAM in 1984, providing a mystificatory front of scientific 'objectivity'. In her attempt to reach an objective understanding of social relations, no point of view is left for the analyst herself, who disappears 'God-like into an invisible all-seeing eye'.

Watson writes that a society which places every human activity before the tribunal of profitability finds it hard to describe the inner workings of music. The Romantics held that music, by opening the door on the sublime, bypasses rational thought. However, Watson says, music is a specific movement of air molecules, objective, collective and recordable. A material event open to scrutiny. Certainly the symphony orchestra is a stunning example of the division of labour. He asks: 'What would a dialectical musicology look like?' The proposal by Theodor Adorno for a socially cognisant musicology, one that sprang from a vision of the social whole, was rejected by British academic departments.

Before the cultural and political turmoil of the 1960s, mass culture was not an occasion for claims and counter-claims which today are the bread and butter of cultural and media studies. The birth of a counter-culture gave pop music its intellectual standing. A spiritual expression of the fact that insurgent populations stopped a major war in Vietnam, which had been waged by imperialist power. And additionally, the events in Paris in 1968. Marvin Gaye, the Beatles, Bob Dylan and Jimi Hendrix brought into the charts political and artistic seriousness. These political facts were omitted by those with designs on academic respectability.

Watson writes that *Performing Rites* by Simon Frith registers a retreat from 1960s militancy. Frith sees music as a wing of the general study of 'popular culture' which includes sport and fashion. 'Rock is the music of youth' were the words which opened his first book (*The Sociology of Rock*, London, 1978). Watson remarks that the English bourgeoisie deem it an indication of immaturity to take either socialism or pop seriously. However, responses to black, American musical forms were initially phrased in adult language — Hermann Hesse's *Steppenwolf*; the jazz poetry of the Beats; Eric Hobsbawm's Marxist jazz criticism. Frith's reduction of non-classical music to a soundtrack for immaturity concedes everything to conservative cultural values.

In 1998 Watson reviewed three new books on Adorno. The first, of a book by Simon Jarvis, was originally written for *Historical Materialism* in 1998. He writes that Jarvis' survey sifts Adorno's thought into a series of carefully-graded positions. Each contention is assessed next to Kant, Hegel, Heidegger, Husserl, Habermas and Derrida. For Jarvis there is only Adorno's philosophy and the patience required to unravel it. Jarvis understands Adorno philosophically rather than politically, and so Adorno's arguments are torn from their moment.

Robert Witkin's account of Adorno focuses on music. However, Witkin emphasises Adorno's Weberian side, ending up with a history of the West as a climax of rationalisation, not the victory of capital. I, myself, was taken aback by Witkin's surmise, quoted by Watson, that a Jewish account of the Holocaust would lack objectivity (!!!). Watson says that this is a direct rebuttal of Adorno's doctrine (and Benjamin's) that the voice of suffering is the voice of truth.

Max Paddison's book, in its conscientious working through, lays the foundation for a materialist musicology, one with revolutionary implications undreamt of by post-modernist apologists for consumer capitalists. Paddison is a musicologist, restoring music as Adorno's primary focus and accentuates his relevance to radical social critique. Paddison translates Adorno's thought into sober musicology, setting up procedures for the music departments for whom the book was written. Paddison explores Adorno's positive response to Béla Bartok, in that the 'folk music' used by romantic composers in industrialised countries was a bourgeois fantasy of class reconciliation, evoking a patriotic never-never land. Watson says that while Paddison acknowledges Adorno's mistakes and lacunae, he finishes with a dialectical observation. Paddison's Adorno is the opposite of the prescriptive mandarin vilified in textbooks.

In the next chapter, Gordon Finlayson responds to Watson's review of Jarvis' book — and with some rancour! Finlayson does not agree with Watson's political, instead of philosophical, reading of Adorno and defends Jarvis. In the next chapter, Watson replies to Finlayson's arguments.

'Frank Zappa: Hollywood Contradiction' consists of a talk Watson gave at Marxism in July 1995 (at which I was present). As Watson writes, during the talk he had criticised statements made by leading comrades of the Socialist Workers Party. They came to hear of this and it almost ended in a punch-up. Watson writes that Zappa is interesting because he presents a mixture of 'high' and 'low' cultural forms. He put genuinely innovative avant-garde music — some of the least popular that has ever existed — into record shops around the world. Watson writes that his interest in Zappa hinges on the fact that he remained loyal to an idea of artistic autonomy and progress in art, associated with modernism. To make his points, Watson considers what Trotsky said about literature, quoting from Trotsky's *Literature and Revolution* of 1924. Trotsky, he wrote, refuses to allow that 'pure art' is in fact possible; art is always an activity which takes place in a concrete social situation. Watson continues by remarking that perhaps music presents the greatest challenge to Marxist criticism. And yet, if Trotsky is right and art, however, abstract, cannot transcend its social function, then a Marxist understanding of society should help us in understanding music.

This book ends with a postscript which uses words as sounds, a type of musical composition of sentences which make a kind of sense, but have to be listened to rather than immediately understood.

The book itself is decorated with black lines, squiggles and blots (the blots reminding me of my schooldays!) which liven up the pages.

I found this book extremely interesting and I agree with Watson's conclusions.

Sheila Lahr

Larry Wayne, *Union Bread. Bagels, Platzels and Chollah: The Story of the London Jewish Bakers' Union*, Jewish Socialist Group and Socialist History Group (SHS Occasional Paper, no 26), London, 2009, pp 114, £6.00

I found this a very interesting study of the Jewish workingmen in the East End, and recommend it without hesitation to readers interested in the social and political history of East London. My own East End ancestry includes a line through the German sugar bakers in Wapping, who had their own distinct identity. The much more numerous Jews came from a range of East European origins — predominantly of course Czarist Russia and its subordinate states — Poland, 'the Ukraine' as it was then called, extinguished Courland and the Baltic statelets.

The richly deserved assassination of Czar Alexander II of Russia in 1881 had as a consequence a savage wave of state-sponsored anti-Semitism across the Russian empire, driving out large numbers of Jews, a significant proportion of whom settled in the East End, changing its ethnic and social character for nearly a century. Among these were bakers of bread, cakes and confectionary, a few of them able to become employers ('masters'), most of them employees, many casual.

Some products are not only essential, but are felt to be essential, and decent people experience a reflex of solidarity with those who produce them. Coal is the most powerful example. Workers in the fishing fleets used to receive the same social benison, but this has been carved away by extreme greens who place the happiness of halibut above that of working families. The men who make and bake good bread have always been popular, and, conversely, there are few more contemptible figures than those who sell adulterated bread during a crisis of supply.

Bread is one of the most special of products. Apparently discovered independently in several parts of the world, its many hundreds of forms are today among the most distinctive marks of cultures and their determination towards continuity. The long-lived 24/7/364 Brick Lane beigel shop (of course I refer to the Jewish original, which favours the old spelling, not the upstart interloper, which I note has taken to describing itself as 'London's original') still frequently provides my drive-to-work breakfast or can't-be-bothered-to-cook-this-late supper, and will do so until Tower Hamlets council (inevitably) stamps on parking rights in the area. I had thought the traditional Jewish baker's shop extinct outside Brick Lane, but the pamphlet reminded me of Rinkoff's in Vallance Road, since when I have called in several times. Elsewhere in London, only a fool passes up the chance to buy Grodzinski's best from one of their branches, though regrettably they are no longer to be found in Whitechapel or Seven Kings. And there are many other fine breads from many cultures — a dozen or more in Brick Lane alone. In the nearby Spitalfields market too, splendid handmade breads can (and should) be purchased. The Turkish breads now available in North-East London deserve to be savoured. The Polish accession population has quickly established its own bakery and distribution networks. In Hanwell where I am employed, there sprouted up, improbably, an Afghani bakery — irregular in its habits, opening hours and production, but well worth finding. All of these remind us of the tastes and textures of risen bread, and the debased quality of the factory 'bread' produced by the 'Chorleywood process'.

The latter is one of the worst aspects of the industrialisation of food that took place in the twentieth century, including meat that is not hung, eggs too old to have any residue of flavour and with whites that spread as thin as water, and 'salads' packed under gas. Years ago when I had an allotment, one of the allotment holders brought and gave out some samples of beans (they have a famous brand name, but to use it would expose this publication to legal hazard, so I will simply drop a mention of avian optics) smuggled out of a contract grower's estate. We all eagerly planted them. Germination was uniform and nearly 100 per cent for all of us. Each plant grew at the same rate regardless of treatment or neglect, to the same height before bursting into flower and setting. Long plump bean pods sprouted, all equal, all ready for machine harvesting. We all picked on the same Saturday and took home bulging bags of beans. We all returned the following Sunday with bulging bags of beans to throw onto our compost heaps. The soggy flavourless quality of retail 'avian optic' beans was not the result of industrial harvesting and freezing — they had bred them that way! It was how they thought they should be, and how they thought we should like them. It was as if our home-brewed beer had come out like Watney's Red Barrel.

The special quality of the baking of bread does not make the baking industry immune from the processes and practices of exploitation of the workers, compelled to sweat out long hours in oppressive conditions. Employers in the bakery business, with a few exceptions, were as hard as any others. In the early stages of the struggle to unionise the bakeries, medical researchers were to attest to the debilitating effects on bakery workers of long hours in appalling conditions. And the fact that the industry was fragmented, with many hundreds of small bakeries across London, meant that the employers often held the stronger hand.

In the auspicious year of 1888 the first recorded strike among East End bakers broke out; its main demand being a reduction in working hours. It was largely a spontaneous affair, and only partially supported among the most recent immigrants, numbers of whom were sleeping on the floors of the bakeries that employed them and consequently unwilling to offend the man who was both boss and landlord. The strike broke down after a couple of days, but had attracted the attention of the AUOB (the Amalgamated Union of Operative Bakers and Confectioners of Great Britain).[1] In the atmosphere of 1888 'new unionism', the unionism of the so-called 'unskilled' was spreading across East London like a brush fire, involving such well-known examples as the Bryant and May matchgirls, the dockers and gas workers.

The AUOB already had a branch for German bakers, and it was not a contentious matter for them to establish a 'Hebrew' branch, which quickly established a membership of about 30. This branch collapsed for a few months, but revived under the inspiration of the dockers' victory of 1889 — John Burns had spoken at the victory rally, calling for a reduction in working hours for the bakers to 60 per week. The resurgent bakers wrung the 10-hour day from the employers at the end of 1889 and marched triumphant behind the Hoxton Town Band, wearing their white aprons and linen jackets with loaves pinned to them. A grand, inspiring sight it must have made. The revived Hebrew Branch was there, with a banner inscribed 'Unity is Strength'.

The tailors had also recently conducted a successful strike, many among them Jews. An attempt was made at a meeting held in the International Workingmen's Club in Berners Street to set up a Jewish trades council, to attempt to cope with the fact that so few of the Jewish workers spoke English. Despite this wave of enthusiasm, the Hebrew Branch again disappeared from the list of active branches, collapsed like an over-risen loaf.

In 1893 a new union — the International Bakers Union — was launched at a mass meeting in Bucks Row. They introduced the tactic of labelling 'union bread', to encourage buyers to limit their purchases to employers who met their conditions. (The first Labour MP, Keir Hardie, speaking at the rally, endorsed this approach.) To achieve the union label, an employer was required to concede the closed shop (union labour exclusively), a 12-hour working day, no work on the Sabbath, and overtime limited to one hour per day. There was an obvious problem here, which the pamphlet does not deal with adequately — the AUOB had stuck to the now decades-old demand for the 10-hour day, while the IBU was prepared to settle for 12. How did this different programme play among the workers? Did they settle for less than the demand they had supported for many years, in order to form a more dynamic and locally responsive union? This central strategic question goes unanswered. What little evidence comes forward suggests that this compromise, if such it were, did not pay off. And how did they deal with the principle 'Unity is Strength' in deciding to start a new union separate from one with a decades-long history, effective organisation and experienced leadership? The IBU seems to have become known as the Jewish bakers union, and although there developed a long tradition of solidarity and joint action between IBU and AUOB, there was *de facto* a division based on religious/ethnic lines.

The IBU approached the Chief Rabbi, but he declined to endorse the union label campaign. Despite the renewed determination that the IBU evidenced, pay and working conditions in the bakeries remained among the very worst that might be encountered, and the gains of the 1889 strike were steadily eroded. The employers were, if anything, better organised than the workers, through a powerful Master Bakers Protection Society.

In a new tactic, the Jewish Bakers set up a cooperative bakery in Spitalfields, which seems to have achieved considerable initial success. Its customers remained loyal despite price cuts from the employers, and the project was enthusiastically supported by other trade unions. The business failed, for reasons that are not elucidated. A repeat of the venture two years later also failed, under the weight of bad debts from its customers.

The AUOB had for many years demanded a legal ban on baking on Sunday, ensuring the bakers at least one day off work each week. Their particular target was German-owned small bakeries. In a test case, a Soho baker was fined 10 shillings for baking on Sunday, and the case threw up the anomaly of the Jewish bakers, for whom the Sabbath was Saturday, when no legal protection of the workers applied. Shortly afterwards, possibly in response to pressure from the German bakers, a Jewish Master Baker in the West End was prosecuted for Sunday baking. A substantial controversy developed, with a number of prosecutions of Jewish Master Bakers, some of them pressed for by the unions. If a law that benefited and protected the workers was not to become a means of oppressing a religious minority, something would have to be changed. However, it became clear that some Jewish Master Bakers were employing workers to bake on the Sabbath simply as a means to achieve seven day a week working, even when severely criticised by Rabbis. While there were numerous successful prosecutions, the magistrates were seemingly unwilling to be drawn into a potentially ugly anti-Semitic campaign and often grudgingly handed down trivial fines. The Christian majority of Master Bakers and the AUOB began to find it an expensive and unrewarding fight, and they abandoned it in 1902. The Jewish Master Bakers baked on Sunday unprosecuted.

A chapter is devoted to the strike for union recognition of 1904, in which the anarchist Rudolf Rocker contributed to the leadership and organisation. Despite determined solidarity and support from Jewish unions as well as the 'English' bakers, after many weeks the union was defeated and effectively destroyed. The story is complex, and involved not only the diversion of solidarity contributions into the attempted cooperative bakery, but also an expensive and unsuccessful court case over the union bread label question.

The union revived itself in 1906, responding to successful struggles by shoemakers and tailors. Recent arrivals from Russia after the failure of the 1905 revolution breathed some life into the labour movement, though often putting forward inappropriately radical demands. A long war of attrition developed between masters and the union, but, however determined, the union was unable to prevail against the well-organised employers. Pay and conditions of work remained wretched. Yet again, in 1913 the Jewish bakers organised for a strike, inspired by the successes of the labour big battalions — dockers, sailors, miners and others. But yet again the masters resisted, eventually starving the journeymen back to work after many bitter months. The long-running differences (over Sunday baking, and the 10-hour day) between the Jewish and 'English' bakers unions contributed to the defeat, and there were accusations (not all unjustified) of scabbing.

The conditions of work hardly changed in the following decade, and inevitably bred the same response from the workers. In the great General Strike of 1926, the Stepney Jewish bakers union leader, Prooth, was sentenced to five months' hard labour, and recommended for deportation, being sent to Russia on his release. The Jewish Bakers union struggled on for decades afterwards, but declined steadily as the East End and the baking industry changed around them. By 1964 the membership had fallen to a mere 12 and it ceased to function. Jewish influence in the inner East End was declining, and starting to become a memory. Since then it has all but vanished, and it is good to have such a well-researched record assembled while there are still a few resonances of this record of brave struggle.

The pamphlet includes an introductory obituary of Larry Wayne, who died in January 2008. Born into an East End Lithuanian-Jewish family, he acquired an education at the Davenant School and subsequently at the LSE. He joined the Communist Party early, and caused family friction by selling the *Daily Worker* on the Sabbath. He was active in the Stepney Branch. After a succession of jobs he became a teacher, and insisted on being posted to a secondary school in what is now Newham, where his talents would be offered to children from deprived and under-privileged backgrounds. His party membership survived the crisis of Khrushchev's 'Secret Speech' in 1956, and the military suppression of the Hungarian revolution of 1956 which broke many of the best long-serving members, but it was eroded away by the failure of the party to function democratically. He continued in political activity, prominently in Medical Aid for Vietnam, and also Jews for Justice for Palestinians. After retirement, with his wife Lily, he set up Redbridge Trade Union and Pensioners Action Group.

JJ Plant

Notes
1. I love those proudly specific names of unions, and their echoes of now often vanished skills. What could seem more incongruous than the advanced militancy in the Russian industrial cities in 1905 of the ribbon-makers. Pretty ribbons make a strange contrast with the scenes of bitter street fighting that ended the 1905 uprising. But their work was gruellingly hard and the pay wretched. Repeatedly they showed themselves capable and determined fighters and organisers.

Mary K Wilmers, *The Eitingons: A Twentieth-Century Story*, Faber and Faber, London, 2009, pp 476, £9.99

My main interest in this book is the story of Leonid (aka Naum) Eitingon, whose long and remarkable career in the NKVD/KGB included a major contribution to the murder of Trotsky, in addition to many other special measures and deceptions. I speculate that, had he died before his posting to Spain, where with Orlov he was involved in operations, some of them murderous, against POUMists, anarchists and other revolutionaries, he might have been regarded as an heroic defender of the Revolution. It is perhaps worthwhile to try to understand how revolutionaries of quality can be transformed into their opposite. But the enquiring reader will get little help on that question from this book.

Much of Eitingon's work was, necessarily, secret and conspiratorial, generating imaginative attempts to fill the gaps and explain apparent inconsistencies. It is not even definitively proven that he was a member of the Eitingon family to which the author belongs, though he certainly originated in the same area of what is now Belarus. The reality of the family connection became a point of contention between Theodore Draper and Stephen Schwartz, the former denying it in as much as it involved the status and honour of Max Eitingon, the latter drawing conclusions bolder than supported by the evidence then available. This controversy came to be conducted in heated tones and involved a number of scholars, among them Pierre Broué. Wilmers, having struggled with a mass of inconsistent and contradictory evidence, concludes that it is 'inconceivable' that Leonid was not a cousin, at whatever remove, of the two other principal subjects of the book, Max and Motty Eitingon, and that their families knew each other. Every family historian and hobby genealogist eventually faces exactly such issues of evidence and has to take a position based on her or his view of the balance of probability. I think she is probably right.

In other circumstances this might be no more than an obscure and even trivial bit of family history. But it allows connections to be drawn among the three extraordinary careers and to fit them into a periodisation of Russian and world history. Motty expanded his international fur business and acquired great wealth through preferential treatment by the Soviet government. Max came to be central to the organisation and financing of the Freudian movement.

Motty had a near miraculous ability to broker deals with the communist-led unions on behalf of the New York fur trade. He was accused more than once of being a communist and of secretly funding the CPUSA and the unions, but the charges could never be made to stick. Wilmers has not been able to prove that Leonid and Motty ever met. However, a now very elderly cousin of Leonid had met Motty, and it was clear not only that he knew Leonid's family but that he knew Leonid was a 'Chekist' (member of the Cheka or one of its descendant security organisations). Leonid's long-time boss, Sudoplatov, mentions, in his memoirs (*Special Measures*) that Leonid's rich relatives in the West had declined to assist him on at least one occasion. It has been argued, not always unconvincingly, that Sudoplatov's book is disinformative. However, effective disinformation needs enough convincing and provable information to make falsehoods that cannot be disproven credible, and plenty in Sudoplatov falls into the convincing and provable categories.

Concerning Max and the relationship Schwartz claims he had with the Soviet secret services, Wilmers points to his long association, friendship with and financial support of Skoblin and Plevitskaya, who were responsible for the kidnap and murder of the White General Miller in Paris in 1937. Max was in their company only two days before the kidnap, and on trial Plevitskaya lied about this contact until confronted with proof of it. Max was at pains to keep this story from Freud, and when it went public he told Freud there was no evidence against Plevitskaya — a flat lie. So we may reasonably conclude that Schwartz was in the right. A line of enquiry that Wilmers might have followed but appears not to have, is Max's role in the expulsion from Freud's movement of Wilhelm Reich. That he was party to the process and the decision seems to be well evidenced, but whether this would have been done on the basis of KGB instructions or with a view to consolidating his influence among the psychoanalysts is still to be assessed. Some of the biographical works on Kim Philby (who like Leonid had a reputation for profligate fornication) have suggested that he had a long-term interest in Reich and his Sex-Pol work, which he may have acquired during his induction into conspiratorial work in Vienna. So there arises a frisson-inducing possibility that two of the most substantial Stalinist spies would have been in opposing camps over the Reich question.

The Eitingons, like a stereotypical Jewish family, were incessantly, insatiably curious about each other's money, but none of them seems to have known the source of Max's bounty. That it dried up at the same time as Motty's fur business hit the buffers is telling.

Wilmers has been able to assemble a great deal of new information on Leonid's life and career, though much of it remains, and probably always will, incomplete, and some of the evidence is contradictory. She has his two official KGB autobiographical statements, and the text of a 2003 biography in Russian (Sharapov). This expands what we knew from Sudoplatov, and the few crumbs we had previously on his work in Spain and Mexico. The provenance of some of Volkogonov's assertions about Eitingon remains unsatisfactory, particularly the claim that he worked with the heroic spy Sorge. And some of the claims to knowledge about Eitingon made by Haynes and Klehr based on the Venona decryptions seem to me to be developed beyond reliability, and nothing brought forward by Wilmers improves them.

As a teenager Leonid joined the Socialist Revolutionaries. Whether he took part in any of their many assassination operations has not been revealed. We don't know when he joined the Bolsheviks, but he joined the Cheka before he was 21 and must by then have been a Bolshevik in good standing. His earliest work was against bandits. Wilmers seeks to describe these as peasants refusing or unable to meet the requisition of basic supplies, but shortly afterwards she describes a real bandit who got the better of the inexperienced Leonid. Diligence, zeal and no small native intelligence won him quick promotion, though he also suffered a short period of expulsion from the party. At some point in his early career, Dzerzhinsky (founder of the Cheka — the first Soviet security organisation) intervened personally on his behalf, by one account to reinstate him after his failure against the bandit. Leonid also seems to have had some part in the grand deception that defeated the White counter-revolutionary Savinkov, though we don't get any detail.

After a period of special training in Moscow he was sent to China in 1925. Initially he was sent to Shanghai, but was in Harbin before Chiang's destruction of the Shanghai communists. There is much still to be discovered on Soviet and other secret operations in Harbin, where a large Russian exile population formed. The following year he was at the Soviet Embassy in Peking when it was raided by a combined force of official police and Manchurian warriors. The latter, followers of the warlord Zhang Zu Chin, were on the roof with fire hoses to prevent the Russians from burning their documents. It appears very likely that Leonid had a hand later in the destruction of Zhang — let us hope so.

Among the damaging revelations was, according to Wilmers, secret British material, which was used to justify the Arcos raid in London a month later. Christopher Andrew (in his 'Official History' of MI5) gives a different account of the origins of the Arcos raid, attributing it to the diligence of MI5 against the 'Ewer ring' and to information received from a disaffected Arcos employee. In a recent paper to the American Historical Association, Alastair Kocho-Williams also states that the Peking raid was the trigger for the Arcos raid, but his explanatory footnote is limited to explaining the Arcos abbreviation.

At some point Leonid returned to Harbin where he had successes in disrupting the Whites among the substantial Russian diaspora. In a brilliant stroke he forged documents that persuaded the Japanese that their network of some 20 White Russian anti-Soviet agents had secretly applied for Soviet citizenship. The zealous Japanese shot their own network.

After a period back in Moscow, Leonid was sent in 1929 to Constantinople. Undoubtedly part of his work was to survey Trotsky's contacts during his Turkish exile. In addition he undertook disruptions against exiled nationalist groups from the southern republics of the USSR. He travelled around the Middle East, as far as Syria, on business that we don't have information on.

Leonid's stepdaughter Zoya is the source of much of Wilmers' new information. She has suggested that the 1931 fire at Trotsky's residence in Prinkipo was Leonid's work, and that the intention was not to destroy the library (which it succeeded in to a large extent), but to kill Trotsky. I don't think this is more than speculative. Wilmers suggests that about this time, the Head of the OGPU, Menzhinsky and his then deputy, soon to be successor, Yagoda, travelled to Constantinople to assess the possibilities of murdering Trotsky. Later, when Trotsky was living in France, she indicates that Shpiegelglass, the chief agent in that country, was ordered to mobilise all his resources for the murder of Trotsky.

By 1936 Leonid was in Spain, with the work-name Kotov, as Deputy Head of the NKVD under Orlov. One of his schemes was to send political rivals such as anarchists and POUMists on the most dangerous missions behind the Francoist lines. During this period he recruited Caridad Mercader and her son Ramón, who was eventually to carry the plot to murder Trotsky to a successful conclusion. Though his family would only speak of it in oblique terms, Leonid was involved in the secret killing of at least tens of Stalin's political opponents. As Orlov's deputy, he almost certainly had a hand in the murder of Andres Nin. Wilmers names Erwin Wolf and Kurt Landau, both prominent Trotskyists, as among those killed on Leonid's orders. She does not, in my estimation, bring forward convincing evidence. But somebody certainly murdered them, and the NKVD had motive and opportunity enough in Spain in 1936 and onward. More convincing is Wilmers' report that Leonid played a key role in the removal of the Spanish Republic's gold reserves to 'safe keeping' in Russia. For some or all of these 'special tasks' he was decorated with the Order of the Red Banner.

After the end of the war in Spain, back in Moscow, Leonid was briefed by Sudoplatov on Stalin's order that Trotsky must be killed. (If it is the case that Stalin had not decided that Trotsky had to be killed until March 1938, some of Wilmers' views on earlier operations cannot be right.) Leonid must have looked like the man for the job; he spoke good Spanish and had his own loyal agents recruited in Spain, including the Mercaders. Wilmers provides some items of information that I think are new, about the organisation and preparation of the murder of Trotsky. I presume this comes in large part from the Sharapov book, but she had also been able to discuss with Sudoplatov and the curators of the KGB records. It appears that Leonid took personal charge of the training of Ramón Mercader. He had an enviable reputation as a fornicator and Wilmers suggests this was useful in preparing Mercader for his seduction of Sylvia Ageloff, through whom he was able to gain access to Trotsky's villa. (I never tire of telling friends that Christopher Andrew, in his first book on Mitrokhin, without a trace of humour, describes Mercader as 'an agent of penetration'.)

Although the killing of Trotsky was the high point of Leonid's career, he remained a very active agent subsequently. After a long and careful return to Russia, when he received the Order of Lenin, he took an important part in organising resistance against the Nazi invasion, and at one point was tasked with assassinating the German General von Papen. He managed a splendid deception, turning a captured Nazi commander and persuading Hitler that a heroic band of his supporters was holding out against huge Soviet numbers. Hitler ordered large supplies of materials to be flown and parachuted to this non-existent band of heroic Nazis.

After the end of the Second World War, although he remained a very busy man, little is known of what he was up to, until his arrest in 1951 for 'nationalist deviations'. He was released within days of Stalin's death, but he was regarded by his rivals as Beria's man, and was marginalised after the death of Beria. In 1957 he was arrested again, for 'high treason', a charge relating to 'special measures' undertaken against Stalin's opponents in the period just after the Second World War — which the powers that came to be chose to regard as unlawful killings. Leonid and Sudoplatov were imprisoned, not to be released until 1964. They both kept up a barrage of appeals for release and rehabilitation, arguing throughout that they had acted from loyalty to the Revolution, and wished only to be allowed back into the service to which they had given their lives.

It really does not seem necessary to convince anybody today that Stalin was the author of Trotsky's murder. But there still remains a great deal of detailed research to be done on how it was achieved, and how the murders of many other revolutionaries and enemies of Stalin were conducted. This book sheds some new light on those questions and deserves to be studied. The author has made of her text a personal journey of exploration into her family roots, and perhaps no other approach would have been viable for her. If that decision produces some frustrations for historians, they will have the compensation of an enjoyable and absorbing text. And at the end of it all, the enigmatic, dedicated figure of Leonid Eitingon still stands challenging the reader, a distillation in human form of all the questions that 1917 produced and failed to answer.

Bridget St Ruth

Alan Woodward, *Life and Times of Joe Thomas: The Road to Libertarian Socialism,* Libertarian Socialists, London, 2010, pp 40, no price stated

To write the life of Joe Thomas is no straightforward project, and Alan Woodward's (and his sources') knowledge of the almost hidden histories of a number of revolutionary groups outside of those tendencies (Stalinism, Trotskyism, Bordigism) that have preserved their own historical records (often tendentiously of course) is of considerable value here. We have available for study a growing collection of Trotskyist memoirs, which allow us to take cross-bearings on the histories of the movement. From the anarchist current there is less, and the most substantial — Albert Meltzer's autobiography — has been attacked by his own side to the extent that it is difficult to assess its reliability as evidence. In Britain there has always been a kind of 'third stream' incorporating Dutch-influenced Council Communism, industry-oriented non-Leninist currents, and what are these days called libertarian socialists (often historical descendants of the anti-parliamentary current that the formation of the Communist Party aimed to snuff out). This complex, often incoherent and conflict-riddled, current has left too little written history; many of Alan

Woodward's references are to personal communications and conversations. This should be seen not as a weakness but a strength of the pamphlet. The job of assembling primary material from sources involved in the action has been done, and will be of permanent value.

Revolutionary History has some interest in Joe Thomas. The late Ernest Rogers, a long-serving and much missed member of the Editorial Board, was closely connected, politically, with Thomas, and wrote an obituary for him that has value as source material and interpretation. Alan Woodward uses information from Rogers, and from Al Richardson — though he expresses doubts about the latter, since it indicates Thomas may have spent some time in membership of the Trotskyist Revolutionary Communist Party.

In fact Thomas' wanderings through numerous small political groups (after his initial period in the Communist Party) form most of the story. How far this nomadic life reflected Thomas' political development and how far it was the consequence of the instability of the groups themselves is difficult to judge. Certainly the group dynamics played a role, as evidenced by the story of Thomas' expulsion from the Workers League, in 1961. Four members purged the other two, on the grounds of 'bureaucracy'! Woodward is right to find this preposterous, but does not draw a benefit from his *tour d'horizon* of left groupings to suggest how things might be done better. It is not easy to resist the conclusion that Thomas was a valuable militant, but that much of his time was wasted in unproductive grouplet politics. Such a conclusion is to be arrived at with sadness, and not without all the necessary self-criticism.

Thomas required his papers to be destroyed, in his will, so it may never be possible to assess his political trajectory with clarity. Woodward does what he can with the available material.

Woodward, like Thomas, has taken his distance from Leninism and Trotskyism, and contributes his energies to the Radical History Network, and to propagating for an alternative socialist direction, which he calls libertarian socialism, or sometimes worker socialism. This approach is based on confidence in the workers' ability to self-organise, and rejects the vanguard party concept. He would have liked to produce a biography of Thomas that would serve as a model or template of political development with a similar trajectory to it. But he is honest and serious enough of an historian to record that it cannot be done with the evidence to hand. Bravo! Such historians are to the taste of this journal.

In clarifying his own position Woodward engages in some sharp criticisms of Lenin and Trotsky, glossing his previous material on workers' councils. Nothing improper in that, of course. But he seems to me sometimes to overstate the strength and quality of the libertarian socialist position. For example, he claims that by the time of Thomas' death (1990) 'there were several thriving bodies all over the UK that could be termed more definitely libertarian socialist'. And again, he states that Thomas' life 'can be regarded as typical of millions of others'. I remember being laughed out of a GMC meeting for saying that the 'winter of discontent' crisis was such that millions of workers would rise up if given a lead by the PLP or TUC. Better had we both been right — but we were not.

For all that, the libertarian socialists have a point that does not go away. The 'gains of October' have thawed into the slush of yesteryear across the planet. The vanguard party gave history its best shot in 1917, and however heroic the old Bolsheviks were (and their heroism remains inadequately stated), its failure in Germany left us all up against the wall nearly a century later.

The small groups in which Thomas spent much of his life contrast starkly with the scale of some of the struggles in which he and his comrades were able to play a role, such as the protracted fight by the print workers at Wapping in the 1980s. Woodward's pamphlet deserves a place in the library of everybody who really hopes to understand how our class and our movement came to be in the deplorable state we are in today. And Thomas may not have been a revolutionary saint, but he was a comrade with determination and intensity who never stopped fighting, and trying to learn from his own experience and that of his class.

Bridget St Ruth

Letters

Trotskyism in Sri Lanka

The following letter was sent by Charles Wesley Ervin to *La Vérité* on 6 May 2009. As it was not published and concerns matters dealt with by *Revolutionary History*, we have agreed for to appear in our pages.

* * *

Dear Friends

I recently read your balance sheet on Trotskyism in Sri Lanka, dated 16 December 2008, reprinted in *Socialist Organizer*. Overall, I agree with your analysis. In this letter I wish to offer a few factual corrections.

First, the article states that when the Indian section of the FI (the BLPI) decided to enter the Socialist Party in 1948, 'The International leadership simply looked the other way.' That is false. In fact, the International Secretariat expressed strong misgivings over the entry proposal. In 1948 the IS instructed the BLPI to postpone the entry decision until a proper discussion could be carried out under the leadership of the FI. (See CW Ervin, *Tomorrow is Ours: The Trotskyist Movement in India and Ceylon 1935-48*, Colombo, 2006.) Unfortunately, the BLPI leaders rejected this good advice and hastily went ahead with the entry. Sadly, the BLPI liquidated itself, just as the British section did a year later, through an inappropriate use of the entry tactic. The IS cannot be blamed for that.

However, as your article states, within a few years Pablo himself became the prophet of entrism. In the 1950s the IS urged the Indian Trotskyists to build a 'centrist' Workers-Peasants Party (Mazdoor Kisan Party), rather than rebuild a 'sectarian' pure Trotskyist party. When that experiment flopped, the Indian Trotskyists launched their own party in 1957. The IS, however, backed a liquidationist faction in that party, and in 1960 the Indian Trotskyists merged with a centrist party, the Revolutionary Communist Party, with the blessings of the Pabloites. That too was a disaster. The Trotskyists were forced to split two years later when the RCP majority backed India in the border war with the China. Then, after the Sino-Soviet split in 1964, Pablo urged the Indian Trotskyists to enter the pro-Peking Communist Party of India (Marxist). The

Stalinists cleverly accepted only the trade unionists. As a result, the Trotskyist movement lost its historic mass base in the coal-fields of West Bengal.

Second, regarding the Third World Congress of the FI (1951), you are right to question the report on the delegation from Ceylon. Robert Gunawardena and Leslie Goonewardene did in fact represent the LSSP. However, contrary to the garbled account in the official proceedings, Philip Gunawardena surely did not.

I suspect that whoever wrote the report was confused by the Sinhalese names. Goonewardene and Gunawardena are different Anglicised spellings for the same name (Gunavardhana in Sinhala). Robert was the younger brother of Philip Gunawardena. To make matters more confusing, 'Robert' was his nickname. His full name was Don Benjamin Rupasinghe Gunawardena. Rupasinghe is their clan name; 'Hupasinghe' is nonsensical.

Politically, Philip wanted nothing to do with the Fourth International at that point. He had split from the LSSP in 1950, formed a rival party, and oriented towards the Stalinist camp. In 1952 he attended the pro-Moscow Congrès des Peuples pour la Paix in Vienna and the Asian Pacific Peace Congress in Peking. Returning from his tours, he publicly pronounced Trotskyism to be a 'dead ideology'. However, it should be noted that on certain key issues, Philip took very Pabloite positions: for example, he held that Stalinism could play a revolutionary role and adopted the theory that the USSR was a 'regenerating workers state'.

Sincerely yours

Charles Wesley Ervin

New from Merlin Press

Immigrants and Intellectuals:
May '68 and the Rise of Anti-Racism in France

Daniel A. Gordon

This book tells, for the first time, the full story of the rise and fall of a cycle of protest movements for the rights of migrant workers from 1961 to 1983.

Based on more than a decade of research in France, including special access to normally closed police archives, it reveals an encounter between two worlds, the immigrant and the intellectual.

Highlighting links to international struggles from Portugal to Senegal, Gordon considers reactions to the massacre of Algerians in Paris in 1961; uncovers the hidden history of migrant worker participation in the general strike of 1968; shows how activists built creches for immigrants' children and asks: how did immigrants view the New Left militants who sought to politicize them? It recounts how a hunger strike by a Tunisian activist leader in 1972 sparked a movement which mobilized some of France's best-known thinkers from Sartre to Foucault, and brought this civil rights campaign into mainstream politics.

After showing how the dreams of '68 were buried and recycled, Gordon concludes with the legacy of this story for the politics of migration and the politics of protest today in France and beyond.

'This book is a fundamental contribution to an understanding of the process which led immigrant workers in France to become politically conscious.' – Professor Alain Romey, University of Nice.

'A significant contribution to our understanding of French political and social history.' – Dr Jim House, Director, Centre for French and Francophone Cultural Studies, University of Leeds.

The bibliography alone is a valuable research resource. Yet while the book is scholarly in the best sense of the term, it is not academic in the worst sense. It is clearly written, without jargon and full of detailed examples, and makes clear the author's passionate personal involvement in his material. – *Revolutionary History*.

ISBN. 978-0-85036-664-8   paperback   £18.95

www.merlinpress.co.uk